HISTORICAL ATLAS

WILLIAM R. SHEPHERD

Late Professor of History, Columbia University

Ninth Edition, 1964

BARNES & NOBLE, INC. NEW YORK

PUBLISHERS • BOOKSELLERS • SINCE 1873

To T. S.
my life's companion
who induced me to go forth
and see the world

Printed in the United States of America

PREFACE TO THE NINTH EDITION

Long a classic in its field, the Shepherd Atlas was out of print for many years, but remained in constant demand. Since the plates, originally made in Germany, were destroyed, this edition was printed by offset lithography. A special supplementary section of historical maps for the period since 1929 was prepared for the new edition by C. S. Hammond & Company.

In his preface to the Seventh Edition, 1929, the author expressed appreciation to Professor Charles H. Haskins, Harvard University; Professor Charles M. Andrews, Yale University; his colleagues, Professors Austin P. Evans, William Linn Westermann and Harry J. Carman, Columbia University; Mr. Harry W. Martin, Horace Mann Boy's School, New York; Dr. Isaiah Bowman and Mr. W. L. G. Joerg, the American Geographical Society; Principal C. Grant Robertson, Birmingham University; Honorary Professor T. F. Tout, Manchester University; Mr. L. Cecil Jane, Aberystwyth College, University of Wales; and the officials of the Library of the British Museum, in particular Mr. F. D. Sladen, Superintendent of the Reading Room.

For suggestions helpful in the preparation of the Eighth Edition, the publisher wishes to thank Mr. James M. Darley, Chief Cartographer of the National Geographic Society; Professor Walther Kirchner, University of Delaware; Professor John A. Krout, Vice President and Provost, Columbia University; Professor Bert James Loewenberg, Sarah Lawrence College; Professor Thomas C. Mendenhall, Yale University; Professor Marshall Smelser, University of Notre Dame.

For their work in the preparation of the Ninth Edition, the publisher is grateful to Professor Erle Leichty, Department of History, University of Minnesota, and Mr. Ronald Abler, Department of Geography, University of Minnesota.

ACKNOWLEDGMENT

Among the works consulted in the preparation of the Atlas the following have been especially serviceable:

R. Altamira y Crevea, Historia de España y de la civilización española. (4 vols. Madrid, 1909—1911)

E. Ambrosius ed., Andrees Allgemeiner Handatlas. (8th ed. 2d imp. Leipzig, 1924)

F. M. Anderson and A. S. Hershey, Handbook for the diplomatic history of Europe, Asia and Africa, 1870—1914. (Washington, 1918)

K. Andree, Geographie des Welthandels. (3 vols. Frankfort, 1910—1913)

Archiv für Eisenbahnwesen. (Berlin, 1878 . . . .)

E. M. Avery, A history of the United States and its people. (7 vols. Cleveland, 1904—1910)

J. G. Bartholomew, An Atlas of economic geography. (London, 1914)

J. G. Bartholomew ed., The Times survey atlas of the world. (London, 1922)

C. R. Beazley, The dawn of modern geography. (3 vols. London, 1897—1906)

E. Bonvalot, Le Tiers État d'après la charte de Beaumont-en-Argonne et ses filiales. (Paris, 1884)

I. Bowman, The new world. (Yonkers, 1926)

J. H. Breasted, A history of Egypt from the earliest times to the Persian conquest. (2d ed. New York, 1909)

J. Brunhes, Human Geography. (New York, 1920)
—, La géographie de l'histoire. (Paris, 1921)

J. Buchan ed., A history of the great war. (4 vols. New York, 1922)

The Cambridge ancient history. (6 vols. Cambridge, 1923 . . . .)

The Cambridge history of British foreign policy, 1783—1919. (3 vols. Cambridge, 1922—1923)

The Cambridge medieval history (5 vols. Cambridge, 1911 . . . .)

The Cambridge modern history (13 vols. Cambridge, 1902—1912).

The Cambridge modern history atlas. (2d ed. Cambridge, 1924)

A del Cantillo, Tratados, convenios y declaraciones de paz y de comercio. (Madrid, 1843)

H. M. Chadwick, The origin of the English nation. (Cambridge, 1907)

C. U. J. Chevalier, Répertoire des sources historiques du moyen-âge; Pt. II: topo-bibliographie. (2 vols. Paris, 1894—1903)

The Colonial Office list. (London, 1862 . . . .)

J. S. Corbett, Drake and the Tudor navy. (2 vols. London, 1899)

H. W. C. Davis, England under the Normans and Angevins. (London, 1915)

E. Debes ed., Neuer Handatlas über alle Teile der Erde. (4th ed. 2d imp. Leipzig, 1914)

L. Dominian, The frontiers of language and nationality in Europe. (New York, 1917)

G. Droysen, Allgemeiner historischer Handatlas. (Leipzig, 1886)

E. M. Earle, Turkey, the great powers and the Bagdad railway. (New York, 1923)

C. Errera, L'epoca delle grandi scoperte geografiche. (Milan, 1902)

Europäischer Geschichtskalender. (Munich, 1860 . . .)

H. J. Fleure, Human geography in western Europe. (2d ed. London, 1919)
—, The treaty settlement of Europe. (London, 1921)

E. Florez, España sagrada. (51 vols. Madrid, 1747—1879)

Foreign Affairs. (New York, 1922)

E. A. Freeman, Historical geography of Europe. (2 vols. 3d ed. London, 1903)

A García Cubas, Cuadro geográfico, estadístico, descriptivo e histórico de los Estados Unidos Mexicanos. (Mexico, 1884)

The Geographical Journal. (London, 1893 . . . .)

The Geographical Review (New York, 1916 . . . .)

W. Götz, Die Verkehrswege im Dienste des Welthandels. (Stuttgart, 1888)
—, Historische Geographie: Beispiele und Grundlinien. (Leipzig, 1904)

A. B. Hart ed., The American nation: a history from original sources by associated scholars. (28 vols. New York, 1904—1918)

C. H. Haskins and R. H. Lord, Some problems of the peace conference. (Cambridge, Mass., 1920)

F. J. Haverfield, The Roman occupation of Britain. (Oxford, 1924)

A. J. Herbertson and O. J. R. Howarth eds, The Oxford survey of the British Empire. (6 vols. Oxford, 1914)

E. Hertslet ed., China treaties (3d ed. London, 1908)
—, The map of Africa by treaty (3d ed. 3 vols. London, 1909)
—, The map of Europe by treaty. (4 vols. London, 1875, 1891)

K. Heussi and H. Mulert, Atlas zur Kirchengeschichte. (Tübingen, 1905)

W. v. Heyd, Histoire du commerce du Levant au moyen-âge. (2 vols. Leipzig, 1885—1886)

ACKNOWLEDGMENT

A. Himly, Histoire de la formation territoriale des états de l'Europe centrale. (2 vols. Paris, 1876)

T. H. Holdich, Boundaries in Europe and the Near East. (London, 1918)

L. Hugues, Cronologia delle scoperte e delle esplorazioni geografiche dall' anno 1492 a tutto il secolo XIX. (Milan, 1903)

C. Huelsen, The Roman forum. (2 d ed. Rome, 1909)

W. W. Hunter, History of British India. (2 vols. London, 1899—1900)

P. Huvelin, Essai historique sur le droit des marchés et des foires. (Paris, 1897)

The imperial gazetteer of India. 3 d ed. 26 vols. Oxford, 1907—1909)

C. Joppen, Historical atlas of India. (London, 1914)

J. S. Keltie, The partition of Africa. (2 d ed. London, 1895)

H. and R. Kiepert, Formae orbis antiqui. (Berlin, 1901 . . . .)

C. G. de Koch and M. S. F. Schoell, Histoire abrégée des traités de paix entre les puissances de l'Europe depuis la paix de Westphalie. (15 vols. Paris, 1817—1818)

C. Kretschmer, Die Entdeckung Amerikas in ihrer Bedeutung für die Geschichte des Weltbildes. (Berlin, 1892)

C. de Lannoy and H. van der Linden, Histoire de l'expansion coloniale des peuples européens. (2 vols. Brussels, 1907—1911)

J. N. Larned ed., History for ready reference. (7 vols. Springfield, 1913)

E. Lavisse, Histoire de France depuis les origines jusqu'à la révolution. (9 vols. Paris, 1900 to 1911)

Lippincott's new gazetteer. (Philadelphia, 1916)

W. J. Loftie, London. (3 d ed. London, 1892)

A. Longnon, Atlas historique de la France. (Paris, 1907)

C. Lucas ed., A historical geography of the British colonies. (12 vols. Oxford, 1905 to 1925)

K. von Martens and F. de Cussy, Recueil manuel et pratique de traités, conventions et autres actes diplomatiques. (7 vols. Leipzig, 1846 to 1857)

L. de Mas-Latrie, Trésor de chronologie d'histoire et de géographie pour l'étude et l'emploi des documents du moyen-âge. (Paris, 1889)

E. Mc Clure, Historical church atlas. (London, 1897)

H. R. Mill, The international geography. (New York, 1909)

C. F. R. de Montalambert, The monks of the west from Saint Benedict to Saint Bernard. (6 vols. New York, 1896)

R. Muir and G. Philip, Philips' New historical atlas for students. (5 th ed. London, 1923)

J. Murdoch and I. Yamagata, A history of Japan. (2 vols. Yokohama, 1903, 1910)

D. P. Myers, Manual of collection of treaties. (Cambridge, Mass., 1922)

H. Nissen, Italische Landeskunde. (2 vols. Berlin, 1883—1902)

A. E. Nordenskiöld, Facsimile atlas to the early history of cartography. (London, 1889)

A. Oakes and R. B. Mowat eds., The great European treaties of the nineteenth century. (Oxford, 1918)

C. W. C. Oman, England before the Norman conquest. (5 th ed. London, 1921)

E. L. Oxenham, Historical atlas of the Chinese Empire. (London, 1898)

P. Pelet, Atlas des colonies françaises. (Paris 1900—1902)

A. Petermanns Mitteilungen aus Justus Perthes' geographischer Anstalt über wichtige neue Erforschungen auf dem Gesamtgebiete der Geographie. (Gotha, 1855 . . . .)

O. F. Peschel, Geschichte des Zeitalters der Entdeckungen. (Stuttgart, 1858)

H. Pirenne, Medieval cities. (Princeton, 1925)

E. Porritt, The unreformed House of Commons. (2 vols. Cambridge, 1903)

R. L. Poole ed., Historical atlas of modern Europe. (Oxford, 1896—1902)

B. Poten ed., Handwörterbuch der Militärwissenschaften. (5 vols. Leipzig, 1877—1880)

F. W. Putzgers Historischer Schul-Atlas (48 th ed. Leipzig, 1928)

H. Rashdall, The universities of Europe in the middle ages. (2 vols. Oxford, 1895)

O. Reclus, Atlas de la plus grande France. (Paris, 1913)

F. P. W. von Richthofen, China: Ergebnisse eigener Reisen und darauf gegründeter Studien. (5 vols. Berlin, 1877—1912)

E. K. A. Riehm, Handwörterbuch des biblischen Altertums. (2 vols. Leipzig, 1898)

W. Z. Ripley, The races of Europe. (New York, 1910)

C. G. Robertson and J. G. Bartholomew, An historical atlas of modern Europe from 1789 to 1922. (2 d ed. London, 1924)

ACKNOWLEDGMENT

C. G. Robertson and J. G. Bartholomew, Historical and modern atlas of the British Empire (with supplement, London, 1905, 1924)

H. T. Robinson, Colonial chronology. (London, 1892)

Royal Asiatic Society of Great Britain and Ireland, Journal. (London, 1834 . . . .)

—, Transactions. (London, 1827 . . . .)

Royal Colonial Institute, Proceedings. (London, 1869 . . . .)

Royal Geographical Society, Journal. (London, 1831 . . . .)

S. Ruge, Die Entwicklung der Kartographie von Amerika bis 1570. (Gotha, 1892)

F. Schrader, Atlas de géographie historique. (Paris, 1911)

F. Seebohm, The English village community. (4th ed. London, 1905)

E. C. Semple, American history and its geographic conditions. (New York, 1903)

W. H. Siebert, The underground railroad from slavery to freedom. (New York, 1898)

W. Sievers, Süd- und Mittelamerika. (3d ed. Leipzig, 1914)

G. A. Smith and J. G. Bartholomew, Atlas of the historical geography of the Holy Land. (London, 1915)

C. von Spruner and T. Menke, Handatlas für die Geschichte des Mittelalters und der neueren Zeit. (Gotha, 1871—1880)

C. von Spruner, Historisch-geographischer Handatlas zur Geschichte Asiens, Afrikas, Amerikas und Australiens. (Gotha, 1855)

The statesman's year-book. (London, 1864 . . . .)

Stielers Handatlas. (Gotha, 1925)

A. M. H. J. Stokvis, Manuel d'histoire, de généalogie et de chronologie de tous les états du globe . . . (3 vols. Leyden, 1888—1893)

A. Supan, Die territoriale Entwicklung der europäischen Kolonien. (Gotha, 1906)

P. Teleki, Atlas zur Geschichte der Kartographie der japanischen Inseln. (Budapest, 1909)

H. W. V. Temperley, ed., A history of the peace conference of Paris. (5 vols. London, 1920 to 1921)

L. Thorndike, The history of medieval Europe. (New York, 1917)

M. Torrente, Historia de la revolución hispano-americana. (3 vols. Madrid, 1829—1830)

The treaties of peace. (2 vols. New York, 1924)

U. S. Bureau of the Census, Statistical atlas of the United States. (Washington, 1903, 1914, 1925)

P. Vidal de la Blache, Histoire et géographie: atlas général Vidal-Lablache. (Paris, 1922)

P. Vinogradoff, The growth of the manor (rev. ed. London, 1911)

—, Villainage in England. (Oxford, 1892)

L. Vivien de Saint-Martin, Atlas universel de géographie (rev. ed. Paris, 1923)

E. A. Walker, Historical atlas of South Africa. (London, 1922)

World atlas of commercial geology: Pt. I, Distribution of mineral production. (Washington, 1921)

World missionary atlas. (London, 1925)

J. K. Wright, Geographical lore at the time of the crusades. (New York, 1924)

H. Yule, Cathay and the way thither (new ed. 4 vols. London, 1915—1916)

A. Zimmermann, Die europäischen Kolonien. (5 vols. Berlin, 1896—1903)

New York, March 1928

W. R. S.

CONTENTS

PAGE

Reference Map of Ancient Egypt 1

Physical Map of Europe, Western Asia and Northern Africa 2. 3

Mycenean Greece, 2100—1300 B. C. 4

The Ancient Near East ca. 1375 B. C. 4

The Assyrian Empire and the Region about the Eastern Mediterranean, 850—625 B. C. 5

Reference Map of Ancient Palestine 6. 7
Insets: Plan of Jerusalem. Dominions of David and Solomon (1025—953 B. C.). Palestine under the later Kings (953—722 B. C.). Palestine under Joshua and the Judges (1250 —1125 B. C.).

The Orient 600—500 B. C. 8
The Oriental Empires about 600 B. C. The Persian Empire about 500 B. C.

The Beginnings of Historic Greece, 700—600 B. C. 8

Vicinity of Troy. The Shores of the Propontis. Plan of Olympia 9

Reference Map of Ancient Greece. Northern Part 10. 11

Greek and Phoenician Settlements in the Mediterranean Basin, about 550 B. C. 12

Greece at the Time of the War with Persia, 500—479 B. C. The Athenian Empire at its Height (about 450 B. C.) 13

Reference Map of Ancient Greece. Southern Part 14. 15
Inset: Crete.

Reference Map of Attica. Plan of Thermopylæ, 480 B. C. 16
Inset: Harbors of Athens.

PAGE

Greece at the Beginning of the Peloponnesian War (431 B. C.). Greece under Theban Headship (362 B. C.) 17

The Macedonian Empire, 336— 323 B. C. 18. 19
Insets: The Ætolian and Achaian Leagues. Plan of Tyre.

Kingdoms of the Diadochi 18. 19
After the Battle of Ipsus (301 B. C.). At the Beginning of the Struggle with Rome (about 200 B. C.).

Reference Map of Asia Minor under the Greeks and Romans 20

Plan of Imperial Rome 22

Plan of Athens 23
Inset: Plan of the Acropolis of Athens.

Plan of Republican Rome 23

Republican Forum. Imperial Forums 24

Reference Map of Ancient Italy. Northern Part 26. 27

The Growth of Roman Power in Italy to 218 B. C. 29

Reference Map of Ancient Italy. Southern Part 30. 31
Insets: Vicinity of Naples. Plan of Syracuse.

Rome and Carthage at the Beginning of the Second Punic War, 218 B. C. 32

The Growth of Roman Power in Asia Minor 33
I, after the Treaty of Apamea, 188 B. C.; II, before the outbreak of the Mithradatic Wars, 90 B. C.; III, as organized by Pompey, 63 B. C.

Territorial Expansion of Rome 34. 35
Insets: Plan of Carthage. Vicinity of Rome. Plan of Alexandria.

CONTENTS

PAGE

Reference Map of the European Provinces of the Roman Empire 38. 39
Insets: Gaul in the Time of Cæsar. The Rhine Country in Roman Times. Country about the Lower Danube in Roman Times.

The Roman Empire about 395 42. 43

Economic Map of the Ancient World 44

Migrations and Conquests, 150—1066 45

Development of Christianity to 1300 46. 47

The Roman and Hunnic Empires about 450 48

Physical Map of the British Isles 49

The Germanic Kingdoms and the East Roman Empire in 486 50

Roman Britain about 410. Britain about 600 51

The Germanic Kingdoms and the East Roman Empire, 526—600 52
The Germanic Kingdoms and the East Roman Empire in 526. Europe and the East Roman Empire, 533—600.

The Califate in 750 53

Growth of Frankish Power, 481—814 53

The Carolingian and Byzantine Empires and the Califate about 814 54. 55
Inset: Northern Austrasia about 814.

Disruption of the Carolingian Empire, 843—888 56

The Peoples of Europe about 900 57

Europe and the Byzantine Empire about 1000 58. 59

England in the Eighth and Ninth Centuries 60
England in the Eighth Century. England in the Ninth Century.

France about 1035 61

Central Europe, 919—1125 62. 63

Italy about 1050 64
Inset: The Patrimony of St. Peter.

Danish Dominions, 1016—1241 64

England 1087—1154 65

Europe and the Mediterranean Lands about 1097 66. 67
Inset: Europe and the Mediterranean Lands by Religions about 1097.

Asia Minor and the States of the Crusaders in Syria, about 1140 68
Insets: Palestine. Plan of Jerusalem about 1187.

France, 1154—1184 69
Inset: Domain, Fiefs and Suzerains of the Count of Champagne in the Twelfth Century.

Europe and the Mediterranean Lands about 1190 70. 71
Inset: Guelf, Hohenstaufen and Ascanian Domains in Germany about 1176.

The Holy Roman Empire under the Hohenstaufen, 1138—1254 72

The Mediterranean Lands after 1204 73

The British Isles, 1200—1450. Plan of London about 1300. Vicinity of London, 1200—1600 74. 75

France in 1328 76
Inset: The Chief Wool-raising Districts of England and Wool-manufacturing Towns of Flanders, Artois and Brabant.

Europe, 1360—1400 77

Central Europe in 1378 78. 79
Inset: Dominions of Ottocar of Bohemia.

Spread of German Settlements to the Eastward, 800—1400 80
Inset: The March of Lusatia.

The Great Schism, 1378—1417 81

France in 1453 81

Spain, 910—1492 82. 83
Spain in 910. Spain in 1037. Spain in 1150. Spain, 1212—1492.

England and France, 1455—1494 84

Decline of the March of Brandenburg under the Houses of Wittelsbach and Luxemburg, 1320—1415 85

The Wettin Lands, 1221—1485 85
Inset: Temporary break-up of the Wettin Lands about 1300.

Central Europe about 1477 86. 87

CONTENTS

PAGE

Decline of German Power in the Baltic Region, 1380—1560   88

The Byzantine Empire, 1265—1355   89
I. The Byzantine Empire in 1265.
II. The Byzantine Empire and the Ottoman Turks in 1355.

Italy about 1494   90
Insets: The Milanese under the Visconti, 1339 - 1402. The Republic of Florence, 1300—1494.

The Swiss Confederation, 1291—1513   91

The Mongol Dominions, 1227—1405   92

The Ottoman Empire, 1451—1481. Constantinople   93

Ecclesiastical Map of Western Europe in the Middle Ages   94. 95
Inset: Vicinity of Naples.

Plan of Rome in the Middle Ages   96

The Roman Suburbicarian (Cardinal) Bishoprics about the 12ᵗʰ Century   96

Ecclesiastical Map of the British Isles in the Middle Ages   97

Mediaeval Commerce (Europe)   98. 99
Insets: England. Hanseatic League in Northern Germany.

Rural Deaneries   100
Part of the bishopric of Winchester showing rural deaneries and religious houses during the Middle Ages.

Mediaeval Universities   100

Ground-Plan of a Monastery (St. Gall, Switzerland)   101

Mediaeval Industry (Western Europe)   102. 103

Plan of a Mediaeval Manor   104

Enfranchisment of Mediaeval Towns   104 A
Expansion of the Charter of Beaumont-en-Argonne, 1182—1300.

Mediaeval Commerce (Asia) 104 B. 104 C
Inset: India.

Europe in 1490   104 D

The West Indies and Central America, 1492—1525   105
Inset: Watling's Island.

The Conquest of Mexico, 1519—1521   106

PAGE

The Expansion of Europe, 1340—1600   107—110

The Conquest of Peru, 1531-1533   111

The Portuguese Colonial Dominions in India and the Malay Archipelago, 1498—1580   112

The Imperial Circles about 1512   113

Central Europe about 1547   114. 115
Insets: Principality of Orange. Wettin Lands, 1485—1554.

The Religious Situation in Europe about 1560   116
The Religious Situation in Central Europe about 1560. The Religious Situation in Europe about 1560.

The Netherlands, 1559—1609   117

Europe about 1560   118. 119

The Religious Situation in Central Europe about 1618   120

Sweden about 1658   120

Principal Seats of War in Europe, 1618—1660   121

Treaty Adjustments, 1648—1660   121
1. Treaty of Westphalia, 1648.
2. Treaty of the Pyrenees, 1659; Peace of Roeskilde-Oliva, 1658, 1660.

Central Europe about 1648   122. 123

Europe in 1648   124

Principal Seats of War in Europe, 1672—1699   125

Treaty Adjustments, 1668—1699   125
Treaties of Aix-la-Chapelle, Nimwegen, St. Germain, Ryswick, Carlowitz.

Extension of the French Frontiers, 1601—1789   126

England an Ireland, 1485—1688   127
England and Wales, 1485—1688. Ireland, 1550—1653. Ecclesiastical England, 1534—1547.

Scotland, 1488—1688   128

The Ottoman Empire, 1481—1683   128 A

The Expansion of Europe, 1600—1700   128 B. 128 C
Insets: Partition of Guiana and the West Indies. India. The Establishment of Dutch Power in the Malay Archipelago, 1602—1641. Guinea Coast.

CONTENTS

PAGE

Principal Seats of War in Europe, 1700—1721   129

Europe about 1740   130. 131
Inset: The Growth of Savoy, 1418—1748.

Principal Seats of War, 1740 —1763   132
Inset: Spain. West Africa. West Indies. Canada. India.

Treaty Adjustments, 1713—1763   133
Treaties of Utrecht, Rastatt, Baden, Stockholm, Frederiksborg, Nystad, Passarowitz, Vienna, Belgrade, Breslau, Dresden, Aix-la-Chapelle, Paris, Hubertusburg.
Insets: Acadia and Newfoundland. Eastern North America.

Central Europe about 1786   134. 135

The Expansion of Europe, 1700 —1763   136
Insets: The West Indies, 1700— 1763. Cook's Voyages in the Southern Pacific.

India, 1700—1792   137

The Growth of Russia in Europe, 1300—1796   138. 139

Typical German States before and since the French Revolution
I. Baden.   142
Insets: County of Sponheim. Lordship of Grävenstein. Baden since 1801.
II. Wurtemberg   143
Insets: County of Horburg and Lordship of Reichenweier. Principality-County of Montbéliard. Wurtemberg since 1495.

France in 1789   146. 147
The "Gouvernements". The Generalities or Intendancies. The Salt tax and the Customs. Laws and Courts.

Ecclesiastical Map of France, 1789 and 1802   148

France in 1791   148

Plans of Versailles and Paris in 1789   149

Napoleon's Campaign in Egypt, 1798   150

PAGE

Northern Italy, 1796 (for the campaigns of 1796—1805)   150

Germany and Italy in 1803   151

Germany and Italy in 1806   151

Treaty Adjustments, 1810—1812   152
Insets: India. Cape Colony.

Principal Seats of War, 1788 —1815   153
Insets: India. Egypt. Napoleon's Campaign in Russia, 1812.

Central Europe in 1812   154. 155
Inset: Europe in 1812.

The Waterloo Campaign. Europe in 1815   156
Plan of the Waterloo Campaign, June 16—18, 1815. Europe in 1815.

Treaty Adjustments, 1814, 1815   157
Inset: Fortresses along the French Frontier.

Central Europe, 1815—1866   158. 159

The German Zollverein (Customs Union) 1828—1872   160
1828 –1834. After 1834.

Germany, 1866—1919   161

Italy, 1815—1924   161

Industrial England since 1750   162

England and Wales in 1832   163

The Ottoman Empire, 1683— 1913   164
Insets: Southwestern Crimea, 1854. Plan of Sevastopol, 1854—1855.

Peoples of Southeastern Europe and Asia Minor in 1913   165

Europe, 1871—1914   166. 167

Peoples of Austria-Hungary in 1914   168

The World at War, 1914—1918   168 A

Principal Seats of War, 1914— 1918   168 B

The Western European Front, 1914—1918   168 C

Treaty Adjustments, 1919—1926   168 D

CONTENTS

PAGE

Treaty Adjustments 1919—1926.
The Rhineland   168 E

Europe in 1929   168 F. 168 G

Peoples of Central Europe in 1929   168 H
Inset: South Tyrol.

The Near East since 1913. I.   168 J. 168 K

The Near East. II.   168 L
Proposed Partitions of the Ottoman Empire, 1915, 1916. The Dardanelles. Partitions of Thrace.
1878—1923. The Religious Situation.

The Growth of European and
Japanese Dominions in Asia
since 1801   170. 171
Inset: Vicinity of Peking.

Australia and New Zealand since
1788   172

The Partition of Africa   174. 175
Insets: The Suez Canal and Lower
Egypt. The Boer Republics till
1902. The Spanish Zone in Morocco.

Distribution of European Lan-
guages   176

European, African and Asiatic
Migration   177

The World in 1929   179—182

Localities in Western Europe,
connected with American History   184

Localities in England, connected
with American History   185

Physical Map of North America   186. 187

The Indians in the United States
to 1905   188

Reference Map of the New Eng-
land Colonies, 1607—1760   189
Insets: Rhode Island. Vicinity of
Boston. Vicinity of New York.

European Exploration and Settlement in the United States,
1513—1776   190. 191
Inset: Principal English Grants,
1606—1665.

Reference Map of the Middle
Colonies, 1607—1760   192
Inset: Settlements on the Dela-
ware River.

Reference Map of the Southern
Colonies, 1607—1760   193
Inset: Settlements on the James
River. The Georgian Coast.

PAGE

The British Colonies in North
America, 1763—1775   194
Inset: Middle Colonies.

Campaigns of the American Revolution, 1775—1781   195
Insets: Vicinity of Boston (1775—
1776). The West and South, 1778—
1781.

The United States, 1783—1803   196
Insets: The State of Franklin,
1784—1788. Early Distribution
of the Public Lands (Ohio).

Territorial Expansion of the
United States since 1803   198. 199
Insets: Alaska. Hawaii. Guam.
Samoa Islands. Wake Island.
Midway Island. Virgin Islands.
Porto Rico. The Philippine Islands.

Campaigns of the War of 1812   200
Campaigns of the War of 1812. The
Southwest. Vicinity of Washing-
ton in 1814.

Campaigns of the Mexican War,
1846—1847   201
Inset: Route from Vera Cruz to
Mexico.

The Organization of Territories
in the United States since 1803   202. 203
I. 1803—1810. II. 1810—1835.
III. 1835—1855. IV. Since 1855.

Slavery and the Staple Agricultural Products in the Southern
States, 1790—1860   204

Slavery and Emancipation in the
United States, 1777—1865   206. 207
Inset: The Region South of the
Great Lakes.

Seat of the Civil War, 1861—1865   204
Inset: Vicinity of Gettysburg.

Westward Development of the
United States   210. 211

Canada and Newfoundland   212
Inset: The Arbitration Boundary
between Canada and Alaska.

Mexico, Central America and
the West Indies   213
Inset: Central Mexico.

South America   214. 215
Inset: South America about 1790.

Hispanic America, 1828—1929   216
Inset: The Chilean — Peruvian —
Bolivian Frontier.

XI

CONTENTS

Maps, since 1929, prepared by C. S. Hammond & Company

Europe, 1930-1939 218

The Far East, 1930-1941 218

European Theater of War
1939-1945 219

Far Eastern Theater of War
1939-1945 219

The World at War, 1939-1945 ...... 220. 221

The World of the United Nations
and the Cold War, 1945-1967 .... 222. 223

Retreat of Colonialism in the
Postwar Period 224. 225

Europe in 1967 226

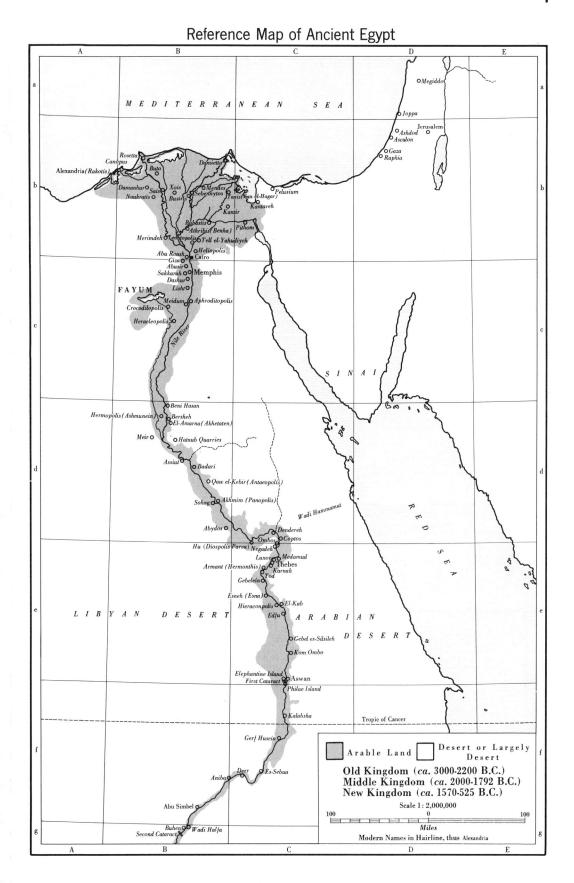

Reference Map of Ancient Egypt

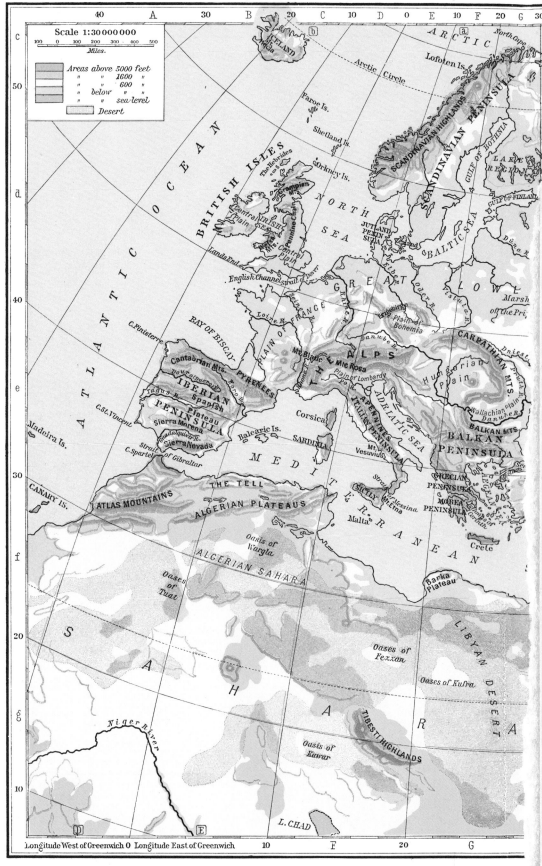

Scale 1:30 000 000

100   0   100   200   300   400   500
Miles.

Areas above 5000 feet
"   "   1600 "
"   "   600   "
"   below   sea-level "
Desert

ATLANTIC OCEAN

ICELAND

Arctic Circle

ARCTIC

North Cape

Lofoten Is.

SCANDINAVIAN HIGHLANDS

SCANDINAVIAN PENINSULA

Faroe Is.

Shetland Is.

GULF OF BOTHNIA

LAKE REGION

BRITISH ISLES

The Hebrides

Orkney Is.

NORTH SEA

GULF OF FINLAND

Grampian

Central Plain

IRISH SEA

Pennine Chain

Central Plain

JUTLAND PENINSULA

BALTIC SEA

Düna R.

Lands End

Elbe R.

Oder R.

Vistula R.

LOW

English Channel Strait of Dover

Marsh of the Pri

GREAT

Loire R.

FRANCE

Seine R.

Plain of Bohemia

CARPATHIAN MTS.

BAY OF BISCAY

PYRENEES

PLAIN OF

C. Finisterre

Mt Blanc Mte Rosa

ALPS

Hungarian Plain

Dniester

Pruth R.

Cantabrian Mts.

Douro or Duero R.

Ebro R.

Rhone R.

Plain of Lombardy
Po R.

Tagus R.

IBERIAN

Spanish

PENINSULA

Plateau

Wallachian Plain
Danube R.

Sierra Morena

APENNINES

ITALIAN PENINSULA

ADRIATIC SEA

BALKAN MTS.

Corsica

BALKAN PENINSULA

C. St. Vincent

Guadalquivir R.

Sierra Nevada

Balearic Is.

SARDINIA

Madeira Is.

Strait of Gibraltar

C. Spartel

MEDITERRANEAN

Mt. Vesuvius

GRECIAN PENINSULA

AEGEAN

CANARY IS.

ATLAS MOUNTAINS

THE TELL

ALGERIAN PLATEAUS

Strait of Messina

SICILY Mt. Etna

Malta

MOREA PENINSULA

Crete

SAHARA

Oasis of Wargla

ALGERIAN SAHARA

Barka Plateau

LIBYAN DESERT

Oases of Tuat

Oases of Fezzan

Oases of Kufra

Niger River

TIBESTI HIGHLANDS

Oasis of Kawar

L. CHAD

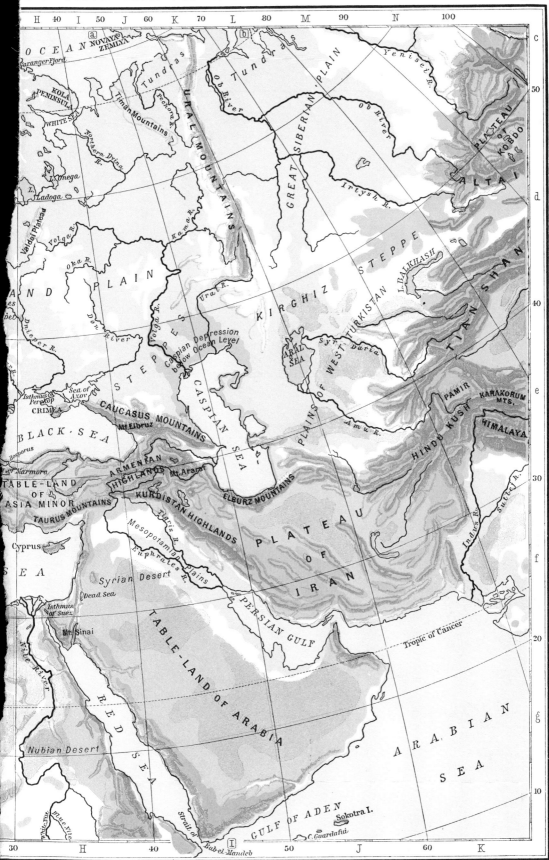

H 40 I 50 J 60 K 70 L 80 M 90 N 100

OCEAN ⓐ NOVAYA ZEMLYA ⓑ c

Varanger Fjord

KOLA PENINSULA

Tundras

Ob Tundras

Yenisei R.

50

WHITE SEA

Timan Mountains

Pechora R.

Northern Dvina R.

URAL MOUNTAINS

Ob River

GREAT SIBERIAN PLAIN

Ob River

Irtysh R.

PLATEAU of KOBDO

ALTAI

d

L. Onega

L. Ladoga

Kama R.

Valdai Plateau

Volga R.

Oka R.

KIRGHIZ STEPPE

L. BALKHASH

TIAN SHAN

AND PLAIN

Dnieper R.

Don River

Ural R.

Volga R.

S T E P P E S

Caspian Depression below Ocean Level

ARAL SEA

Syr Daria

PLAINS OF WEST-TURKISTAN

40

PAMIR

KARAKORUM MTS.

e

Sea of Azov

Isthmus of Perekop

CRIMEA

CAUCASUS MOUNTAINS

Mt Elbruz

CASPIAN SEA

Amu R.

HINDU KUSH

HIMALAYA

BLACK SEA

Bosporus

ARMENIAN HIGHLANDS

Mt.Ararat

ELBURZ MOUNTAINS

30

Sea of Marmora

TABLE-LAND OF ASIA MINOR

KURDISTAN HIGHLANDS

Indus R.

Sutlej R.

TAURUS MOUNTAINS

Tigris R.

P L A T E A U

Cyprus

Mesopotamian Plains

Euphrates R.

OF

f

SEA

Syrian Desert

I R A N

Dead Sea

Isthmus of Suez

PERSIAN GULF

20

Mt. Sinai

Tropic of Cancer

Nile River

TABLE-LAND OF ARABIA

RED SEA

g

Nubian Desert

A R A B I A N

S E A

10

White Nile

Blue Nile

Strait of Bab-el-Mandeb

ⓘ

GULF OF ADEN

Sokotra I.

C. Guardafui

30 H 40 50 J 60 K

Mycenean Greece and The Orient, 2100—1300 B.C.

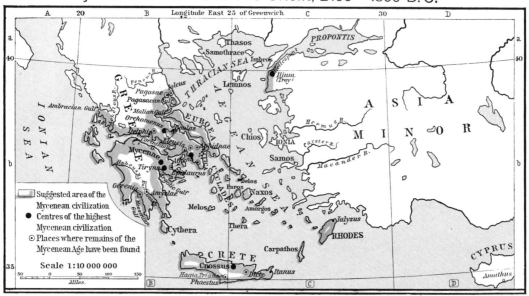

The Ancient Near East ca. 1375 B.C.

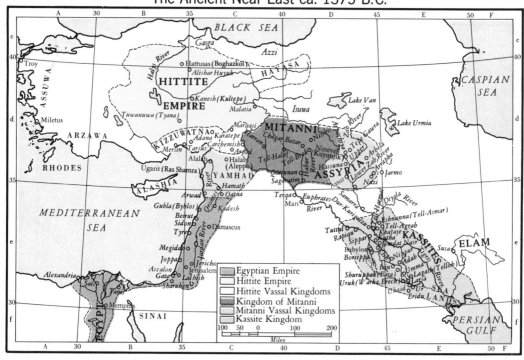

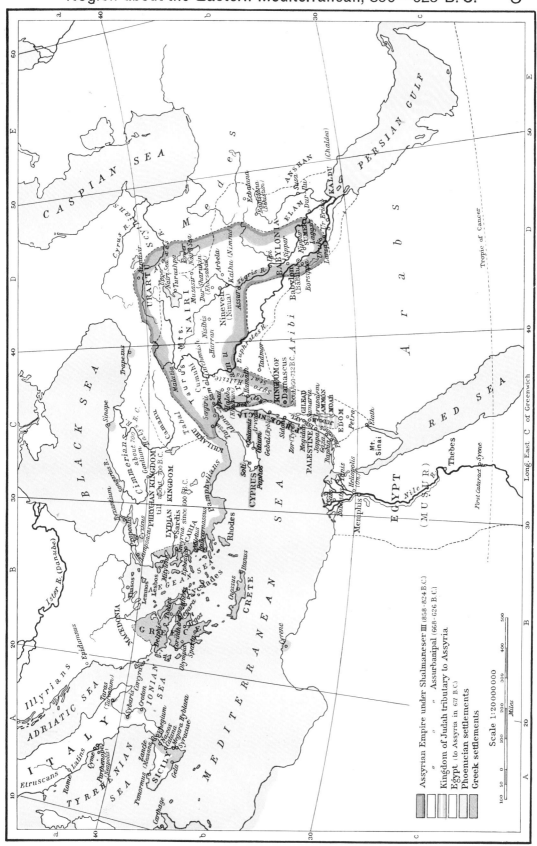

Scale 1:20000000

Assyrian Empire under Shalmaneser III (858-824 B.C.)
"   " Assurbanipal (668-626 B.C.)
Kingdom of Judah tributary to Assyria.
Egypt (to Assyria in 671 B.C.)
Phoenician settlements
Greek settlements

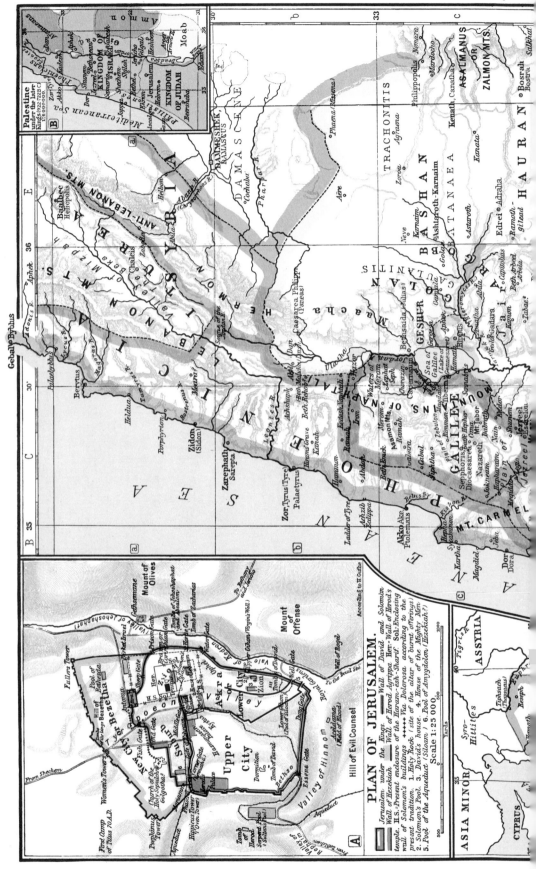

PLAN OF JERUSALEM.

Jerusalem under the Kings: ▬▬ Wall of David and Solomon.
Wall of Hezekiah. ▬▬ Wall of Herod Agrippa. Herr. Wall of Herod's
temple. H.S.=Present enclosure of the Haram-esh-Sharif. Sol.=Enclosing
wall of Solomon's buildings. +++++ Via Dolorosa, according to the
present tradition. 1. Holy Rock (site of the altar of burnt offerings)
2. Solomon's Pool. 3. David's house. 4. House of the Mighty Men
5. Pool of the Aqueduct (Siloam) 6. Pool of Amygdalon (Hezekiah?)

Scale 1:25,000.

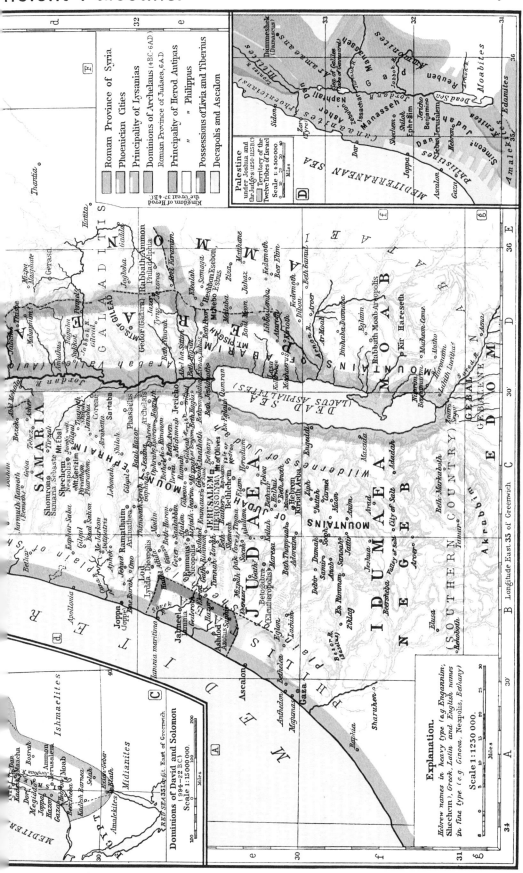

Palestine under Joshua and the Judges 1250-1125 B.C.
Scale 1:4500000
Territory of the Twelve Tribes of Israel

Roman Province of Syria
Phoenician Cities
Principality of Lysanias
Dominions of Archelaus (4 BC-6 AD)
Roman Province of Judaea, 6 AD
Principality of Herod Antipas and Tiberius
"   " Philippus
Possessions of Livia and Ascalon
Decapolis and Ascalon
Kingdom of Herod the Great 37-4 BC.

Dominions of David and Solomon (994-22 BC)
Scale 1:15000000

Explanation.
Hebrew names in heavy type (e.g. Engannim, Shechem), Greek, Latin and English names in fine type (e.g. Ginæa, Neapolis, Bethany)
Scale 1:1250000.

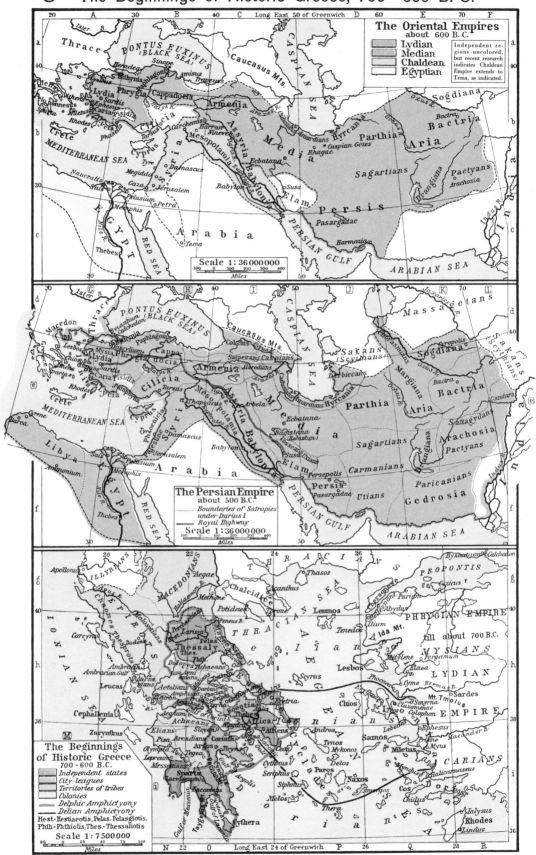

The Oriental Empires
about 600 B. C.

Lydian
Median
Chaldean
Egyptian

Independent regions uncolored, but recent research indicates Chaldean Empire extends to Tema, as indicated.

Scale 1:36000000

The Persian Empire
about 500 B. C.
.... Boundaries of Satrapies under Darius I
——— Royal Highway
Scale 1:36000000

The Beginnings of Historic Greece
700-600 B. C.
Independent states
City-leagues
Territories of tribes
Colonies
——— Delphic Amphictyony
——— Delian Amphictyony
Hest.-Hestiaeotis, Pelas.-Pelasgiotis, Phth.-Phthiotis, Thes.-Thessaliotis
Scale 1:7500000

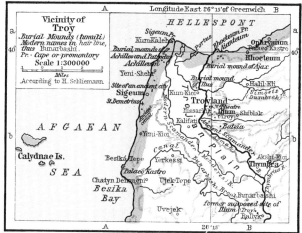

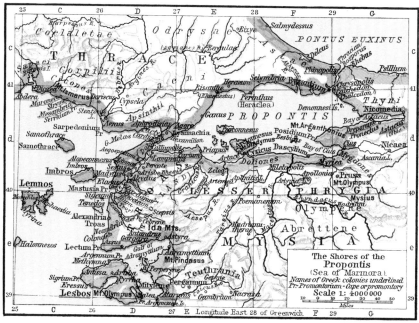

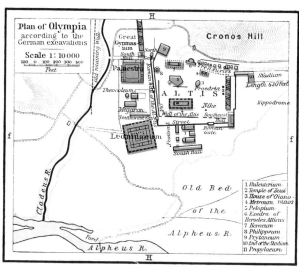

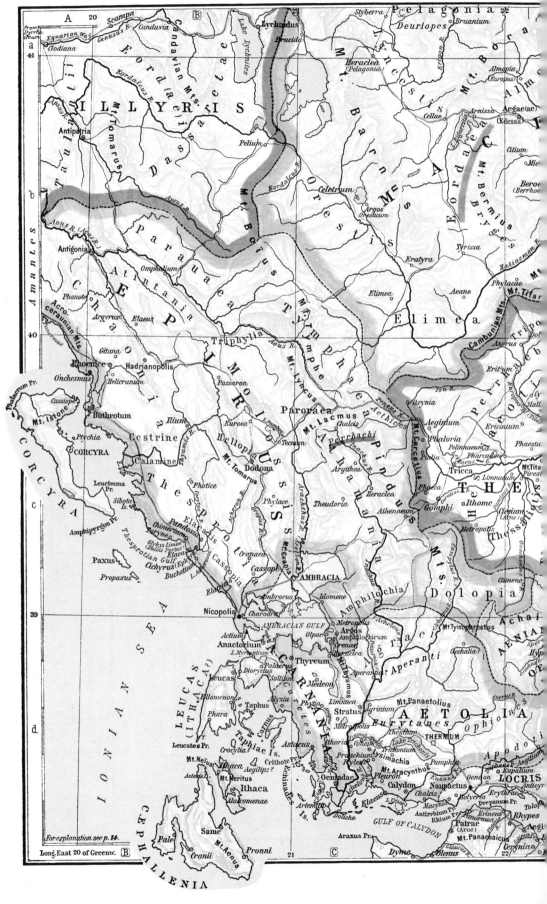

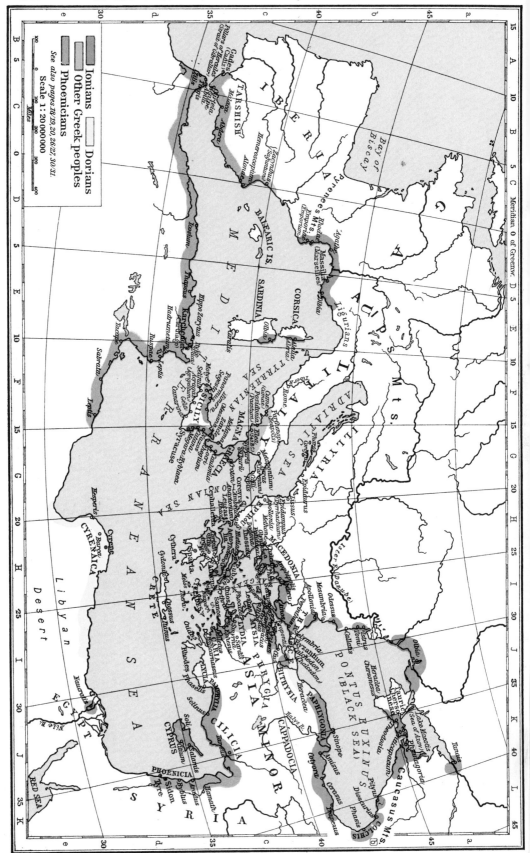

Greece at the Time of the War with Persia.
The Athenian Empire at its Height.

13

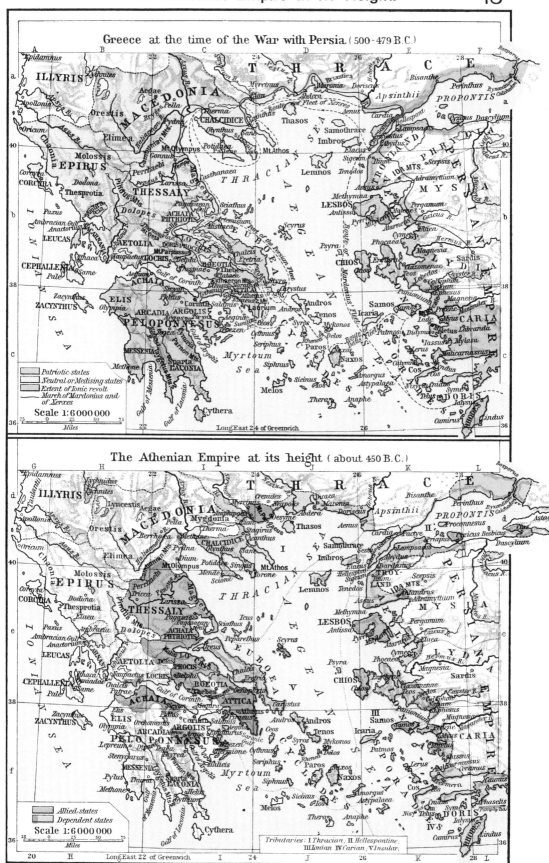

Greece at the time of the War with Persia. (500-479 B.C.)

Patriotic states
Neutral or Medising states
Extent of Ionic revolt
March of Mardonius and of Xerxes

Scale 1:6 000 000

The Athenian Empire at its height (about 450 B.C.)

Allied states
Dependent states

Scale 1:6 000 000

Tributaries: I Thracian, II Hellespontine, III Ionian, IV Carian, V Insular.

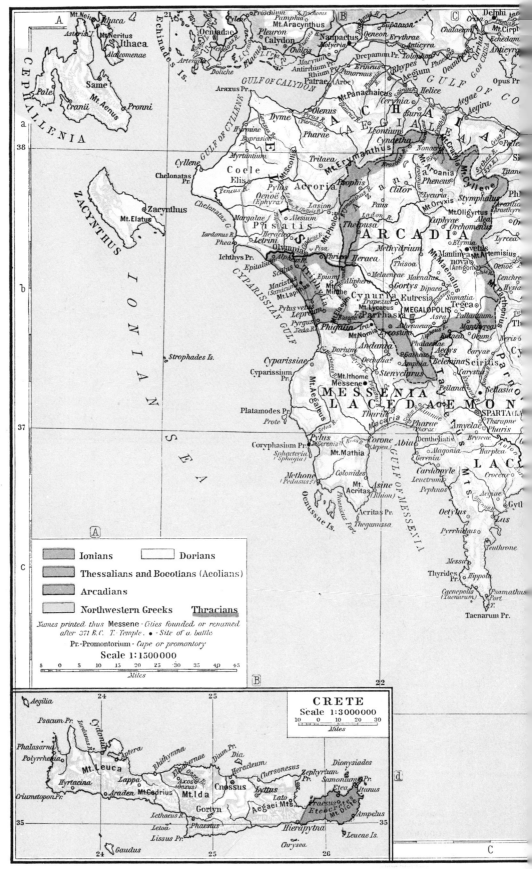

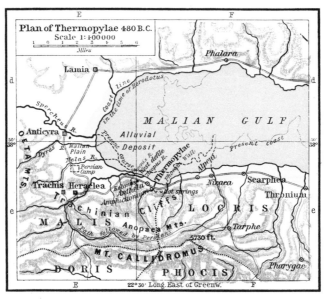

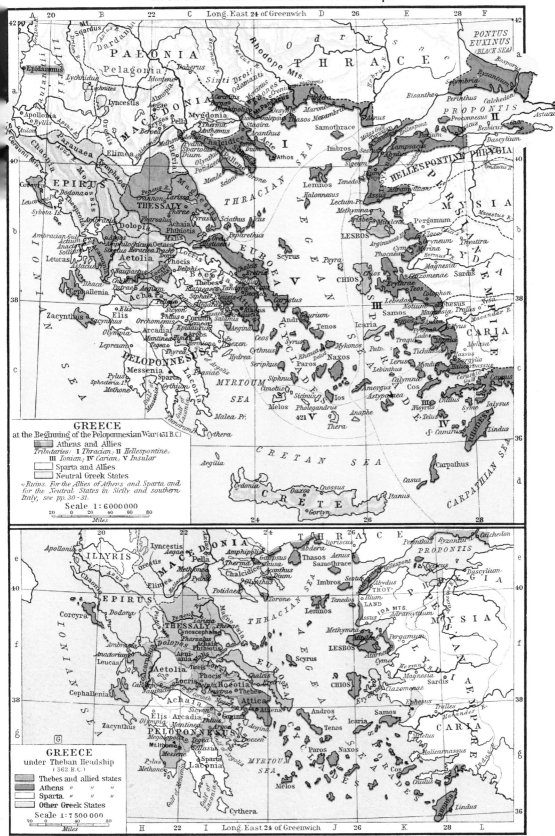

GREECE
at the Beginning of the Peloponnesian War (431 B.C.)
Athens and Allies
Tributaries: I *Thracian*; II *Hellespontine*;
III *Ionian*; IV *Carian*; V *Insular*
Sparta and Allies
Neutral Greek States
∴ *Ruins. For the Allies of Athens and Sparta, and*
for the Neutral States in Sicily and southern
Italy, see pp. 30–31.
Scale 1: 6000000
20 0 20 40 60 80
Miles

GREECE
under Theban Headship
(362 B.C.)
Thebes and allied states
Athens " " "
Sparta " " "
Other Greek States
Scale 1: 7500000
20 0 40 80
Miles

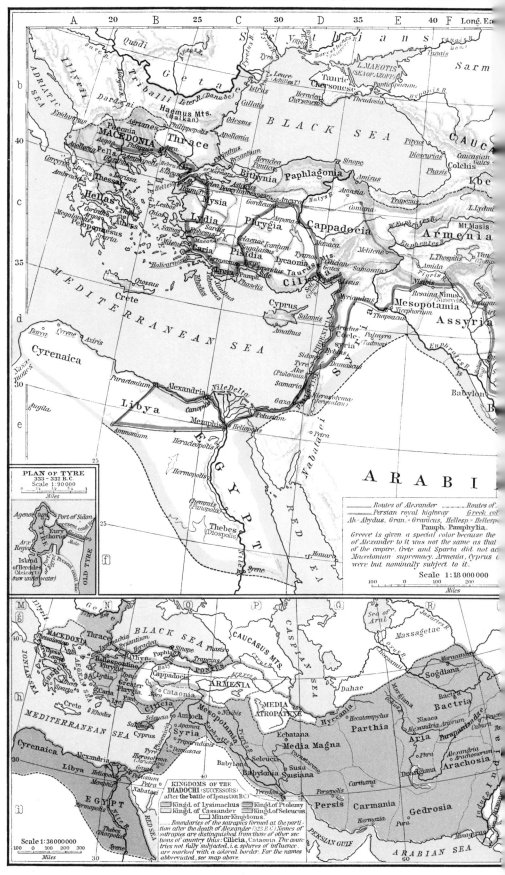

PLAN OF TYRE
333 - 332 B.C.
Scale 1:90 000

KINGDOMS OF THE
DIADOCHI (SUCCESSORS)
after the battle of Ipsus (301 B.C.)
Kingd. of Lysimachus — Kingd. of Ptolemy
Kingd. of Cassander — Kingd. of Seleucus
Minor Kingdoms.
Boundaries of the satrapies formed at the partition after the death of Alexander (323 B.C.) Names of
satrapies are distinguished from those of other sections of country thus: Cilicia, Catania. The countries not fully subjected, i.e. spheres of influence,
are marked with a colored border. For the names
abbreviated, see map above.

Scale 1:36 000 000

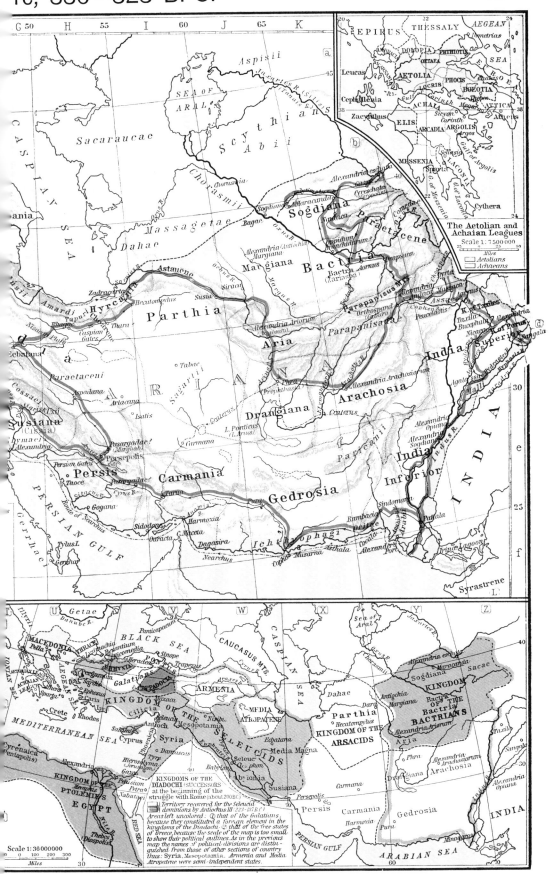

The Aetolian and
Achaian Leagues
Scale 1:7 500 000

KINGDOMS OF THE
DIADOCHI (SUCCESSORS)
at the beginning of the
struggle with Rome (about 200 B.C.)
Territory recovered for the Seleucid
dominions by Antiochus III (223-187 B.C.)
Areas left uncolored: ① that of the Galatians
because they constituted a foreign element in the
kingdoms of the Diadochi; ② that of the free states
of Greece, because the scale of the map is too small
to show their political outlines. As in the previous
map the names of political divisions are distinguished from those of other sections of country:
thus, Syria, Mesopotamia, Armenia and Media
Atropatene were semi-independent states.

Scale 1:36 000 000
0   100   200   300
Miles

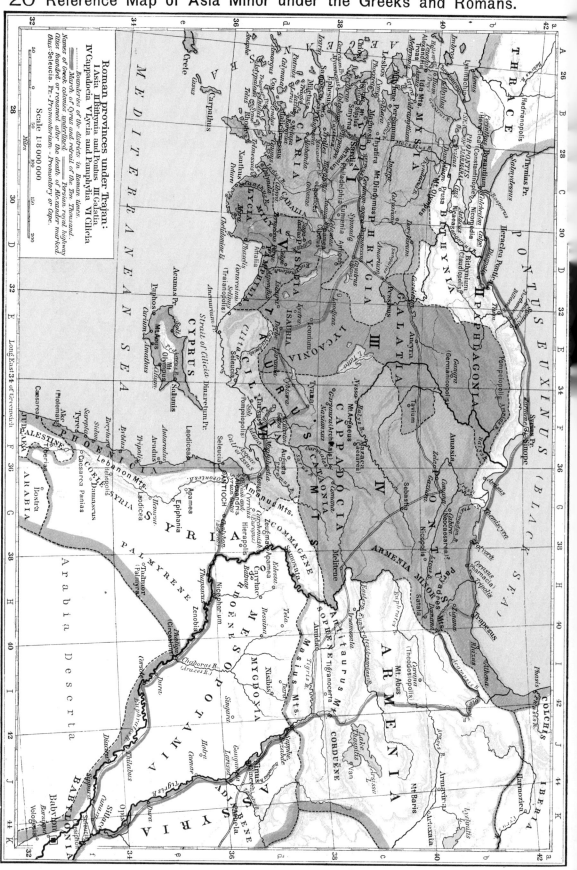

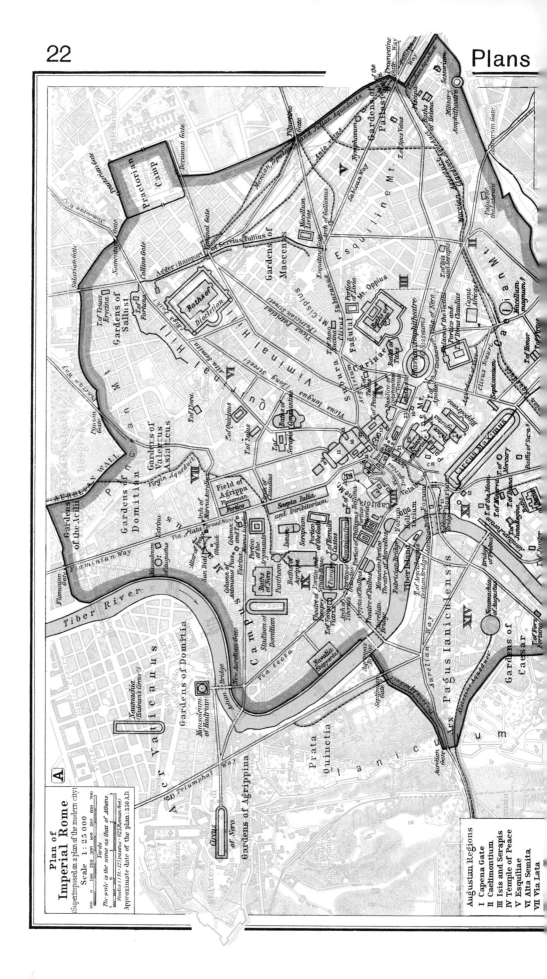

Plan of
Imperial Rome
(Superimposed on a plan of the modern city)
Scale 1 : 25 000

The scale is the same as that of Athens.
Stadia 1 St.=125 passus =625 Roman ft.
Approximate date of the plan : 350 A.D.

Augustan Regions
I Capena Gate
II Caelimontium
III Isis and Serapis
IV Temple of Peace
V Esquiliae
VI Alta Semita
VII Via Lata

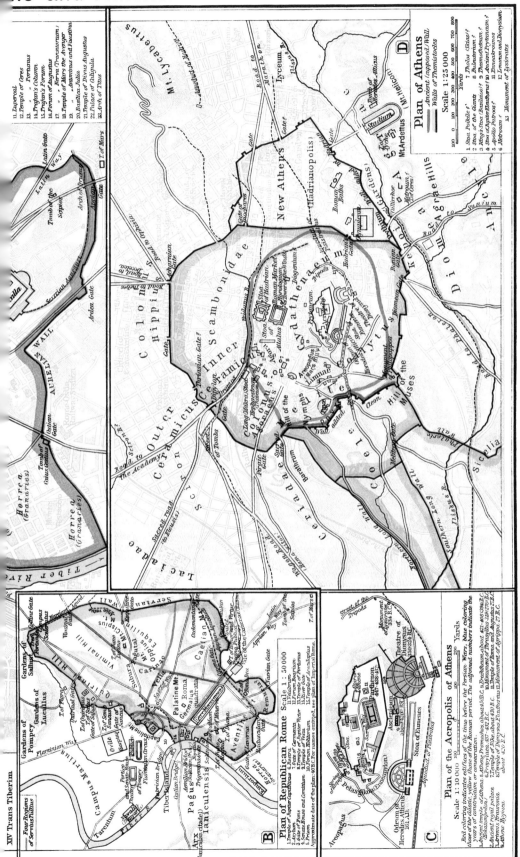

Plan of Athens

Ancient (supposed) Wall
Walls of Themistocles

Scale 1:25 000

Yards
0 100 200 300 400 500 600 700 800

1 Stoa Pœcile?
2 Stoa of the Giants
3 King's Stoa (Basileios)?
4 Stoa of Jupiter Eleutherios?
5 Stoa of Jupiter Eleutherios?
6 Metroum?

7 Tholos (Skias)?
8 Buleuterium?
9 Thesmotheteum?
10 Ancient Prytaneum?
11 Eneacrounos
12 Leneum and Dionysium
13 Monument of Lysicrates

Plan of Republican Rome   Scale 1:50 000

1 Temple of Jupiter Capitolinus
2 Rostra
3 Gate of Janus
4 Senate House and Comitium
5 Prison

6 Dosra
7 Temple of Vesta
8 Temple of Castor
9 Temple of Vesta
10 Forum Boarium

11 Velabrum
12 Temple of Carmenta
13 Temple of Jupiter Victor
14 Temple of Portunus
15 Temple of Aesculapius

Approximate date of the plan: 40 B.C. For names omitted, see plan of Imperial Rome.

Plan of the Acropolis of Athens

Scale 1:10 000   Yards

Red coloring indicates edifices of the time before the Persian Wars, blue coloring those of the classic, yellow those of the Roman period. The adjoined numbers indicate the
1 Ancient temple of Athena
(Hekatompedon)
2 Ancient royal palace
3 Temenos Pandrosia
4 Altar Hyecœus

5 Athene Promachos about 450 B.C.
6 Propylaea 437–432 B.C.
7 Temple of Nike about 430 B.C.
8 Temple of Dionysus Eleuthereus
about 420 B.C.

9 Erechtheum about 421–408 B.C.
10 Monument of Thrasyllus 319/270 B.C.
11 Temple of Roma and Augustus 27 B.C.
12 Monument of Agrippa 27 B.C.

XIV Trans Tiberim

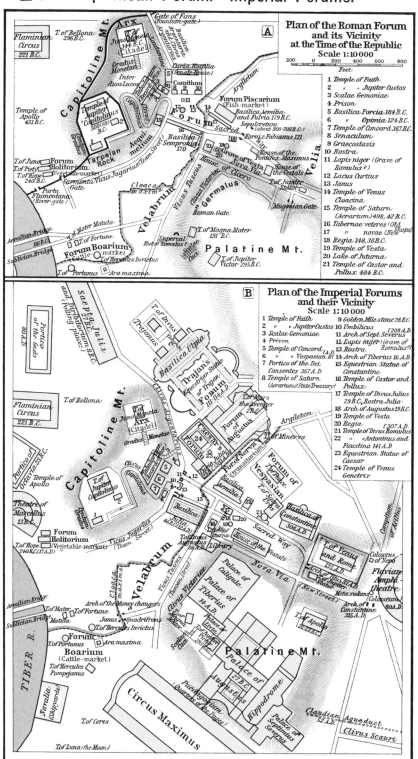

**Plan of the Roman Forum
and its Vicinity
at the Time of the Republic**
Scale 1:10 000

200   0   200   400   600   800
Feet

1. Temple of Faith
2.   "   " Jupiter Custos
3. Scalae Gemoniae
4. Prison
5. Basilica Porcia 184 B.C.
6.   "   Opimia 124 B.C.
7. Temple of Concord 367 B.C.
8. Senaculum
9. Graecostasis
10. Rostra
11. Lapis niger (Grave of Romulus ?)
12. Lacus Curtius
13. Janus
14. Temple of Venus Cloacina
15. Temple of Saturn (Aerarium) 498, 42 B.C.
16. Tabernae veteres (Old Shops)
17.   "   novae (New Shops)
18. Regia 148, 36 B.C.
19. Temple of Vesta
20. Lake of Juturna
21. Temple of Castor and Pollux 484 B.C.

**Plan of the Imperial Forums
and their Vicinity**
Scale 1:10 000

1. Temple of Faith
2.   "   " Jupiter Custos
3. Scalae Gemoniae
4. Prison
5. Temple of Concord   [203 A.D.
6.   "   " Vespasian 81
7. Portico of the Dei Consentes 367 A.D.
8. Temple of Saturn (Aerarium)(State Treasury)
9. Golden Milestone 28 B.C.
10. Umbilicus
11. Arch of Sept. Severus
12. Lapis niger (Grave of Romulus ?)
13. Rostra
14. Arch of Tiberius 16 A.D.
15. Equestrian Statue of Constantine
16. Temple of Castor and Pollux
17. Temple of Divus Julius 29 B.C., Rostra Julia
18. Arch of Augustus 19 B.C.
19. Temple of Vesta
20. Regia   [307 A.D.
21. Temple of Divus Romulus
22.   "   " Antoninus and Faustina 141 A.D.
23. Equestrian Statue of Caesar
24. Temple of Venus Genetrix

The dates given are those of the construction or consecration of the buildings.

Scale 1:2 500 000

10   0   10   20   30   40   50
Miles

Greek colonies   Phoenician colonies
Roman colonies before the civil wars (See also p. 29)
Of the two northern boundaries of Italy and of
Etruria, the more southerly is that of the
period before Augustus, and the more northerly
that of the period after Augustus.
Modern names of passes thus [Julier]
Pr.-Promontorium - Cape or promontory

The Growth of Roman Power in Italy to 218 B.C.

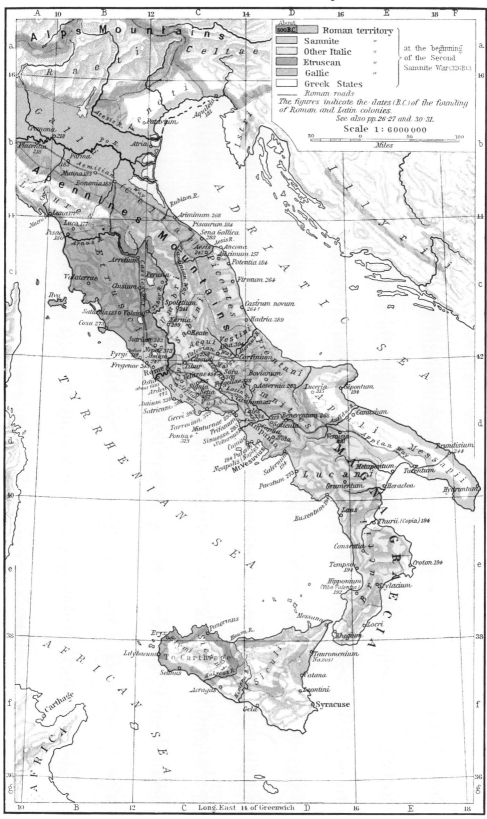

About 500 B.C. ▨ **Roman territory** "
◻ **Samnite** "
◻ **Other Italic** "
◼ **Etruscan** "
◼ **Gallic** "
◻ **Greek States**

at the beginning of the Second Samnite War (326 B.C.)

— — Roman roads

The figures indicate the dates (B.C.) of the founding of Roman and Latin colonies.
See also pp. 26-27 and 30-31.

Scale 1 : 6 000 000

Miles

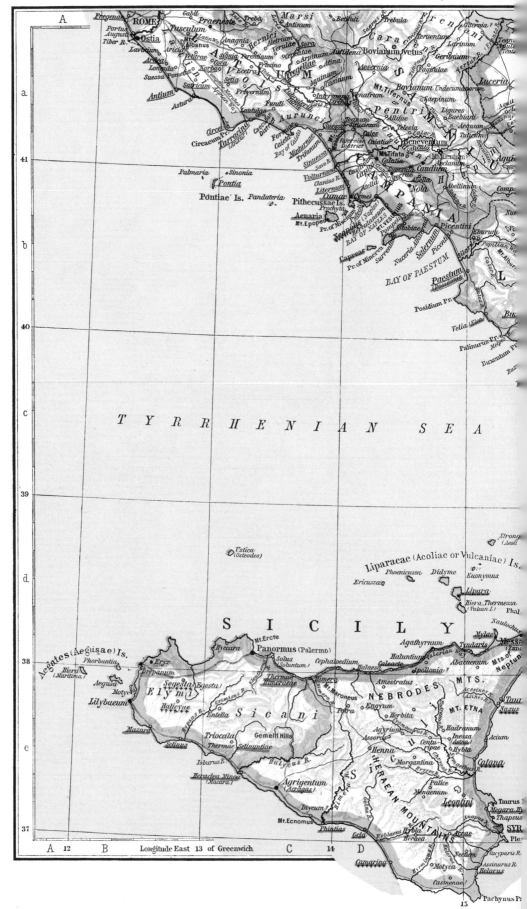

Map labels (clockwise and by region):

F 17 G 18 H 19 I

Merinum
Apenestae
Garganum Pr.
GANUS
Matinum
Sipontum
L. of Salapia
Salapia
Aufidena
Barduli
Cannae Turenum
Canusium
AUFIDUS
Rubi
Butuntum
Grumum
Barium
Caelia
Neapolis
Axetium
Gnatia (Egnatia)
APPIAN WAY
Silvium
Blera
PEUCETII
APULIA
Bantia
Bradanus R.
Casuentus R.
Genusia
Anxia
Acalander R.
Metapontum
Pandosia
Aciris R.
Siris R.
Heraclea
Siris
Nerulum
Muranum
Interamnium
Cuprasia
Sybaris
Crathis R.
Thurii (Col. Copia)
Roscianum
Paternum
Crimisa Pr.
Crimisa
Consentia
Petelia
Neaethus R.
Ad Sabatum
Croton
Lacinium Pr.
Dioscurias Pr.
Castra Hannibalis
Scolacium (Scylacium)
GULF OF SCYLACIUM
Cocynthum Pr.
Caulonia
Mamertium
Locri Epizephyrii
Zephyrium Pr.
Pr. of Hercules
Sturni Trajan's Way
Caelia
CALABRIA
Brundisium
Barra I.
Tarentum (Taras)
(Col. Neptunia)
Uria
Manduria
Rudiae
Lupiae
Neretum
Callipolis (Calata)
Aletium
Uxentum
Veretum (Baris)
Leuca
Sallentinum (Iapygium) Pr.
APPIAN WAY
MESSAPII SALLENTINI
Valetium (Balesium)
Hydruntum
Castrum Minervae
Oricum

ADRIATIC SEA

GULF OF TARENTUM

ILLYRICUM
Lissus
Drilon R.
Mathis R.
Bassania
Pistum
Dyrrhachium (Epidamnus)
EGNATIAN WAY
Clodiana
Genusus R.
Arnisus
Marusium
Apsus
Apsus R.
Apollonia
Aous R.
Sason
Byllis
Acroceraunia Pr.
Aulon
ACROCERAUNIAN MTS.

a
41
b
40
c

H   I

Vicinity of Naples   [A]

Phlegraean Fields
Mt.Gaurus
Cyme Cumae
Astroni
Mte Nuovo
Naples
Avernus L.
Lucrinus L.
Acherusia L.
Forum Vulcani (Solfatara)
Palaeopolis
Megaris
Vergil's Grave
Bauli
Baiae
Dicaearchia, Puteoli
Nesis
Mte Posilipo
Harbor of Misenum
Pausilypum
Prom. of Misenum

Scale 1:300 000
Miles
Present area of Naples
Modern names in hair-line

Plan of Syracuse   [B]

At the time of the Peloponnesian War (431–404 B.C.)
Extension under Dionysius I (405–367 B.C.)

Leontine Way
Trogilus Port
Labdalum
Euryalus EPIPOLAE
Aqueduct
TYCHA
ACHRADINA
NEAPOLIS
Temenites
ORTYGIA (NASOS)
Lysimelian Marsh
Anapus
Great Harbor
Shrine of Cyana
Olympieum
Cyane R. POLICHNE
Dascon
Helorine Way
Little Harbor
Greek theatre
PLEMMYRIUM

Scale 1:200 000
Miles

1 Arethusa Spring
2 Temple of Athene
3   "   " Artemis
4 Citadel of Dionysius
5 Pentapylum
6 Forum
7 Stone quarries (Latomiae)
8 Roman amphitheatre
9 Greek theatre
10 Heracleum
11 Hexapylum
12 Temple of Demeter and Persephone

Neapolis Allies of Athens during the
Syracuse   "   " Sparta Peloponnesian War
Croton   Neutral States (431–404 B.C.)
For scale and explanation, see p. 26–27.

Rome and Carthage at the
Beginning of the Second Punic War, 218 B. C.

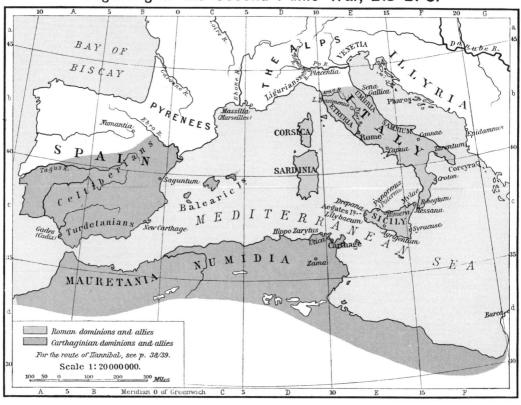

Roman dominions and allies
Carthaginian dominions and allies
For the route of Hannibal, see p. 38/39.
Scale 1 : 20 000 000.
100 50 0 100 200 300 Miles
Meridian 0 of Greenwich

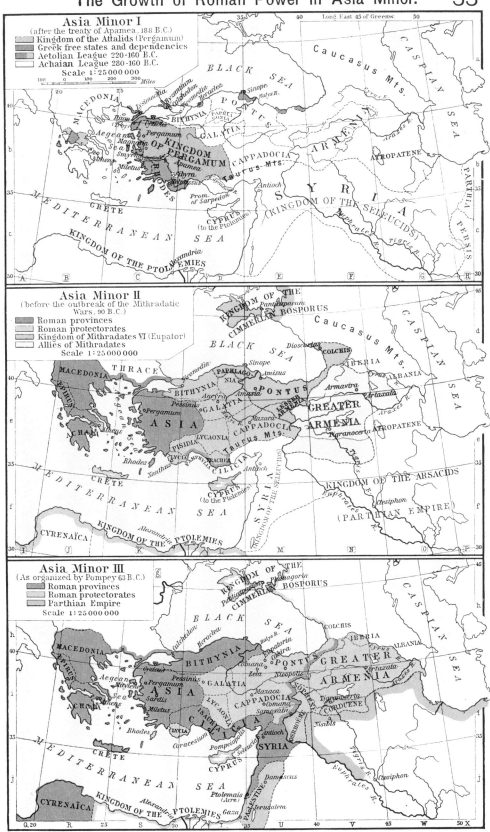

Asia Minor I
(after the treaty of Apamea, 188 B.C.)
- Kingdom of the Attalids (Pergamum)
- Greek free states and dependencies
- Aetolian League 220-160 B.C.
- Achaian League 280-160 B.C.
Scale 1:25 000 000

Asia Minor II
(before the outbreak of the Mithradatic Wars, 90 B.C.)
- Roman provinces
- Roman protectorates
- Kingdom of Mithradates VI (Eupator)
- Allies of Mithradates
Scale 1:25 000 000

Asia Minor III
(As organized by Pompey 63 B.C.)
- Roman provinces
- Roman protectorates
- Parthian Empire
Scale 1:25 000 000

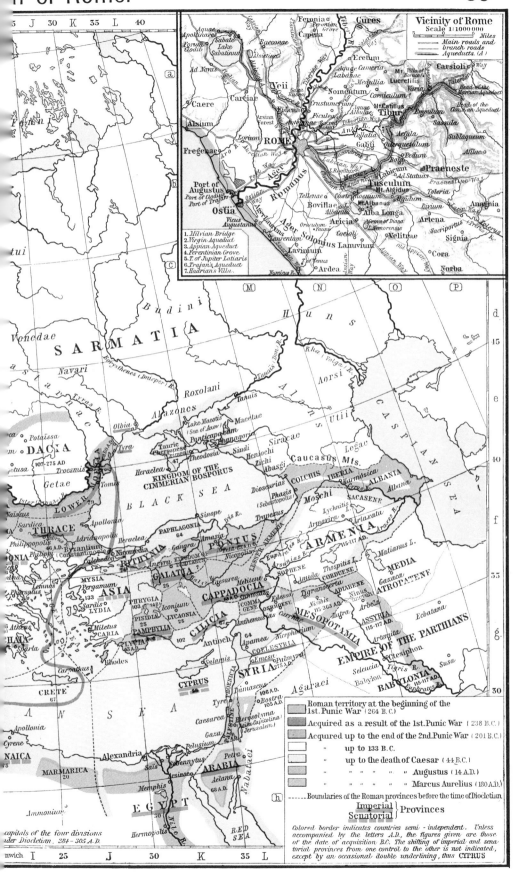

Vicinity of Rome
Scale 1:1000000

Miles

— Main roads and
  branch roads
---- Aqueducts (A)

Feronia
Faustini Grove
Capena
Cures
Eretum
Bucconae
Veii
Carciae
Caere
Fidenae
Alsium
Nomentum
Cumerian Way
Labicana
Mt. Villa of Horace's
Lucretilis
Varia
Corniculum
Crustumerium
Ficulea
Tibur
Emporium
Carsioli
Vale
Head of the Marcian Aqueduct
Head of the Anician Aqueduct
Sassula
Subiaculum
Aefula
Afile
Fregenae
Lorium
ROME
Gabii
Bola
Querquetulum
Pedum
Praeneste
Port of Augustus
Port of Claudius
Port of Trajan
Ostia
Vicus Augustanus
Ager Romanus
Collatia
Labicum
Tusculum
Mt. Algidus
Algidum
Toleria
Bovillae
Mt. Albanus
Alba Longa
Corbio
Livium
Anagnia
Tellenae
Aricia
Grove of Diana
Sacriportus
Artena
Signia
Laurentum
Corioli
Velitrae
Lanuvium
Lavinium
Ardea
Cora
Norba

1. Milvian Bridge
2. Virgin Aqueduct
3. Appian Aqueduct
4. Ferentinian Grove
5. T. of Jupiter Latiaris
6. Trajan's Aqueduct
7. Hadrian's Villa.

Budini
HUNS
SARMATIA
Venedae
Navari
Borysthenes (Dnieper) R.
Roxolani
Alazones
Tyras R.
Olbia
Tyra
Aorsi
Alans
Utii
CASPIAN SEA
Legae
DACIA
107-275 AD
Getae
Troesmis
Tomis
Tauric Chersonese
Theodosia
Panticapaeum
Phanagoria
Lake Maeotis (Sea of Azov)
Maeotae
Siracae
Henochi
Zichi
Abasci
Caucasus Mts.
Albani
ALBANIA
Heraclea
KINGDOM OF THE CIMMERIAN BOSPORUS
Dioscurias (Sebastopolis)
Phasis
COLCHIS
IBERIA
Harmozica
SACASENE
Moschi
BLACK SEA
Sinope
Iris R.
Trapezus
Lychnitis L.
Artaxata
Araxes R.
Naissus
Sardica
THRACE
Apollonia
Adrianopolis
Heraclea
PAPHLAGONIA
Amasia
PONTUS
LESSER ARMENIA
Armavira
ARMENIA
115-117 AD
Matianus L.
Philippopolis
Byzantium
Calchedon
Nicomedia
BITHYNIA
Ancyra
Gangra
KINGDOM OF DEIOTARUS
Nicopolis
Euphrates R.
Arsanias R.
SOPHENE
Thospitis L.
MEDIA
ATROPATENE
Gazaca
MYSIA
Pergamum
ASIA
Caesarea
Melitene
CAPPADOCIA
Amula
CORDUENE
Nisibis
ADIABENE
Arbela
Ecbatana
Sardis
LYDIA
PHRYGIA
Iconium
LYCAONIA
COMMAGENE
Samosata
Edessa
OSRHOENE
Carrhae
MESOPOTAMIA
ASSYRIA
115-117 AD
Ninus
Artemita
Athens
Pharsalus
Miletus
CARIA
PISIDIA
PAMPHYLIA
LYCIA
CILICIA
Anthemusias
Nicephorium
Apamea
COELESYRIA
EMPIRE OF THE PARTHIANS
Ctesiphon
Sparta
Rhodes
Antioch
Palmyra
Seleucia
Tigris R.
Susa
Carpathus
CRETE
SYRIA
Emesa
Babylon
Euphrates R.
BABYLONIA
115-117 AD
Salamis
CYPRUS
PHOENICIA
Tyre
Damascus
Bostra
Agaraei
Apollonia
Cyrene
Caesarea
Gaza
PALESTINE
Hierosolyma (Aelia Capitolina) Jerusalem
Petra
ARABIA
Nabataei
CYRENAICA
Alexandria
Sais
Pelusium
MARMARICA
Sebennytus
Arsinoe
Aelana
Memphis
Ammonium
EGYPT
Hermopolis
RED SEA
Nile R.

Roman territory at the beginning of the
1st. Punic War (264 B.C.)

Acquired as a result of the 1st. Punic War (238 B.C.)

Acquired up to the end of the 2nd. Punic War (201 B.C.)

"   "   up to 133 B.C.

"   "   up to the death of Caesar (44 B.C.)

"   "   "   "   "   Augustus (14 A.D.)

"   "   "   "   "   Marcus Aurelius (180 A.D.)

----- Boundaries of the Roman provinces before the time of Diocletian

Imperial } Provinces
Senatorial }

capitals of the four divisions
under Diocletian, 284-305 A.D.

Colored border indicates countries semi-independent. Unless
accompanied by the letters A.D., the figures given are those
of the date of acquisition B.C. The shifting of imperial and senatorial provinces from one control to the other is not indicated,
except by an occasional double underlining, thus CYPRUS

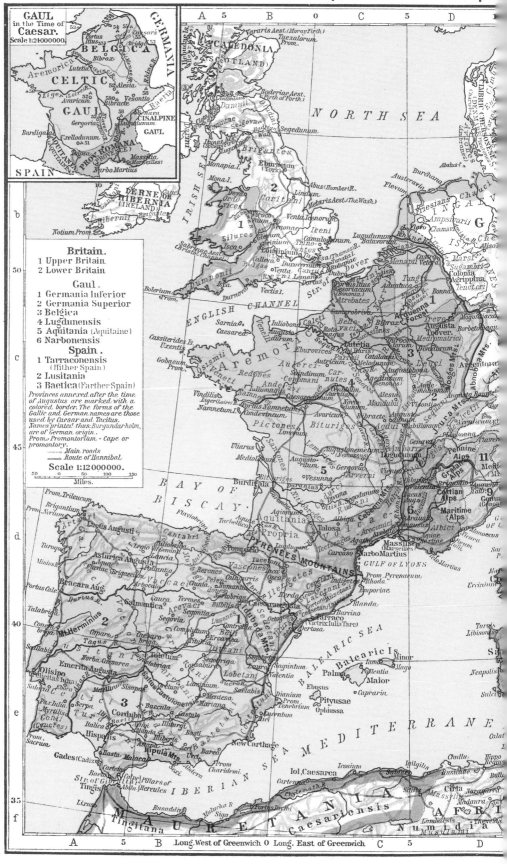

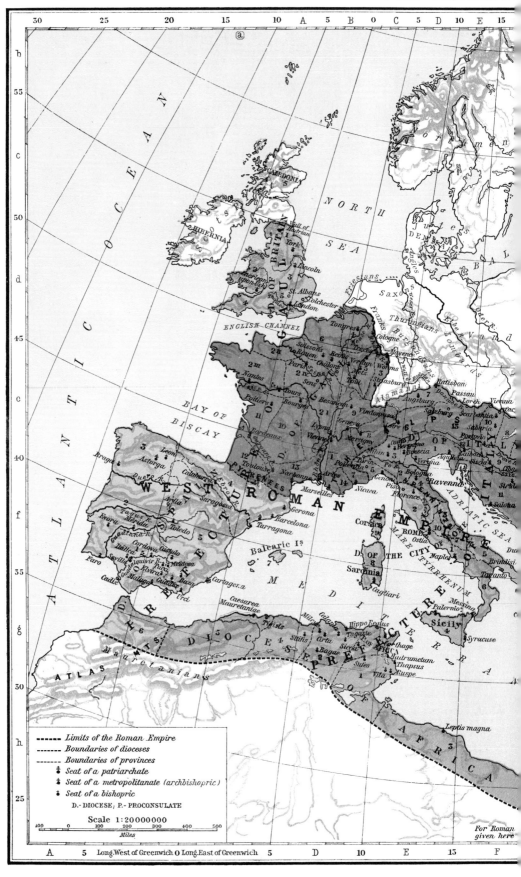

Scale 1:20000000

Limits of the Roman Empire
Boundaries of dioceses
Boundaries of provinces
⚜ Seat of a patriarchate
⚜ Seat of a metropolitanate (archbishopric)
⚜ Seat of a bishopric

D.- DIOCESE; P.- PROCONSULATE

100 0 100 200 300 400 500
Miles

For Roman
given here

A 5 Long. West of Greenwich 0 Long. East of Greenwich 5 D 10 E 15 F

Provinces

PREFECTURE OF GAUL

DIOCESE OF SPAIN
1. *Baetica*, 2. *Lusitania*, 3. *Galicia*, 4. *Tarraconensis*, 5. *Carthaginiensis*, 6. *Mauretania Tingitana* 7. *Balearic Isles.*

DIOCESE OF GAUL
1. *Viennensis*, 2. *Lugdunensis*, 3, 4. *Germania I. II,* 5, 6. *Belgica I. II,* 7. *Maritime Alps,* 8. *Pennine and Graian Alps,* 9. *Maxima Sequanorum,* 10, 11. *Aquitaine I. II,* 12. *Novempopulana,* 13, 14. *Narbonnensis I. II,*

DIOCESE OF BRITAIN
1. *Maxima Caesariensis,* 2. *Valentia,* 3, 4. *Britain I. II,* 5. *Flavia Caesariensis.*

PREFECTURE OF ITALY

DIOCESE OF AFRICA
1. *Byzacium,* 2. *Numidia,* 3. *Tripolitana,* 4. *Mauretania Sitifensis* 5. *Mauretania Caesariensis*

DIOCESE OF THE CITY OF ROME
1. *Campania,* 2. *Tuscany and Umbria,* 3 *Picenum Suburbicarium,* 4. *Sicily,*

5. *Apulia and Calabria,* 6. *Bruttia and Lucania,* 7. *Samnium,* 8. *Sardinia,* 9. *Corsica,* 10. *Valeria.*

DIOCESE OF ITALY
1. *Venetia and Istria,* 2. *Aemilia,* 3. *Liguria,* 4. *Flaminia and Picenum Annonarium,* 5. *Cottian Alps,* 6, 7. *Raetia I. II,* 8. *Pannonia II,* 9. *Savia,* 10. *Pannonia I,* 11. *Dalmatia,* 12. *Noricum mediterraneum,* 13. *Noricum ripense,* 14. *Valeria ripensis*

PROCONSULATE of AFRICA

PREFECTURE of ILLYRICUM

DIOCESE OF MACEDONIA
1. *Macedonia,* 2. *Crete,* 3. *Thessaly,* 4. *Epirus vetus,* 5. *Epirus nova,* 6. *Macedonia Salutaris.*

DIOCESE OF DACIA
1. *Dacia mediterranea,* 2. *Moesia I,* 3. *Praevalitana,* 4. *Dardania,* 5. *Dacia ripensis.*

PROCONSULATE of ACHAIA

PREFECTURE OF THE EAST

DIOCESE OF EGYPT
1. *Upper Libya,* 2. *Lower Libya,* 3. *Thebais,* 4. *Egypt,* 5. *Arcadia,* 6. *Augustamnica.*

DIOCESE OF THE EAST
1. *Palestine I,* 2. *Phoenicia,* 3. *Syria I,* 4. *Cilicia I,* 5. *Cyprus,* 6. *Palestine II,* 7. *Palestine Salutaris,* 8. *Phoenicia Libani,* 9. *Eufratensis,* 10. *Syria Salutaris,* 11. *Osrhoëne,* 12. *Mesopotamia,* 13. *Cilicia II,* 14. *Isauria,* 15. *Arabia.*

DIOCESE OF PONTUS
1. *Bithynia,* 2. *Galatia,* 3. *Paphlagonia,* 4. *Honorias,* 5. *Galatia Salutaris,* 6, 7. *Cappadocia I. II,* 8. *Helenopontus,* 9. *Pontus Polemoniacus.* 10, 11. *Armenia I. II,*

DIOCESE OF ASIA
1. *Pamphylia,* 2. *Lydia,* 3. *Caria,* 4. *Lycia,* 5. *Lycaonia,* 6. *Pisidia,* 7. *Phrygia Pacatiana,* 8. *Phrygia Salutaris.*

DIOCESE OF THRACE
1. *Europe,* 2. *Thrace,* 3. *Haemimontium,* 4. *Rhodope,* 5. *Moesia II,* 6. *Scythia.*

PROCONSULATE OF ASIA

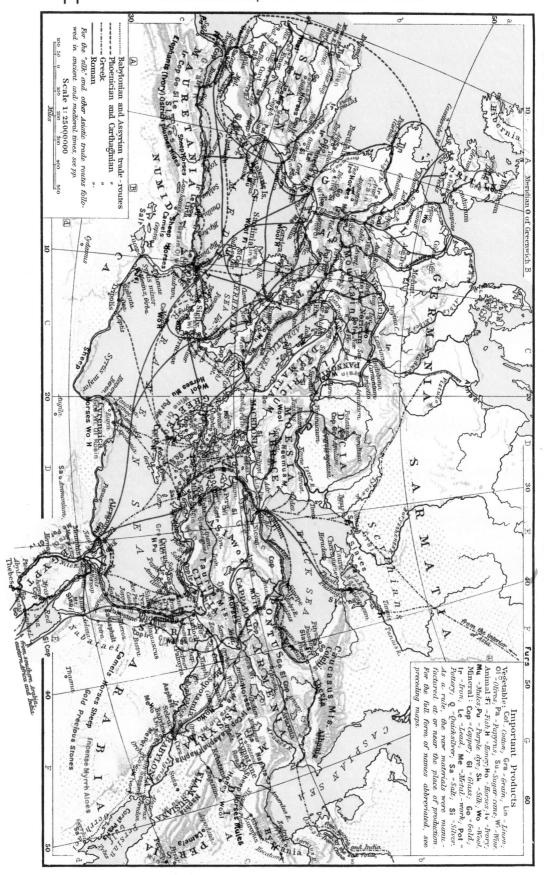

Important Products

Vegetable: Cot=Cotton; Gra=Grain; Lin=Linen;
Ol=Olives; Pa=Papyrus; Su=Sugar-cane;
W.=Wine; Animal: Fi=Fish; H=Honey; Ho=Horses; Iv=Ivory;
Mu=Mules; Pu=Purple dye; Sk=Silk; Wo=Wool;
Mineral: Cop=Copper; Gl=Glass; Go=Gold;
Ir=Iron; Le=Lead; Me=Metal-work; Pot=
Pottery; Q=Quicksilver; Sa=Salt; Si=Silver;
As a rule, the raw materials were manu-
factured at or near the place of production.
For the full form of names abbreviated, see
preceding maps.

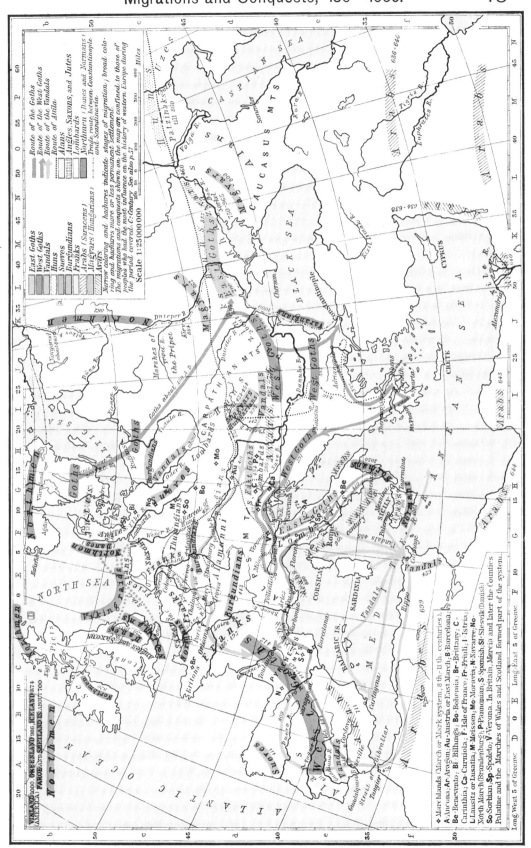

Extent of Christianity about 600 (pontificate of
Gregory I, the Great, 590 - 604)
Area Christianized   600 - 800
"   "   800 - 1100
"   "   1100 - 1300
Damascus   Churches of the apostolic period (33 - 100)
Nicaea   Principal churches of the post apostolic period (100 - 311)
Alexandria   Mission centres in both periods
Antioch
           Journeys of the Apostle Paul
           Peoples converted from Arianism to Catholicism
Figures indicate approximate dates of conversion to Christianity

Scale 1 : 20 000 000

100   0   100   200   300   400
Miles

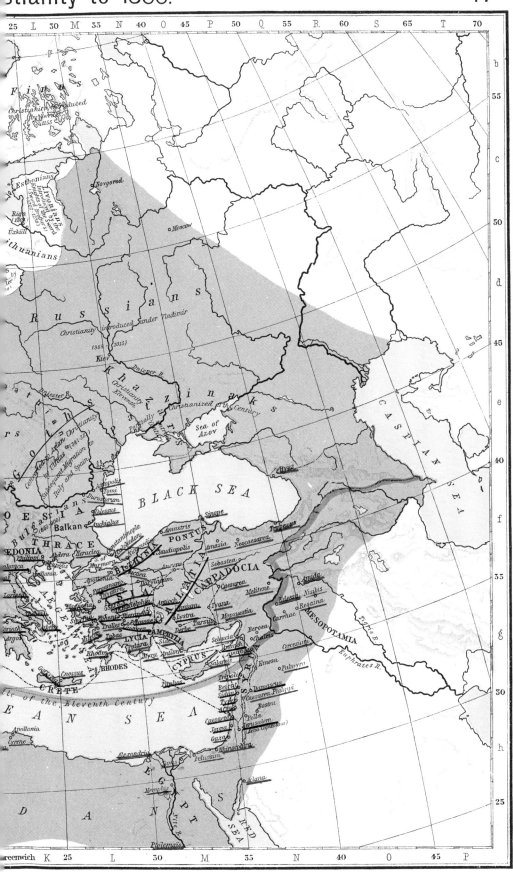

L 30 M 35 N 40 O 45 P 50 Q 55 R 60 S 65 T 70

Fin...

Christianity introduced
Denmark
1155

Estonians

Livonians
Knights of the Sword
Riga
1201
Üxküll

Lithuanians

Novgorod

Moscow

R u s s i a n s

Christianity introduced under Vladimir
(988 1015)

Kiev

Dnieper R.

K h a z a r s

Christianity introduced

Petzinaks

Partially Christianized in 10th Century

Dniester R.

Sea of
Azov

CASPIAN SEA

G o t h s

Converted to Arian Christianity by Ulfilas (341-38)
Subsequent Migration to Italy and Spain

B u l g a r i a n s
(865-000)

BLACK SEA

Halys

Tomi
Durostorum
Odessus
Anchialus
Balkan
THRACE

Abdera Heraclea
Aenus

EDONIA
Philippi
Thessalonica
Apollonia

LARISSA
Madytus
Pergamum

Chios
Smyrna

Corinth
Argos
Ephesus

Miletus
Tralles

RHODES

Cnossus
CRETE

of the Eleventh Century

Apollonia
Cyrene

Sinope

Amastris
Constantinople
Chalcedon
Nicomedia
Nicaea
Claudiopolis

PONTUS
Amasia
Neocaesarea
Trapezus

BITHYNIA

Ancyra
Pessinus

Sardis
Philadelphia
Colossae
Antioch
Iconium
Lystra
Derbe
LYCIA
Patara
Myra
PAMPHYLIA
Side
Attalia
CYPRUS
Paphos
Salamis

GALATIA

Sebastea
CAPPADOCIA
Caesarea
Tyana
Mopsuestia
Tarsus
Seleucia

Antioch
Apamea

Tripolis
Beirut
Sidon
Tyre
Ptolemais
Caesarea
Joppa
Gaza

Amida
Edessa Nisibis
Resaina
Carrhae

MESOPOTAMIA

Berea
Chalcis

Circesium

Euphrates R.

Emesa
Palmyra

Damascus
Caesarea Philippi
Bostra
Pella
Jerusalem
(Aelia Capitolina)

Tigris R.

S
Y
R
I
A

A E G E

Alexandria
Taposiris
Pelusium

E G Y P T

Arsinoe

Memphis

Nile R.

ADANA
S E A

D

Aduna

S
RED
SEA

Ptolemais

Greenwich K 25 L 30 M 35 N 40 O 45 P

b
c
55
50
d
45
e
40
f
35
g
30
h
25

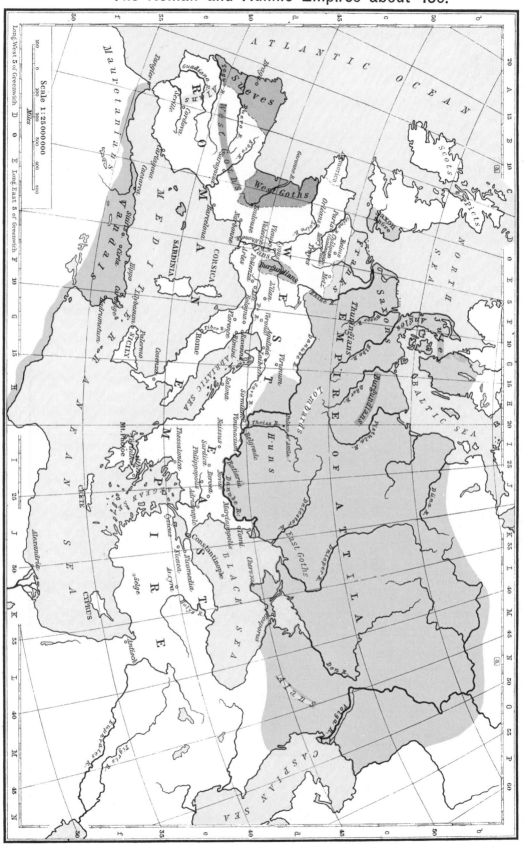

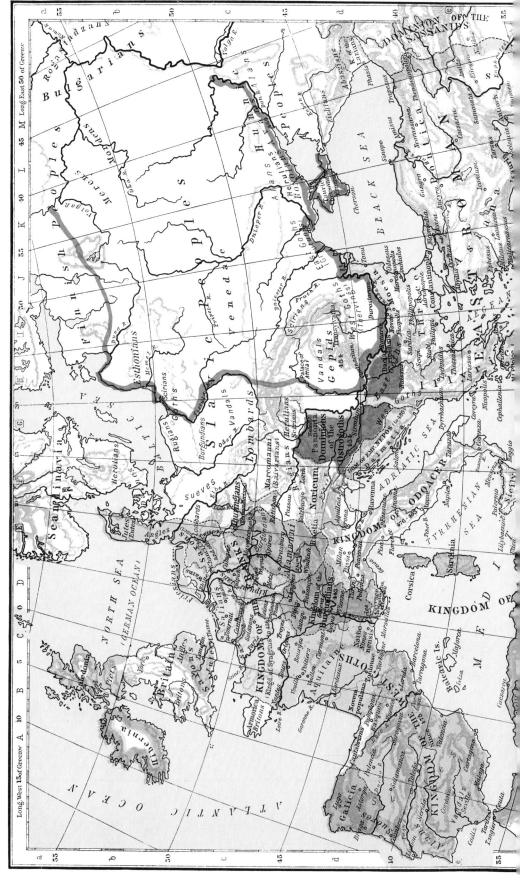

Roman Britain
about 410.

1......2 Routes of Caesar's
expeditions to Britain
(55-54 B.C.)
Roman roads
Names of native tribes thus:
Brigantes
Scale 1:5 000 000

Settlements
of Angles, Saxons and Jutes
in Britain about 600.
See, also, p. 60
Scale 1:10 000 000

The Germanic Kingdoms and the East Roman Empire in 526

The headship of Theodoric and the East Goths over the West Goths is indicated by underlining the name of the latter in white. The colorings of the district occupied by the Alamanni are intended to show how checkered their career was. Of this district the area bordered in green, corresponds roughly to that of the later duchy of Franconia.

Scale 1:30000000

Longitude East 10 of Greenwich

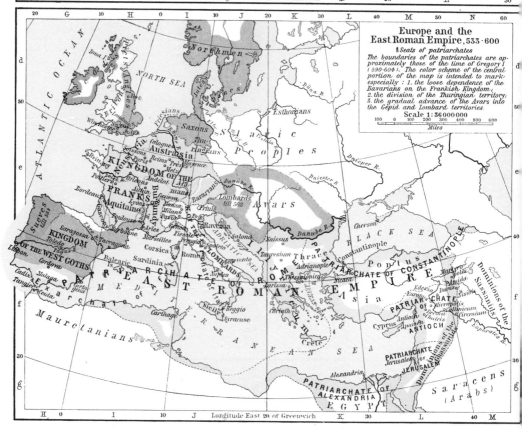

Europe and the East Roman Empire, 533·600

‡ Seats of patriarchates

The boundaries of the patriarchates are approximately those of the time of Gregory I (590-604). The color scheme of the central portion of the map is intended to mark especially: 1. the loose dependence of the Bavarians on the Frankish Kingdom; 2. the division of the Thuringian territory; 3. the gradual advance of the Avars into the Gepid and Lombard territories.

Scale 1:36000000

Longitude East 20 of Greenwich

The Califate in 750. Growth of Frankish Power, 481—814.

The Califate about 750

Conquests of the Arabs (Saracens) up to the death of Mohammed, 632
" " " under the first three Califs, 632-656
" " " Ommiad Califs, 661-750
Boundary of the Califate
" " " East Roman (Byzantine) Empire
The dates are those of conquest

Scale 1 : 50 000 000

100 0 100 200 300 400 500 600 700 800 900 1000
Miles

Growth of Frankish Power 481-814

Frankish territory in 481
Conquests of Clovis, 486-511
Conquests, 531-614
" 714-768
" of Charlemagne, 768-814
Peoples tributary to Charlemagne

Scale 1 : 20 000 000

100 50 0 100 200 300 400
Miles

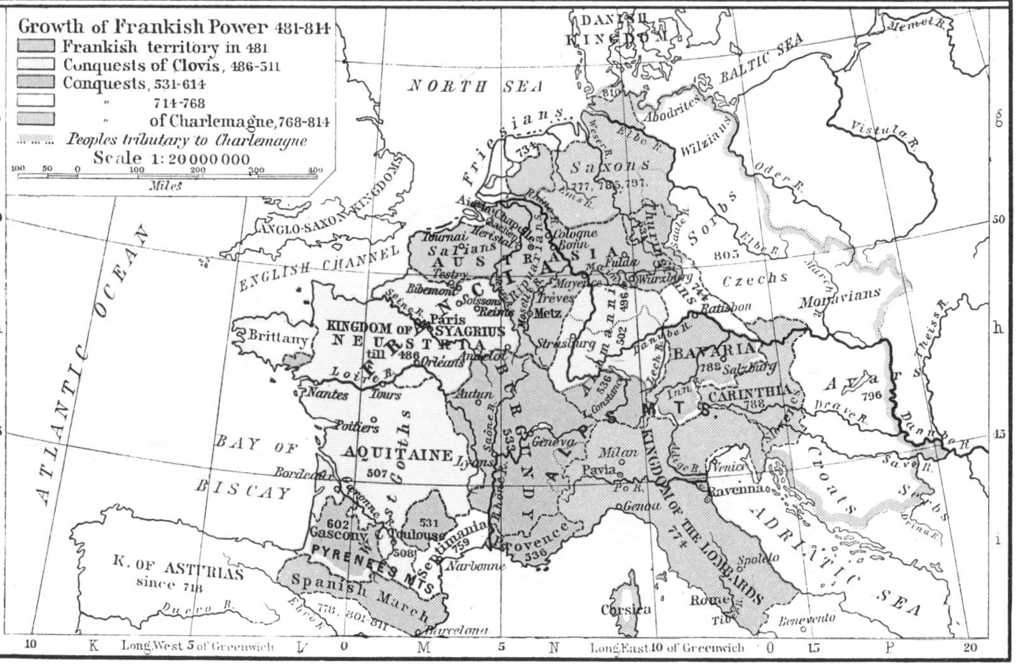

The Carolingian Empire
Slavic peoples tributary to Charlemagne
Slavs   Celts
The Byzantine Empire
The Califate
Boundary of the Patrimony of St. Peter,
as determined in 774

Frontier station for trade with Slavs and Avars thus: Schesel
Site of important event thus: Poitiers

‡ *Seat of an archbishopric* ⎫ *In the East Frankish dominions*
†   " " a *bishopric* ⎬ *about the end of the ninth century.*
□ *Monastery* ⎭ ◇ *Castle or stronghold*

Scale 1 : 20 000 000
100 50 0   100   200   300   400   500
Miles

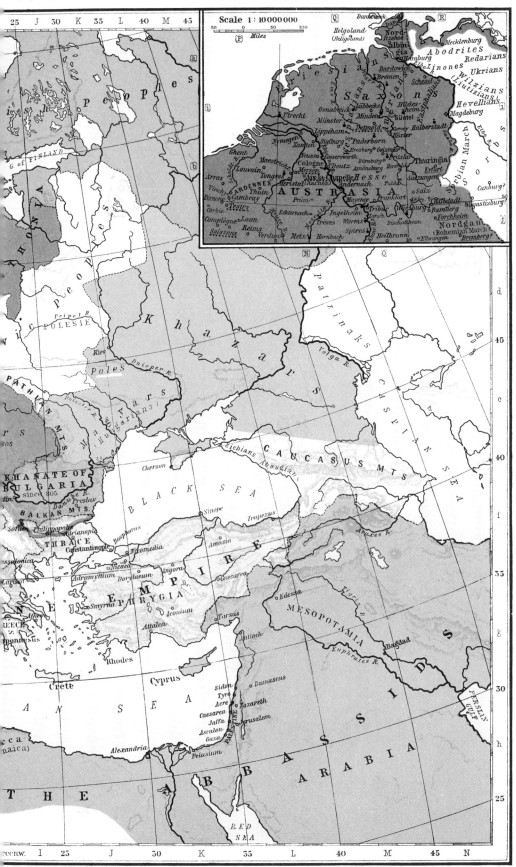

Scale 1 : 10 000 000

Helgoland
(Heligoland)

AUSTRASIA

Saxons
Westphalians
Eastphalians
Thuringia
Hesse

Nordgau
(Bohemian March)

Sorbian March

Serbs

Mecklenburg
Abodrites
Redarians
Ukrians
Wilzians
(Liutizians)
Hevellians
Magdeburg
Halberstadt
Erfurt
Salzungen
Fulda
Forchheim
Bamberg
Canburg?
Wogastisburg?
Brenberg?

Hamburg
Bardwick
Bremen
Osnabrück
Lübbecke
Minden
Hildesheim
Süntel
Höxter
Detmold
Paderborn
Ersburg
Geismar
Corvey
Münster
Utrecht
Lippeham
Nymegen
Xanten
Sigiburg
Neuss
Kaiserswerth
Deutz
Amöneburg
Cologne
Mersen
Maestricht
Aix-la-Chapelle
Andernach
Prüm
Echternach
Tribur
Worms
Ingelheim
Treves
Mayence
Frankfort
Salz
Würzburg
Hornbach
Spires
Heilbronn
Ellwangen
Bischofsheim

Ghent
Louvain
Tongres
Arras
Vinchy
ARDENNES
Cambray
Corbie
Festry
Compiègne
Laon
Reims
Soissons
Verdun
Metz

THE ABBASSIDS

Finland

Lithuanian Peoples

POLESIE
Pripet R.
Kiev
Dnieper R.
Poles

Khazars
Volga R.
Patzinaks

CASPIAN SEA

Magyars
Hungarians

KHANATE OF BULGARIA
since 805
Preslav
Danube R.
BALKAN MTS.
Sofia
Philippopolis
Adrianople
THRACE
Constantinople
Nicomedia
Bosphorus
Cherson
Zichians
Abasgians
CAUCASUS MTS.
Araxes R.

BLACK SEA

Sinope
Trapezus
Amasia
Nicaea
Dorylaeum
Angora
Caesarea
Adramyttium
PHRYGIA
Smyrna
Iconium
Tarsus
Attalea
EMPIRE
Athens
Peloponnesus

MESOPOTAMIA
Edessa
Tigris R.
Euphrates R.
Bagdad

Rhodes
Crete
Cyprus

SEA

Sidon
Tyre
Acre
Caesarea
Jaffa
Ascalon
Gaza
Damascus
Nazareth
Jerusalem
PALESTINE
PERSIAN GULF

Alexandria
Pelusium

ARABIA

RED SEA

Greenw.

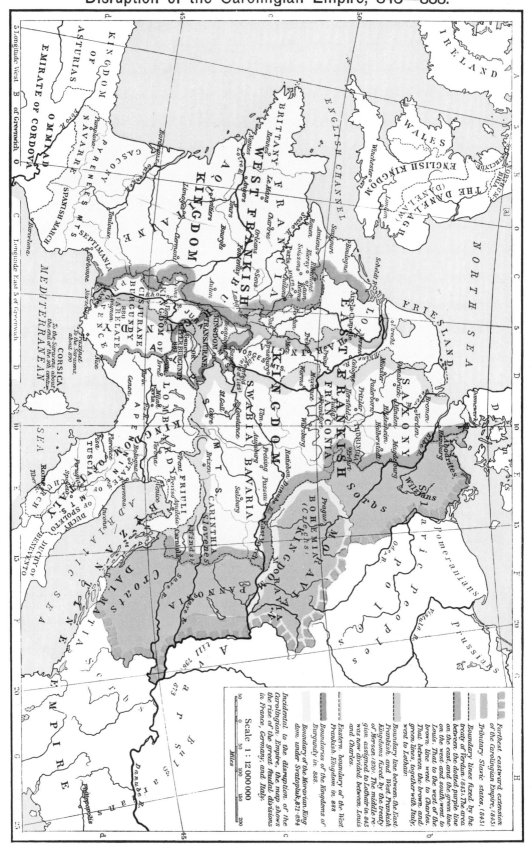

The Peoples of Europe, about 900.

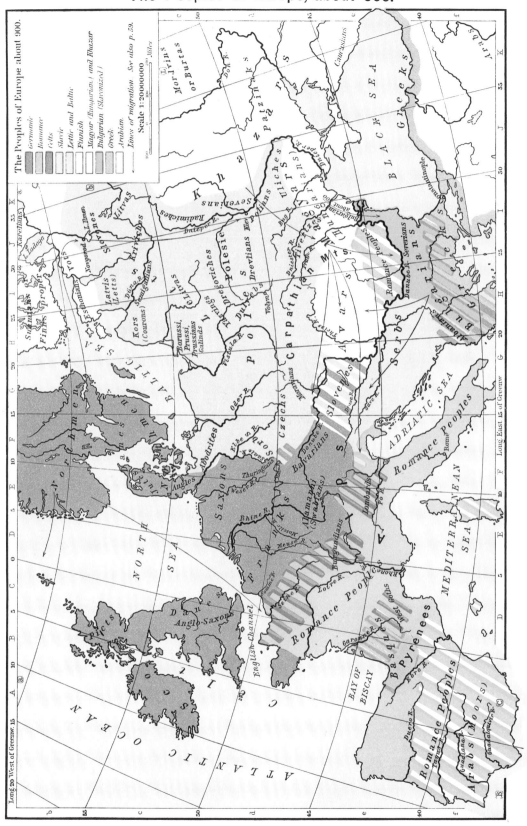

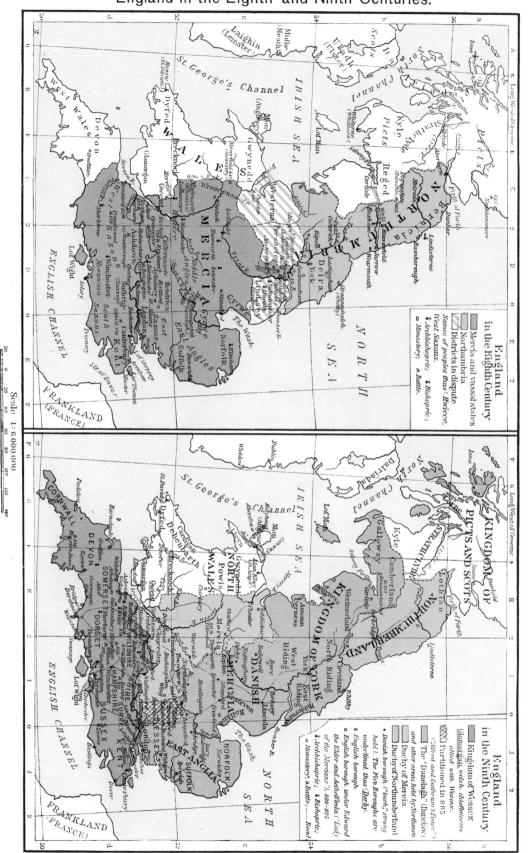

France about 1035.

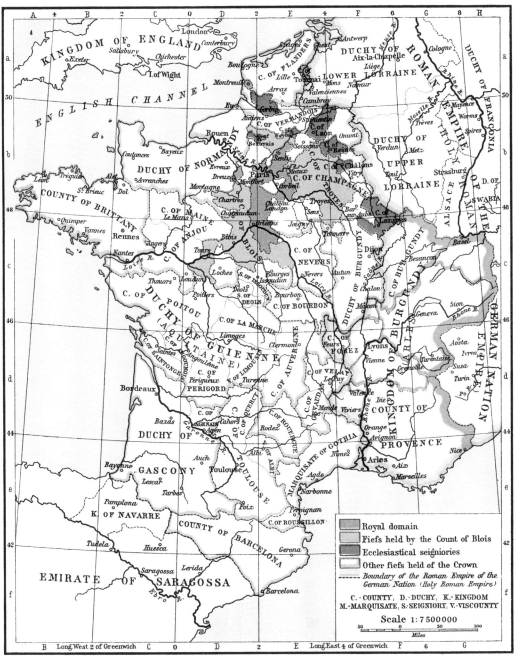

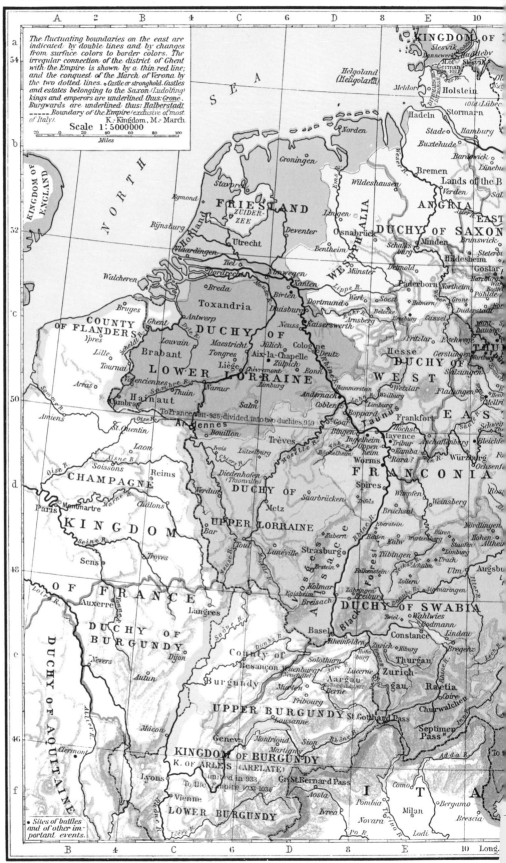

The fluctuating boundaries on the east are indicated by double lines and by changes from surface colors to border colors. The irregular connection of the district of Ghent with the Empire is shown by a thin red line; and the conquest of the March of Verona by the two dotted lines. ○ Castle or stronghold. Castles and estates belonging to the Saxon (Ludolfing) kings and emperors are underlined. Thus: Grone. Burgwards are underlined thus: Halberstadt.
— — — Boundary of the Empire (exclusive of most of Italy). K. Kingdom, M. March.

Scale 1:5000000
Miles

NORTH SEA

KINGDOM OF ENGLAND

KINGDOM OF

Slesvik
Dannewerk
A. of German
Slesvik
Meldorf
Holstein
(Old Lübeck
Hadeln
Stormarn
Stade
Hamburg
Buxtehude
Bardewick
Lüneburg
Bremen
Verden
Lands of the B

Helgoland
(Heligoland)
Norden

Groningen
Lingen
Osnabrück
Wildeshausen
Schalks-
burg
Minden
Brunswick
Steterbu
Hildesheim
Goslar

ANGRIA
EAST
DUCHY OF SAXON

FRIESLAND
ZUIDER-
ZEE
Stavoren
Egmond
Rijnsburg
Deventer
Bentheim
Münster
Detmold
Paderborn
Northeim
Grone
Pöhlde
Duderstad

Utrecht

WESTPHALIA

Walcheren
Breda
Nimwegen
Xanten
Lippe R.
Werl
Soest
Belecke
Arnsberg
Cassel
Eresburg
Helmern

Vlaardingen
Dordrecht
Tiel
Birten
Dortmund

Toxandria
Antwerp
Duisburg
Neuss
Kaiserswerth

COUNTY
OF FLANDERS
Ypres
Ghent
DUCHY OF
Jülich
Cologne
Deutz
Aix-la-Chapelle
Zülpich
Bonn

Bruges
Lille
Louvain
Brabant
Maestricht
Tongres
Liège
Chèvremont
Limburg
HESSE
DUCHY OF
WEST
Gerstungen
Salzungen

Tournai
LOWER LORRAINE
Namur
Salm
Andernach
Coblenz
Boppard
St. Goar
Bingen
WETZLAR
Weilburg
Lahn R.
Frankfurt
TAUNU
EAST

Arras
Valenciennes
Thuin
To France 911-925; divided into two duchies, 959
Ardennes
Bouillon
Trèves
Ingelheim
Oppen-
heim
Mayence
Tribur
Höchst
Aschaffenburg
Kamba
Rara?
Würzburg
FRANCONIA

Amiens
St. Quentin
Hainaut
Cambrai
Lützelburg
Diedenhofen
(Thionville)
Worms
Spires

Laon
Soissons
Reims
DUCHY OF
Verdun
Saarbrücken
Trifels
Wimpfen
Weinsberg
Nördlingen

CHAMPAGNE
Châlons
Metz
Bar
Eberstein
Bruchsal
Hohen-
Altheit

Paris
Montmartre
KINGDOM
UPPER LORRAINE
Toul
Lunéville
Strasburg
Baden
Kulm
Wartenberg
Tübingen
Staufen
Limburg
Ulm
Augsbu

Sens
Troyes
Zabern
Erstein
Egisheim
Kolmar
Zollern
Sigmaringen

OF FRANCE
Auxerre
Langres
Breisach
Zähringen
Freiburg
DUCHY OF SWABIA
Biel
Wahlwies
Bodmann
Lindau
Bregenz

DUCHY OF
BURGUNDY
Nevers
Dijon
Autun
County of
Besançon
Neuenburg
Neuchâtel
Solothurn
Basel
Rheinfelden
Zurich
Kiburg
Lucerne
Aargau
Zurich
gau
Raetia
Coire
Churwalchen

DUCHY OF AQUITAINE
Mâcon
Burgundy
Murten
Berne
Fribourg
Lausanne
UPPER BURGUNDY
St. Gothard Pass
Septimer
Pass

Clermont
Geneva
Montrigod
Martigny
Sion
KINGDOM OF BURGUNDY
Lyons
K. OF ARLES (ARELATE)
limited in 933
To the Empire 1032-1034
Gr. St. Bernard Pass
Aosta
Pombia
Como
Bergamo
Milan
Brescia
ITALY

Vienne
LOWER BURGUNDY
Ivrea
Novara
Lodi
Po R.

● Sites of battles and of other important events.

BALTIC SEA

Rügen
Arkona
Jolin (Jomsburg)
Kolberg
Danzig

Prussians

M·ARCH
Wolgast
Demmin
Usedom
Wollin
Belgard
Nakel

POMERANIA

LUNGS
Stettin
Redarians
Rhetra ?
Garz
Pyritz
Ukrians

Gnesen

Wilzians
(Liutizians)
Prizlawa
Havelberg
Hevellians
Lebus
Posen

POLAND
Kingdom, 1025

NORTH MARCH
(NORDMARK)
Brandenburg
Krossen

EAST MARCH
(OSTMARK)
Zerbst
Jüterbog
Lebusa
Niemitsch
Sagan
Gloyau
Breslau
Liegnitz

Lusatians
March of Lusatia
Dobrilugk
Polish
March of Meissen
Görlitz
Bautzen
Meissen
Schweidnitz

MARCH OF THURINGIA
Strehla
Miltzenians

Under Poland since 999

CHROBATIA
Cracow

Miriquidi
Leitmeritz
Glatz
Warthe

Brüx
Melnik
Nimburg
Saaz
Bunzlau
Elbe R.
Prague
Leitomischl

DUCHY OF BOHEMIA
Under Poland, 1003-1004

Pilsen
Klattau
Netolitz

MORAVIA
Under Poland, 1003-1029
Olmütz
Brünn
Trencsin

Ratisbon
Zpaym

Mailberg

BAVARIAN EAST MARCH
(OSTMARK)
(MARGRAVATE OF AUSTRIA)

Passau
Linz
Melk
Tulln
Vienna
Hainburg
Presburg

Mühldorf
Wels
Pöchlarn
St. Pölten
Hungarians 907-955
Duchy, 1156

DUCHY OF BAVARIA
Salzburg
Ödenburg
(Sopron)
Buda
(Ofen)

HUNGARY

MARCH OF
Established 970 ?
Detached from Carinthia 1035

Friesach
CARINTHIA

DUCHY OF CARINTHIA
Villach
Detached from Bavaria 976
From 1055
1180, Duchy
M. of STYRIA

Friuli
OF VERONA
Laibach
MARCH OF CARNIOLA
to Carinthia, 976
Aquileia
Trieste
Detached from Carinthia 1040
Grado

MARCH OF
ISTRIA
Duchy of Venice

CROATIA

Danube R.
Save R.

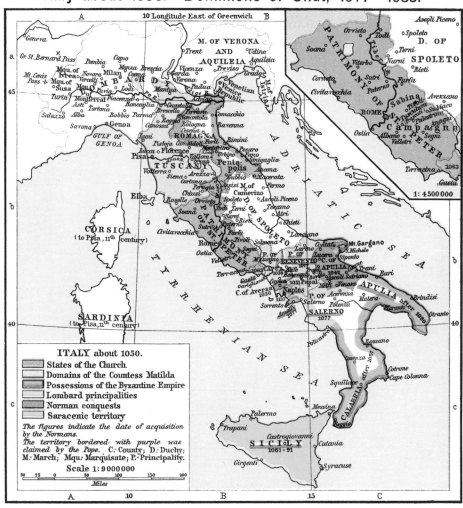

ITALY about 1050.
States of the Church
Domains of the Countess Matilda
Possessions of the Byzantine Empire
Lombard principalities
Norman conquests
Saracenic territory

The figures indicate the date of acquisition by the Normans.
The territory bordered with purple was claimed by the Pope. C. County; D. Duchy; M. March; Mqu. Marquisate; P. Principality.

Scale 1:9000000

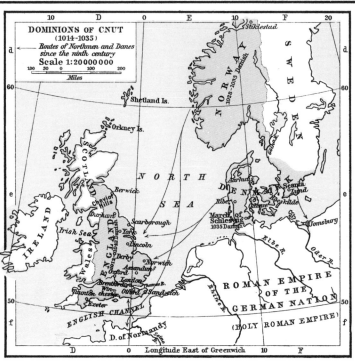

DOMINIONS OF CNUT
(1014-1035)
Routes of Northmen and Danes since the ninth century
Scale 1:20000000

England, 1087—1154.

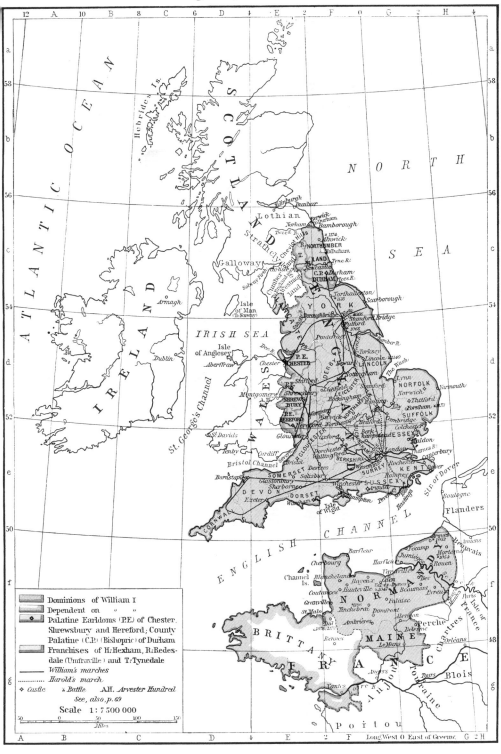

Dominions of William I
Dependent on   "   "
Palatine Earldoms (P.E.) of Chester,
Shrewsbury and Hereford; County
Palatine (C.P.) (Bishopric) of Durham
Franchises of H:Hexham, R:Redes-
dale (Umfraville) and T:Tynedale
William's marches
Harold's march
◇ Castle   ▴ Battle   A.H. Arvester Hundred
See, also, p. 69
Scale 1 : 7 500 000

Routes of the leaders of the first Crusade
(1096-1099)

Godfrey of Bouillon
Adhemar of Puy and Raymond of Toulouse
Bohemond and Tancred
Robert of Flanders and Hugh of Vermandois
Route of the combined forces. C-County; D.-Duchy;
P.-Principality.

Scale 1:20 000 000

100 50 0 100 200 300 400 500
Miles

The Growth of Islamic Power, 632-1097

Under Mohammed, up to 632
632 - 700
701 - 800
801 - 900
To 1097

Scale 1:90 000 000

Europe and the Mediterranean
Lands by Religions about 1097.

Christians:
Belonging to the Roman Church
   "   "   " Greek   "

Mohammedans:
Under the Calif of Bagdad (Abbasid)
   "   "   " Cairo (Fatimite)
Dates are those of conversion to Christianity

Asia Minor and the States of the Crusaders in Syria, about 1140.

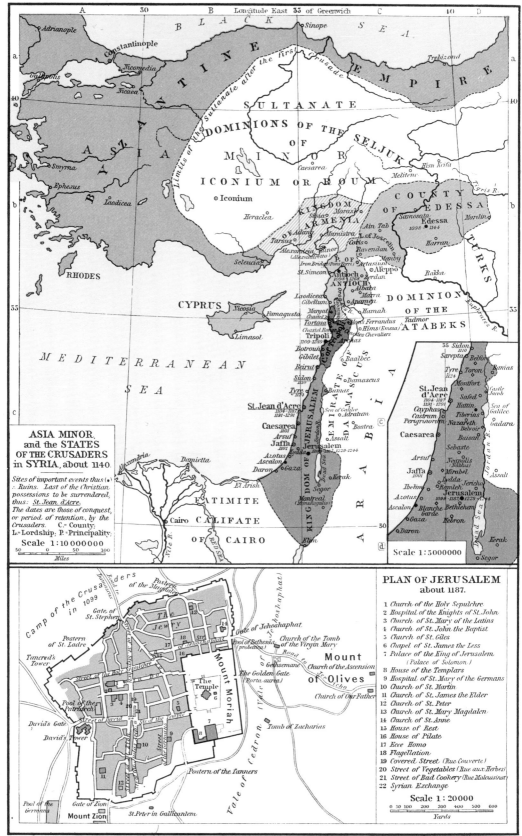

ASIA MINOR and the STATES OF THE CRUSADERS in SYRIA, about 1140.

Sites of important events thus (•).
Ruins. Last of the Christian possessions to be surrendered, thus: _St. Jean d'Acre._
The dates are those of conquest, or period of retention, by the Crusaders. C.= County; L.= Lordship; P.= Principality;

Scale 1:10 000 000

50   0   50   100
Miles

Scale 1:5000000

PLAN OF JERUSALEM about 1187.

1 Church of the Holy Sepulchre
2 Hospital of the Knights of St. John
3 Church of St. Mary of the Latins
4 Church of St. John the Baptist
5 Church of St. Giles
6 Chapel of St. James the Less
7 Palace of the King of Jerusalem (Palace of Solomon)
8 House of the Templars
9 Hospital of St. Mary of the Germans
10 Church of St. Martin
11 Church of St. James the Elder
12 Church of St. Peter
13 Church of St. Mary Magdalen
14 Church of St. Anne
15 House of Rest
16 House of Pilate
17 Ecce Homo
18 Flagellation
19 Covered Street (Rue Couverte)
20 Street of Vegetables (Rue aux Herbes)
21 Street of Bad Cookery (Rue Malcuisinat)
22 Syrian Exchange

Scale 1 : 20000

0 50 100   200   300   400   500   600
Yards

France, 1154—1184.

Scale 1:7,500,000

Domain, Fiefs and Suzerains of the Count of Champagne in the Twelfth Century.

Scale 1:5,000,000

De Cl. = De Clare, De Co. = De Courcy, De L. = De Lacy (Anglo-Norman Earldoms
in Ireland); DOM. = Dominion, K. = Kingdom, PRINC. = Principality,
W.M.E. = Welsh Marcher Earldoms, W.P. = Welsh Principalities.
—— Crusade of Louis VII and Conrad III (1147-1149)
—— Crusade of Richard I, Philip II (Augustus) and
Frederick I (Barbarossa) (1189-1191)

Scale 1:20000000

100 50 0   100   200   300   400   500

Miles

Guelf, Hohenstaufen and Ascanian domains
in Germany about 1176

☐ Guelf   ☐ Hohenstaufen   ☐ Ascanian

Scale 1:15 000 000

*The dark coloring indicates hereditary or imperial domains;
light coloring, feudal territories, and border coloring, suzerainty.*

Boundary of the Empire
The thin blue line in the north
east shows that Pomerania,
Pomerelia and Prussia were
added to the Empire during
the Hohenstaufen period.
Within Pomerania it indicates
the boundary of the Ascanian
possessions about 1300. The
territory in Italy claimed by
the Pope is shown by the purple
line. ◦ Monastery ◦ Castle
Cities (including Lodi and Parma)
that belonged to the Lombard
League in 1177 are underlined
thus: Milan. Imperial cities
thus: Pavia
C.=County; D.=Duchy; K.=Kingdom;
L.=Landgraviate; M.=March or
Margravate. Sites of battles and
of other important events are
indicated by the signs (●●)

Scale 1:9 000 000
50   0   50   100
Miles

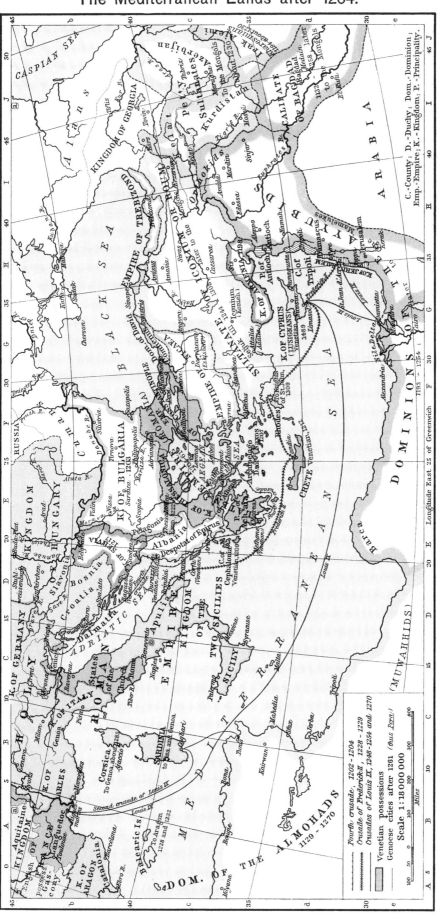

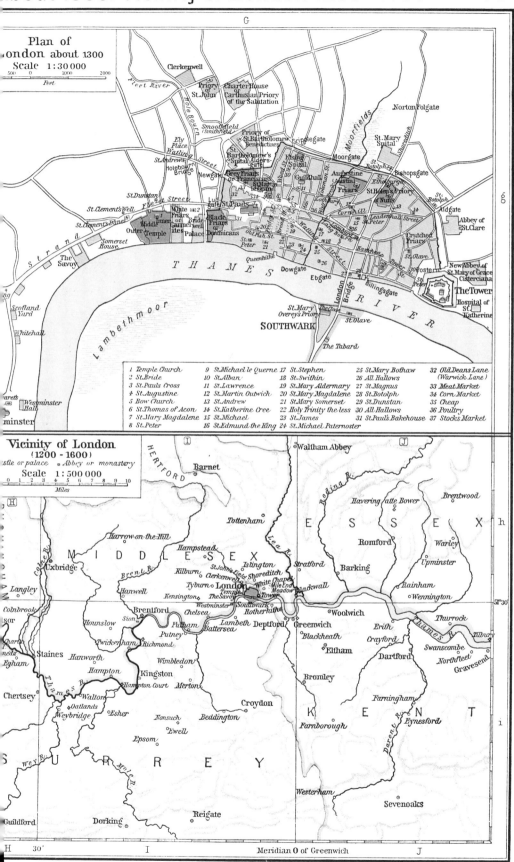

Plan of London about 1300
Scale 1 : 30 000
500 0   1000   2000
Feet

Clerkenwell

Fleet River

Hoseborn

Priory of St.John

Charterhouse Carthusian Priory of the Salutation

Norton Folgate

Smoothfield (Smithfield)

Moorfields

St.Mary Spital

Ely Place
Watling Street

Priory of St.Bartholomew Benedictines

St.Andrew

St.Bartholomew's Spital Aldersgate
Cripplegate

St.Botolph

Bishopsgate

St.Ethelburga

Holeborn Bridge

Newgate

Grey Friars or Franciscans
St.Martin le Grand

Rising Spital

Guildhall

Augustine (Austin) Friars

St.Helen's Priory of Nuns

St.Dunstan

Fleet Street
St.Pauls

Lothbury

Cornhill

Leadenhall Street
St.Peter

Aldgate

St.Clement's Well
St.Clement's Danes

White Friars or Carmelites

Inner Temple
Middle Temple
Outer Temple

Lud gate
Bride well Palace

Black Friars or Dominicans

Old Fish St.

Watling St.

Long Acre Lane

Crutched Friars

Abbey of St.Clare

Somerset House

St.Peter

Queenhithe

Eastcheap

Tower St.

St.Olave

Eastern

New Abbey of St.Mary of Grace Cisterciana

The Savoy

Dowgate

Ebgate

London Bridge

St.Peter

The Tower

THAMES RIVER

Scotland Yard

Whitehall

Lambethmoor

St.Mary Overey's Priory
St.Olave

Billingsgate

Hospital of St.Katherine

Westminster Hall
minster

SOUTHWARK

The Tabard

1 Temple Church	9 St.Michael le Querne	17 St.Stephen	25 St.Mary Bothaw	32 Old Deans Lane
2 St.Bride	10 St.Alban	18 St.Swithin	26 All Hallows	(Warwick Lane)
3 St.Pauls Cross	11 St.Lawrence	19 St.Mary Aldermary	27 St.Magnus	33 Meat Market
4 St.Augustine	12 St.Martin Outwich	20 St.Mary Magdalene	28 St.Botolph	34 Corn Market
5 Bow Church	13 St.Andrew	21 St.Mary Somerset	29 St.Dunstan	35 Cheap
6 St.Thomas of Acon	14 St.Katherine Cree	22 Holy Trinity the less	30 All Hallows	36 Poultry
7 St.Mary Magdalene	15 St.Michael	23 St.James	31 St.Pauls Bakehouse	37 Stocks Market
8 St.Peter	16 St.Edmund the King	24 St.Michael Paternoster		

Vicinity of London
(1200 - 1600)
☐ Castle or palace   ○ Abbey or monastery
Scale 1 : 500 000
0 1 2 3 4 5 6 7 8 9 10
Miles

HERTFORD

Waltham Abbey

Barnet

Roding R.

Havering atte Bower

Brentwood

Tottenham

ESSEX

Harrow-on-the-Hill

Hampstead

Romford

Warley

Islington

Stratford

Upminster

Brent R.

Kilburn

Clerkenwell
Shoreditch

Barking

Hanwell

Tyburn

London
Temple
The Savoy

White Chapel
Mile End
Meadow

Blackwall

Rainham

Wennington

Uxbridge

MIDDLESEX

Langley

Kensington

Westminster
Chelsea

Southwark
Tower

Woolwich

Thurrock

Colnbrook

Brentford

Fulham
Battersea
Lambeth

Rotherhithe

Deptford

Greenwich

Erith

Tilbury

Hounslow

Sion

Putney

Blackheath

Crayford

Swanscombe

Staines

Twickenham
Richmond

Eltham

Dartford

Northfleet
Gravesend

Egham

Hanworth

Wimbledon

Hampton

Kingston

Bromley

Farningham

Eynesford

Chertsey

Walton
Oatlands
Weybridge

Esher

Hampton Court
Merton

Croydon

KENT

Nonsuch

Beddington

Farnborough

Ewell

Epsom

SURREY

Mole R.

Wey R.

Westerham

Sevenoaks

Guildford

Dorking

Reigate

France in 1328

Domain of the French Crown, and ecclesiastical seigniories

Appanages of princes descended from Louis IX [Crown

Other fiefs held of the French

Immediate fiefs thus: C.of FOREZ
Rerefiefs thus: C. of Porhoët

The English possessions in France
Held in 1188
Held in 1328

Scale 1:6000000
20   0   20   40   60   80
Miles

Route of Edward III. 1346 •Castle
C.- County; D.-Duchy; DAUPH.-Dauphiny;
K.- Kingdom; S.- Seigniory; V.-Viscounty
GIM.- GIMOËS; P.G.-PERCHE-GOUET

The Chief Wool-raising Districts of England and Wool-manufacturing Towns of Flanders, Artois and Brabant

Abbreviations.
C.- County; D.-Duchy; K.- Kingdom
H.- HUNTINGDON; R.- RUTLAND

Scale 1:6000000
20   0   20   40   60   80

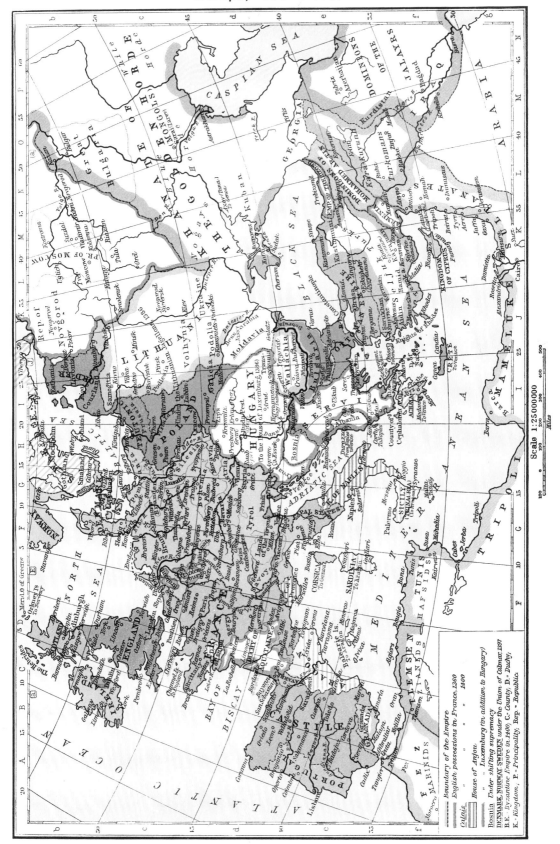

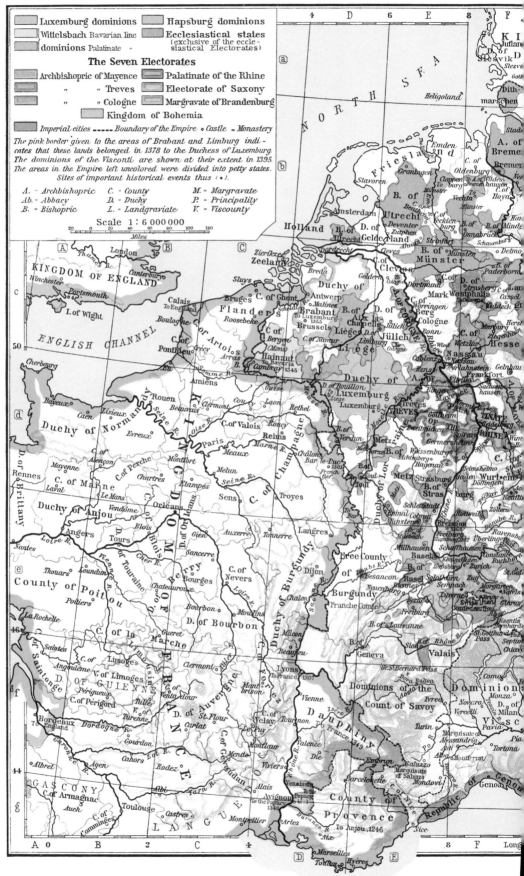

The Seven Electorates

- Luxemburg dominions
- Wittelsbach Bavarian line
- dominions Palatinate „
- Hapsburg dominions
- Ecclesiastical states (exclusive of the ecclesiastical Electorates)

- Archbishopric of Mayence
- „ „ Treves
- „ „ Cologne
- Palatinate of the Rhine
- Electorate of Saxony
- Margravate of Brandenburg
- Kingdom of Bohemia

Imperial cities ----- Boundary of the Empire ○ Castle ▢ Monastery

The pink border given to the areas of Brabant and Limburg indicates that these lands belonged in 1378 to the Duchess of Luxemburg. The dominions of the Visconti are shown at their extent in 1395. The areas in the Empire left uncolored were divided into petty states. Sites of important historical events thus (•).

A. = Archbishopric	C. = County	M. = Margravate
Ab. = Abbacy	D. = Duchy	P. = Principality
B. = Bishopric	L. = Landgraviate	V. = Viscounty

Scale 1 : 6 000 000

Dominions of Ottocar of Bohemia

☐ Bohemia and Moravia
☐ Acquisitions of Ottocar

Scale 1 : 12 000 000

Spread of German Settlements to the Eastward, 800—1400.

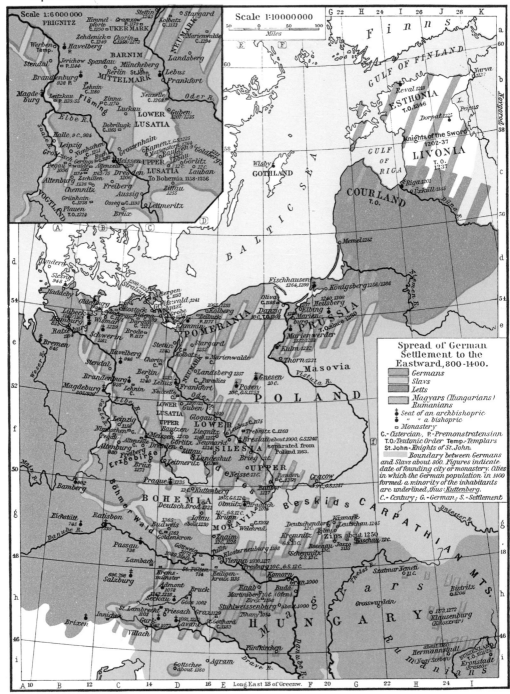

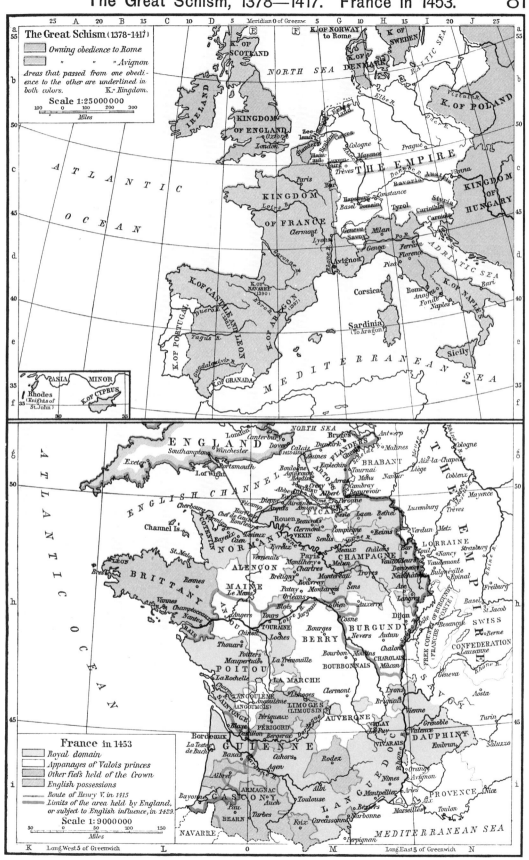

The Great Schism (1378-1417)

Owning obedience to Rome

" " " Avignon

Areas that passed from one obedience to the other are underlined in both colors.   K.= Kingdom.

Scale 1:25000000

France in 1453

Royal domain

Appanages of Valois princes

Other fiefs held of the Crown

English possessions

Route of Henry V. in 1415

Limits of the area held by England, or subject to English influence, in 1429.

Scale 1:9000000

Spain in 910
Kingdom of León
Kingdom of Navarre
County of Barcelona
Emirate of Cordova
Independent Moorish S
C.= County; K.= Kingdom.
Scale 1:9 000 000

Spain in 1150
Kingdoms of León and Castile
Kingdom of Navarre
Kingdom of Aragon and its dependa
Kingdom of Portugal (1140)
Dominion of the Almohads
The dates in parentheses are those of Chr
conquests of Moorish territory.
Scale 1:9 000 000

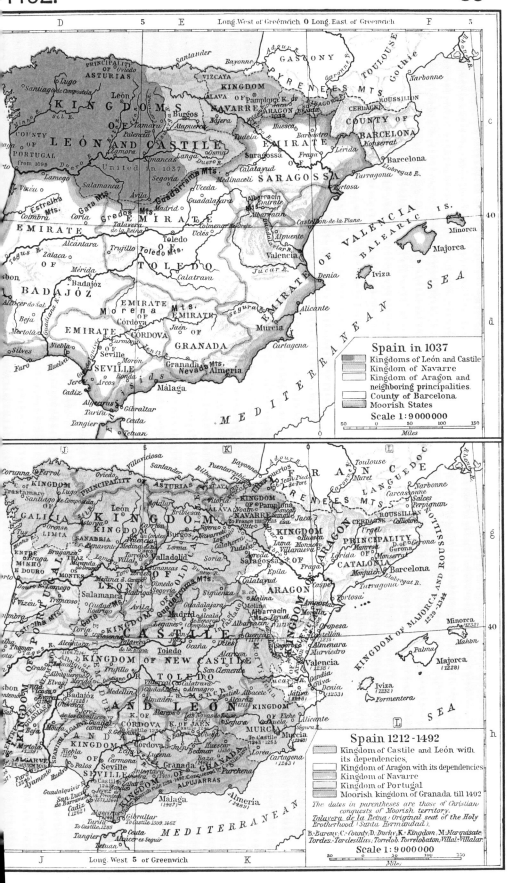

Spain in 1037

Kingdoms of León and Castile
Kingdom of Navarre
Kingdom of Aragon and
neighboring principalities.
County of Barcelona
Moorish States

Scale 1:9 000 000

Spain 1212-1492

Kingdom of Castile and León with
its dependencies.
Kingdom of Aragon with its dependencies
Kingdom of Navarre
Kingdom of Portugal
Moorish kingdom of Granada till 1492

The dates in parentheses are those of Christian
conquests of Moorish territory.
Talavera de la Reina: Original seat of the Holy
Brotherhood (Santa Hermandad).

B.=Barony; C.=County; D.=Duchy; K.=Kingdom; M.=Marquisate.
Tordes.=Tordesillas; Torrelob.=Torrelobaton; Villal.=Villalar.

Scale 1:9 000 000

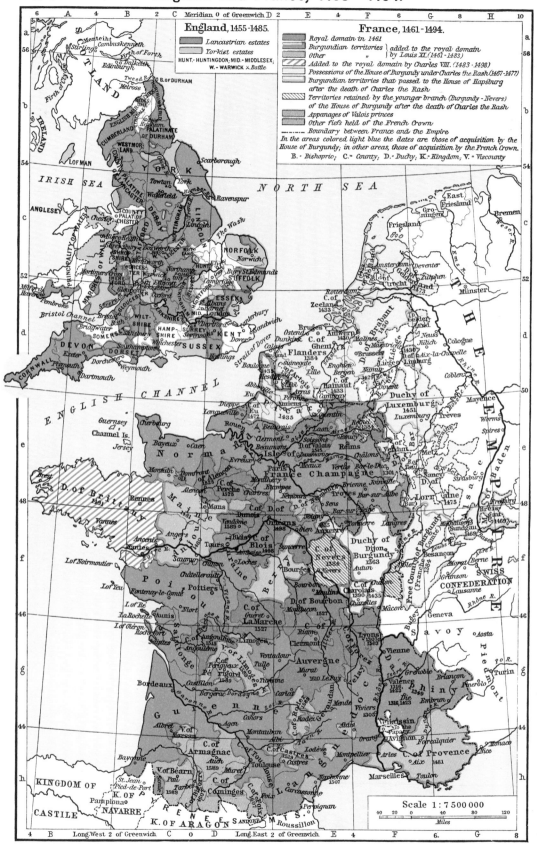

England, 1455-1485.
- Lancastrian estates
- Yorkist estates
- HUNT.- HUNTINGDON; MID.- MIDDLESEX;
- W.- WARWICK × Battle

France, 1461-1494.
- Royal domain in 1461
- Burgundian territories } added to the royal domain
- Other " } by Louis XI. (1461-1483)
- Added to the royal domain by Charles VIII. (1483-1498)
- Possessions of the House of Burgundy under Charles the Rash (1467-1477)
- Burgundian territories that passed to the House of Hapsburg after the death of Charles the Rash
- Territories retained by the younger branch (Burgundy-Nevers) of the House of Burgundy after the death of Charles the Rash
- Appanages of Valois princes
- Other fiefs held of the French Crown
- Boundary between France and the Empire

In the areas colored light blue the dates are those of acquisition by the House of Burgundy; in other areas, those of acquisition by the French Crown.

B.- Bishopric; C.- County; D.- Duchy; K.- Kingdom; V.- Viscounty.

Scale 1 : 7 500 000

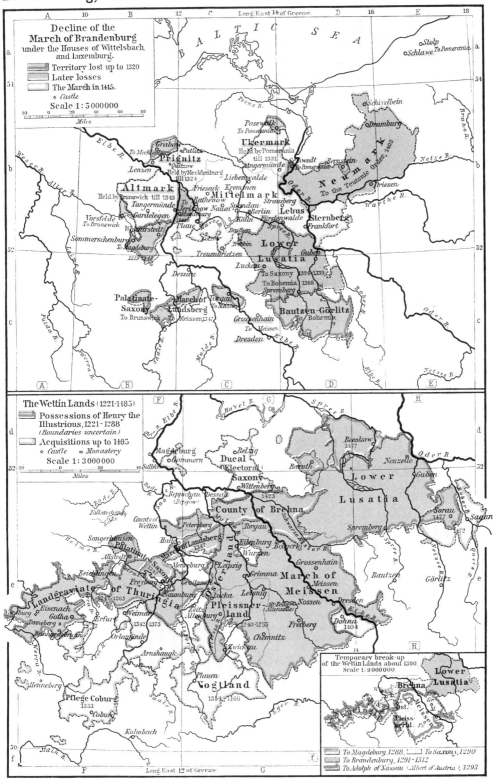

Decline of the
March of Brandenburg
under the Houses of Wittelsbach
and Luxemburg.

Territory lost up to 1320
Later losses
The March in 1415.
◇ *Castle*
Scale 1 : 5 000 000

The Wettin Lands (1221-1485)
Possessions of Henry the
Illustrious, 1221- 1288
(*Boundaries uncertain*)
Acquisitions up to 1485
◇ *Castle*   □ *Monastery*
Scale 1 : 3 000 000

Temporary break-up
of the Wettin Lands about 1300.
Scale 1 : 9 000 000

To Magdeburg, 1288,   To Saxony, 1290
To Brandenburg, 1291-1312
To Adolph of Nassau (Albert of Austria), 1293

Meridian 0 of Greenw.

N O R T H S E A

KINGDOM OF ENGLAND

ENGLISH CHANNEL

KINGDOM OF FRANCE

Normandy

Maine

Poitou

Anjou

C. of Flanders

Brabant

D. of Gelderland

Friesland

B. of Utrecht

B. of Münster

Duchy of Luxemburg

Champagne

Lorraine

PAL. OF THE RHINE

Alsace

DUCHY OF BURGUNDY

FREE COUNTY (FRANCHE COMTÉ)

SWISS CONFEDERATION

Savoy

DUCHY OF SAVOY

Piedmont

Dauphiny

County of Provence

Republic of Genoa

☐ **Dominions of the House of Hapsburg**
☐ **Dominions of the House of Burgundy**
☐ **Possessions of Charles the Rash**
        "   " the Burgundy-Nevers line

The possessions of Charles the Rash held of the French Crown are given a wide border; those of the Burgundy-Nevers line, similarly, a narrow border.

☐ **Ecclesiastical States**   ☐ **Imperial Cities**
------ *Boundary of the Empire*

The two colorings given to the Bohemian region are intended to show that in 1477 a Polish Jagellon was reigning in Bohemia; and that Moravia and Silesia were subject to Hungary, but were reunited with Bohemia in 1490. The areas in the Empire left uncolored were divided into petty states.

Abbreviations

A: Archbishopric; Ab: Abbacy; B: Bishopric; C: County; D: Duchy; Lg: Landgraviate; M: Margravate; Marq: Marquisate; P: Principality; Pal: Palatinate; Rep: Republic; ○ Castle ▫ Monastery.

Scale 1:6 000 000

20 0 20 40 60 80 100 120 140
Miles

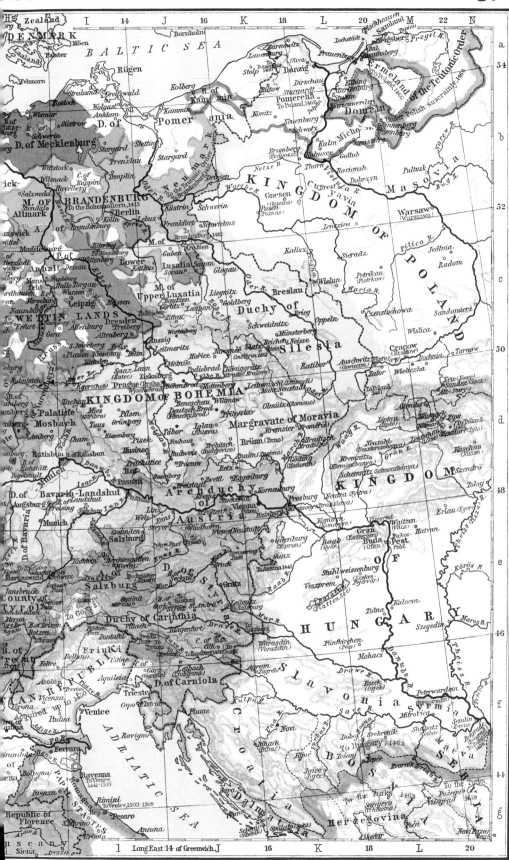

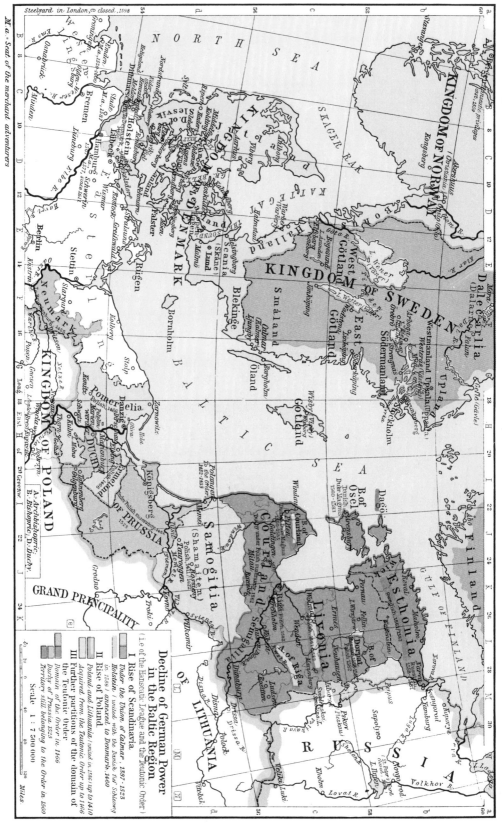

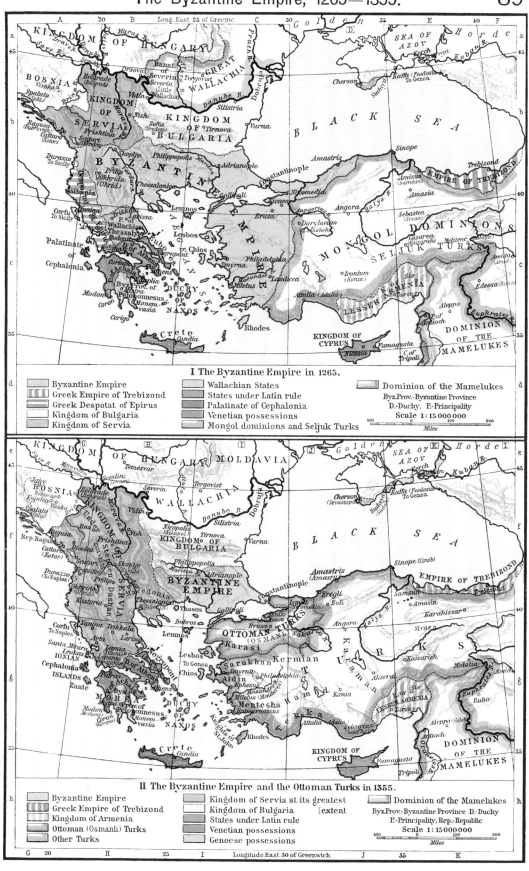

I The Byzantine Empire in 1265.

Byzantine Empire
Greek Empire of Trebizond
Greek Despotat of Epirus
Kingdom of Bulgaria
Kingdom of Servia
Wallachian States
States under Latin rule
Palatinate of Cephalonia
Venetian possessions
Mongol dominions and Seljuk Turks
Dominion of the Mamelukes
Byz.Prov.-Byzantine Province
D.-Duchy; P.-Principality
Scale 1: 15 000 000

II The Byzantine Empire and the Ottoman Turks in 1355.

Byzantine Empire
Greek Empire of Trebizond
Kingdom of Armenia
Ottoman (Osmanli) Turks
Other Turks
Kingdom of Servia at its greatest extent
Kingdom of Bulgaria
States under Latin rule
Venetian possessions
Genoese possessions
Dominion of the Mamelukes
Byz.Prov.-Byzantine Province D.-Duchy
P.-Principality; Rep.-Republic
Scale 1: 15 000 000

The Milanese under the Visconti,
1339-1402.

Dominions of Azzo Visconti (1329-1339)
Acquired by Luchino and Giovanni Visconti (1339-54)
"   " Bernabò and Galeazzo Visconti (1354-85)
"   " Gian Galeazzo Visconti (1385-1402)

Areas given a border coloring are those which became dow-
ries for Visconti heiresses, or were otherwise lost, before 1402.

Scale 1:5000000   20   0   20   40   60   80
                                                      Miles

The
Republic of Florence,
1300-1494.
- - - - - Boundaries of the
Tuscan States in 1500
The Republic of Florence
□ In 1300
□ Acquired, 1300 – 1377
□   " ,1377 – 1435
□   " ,1435 – 1494
□ Protected States
Scale 1:5000000   15 0   15   30   45   60
                                              Miles

In the States of the Church the
areas given a surface coloring
of violet were under effective
control.

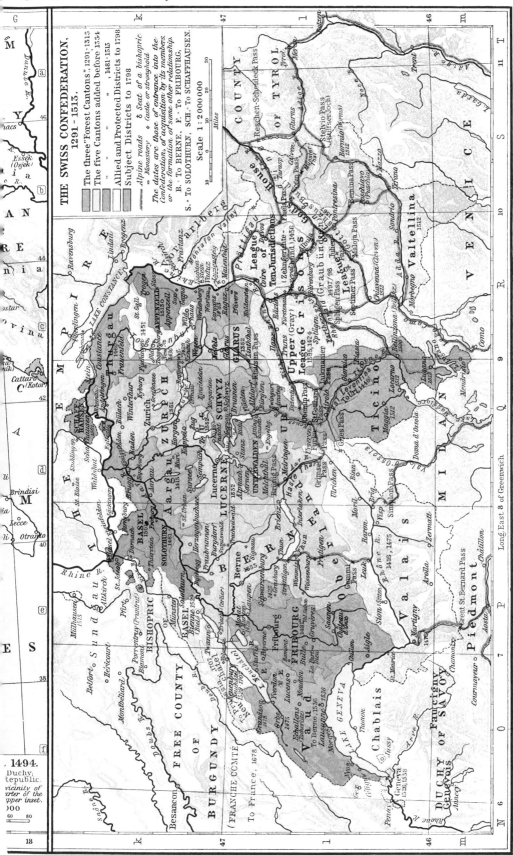

THE SWISS CONFEDERATION,
1291-1513.

The three "Forest Cantons", 1291-1315
The five Cantons added before 1354
"   "   "   , 1481-1513
Allied and Protected Districts to 1798
Subject Districts to 1798

Alpine roads   ‡ Seat of a bishopric
= Monastery   ○ Castle or stronghold
The dates are those of entrance into the
Confederation, of acquisition by its members,
or the formation of some other relationship.
B.= To BERNE.   F.= To FRIBOURG.
S.= To SOLOTHURN.   SCH.= To SCHAFFHAUSEN.

Scale 1 : 2 000 000

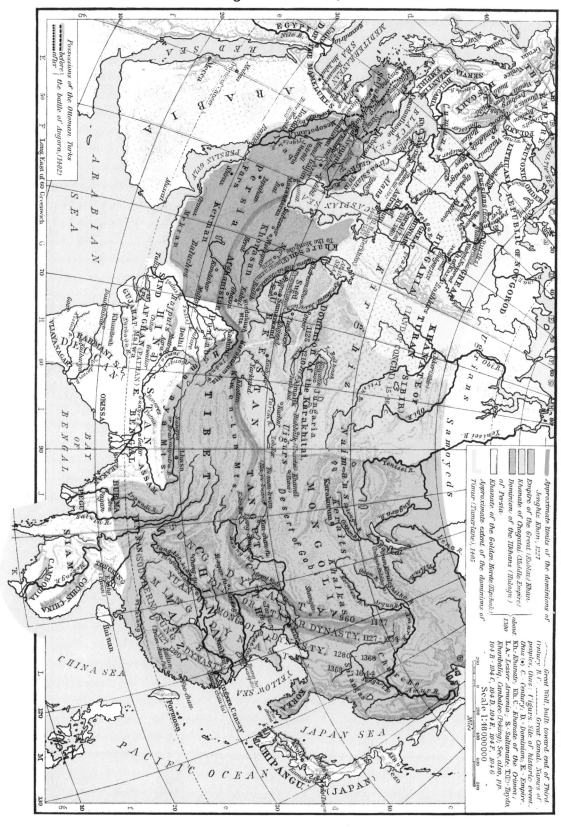

The Ottoman Empire 1451 - 1481

Remnant of the Byzantine Empire and its dependencies in the Morea (Peloponnesus)

Greek Empire of Trebizond

Servia

Bosnia, Herzegovina, Montenegro

Albania under George Castriota (Scanderbeg) [1443-1468]

States under Latin rule

Venetian possessions

Genoese possessions

Dominion of the Circassian Mamelukes

Dominions of the Ottoman Turks

Dominions of the Ottoman Turks acquired between 1451 and 1481

D.-Duchy; Desp.-Despotat; Rep.-Republic

The dates are those of acquisition by the Turks   × Battle

Scale 1:15 000 000   100   0   100   200 Miles

CONSTANTINOPLE

Scale 1:125 000   0   ½   1   1½ Miles

Byzantine names in thin type, thus: Cosmidion. 1 - St. Sophia. 2 - *Statue of Justinian.* 3 - *Serpent Column.* 4 - *Burnt Column (of Constantine).* 5 - Mosque of Bajazet 6 - Mosque of Sultan Valideh 7 - *Grave of the last Byzantine emperor* 8 - *Greek Patriarchate* 9 - *Prison of Anemas* 10 - Old Mahmoud Bridge 11 - New (Valideh) Bridge 12 - *Tomb of Khair-ed-Din Barbarossa* 13 - *Column of Arcadius.* ═══ *Route over which the ships of Mohammed II. were drawn.*

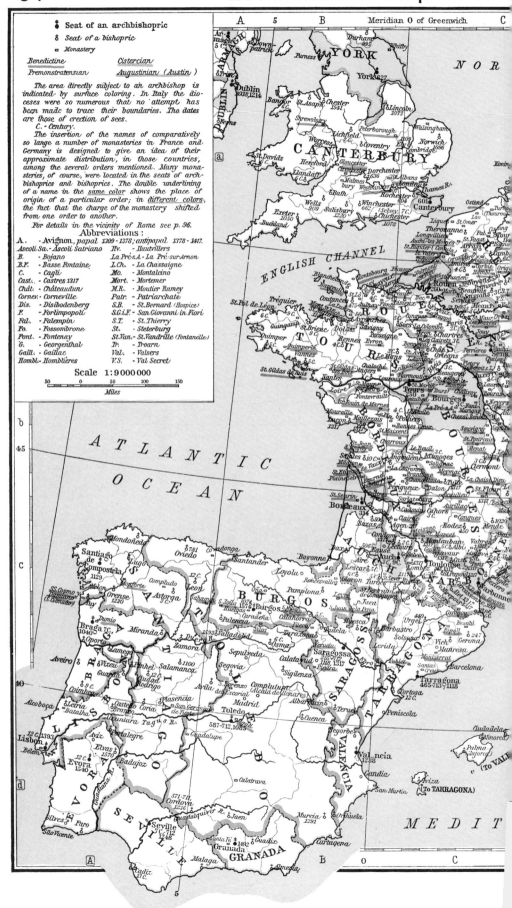

Plan of Rome in the Middle Ages.
The Roman Suburbicarian Bishoprics.

96

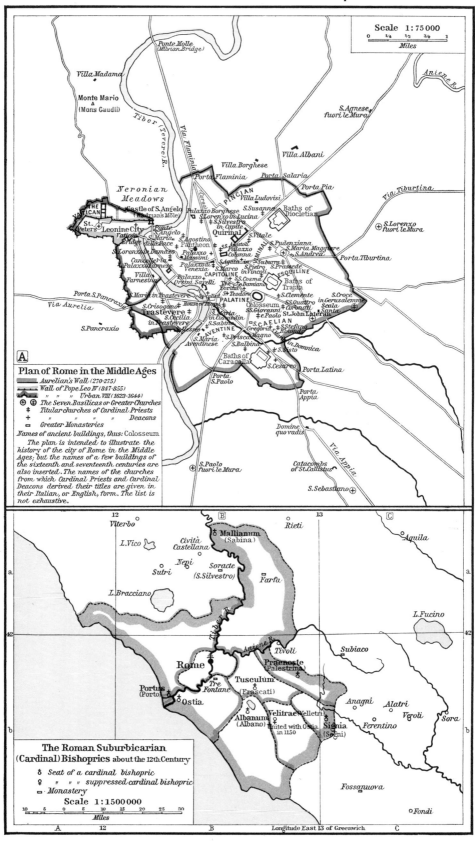

Scale 1:75000

0   ¼   ½   ¾   1
Miles

A

Plan of Rome in the Middle Ages

▬▬▬ Aurelian's Wall (270-275)

▬▬▬ Wall of Pope Leo IV (847-855)

" " " Urban VIII (1623-1644)

⊕ ⊕ The Seven Basilicas or Greater Churches

‡ Titular churches of Cardinal Priests

+ " " " " Deacons

▱ Greater Monasteries

Names of ancient buildings, thus: Colosseum

The plan is intended to illustrate the history of the city of Rome in the Middle Ages; but the names of a few buildings of the sixteenth and seventeenth centuries are also inserted. The names of the churches from which Cardinal Priests and Cardinal Deacons derived their titles are given in their Italian, or English, form. The list is not exhaustive.

The Roman Suburbicarian
(Cardinal) Bishoprics about the 12th Century

☿ Seat of a cardinal bishopric

♀ " " " suppressed cardinal bishopric

▱ Monastery

Scale 1:1500000

10 5 0 5 10 15 20 25 30
Miles

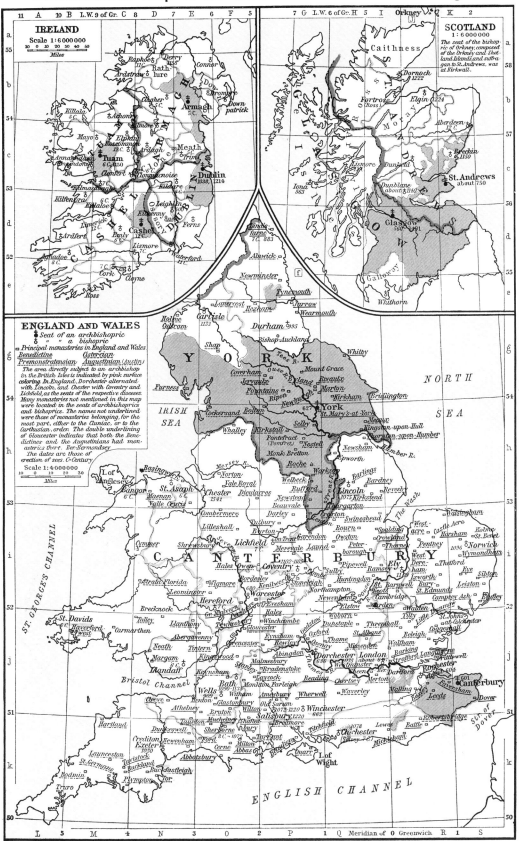

IRELAND
Scale 1:6 000 000
10 0 10 20 30 40 50
Miles

SCOTLAND
1:6 000 000
The seat of the bishop-
ric of Orkney, composed
of the Orkney and Shet-
land Islands and suffra-
gan to St. Andrews, was
at Kirkwall.

ENGLAND AND WALES
⚜ Seat of an archbishopric
⚜ " " a bishopric
□ Principal monasteries in England and Wales
Benedictine — *Cistercian*
Premonstratensian — *Augustinian (Austin)*
The area directly subject to an archbishop
in the British Isles is indicated by pink surface
coloring. In England, Dorchester alternated
with Lincoln, and Chester with Coventry and
Lichfield, as the seats of the respective dioceses.
Many monasteries not mentioned in this map
were located in the seats of archbishoprics
and bishoprics. The names not underlined
were those of monasteries belonging, for the
most part, either to the Cluniac, or to the
Carthusian, order. The double underlining
of Gloucester indicates that both the Benedictines and the Augustinians had monasteries there. Ber-Bermondsey.
The dates are those of
erection of sees. C.=Century.
Scale 1:4 000 000
10 0 10 20 30
Miles

NORTH SEA

IRISH SEA

ST. GEORGES CHANNEL

Bristol Channel

Y O R K

C A N T E R B U R Y

ENGLISH CHANNEL

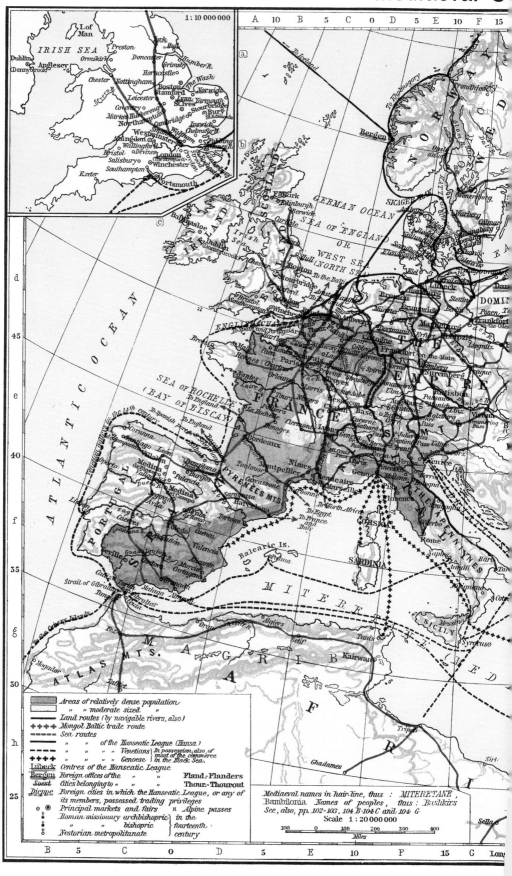

Scale 1:10 000 000

I. of Man

IRISH SEA

Dublin — Anglesey
(Donnybrook)

York *Preston* *Hull* *Humber R.*
Ormskirk *Doncaster* *Grimsby*
Chester *Nottingham* *Horncastle* *The Wash*
Leicester *Boston* *Norwich*
Coventry *Stamford* *Lynn* *St Ives* *Yarmouth*
Market Hill *Northampton* *Stourbridge*
Cambridge *Inswich*
Westminster *Walsingham* *Chelmsford*
Abingdon *Devizes* *London*
Bristol *Wallingford* *The Steelyard*
Salisbury *Winchester*
Exeter *Southampton*
Portsmouth

ATLANTIC OCEAN

GERMAN OCEAN

SEA OF ENGLAND

OR

WEST SEA
(NORTH SEA)

NORWAY

Bergen

SKAGER

SEA OF ROCHELLE
(BAY OF BISCAY)

FRANCE

PORTUGAL

PYRENEES MTS.

Bordeaux

Toulouse
Montpellier
Nimes
Marseilles

Balearic Is.

Strait of Gibraltar

M A G R I B

ATLAS MTS.

MITERE

SARDINIA

CORSICA

Rome

SICILY

Ghadames

Tripoli

Legend:

Areas of relatively dense population

" " moderate sized "

Land routes (by navigable rivers, also)

Mongol Baltic trade route

Sea routes

" " of the Hanseatic League (Hansa)

" " " " Venetians } In possession, also, of
" " " " Genoese } most of the commerce
in the Black Sea.

Lübeck Centres of the Hanseatic League

Bergen Foreign offices of the " "   **Fland.=Flanders**

Soest Cities belonging to " "   **Thour.=Thourout**

Dieppe Foreign cities in which the Hanseatic League, or any of
its members, possessed trading privileges

⊙ ◉ Principal markets and fairs   ⋉ Alpine passes

Roman missionary archbishopric } in the
" " bishopric } fourteenth
Nestorian metropolitanate } century

Mediaeval names in hair-line, thus : MITERETANE,
Bambilonia. Names of peoples, thus : Bashkirs
See, also, pp. 102-103, 104 B-104 C and 104 G

Scale 1 : 20 000 000

100   0   100   200   300   400
Miles

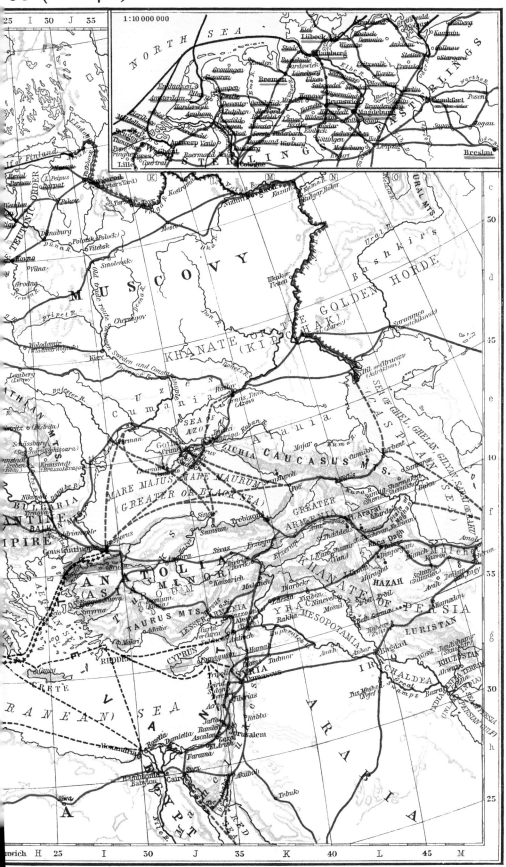

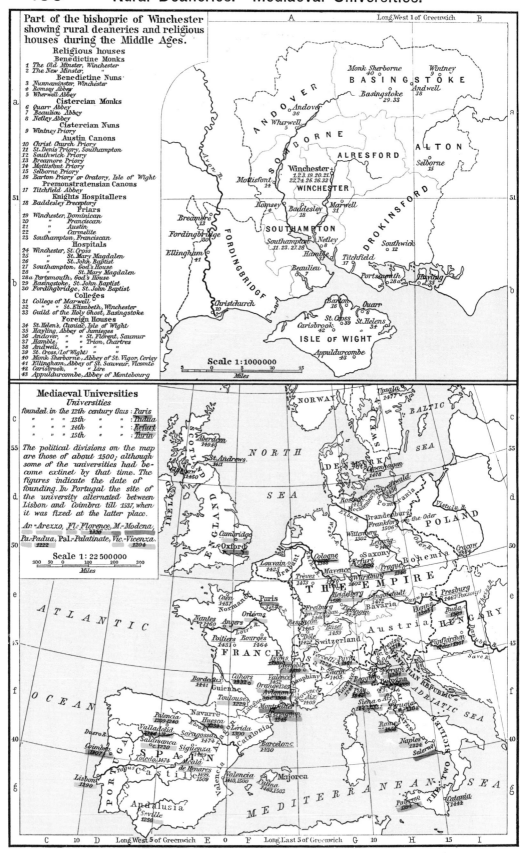

Part of the bishopric of Winchester showing rural deaneries and religious houses during the Middle Ages.

Religious houses
Benedictine Monks
1 The Old Minster, Winchester
2 The New Minster,
Benedictine Nuns
3 Nunnaminster, Winchester
4 Romsey Abbey
5 Wherwell Abbey
Cistercian Monks
6 Quarr Abbey
7 Beaulieu Abbey
8 Netley Abbey
Cistercian Nuns
9 Wintney Priory
Austin Canons
10 Christ Church Priory
11 St.Denis Priory, Southampton
12 Southwick Priory
13 Breamore Priory
14 Mottisfont Priory
15 Selborne Priory
16 Barton Priory or Oratory, Isle of Wight
Premonstratensian Canons
17 Titchfield Abbey
Knights Hospitallers
18 Baddesley Preceptory
Friars
19 Winchester, Dominican
20   "   Franciscan
21   "   Austin
22   "   Carmelite
23 Southampton, Franciscan
Hospitals
24 Winchester, St.Cross
25   "   St.Mary Magdalen
26   "   St.John Baptist
27 Southampton, God's House
28   "   St.Mary Magdalen
28a Portsmouth, God's House
29 Basingstoke, St.John Baptist
30 Fordingbridge, St.John Baptist
Colleges
31 College of Marwell.
32   "   St.Elisabeth, Winchester
33 Guild of the Holy Ghost, Basingstoke
Foreign Houses
34 St.Helen's, Cluniac, Isle of Wight
35 Hayling, Abbey of Jumieges
36 Andover,   "   St. Florent, Saumur
37 Hamble,   "   Trion, Chartres
38 Andwell,   "   "
39 St. Cross,(I.of Wight)   "   "
40 Monk Sherborne, Abbey of St. Vigor, Cerisy
41 Ellingham, Abbey of St. Sauveur, Vicomte
42 Carisbrook,   "   Lire
43 Appuldurcombe, Abbey of Montebourg

Scale 1:1000000

Mediaeval Universities
Universities
founded in the 12th century thus : Paris
   "   "   13th   "   "   : Padua
   "   "   14th   "   "   : Erfurt
   "   "   15th   "   "   : Turin

The political divisions on the map are those of 1500; although some of the universities had become extinct by that time. The figures indicate the date of founding. In Portugal the site of the university alternated between Lisbon and Coimbra till 1537, when it was fixed at the latter place.

Ar.-Arexxo, Fl.-Florence, M.-Modena, Pa.-Padua, Pal.-Palatinate, Vic.-Vicenxa.

Scale 1: 22500000

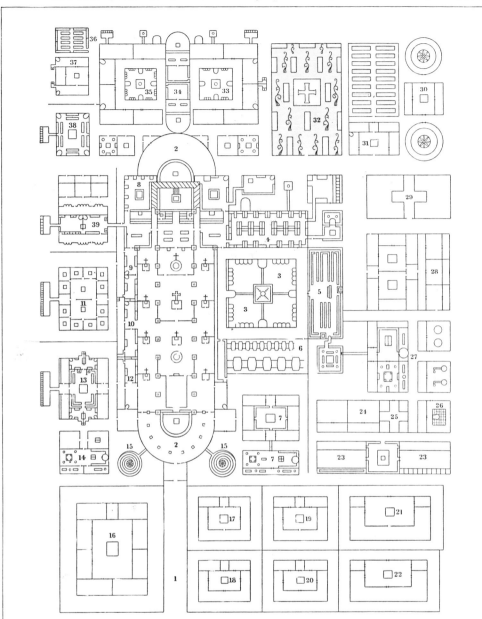

Explanation

This ground-plan is a reduced copy from the ninth century original preserved in the present monastery library. It represents an ideal Benedictine house, and was probably not carried out in complete detail. The enclosure, surrounded by a wall, was about four hundred feet long by about three hundred wide. - 1. Entrance to the church from outside the walls. 2. Church with two apses and numerous altars. 3. Main cloister, showing arches. 4. Dormitory above, room with heating apparatus below. 5. Refectory below, wardrobe above. 6. Cellar with storehouses above. 7. House for pilgrims and poor travellers, with brewery and bakery adjoining. 8. Writing-room below; library above. 9. Living-room and dormitory for visiting monks. 10. Schoolmaster's lodging. 11. School-room for ordinary pupils with lodgings for the teachers. 12. Porter's lodge. 13. Quarters for guests of quality. 14. Brewery and bakery belonging to 13. 15. Towers with spiral staircases, overlooking the whole place. 16. Large building of unknown use. 17. Sheep-stall. 18. Servants' quarters. 19. Goat-stall with goatherds' quarters. 20. Swine-stall with swineherds' quarters. 21. Cattle-shed with cowherds' quarters. 22. Horse-barn with grooms' quarters. 23. Stable for mares and oxen with hay-lofts above and quarters for servants in the middle. 24. Workshops of coopers and turners. 25. Storehouse for brewery-grain. 26. Fruit-drying house. 27. Brewery and bakery for the resident monks, showing mortars and hand-mills. 28. Workshops of shoemakers, saddlers, sword and shield-makers, carvers, turners, goldsmiths, blacksmiths, fullers. 29. Granary and threshing-floor. 30. House of poultry-keeper, hen-house and goose-pen adjoining. 31. House of the gardener, kitchen-garden adjoining. The original gives names of vegetables on the several beds. 32. Burying-ground. 33. Cloister and living-rooms of the "oblati" and their teacher, and of convalescents. 34. Church for the novices and the ill. 35. Cloister and living-rooms, especially for the seriously ill. 36. Hospital-garden. 37. Physician's quarters, apothecary-shop and rooms for patients. 38. Additional building for surgical purposes. 39. Abbot's house, showing entrance to church and to main cloister.

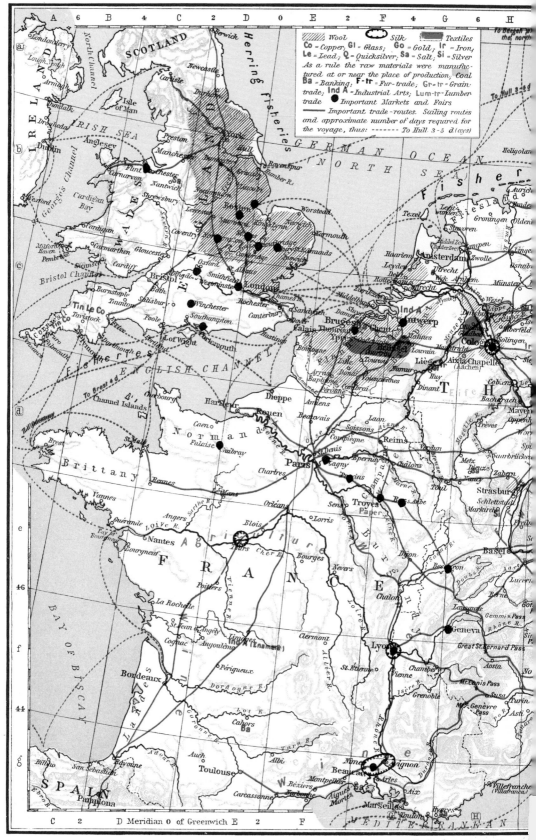

Scale 1:7000000

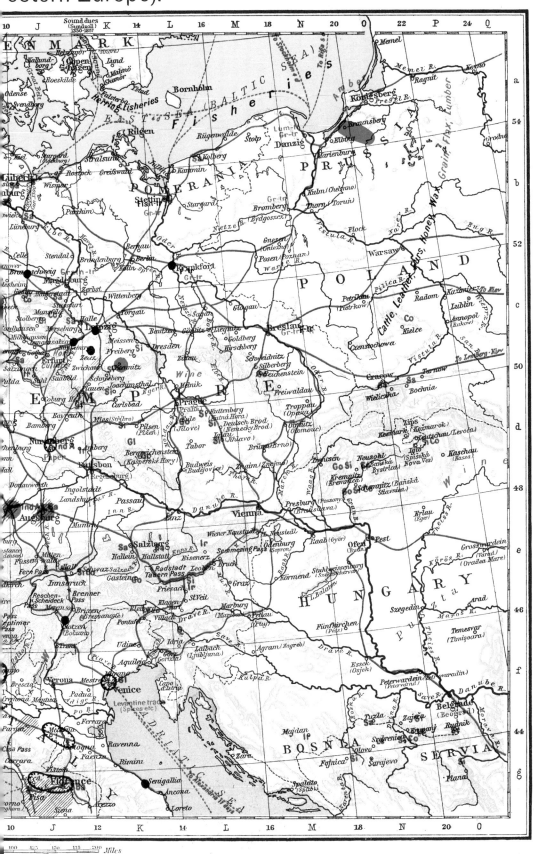

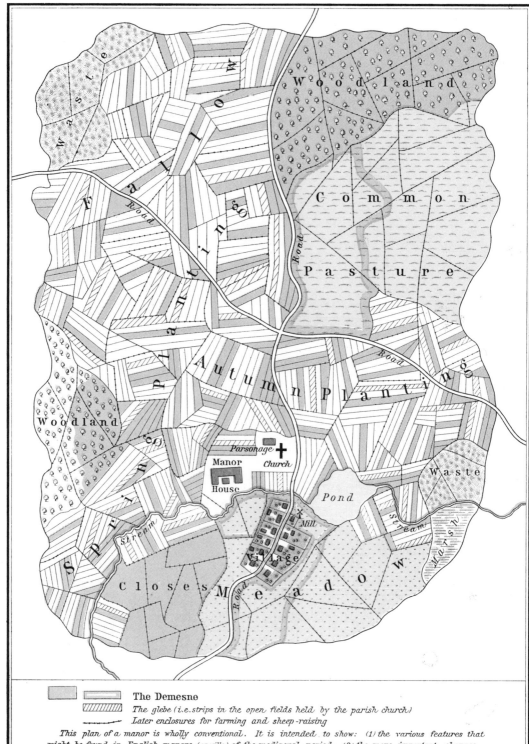

The Demesne

////// The glebe (i.e. strips in the open fields held by the parish church)

Later enclosures for farming and sheep-raising

This plan of a manor is wholly conventional. It is intended to show: (1) the various features that might be found in English manors (or vills) of the mediaeval period; (2) the more important changes in the agricultural system which occurred in England from the fourteenth century onward. Many of these manorial features, of course, appeared in similar domains on the continent.

Enfranchisement of Mediaeval Towns: Expansion of the Charter of Beaumont-en-Argonne, 1182—1300.

104ᴬ

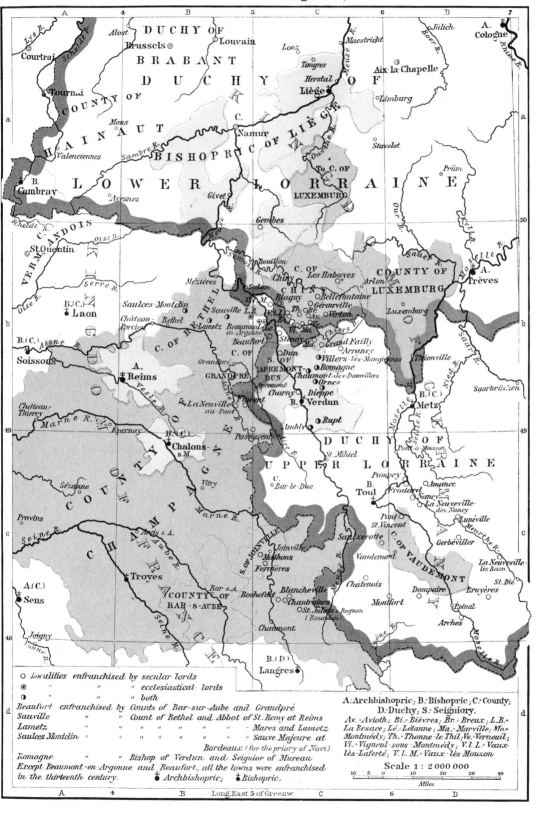

○ *Localities enfranchised by secular lords*
◉   "   "   " *ecclesiastical lords*
◑   "   "   " *both*

Beaufort *enfranchised by Counts of Bar-sur-Aube and Grandpré*
Sauville   "   " *Count of Rethel and Abbot of St. Remy at Reims*
Lametz   "   "   "   "   "   " *Mares and Lametz*
Saulces Montclin "   "   "   "   "   " *Sauve Majeure at*
                                        Bordeaux (for the priory of Novi)
Romagne   "   " *Bishop of Verdun and Seignior of Mureau*
Except Beaumont-en-Argonne and Beaufort, all the towns were enfranchised
in the thirteenth century.   ✝ *Archbishopric;* ✟ *Bishopric.*

A. Archbishopric; B. Bishopric; C. County;
D. Duchy, S. Seigniory.

Av. = Avioth; *Bi.* = Bièvres; *Br.* = Breux; *L.B.* =
La Besace; *Lé.* = Létanne; *Ma.* = Marville; *Mo.* =
Montmédy; *Th.* = Thonne-le-Thil; *Ve.* = Verneuil;
Vi. = Vigneul-sous-Montmédy; *V.l.L.* = Vaux-
lès-Laferté; *V.l.M.* = Vaux-lès-Mouxon

Scale 1 : 2 000 000
10 5 0   10   20   30   40
Miles

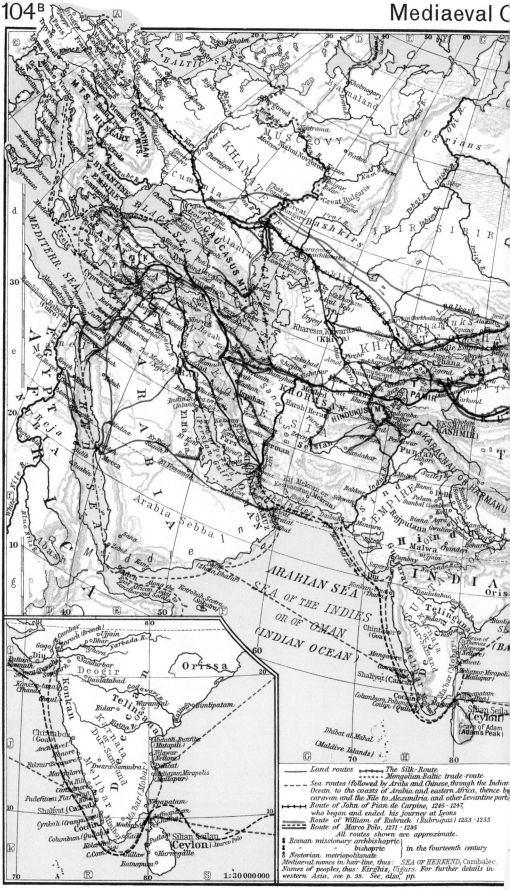

Land routes 　　　　　The Silk-Route
Mongolian-Baltic trade-route
Sea routes (followed by Arabs and Chinese, through the Indian
Ocean. to the coasts of Arabia and eastern Africa, and thence by
caravan. and the Nile to Alexandria, and other Levantine port.
Route of John of Pian de Carpine, 1245-1247,
who began and ended. his journey at Lyons
Route of William of Rubruck (Rubruquis) 1253-1255
Route of Marco Polo, 1271-1295
All routes shown are approximate.
Roman missionary archbishopric
" 　" 　bishopric　in the fourteenth century
Nestorian metriopolitanate
Mediaeval names in hair-line, thus:　SEA OF HERKEND; Cambalec.
Names of peoples, thus: Kirghiz, Uigurs. For further details in
western Asia, see p. 99. See, also, pp.

1:30 000 000

Scale 1:40000000

Greenwich J 100

400 600 800 *Miles*

Europe in 1490.

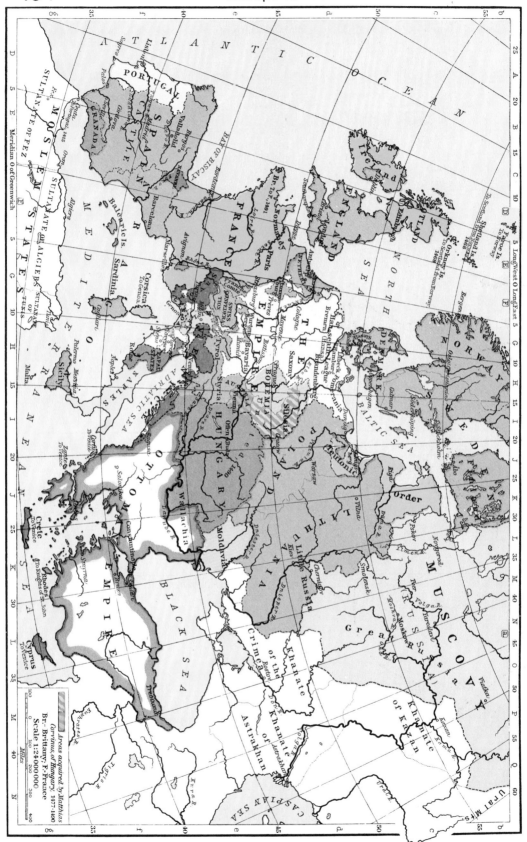

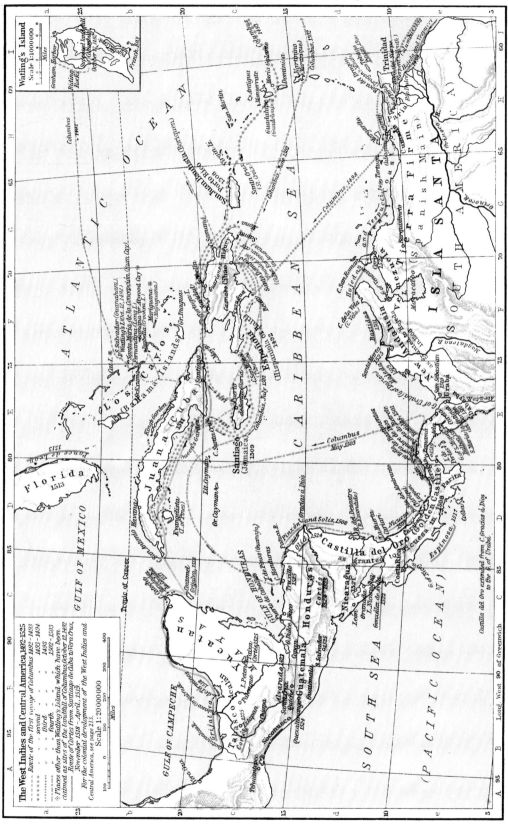

The

The Conquest of Mexico, 1519—1521.

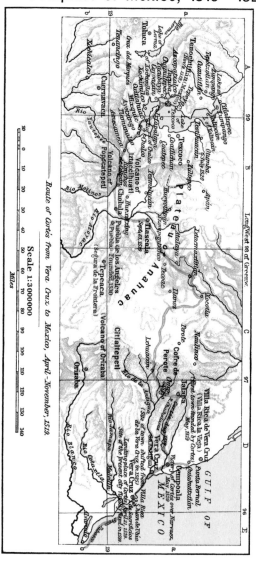

Scale 1:3000000

Route of Cortés from Vera Cruz to Mexico, April.-November, 1519.

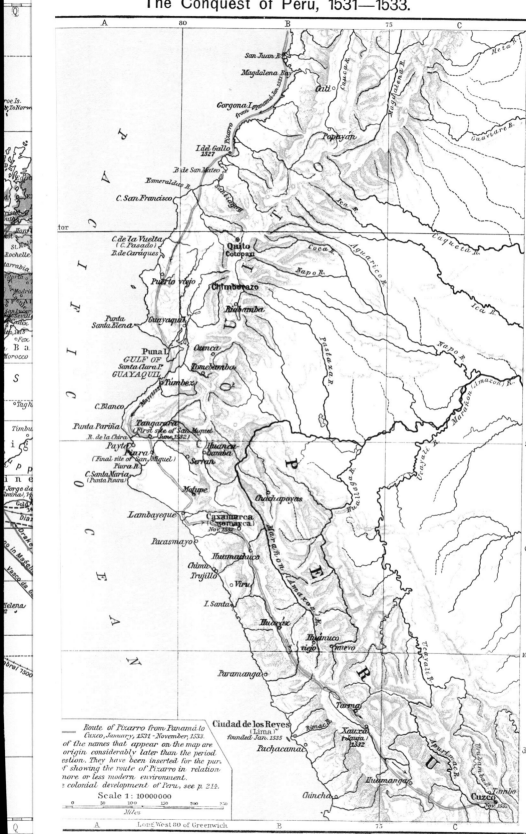

The Conquest of Peru, 1531—1533.

Route of Pizarro from Panamá to Cuzco, January, 1531 - November, 1533.
... of the names that appear on the map are ... origin considerably later than the period ... estion. They have been inserted for the pur... f showing the route of Pizarro in relation ... nore or less modern environment.
... colonial development of Peru, see p. 214.

Scale 1 : 10000000

Miles

Long West 80 of Greenwich

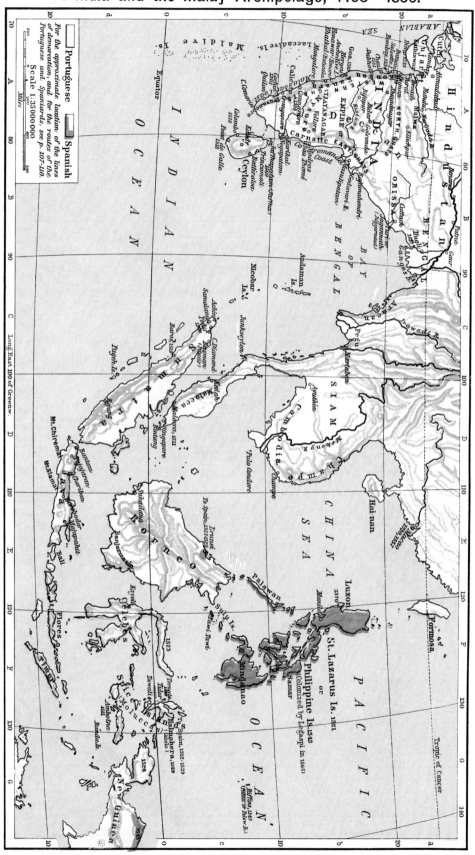

The Portuguese Colonial Dominions in India and the Malay Archipelago, 1498—1580.

Scale 1:35000000

For the approximate location of the lines of demarcation, and for the routes of the Portuguese and Spaniards, see p. 107–110.

Portuguese

Spanish

The Imperial Circles about 1512.

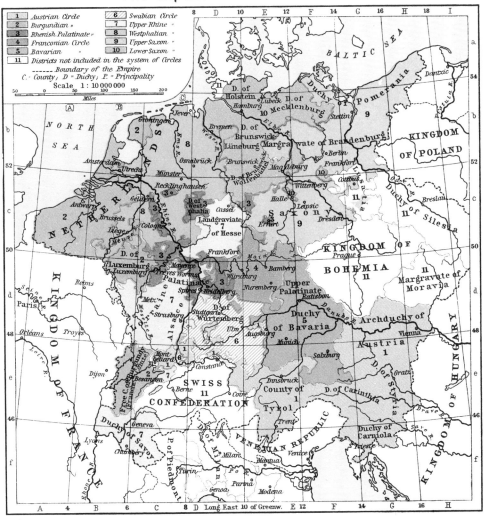

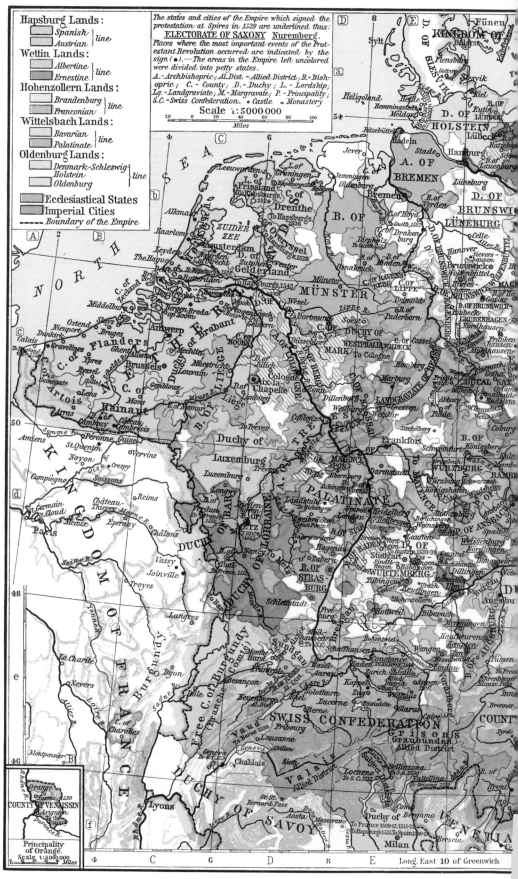

Hapsburg Lands:
    Spanish } line
    Austrian

Wettin Lands:
    Albertine } line
    Ernestine

Hohenzollern Lands:
    Brandenburg } line
    Franconian

Wittelsbach Lands:
    Bavarian } line
    Palatinate

Oldenburg Lands:
    Denmark-Schleswig
    Holstein } line
    Oldenburg

Ecclesiastical States
Imperial Cities
- - - - Boundary of the Empire

The states and cities of the Empire which signed the
protestation at Spires in 1529 are underlined thus:
ELECTORATE OF SAXONY Nuremberg.
Places where the most important events of the Prot-
estant Revolution occurred are indicated by the
sign (●).—The areas in the Empire left uncolored
were divided into petty states.
A.-Archbishopric; Al.Dist.-Allied District; B.-Bish-
opric; C.-County; D.-Duchy; L.-Lordship;
Lg.-Landgraviate; M.-Margraviate; P.-Principality;
S.C.-Swiss Confederation. ◆ Castle ■ Monastery

Scale 1:5000000

Principality of Orange.
Scale 1:5000000

Long. East 10 of Greenwich

The Netherlands, 1559—1609.

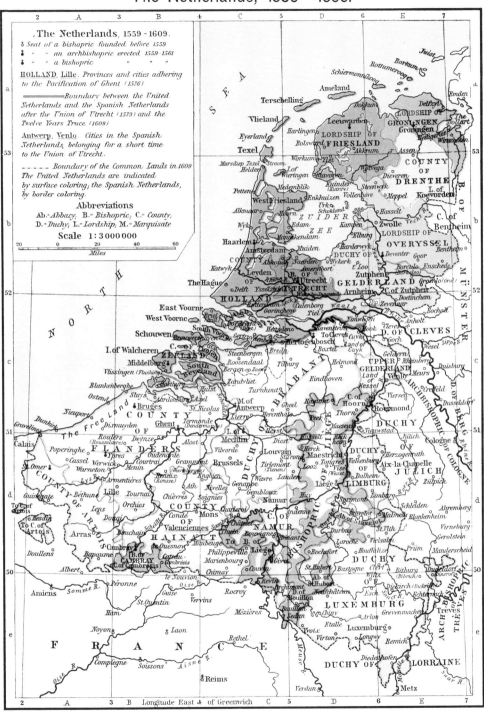

Possessions of the House of Hapsburg:
  Spanish line ⎫ in surface
  Austrian line ⎭ coloring
  European empire of Charles V
    about 1526
Possessions of the House of Bourbon:
  Hereditary lands of Henry of
    Bourbon-Navarre (later Henry IV.)
  Lands of Charles of Bourbon-
    Montpensier (the Constable)

*The underlining of Metz, Toul and Verdun
indicates that, while these cities legally
formed part of the Empire after 1552, they
were actually held by France.
Montferrat belonged to Mantua, and the
papal territory of Ferrara to Modena.
Sites of important events are indicated
by the sign (•).*
- - - - - - - Route of the Armada 1588.
× Battle   ◦ Castle   ▫ Monastery
Abbreviations:
D.= Duchy. Dom.= Domain. K.= Kingdom.
L.N.= Lower Navarre. M.= Margravate.
P.= Principality. Rep.= Republic. U.N.= Upper
Navarre.

Scale 1:15 000 000
100   0   100   200
          Miles

The Religious Situation in Central Europe about 1618.
Sweden about 1658.

120

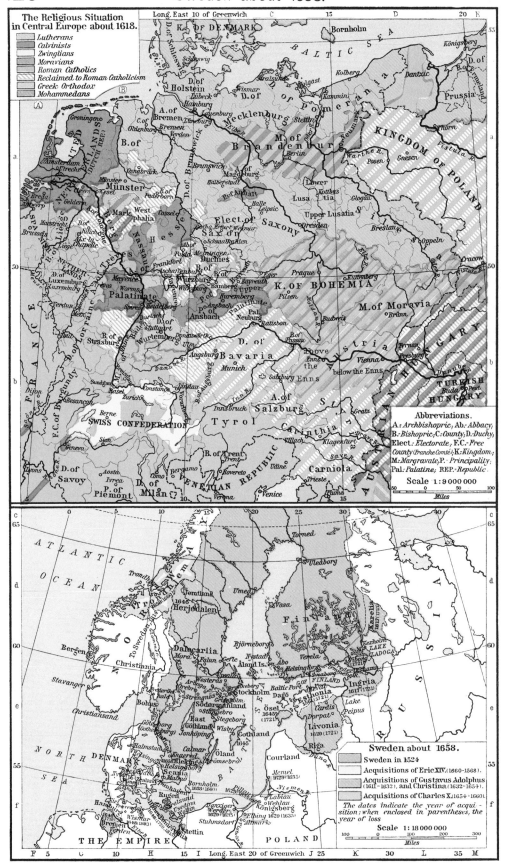

The Religious Situation in Central Europe about 1618.

- Lutherans
- Calvinists
- Zwinglians
- Moravians
- Roman Catholics
- Reclaimed to Roman Catholicism
- Greek Orthodox
- Mohammedans

Abbreviations.

A: Archbishopric; Ab: Abbacy;
B: Bishopric; C: County; D: Duchy;
Elect: Electorate; F.C: Free
County (Franche Comté); K: Kingdom;
M: Margravate; P: Principality;
Pal: Palatine; REP: Republic.

Scale 1: 9 000 000

Sweden about 1658.

- Sweden in 1524
- Acquisitions of Eric XIV. (1560-1568).
- Acquisitions of Gustavus Adolphus (1611-1632), and Christina (1632-1654).
- Acquisitions of Charles X. (1654-1660).

The dates indicate the year of acquisition: when enclosed in parentheses, the year of loss.

Scale 1: 18 000 000

Principal Seats of War, 1618—1660.
Treaty Adjustments, 1648—1660.

121

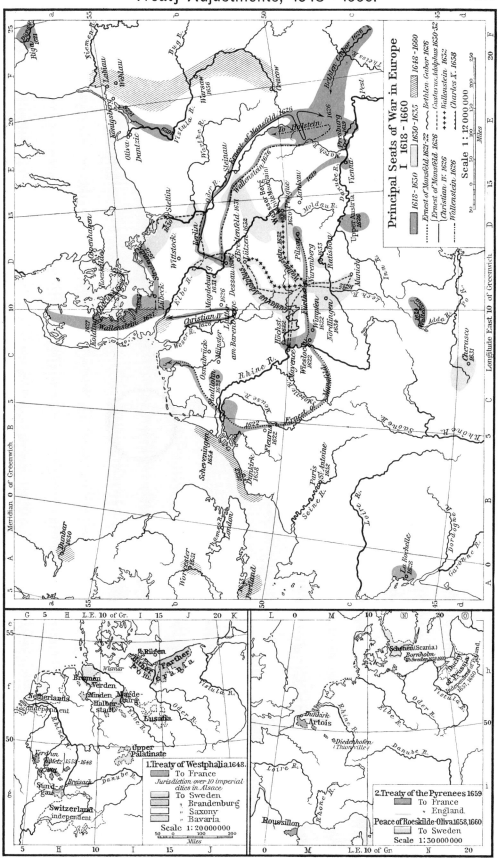

Principal Seats of War in Europe

I 1618 - 1660

1618-1630	1630-1635	1648-1660

.... Ernest of Mansfeld 1621-22 ——— Bethlen Gabor 1626
.... Ernest of Mansfeld 1626 ———— Gustavus Adolphus 1630-32
——— Christian IV. 1626 ++++ Wallenstein 1632
——— Wallenstein 1626 ———— Charles X. 1658

Scale 1:12000000

1. Treaty of Westphalia, 1648.
To France
Jurisdiction over 10 imperial cities in Alsace
To Sweden
" Brandenburg
" Saxony
" Bavaria
Scale 1:20000000

2. Treaty of the Pyrenees 1659
To France
" England
Peace of Roeskilde-Oliva 1658,1660
To Sweden
Scale 1:30000000

Hapsburg Lands:
   Austrian } line
   Spanish
Hohenzollern Lands:
   Brandenburg } line
   Franconian
Wettin Lands:
   Albertine } line
   Ernestine
Wittelsbach Lands:
   Bavarian } line
   Palatinate
Oldenburg Lands:
   Denmark (royal portion) and Oldenburg
   Holstein-Gottorp (ducal portion)
   Ecclesiastical States
   Imperial Cities
- - - - - Boundary of the Empire

The chief territorial changes in the seventeenth century
are indicated by narrow colored borders. The color
scheme, furthermore, shows how the Saxon portion of the
County of Henneberg, held in common by the Albertines and
the Ernestines till 1660, was divided between them at that
time; also, how the County of Sponheim, held in common by
Baden and the Palatinate, was divided between them in
1707 and 1776. The areas in the Empire left uncolored were
divided into petty states.
Sites of the most important battles and diplomatic nego-
tiations are given the sign ●
The states and cities to which the Edict of Restitution (1629)
applied are underlined, thus: Strasburg
Abbreviations
A.=Archbishopric. A.Z.=Anhalt Zerbst. Ab.=Abbacy. B.=Bishopric.
Bav.=Bavaria. Brand.=Brandenburg. C.=County. D.=Duchy.
Fr.W.C.=Frederick William Canal. H.C.=Hesse-Cassel. L.=Lordship.
Lg.=Landgraviate. M.=Margravate. Meck.=Mecklenburg.
P.=Principality. Pal.=Palatinate.
◇=Castle.   ✠=Monastery.
Scale 1:5 000 000
Miles.

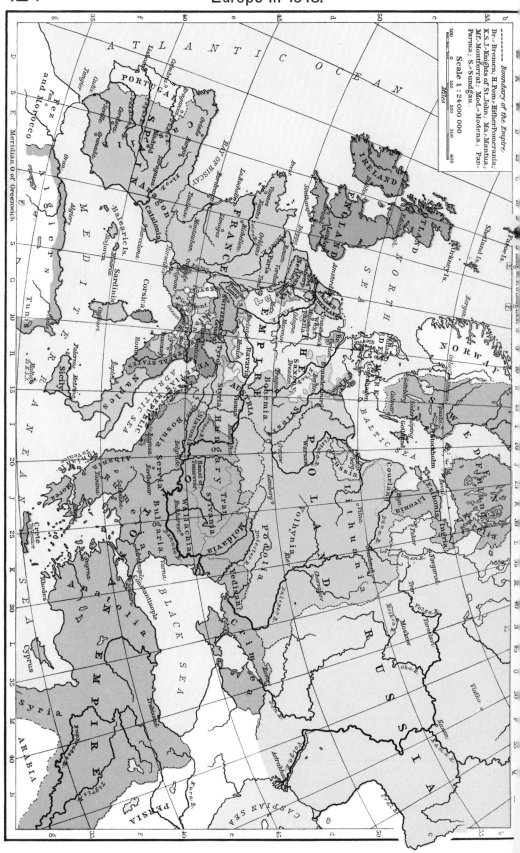

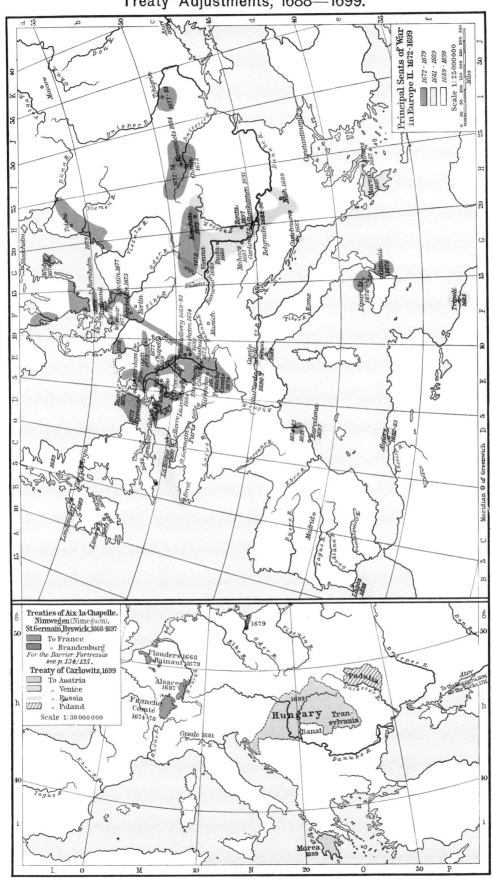

Principal Seats of War
in Europe II. 1672-1699

1672 - 1679
1681 - 1689
1689 - 1699

Scale 1:25000000

Miles

Meridian 0 of Greenwich

Treaties of Aix-la-Chapelle,
Nimwegen (Nimeguen),
St.Germain,Ryswick,1668-1697
  To France
  „ Brandenburg
For the Barrier Fortresses
  see p. 134/135.
Treaty of Carlowitz, 1699
  To Austria
  „ Venice
  „ Russia
  „ Poland
  Scale 1:30000000

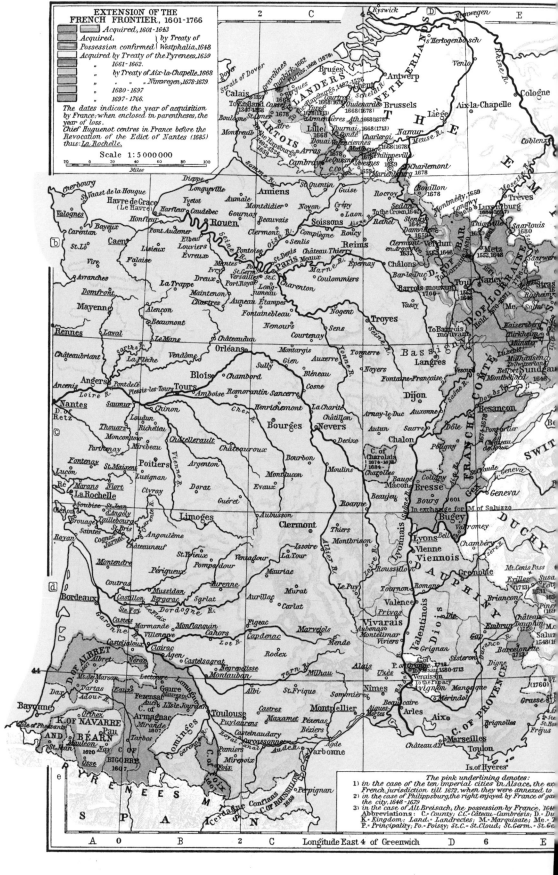

EXTENSION OF THE
FRENCH FRONTIER, 1601-1766

Acquired, 1601-1643
Acquired,   } by Treaty of
Possession confirmed } Westphalia, 1648
Acquired by Treaty of the Pyrenees, 1659
"   1661-1662.
"   by Treaty of Aix-la-Chapelle, 1668
"   "   Nimwegen, 1678-1679
"   1680-1697
"   1697-1766.

The dates indicate the year of acquisition
by France; when enclosed in parentheses, the
year of loss.
Chief Huguenot centres in France before the
Revocation of the Edict of Nantes (1685)
thus: La Rochelle.

Scale 1:5 000 000

Miles

The pink underlining denotes:
1) in the case of the ten imperial cities in Alsace, the ex
French jurisdiction till 1672, when they were annexed to
2) in the case of Philippsburg, the right enjoyed by France of ga
the city, 1648-1679
3) in the case of Alt Breisach, the possession by France, 1648
Abbreviations: C.· County; C.C.· Cāteau-Cambrésis; D.· Du
K.· Kingdom; Land.· Landrecies; M.· Marquisate; Me.· T
P.· Principality; Po.· Poissy; St.C.· St.Cloud; St.Germ.· St.Ge

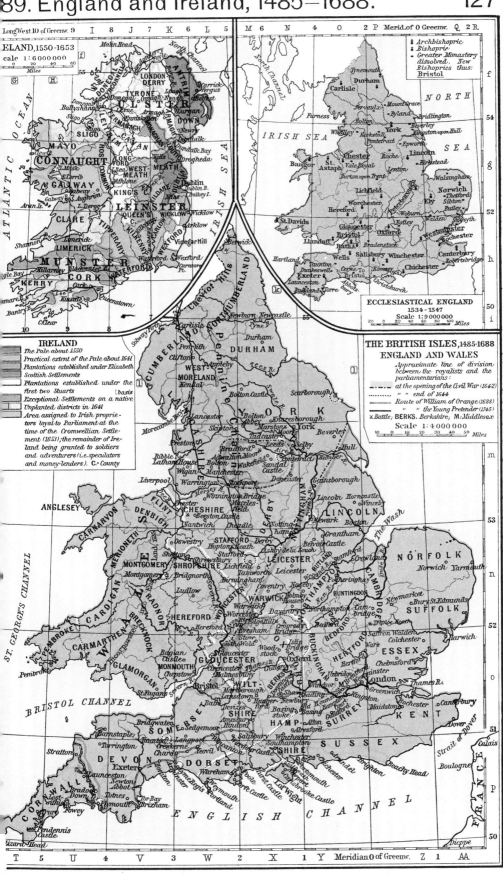

ECCLESIASTICAL ENGLAND
1534–1547
Scale 1:9 000 000

IRELAND
The Pale about 1550
Practical extent of the Pale about 1641
Plantations established under Elizabeth
Scottish Settlements
Plantations established under the
first two Stuarts   basis
Exceptional Settlements on a native
Unplanted districts in 1641
Area assigned to Irish proprie-
tors loyal to Parliament at the
time of the Cromwellian Settle-
ment (1653); the remainder of Ire-
land being granted to soldiers
and adventurers (i.e. speculators
and money-lenders). C.=County

THE BRITISH ISLES, 1485–1688
ENGLAND AND WALES
Approximate line of division
between the royalists and the
parliamentarians:
———— at the opening of the Civil War (1642)
·········· ″ ″ end of 1644
——— Route of William of Orange (1688)
″ ″ the Young Pretender (1745)
x Battle; BERKS. Berkshire; M. Middlesex
Scale 1:4 000 000

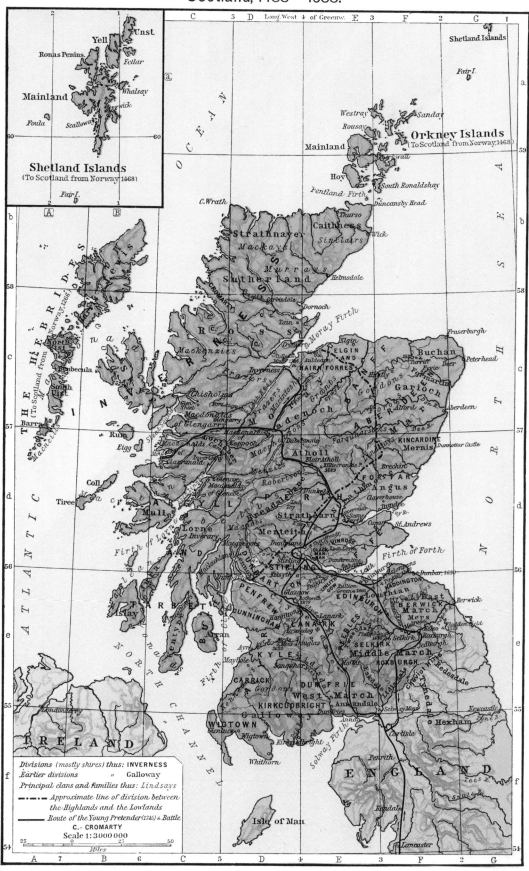

Shetland Islands
(To Scotland from Norway 1468)

Orkney Islands
(To Scotland from Norway, 1468)

Divisions (mostly shires) thus: INVERNESS
Earlier divisions   "   Galloway
Principal clans and families thus: Lindsays
— · — · — Approximate line of division between
the Highlands and the Lowlands
———— Route of the Young Pretender (1745) & Battle
C.= CROMARTY
Scale 1:3 000 000

The Ottoman Empire, 1481—1683.

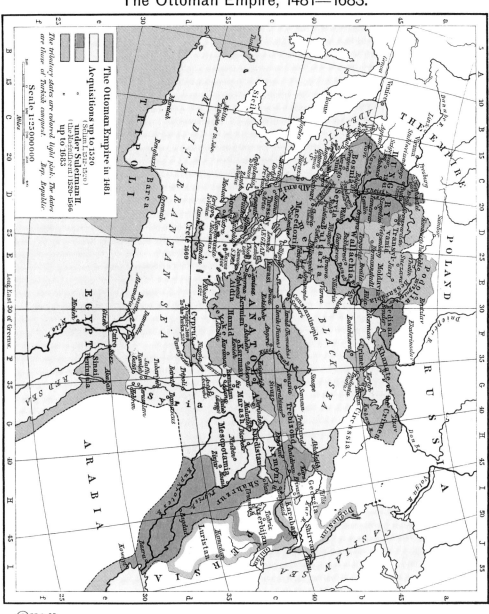

Partition of Guiana and the West Indies (1600-1700)

English — French
Dutch — Spanish

⌐ *Haunts of the Buccaneers.*
Scale along the Equator 1:40000000

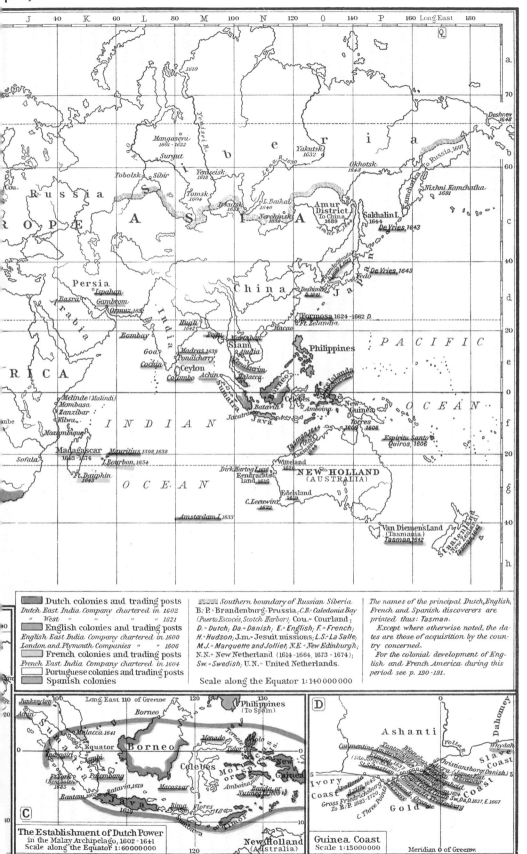

Dutch colonies and trading posts
Dutch East India Company chartered in 1602
  "   West   "   "   "   1621
English colonies and trading posts
English East India Company chartered in 1600
London and Plymouth Companies " 1606
French colonies and trading posts
French East India Company chartered in 1604
Portuguese colonies and trading posts
Spanish colonies

Southern boundary of Russian Siberia
B. P.= Brandenburg-Prussia.; C.B.= Caledonia Bay
(*Puerto Escocés, Scotch Harbor*); Cou.= Courland;
D.= Dutch; Da.= Danish; E.= English; F.= French;
H.= Hudson; J.m.= Jesuit missions; L.S.= La Salle;
M.J.= Marquette and Jolliet; N.E.= New Edinburgh;
N.N.= New Netherland (1614-1664, 1673 - 1674).;
Sw.= Swedish; U.N.= United Netherlands.

Scale along the Equator 1:140 000 000

The names of the principal Dutch, English,
French and Spanish discoverers are
printed thus: Tasman.
  Except where otherwise noted, the da-
tes are those of acquisition by the coun-
try concerned.
  For the colonial development of Eng-
lish and French America during this
period see p. 190-191.

The Establishment of Dutch Power
in the Malay Archipelago, 1602 - 1641
Scale along the Equator 1:60 000 000

Guinea Coast
Scale 1:15 000 000

Meridian 0 of Greenw.

Principal Seats of War in Europe, 1700—1721.

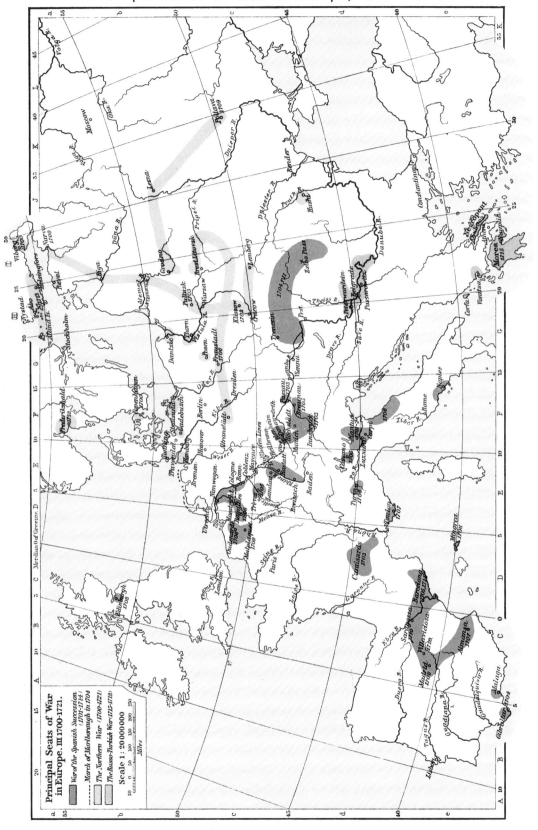

Principal Seats of War
in Europe. III 1700-1721.

War of the Spanish Succession
(1701-1714)
March of Marlborough in 1704
The Northern War (1700-1721)
The Russo-Turkish War (1715-1718)

Scale 1 : 20000000

Miles
50 0 50 100 150 200 250

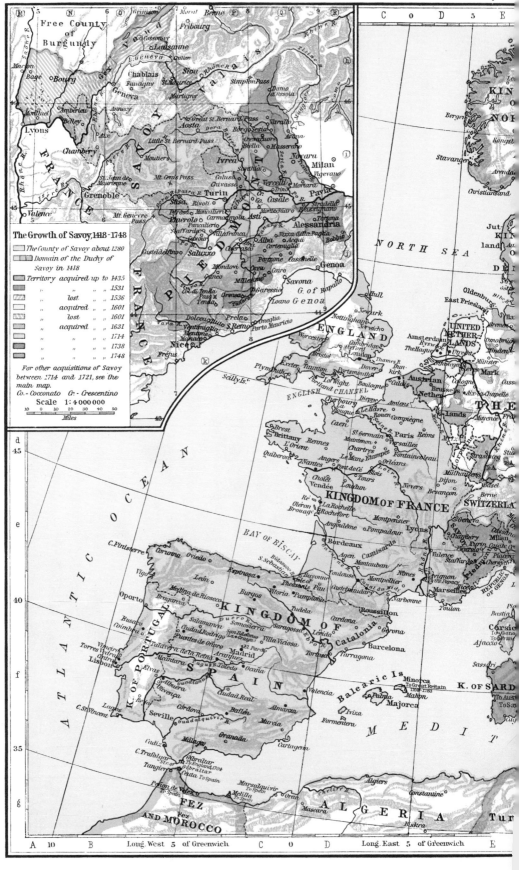

House of Bourbon
House of Hapsburg-Lorraine
Kingdom of Prussia
and its dependencies
House of Savoy
------- Boundary of the Empire
◇ ✩ Castle or fortress ▭ Monastery
Abbreviations.
A.= Austria. D.= Duchy. Govt.= Government.
GR.D.= Grand Duchy. Gr.P.= Grand Principali-
ty. H.= Holstein-Gottorp. K.= Kingdom.
P.= Principality. REP.= Republic.

Sites of battles, diplomatic negotiations and other events of historical
importance are indicated by the sign ◇.

Scale 1:15000000
0   100   200   300   400   500
Miles

Principal Seats of War, 1740—1763.

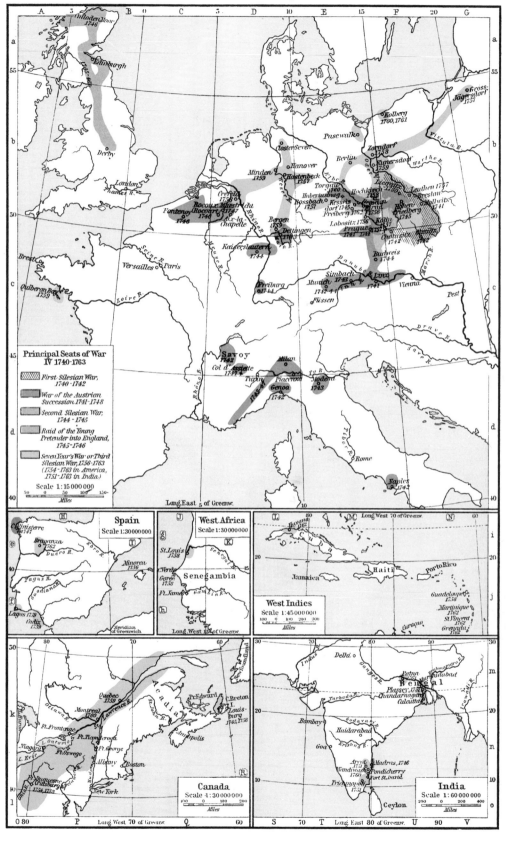

**Principal Seats of War
IV 1740-1763**

First Silesian War,
1740-1742

War of the Austrian
Succession 1741-1748

Second Silesian War,
1744-1745

Raid of the Young
Pretender into England,
1745-1746

Seven Year's War or Third
Silesian War, 1756-1763
(1754-1763 in America,
1751-1763 in India.)

Scale 1:15 000 000

Spain
Scale 1:30 000 000

West Africa
Scale 1:30 000 000

Senegambia

West Indies
Scale 1:45 000 000

Canada
Scale 1:30 000 000

India
Scale 1:60 000 000

Treaty Adjustments, 1713—1763.

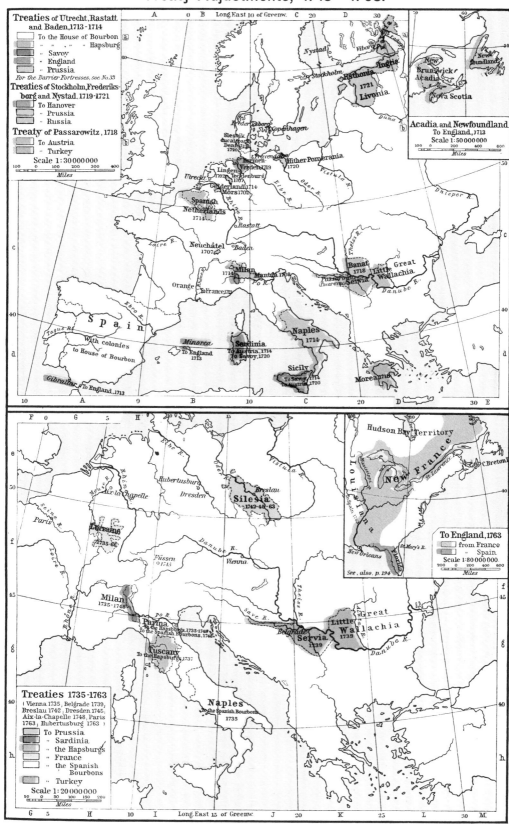

Treaties of Utrecht, Rastatt and Baden, 1713-1714
- To the House of Bourbon
- " " " Hapsburg
- " Savoy
- " England
- " Prussia

For the Barrier Fortresses, see No.33

Treaties of Stockholm, Frederiksborg and Nystad, 1719-1721
- To Hanover
- " Prussia
- " Russia

Treaty of Passarowitz, 1718
- To Austria
- " Turkey

Scale 1:30 000 000

100   0   100   200   300   400
Miles

Acadia and Newfoundland
To England, 1713
Scale 1:50 000 000

100   0   200   400   600
Miles

New Brunswick
Acadia
Nova Scotia
New Foundland

Nystad
Viborg
Ingria
Stockholm
Esthonia
1721
Livonia
Düna R.
Dnieper R.

Frederiksborg
Copenhagen
Sleswik
duca. prov.
Denmark
1720
Gravendeel
Wesel 1719
Hither Pomerania
1720
Oder R.
Vistula R.
Lingen 1702
Tecklenburg
Geldernland 1714
Mörs 1702
Elbe R.
Utrecht
1707

Spanish
Netherlands
1714
Rhine R.
Rastatt

Loire R.
Neuchâtel 1707
Baden
Rhone R.
Theiss R.
Banat
1718
Little Great
Wallachia
Passarowitz
Servia
Danube R.

Orange
To France 1713
Milan
1714
Mantua 1708
Po R.

Spain
With colonies
to House of Bourbon
Tagus R.
Ebro R.

Minorca
To England
1713
Sardinia
To Austria, 1714
To Savoy, 1720
Naples
1714

Gibraltar. To England, 1713
Sicily
To Savoy 1714
To Austria 1720
Morea 1714

Hudson Bay Territory

New France
St. Lawrence R.
C. Breton

Louisiana
Mississippi R.
Spain R.

To England, 1763
from France
Spain
Scale 1:80 000 000
200   0   200   400   600
Miles

New Orleans
St. Mary's R.
Florida

See, also, p. 194

Elbe R.
Oder R.
Vistula R.
Hubertusburg
Breslau
Dresden
Silesia
1742-48-63

Rhine R.
Maas R.
Aix-la-Chapelle
Seine R.
Paris
Lorraine
1735-66
Loire R.

Füssen
1745
Danube R.
Vienna

Milan
1735-1748
Rhine R.
Parma
To the Hapsburgs 1735-1748
To the Spanish Bourbons, 1748
Tuscany
To the Hapsburgs 1737
Po R.
Save R.
Theiss R.
Belgrade
Servia
1739
Little
Great
Wallachia
1739
Danube R.

Naples
To the Spanish Bourbons
1735

Treaties 1735-1763
(Vienna 1735, Belgrade 1739, Breslau 1742, Dresden 1745, Aix-la-Chapelle 1748, Paris 1763, Hubertusburg 1763)
- To Prussia
- " Sardinia
- " the Hapsburgs
- " France
- " the Spanish Bourbons
- " Turkey

Scale 1:20 000 000
50   0   50   100   150   200
Miles

Long. East 10 of Greenw.
Long. East 15 of Greenw.

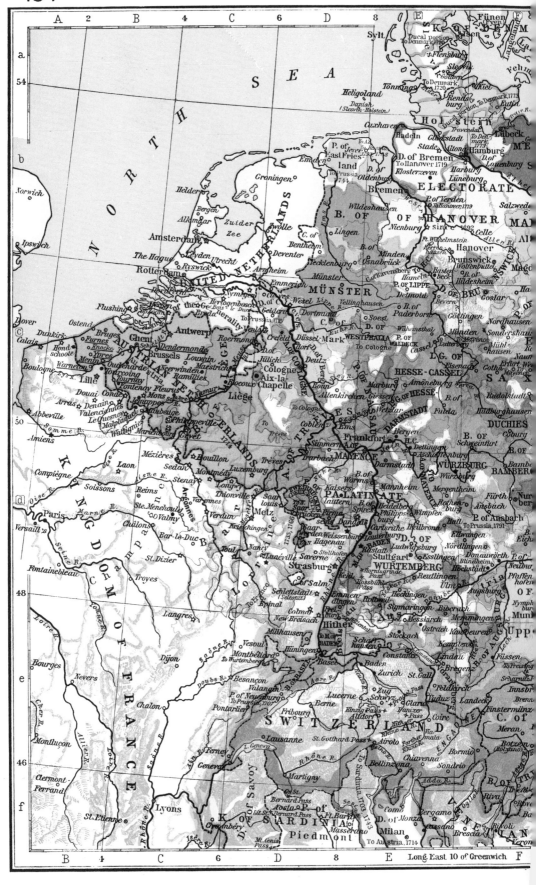

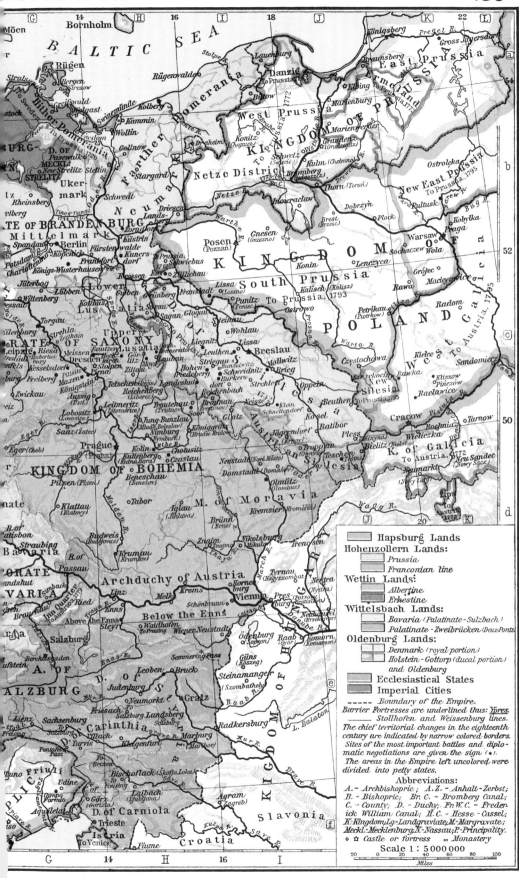

Hapsburg Lands
Hohenzollern Lands:
  Prussia
  Franconian line
Wettin Lands:
  Albertine
  Ernestine
Wittelsbach Lands:
  Bavaria (Palatinate-Sulzbach)
  Palatinate-Zweibrücken (DeuxPonts)
Oldenburg Lands:
  Denmark (royal portion)
  Holstein-Gottorp (ducal portion)
    and Oldenburg
Ecclesiastical States
Imperial Cities
----- Boundary of the Empire.
Barrier Fortresses are underlined thus: Ypres.
—— Stollhofen and Weissenburg lines.
The chief territorial changes in the eighteenth
century are indicated by narrow colored borders.
Sites of the most important battles and diplo-
matic negotiations are given the sign (•).
The areas in the Empire left uncolored were
divided into petty states.
Abbreviations:
A. = Archbishopric; A.Z. = Anhalt-Zerbst;
B. = Bishopric; Br. C. = Bromberg Canal;
C. = County; D. = Duchy; Fn.W.C. = Freder-
ick William Canal; H. C. = Hesse-Cassel;
K. Kingdom; Lg. Landgraviate; M. Margravate;
Meckl. Mecklenburg; N. Nassau; P. Principality.
◇ ☆ Castle or fortress   • Monastery
Scale 1 : 5000000
20 0   20   40   60   80 100
Miles

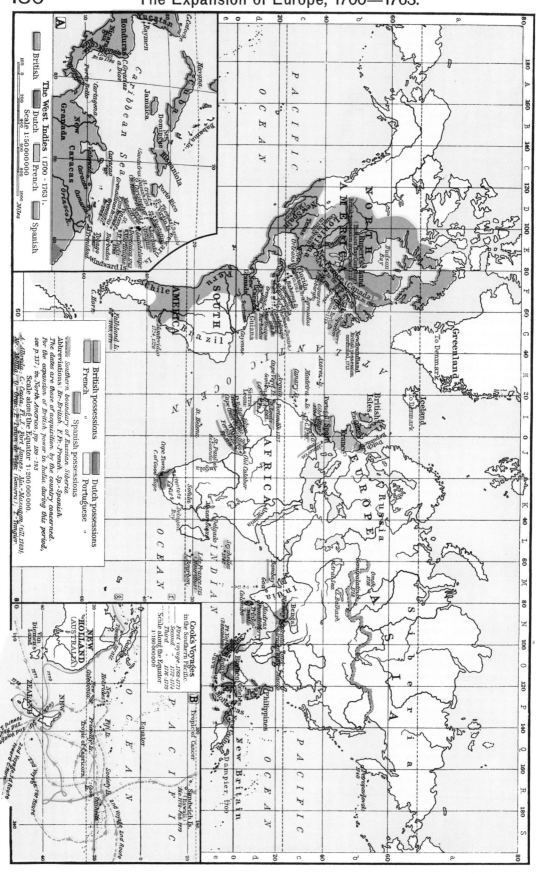

A

The West Indies
(1700 - 1763).

Scale 1:50,000,000

British   French   Spanish

Dutch

British possessions   Spanish possessions

French   "   Portuguese "

Dutch possessions

Southern boundary of Russian Siberia.
Abbreviations: Br.-British. F.Fr.-French. Sp.-Spanish.
The dates are those of acquisition by the country concerned.
For the expansion of British power in India during this period,
see p. 137; tr. North America, pp. 189 - 193.

Scale along the Equator 1:200,000,000.

A: Albrolho; C: Cayta; F.J.: Port James; Alc: Mezagan, (till 1769);
Mc: Melilla; O: Oran; P: Return de Vélez. (Gomera); T: Tangier.

B

Cook's Voyages
in the Southern Pacific.

First voyage 1768-1771
Second " 1772-1774
Third " 1776-1779

Scale along the Equator
1:180,000,000

India, 1700—1792.

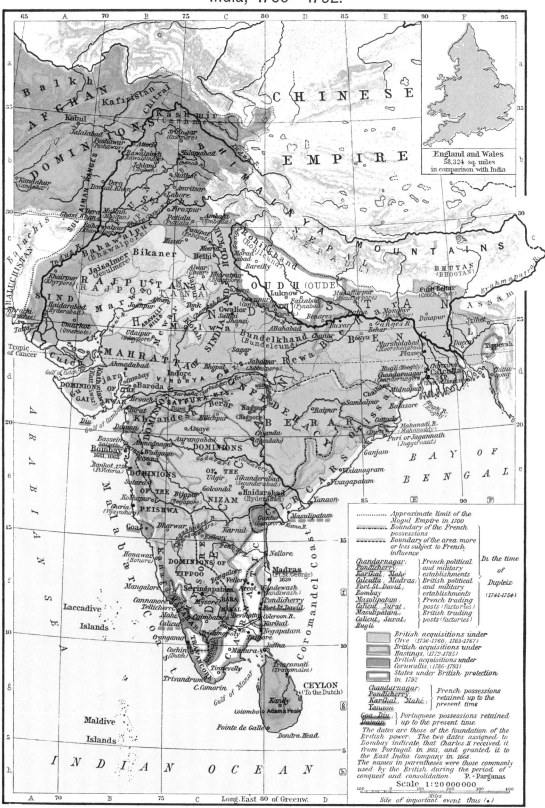

England and Wales
58,324 sq. miles
in comparison with India

Legend:

.... Approximate limit of the Mogul Empire in 1700

–·–·–·– Boundary of the French possessions

– – – – Boundary of the area more or less subject to French influence

		In the time of Dupleix (1741–1754)
Chandarnagar, Pondicherry, Karikal, Mahé	French political and military establishments
Calcutta, Madras, Fort St. David, Bombay	British political and military establishments
Masulipatam; Calicut, Surat;	French trading posts (factories)
Masulipatam; Calicut, Surat; Hugli	British trading posts (factories)

British acquisitions under Clive (1756–1760, 1765–1767)

British acquisitions under Hastings, (1772–1785)

British acquisitions under Cornwallis, (1786–1793)

States under British protection in 1792

Chandarnagar, Pondicherry, Karikal, Mahé, Yanaon — French possessions retained up to the present time

Goa, Diu, Daman — Portuguese possessions retained up to the present time

The dates are those of the foundation of the British power. The two dates assigned to Bombay indicate that Charles II received it from Portugal in 1661, and granted it to the East India Company in 1668. The names in parentheses were those commonly used by the British during the period of conquest and consolidation. P.-Parganas

Scale 1:20 000 000

Long. East 80 of Greenw.

Miles

Site of important event thus (•)

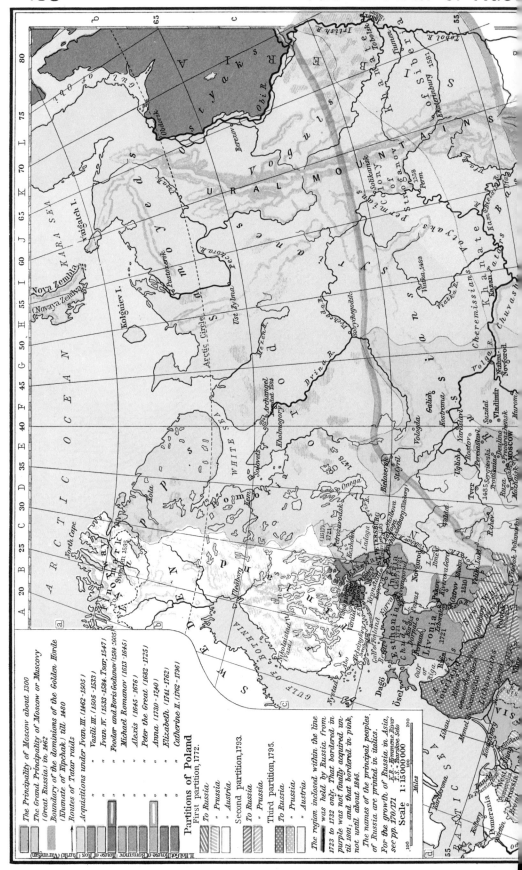

The Principality of Moscow about 1300

The Grand Principality of Moscow or Muscovy
(Great Russia) in 1462

Boundary of the dominions of the Golden Horde
(Khanate of Kipchak) till 1480

Routes of Tatar raids

Acquisitions under Ivan III. (1462–1505)

"   "   " Vasili III. (1505–1533)

"   "   " Ivan IV. (1533–1584. Tsar 1547)

"   "   " Feodor and Boris Godunov (1584–1605)

"   "   " Michael Romanov (1613–1645)

"   "   " Alexis (1645–1676)

"   "   " Peter the Great (1682–1725)

"   "   " Anna (1730–1740)

"   "   " Elizabeth (1741–1762)

"   "   " Catherine II. (1762–1796)

Partitions of Poland
First partition, 1772.

To Russia.
" Prussia.
" Austria.

Second partition, 1793.

To Russia.
" Prussia.

Third partition, 1795.

To Russia.
" Prussia.
" Austria.

The region inclosed within the line
was held by Russia. From
1723 to 1732 only. That bordered in
purple was not finally acquired until 1801; and that bordered in pink,
not until about 1815.

The names of the principal peoples
of Russia are printed in italics.

For the growth of Russia in Asia,
see pp. 170/171.
K.R.= Kamenne River
T.S.= Tsarskoe Selo
Scale 1:15000000

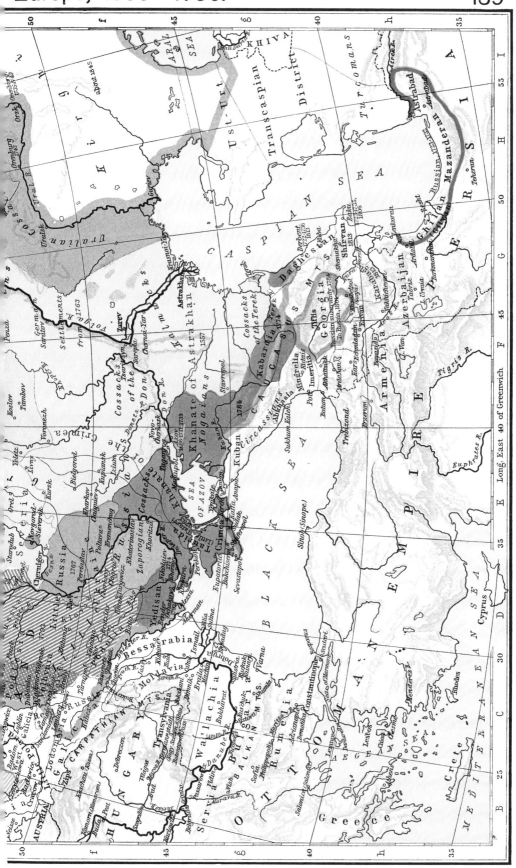

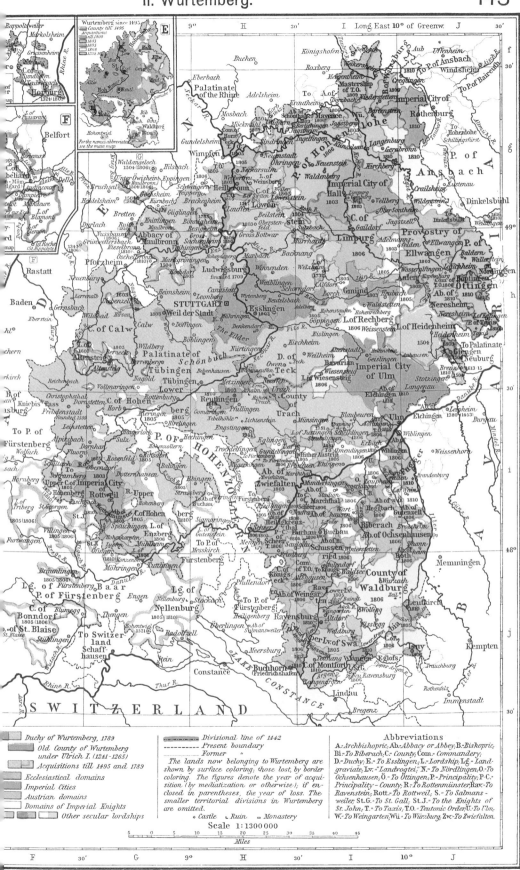

144

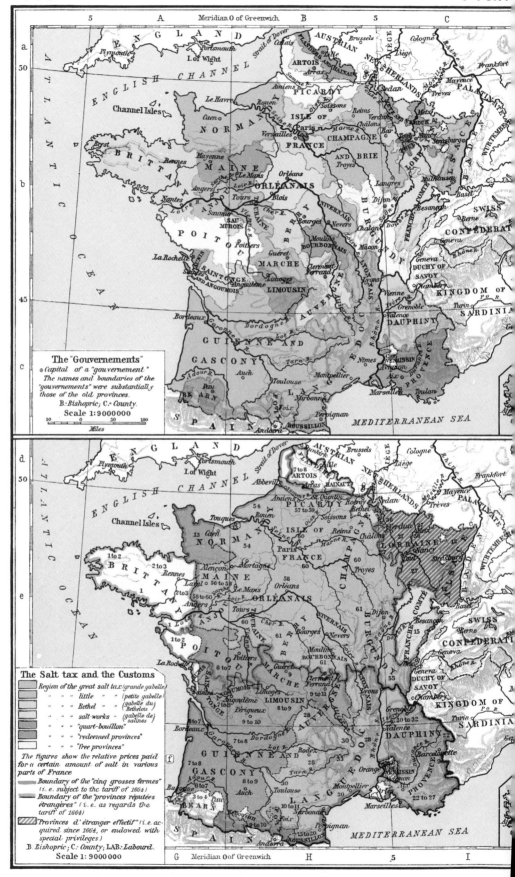

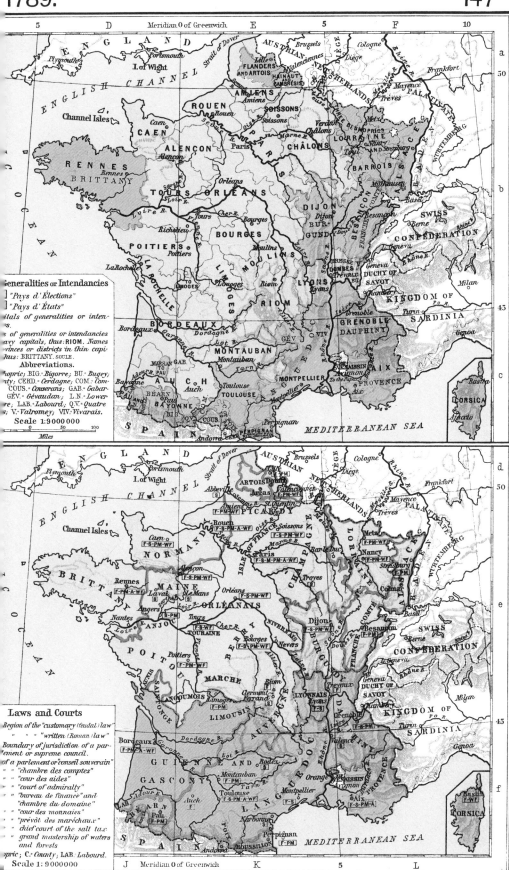

Generalities or Intendancies

□ "Pays d'Élections"
□ "Pays d'États"
... itals of generalities or inten-
...s.
...s of generalities or intendancies
...avy capitals, thus: RIOM. Names
...vinces or districts in thin capi-
...tals: BRITTANY. SOULE.

Abbreviations.

...hopric; BIG.·Bigorre; BU.·Bugey;
...nty; CERD.·Cerdagne; COM.·Com-
...COUS.·Conserans; GAB.·Gabar-
...GÉV.·Gévaudan; L.N.·Lower
...re, LAB.·Labourd; Q.V.·Quatre
...s; V.·Valromey; VIV.·Vivarais.

Scale 1:9 000 000
0   50   100
Miles

Laws and Courts

... Region of the "customary (feudal) law"
"   "   "written (Roman) law"
Boundary of jurisdiction of a par-
...ement or supreme council.
...of a parlement or "conseil souverain"
"   "   "chambre des comptes"
"   "   "cour des aides"
"   "   "court of admiralty"
"   "   "bureau de finance" and
          "chambre du domaine"
"   "   "cour des monnaies"
"   "   "prévôt des maréchaux"
"   "   chief court of the salt tax
"   "   grand mastership of waters
          and forests
...opric; C.·County; LAB.·Labourd.

Scale 1: 9 000 000

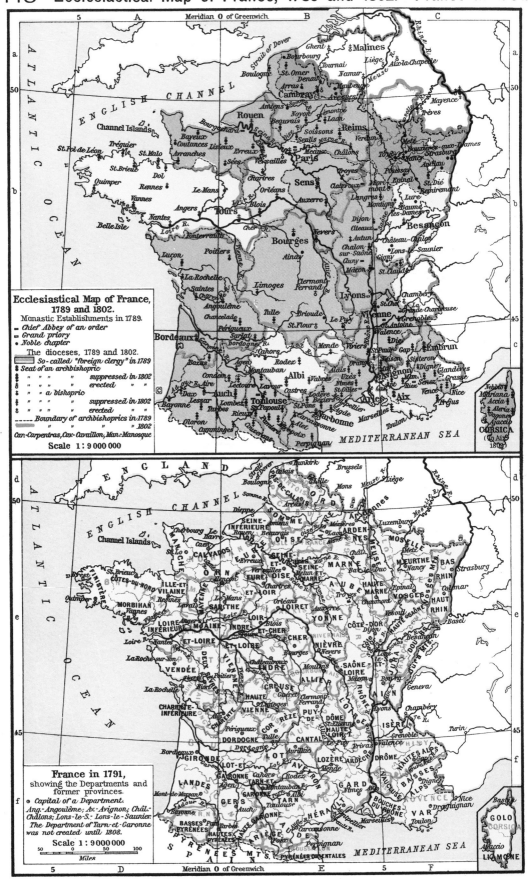

Ecclesiastical Map of France, 1789 and 1802.
Monastic Establishments in 1789.
■ Chief Abbey of an order
▪ Grand priory
• Noble chapter
The dioceses, 1789 and 1802.
So-called "foreign clergy" in 1789
☩ Seat of an archbishopric
☩ " " " suppressed in 1802
☩ " " " erected " "
☩ " " a bishopric
☩ " " " suppressed in 1802
☩ " " " erected " "
——— Boundary of archbishoprics 1789
▬▬▬ " " " 1802
Can-Carpentras, Cav-Cavaillon, Man-Manosque
Scale 1 : 9 000 000

France in 1791,
showing the Departments and former provinces.
• Capital of a Department.
Ang-Angoulême; Av-Avignon; Châl-Châlons; Lons-le-S- Lons-le-Saunier.
The Department of Tarn-et-Garonne was not created until 1808.
Scale 1 : 9 000 000
50   0   50   100
Miles

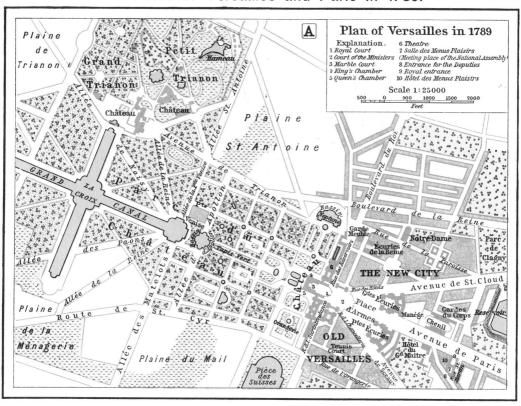

Plan of Versailles in 1789

Explanation.
1 Royal Court
2 Court of the Ministers
3 Marble Court
4 King's Chamber
5 Queen's Chamber
6 Theatre
7 Salle des Menus Plaisirs (Meeting place of the National Assembly)
8 Entrance for the Deputies
9 Royal entrance
10 Hôtel des Menus Plaisirs

Scale 1:25000
500   0   500   1000   1500   2000
Feet

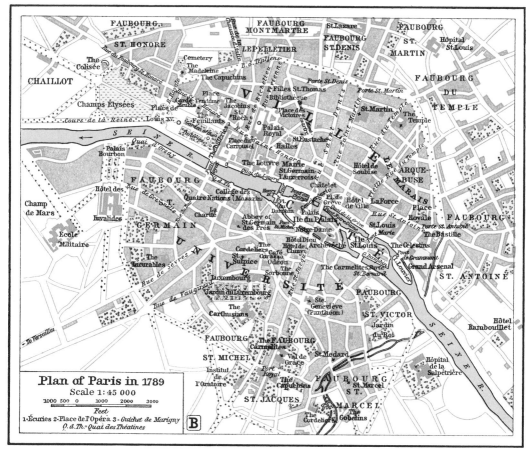

Plan of Paris in 1789

Scale 1:45 000
1000 500 0   1000   2000   3000
Feet
1-Écuries 2-Place de l'Opéra 3-Guichet de Marigny
Q. d. Th.-Quai des Théatines

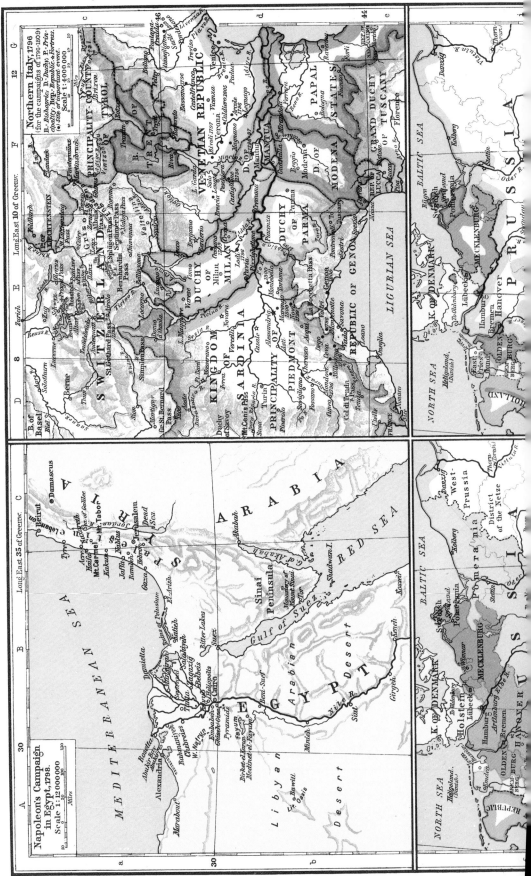

Northern Italy, 1796
(for the campaigns of 1796-1809)
B.=Bishopric; D.=Duchy; P.=Prin-
cipality; Rep.=Republic; ★ Fortress.
(•) Site of important event.
Scale 1:4,000,000

Napoleon's Campaign
in Egypt, 1798.
Scale 1:12,000,000

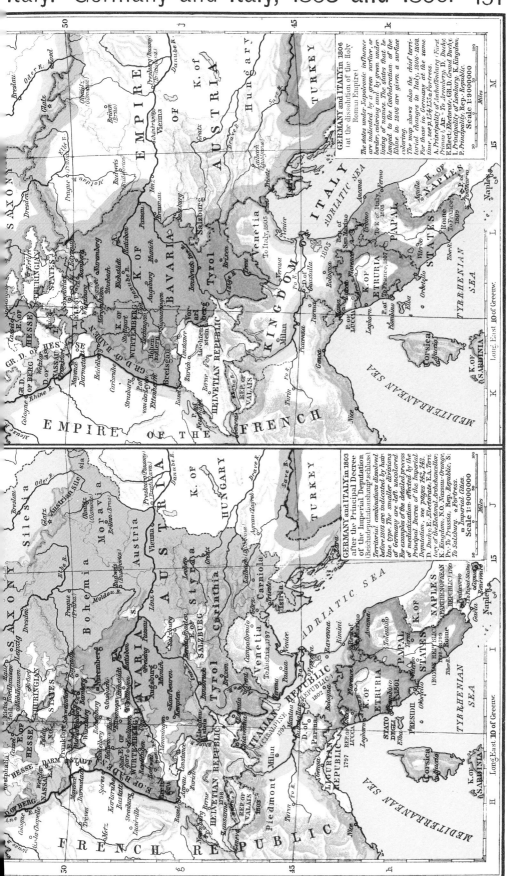

Treaty Adjustments, 1801—1812.

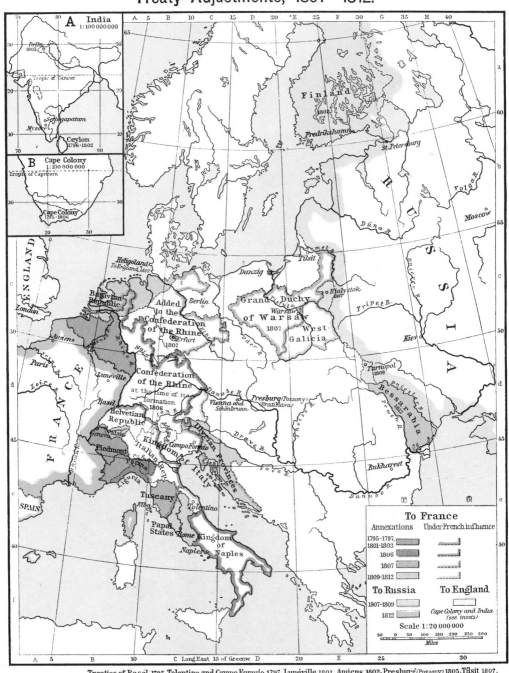

Treaties of Basel, 1795, Tolentino and Campo Formio, 1797, Lunéville, 1801, Amiens, 1802, Presburg (Pozsony), 1805, Tilsit 1807, Fredrikshamn and Vienna (Schönbrunn), 1809, Bukharest, 1812.

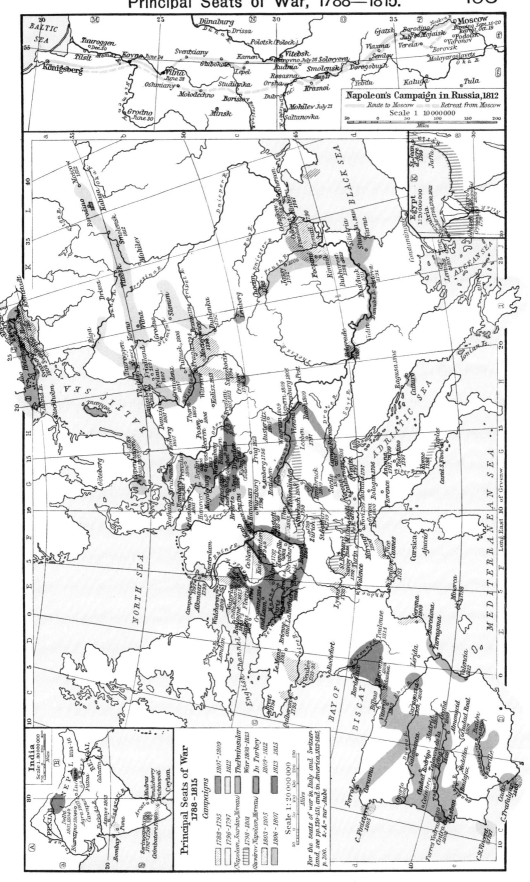

Napoleon's Campaign in Russia, 1812
Route to Moscow — — Retreat from Moscow
Scale 1 : 10 000 000

BLACK SEA

ADRIATIC SEA

MEDITERRANEAN SEA

NORTH SEA

BALTIC SEA

BAY OF BISCAY

AEGEAN SEA

Egypt
1:20 000 000

India
Scale 1:30 000 000

Principal Seats of War
1788—1815
Campaigns

1788–1795	1807–1809
1796–1797	1812
(Napoleon, Jourdan, Moreau)	The Peninsular War 1808–1813
1798–1801	In Turkey
(Suvarov, Napoleon, Moreau)	1809–1812
1803–1805	1813–1815
1806–1807	

Scale 1:20 000 000

For the seats of war in Italy and Switzerland, see pp. 150–151, and in America, 1812-1815,
p. 200. S.-A.= sur-Aube

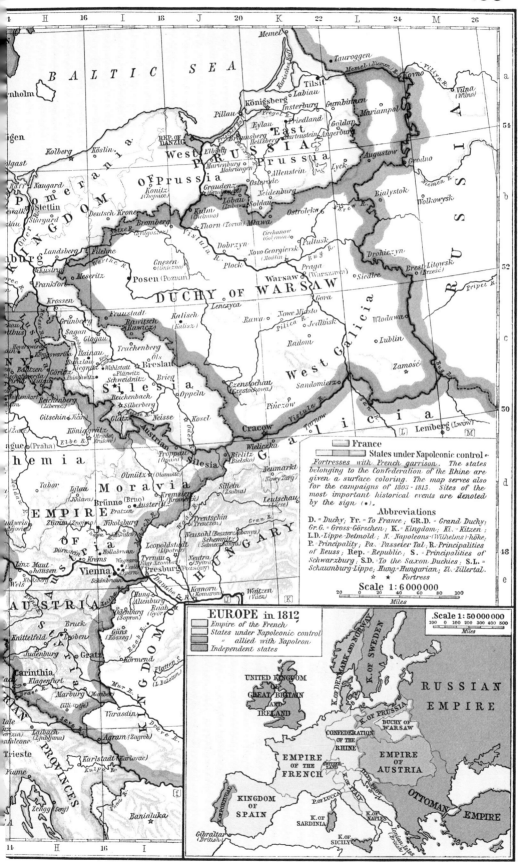

Abbreviations

D. = Duchy; Fr. = To France; GR.D. = Grand Duchy; Gr.G. = Gross-Görschen; K. = Kingdom; Ki. = Kitzen; L.D. = Lippe-Detmold; N. = Napoleons-(Wilhelms)-höhe; P. = Principality; Pa. = Passeier Tal; R. = Principalities of Reuss; Rep. = Republic; S. = Principalities of Schwarzburg; S.D. = To the Saxon Duchies; S.L. = Schaumburg-Lippe; Hung. = Hungarian; Zl. = Zillertal. ☆ = Fortress

Scale 1 : 6 000 000

EUROPE in 1812
Scale 1 : 50 000 000

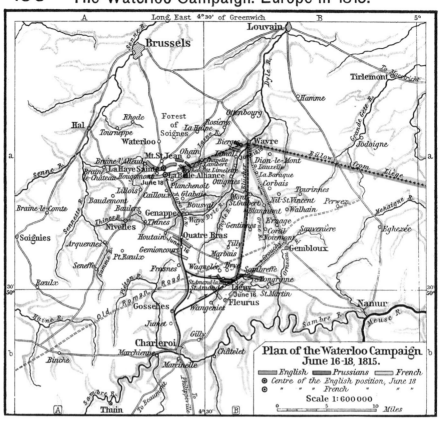

Plan of the Waterloo Campaign.
June 16-18, 1815.

English   Prussians   French
⊙ Centre of the English position, June 18
⊙ " " " French " "

Scale 1:600 000

0   5   10   Miles

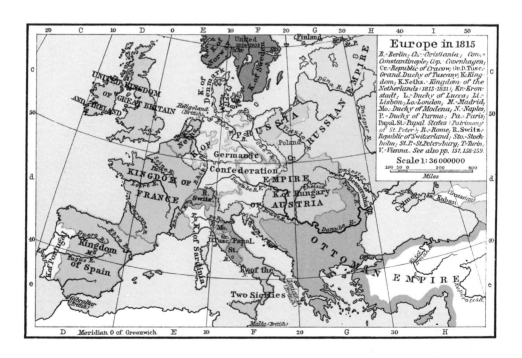

Europe in 1815

B.=Berlin; Chr.=Christiania; Con.=
Constantinople; Cop.=Copenhagen;
Cr.=Republic of Cracow; Gr.D.Tusc.=
Grand Duchy of Tuscany; K.=King-
dom; K.Neths.=Kingdom of the
Netherlands (1815-1831); Kr.=Kron-
stadt; L.=Duchy of Lucca; Li.=
Lisbon; Lo.=London; M.=Madrid;
Mo.=Duchy of Modena; N.=Naples;
P.=Duchy of Parma; Pa.=Paris;
Papal St.=Papal States (Patrimony
of St. Peter); R.=Rome; R.Switz.=
Republic of Switzerland; Sto.=Stock-
holm; St.P.=St.Petersburg; T.=Turin;
V.=Vienna. See also pp. 157, 158, 159.

Scale 1:36 000 000

100 50 0   200   400
Miles

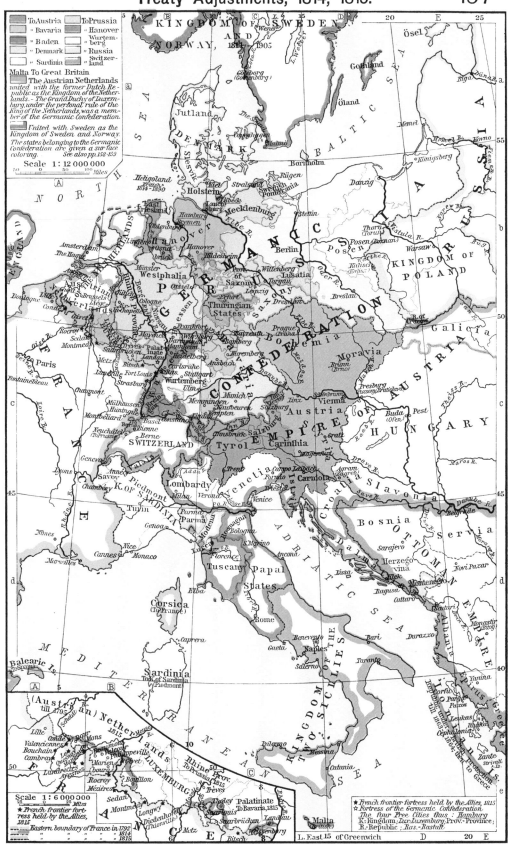

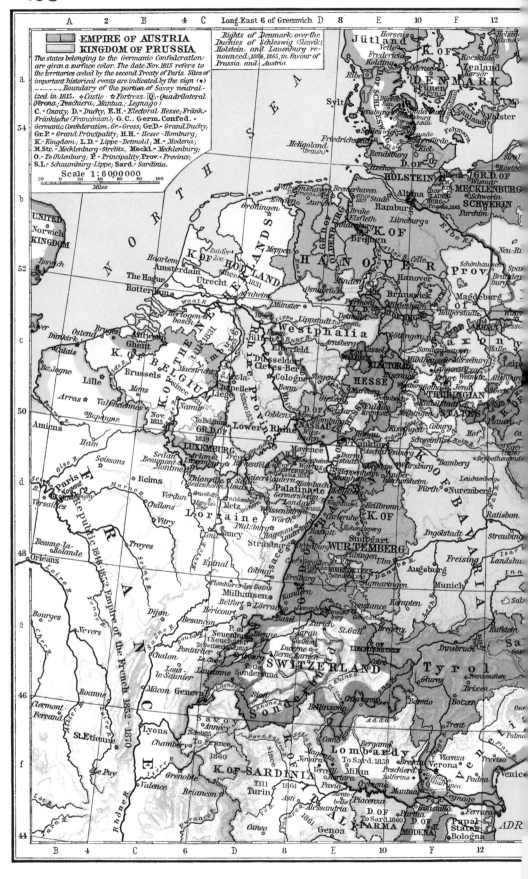

EMPIRE OF AUSTRIA
KINGDOM OF PRUSSIA

The states belonging to the Germanic Confederation are given a surface color. The date Nov. 1815 refers to the territories ceded by the second Treaty of Paris. Sites of important historical events are indicated by the sign (•)
—— Boundary of the portion of Savoy neutralized in 1815. ◇ Castle. ☆ Fortress. ▢ Quadrilateral (Verona; Peschiera; Mantua; Legnago)
C. = County, D. = Duchy, E.H. = Electoral Hesse, Fränk. = Fränkische (Franconian), G.C. = Germ. Confed. = Germanic Confederation, Gr. = Gross, Gr.D. = Grand Duchy, Gr.P. = Grand Principality, H.H. = Hesse-Homburg, K. = Kingdom, L.D. = Lippe-Detmold, M. = Modena, M.Str. = Mecklenburg-Strelitz, Meckl. = Mecklenburg, O. = To Oldenburg, P. = Principality, Prov. = Province, S.L. = Schaumburg-Lippe, Sard. = Sardinia.

Scale 1:6 000 000

Rights of Denmark over the Duchies of Schleswig (Slesvik), Holstein and Lauenburg renounced, 1864, 1865, in favour of Prussia and Austria.

The German Zollverein (Customs-Union), 1828—1872.

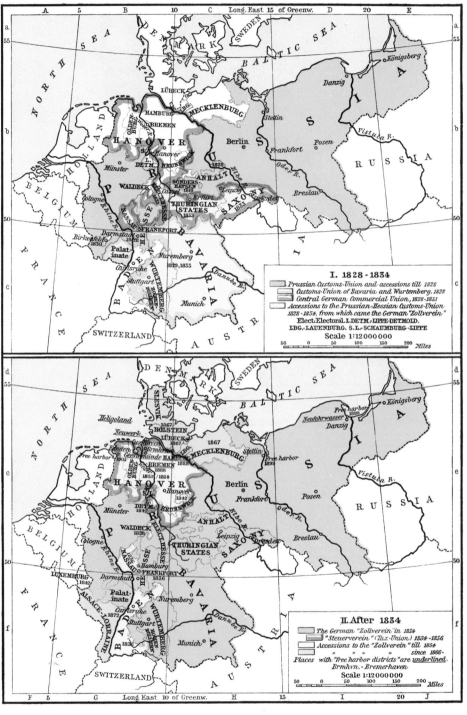

I. 1828 - 1834
Prussian Customs-Union and accessions till 1828
Customs-Union of Bavaria and Wurtemberg, 1828
Central German Commercial Union, 1828-1831
Accessions to the Prussian-Hessian Customs-Union
1828-1834, from which came the German "Zollverein"
Elect.Electoral. L.DETM.= LIPPE-DETMOLD.
LBG.= LAUENBURG. S.L.= SCHAUMBURG-LIPPE.
Scale 1:12000000
50   0   50   100   150   200   Miles

II. After 1834
The German "Zollverein" in 1834
"Steuerverein" (Tax-Union) 1834-1836
Accessions to the "Zollverein" till 1854
"   "   "   since 1866
Places with "free harbor districts" are underlined.
Brmhvn.= Bremerhaven.
Scale 1:12000000
50   0   50   100   150   200   Miles

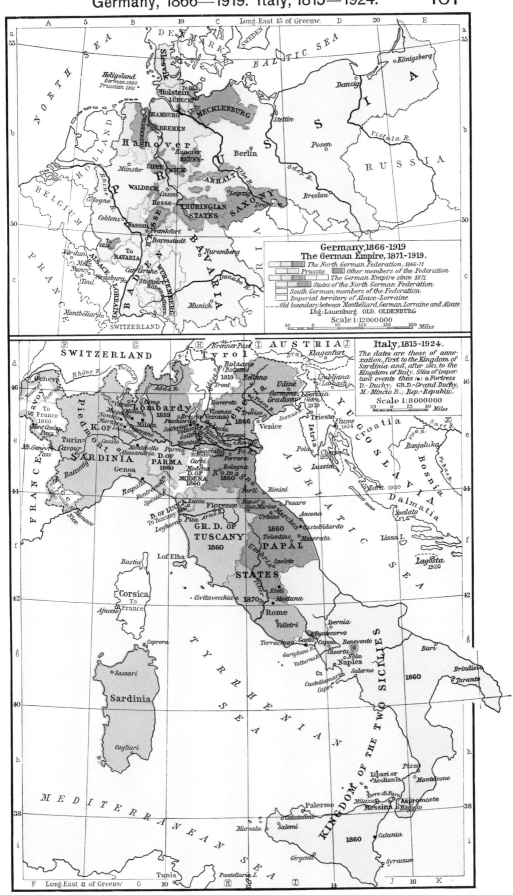

Germany, 1866-1919
The German Empire, 1871-1919.

The North German Federation, 1866-71
Prussia
The German Empire since 1871
States of the North German Federation
South German members of the Federation
Imperial territory of Alsace-Lorraine
Old boundary between Montbéliard, German Lorraine and Alsace
Lbg.=Lauenburg. OLD.=OLDENBURG
Scale 1:12 000 000

Italy, 1815-1924.
The dates are those of anne-
xation, first to the Kingdom of
Sardinia and, after 1861, to the
Kingdom of Italy. Sites of impor-
tant events thus (●) ☆Fortress
D.=Duchy; GR.D.=Grand Duchy;
M.=Mincio R.; Rep.=Republic.
Scale 1:8 000 000

Map legend:

Centres of population
Chief manufacturing centres
Districts in which manufacturing was carried on jointly with agriculture
Coalfields about 1800
Canals

Centres of population
Important manufacturing centres
Principal districts in which manufacturing is carried on

The names of the more important products and manufactures of England at the present time are printed thus

The violet coloring indicates that the areas concerned were centres of population both in 1750 and at the present time

Scale 1 : 3 700 000
20 10 0   20   40   60
Miles

England and Wales in 1832.

Meridian 0 of Greenw. 0

Ab. = Abingdon
Am. = Amersham
And. = Andover
Ayl. = Aylesbury
B.A. = Bere Alston
Blet. = Bletchingley

Chelt. = Cheltenham
Chipp. = Chippenham
Ch.Wyc. = Chipping Wycombe
Chr. = Christchurch
Crenc. = Cirencester
Crick. = Cricklade
E. = East
E.S. = East Surrey
Finsb. = Finsbury
Gat. = Gatton
Greenw. = Greenwich
Gr.M. = Great Marlow
Guildf. = Guildford

Heyt. = Heytesbury
Hind. = Hindon
Hudd. = Huddersfield
Kidderm. = Kidderminster
Lamb. = Lambeth
Lisk. = Liskeard

Malm. = Malmesbury
Marlb. = Marlborough
Maryleb. = Marylebone
MIDD. = Middlesex
Milb. = Milborne Port
N. = North
New Wood. = New Woodstock
NOTT. = Nottingham
Old S. = Old Sarum
Petersf. = Petersfield
Read. = Reading

S. = South
Salf. = Salford
Salisb. = Salisbury
Sherb. = Sherborne
Southw. = Southwark

Tewkesb. = Tewkesbury

W. = West
Wall. = Wallingford
Warr. = Warrington
W.B. = Wootton Bassett
We. = Wendover
Westm. = Westminster

Winch. = Winchester
Wolv. = Wolverhampton
Worc. = Worcester

ENGLAND AND WALES

showing the system of representation in the House of Commons before and after the Reform Act of 1832

○ Haslemere   Borough returning two members before 1832 } disfranchised in 1832
● Higham Ferrers   „   „   one member   „
○ St. Ives   „   that had its representation reduced in 1832
● Birmingham   „   enfranchised in 1832, and returning two members
○ Tynemouth   „   „   „   „   „   „   one member
○ Nottingham   „   returning two members before and after 1832
○ Abingdon   „   „   one member   „   „   „   „

OXFORD   County   three members after 1832
BEDFORD   „   two   „   „   „
SOUTH DEVON. Division of county returning two members after 1832.
Before 1832 each county in England returned two members, and each county in Wales one member; after 1832 nine counties in Wales, only, returned one member.

Scale 1:3700000   Miles

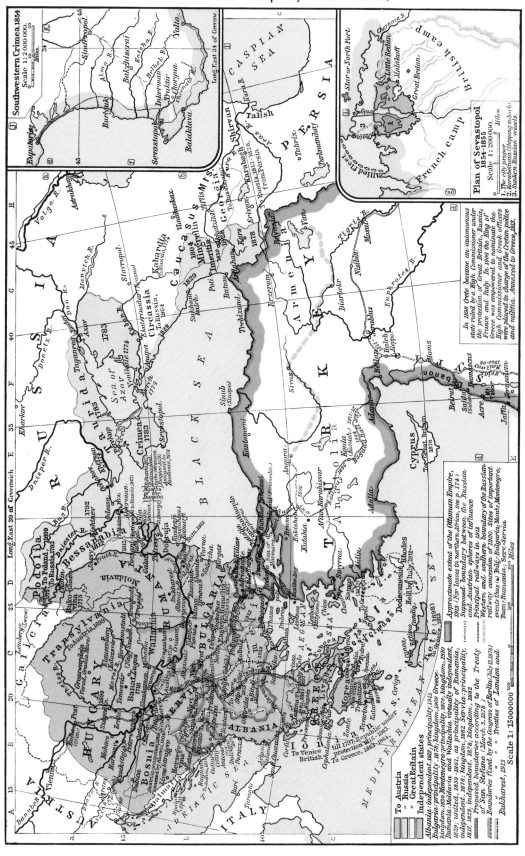

Peoples of Southeastern Europe and Asia Minor in 1913.

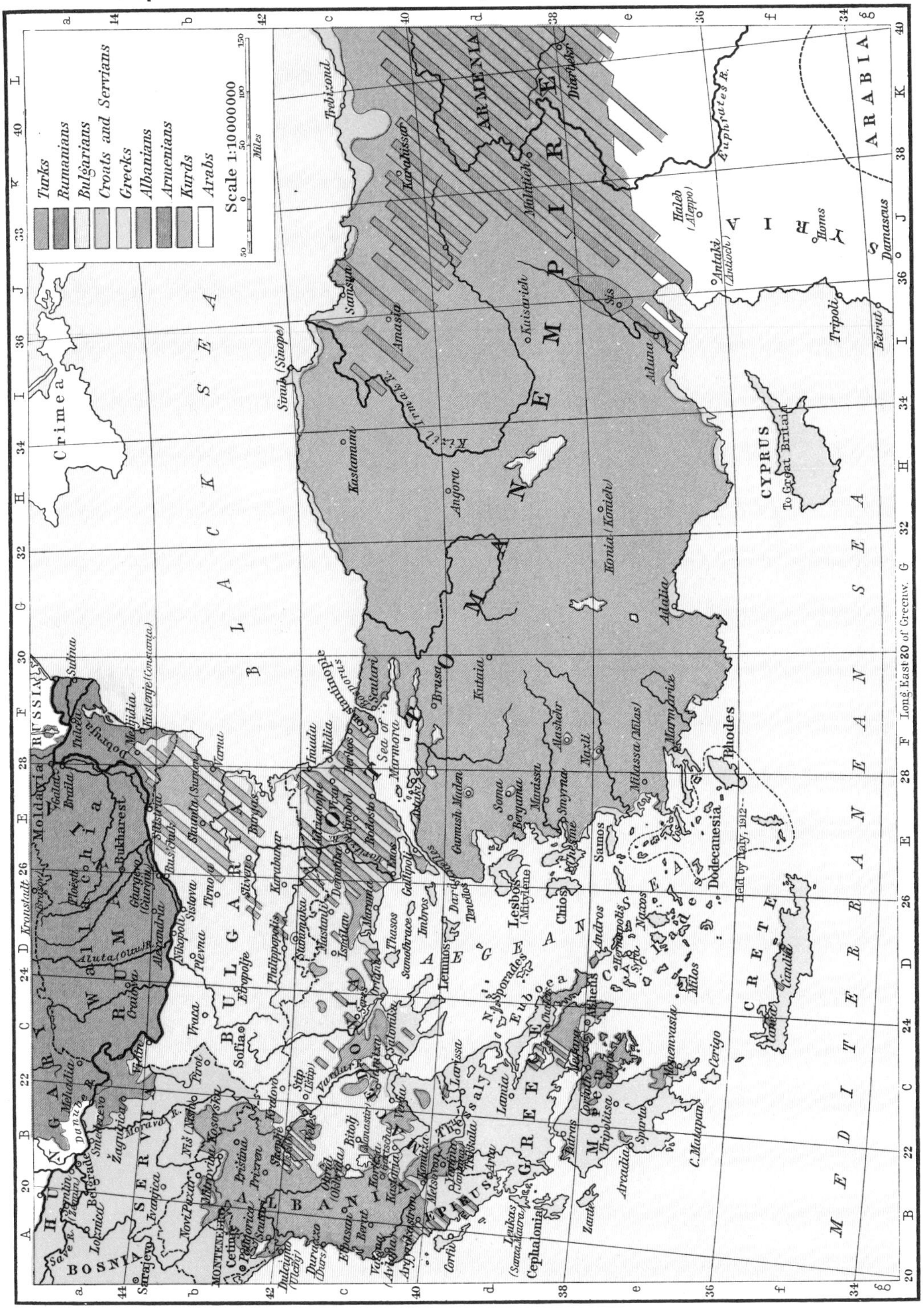

Turks
Rumanians
Bulgarians
Croats and Servians
Greeks
Albanians
Armenians
Kurds
Arabs
Scale 1:10000000
Miles
BLACK SEA
MEDITERRANEAN SEA
AEGEAN SEA
OTTOMAN EMPIRE
ARMENIA
ARABIA
SYRIA
CYPRUS
To Great Britain
CRETE
Rhodes
Dodecanesia
Held by Italy, 1912
BULGARIA
RUMANIA
SERVIA
MONTENEGRO
BOSNIA
ALBANIA
GREECE
Crimea
Long. East 30 of Greenw.

Illinois, 56,650 sq. miles
in comparison with Europe

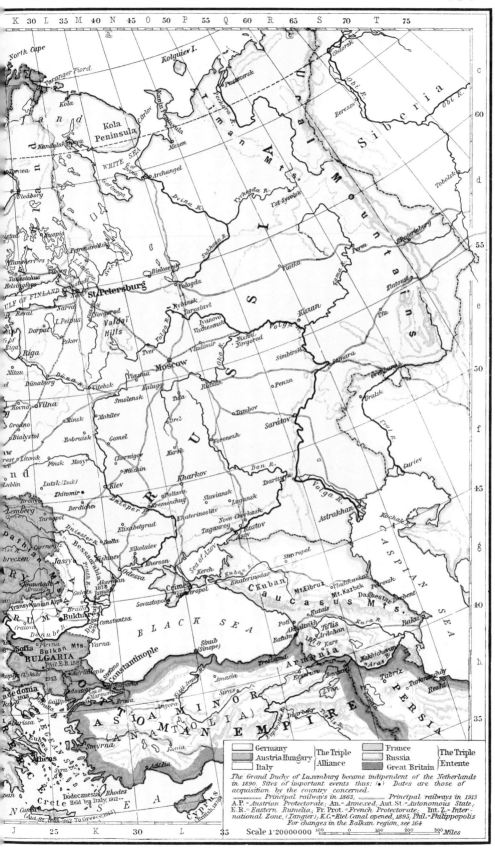

K 30 L 35 M 40 N 45 O 50 P 55 Q 60 R 65 S 70 T 75

North Cape

Kolguïev I.

Obdorsk

Varanger Fiord

Puskozersk

c

Obi R.

Siberia

60

Kola

Kola Peninsula

Berezov

Kanitalak ya

Cortov

Mezen

Obi R.

Tobolsk

d

WHITE SEA

Archangel

Dvina R.

Uleåborg

G.of Onega

Tschgda R.

Ust Sysolsk

Ekaterinburg

55

Kuopio

Onega

Sukhona R.

Viatka

Perm

Zlatoust

Bieloseck

Vologda

Kama R.

Ufa

e

St.Petersburg

Novgorod

Rybinsk

Yaroslavl

Kazan

Narva

Valdai Hills

Ivanovo Voznesensk

Nizhni Novgorod

Simbirsk

Samara

Orenburg

50

Dorpat

L.Peipus

Pskov

Tver

Vladimir R.

Volga R.

Ural R.

Riga

Düna R.

Moscow

Kaluga

Riazan

Penza

Uralsk

Mitan

Vitebsk

Viazma

f

Vilna

Smolensk

Tula

Orel

Tambov

Saratov

Guriev

Minsk

Mohilev

Bobruisk

Gomel

Voronezh

Grodno

Bialystok

Chernigov

Kursk

Don R.

Tsaritsin

45

Pinsk

Mosyr

Nezhin

Lublin

Kiev

Kharkov

Volga R.

Astrakhan

Lutsk (Luck)

Zhitomir

Pollava

Slaviansk

Lugansk

Kochak

g

Lemberg

Berdichev

Dnieper R.

Kremenchug

Novo Cherkask

Dniester R.

Elizabetgrad

Ekaterinoslav

Tagaurog

Rostov

CASPIAN SEA

Czernovitz

Bessarabia

Balta

Nikolaiev

Sea of Azov

Stavropol

Kherson

Odessa

Akkerman

Kuban R.

Ekaterinodar

C Kuban

Mt.Elbruz

40

Brăila

Crimea

Simferopol

Kerch

Vladikavkaz

Mt.Kazbek

Perovsk

Bukharest

Sevastopol

Poti

Kutais

Caucasus Mts.

Daghestan Derbent

Baku

BLACK SEA

Batum

Tiflis

Kura R.

BULGARIA

Varna

Sinub (Sinope)

Armenia

Nakhichevan

Aras R.

h

Constantinople

Adrianople

Amasia

Erzerum

Tabriz

Resht

ASIA MINOR (ANATOLIA)

OTTOMAN EMPIRE

PERSIA

35

Smyrna

Crete

CYPRUS

Dodecanesia Rhodes

AEGEAN SEA

J 25 K 30 L 35

Scale 1:20000000

Germany
Austria-Hungary The Triple Alliance
Italy
France
Russia The Triple Entente
Great Britain

The Grand Duchy of Luxemburg became independent of the Netherlands in 1890. Sites of important events thus: (•) Dates are those of acquisition by the country concerned.
—— Principal railways in 1863, —— Principal railways in 1913
A.P. = Austrian Protectorate; An. = Annexed, Aut.St. = Autonomous State;
E.R. = Eastern Rumelia; Fr.Prot. = French Protectorate; Int.Z. = International Zone, (Tangier); K.C. = Kiel Canal opened, 1895, Phil. = Philippopolis
For changes in the Balkan region, see 164

Peoples of Austria-Hungary in 1914.

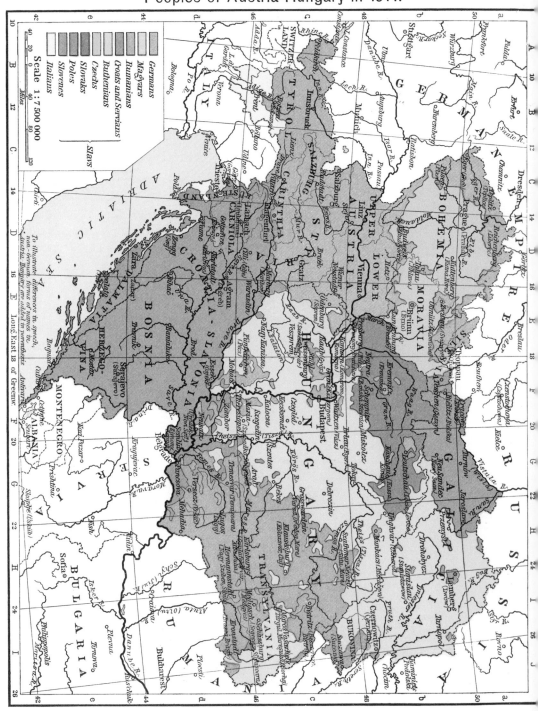

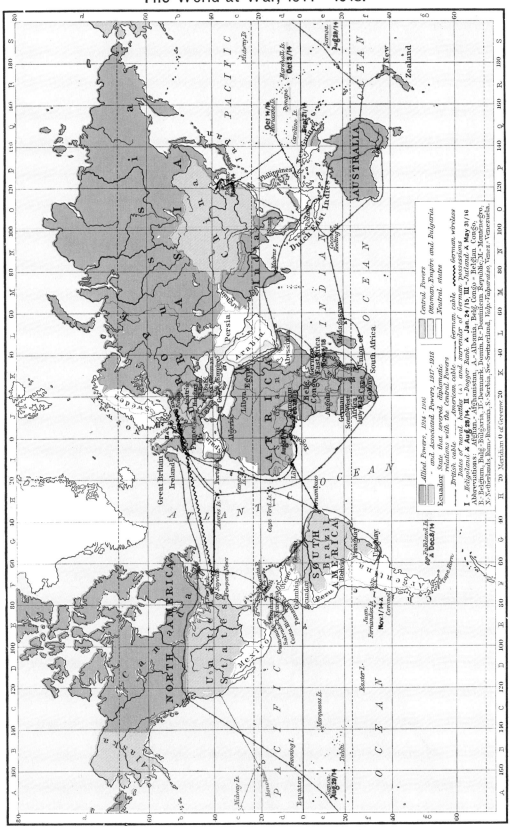

Principal Seats of War, 1914—1918.

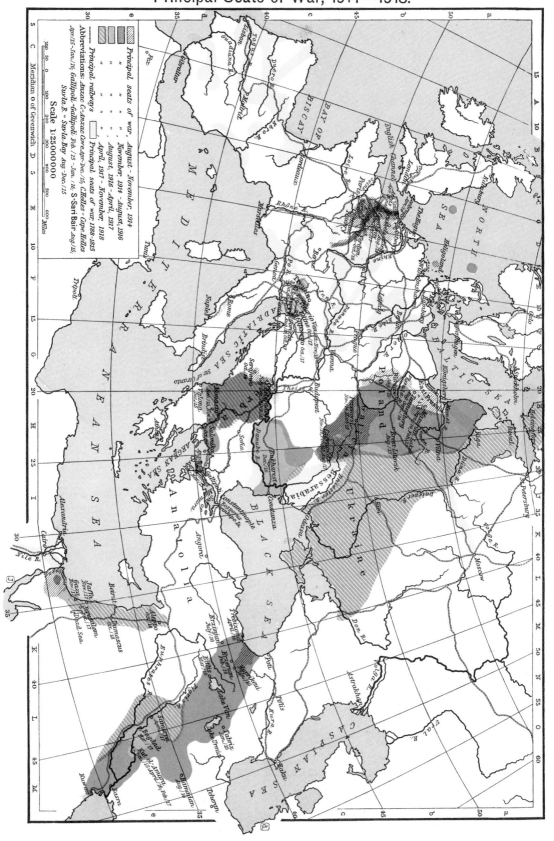

The Western European Front, 1914—1918.

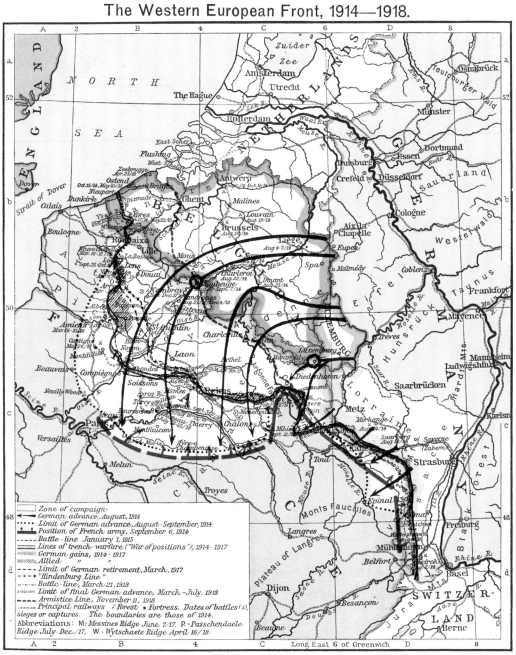

Scale 1: 4 000 000

Miles

Treaty Adjustments, 1919—1926.

Legend:

- Ceded by Germany
- " " Austria-Hungary
- " " Bulgaria
- " " Russia
- German areas demilitarized
- Rhineland zone of Allied occupation
- Plebiscite areas ceded or retained through popular vote, assignment by the League of Nations or decision of the Allied Council of Ambassadors, 1920-1922

.... Boundaries in 1914
AUSTRIA-HUNGARY: Name indicative of extent of territory held in 1914
-------- Boundaries in 1926

"Succession States" } "Little Entente": Czechoslovakia, Yugoslavia, Rumania, 1920; 1921. Poland, Austria, Hungary.

Rivers internationalized: Danube, below Ulm; Elbe (Labe) - Moldau (Vltava), below Prague; Niemen (Nyeman, Memel), below Gardinas (Grodno); Oder (Odra), below Oppeln.
Treaties of Versailles, St.Germain-en-Laye, Neuilly, Paris, 1919; Trianon (Versailles), Sèvres, Riga, Tartu (Dorpat), Rapallo, 1920; Lausanne, 1923; Locarno, 1925. Dates associated with the names of new states are those of independence. For mandated territories, see pp 168^F-168^G 168^I-168^L; 170-175; 179-182. A.=Austria; Aut. A.=Autonomous Area under the League of Nations; B.=Belgium; Cs.=Czechoslovakia; D.=Denmark; E.=Eupen; F.C.T.=Free City and Territory under the League of Nations; G.=Germany; Ind.=Independent; L.=Lithuania; P.=Poland; P.C.="Polish Corridor"; R.V.=Ruhr Valley; S.B.=Saar Basin; Ys.=Yugoslavia.

Scale 1:17000000

100   0   100   200
Miles

For the Rhineland see p 168^E

Treaty Adjustments, 1919—1926. The Rhineland.

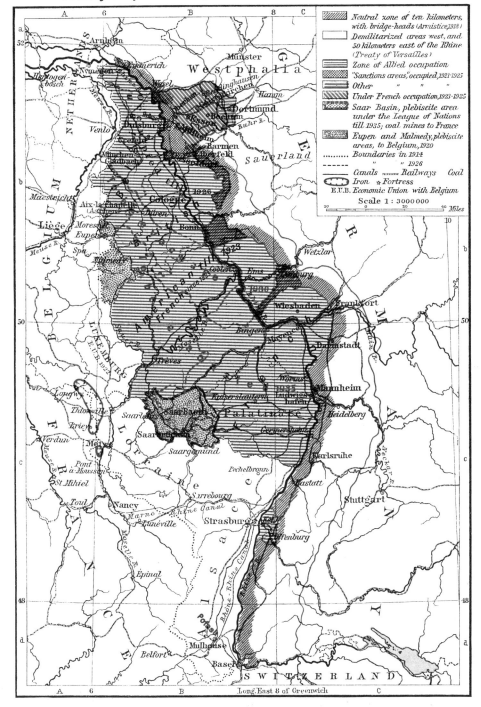

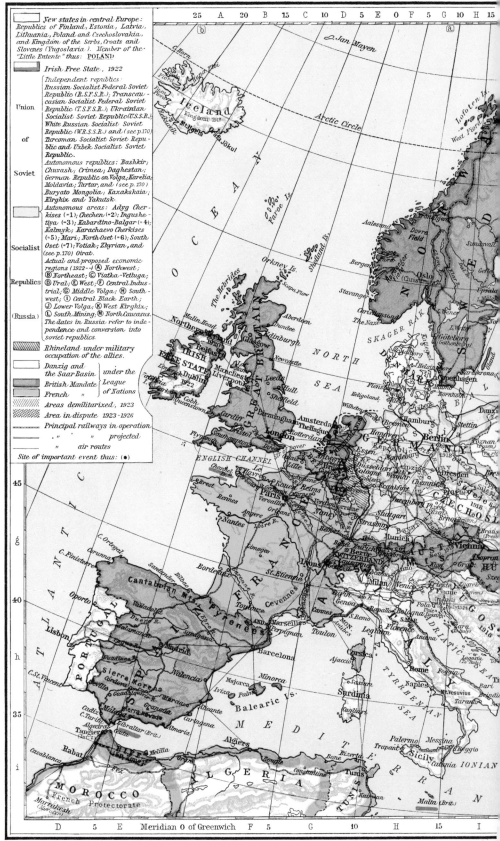

New states in central Europe: Republics of Finland, Estonia, Latvia, Lithuania, Poland and Czechoslovakia, and Kingdom of the Serbs, Croats and Slovenes (Yugoslavia). Member of the "Little Entente" thus: POLAND)

Irish Free State, 1922

Independent republics: Russian Socialist Federal Soviet Republic (R.S.F.S.R.); Transcaucasian Socialist Federal Soviet Republic (T.S.F.S.R.); Ukrainian Socialist Soviet Republic (U.S.S.R.); White Russian Socialist Soviet Republic (W.R.S.S.R.) and (see p.170) Turcoman Socialist Soviet Republic and Uzbek Socialist Soviet Republic.
Autonomous republics: Bashkir; Chuvash; Crimea; Daghestan; German Republic on Volga; Karelia; Moldavia; Tartar, and (see p. 170) Buryato Mongolia; Kazakskaia; Kirghix and Yakutsk.
Autonomous areas: Adyg Cherkises (=1); Chechen (=2); Ingushetiya (=3); Kabardino-Balgar (=4); Kalmyk; Karachaevo Cherkises (=5); Mari; North-Oset (=6); South Oset (=7); Votiak; Zhyrian, and (see p.170) Oirat.
Actual and proposed economic regions (1922–) Ⓐ Northwest; Ⓑ Northeast; Ⓒ Viatka-Vetluga; Ⓓ Ural; Ⓔ West; Ⓕ Central Industrial; Ⓖ Middle Volga; Ⓗ Southwest; Ⓘ Central Black Earth; Ⓙ Lower Volga; Ⓚ West Kirghix; Ⓛ South Mining; Ⓜ North Caucasus.
The dates in Russia refer to independence and conversion into soviet republics.

Union of Soviet Socialist Republics (Russia)

Rhineland under military occupation of the allies.

Danzig and the Saar Basin — under the League of Nations
British Mandate
French   "

Areas demilitarized, 1923
Area in dispute 1923–1926

Principal railways in operation
     ." "   " projected
     " " air routes

Site of important event thus: (●)

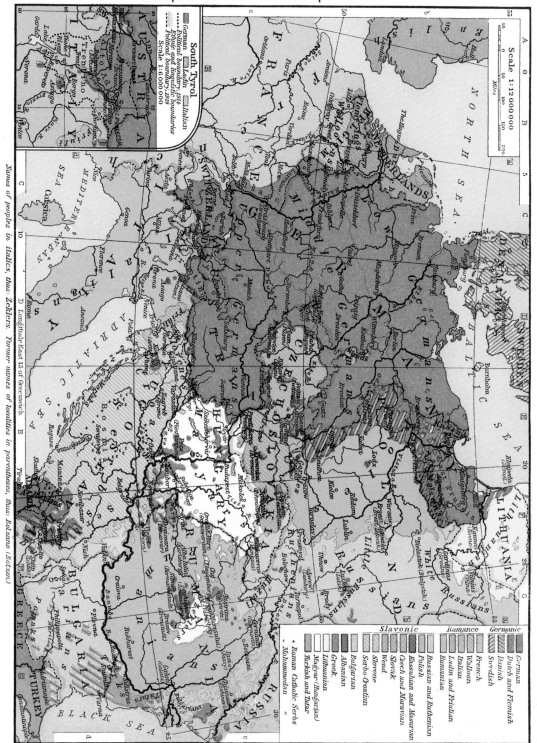

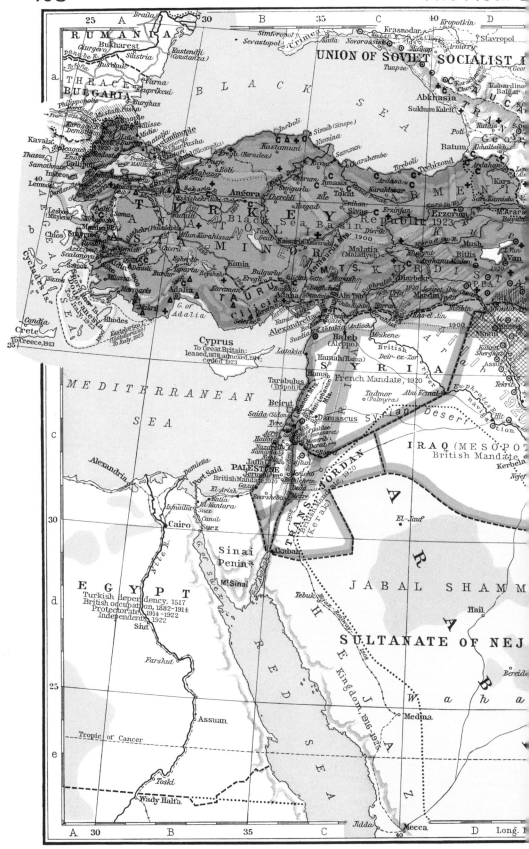

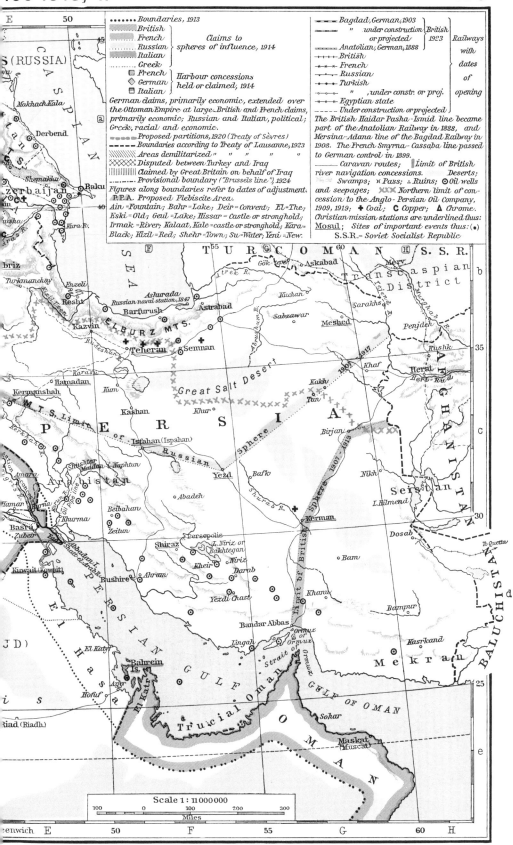

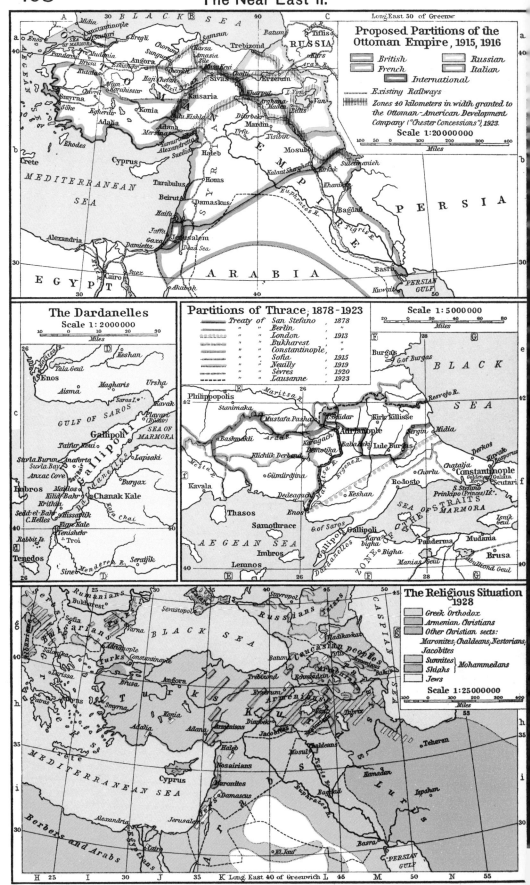

Proposed Partitions of the Ottoman Empire, 1915, 1916

- British
- French
- Russian
- Italian
- International
- Existing Railways
- Zones 40 kilometers in width granted to the Ottoman-American Development Company ("Chester Concessions"), 1923.

Scale 1:20 000 000

The Dardanelles
Scale 1:2 000 000

Partitions of Thrace, 1878–1923
Scale 1:5 000 000

Treaty of	San Stefano	1878
" "	Berlin	"
" "	London	1913
" "	Bukharest	"
" "	Constantinople	"
" "	Sofia	1915
" "	Neuilly	1919
" "	Sèvres	1920
" "	Lausanne	1923

The Religious Situation 1928

- Greek Orthodox
- Armenian Christians
- Other Christian sects: Maronites, Chaldeans, Nestorians, Jacobites
- Sunnites } Mohammedans
- Shiahs
- Jews

Scale 1:25 000 000

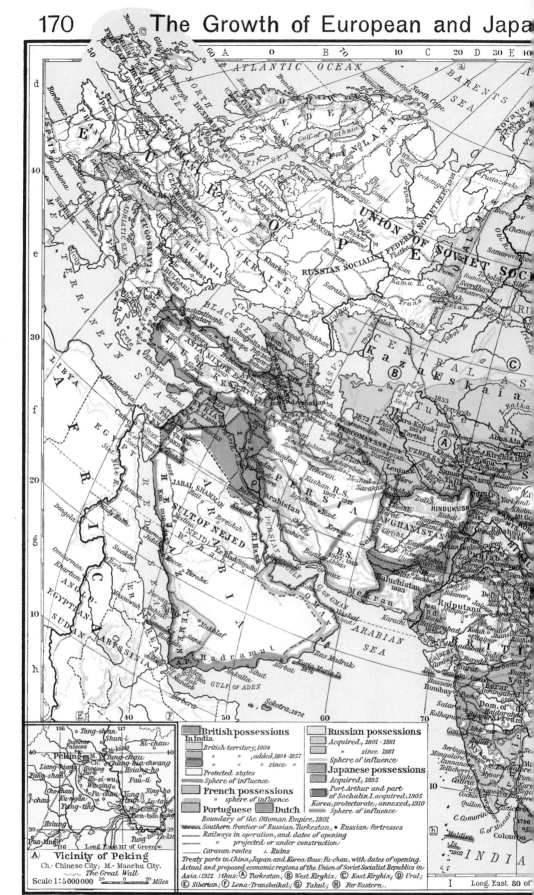

British possessions
In India
  British territory, 1804
  "   "   , added, 1804-1857
  "   "   "   since   "
  Protected states
  Sphere of influence
French possessions
  "   sphere of influence
Portuguese   Dutch
Russian possessions
  Acquired, 1801-1881
  "   since 1881
  Sphere of influence
Japanese possessions
  Acquired, 1895
  Port Arthur and part
  of Sachalin I. acquired, 1905
  Korea, protectorate; annexed, 1910
  Sphere of influence

Boundary of the Ottoman Empire, 1801
Southern frontier of Russian Turkestan, ♦ Russian fortresses
Railways in operation, and dates of opening
  "   projected or under construction
  Caravan routes   ∴ Ruins
Treaty ports in China, Japan and Korea thus: Fu-chau, with dates of opening.
Actual and proposed economic regions of the Union of Soviet Socialist Republics in
Asia (1922) thus: Ⓐ Turkestan; Ⓑ West Kirghix; Ⓒ East Kirghix; Ⓓ Ural;
Ⓔ Siberian; Ⓕ Lena-Transbaikal; Ⓖ Yakul; Ⓗ Far Eastern.

Ⓐ Vicinity of Peking
  Ch.- Chinese City; M.- Manchu City.
      The Great Wall
  Scale 1:5 000 000   20   0   20 Miles

Long. East 80 of

Abbreviations: A.A.- Autonomous (Socialist Soviet) Area; A.P.- Aden Protectorate; A.R.- Autonomous (Socialist Soviet) Republic; ALB.- Alba
EST.- Estonia; E.M.S.- Federated Malay States; F.M.- French Mandate; J.- Japan; LEB.- Lebanon; LITH.- Lithuania; PAL- Palestine; R.- Rus

B.M.=British Mandate; Bur.Mong.=Buryato Mongolia; Cr.=Crimea; Dom.=Dominions; Sphere; REP.=Republic; S.S.R.=Socialist Soviet Republic; SULT.=Sultanate.

Scale 1:40 000 000

Miles

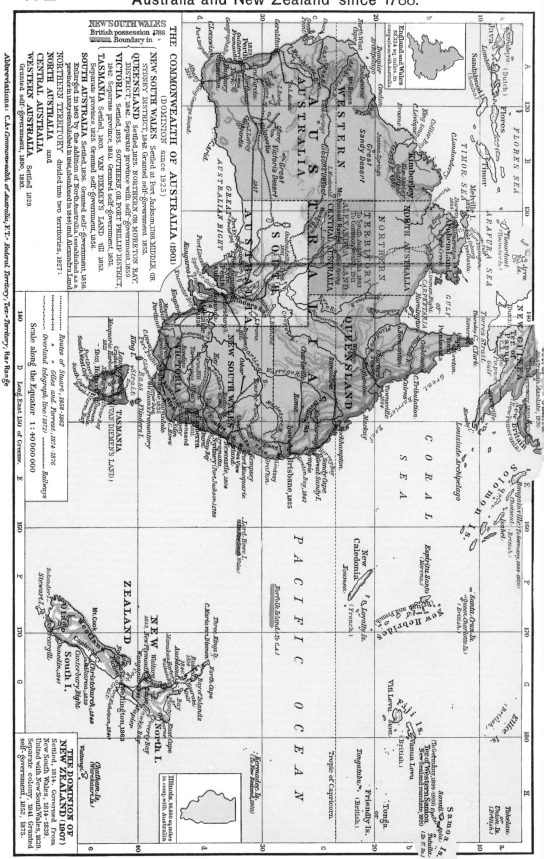

THE COMMONWEALTH OF AUSTRALIA (1901) AND THE DOMINION OF NEW ZEALAND (1907)

THE COMMONWEALTH OF AUSTRALIA (1901)
(DOMINION since 1925)

NEW SOUTH WALES Settled at Port Jackson,1788.
SYDNEY DISTRICT,1842.Granted self-government 1855.

QUEENSLAND Settled,1825. NORTHERN OR MORETON BAY.
DISTRICT, 1842. Separate province with self-government,1859.

VICTORIA Settled,1835. SOUTHERN OR PORT PHILIP DISTRICT,
1842. Separate province, 1851. Granted self-government,1855.

TASMANIA Settled, 1803. VAN DIEMEN'S LAND till 1853.
Separate province 1825. Granted self-government, 1856.

SOUTH AUSTRALIA Settled,1836. Granted self-government 1856.
Enlarged in 1863 by the addition of North Australia (established as a
province in 1863) and extended in 1864, abandoned in 1849) and Alexandra Land.

NORTHERN TERRITORY divided into two territories, 1927:
NORTH AUSTRALIA and
CENTRAL AUSTRALIA

WESTERN AUSTRALIA Settled 1829.
Granted self-government, 1890, 1893.

Abbreviations: C.A= Commonwealth of Australia; F.T.= Federal Territory; Ter= Territory; Ra= Range

Routes of Stuart, 1858–1862
Giles and Forrest, 1874–1876
Overland telegraph line, 1872
Railways

Scale along the Equator 1 : 40 000 000

THE DOMINION OF
NEW ZEALAND (1907)
Settled, 1814. Governed from
New South Wales, 1814–1839.
United with New South Wales, 1839.
Separate colony, 1841. Granted
self-government, 1852, 1875.

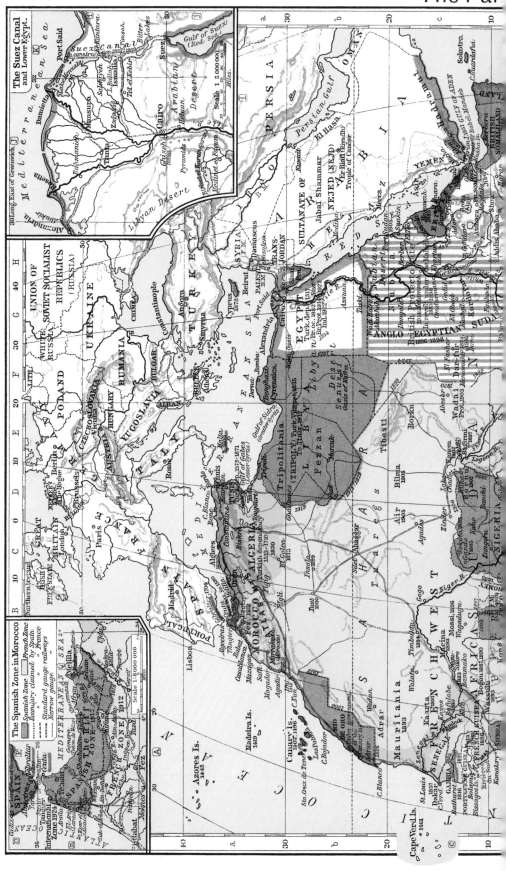

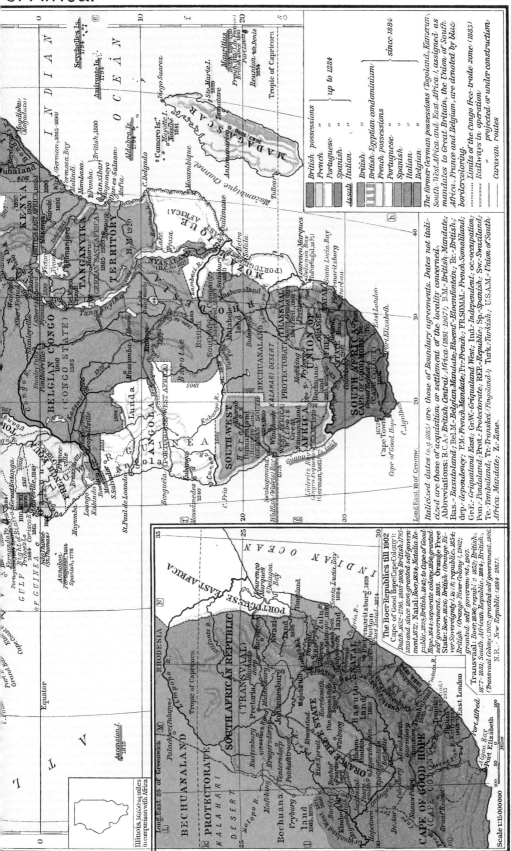

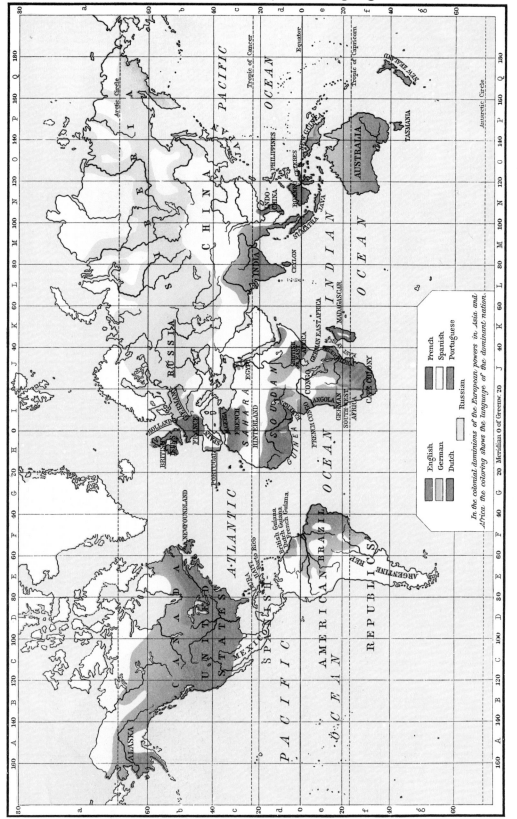

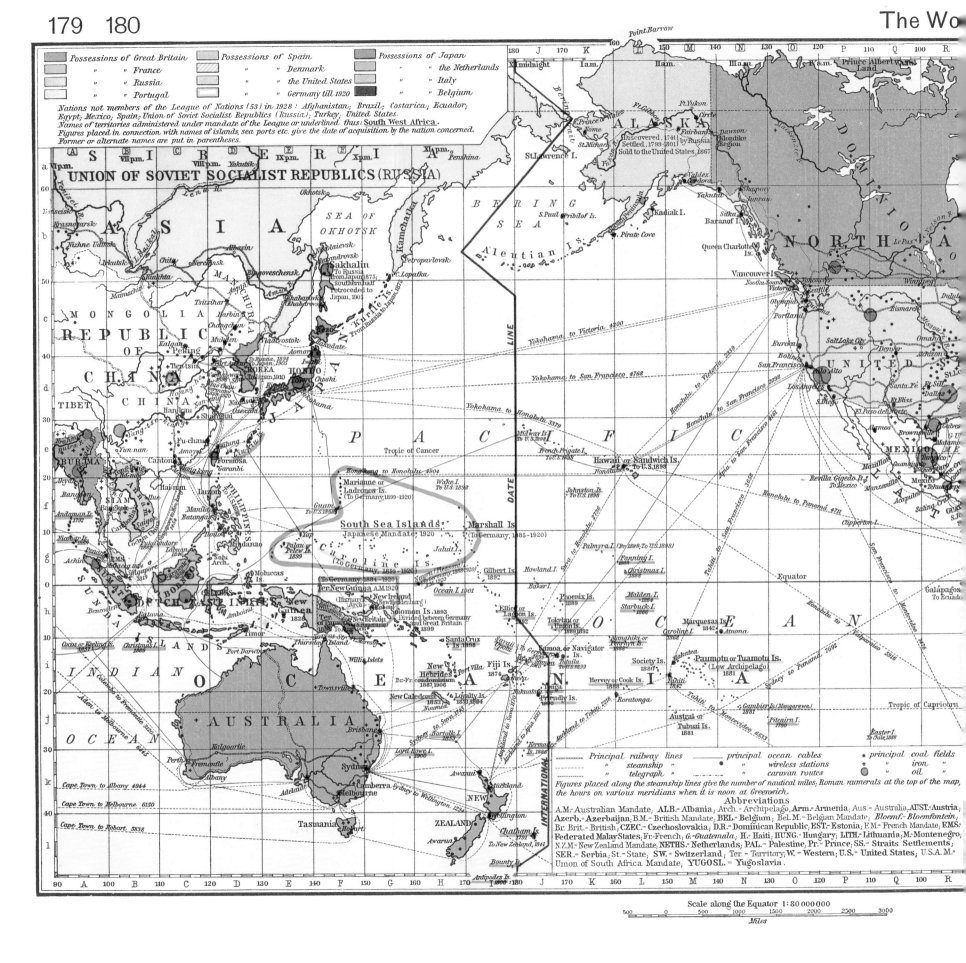

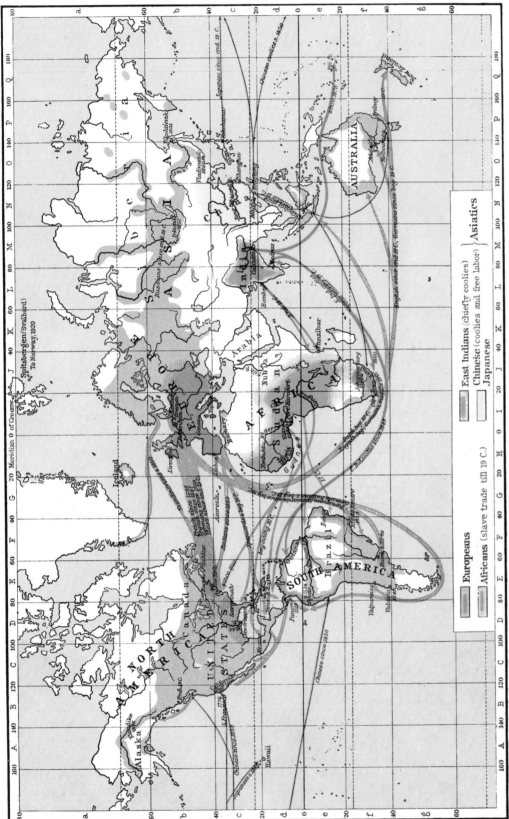

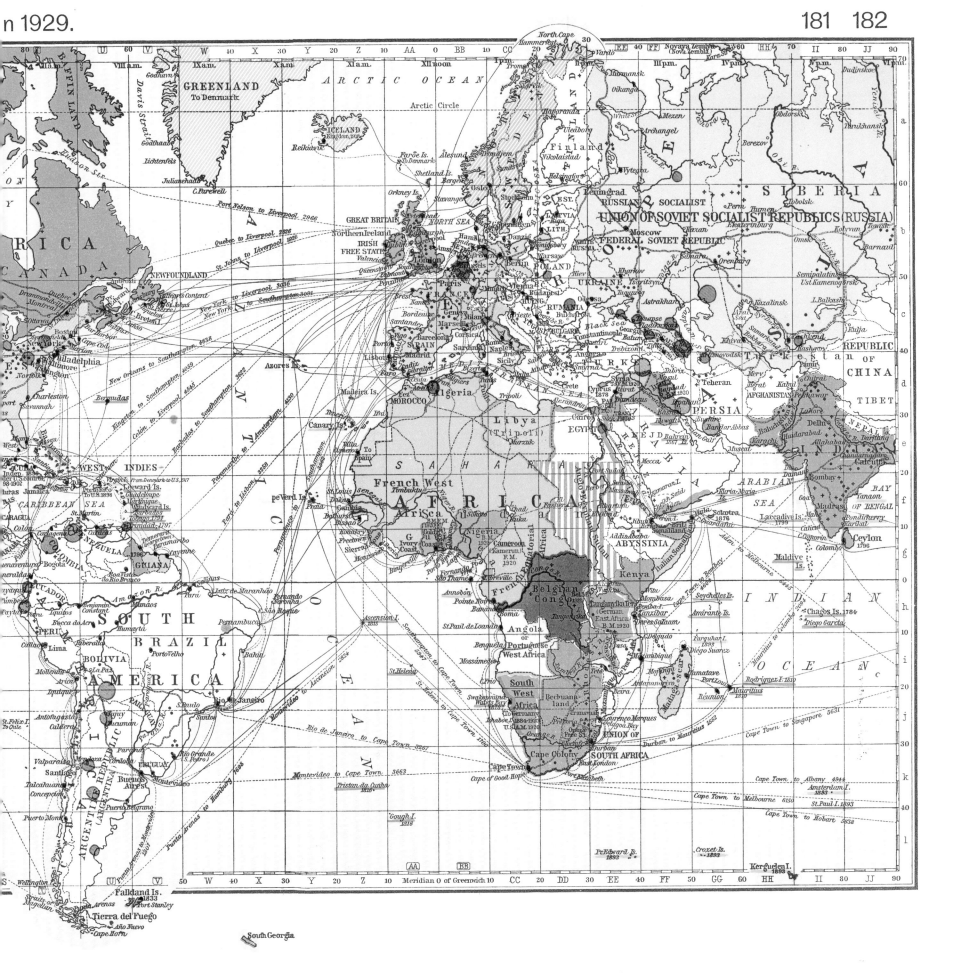

Localities in Western Europe, connected with American History

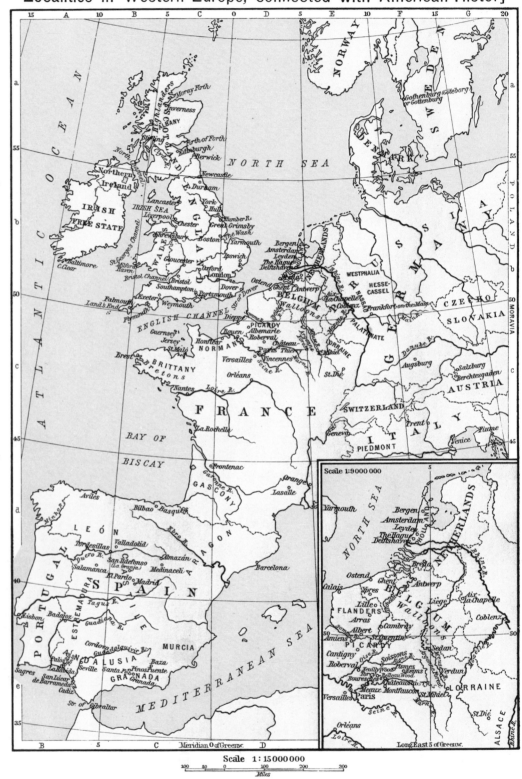

Scale 1 : 15 000 000

Miles

Localities in England, connected with American History.

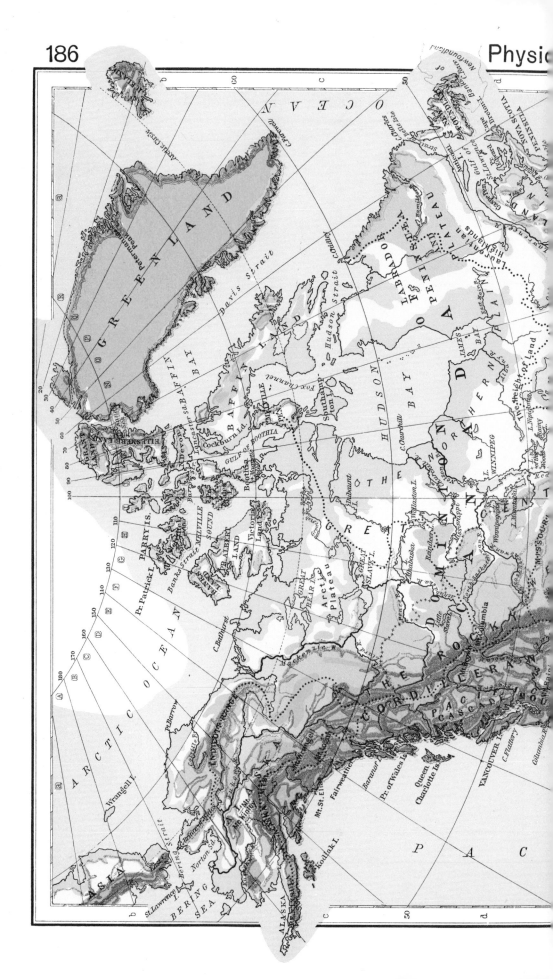

Scale 1 : 30 000 000

Areas above 5000 feet
  "   "   1600 "
  "   "   600 "
  "   below sea-level

......Drainage divide
+++++ Approximate boundary between the eastern
forests and the western prairies and plains.

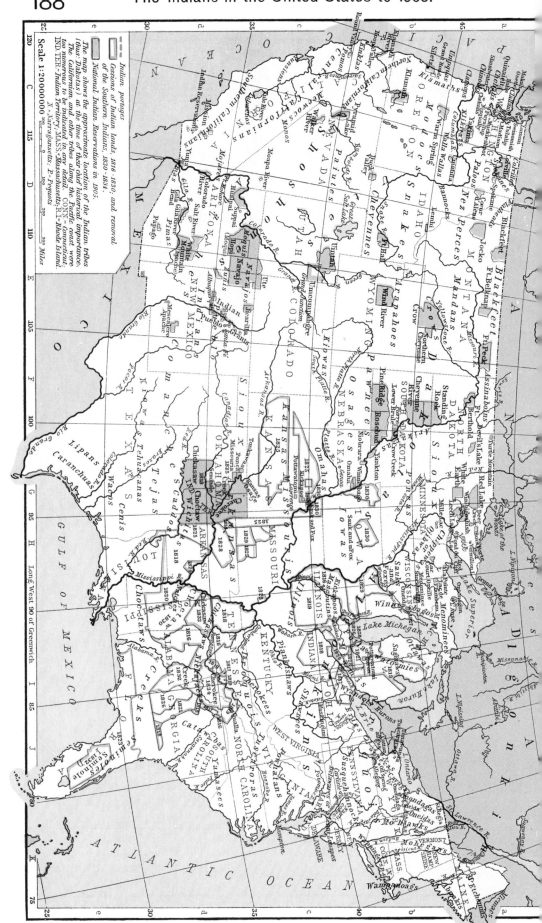

Indian portages

Cessions of Indian lands, 1816–1830, and removal of the Southern Indians, 1830–1834.

National Indian Reservations in 1905.

The map shows the approximate location of the Indian tribes (thus: *Dakotas*) at the time of their chief historical importance. The Californian and other tribes along the Pacific coast were too numerous to be indicated in any detail. CONN.=Connecticut, IND.TER.=Indian Territory, MASS.=Massachusetts, R.I.=Rhode Island. N.=Narragansetts; P.=Pequots.

Scale 1:20000000

English possessions about 1750
Approximate area of settlement in 1660
" " " " 1750
" " " frontier of the New England Confederation; 1643-1684
Dutch possessions, 1613-1664, 1673-1674
French possessions about 1750

MASSACHUSETTS BAY
Corporate colony under patent from the Council for New England, 1628, and under royal charter, 1629; charter annulled, 1684; royal Province under new charter, 1691; charter practically abrogated by Parliament, 1774.

New Plymouth
Corporate colony under patent from the London Company, 1620, and from the Council for New England, 1621, 1630; added to Massachusetts Bay, 1691.

MAINE : (between the Merrimac and Kennebec Rivers)–
Proprietary colony under patent from the Council for New England, 1622
": (between the Piscataqua and Kennebec Rivers)–
Proprietary colony under royal charter, 1637; held by Massachusetts Bay, 1651-1665, 1667-1679; nominally a royal province, but actually held by Massachusetts Bay, 1679-1686, 1689-1696
": (between the Kennebec and St. Croix Rivers)–
Proprietary colony under royal charter, 1664-1691.
": (between the Piscataqua and St. Croix Rivers)–
Added to Massachusetts Bay, 1691.

NEW HAMPSHIRE
*Proprietary colony (part of MAINE) under patent from the Council for New England, 1622; proprietary colony of **New Hampshire** (between the Merrimac and Piscataqua Rivers) under patent from the Council for New England, 1629; held by Massachusetts Bay, 1641-1679, 1690-1692; royal province, 1679-1690, 1692-1698; under same governor as Massachusetts Bay, 1698-1741; separate province, 1741–*

CONNECTICUT
Corporate colony under royal charter, 1662.

New Haven
United with Connecticut, 1664.

RHODE ISLAND
Corporate colony under charter from Parliament, 1644, and under royal charter, 1663.

Massachusetts Bay and the area in Maine subject to its control	1686-1689	
New Plymouth	"	under the rule
New Hampshire	"	of a royal
Rhode Island	"	
Connecticut	1687-1689	governor-general
New York	1688-1689	
East and West New Jersey	"	

The map is designed to serve as an index to localities in the New England Colonies which for lack of space could not be inserted in the map of European Exploration and Settlement in the United States, 1513 - 1776 (pages 190-191). The list of names given is not exhaustive. For names of Indian tribes, see page 188.

Dates associated with the names of localities having the sign (⊙⊙) are those of settlement, or of change of name, e.g.: Agawam, 1633; Ipswich, 1634. In the case of Corlaer or Schenectady, Agamenticus, Casco or Ft. Loyal, Pemaquid, and Penobscot or Ft. Pentagöet, the dates of settlement are underlined.

✦ Fort, with date of construction. ✕ Site of event in colonial warfare (1689-1760), with date of occurence. Other localities and dates of importance during the period of warfare in question are: Quebec, 1690, 1759; Port Royal (Acadia), 1690, 1707, 1710; Grand Pré, 1704; Canso, 1744; Louisburg, 1745, 1758; and St. Johns (Newfoundland),1696,1705,1709. See p.194.

To the extent shown in the map, the artificial boundaries (┅┅) are those of the present States of Massachusetts, New Hampshire, Connecticut and Rhode Island. Boundary disputes are not indicated. For the extent of the various grants by royal charter, see pp. 190-191 (inset).

Abbreviations: C.-To Connecticut till 1664; Dart.- Dartmouth; Ki.-Kittery,1624; M.B.- To Massachusetts Bay; Mid.- Middleborough; N.Hv.-To New Haven till 1664; Nor.- Norwich; Rich.- Richmond I.; Salisb.- Salisbury; S.B.- South Berwick; Sudb.- Sudbury; Th.R.-Thames R.

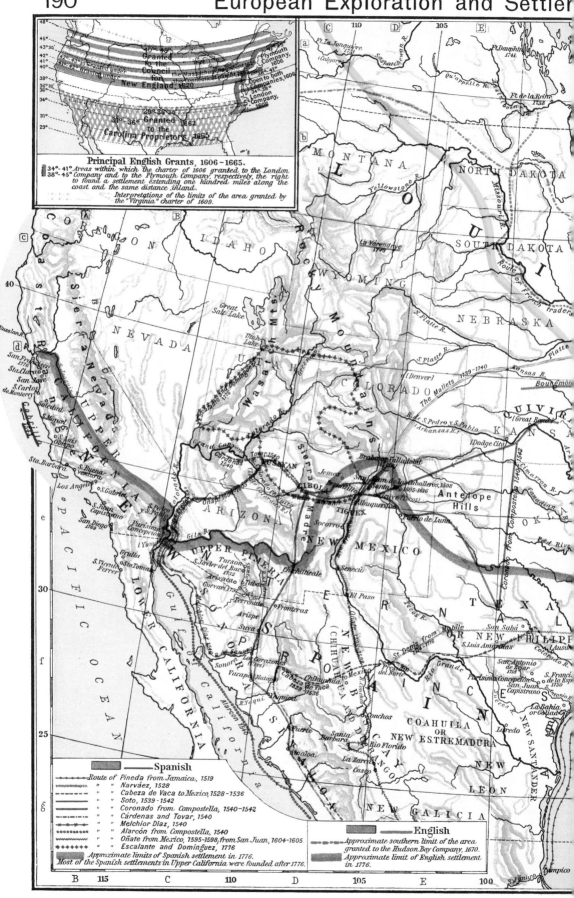

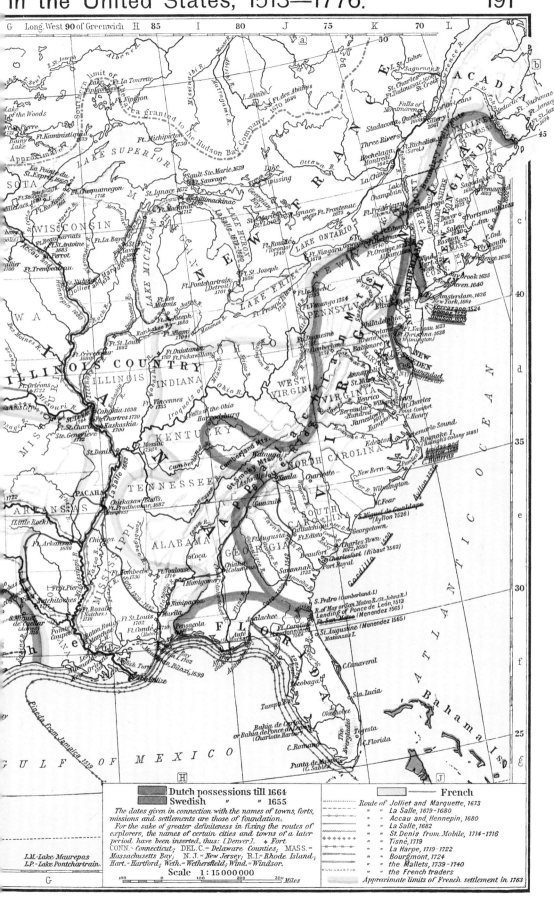

Reference Map of the Middle Colonies, 1607—1760.

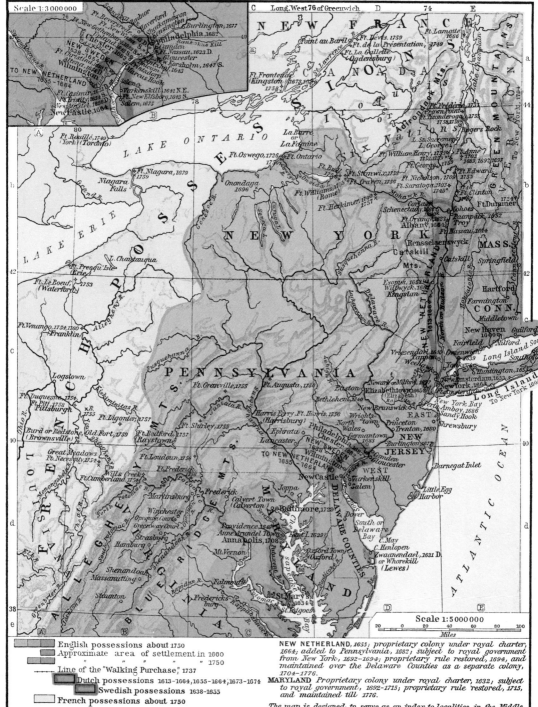

Scale 1:3 000 000

Long.West 76 of Greenwich

Scale 1:5 000 000

English possessions about 1750
Approximate area of settlement in 1660
"   "   "   " 1750
Line of the "Walking Purchase", 1737
Dutch possessions 1613-1664, 1655-1664, 1673-1674
Swedish possessions 1638-1655
French possessions about 1750

NEW YORK   As NEW NETHERLAND, under Dutch rule, 1623-1664, 1673-1674;
proprietary colony under royal charter, 1664-1685; royal province,
1685-1688; united with the New England colonies under royal governor-
general, 1688-1689; separate province, 1689-

NEW JERSEY Proprietary colony under royal charter, 1664, and under
patent from the Duke of York, 1664-1674; divided into East New Jersey
and West New Jersey, 1676; united with the New England colonies
under royal governor-general, 1688-1689; proprietary colonies of
East New Jersey and West New Jersey, 1689-1702; royal province of
New Jersey, 1702; under same governor as New York, 1702-1738;
separate province, 1738-

PENNSYLVANIA Proprietary colony under royal charter, 1681;
subject to royal government from New York, 1692-1694; proprietary
rule restored, 1694, and maintained till 1776

DELAWARE COUNTIES (The Three Lower Counties on the Delaware)
As NEW SWEDEN, under Swedish rule, 1638-1655; annexed to

NEW NETHERLAND, 1655; proprietary colony under royal charter,
1664; added to Pennsylvania, 1682; subject to royal government
from New York, 1692-1694; proprietary rule restored, 1694, and
maintained over the Delaware Counties as a separate colony,
1704-1776.

MARYLAND Proprietary colony under royal charter, 1632; subject
to royal government, 1692-1715; proprietary rule restored, 1715,
and maintained till 1776.

The map is designed to serve as an index to localities in the Middle
Colonies which for lack of space could not be inserted in the map
of European Exploration and Settlement in the United States,
1513-1776 (pages 190/191). The list of names given is not exhaustive. For names of Indian tribes, see p. 188.

Dates associated with the names of localities having the sign (oo)
are those of settlement, or of change of name.

✦Fort, with date of construction. ✕ Site of event in colonial warfare
(1689-1760), with date of occurrence.

To the extent shown in the map, the artificial boundaries (..........)
are those of the present States of New York, New Jersey,
Pennsylvania, Delaware and Maryland. Boundary disputes
are not indicated. For the extent of the various grants by royal
charter, see p. 190 (inset).

Abbreviations: B.= Site of Braddock's defeat; CONN.= CONNECTICUT,
D.= Founded or renamed by the Dutch; MASS.= MASSACHUSETTS,
N.E.= Settled from New England; S.= Founded or renamed by the Swedes.

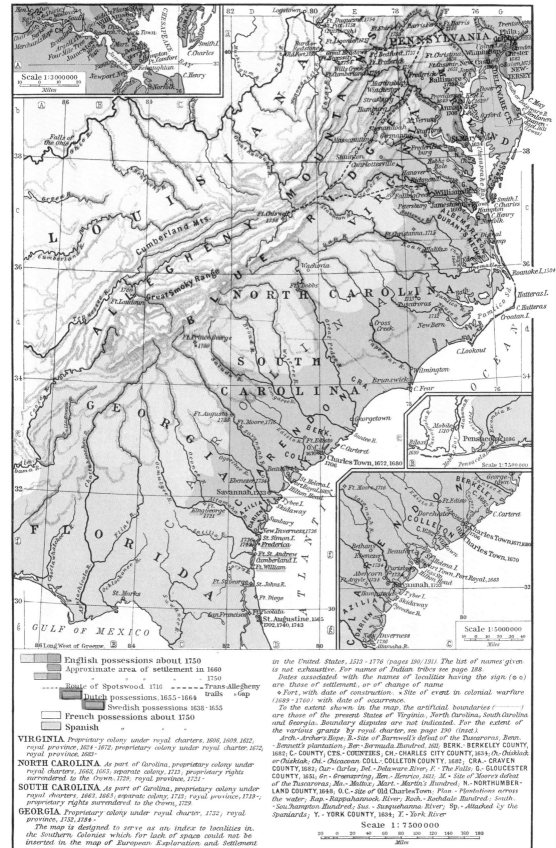

English possessions about 1750
Approximate area of settlement in 1660
······· Route of Spotswood 1716 ----- Trans-Allegheny
Dutch possessions, 1655-1664 trails »Gap
Swedish possessions 1638-1655
French possessions about 1750
Spanish " " "

VIRGINIA *Proprietary colony under royal charters, 1606, 1609, 1612; royal province, 1624-1672; proprietary colony under royal charter, 1672; royal province, 1683-*

NORTH CAROLINA *As part of Carolina, proprietary colony under royal charters, 1663, 1665; separate colony, 1713; proprietary rights surrendered to the Crown, 1729; royal province, 1731-*

SOUTH CAROLINA *As part of Carolina, proprietary colony under royal charters, 1663, 1665; separate colony, 1713; royal province, 1719-; proprietary rights surrendered to the Crown, 1729.*

GEORGIA *Proprietary colony under royal charter, 1732; royal province, 1752, 1754 -*
The map is designed to serve as an index to localities in the Southern Colonies which for lack of space could not be inserted in the map of European Exploration and Settlement

in the United States, 1513 - 1776 (pages 190/191). The list of names given is not exhaustive. For names of Indian tribes see page 188.
Dates associated with the names of localities having the sign (⊙ ⊙) are those of settlement, or of change of name
◆ Fort, with date of construction. × Site of event in colonial warfare (1689 - 1760) with date of occurrence.
To the extent shown in the map, the artificial boundaries (·········) are those of the present States of Virginia, North Carolina, South Carolina and Georgia. Boundary disputes are not indicated. For the extent of the various grants by royal charter, see page 190 (inset).
Arch.-Archer's Hope; B.- Site of Barnwell's defeat of the Tuscaroras, Benn.- Bennett's plantation; Ber.- Bermuda Hundred, 1611; BERK.- BERKELEY COUNTY, 1682; C.- COUNTY; CTS.- COUNTIES; CH.- CHARLES CITY COUNTY, 1634; Chi.- Chisklack or Chiskiak; Chi.- Chicacoan; COLL.- COLLETON COUNTY, 1682; CRA.- CRAVEN COUNTY, 1682; Cur.- Curles; Del.- Delaware River; F.- The Falls; G.- GLOUCESTER COUNTY, 1651; Gr.- Greenspring; Hen.- Henrico, 1611; M.- Site of Moore's defeat of the Tuscaroras; Ma.- Mattox; Mart.- Martin's Hundred; N.- NORTHUMBER- LAND COUNTY, 1648; O.C.- Site of Old CharlesTown; Plan.- Plantations across the water; Rap.- Rappahannock River; Roch.- Rochdale Hundred; South.- - Southampton Hundred; Sus.- Susquehanna River; Sp.- Attacked by the Spaniards; Y.- YORK COUNTY, 1634; Y.- York River

Scale 1 : 7 500 000
20 0 20 40 60 80 100 120 140 160 180
Miles

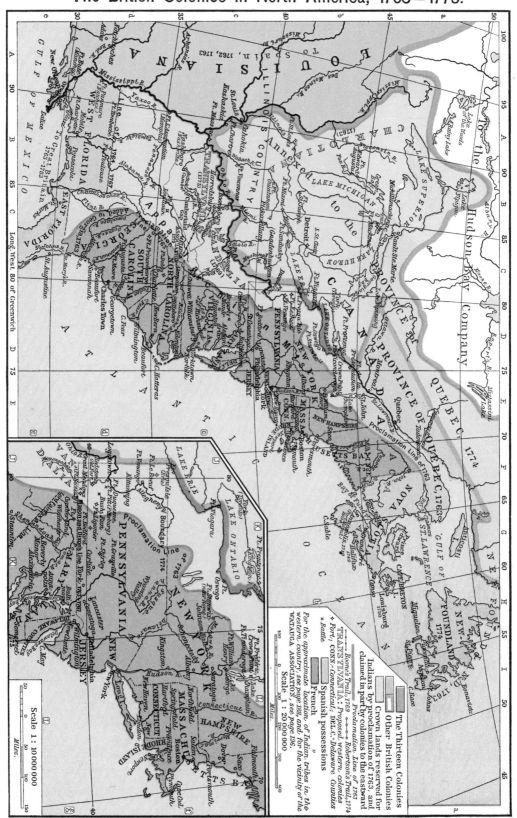

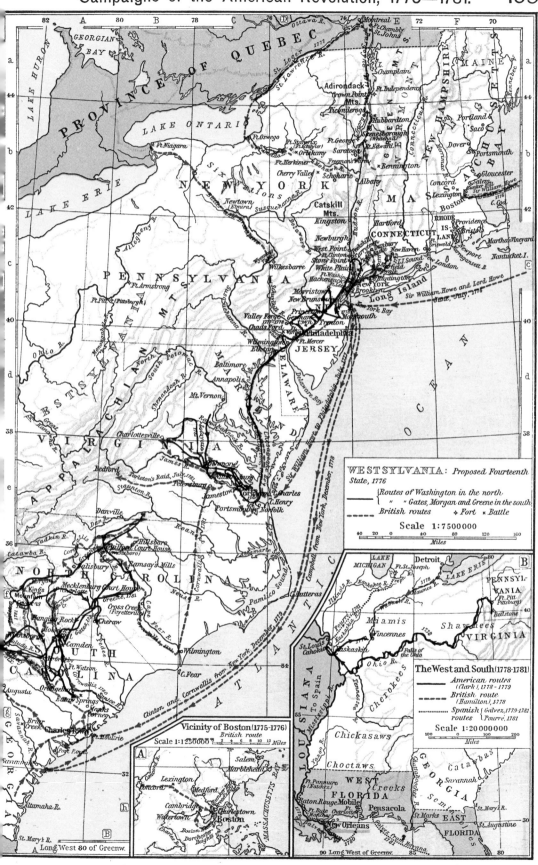

The United States, 1783—1803.

Early Distribution of the Public Lands.
The rectangular system of surveying, partially shown in the map, was adopted in 1785
Scale 1:6 000 000

Legend:

Treaty line of 1783
Acquired from Great Britain 1783
States having no claim to the western territory
Claimed by Virginia; ceded in 1784
Area disputed with Great Britain
British posts in the territory of the United States held until the treaty of 1794
British possessions   ◆ Fort
Spanish   ✕ Battle

C.D.·Cumberland District or District of Miro; F.·Franklin;
S.P.·Sold to Pennsylvania; W.S.·Watauga Settlements; WEST.·WESTERN.
For the approximate location of Indian tribes in the western territory, see p. 188.

Scale 1:15 000 000
100 50 0   100   200   300
Miles

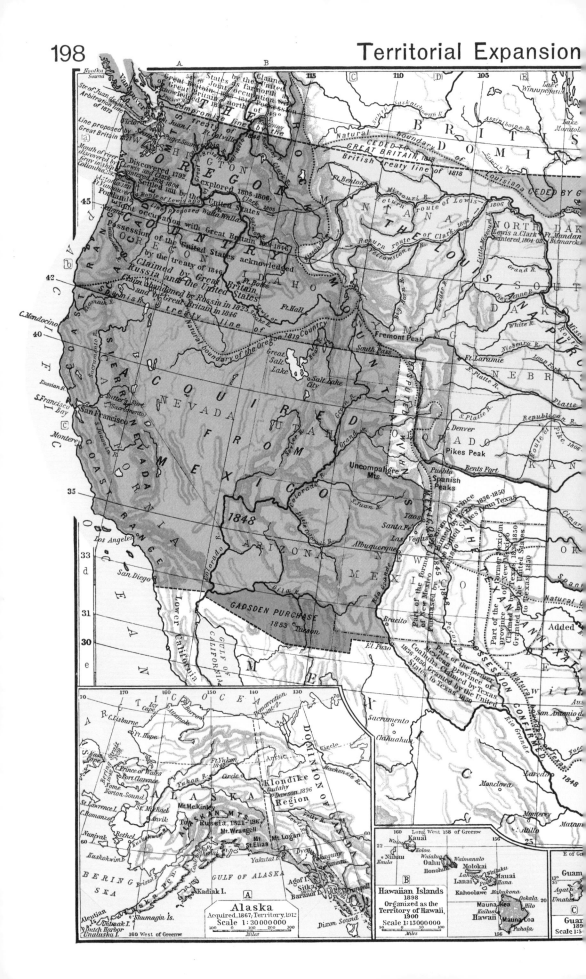

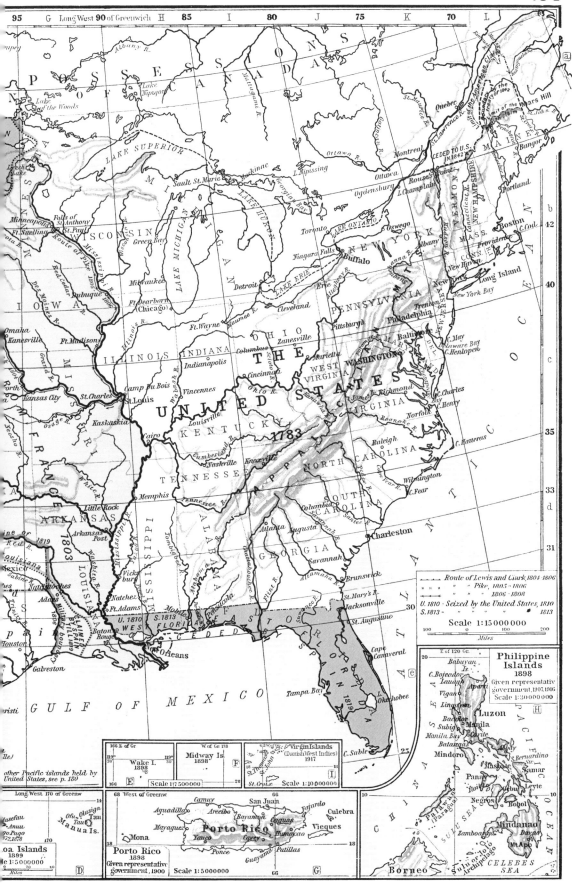

Route of Lewis and Clark 1804-1806
"   "   Pike, 1805-1806
"   "   " 1806-1808
U. 1810 - Seized by the United States, 1810
S.1813 -   1813

Scale 1:15000000
100   0   100   200
Miles

Philippine Islands 1898
Given representativ government, 1907-1916
Scale 1:30000000

Wake I. 1898
Scale 1:7500000

Midway Is. 1898

Virgin Islands (Danish West Indies) 1917
Scale 1:10000000

oa Islands 1899
1:5000000

Porto Rico 1898
Given representative government, 1900
Scale 1:5000000

other Pacific islands held by United States, see p. 180

200

Campaigns of the War of 1812.

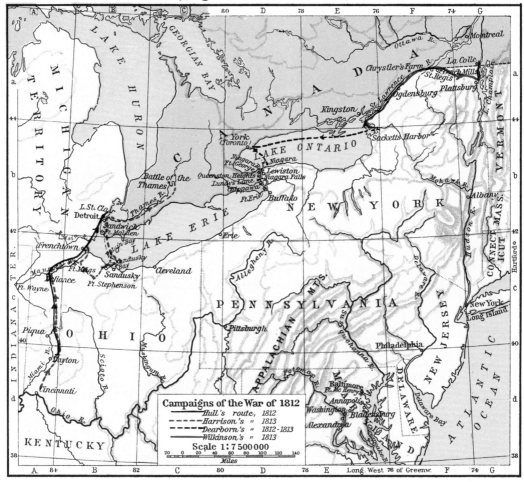

MASS.= MASSACHUSETTS; TER.= TERRITORY. ◆ Fort ✕ Battle

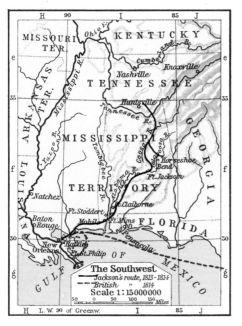

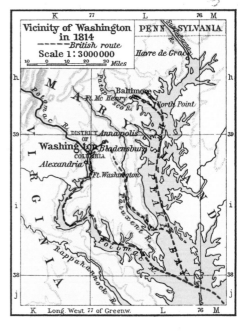

Campaigns of the Mexican War, 1846—1847.

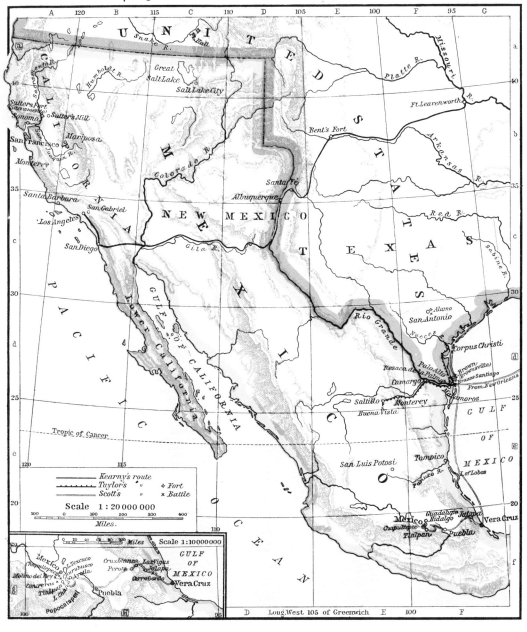

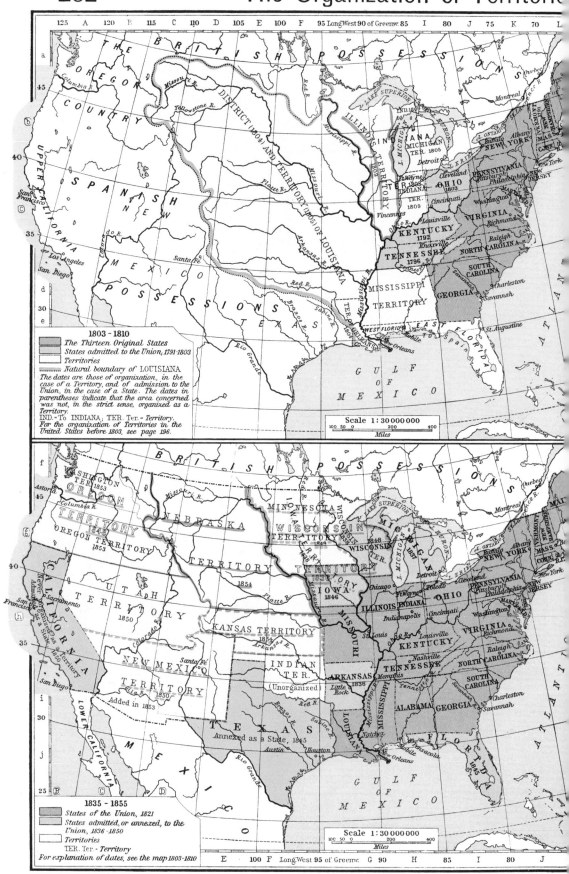

1803 - 1810
The Thirteen Original States
States admitted to the Union, 1791-1803
Territories
Natural boundary of LOUISIANA
The dates are those of organization, in the
case of a Territory, and of admission to the
Union, in the case of a State. The dates in
parentheses indicate that the area concerned
was not, in the strict sense, organized as a
Territory.
IND. - To INDIANA ; TER. Ter. - Territory.
For the organization of Territories in the
United States before 1803, see page 196.

Scale 1:30 000 000
100 50 0   200   400
Miles

1835 - 1855
States of the Union, 1821
States admitted, or annexed, to the
Union, 1836-1850
Territories
TER. Ter - Territory
For explanation of dates, see the map 1803-1810

Scale 1:30 000 000
100 50 0   200   400
Miles

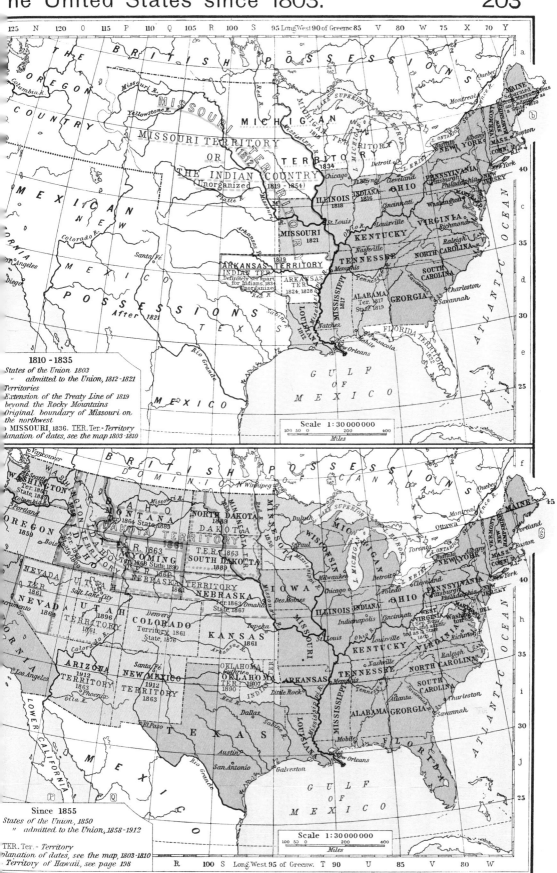

Slavery and the Staple Agricultural Products in the Southern States, 1790—1860.

Staple Agricultural Products in the Southern States, 1790-1860

Legend: Slaves · Cotton · Tobacco · Rice · Sugar-cane

Year	Product	ALABAMA	ARKANSAS	FLORIDA	GEORGIA	KENTUCKY	LOUISIANA	MARYLAND	MISSISSIPPI	MISSOURI	N.CAROLINA	S.CAROLINA	TENNESSEE	TEXAS	VIRGINIA	Totals
1860	Cotton	395,982,200	146,957,200	26,061,200	280,736,000		311,095,200		481,002,800	16,475,200	58,205,800	141,364,800	118,585,600	172,585,200	5,090,800	2,154,141,600
1860	Tobacco	232,914	989,980	828,815	919,318	108,126,840	39,940	38,410,965	809,082	25,086,196	32,853,250	104,412	43,448,097	97,914	123,968,312	375,266,094
1860	Rice	493,465	16,831	223,704	52,507,652		6,331,257	9,767	506,000	402,000	7,593,796	119,100,528	40,372	88,203	198,000	187,160,710
1860	Sugar-cane	1,669,000		1,167,000	1,167,000		221,726,000		506,000			198,000		5,099,000		230,982,000
1860	Slaves	435,080	111,115	61,745	462,198	225,483	331,726	87,189	436,631	114,931	331,059	402,406	275,719	182,566	490,865	3,948,713
1850	Cotton	225,573,600	26,137,600	18,052,400	199,636,400		71,494,800		193,716,800	423,924	29,538,000	120,360,400	77,812,800	23,228,800	1,578,800	987,635,600
1850	Tobacco	164,990	218,936	998,614	423,924	55,501,196	26,878	21,407,497	49,960	17,113,784	11,984,786	74,285	20,148,932	66,897	56,803,227	185,083,906
1850	Rice	2,312,252	63,179	1,075,090	38,950,691		4,425,349	700	2,719,856		5,465,868	159,930,613	258,854	88,203	17,154	215,313,397
1850	Sugar-cane	8,242,000		2,750,000	1,642,000		226,001,000		388,000					7,351,000		247,583,000
1850	Slaves	342,844	47,100	39,310	381,682	210,981	244,809	90,368	309,878	87,422	288,548	384,984	239,459	58,161	472,528	3,198,074
1840	Cotton	117,138,823	6,028,642	12,110,533	163,392,396	691,456	152,555,368	5,673	193,401,577	121,121	51,926,190	61,710,274	27,701,277		3,494,483	790,277,213
1840	Tobacco	273,302	148,439	75,274	162,894	53,436,909	119,824	24,816,012	83,471	9,067,913	16,772,359	51,519	29,550,432		75,347,106	209,905,454
1840	Rice	5,454	481,420		12,384,732	16,736	3,604,534	274,853	77	50	2,820,388	60,590,861	7,977		2,956	80,841,322
1840	Sugar-cane	10,143	1,542	275,337	329,744		119,947,720	36,266			30,000	258,073			1,541,833	124,100,566
1840	Slaves	253,532	19,935	25,717	280,944	182,258	168,452	89,737	195,211	58,240	245,817	327,038	183,059		449,087	2,479,027
1830	Slaves	117,549	4,576	15,501	217,531	165,213	109,588	102,994	65,659	25,091	245,601	315,401	141,603		469,757	1,996,065
1820	Slaves	47,439	1,617		149,656	126,732	69,064	107,398	32,814	10,222	205,017	258,475	80,107		425,153	1,513,694
1810	Slaves				105,218	80,561	34,660	111,502	17,088	3,011	168,824	196,365	44,535		392,518	1,154,282
1800	Slaves				59,404	40,343		105,635	3,489		133,296	146,151	13,584		345,796	847,698
1790	Slaves				29,264	11,830		103,036			100,572	107,094	3,417		293,427	648,640

The shorter strips are proportioned in size to this representation of the maximum number. In the absence of any strip, the figures alone mean that the number of slaves, or of pounds of a certain agricultural product, was less than one tenth of the maximum.

By reference to the figures in each column, it will be seen that the colored strips extending from one vertical line to another indicate the maximum number of slaves, or of pounds of a certain agricultural product, recorded during any of the decennial years.

The purpose of this chart is to suggest a possible relation between the sectionalization of slavery and the growth of the staple agricultural products in the Southern States. Unfortunately the Reports of the United States, from which the figures are taken, do not supply agricultural statistics before 1840.— Although a slave-holding State, Delaware is not included in the list, because the amount of any of the staple agricultural products raised there was too small for the purpose of comparison.

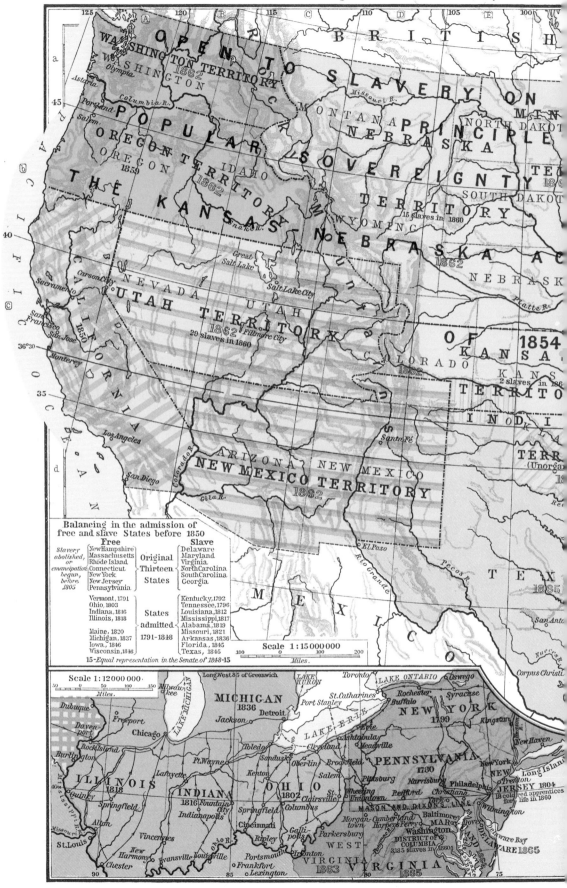

Balancing in the admission of
free and slave States before 1850

Free		Slave
Slavery abolished, or emancipation begun, before 1805.	New Hampshire Massachusetts Rhode Island Connecticut New York New Jersey Pennsylvania	*Original Thirteen States*	Delaware Maryland Virginia North Carolina South Carolina Georgia
	Vermont, 1791 Ohio, 1803 Indiana, 1816 Illinois, 1818	*States admitted 1791-1848*	Kentucky, 1792 Tennessee, 1796 Louisiana, 1812 Mississippi, 1817 Alabama, 1819 Missouri, 1821 Arkansas, 1836 Florida, 1845 Texas, 1845
	Maine, 1820 Michigan, 1837 Iowa, 1846 Wisconsin, 1848		

15=Equal representation in the Senate of 1848-15

Scale 1:15 000 000

Scale 1:12 000 000

Seat of the Civil War, 1861—1865.

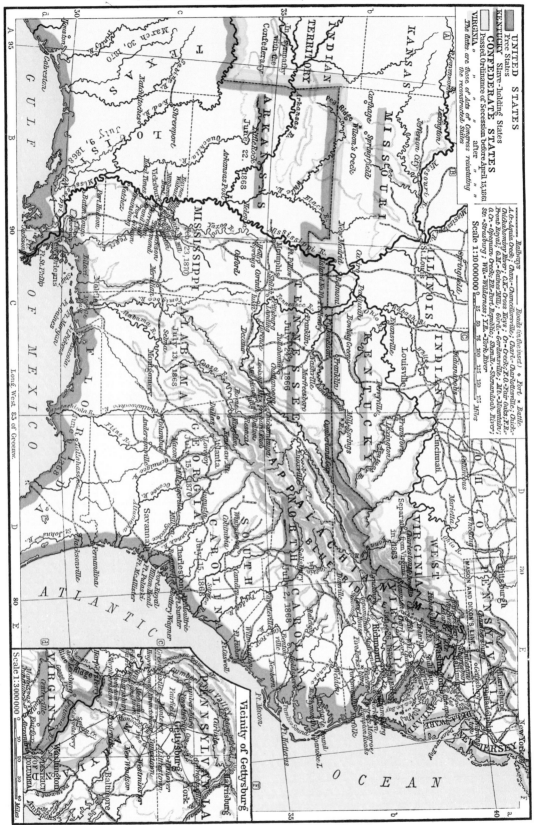

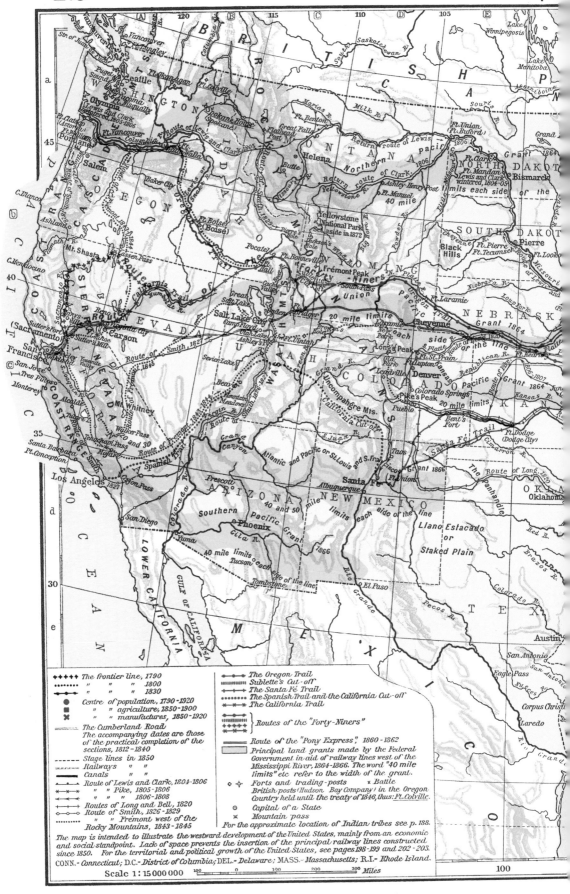

The map is intended to illustrate the westward development of the United States, mainly from an economic and social standpoint. Lack of space prevents the insertion of the principal railway lines constructed since 1850. For the territorial and political growth of the United States, see pages 198-199 and 202-203.

CONN.- Connecticut; D.C.- District of Columbia; DEL.- Delaware; MASS.- Massachusetts; R.I.- Rhode Island.

Scale 1:15 000 000

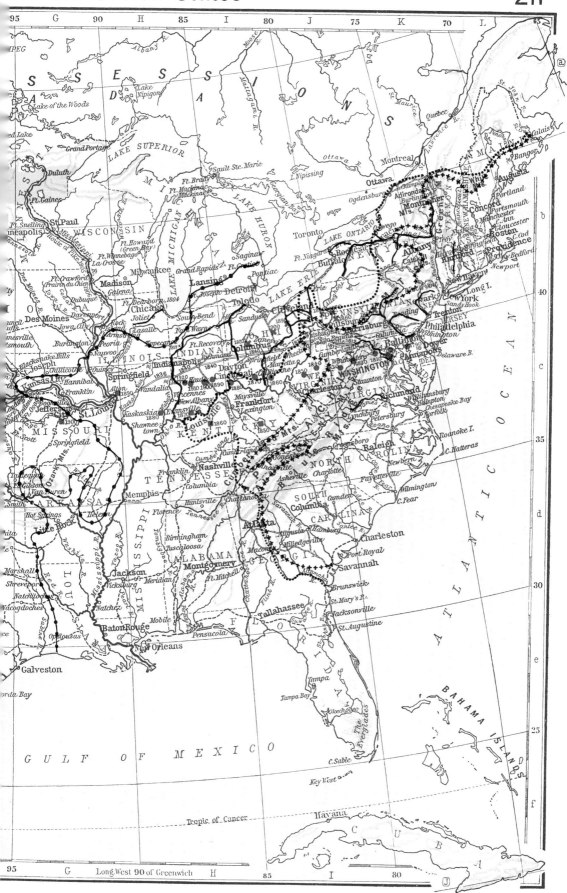

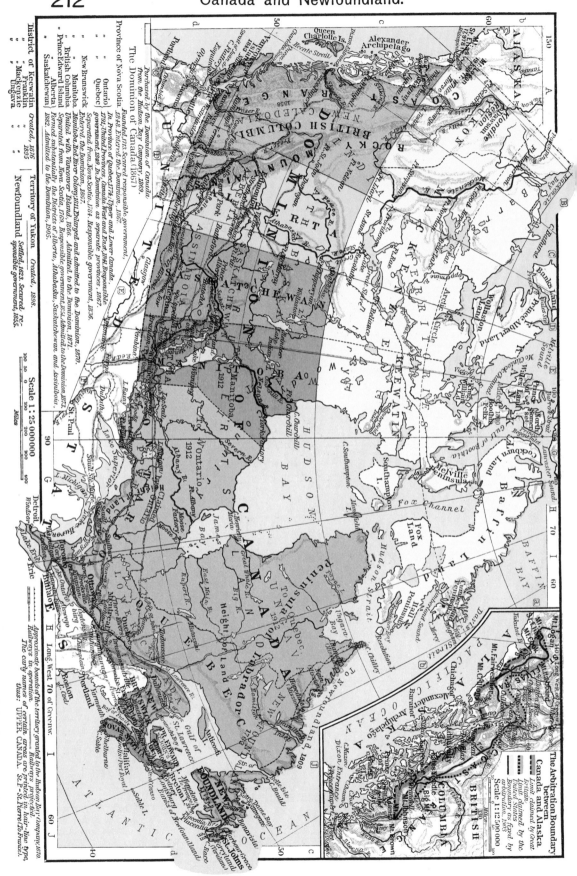

The Arbitration Boundary
between
Canada and Alaska.

Scale 1:12,500,000

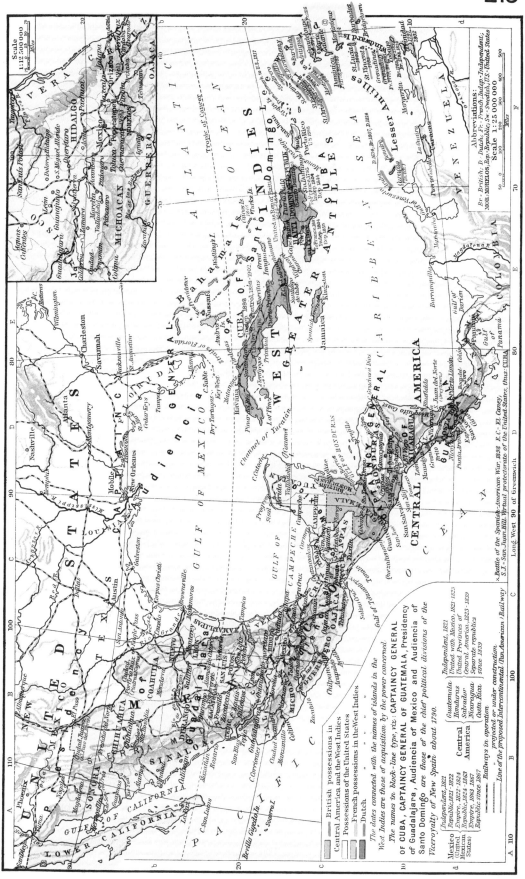

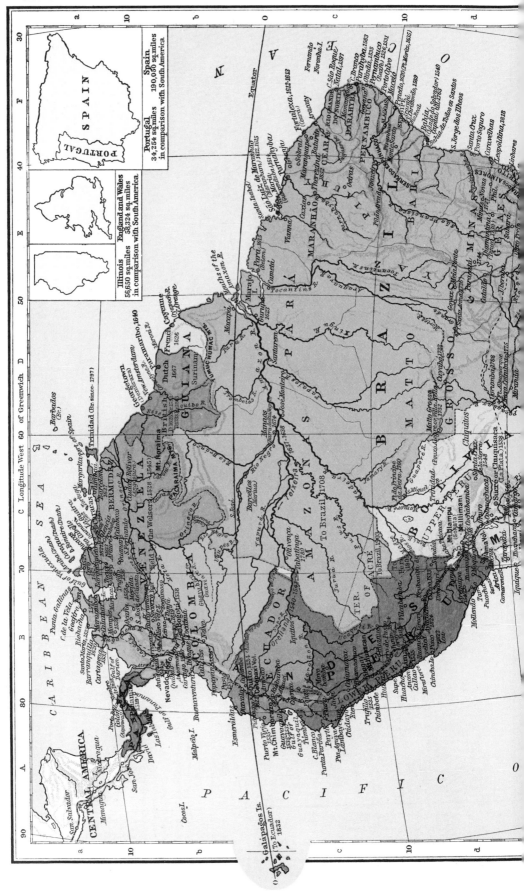

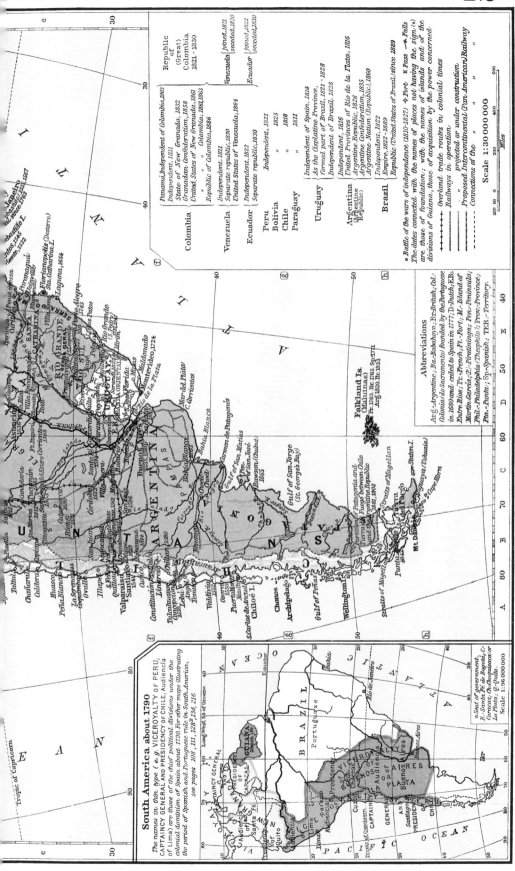

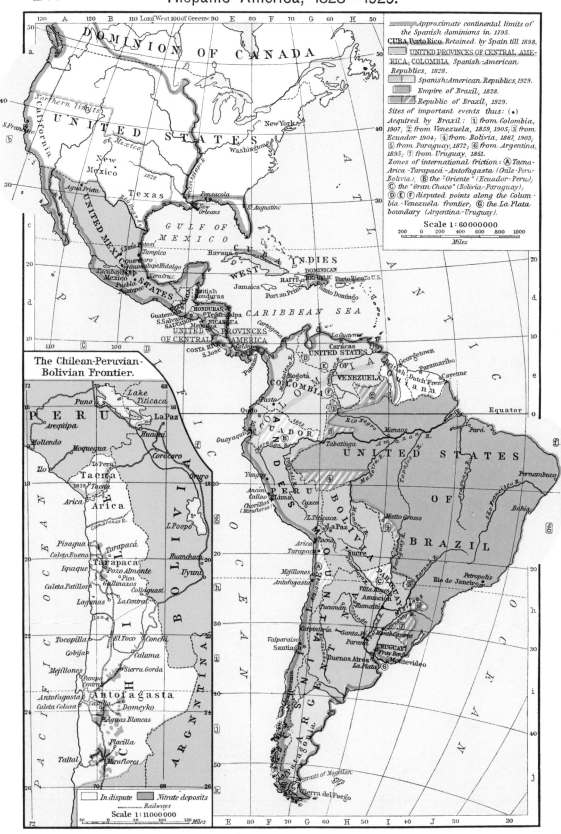

The Chilean-Peruvian-Bolivian Frontier.

In dispute   Nitrate deposits

Railways

Scale 1: 11000000

MAPS SINCE 1929

PREPARED BY C. S. HAMMOND & COMPANY

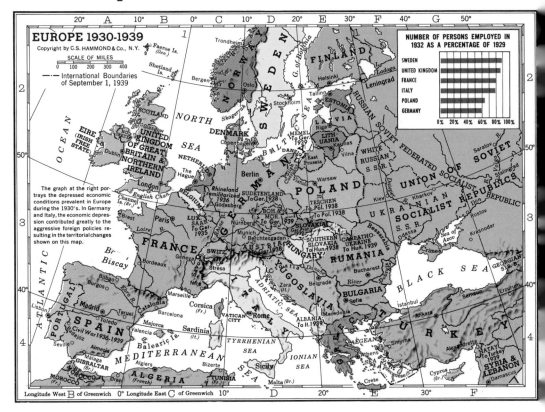

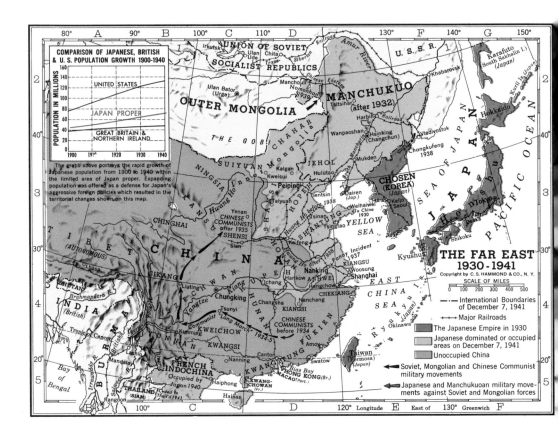

European Theater of War 1939-1945.

Far Eastern Theater of War 1939-1945.

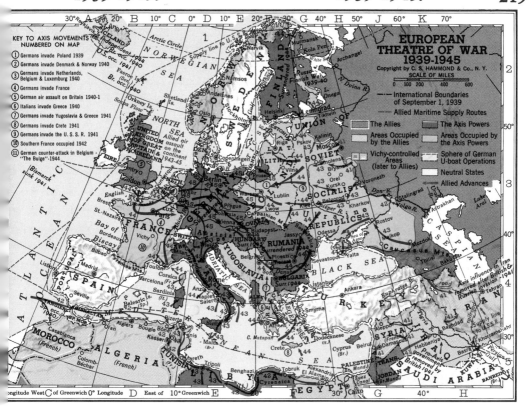

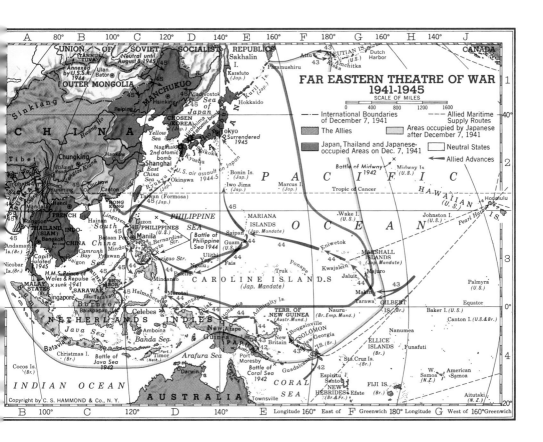

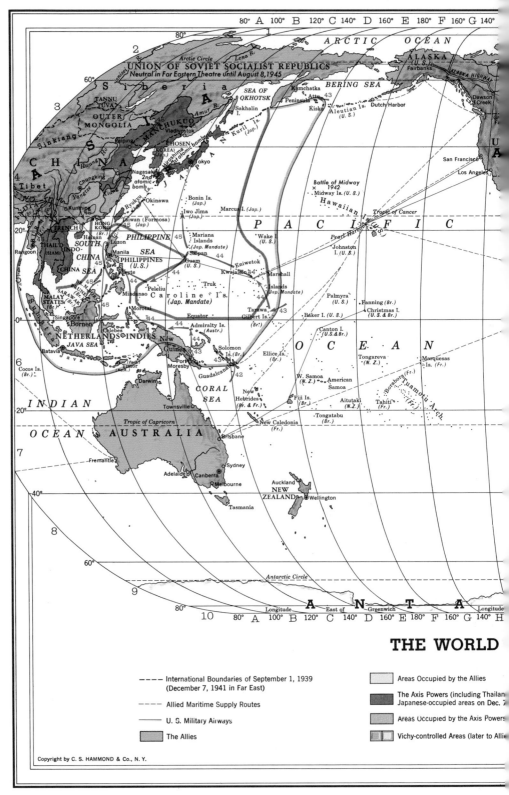

THE WORLD

---- International Boundaries of September 1, 1939
      (December 7, 1941 in Far East)

----- Allied Maritime Supply Routes

—— U. S. Military Airways

█ The Allies

Areas Occupied by the Allies

The Axis Powers (including Thailan
Japanese-occupied areas on Dec. 7

Areas Occupied by the Axis Powers

Vichy-controlled Areas (later to Allie

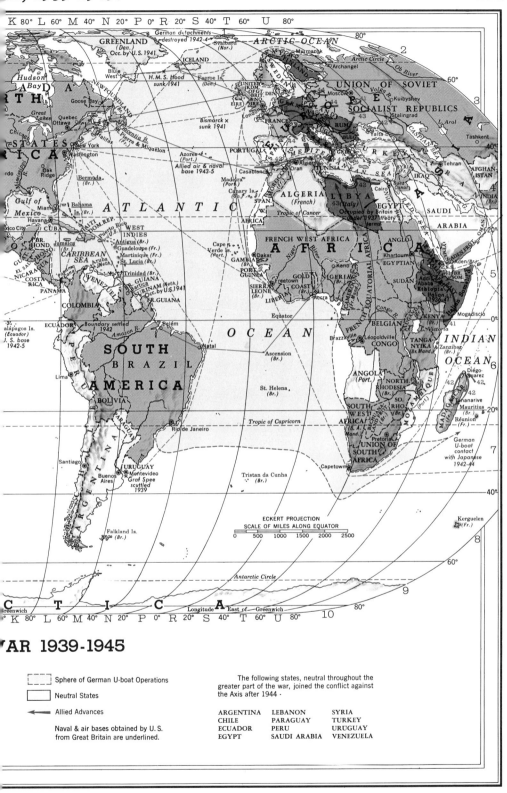

WAR 1939-1945

⬚ Sphere of German U-boat Operations	The following states, neutral throughout the greater part of the war, joined the conflict against the Axis after 1944 -
▭ Neutral States	
⬅ Allied Advances	

Naval & air bases obtained by U.S. from Great Britain are underlined.

ARGENTINA	LEBANON	SYRIA
CHILE	PARAGUAY	TURKEY
ECUADOR	PERU	URUGUAY
EGYPT	SAUDI ARABIA	VENEZUELA

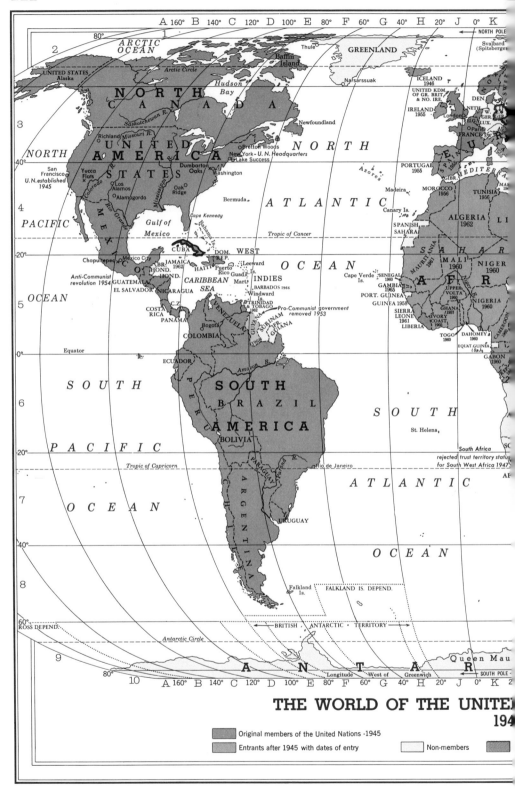

THE WORLD OF THE UNITE[
194[

TIONS AND THE COLD WAR

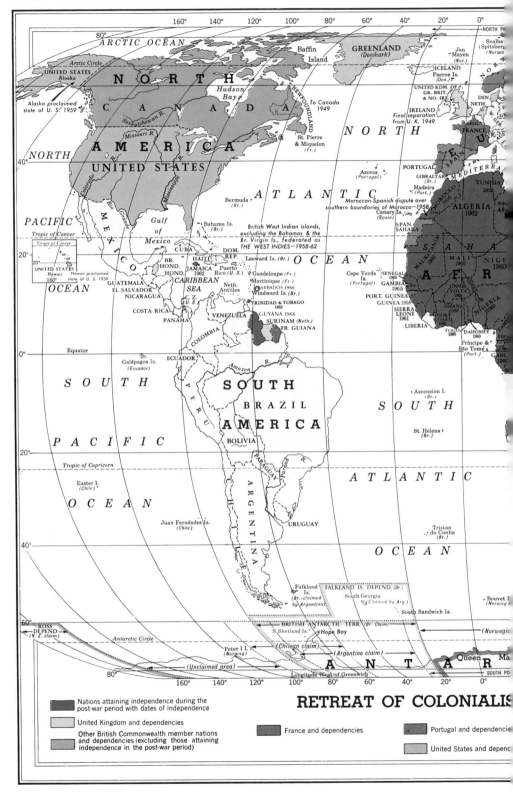

RETREAT OF COLONIALIS

Nations attaining independence during the post-war period with dates of independence

United Kingdom and dependencies

Other British Commonwealth member nations and dependencies (excluding those attaining independence in the post-war period)

France and dependencies

Portugal and dependencie

United States and depenc

THE POST-WAR PERIOD

Netherlands and dependencies	Norway and dependencies
Spain and dependencies	Denmark and dependency

Other countries

Areas of the Soviet Union in which Great Russians constitute a majority of the population. Names of other peoples are underlined.

Copyright by C. S. HAMMOND & Co., N. Y.

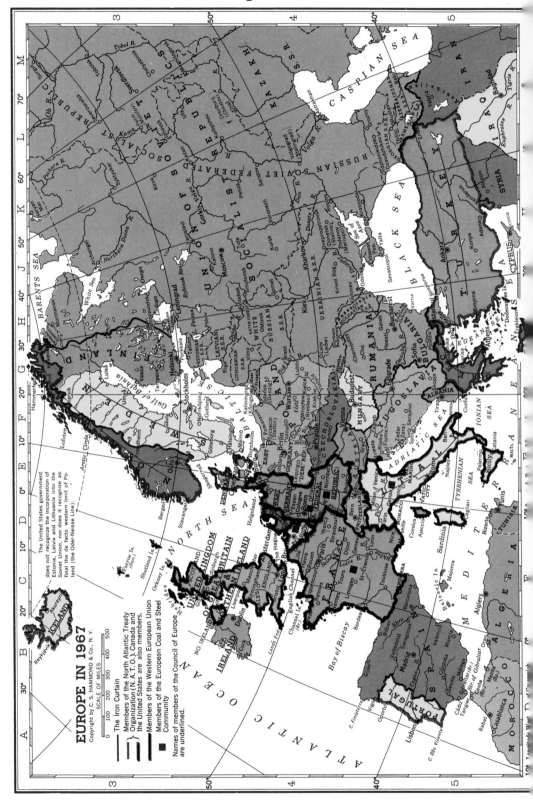

EUROPE IN 1967

Copyright by C. S. HAMMOND & Co., N. Y.

SCALE OF MILES

0 100 200 300 400 500

The Iron Curtain

Members of the North Atlantic Treaty Organization (N.A.T.O.). Canada and the United States are also members.

Members of the Western European Union

Members of the European Coal and Steel Community

Names of members of the Council of Europe are underlined.

The United States government does not recognize the incorporation of Estonia, Latvia and Lithuania into the Soviet Union, nor does it recognize as final the de facto western limit of Poland (the Oder-Neisse Line).

INDEX

UNLESS otherwise indicated, the names given are those of towns. The Index does not furnish a complete set of references to the more important countries at successive periods of time. The maps needful for this purpose may be found by consulting the Table of Contents.

Modern names of ancient localities and different spellings of the same name are sometimes inclosed in parentheses, sometimes noted by cross-references. Though not appearing on the maps themselves, a considerable number of classical and medieval Latin names, and of different spellings of the same name, have been inserted in the Index with the proper cross-reference to the modern or customary form of such names.

If not accompanied by the letters B. C., the dates cited are A. D.

The number following a name refers to the page on which the name appears. The capital letter or letters following this number usually refer to a strip on that page inclosed by lines of longitude, and the small letter or letters, to a strip inclosed by lines of latitude. The name itself lies within the block formed by the intersection of the two strips. Thus the name *Madrid* 83 K g will be found on page 83, within the block formed by the intersection of the strip lettered K and the strip lettered g. In some cases, however, the letter or letters refer to a particular plan or inset on the page concerned.

Names which appear in the original Index without indication of the block in which they lie, are repeated with full information in the Index-Supplement. Names contained in the maps for the period 1911-1929 also appear in the Index-Supplement, as well as a number of names for the old maps which were omitted in the original Index. Place names followed by an asterisk (*) have been deleted from the maps because of recent archaeological discoveries. Note that other changes based on recent researches are listed on page 115.

ABBREVIATIONS

ab. = abbacy
abp. = archbishopric
Arg. Rep. = Argentine Republic
Aug. Reg. = Augustan Region
auton. = autonomous
bldg. = building
bp. = bishopric
Cal. = California
calif. = califate
cap. = captaincy
cent. = century
ch. = church
col. = colony
Conn. = Connecticut
cty. = county
cy. = city
dept. = department
desp. = despotat
dioc. = diocese
dist. = district
dom. = dominion(s)
E. = East
elect. = electorate
emir. = emirate
emp. = empire
exarch. = exarchate
fam. = family or clan
for. off. = foreign office

Frank. = Frankish
gen. = general or generality
gouv. = gouvernement
gov. = government
gr. = grand
Hanse. = Hanseatic
imp. = imperial
Ind. Res. = Indian Reservation
ins. = inset
isl. = island(s)
khan. = khanate
km. = kingdom
landgr. = landgraviate
leg. = legend
loc. = locality
margr. = margravate
marq. = marquisate
Mass. = Massachusetts
Miss. = Mississippi
mon. = monastery
mt., mts. = mountain(s)
N. = North
Ore. = Oregon
Pa. = Pennsylvania
palat. = palatinate
parl. bor. = parliamentary borough
patr. = patriarchate
pen. = peninsula

poss. = possessions
pref. = prefecture
pres. = presidency
princ. = principality
proc. = proconsultate
prom. = promontory
prot. = protectorate
prov. = province
R. = River
reg. = region
rep. = republic
Rom. = Roman
S. = South
satr. = satrapy
S. C. = South Carolina
seign. = seigniory
sen. = senatorial
set. = settlement
str. = strait
ter. = territory
univ. = university
U. S. = United States
Va. = Virginia
viscty. = viscounty
vol. = volcano
W. = West or Western

Aach 142   C e
Aachen (Aix-la-Chapelle) . . . 55   Q i
Aalborg 88   C c
Aalen 143   J h
Aalesund 166   G c
Aarau 91   Q k
Aardenburg 117   B c
Aar or Aare River 91   Q k
Aargau, distr. 91   Q k
Aargau, region 62   D e
Abacaenum 30   E d
Abæ 11   D d
Aballo, see Avallon
Abalus (Helgoland), isl. 38   D b
Abana River 6   E a
Abarim, Mountains of 7   D f
Abaris, promontory 9   B c
Abasgi, people. 35   M e
Abasgians, people. 50   L d
Abbassids, Calif. of the 55   K h
Abbeville 76   D a
Abbotsbury, mon. 97   O k
Abdera, in Spain 12   C c
Abdera, in Thrace 12   H b
Abejar 82   B a
Abel 6   D h
Abel-Keramin 7   D e
Abella 30   D b
Abellinum 30   D b
Abensberg 154   F d
Abercorn, in Georgia . . . . . 193 ins. C
Abercorn, in Scotland 185   C b
Aberdeen
Aberdeen, bp. 97   K b
Aberdeen, cty.
Aberdeen, univ. 100   E c
Aberffraw
Abergavenny
Abergavenny, mon. 97   O j
Aberystwith, parl. bor.
Abeshr. 174   F c
Abia 14   C c
Abila, in Gilead 6   D c
Abila, in Mauretania 38   A e
Abila, in Syria 6   E a
Abingdon, in England . . . . . 98 ins. A
Abingdon, mon. 97   P j
Abingdon, parl. bor. . . . . . 163 M f (Ab.)
Abingdon, in Virginia . . . . . 196 ins. A
Abittibi, lake 188   J a
Abittibi, river 188   J a
Abkhasia, reg. 119   L e
Abkoude 117   C b
Abnakis, people. 188   M b
Abnoba Mountains 38   D c
Abo 120   J d
Abodrites, people. 55   R i
Abomey 174   D d
Abrincas or Abrincates, see
Avranche
Abruzzi, dist. 90   D c
Abruzzo, bp. 95   E c
Absalom, Tomb of . . . . 6 ins. A
Abukir 174   J i
Abukir Bay 150   A a
Abus, mt. 20   I c
Abus Fluvius (Humber River).
Abu Simbel 1   B f
Abusina 38   E c
Abydos, in Egypt 1   B d
Abydos, on the Hellespont . . .
Abyssinia, reg. 109   U g
Abyssinia, cty. 174   G d
Acadia, reg. 194   F a
Acalander River 31   F b
Acamas, prom. 20   E e
Acambaro . . . . 213 ins.
Acampsis River 20   I b
Acanthian Gulf 11   E b
Acanthus 11   E b
Acapulco . . . . 107, 108   H f
Acarnania, reg. 10   B d
Accau, route of 191   G c

Acci 38   B e
Accia 148   C c
Accomack, cty. . . . . 193 ins. A
Accra 175   C d
Aceldama, loc. near Jerusalem . 6 ins. A
Acelum 26   F b
Acerenza 64   C b
Acerenza, abp. 95   F c
Acerra, bp. . . . . 95 ins.
Acerræ, in Campania 30   D b
Acerræ, in Venetia. 26   D b
Aceruntia 30   E b
Acervo 27   I b
Acesines River, in India 19   L d
Acesines River, in Sicily 30   E e
Achaia, dioc. 43   G f
Achaia, princ. 89   B c
Achaia, prov. 35   I f
Achaia, reg. 14   B a
Achaia (Phtiotis), reg. 11   D c
Achaia, state 13   B b
Achaian, League . . . . 19 ins. A
Achaian Mountains 10   D d
Achalm, castle 62   E d
Achalm, ruin 143   H h
Acharnae 15   D a
Acharnian Gate 23   D
Achelous River 10   C d
Achern 142   B c
Acheron River 10   B c
Acherusia, lake in Campania . 31 ins. A
Acherusia, lake in Epirus . . . 10   B c
Achilles, Burial mound of . . .
Achilleum . . . .
Achillis Island. 18   D a
Achin 112   C c
Achonry, bp. 97   C b
Achradina, quarter in Syracuse . 31 ins. B
Achrida 59   I e
Achshaph 6   C b
Achzib. 6   C b
Acilii, Gardens of the 22   A
Aciris (Agri) River. 31   F b
Acium 30   E c
Acla 105   E e
Acoma 190   D e
Aconcagua, mt. 215   C f
Acqui 90   I h
Acqui, bp. 95   D c
Acræ 30   D e
Acraephia. 11   E d
Acragas (Girgenti) 30   C e
Acre, see Saint Jean d'Acre. . 73   G d
Acre, ter. 214   B c
Acriæ 15   C c
Acritas, mt. 14   B c
Acritas, prom. 14   B c
Acroceraunia, prom 31   I b
Acroceraunia, reg. 17   A a
Acroceraunian Mountains. . . . 10   A b
Acrocorinthus 15   C b
Acropolis of Athens, plan of the 23   C
Acroria, reg. 14   B b
Acrothoi 11   F b
Acte, reg. in Argolis 15   D b
Acte, reg. in Attica 16   D c
Acte, reg. in Chalcidice 11   F b
Actium 10   B d
Aculco . . . . 213 ins.
Adadah 7   C f
Adaes 191   G e
Adalia 77   K e
Adams, Fort, in Mississippi . . 199   G d
Adams, Fort, in Ohio . . . . . 196 ins. B
Adams, mt. . . . . 212 ins.
Adamawa, Adamaua, reg. . . . 174   E d
Adana 20   F d
Ad Aquilam 27   F d
Ad Castores 26   E b
Adda River 90   I h
Addis Abeba . . . .
Addua (Adda) River 26   D a
Adelaide 172   C d
Adelberg, mon. 143   I h

Adelmannsfelden 143   I
Adelsberg 159   H
Adelsheim 142   D
Adelsreuthe 142   E
Aden. . . . .
Aden, Gulf of 170   F
Aden Protectorate . . . . 170 F g (A.P.)
Ad Fines
Adiabene, reg. 20   J
Adige River 90   J
Adirondack Mountains. 192   D
Adis Ababa
Admiralty Island . . . . 212 ins.
Admont, mon. 80   D
Ad Novas, on Lake Sabatinus . 35 ins. E
Ad Novas, near L. Trasimenus . 27   F c
Adoraim. 7   C
Adour River 76   C
Adowa 174   G
Ad Padum 27   G
Adra 82   B
Adraha 6   E c
Adramyttium
Adramyttium, Gulf of . . . . .
Adrana River 39   J h
Adrar, reg. 174   B
Adratum 68   C c
Adria 64   B a
Adria, bp. 95   E b
Adrianople 43   H e
Adrianopolis 35   J e
Adrianus River 27   F b
Adriatic Sea 2   E d
Ad Sabatum 31   F c
Adsalluta River 27   I a
Ad Sextum 27   F d
Ad Statuas . . . . 35 ins. B
Adua see Adowa
Aduatuca 39   H h
Aduatuci, people 39   H h
Adula, mt. 26   C a
Adullam 7   B e
Adwalton Moor 127   X m
Æane 10   C b
Æas River 10   A b
Æcæ 30   E a
Æclanum 30   D a
Ædepsus 11   E d
Ædro, Portus 27   G b
Ædui, see Autun
Ædui, people 38   C c
Æfula . . . . 35 ins. B
Ægæ, in Achaia 14   C a
Ægæ, in Euboea 11   E d
Ægæ or Agææ, in Macedonia . 10   D b
Ægaleos, mountain in Attica . 16   B b
Ægaleus, mountain in Messenia 14   B b
Ægates, isl. 30   B d
Æge 11   E c
Ægeae 20   F d
Ægean Islands, Theme of the . 59   I f
Ægean Sea 2   G e
Ægiæ 14   C c
Ægialea, reg. 14   B a
Ægilia, in Attica 16   B b
Ægilia, island near Crete . . . 15   D d
Ægilia, island near Euboea . . 15   E a
Ægilips, isl. 10   B d
Ægilos, isl. 26   D d
Ægina 15   D b
Ægina, isl. 15   D b
Æginium 10   C c
Ægira 14   C a
Ægitium 10   D d
Ægium 14   C a
Ægospotami River . . . .
Ægosthena 15   D a
Ægusa, isl. 30   B e
Ægyptus, Rom. prov., see Egypt 35   J h
Ægys 14   C b
Ælana 35   K h
Ælia Capitolina (Jerusalem) . . 35   L g
Ælian Bridge 22   A
Ælmere, bay, see Zuider Zee

Æmilia, reg.	26	E c
Æmilia, Rom. prov.	42	E e (2)
Æmilia, Basilica, bldg.	24	B
Æmilian Bridge	24	A
Æmilian Portico	22	A
Æmilian Way, road	26	C c
Æmilian Way of Scaurus, road	26	D c
Ænaria, (Ischia), isl.	30	C b
Ænea	11	D b
Æneum, prom.	11	D b
Æniania, reg.	10	D d
Ænis, reg.	8	N h
Ænona	27	J c
Ænus		
Ænus, mt.	10	B d
Ænus (Inn) River	38	E c
Ænyra	11	F b
Æoli, (Stromboli), isl.	30	E d
Æoliæ, (Lipari), isl.	30	D d
Æolian Islands	90	E e
Æolians, people	8	O h
Æolis, reg.	8	Q h
Æpea	14	B c
Æqui, people	27	H e
Æquians, people		
Æquimelium	24	A
Æquum Tuticum	30	E a
Ærarium, bldg. in Rome		
Aëre	6	E b
Æsar River	31	G c
Æsculapius, Temple of, in Carthage	34 ins. A (5)	
Æsculapius, Temple of, in Rome	22	A
Æsepus River		
Æsernia	30	D a
Æsis	27	H d
Æsis (Esino) River	27	H d
Æsium, see Jesi		
Æson River	11	D b
Æstui, people	38	G a
Æthalia, (Elba), isl.	26	E e
Æthices, people	10	C c
Ætna	30	D e
Ætna, mt., see Etna		
Ætolia, reg.	10	C d
Ætolian League	19 ins. A	
Æxone	16	B b
Afghanistan, cty.	170	H e
Afghans, people		
Africa, continent	174, 175	
Africa, dioc.	42	
Africa, exarch.	52	I f
Africa, Proconsular, Rom. prov.	34	F f
Africa, prov.	38	D e
Agade	4	G c
Agades	174	D c
Agalassa	19	L d
Agamenticus	189	C c
Agaña	198 ins. C	
Agaraci, people	35	L g
Agat	198 ins. C	
Agatha, Agathe (Agde)	12	D b
Agathyrnum	30	D b
Agawam (Ipswich, Mass.)	189	C c
Agawam (Springfield, Mass.)	189	B c
Agde	61	E e
Agedincum (Sens)	38	C c
Agen	46	G e
Agen, bp.	94	C c
Agen, cty.	69	D d
Agenais, cty.	61	D d
Agennum, see Agde		
Agenorium	18 ins. B	
Ager Gallicus, dist.	27	G d
Ager Romanus, dist.	35 ins. B	
Ager Solonius, dist.	35 ins. B	
Ager Vaticanus, dist.	22	A
Aggershuus (Christiania)		
Aghadoe, bp.	97	B d
Aghlabids, Dom. of the	54	G g
Agida	27	H b
Agincourt	81	M g
Aginnum (Agen)	38	C d
Agnadello	90	I h
Agnus	16	B b
Agogna River	90	I h
Agora (Lysimachia)		
Agordo	90	J g
Agostinho, Cape	108	R i
Agra	137	C c
Agræ	16	B b
Agræ, reg.	23	D
Agræi, people	10	C d
Agræna	6	E c
Agram	72	D b
Agram, bp.	95	F b
Agrianes, people	18	B b
Agri Decumates (Tithe Lands), distr.	39	J i
Agrigentum (Girgenti)	30	C e
Agrinium	10	C d
Agrippa, Baths of	22	A
Agrippa, Field of	22	A
Agrippa, Monument of	22	A
Agrippa's Bridge	22	A
Agrippina, Gardens of	22	A
Agryle	16	B b
Aguadilla	199 ins. G	
Aguantum	27	G a
Aguarico River	111	B b
Agua Salud River		
Aguas Blancas	215	B e
Aguas Calientes	213 ins.	
Aguilar	83	K g
Aguilas	82	B b
Aguinum	30	C a
Agulhas, Cape	175	E h
Aguya, Punta	214	A c
Agyrium	30	D e
Ahausen	122	F d
Ahmadabad	137	B d
Ahmadnagar	137	B e
Ahorca Lagarto		
Ahremberg	117	E d
Ahwaz	99	M g
Ai	7	C e
Aianteion, quarter	93	G e
Aianteum		
Aibar	83	K g
Aidin	164	D c
Aidin, reg.	77	J e
Aigle	91	P l
Aigues-mortes	73	A b
Aiguillon	76	D d
Aigun	171	N c
Aimores, Serra dos	214	E d
Ain, dept.	148	F e
Ain River	126	D c
Ainay, mon.	148	B b
Aini	99	L e
Ainos	12	I b
Ain-Tab	68	C b
Aiquebelle, mon.	95	D c
Air, reg.	174	D c
Airaines	76	D b
Aird's Moss		
Aire	126	C a
Aire, bp.	94	B c
Aire River	127	X m
Airebolu	165	E c
Airolo	91	Q l
Aisne, dept.	148	E e
Aisne River	126	C b
Aix	61	F e
Aix, (Aix-les-Bains)	130	N i
Aix, abp.	95	D c
Aix, gen.	147	F c
Aix, univ.	100	G f
Aix-la-Chapelle (Aachen)	55	Q i
Aix-la-Chapelle, imp. cy.	78	D c
Ajaccio	72	B c
Ajaccio, bp.	95	D c
Ajalon	7	C e
Ajana, reg.		
Ajax, Burial mound of		
Ajmere	137	B c
Akabah	99	K h
Akabah, Gulf of	99	J h
Akaroa	172	G e
Akasheh	174	F b
Ake	6	C c
Akerman	99	J d
Akhalzikh	164	G b
Akhsi		
Akkad, reg.	4	G c*
Akko	6	C c
Akkrum	117	D a
Akra	6 ins. A	
Akrabbi	7	C d
Akrabbim, mts	7	B g
Akserai	89	J g
Akshehr	93	D c
Akshi-Kioi		
Aksu		
Akureyri	166	B b
Alabama River	187	K e
Alabama, state	203	U d
Alabama, ter.	203	U d
Alabanda	20	C d
Alagoas, state	214	F c
Alagonia	14	C c
Alais	76	E d
Alalcomenæ	10	B d
Alalia	12	E b
Alamance, battle	194	D c
Alamanni, people in 486	50	E c
Alamanni, people about 900	57	E d
Alamannia, duchy about 1000	58	F d
Alamannia, Frank. prov.	53	N h
Alamannia, reg.	54	F d
Alamo, battle	201	F d
Alamos	213	B b
Alamos de Catorce	213	B b
Alamut	92	F d
Alancione, see Alençon		
Åland Islands	120	I d
Alans, people in Russia		
Alans, people in France	48	F d
Alans, people in Spain	45	C e
Alara River	39	J g
Alarcon	82	B b
Alarcon, route of	190	C f
Alashehr	93	C c
Alaska, Gulf of	198 ins. A	
Alaska, dist.	186	D b
Alaska Mountains	186	D b
Alaska Peninsula	186	D c
Alatri, bp.	95	E c
Alausi	214	B c
Alava, cty.	82	B a
Alava, reg.	83	K g
Alazones, people	35	K d
Alba River, see Aube River		
Alba	90	I h
Alba, bp.	95	D c
Albacete	83	K h
Alba Fucens	27	H e
Alba Longa	35 ins. B	
Alba Mountains	38	D c
Albana	35	N e
Albania, princ.	93	A b
Albania, reg. in Caucasia	19	G b
Albania, reg. in Epirus	73	E b
Albanian Principalities	77	I d
Albanians, people	165 leg.	
Albano	64 ins.	
Albano, bp.	96	B b
Albanum, bp.	96	B b
Albanus, lake	35 ins. B	
Albanus, mt.	30	B a
Albany, in W. Australia	172	A d
Albany, in New York	192	D b
Albany, Fort	212	G c
Albany, New	211	H c
Albany River	186	K c
Alba Pompeia	26	C c
Albara	68	C b
Albarracin	82	B a
Albarracin, emir.	83	E c
Albasin	171	N c
Albay	199 ins. H	
Albemarle	184	D c

Albemarle, reg. . . . . 193 F c
Albemarle Sound . . . . 193 F c
Albenga . . . . 90 B b
Albenga, bp. . . . . 95 D c
Albert . . . . 81 M g
Alberta, prov. . . . . 212 D c
Albert Edward Nyanza lake, see
  Edward Nyanza
Albert Nyanza, lake . . . . 175 F d
Albi . . . . 61 E e
Albi, abp. . . . . 148 B c
Albi, bp. . . . . 94 C c
Albi, viscty. . . . . 61 E e
Albici, people . . . . 38 D d
Albiga (Albi) . . . . 38 C d
Albigeois, cty. . . . . 69 E e
Albingaunum . . . . 26 C c
Albinia River . . . . 27 F e
Albintimilium . . . . 26 B d
Albion, name applied at first to
  Britain, later to England
Albis (Elbe) River . . . . 38 E b
Albon, cty. . . . . 69 F d
Albret, castle . . . . 76 C d
Albret, duchy . . . . 126 A d
Albret, seign. . . . . 69 C d
Albuera . . . . 130 B f
Albula Pass . . . . 91 R l
Albuquerque, in New Mexico . 188 E d
Albuquerque, in Spain . . . . . 83 J h
Albuquerque, duchy . . . . . . 83 J h
Albuquerque, Fort . . . . 214 D d
Albuquerque, route of . . . . . 109 X h,
                              110 BB h
Alburnus, mt. . . . . 30 C c
Albury . . . . 172 D d
Alcácer do Sal . . . . 82 A b
Alcácer es Seguir . . . . 83 J h
Alcalá de Henares . . . . 82 B a
Alcalá de Henares, univ. . . . 100 E f
Alcalá la Real . . . . 82 B b
Alcalde . . . . 210 A c
Alcañiz . . . . 82 B a
Alcántara . . . . 82 A b
Alcantarilla . . . . 82 B b
Alcaráz . . . . 82 B b
Alcázar . . . . 82 H f
Alcluyd
Alcmona River, see Altmühl R.
Alcoboça, mon. . . . . 94 A d
Alcoraz . . . . 66 F e
Alcyonian Gulf . . . . 15 D a
Aldabra Islands . . . . 175 H e
Aldan River . . . .
Aldborough, parl. bor. . . . . . 163 M c
Aldeburgh, parl. bor. . . . . . 163 P e
Alderney, isl. . . . . 69 B b
Aldersbach, mon. . . . . 95 E b
Aldersgate, in London . . . . . 75 G g
Aldgate, in London . . . . 75 G g
Aldobrandeschi, fam. . . . . . . 90 L j
Alea . . . . 14 C b
Alemtejo, reg. . . . . 82 G f
Alençon . . . . 76 D b
Alençon, cty. . . . . 76 D b
Alençon, duchy . . . . 84 D e
Alençon, gen. . . . . 147 D b
Alençon, reg. . . . . 81 L h
Alençon, seign. . . . . 69 H f
Aleppo . . . . 68 C b
Alerheim . . . . 122 F d
Aleria . . . . 26 D e
Aleria, bp. . . . . 148 C c
Aleshki . . . . 131 J d
Alesia . . . . 38 C c
Alesium . . . . 14 C c
Alessandria . . . . 78 F f
Alessandria, bp. . . . . 95 D c
Alet . . . . 61 C b
Alet, bp. . . . . 94 C c
Aletium . . . . 31 H b
Aletrium . . . . 30 C a
Aletum, see Alet
Aleutian Islands . . . . 179 I b

Alexander Archipelago . . . . . 212 ins.
Alexander's Mole . . . . 18 ins. B
Alexandra Land, reg. . . . . . . 172 C c
Alexandretta . . . . 68 C b
Alexandria, in Babylonia . . . 19 G d
Alexandria, in Egypt . . . . . . 1 A b
Alexandria, in India Superior. 19 L d
Alexandria, near Parapanisus
  Mts. . . . . 19 K c
Alexandria, in Rumania . . . . 165 D b
Alexandria, in Syria (Iscan-
  derum) . . . . 20 G d
Alexandria, in Virginia . . . . 194 K g
Alexandria, plan of . . . . . . 34 ins. C
Alexandria, patr. . . . . 52 K f
Alexandria Arachosiorum . . . 19 K d
Alexandria Ariorum . . . . . . 19 J d
Alexandria eschata . . . . 19 K b
Alexandria Margiana . . . . . . 19 J c
Alexandria minor (Alexandretta) 68 C b
Alexandria Opiana . . . . 19 L e
Alexandria Oxiana . . . .
Alexandria Sogdiana . . . . . . 19 K e
Alexandria Troas . . . .
Alexandrine Aqueduct . . . . . 35 ins. B
Alexinatz . . . . 164 C b
Alfdorf . . . . 143 I h
Alford . . . .
Algarve, dist. . . . . 82 G f
Algarve, Spanish, dist. . . . . 83 J h
Algarve de Aquem Mar, dist. 83 J h
Algeciras . . . . 82 A b
Algeria, col. . . . . 174 D a
Algeria, reg. . . . .
Algeria, state . . . . 118 E g
Algerian Plateaus . . . . 2 E e
Algerian Sahara . . . . 2 E e
Algidus, mt. . . . . 35 ins. B
Algiers . . . . 58 E f
Algoa Bay . . . . 175 M m
Algonkins, tribes . . . . 188 I b
Alhama, near Granada . . . . . 82 B b
Alhama, near Murcia . . . . . . 82 B b
Alibunar . . . . 159 K f
Alicante . . . . 82 B b
Alice Spring Station . . . . . 172 C c
Alife . . . . 64 B b
Alife, bp. . . . . 95 ins.
Aligarh . . . . 170 I f
Aliphera . . . . 14 B b
Aliso . . . . 39 I h and J h
Aliwal . . . . 170 I e
Aliwal North . . . . 175 M m
Aljubarrota . . . . 83 J h
Alkmaar . . . . 117 C b
Allahabad . . . . 137 D c
Allaine River . . . . 143 ins. F
Allegany, Ind. Res. . . . . . . 188 K b
Alleghany Mountains . . . 193 B d-E a
Allegheny Plateau . . . . 187 K e
Allegheny River . . . . 192 B c
Allenstein . . . . 155 K b
Allerheiligen, mon. . . . . . . 142 B c
Alle River (Allaine R.) . . . . 143 ins. F
Alle River (Prussia) . . . . . 115 K a
Aller River . . . . 78 F b
All Hallows, church in London 75 G g
                              (26.30)
Allier, dept. . . . . 148 E e
Allier River . . . . 76 E d
Allifae . . . . 30 D a
Allobroges, people . . . . 26 A b
Allstedt . . . . 63 F c
Almada . . . . 82 A b
Almagro . . . . 83 K h
Almagro, route of . . . . 108 K i
Almalik . . . . 92 I c
Almansa . . . . 130 C f
Alma River . . . . 164 J f
Almazan . . . . 184 C d
Almeida . . . . 214 F d
Almendingen . . . . 143 I i
Almería . . . . 82 B b
Almería, bp. . . . . 94 B d

Almirante, Bahia del, bay . . . 105 D
Almissa, bp. . . . . 95 F
Almodóvar del Campo . . . . . 82 B
Almohads, Dom. of the . . . . 70 H
Almopia . . . . 10 D
Almopia, reg. . . . . 10 D
Almoravids, Dom. of the . . . .
Almuñecar . . . . 82 B
Alnwick . . . .
Alnwick, mon. . . . . 97 P
Alonæ . . . . 12 C
Alope, in Locris . . . . 11 D
Alope, in Phthiotis . . . . . . 11 D
Alopece . . . . 16 B
Alorus . . . . 11 D
Alost . . . . 117 B
Alpeni . . . . 16 F
Alpheus River . . . . 14 B
Alpirsbach . . . . 143 F
Alpirsbach, mon. . . . . 95 D
Alpis Graia, pass . . . . 26 A
Alpis Poenina, pass . . . . . . 26 B
Alpnach . . . . 91 Q
Alps, The, mts. . . . . 2 E
Alpuente . . . . 83 E c
Alpujarras, mts. . . . . 83 K
Alresford . . . . 127 X c
Alresford, parl. bor. . . . . .
Alsace, gen. . . . . 147 F
Alsace, gouv. . . . . 146 C b
Alsace, prov. . . . . 148 F c
Alsace - Lorraine, imp. ter. . . 161 B c
Alsek River . . . . 212 ins.
Alsen, isl. . . . . 114 F
Alsietinus, lake . . . . 35 ins. B
Alsietine Aqueduct . . . . 35 ins. B
Alsium . . . .
Altai Mountains . . . . 102 I c
Altamaha River . . . . 193 C f
Altamura . . . . 90 F d
Alta Ripa . . . . 39 J i
Alta Semita, loc. in Rome . . . 22 A
Alt - Breisach . . . . 142 A d
Altdorf, near Nuremberg . . . 114 F d
Altdorf, in Swabia . . . . . . 143 I j
Altdorf, in Switzerland . . . . 91 Q l
Altefóhr . . . . 123 G a
Alteia . . . . 39 I i
Altena (Wilmington) . . . . . 192 ins.
Altenburg, in Hungary . . . . 72 D b
Altenburg, in Thuringia . . . 72 C a
Altenburg, mon. in Austria . . 95 F b
Altenkirchen . . . . 134 D c
Altenstadt . . . . 143 I h
Altensteig . . . . 143 G h
Altensteig, lordship . . . . . 143 G h
Altenzaun . . . . 154 F b
Altenzella, mon., near Würzburg 95 D b
Altenzelle, mon., near Meissen 85 G c
Alternus River . . . . 27 H e
Altheim, Hohen- . . . . 62 F d
Altinum . . . . 27 G b
Altis, loc. in Olympia . . . . .
Alt - Lussheim . . . . 142 C b
Altmark, reg. . . . . 79 G b
Altmühl River . . . . 62 F d
Altomünster, mon. . . . . 95 E b
Alton, in England . . . . 127 Y c
Alton, in Illinois . . . . 211 G c
Alton, parl. bor. . . . .
Altona . . . . 122 E b
Altorf (Altdorf), in Switzerland 150 E c
Alt - Ötting . . . . 123 G e
Altötting, mon. . . . . 95 E b
Altranstädt . . . . 135 G c
Altshausen . . . . 143 I j
Altsohl . . . . 159 J d
Aluta River . . . . 73 E a
Alutus River (Aluta R.) . . . . 39 M l
Alvarado . . . . 213 ins.
Alvarado, route of . . . . 105 B c
Alvaro de Saavedra, route of . 110 I f
Alvona . . . . 27 I b
Alwar . . . . 137 C c

Name	Page	Grid
Alyzia	10	B d
Amadeus, lake	172	C c
Amalekites, people	7	ins. C
Amalfi	64	B b
Amalfi, abp.	95	E c
Amalphis, see Amalfi		
Amanus Mountains	20	G d
Amapuemecan		
Amardi, people	19	H c
Amardians, people	8	D b
Amasea	35	K e
Amaserah	93	D b
Amasia	20	F b
Amastra	59	K e
Amastris	47	M e
Amatha	6	D c
Amathus, in Cyprus	20	E e
Amathus, in Peræa	7	D d
Amaya	82	H e
Amazonas, state	214	C c
Amazon River	214	D c
Amba Alaji, mt.	174	G c
Ambacia, see Amboise		
Ambala	137	C b
Amharri, people	38	D c
Ambato	214	B c
Amberg	122	F d
Ambérieu	130	N i
Ambert	76	E d
Ambiani or Ambianis, see Amiens		
Amboise	69	H g
Amboyna, isl.	112	F d
Ambracia (Arta)	10	C c
Ambracia, state	13	B b
Ambracian Gulf (Gulf of Arta)	10	B d
Ambracus	10	B c
Ambras, castle	122	F e
Ambrières	65	F f
Ambrysus	11	D d
Ameland, isl.	117	D a
Amelia Island	207	I d
Ameria	27	G e
America, name on Waldsee-müller map	108	K j
America, Central, reg.	213	D c
America, North, continent	186, 187	
America, South, continent	214, 215	
Amersfoert	189	ins. C
Amersfoort	117	D b
Amersham, parl. bor.	163	N f (Am.)
Amesbury	127	X o
Amesbury, mon.	97	P j
Amestratus	30	D e
Amhara, reg.	174	G c
Amherstburg	212	I d
Amichel, reg.	191	F f
Amid or Amida (Diarbekr)	4	G c
Amida, abp.	43	K f
Amidas, route of	191	J d
Amiens	46	G d
Amiens, bp.	94	C b
Amiens, cty.	69	I f
Amiens, gen.	147	E b
Amirante Islands	175	I e
Amisia (Ems) River	38	G b
Amisus	20	G b
Amiternum	27	H e
Amjhera		
Ammon, reg.	4	F c*
Ammonites, people	7	ins. D
Ammonium	18	C e
Amnias River	20	F b
Amol, in Persia		
Amol, in Turkestan		
Amöneburg	134	E c
Amöneburg, mon.	95	D a
Amorbach	142	D a
Amorbach, mon.	95	D b
Amorgos, isl.	4	C b
Amorgus	13	D c
Amorium	20	D c
Amoy	171	M f
Ampelus, prom. in Chalcidice	11	E c
Ampelus, prom. in Crete	14	ins.
Ampfing	79	H d
Amphaxitis, reg. in Mygdonia	11	D b
Amphaxitis, reg. in Pæonia		
Amphia	14	C b
Amphiale, prom.	16	B b
Amphiaræum	16	B a
Amphicæa	11	D d
Amphictionium	16	F e
Amphilochia, reg.	10	C c
Amphipagus, prom	10	A c
Amphipolis	11	E b
Amphissa	11	D d
Amphitrope	16	C b
Amposta	83	L g
Ampsivarii, people	38	D b
Amritsar	137	B b
Amselfeld, battle	93	B b
Amsteg	91	Q l
Amsterdam	117	C b
Amsterdam, Hanse. cy.	99	ins. B
Amsterdam, Fort (New York)	189	ins. C
Amsterdam, New, in Dutch Guiana	214	D b
Amsterdam, New (New York)	189	ins. C
Amu-Daria River		
Amur District	171	N c
Amur River		
Amyclæ	14	C b
Amygdolon, Pool of	6	ins. A (6)
Amyrus	11	D c
Amyrus River	11	D c
Anab	7	B f
Anacæa	16	B a
Anactorium	10	B d
Anæa	17	E c
Anagni	90	D d
Anagni, bp.	95	E c
Anagnia (Anagni)	30	C a
Anagyrus	16	B b
Anah	99	L g
Anahuac, Plateau of	106	C a
Anam		
Anamari, people	26	D c
Anamis River	19	I e
Anaphe, isl.	13	D c
Anaphlystus	15	D b
Anapus River, in Acarnania	10	C d
Anapus River, in Sicily	30	E e
Anas (Guadiana) River	38	A e
Anathoth	7	C e
Anatolia, reg.	99	I f
Anatolic Theme	59	K f
Anaua	20	C d
Anauni, people	26	E a
Anaunium	26	E a
Anazarbus	43	J f
Anbar	99	L g
Ancenis	84	C f
Anchedive Island		
Anchesmus, mt.	16	B a
Anchialus	43	H e
Ancón	214	B d
Ancona	27	H d
Ancona, bp.	95	E c
Ancona, march	72	C c
Ancúd, San Carlos de	215	B g
Ancyra, in Galatia	20	E c
Ancyra, in Mysia	20	C c
Andaca	19	L d
Andagoya, route of	108	J g
Andahan		
Andalos, reg.	53	B b
Andalusia, reg.	83	J h
Andaman Islands	103	J f
Andania	14	C b
Andaraba		
Andecavi, see Angers		
Andecavi, people	38	B c
Andechs, castle	72	C b
Andechs, mon.	95	E b
Andegavis, see Angers		
Andelfingen, castle	91	Q k
Andelaus, see Andelot		
Andelot	53	N h
Andelys	69	H f
Andematunnum	39	H j
Andenne	117	D d
Anderida or Anderidæ (Pevensey)	51	Q i
Anderitum, see Javols		
Andermatt	150	E c
Andernach	62	D c
Andersonville	208	D c
Andes	26	E b
Andes Mountains	214	B bg
Andijan		
Andlau, mon.	148	C b
Andorra	82	C a
Andover, in Mass.	189	C c
Andover, deanery, in England	100	A a
Andover, mon.	100	A a
Andover, parl. bor.	163	M f (And.)
Andoverpis, see Antwerp		
Andros	15	E b
Andros, isl., Cyclades	15	E b
Andros Islands, Bahama Is.	213	E b
Androscoggin River	189	C b
Andrussov	138	C c
Andújar	82	B d
Andwell, mon.	100	B a
Anemas, Prison of	93	G e (9)
Anemo River	27	F c
Anemoria	11	D d
Anemurium, prom.	20	E d
Angara River		
Angele	16	B b
Angerburg	155	K a
Angeriacus, see Saint Jean-d'Angély		
Angermünde	85	D b
Angers	61	C c
Angers, bp.	94	B b
Angers, univ.	100	E e
Anghiari	90	M j
Angites River	11	E b
Angles, people, in Britain	51	R k
Angles, people, in Holstein	38	D b
Angles, people, about 900	57	E c
Anglesey, isl.	49	D e
Anglesey, cty.	127	U m
Anglesey, parl. dist.	163	J d
Anglo-Egyptian Sudan, reg.	174	F c
Anglo-Saxon kingdom, about 1000		
Anglo-Saxon kingdoms, about 814	54	D c
Angol	215	B f
Angola, dist.	175	E e
Angora	55	K f
Angostura	214	C b
Angoulême	61	D d
Angoulême, bp.	94	C b
Angoulême, cty.	69	D d
Angoumois, cty.	61	C d
Angoumois, prov.	148	D e
Angra das Voltas	108	S j
Angra Pequena, bay	175	E g
Angria, reg.	62	E b
Angrians, people	55	Q i
Angrivarii, people	39	J g
Anguilla, isl.	213	F c
Angus, cty.		
Angus, reg.		
Anhalt, castle	71	S j
Anhalt, princ.	79	G c
Anhausen, mon.	143	J h
Anholt	117	E c
Ani	67	O e
Aniane, mon.	94	C c
Anicium, see Le Puy		
Aniene River	96	B b
Anio River	27	G f
Anio novus, aqueduct	35	ins. B
Anisus River, see Enns River		
Anjou, cty.	61	C c
Anjou, duchy	78	B e
Anjou, gouv.	146	A b
Anjou, prov.	148	D e
Anklam	87	I b
Anklam, Hanse. cy.	99	ins. B

Ann, Cape . . . . 189 C c
Annaburg, castle . . . . 115 ins. B
Annandale, reg. . . . .
Annapolis, in Maryland . . . . 192 C d
Annapolis, in Nova Scotia . . 212 I d
Anne, Fort . . . . 192 E b
Anne Arundel Town . . . . . 192 C d
Annecy . . . . 130 O i
Anneianum, in Etruria . . . . 27 F d
Anneianum, in Venetja . . . . 27 F b
Annobon, isl. . . . . 175 D e
Anopæa Mountains . . . . . 16 F e
Ansbach . . . . 114 F d
Ansbach, princ. . . . . 114 F d
Anserma . . . . 214 B b
Antaki . . . .
Antananarivo . . . . 175 H f
Antandrus . . . .
Antaradus . . . . 20 F e
Antelope Hills . . . . 190 E d
Antemnæ . . . . 35 ins. B
Antequera . . . . 82 B b
Anthedon, in Bœotia . . . . . 11 E d
Anthedon, in Philistæa . . . . 7 A e
Anthela . . . . 16 F e
Anthemus . . . . 11 E b
Anthemus, reg. . . . . 11 E b
Anthemusias . . . . 35 L f
Anthena . . . . 15 C b
Antian Way, road . . . . . . 35 ins. B
Antibes . . . . 126 E e
Anticosti, isl. . . . . 186 M d
Anticyra, in Locris Ozolis . . . 10 D d
Anticyra, in Malis . . . . . . 11 D d
Anticyra, in Phocis . . . . . . 11 D d
Antietam, battle . . . . 208 ins.
Antietam River . . . . 208 ins.
Antigonia, in Arcadia . . . . . 14 C b
Antigonia, in Chalcidice . . . 11 E b
Antigonia, in Epirus . . . . . 10 A b
Antigua, isl. . . . . 105 H c
Antigua, Rio de la, river . . . 106 D a
Anti-Lebanon Mountains . . . 6 E a
Antinoë . . . . 43 I h
Antinum . . . . 27 H f
Antioch, in Phrygia . . . . . . 20 D c
Antioch, in Syria . . . . 20 G d
Antioch, patr. . . . . 52 L f
Antioch, princ. about 1140 . . 68 C b
Antioch, princ. about 1190 . . 71 N f
Antioch, theme . . . . 59 L f
Antiochia, in Asia Minor . . . 43 I f
Antiochia, in Margiana . . . . 19 J c
Antioquia . . . . 214 B b
Antipatria . . . . 10 A b
Antipatris . . . . 7 B d
Antipodes Islands . . . . . . 179 I l
Antipolis . . . . 26 B d
Antirrhium, prom. . . . . . . 10 C d
Antirrhodus, isl. . . . . . . 34 ins. C (2)
Antissa . . . . 13 D b
Antitaurus Mountains . . . . 20 I c
Antium . . . . 30 B a
Antivari . . . . 164 B b
Antivari, abp. . . . . 95 F c
Antofagasta . . . . 215 B e
Antonine, Wall of . . . . . . 51 O g
Antoninus Pius, Column of . . 22 A
Antonius, Temple of . . . . . 24 B (19)
Antrim, cty. . . . . 127 K f
Antron . . . . 11 E d
Antunnacum . . . . 39 I h
Antwerp . . . . 117 C c
Antwerp, Hanse. for. cy. . . . 99 ins. B
Antwerp, marg. . . . . 117 C c
Anuu, isl. . . . . 199 ins. D
Anvik . . . . 198 ins. A
Anxa . . . . 31 G b
Anxanum . . . . 27 I e
Anxia . . . . 30 E b
Anxur (Terracina) . . . . . . 30 C a
Anydrus, mt. . . . . 16 B b
Ansican, reg. . . . . 109 S h
Aomori . . . . 171 P d

Aornus, in Bactria . . . . . . 19 K c
Aornus, in India . . . . 19 L d
Aorsi, people . . . . 35 N d
Aosta . . . . 90 A b
Aosta bp. . . . . 95 D b
Aous mt. . . . . 20 E e
Aous River . . . . 10 A b
Apacue, Ind. Res. . . . . . . 188 E d
Apaches, tribe . . . . 188 D c
Apalachee . . . . 191 I e
Apalachee Bay . . . . 191 I f
Apalachicola River . . . . . . 193 B f
Apamea, in Osrhoëne . . . . . 20 G d
Apamea, in Syria . . . . 20 G e
Apamea Cibotus . . . . 20 D c
Aparri . . . . 199 ins. H
Apenestae . . . . 31 F a
Apennines, mts. . . . . 2 F d
Aperanti, people . . . . 10 C d
Aperantia . . . . 10 C d
Aperopia (Doko), isl. . . . . 15 D b
Aphek . . . .
Aphetæ . . . . 11 E c
Aphidnæ . . . . 16 B a
Aphnitis Lake . . . .
Aphrodisias . . . . 43 H f
Aphrodisium . . . . 16 D c (4)
Aphytis . . . . 11 E b
Apia . . . . 172 H b
Apidanus River . . . . 10 D c
Apo, mt. . . . . 199 ins. H
Apodoti, people . . . . 10 C d
Apollo, Cave of . . . . 23 C
Apollo, Temple of . . . . . . 24 A
Apollon, Allée d' . . . . . . 149 A
Apollonia, in Illyricum . . . . 31 I b
Apollonia, in Mysia . . . . . .
Apollonia, in Palestine . . . . 7 B d
Apollonia, in Pieria . . . . . 11 F b
Apollonia, in Sicily . . . . . 30 D d
Apollonia, in Thrace . . . . . 12 I b
Apollonia Chalcidice . . . . . 11 E b
Apollonia Mygdonia . . . . . 11 E b
Aponus . . . . 26 F b
Apostles, Church of the . . . 93 G e
Appalachian Highland . . . . 187 K e
Appenweier . . . . 142 A c
Appenzell . . . . 91 R k
Appenzell, canton . . . . . . 91 R k
Appian Aqueduct . . . . . . 35 ins. B (3)
Appian Gate . . . . 22 A
Appian Way, road . . . . . . 30 B a
Appian Way, Old, road . . . . 35 ins. B
Appleby . . . . 127 W l
Appleby, dist. . . . . 84 B b
Appomattox Court House . . . 208 E b
Appomattox River . . . . . . 193 E c
Appuldurcombe, mon. . . . . 100 A b
Apsinthii, people . . . .
Apsorus . . . . 27 I c
Apsorus, isl. . . . . 27 I c
Apsus . . . . 31 I b
Apsus River . . . . 10 A b
Apt, bp. . . . . 95 D c
Apta or Apta Iulia, see Apt
Apuani, people . . . . 26 D c
Apulia, cty. . . . . 64 C b
Apulia, duchy . . . . 70 I e
Apulia, reg. . . . . 30 E a
Apulia and Calabria, Aug. Reg. 38 F d (2)
Apulia and Calabria, prov. . . 42 F e (5)
Apulum . . . . 35 I d
Apure River . . . . 214 C b
Apurimac River . . . . 111 C d
Aquæ, see Aquæ Sextiæ
Aquæ, see Dax
Aquæ . . . . 39 J j
Aquæ Albulæ . . . . 35 ins. B
Aquæ Apollinares . . . . . . 35 ins. B
Aquæ Aureliæ . . . . 39 J i
Aquæ Bormiæ . . . . 26 E a
Aquæ Cutiliæ . . . . 27 G e
Aquæ Grani or Aquæ Granni,
see Aix-la-Chapelle

Aquæ Mattiacæ . . . . 39 J h
Aquæ Pisanæ . . . . 26 E d
Aquæ Populoniæ . . . . 26 E d
Aquæ Sextiæ (Aix) . . . . . . 38 D d
Aquæ Solis or Aquæ Sulis (Bath) 51 O i
Aquæ Statiellæ . . . . 26 C c
Aquæ Volaterranæ . . . . . . 26 E d
Aquia Creek . . . . 208 E b (A. Cr.)
Aquidaban River . . . . 215 D e
Aquidneck Island . . . . . . 189 ins. A
Aquila . . . . 90 D c
Aquileia, in Germany . . . . . 39 J i
Aquileia, in Venetia . . . . . 27 H b
Aquileia, abp. . . . . 95 E b
Aquileia, march. . . . . 64 B a
Aquileia, patr. . . . . 79 H e
Aquilonia, in E. Samnium . . .
Aquilonia, in W. Samnium . . .
Aquilo River . . . . 30 E a
Aquincum (Budapest) . . . . 38 F c
Aquino, bp. . . . . 95 E c
Aquis, see Aquæ Sextiæ (Aix)
Aquis, see Dax
Aquis Granum, see Aix-la-Cha-
pelle
Aquitaine, duchy, 11 cent. . . . 61 C c d
Aquitaine, duchy, 14 cent. . . . 77 D d
Aquitaine, reg., about 814 . . 54 E d
Aquitaine (Aquitania), Rom.
prov. . . . . 38 C c (5)
Aquitaine I, Rom. prov. . . . 42 C d (10)
Aquitaine II, Rom. prov. . . . 42 B d (11)
Aquitania (Aquitaine), Rom.
prov. . . . . 38 C c (5)
Aquitania Propria, reg. . . . . 38 B d
Arabah Valley . . . . 7 D e
Arabia, Rom. prov. . . . . . 43 Y g (15)
Arabia, pen. . . . . 170 F f
Arabia, Rom. prov. . . . . . . 35 K g
Arabia, reg. . . . . 53 G d
Arabia, table land . . . . . . 3 I f
Arabia Deserta, reg. . . . . . 20 H f
Arabian Desert, in Egypt . . . 150 B b
Arabian Sea . . . .
Arabii, people . . . . 19 K e
Arabius River . . . . 19 K e
Arab raids, 9 cent. . . . . . . 45 G d
Arabs, people, in Arabia . . . 4 G d
Arabs, people, in North Africa 45 D I-f
Arabs, people, in Sicily . . . . 45 G e
Arabs, people, in S. France . . 45 EF d
Arabs, people, in Spain, 711 . . 45 D e
Arabs, people, in Spain, about 900 57 B f
Aracajú . . . . 214 F d
Aracan . . . . 136 N c
Aracan, reg. . . . . 112 C a
Aracaty . . . . 214 F c
Arachnæus, mt. . . . . 15 C b
Arachosia, prov. . . . . 19 K d
Arachosia, satr. . . . . 18 R h
Arachotus . . . . 8 E b*
Arachotus River . . . . 19 K d
Arachthus River . . . . 10 C c
Aracynthus, mt. . . . . 10 C d
Arad, in Hungary . . . . . . 77 I c
Arad, in Palestine . . . . . . 7 C f
Arad, reg. . . . . 53 G b
Araden . . . . 14 ins.
Aradus . . . . 12 K d
Aræ Flaviæ . . . . 39 J i
Aræthyrea . . . . 14 C b
Arafura Sea . . . . 172 C a
Aragon, km., 12 cent. . . . . . 82 H e
Aragon, km., 13–15 cent. . . . 83 L g
Aragon, distr. . . . . 82 H e
Araguaya River . . . . 214 E c
Arakan, reg. . . . . 92 J e
Aral Sea . . . . 3 J d
Aramæans, people . . . . . . 7 ins. D
Ara Maxima . . . . 24 A
Aran Islands . . . . 127 H h
Arantia . . . . 14 C b
Arapahœs, tribe . . . . 188 E b
Araphen . . . . 15 E b

Ararat, mt. . . . . 3 I e
Arar River . . . . 38 C c
Araris River, see Aar or Aare River
Aras River . . . . 73 J c
Araucanians, people . . . . . . 215 B f
Araure. . . . . 214 C b
Arausio or Arausione (Orange) 38 D d
Aravalli Hills . . . . 137 B c
Araxes River, in Armenia . . . 5 D b
Araxes River, in Mesopotamia . 20 I e
Araxes River, in Persis . . . . 19 H d
Araxus prom. . . . . 14 B a
Arba, isl. . . . . 27 I c
Arbe, bp. . . . . 95 E c
Arbela . . . . 4 D d
Arbela, abp. . . . . 43 K f
Arboga . . . . 88 F b
Arbor Felix . . . . 39 J j
Arc . . . . 81 N h
Arcadia, Rom. prov. . . . . . 43 I h (5)
Arcadia, reg. . . . . 14 C b
Arcadia, state . . . . 13 B c
Arcadius, Column of . . . . . 93 Ge(13)
Archangel. . . . . 128 F c
Archas . . . . 68 C c
Archelaïs (Akserai), in Cappadocia . . . . 20 F c
Archelaïs in Palestine . . . . . 7 C d
Archers Hope . . . . . . 103 ins. A (Arch.)
Archidona . . . . 82 B b
Arcis-sur-Aube . . . . 154 C d
Arcole . . . . 150 F d
Arcos . . . . 82 A b
Arcot . . . . 137 C f
Arctic Ocean . . . . 2 E a
Arctic Plateau . . . . 186 H b
Ardabil . . . . 92 E d
Ardagh, bp. . . . . 97 D c
Ardea . . . . 30 B a
Ardea Gate. . . . . 22 A
Ardèche, dept. . . . . 148 E f
Arden, forest. . . . . 49 F e
Ardenne, mon. . . . . 94 B b
Ardennes, dept. . . . . 148 E e
Ardennes, mts. . . . . 62 C d
Ardettus, mt. . . . . 23 B
Ardfert, bp. . . . . 97 B d
Ardmore . . . . 210 F d
Ardstraw, bp. . . . . 97 D b
Arduenna Forest . . . . 39 H i
Arebrigium. . . . . 26 B b
Arecibo . . . . 199 ins. G
Arelate . . . . 38 C d
Arelate (Arles), km. . . . . . 61 D f
Aremberg, dist. . . . . 151 H f
Aremorica, reg. . . . . 38 B c
Arenacum . . . . 39 H f
Arenas, Punta, in Chile . . . . 215 B l
Arenas, Punta, in Costa Rica . 213 D d
Arendal . . . . 130 E b
Arenenberg, castle . . . . . . 158 E e
Arensburg . . . . 119 I b
Areopagus (Mars Hill) . . . . .
Areopolis . . . . 7 D f
Arequipa . . . . 214 B d
Arethon River . . . . 10 C c
Arethusa . . . . 11 E b
Arevaci, people . . . . 38 B d
Arezzo . . . . 90 L j
Arezzo, bp. . . . . 95 E c
Arezzo, univ. . . . . . . 100 H f (Ar.)
Argæus, mt. . . . . 20 F c
Argall's Town . . . . . . 193 ins. A
Argen River . . . . 143 I j
Argen River, Lower . . . . . . 143 I j
Argen River, Upper . . . . . . 143 I j
Argentan . . . . 76 C b
Argentarius, mt. . . . . 27 F e
Argenteus River . . . . 26 A d
Argentina, see Argentoratum (Strasburg)
Argentina, or the Argentine Republic, cty. . . . . 215 C ef

Argenton . . . . 126 B c
Argentoratum (Strasburg) . . . 39 I i
Argiletum, street . . . . 22 A
Argilus . . . . 11 E b
Arginussæ Islands . . . . 17 E b
Argithea . . . . 10 C c
Argob, reg. . . . .
Argolic Gulf . . . . 4 B b
Argolis, reg. . . . . 15 C b
Argonauts, Portico of the . . . 22 A
Argonnes, mts. . . . . 134 C d
Argos . . . . 14 C b
Argos Amphilochicum . . . . . 10 C d
Argos Oresticum . . . . 10 C b
Argous Portus . . . . 26 E e
Arguin, isl. . . . .
Argun Islands . . . . 108 P e
Argun River . . . . 92 L b
Argura . . . . 11 D c
Argyle, bp. in Scotland . . . .
Argyle, cty. . . . .
Argyle, dist. . . . .
Argyle, Fort . . . . 193 ins. C
Argyrus (Argyrokastron) . . . 10 B b
Aria, prov. . . . . 19 J d
Aria, reg. . . . . 8 E b
Aria, satr. . . . . 18 R h
Arialbinnum, see Basel
Ariana, reg. . . . . 19 H d
Ariano, bp. . . . . 95 F c
Arica . . . . 214 B d
Aricia . . . . 30 B a
Arid, Cape . . . . 172 A d
Ariège, dept. . . . . 148 E f
Arikaras, tribe . . . . 188 G b
Arilica . . . . 26 E b
Arimathea . . . . 7 C d
Ariminum . . . . 27 G c
Ariminus River . . . . 27 G c
Ariola . . . . 39 H i
Ariolica, in Gaul . . . . 39 I j
Ariolica, in Italy . . . . 26 B b
Arisbe . . . .
Arispe . . . . 190 C e
Aristonautæ . . . . 14 C a
Arius, lake . . . . 19 J d
Arius River . . . . 19 J d
Arivaca . . . . 190 C e
Arizona, ter. . . . . 203 P h
Arkansas, Fort . . . . 191 D d
Arkansas, tribe . . . . 188 G c
Arkansas, state . . . . 202 G h
Arkansas, ter. 1819 . . . . . . 203 S c
Arkansas, ter. 1824 . . . . . . 203 T d
Arkansas Post . . . . 199 G d
Arkansas Post, battle . . . . . 208 B c
Arkansas River . . . . 190 E d
Arklow . . . .
Arkona . . . . 63 G a
Arles . . . . 61 F e
Arles, abp. . . . . 94 C c
Arles, km., about 1035 . . . . 61 F d
Arles, km., 13 cent. . . . . . . 72 B b
Arlon . . . . 117 D e
Armagh . . . .
Armagh, abp. . . . . 97 D c
Armagh, cty. . . . . 127 K g
Armagnac, cty. 12 cent. 69 C e (Arm.)
Armagnac, cty. 14 cent. . . . 76 D e
Armagnac, cty. 17 cent. . . . 126 B e
Armagnac, dist. . . . . 81 M i
Armavir, Armavira . . . . . . 20 J b
Armenia, km., about 1140 . . . 68 C b
Armenia, km., about 1340 . . .
Armenia, km., 14 cent. . . . .
Armenia, reg., about 600 B.C. . 8 C b
Armenia, reg., about 750 . . . 53 G c
Armenia, reg., about 1097 . . . 67 O f
Armenia, satr. . . . . 8 I e
Armenia I, Rom. prov. . . . . 43 J f(10)
Armenia II, Rom. prov. . . . . 43 J f(11)
Armenia, Great, reg. . . . . . 99 L e
Armenia, Lesser, reg. in Cilicia 99 J f
Armenia, Lesser, reg. in Pontus 35 L f

Armenia minor, reg. . . . . . . 20 H c
Armeniac Theme . . . . 59 L e
Armenian Highlands . . . . . . 3 I d
Armenians, people
Armenta River . . . . 27 F e
Armentières . . . . 117 A d
Armstrong, Fort, in Illinois . . 211 G b
Armstrong, Fort, in Pa. . . . . 195 B c
Arnay-le-Duc . . . . 126 D c
Arne . . . . 10 D c
Arneburg . . . . 63 F b
Arnheim . . . . 117 D b
Arnhem, Hanse. cy. . . . . . 99 ins. B
Arnhem Land, reg. . . . . . . 172 C b
Arnissa, in Illyricum . . . . . 31 I b
Arnissa, in Macedonia . . . . 10 C b
Arno River . . . . 90 L j
Arnon River . . . . 7 D f
Arnsberg . . . . 62 D c
Arnshaugk . . . . 85 F e
Arnstadt . . . . 62 F c
Arnus (Arno) River . . . . . . 26 E d
Aro River . . . . 27 G f
Aroania, mt. . . . . 14 C b
Aroanius River . . . . 14 C b
Aroë . . . . 14 B a
Arœr, in Idumæa . . . . 7 C f
Arœr, in Peræa . . . . 7 D f
Arogas River . . . . 31 F c
Arolla . . . . 91 P l
Arolsen . . . . 154 E c
Arona . . . . 90 I h
Arouaise, mon. . . . . 94 C a
Arpad (Tel-Erfâd) . . . .
Arpi . . . . 30 E a
Arpinum (Arpino) . . . . 30 C a
Arquebuse . . . . 149 B
Arquennes . . . . 156 A a
Arques, castle . . . . 76 D b
Arrabo River, see Raab River
Arrabona . . . . 38 F c
Arran, isl. . . . .
Arras . . . . 117 A d
Arras, bp. . . . . 94 C a
Arraticum, see Arras
Arretium (Arezzo) . . . . 27 F d
Arru Islands . . . . 172 C a
Arsacids, Kingdom of the, about 200 B.C. 19 X k
Arsacids, Kingdom of the, about 90 B.C. 33 N f
Arsamosata . . . . 20 H c
Arsanias River . . . . 20 I c
Arsia (Arsa) River . . . . . . 27 I b
Arsian Forest . . . . 35 ins. B
Arsinoë, in Cyrenaica . . . . . 34 H g
Arsinoë, on L. Mœris . . . . . 4 ins. *
Arsinoë, on the Red Sea . . . 35 K g
Arsissa Lake . . . . 20 J c
Arsuf . . . . 68 ins. A
Arta . . . . 73 E c
Artabri, people . . . . 38 A d
Artacana . . . . 19 H d
Artace . . . .
Artacoana . . . . 19 J d
Artaki . . . . 165 E c
Artasium . . . . 68 C c
Artaxata . . . . 20 K c
Artemis, Temple of . . . . . 31 ins. B(3)
Artemis Agrotera, temple . . . 23 D
Artemis Brauronia, temple . . 23 C(3)
Artemisium, prom. . . . . . . 11 E c
Artemisius, mt. . . . . 14 C b
Artemita . . . . 35 M g
Artemita, isl. . . . . 10 C d
Artena . . . . 35 ins. B
Artlenburg . . . . 122 F b
Artois, cty. 14 cent. . . . . . 76 E a
Artois, cty. 16 cent. . . . . . 117 A d
Artois, gouv. . . . . 146 B a
Artois, reg. . . . . 148 E d
Artynia Lake . . . .
Aruba, isl. . . . . 214 C a
Arundel . . . . 127 Y p

Arundel, castle	65	F	e
Arundel, mon.	74	E	f
Arundel, parl. bor.	163	N	g
Arupium	27	J	c
Arurius (Aar or Aare) River	39	I	j
Arvad	4	F	c *
Arverni, see Clermont-Ferrand			
Arverni, people	38	C	c
Arx (citadel) on Capitoline Mt.	24	A	
Arx (citadel) on the Janiculum	22	A	
Arx Regia, in Tyre	18 ins.	B	
Asabara	7	D	e
Asalmanus Mountains	6	F	c
Asamon Mountains	6	C	c
Asbach, mon.	95	E	b
Ascalon			
Ascania Lake			
Ascanian Domains	71 ins.		
Ascension Island	108	P	h
Aschaffenburg	86	G	d
Aschaffenburg, princ.	151	K j (A)	
Aschersleben, Hanse. cy.	99 ins.	B	
Asciburgium	39	I	h
Asciburgius Mountains	38	F	b
Asclepieum	23	C	
Ascoli Piceno	64	B	b
Ascoli Piceno, bp.	95	E	c
Ascoli Satriano	64	C	b
Ascoli Satriano, bp.	95	F	c
Ascordus River	11	D	b
Ascra	11	E	d
Asculum (Ascoli Piceno)	27	H	e
Ascuris	11	D	c
Asea	14	C	b
Ashanti, reg.	174	C	d
Ashburton, parl. bor.	163	K	g
Ashburton River	172	A	c
Ashby de la Zouch	127	X	n
Ashdod	7	B	e
Ashdown			
Asher	7	C	d
Asher, tribe	7 ins.	D	
Asheville	211	I	c
Ashland	210	A	b
Ashley River	193 ins.	C	
Ashley-Henry Post	210	D	a
Ashley's Post	210	C	c
Ashtabula	206 ins.		
Ashtaroth-Karnaim	6	E	c
Ashton, parl. bor	163	L	d
Ashurada	170	G	e
Asia, continent	170, 171		
Asia, Rom. dioc.	43	I	f
Asia, East Rom. prov.	43	H	f
Asia, Rom. prov.	35	J	f
Asia Minor, reg.	20		
Asia Minor, table-land	3	H	e
Asiana, reg.	50	I	e
Asinarian Gate	22	A	
Asine, in Argolis	15	C	b
Asine, in Messenia	14	B	c
Asines River	30	E	e
Asir, reg.	170	F	g
Asisium	27	G	d
Askabad			
Asmak River			
Asmara	174	G	c
Asmonæan Palace	6 ins. A *		
Asola	90	J	h
Asopus	15	C	c
Asopus River, in Bœotia	11	E	d
Asopus River, in Corinth	14	C	b
Asopus River, in Malis	14	D	d
Aspadana (Ispahan)	19	H	d
Aspara			
Aspern	155	I	d
Aspinwall			
Aspisii, people	19	J	a
Aspledon	11	D	d
Aspona			
Aspromonte, mt.	161	K	h
Assa	11	E	b
Assab	174	H	c
Assaba	174	D	d
Assaceni, people	19	L	d
Assalt	68 ins.	A	
Assam, prov.	171	K	f
Assam, reg.	92	J	e
Assandun	64	E	e
Assassins, sect, in Persia	92	F	d
Assassins, sect, in Syria	68	C	b
Assaye	137	C	d
Assen	117	E	a
Assenisipia, proposed state in U. S.	196	B	b
Assens	88	D	d
Assera	11	E	b
Asseria	27	J	c
Asseritis, reg.	11	E	b
Assinaboins, tribe	188	F	a
Assinarus River	30	E	e
Assiniboia, prov.	212	E	c
Assiniboine River			
Assisi	90	D	c
Assisi, bp.	95	E	c
Assisium, see Assisi			
Assorus	30	D	e
Assuan	174	G	b
Assur	4	D	d
Assus	11	E	b
Assyria, prov.	18	F	c
Assyria, reg.	8	C	b
Assyria, satr.	8	I	e
Assyrian Empire	5		
Asta, see Asti			
Astacus, in Acarnania	10	C	d
Astacus, in Bithynia	9	E	c
Astacus, bay of	9	E	c
Astæ, people	9	D	b
Astapa	38	B	e
Astarac, cty.	76	D	e
Astauene, reg.	19	I	c
Asteris, isl.	10	B	d
Asthala, isl.	19	J	d
Asti	90	I	h
Asti, bp.	95	D	b
Aston Manor	162	E	e
Astorga	82	A	a
Astorga, abp.	42	A	e
Astorga, bp.	94	A	c
Astoria	198	A	a
Astrabad			
Astrabad, reg.	139	H	h
Astrakhan	139	G	f
Astrakhan, Khanate of	139	F	f
Astroni, crater	31 ins.	A	
Astura	30	B	a
Astures, people	38	A	d
Asturias, cty.	82	A	a
Asturias, Kingdom of	54	C	e
Asturias, princ.	83	D	c
Asturias, reg.	58	C	e
Austurica Augusta (Astorga)	38	A	d
Astypalæa, isl.	13	E	c
Astypalæa, prom.	16	B	b
Astyra			
Asunción	215	D	e
Asylum	24	A	
Atabeks, Dom. of the	68	C	c
Atabeks, Ildijiz, dom.	71	P	f
Atabeks, Zengid, dom.	71	O	f
Atabeks of Irbil, dom.	71	O	f
Atacama, Desert of	215	C	e
Atacama, reg.	108	K	j
Atalante	11	D	a
Atalante, isl. near Locris Opuntia	11	E	d
Atalante, isl. near Salamis	16	B	b
Atalia	26	D	e
Atapuerca	83	A	a
Atarneus			
Ataroth	7	D	e
Atbara River	174	G	c
Atchison	210	F	c
Atella, in Basilicata	90	E	d
Atella, in Campania	30	D	b
Aternum (Pescara)	27	I	e
Aternus (Pescara) River	27	H	e
Ateste (Este)	26	F	b
Atn	117	B	d
Athabaska, lake	186	H	c
Athabaska, prov.	212	D	c
Athabaska River	186	H	c
Athamania, reg.	10	C	c
Athelney			
Athelney, mon.	97	O	j
Athena	20	I	b
Athena, Temple of, in Athens	23	C (1)	
Athenæ	16	B	b
Athenæ Diades	11	E	d
Athenæum, in Arcadia	14	C	b
Athenæum, in Epirus	10	C	c
Athene, Temple of, in Syracuse	31 ins. B (2)		
Athene Promachos, monument	23	C (5)	
Athenian Empire	13		
Athenopolis	26	A	d
Athens, in Attica	15	D	b
Athens, bp.	43	G	f
Athens, duchy, 13 cent.	73	G	f
Athens, duchy, 15 cent.	93	B	c
Athens, plan of ancient	23	D	
Athens, plan of modern	23	D	
Athesis (Adige) River	26	E	a
Athlone			
Athmonum	16	B	a
Athol, reg.			
Athos, mt.	11	F	b
Athyras River			
Atienza	82	B	a
Atina, in Latium	30	C	a
Atina, in Lucania	30	E	b
Atintania, reg.	10	B	b
Atkinson, Fort	210	F	b
Atlanta	211	I	d
Atlantic and Pacific Railroad Grant	210	C	c
Atlantic Ocean	108	Nc-Pk	
Atlantic Plain	187	K	e
Atlas Mountains	2	D	e
Atmeidan	93	C	e
Atoyac River			
Atrans	27	I	a
Atrato River	105	E	e
Atrax	11	D	c
Atrebates or Atrebatis, see Arras			
Atrebates, people, in Britain	51	P	i
Atrebates, people, in Gaul	38	C	b
Atrectian Alps, mts.	26	B	b
Atri	90	D	c
Atri, bp.	95	E	c
Atria	26	F	b
Atropatene, Media, reg.	35	N	f
Atropatene, Media, satr.	18	P	h
Attalea	59	K	f
Attalia	20	D	d
Attalids, Kingdom of the	33 legend		
Attalus, Stoa of	23	D	
Attamok	198 ins. A		
Attica, reg.	16		
Attidium	27	G	d
Attila, Empire of	48	F L b	
Attilla, Palace of	48	I	c
Attinghausen	91	Q	l
Attium, prom.	26	C	e
Attock	137	B	b
Atur or Aturius (Adour) River	38	B	d
Atwood Cay	105	F	b
Aube, dept.	148	E	e
Aube River	69	I	f
Aubenas	126	D	d
Aubeterre, mon.	94	B	b
Aubusson	76	E	d
Auch	61	D	e
Auch, abp.	94	B	c
Auch, gen.	147	D	c
Auchi-les-Moines, mon	94	C	a
Auckland	172	G	d
Aude, dept.	148	E	f
Aude River	126	C	e
Audincourt	143 ins. F		
Auerstädt	154	F	c
Aufidena, in Apulia	31	F	a
Aufidena, in Samnium	31	D	a

Aufidus, Bridge of . . . . 30 E a
Aufidus (Ofanto) River . . . . 31 F a
Aufinum . . . . 27 H e
Aughrim . . . . 127 I h
Augila . . . . 18 B e
Augsburg . . . . 62 F d
Augsburg, bp. . . . . 79 G e
Augsburg, imp. city . . . . . . 79 G d
Augusta, in Cilicia . . . . 20 F d
Augusta, in Maine . . . . 211 L b
Augusta, in Sicily . . . . 131 G f
Augusta, in S. C. . . . . 196 C d
Augusta, Asturica (Astorga) . . 38 A d
Augusta, Bracara (Braga) . . . 38 A d
Augusta, Emerita (Mérida) . . . 38 A e
Augusta, Fort, in Georgia . . . 193 D e
Augusta, Fort, in Pa. . . . . . 192 C c
Augusta Bagiennorum (Bene) . 26 B c
Augusta Prætoria (Aosta) . . . 26 B b
Augusta Rauricorum (Augst) . . 39 I j
Augusta Suessionum, see Soissons
Augusta Taurinorum (Turin) . 26 B b
Augusta Treverorum (Trèves) . 39 I i
Augusta Vindelicorum (Augsburg) 38 E c
Augustamnica, Rom. prov. . . . 43 I g (6)
Augustan Canal . . . . 27 G c
Augustanus, Vicus . . . . 35 ins. B
Augusti, Lucus (Luc-en-Die) . 38 D d
Augusti, Lucus (Lugo) . . . . . 38 A d
Augusti, Portus . . . . 27 G f
Augustine Friars, mon. of . . . 75 G g
Augustobona (Troyes) . . . . . 38 C c
Augustobriga (Talavera la Vieja) 38 B e
Augustodunum (Autun) . . . . 38 C c
Augustodurum (Bayeux) . . . . 38 B c
Augustonemetum (Clermont-
Ferrand) . . . . 38 C c
Augustoritum (Limoges) . . . . 38 C c
Augustowo . . . . 155 L b
Augustus, Arch of . . . .
Augustus, Forum of . . . . . . 24 B
Augustus, Mausoleum of . . . . 22 A
Augustus,, Naumachia of . . . . 22 A
Augustus, Palace of . . . . . . 24 B
Augustus, Port of . . . . 35 ins. B
Augustus, Temple of
Aujila . . . . 99 H h
Auldearn . . . . 127 Q g
Aulendorf . . . . 143 I j
Aulerci Cenomani, people . . . 38 B c
Aulis . . . . 11 E d
Aulnay . . . . 76 C c
Aulnay, mon. . . . . 94 B b
Aulon . . . . 31 I b
Aulon, valley in Laconia . . . . 14 C c
Aulon, valley in Macedonia . . 11 E b
Aulon, valley in Palestine . . . 7 D d
Aumale . . . . 76 D b
Aumône, L', mon. . . . . 94 C b
Auneau . . . . 126 B b
Aunis, gouv. . . . . 146 A b
Aunis, prov. . . . . 148 D e
Aurangabad . . . . 137 C e
Auranitis, reg. . . . . 7 E d
Auray . . . . 76 B c
Aureus, Mt. . . . . 26 C e
Aurelian Bridge . . . . 22 A
Aurelian Gate . . . . 22 A
Aurelian Gate, New . . . . . . 22 A
Aurelian Wall . . . . 22 A
Aurelian Way, road . . . . . . 26 E d
Aureliani or Aurelianis (Orléans) 38 C c
Aurelii, Forum . . . . 27 F e
Aureoli, Pons . . . . 26 D b
Aurich . . . . 158 D b
Aurillac . . . . 69 E d
Aurillac, mon. . . . . 94 C c
Aurunci, people . . . . 30 C a
Ausava . . . . 39 I h
Auscii or Ausciis, see Auch
Ausculum . . . . 30 E a
Ausetani, people . . . . 38 C d
Auser River . . . . 26 E c
Ausonians, people . . . . 29 C d

Aussig . . . . 87 J c
Austerfield . . . . 185 E d
Austerlitz . . . . 155 I d
Austin . . . . 210 F d
Austin, Lake . . . . 172 A c
Austral Islands . . . . 180 M j
Australia, continent 172
Australia, North, reg . . . . . 172 C b
Australian Alps . . . . 172 D d
Australian Bight, Great . . . . 172 B d
Austrasia, reg. . . . . 54 F c
Austria, archduchy . . . . . . 87 J d
Austria, duchy, 12 cent. . . . . 72 D b
Austria, duchy, 13 cent. . . . . 79 I d
Austria, empire, 1806 . . . . . 151 M j
Austria, empire, 1812 . . . . . 155 ins.
Austria, empire, 1815 158–159
Austria, march . . . . 59 H d
Austria, margr. . . . . 63 I d
Austria, Lower, dist . . . . . . 159 H d
Austria, Upper, dist . . . . . . 159 H d
Austrian Netherlands, prov. . . 134 C c
Austrian Silesia, dist. . . . . . 135 I c
Ausugum . . . . 27 F a
Autariatæ, people . . . . 39 L l
Auté . . . . 191 I e
Autessiodurum or Autissiodu-
rum, see Auxerre
Autricum (Chartres) . . . . . . 38 C c
Autrigones, people . . . . . . 38 B d
Autun . . . . 61 F c
Autun, bp. . . . . 94 C b
Auvergne, cty. . . . . 61 E d
Auvergne, duchy . . . . 78 C f
Auvergne, gouv. . . . . 146 B b
Auvergne, prov. . . . . 148 C c
Auxerre . . . . 69 E c
Auxerre, bp. . . . . 69 I g
Auxerre, cty. . . . . 76 E c
Auxerre, dist. . . . . 84 E f
Auximum (Osimo) . . . . . . 27 H d
Auxonne . . . . 126 D c
Ava . . . . 103 J e
Ava, reg. . . . . 102 J e
Avah . . . . 99 M f
Avallon, Avallone . . . . 76 F c
Avalon Peninsula . . . . 212 J d
Avaricum (Bourges) . . . . . . 38 C c
Avars, people . . . . 54 H d
Avasgians, people . . . . 55 M e
Aveia . . . . 27 H e
Aveiro . . . . 82 A a
Avellino . . . . 90 E d
Avellino, bp. . . . . 95 ins.
Avendo . . . . 27 J c
Avenio or Avenione, see Avignon
Avens River . . . . 27 H e
Aventicum (Avenches) . . . . . 39 I j
Aventine, quarter . . . . 96 A
Aventine, Augustan, Region of
Rome . . . . 22 A
Aventine Mount . . . . 22 A
Avenue de Paris, Versailles . . 149 A
Avenue de Saint Cloud, Ver-
sailles . . . . 149 A
Avenue de Trianon, Versailles 149 A
Averni, see Clermont, in
Auvergne
Avernus Lake . . . . 31 ins. A
Aversa . . . . 90 E d
Aversa, bp. . . . . 95 ins.
Aversa, cty. . . . . 64 B b
Avesica . . . . 27 H b
Avesnes . . . . 69 F a
Avesnes, mon. . . . . 148 B a
Aveyron, dept. . . . . 148 E f
Avezzano . . . . 64 ins.
Avignon . . . . 61 F d
Avignon, bp. . . . . 94 C c
Avignon, papal dom. . . . . . 78 D f
Avignon, univ. . . . . 100 F f
Ávila . . . . 82 B a
Avila, bp. . . . . 94 B c
Avilés . . . . 82 A a

Aviones, people . . . . 38 D a
Aviz . . . . 94 A d
Avlona . . . . 164 B b
Avola . . . . 90 E f
Avona River . . . . 38 B b
Avon River . . . . 127 W n
Avranches . . . . 61 C b
Avranches, bp. . . . . 94 B b
Avranches, cty. . . . . 69 C b
Axbridge, parl. bor. . . . . . .
Axel . . . . 117 B c
Axima . . . . 26 A b
Axiupolis . . . . 43 H e
Axius (Vardar) River . . . . . 11 D b
Axminster . . . . 127 V p
Axona River, see Aisne River
Axtopolis . . . . 47 L e
Axuenna . . . . 39 H i
Axuenna River, see Aisne River
Ayacucho, battle . . . . 214 B d
Ayamonte . . . . 83 J h
Ayas . . . . 99 K f
Ayerbe . . . . 82 B a
Aylesbury, parl. bor. . . . . . 163 N f (Ayl.)
Aylesbury, parl. dist . . . . . 163 N f (Ayl.)
Ayllon, route of . . . . 191 J e
Ayotta . . . . 201 H g
Ayr . . . .
Ayr, cty. . . . . 127 P i
Ayr, reg. . . . .
Ayuthia . . . .
Ayutla . . . . 213 C c
Ayyubids, Dominion of the . . 73 H d
Azania, reg. . . . . 14 B b
Azenia . . . . 16 B b
Azerbijan, reg. . . . .
Azetium . . . . 31 F b
Azilia, dist. . . . . 193 ins. C
Asiris . . . . 18 B d
Azores Islands . . . . 175 A a
Azorus . . . . 10 D c
Azotus . . . . 7 B e
Azov . . . . 139 E f
Azov, Sea of . . . . 3 H d
Aztecs, Dominion of the . . . 107 G e
Azzo Visconti, Dominion of . . 90 I h

Baalbec . . . . 6 E a
Baal Gad . . . . 6 D b*
Baar, landgr. . . . . 142 B e
Babadagh . . . . 131 I e
Babahoyo . . . . 214 B c (Ba)
Baba Mahal, reg. . . . .
Bab el Mandeb, strait . . . . . 170 F g
Babenberg, see Bamberg . . . 62 F d
Babuyan Islands . . . . 171 N g
Babylon . . . . 4 D e
Babylonia, prov. . . . . 18 G d
Babylonia, reg. . . . . 8 C b
Babylonia, satr. . . . . 8 I e
Bacallaos, Tierra de los . . . . 108 L c
Bacanore . . . .
Bacca . . . . 77 L e
Bacenis Forest . . . . 39 J h
Backnang . . . . 143 H h
Back's River . . . . 212 E b
Bac-ninh . . . . 171 L f
Bacolor . . . . 199 ins. H
Bacs, reg. . . . .
Baotra . . . . 8 E b
Bactria, prov. . . . . 19 K c
Bactria, reg. . . . . 8 E b
Bactria, satr. . . . . 8 K e
Bactrians, Kingdom of the . . 19 Y k
Badajóz . . . . 83 D d
Badajóz, bp. . . . . 94 A d
Badajór, emir. . . . . 83 D d
Badakshan, reg. . . . .
Baddesley, preceptory . . . . 100 A b
Baden, in Baden . . . . 142 E d
Baden, in Switzerland . . . . . 91 Q k
Baden, near Vienna . . . . . . 79 J c
Baden, castle . . . . 62 E d
Baden, elect. . . . . 151 H g

Baden	INDEX	Basman
Baden, gr. duchy . . . . 151 K j	Ballaarat . . . 172 D d	Bard, Fort . . . . 150 D d
Baden, margr. . . . . . . 86 G d	Ballah, lake . . . . 174 K i	Bardenwick, see Bardowiek
Badenoch, reg.	Ballenstedt . . . 62 F c	Bardney, mon. . . . . . . 97 Q h
Badenweiler . . . . 142 A e	Ballinasloe . . . 98 B c	Bardo
Badenweiler, lordship . . . . 142 A e	Ballyshannon . . . . . . 127 I g	Bardowiek . . . . 62 F b
Badiæ . . . . 46 H g	Balsas, Rio de las, R. . . . 213 ins.	Bardstown . . . . . . 196 B c
Bæbiani . . . . 30 D a	Balta . . . . 139 C f	Barduli . . . . 31 F a
Bæcula . . . . 38 B e	Baltic Port . . . 120 J e	Bardulia, cty. . . . . 82 B a
Bæterræ, see Béziers	Baltic Sea . . . . 2 F c	Barea . . . . 38 B e
Bætica, West Rom. prov. . . . . 42 A f(1)	Baltimore, in Ireland . . . 184 B b	Bareilly . . . . . 137 C c
Bætica, Farther, senat. prov. . . . 34 C f	Baltimore, in Maryland . . . . 192 C d	Bärenburg, castle . . . . 91 R l
Bætica (Farther Spain) Augustan prov. . . . . 38 A e(3)	Baltischport (Baltic Port) . . . . 120 J e	Barfleur . . . . 65 F f
Bætica, Hither, senat. prov. . . . 34 D f	Baluches, people . . . . 92 G e	Barga . . . . 90 L i
Bætis River (Guadalquivir) . . . 38 A e	Baluchistan, state . . . . 170 H f	Bargu, reg.
Bæto . . . . 38 A e	Balyra River . . . . 14 B b	Bargylia . . . 17 E c
Bæza . . . . 82 B b	Bamberg . . . 62 F d	Bari . . . . 64 C b
Baffin Bay . . . . 186 L a	Bamberg, bp. . . . 79 G d	Bari, abp. . . . 95 F c
Baffin Land . . . . 186 L a	Bamborough	Baris . . . . 31 H c
Bafulabe . . . . 174 B c	Bamborough, parl. bor. . . .	Barium . . . . 31 F a
Bagæ . . . . 42 D f	Bambuk, reg. . . . . 174 B c	Barka Plateau . . . 2 G e
Bagamoyo . . . . 175 G e	Bamian . . . . 102 G d	Barkhalikend.
Bagdad . . . . 53 G c	Bammako . . . . 174 C c	Barking . . . . 75 J h
Bagdad, calif. . . . . 73 I d	Banat, reg. . . . . 159 K f	Barking, mon. . . . 97 R j
Bagé, in Brazil . . . . . 215 D f	Banbury, parl. bor. . . . . . 163 M e	Barkly . . . . 175 L l
Bagé, in France . . . . 130 M h	Banda, isl. . . .	Barkul
Bagienni, people . . . . 26 B c	Banda Oriental, prov. . . . . . 215 D f	Barlee, lake . . . . 172 A c
Bagirmi, reg. . . . . . 174 E c	Bandar Abbas . . . . 170 G f	Barletta . . . . 90 F d
Bagistana (Behistun)	Bandusia, Fount of . . . . 30 E b	Barlings, mon. . . . 97 Q k
Bagno di Romagna . . . . . . 90 M j	Banff, cty.	Barlow, route of . . . 191 J d
Bagnolo . . . . 90 J h	Banff Park, town . . . . 212 D c	Barnegat Inlet . . . . 192 D d
Bagnorea, bp. . . . . 95 E c	Bangalore . . . . . 137 C f	Barnet . . . . 75 I h
Bagradas River . . . . 38 D e	Bangkok . . . . . 171 K g	Barnim, reg. . . . 80 ins.
Bahama Islands . . . . 105 E b	Bangor, in Maine . . . 199 L b	Barnsley . . . . 162 E d
Bahawalpur . . . . 137 B c	Bangor, in Wales. . . .	Barnstable . . . . 189 C d
Bahawalpur, reg. . . . . 137 B c	Bangor, bp. . . . . . 97 M h	Barnstaple . . . . 65 D e
Bahia . . . . 214 F d	Bangweolo, lake . . . . 175 F f	Barnstaple, parl. bor. . . . 163 J f
Bahia, cap. . . . . 108 M i	Banialuka . . . . 159 I f	Barnus, mt. . . . 10 C b
Bahia, state. . . . . 214 E d	Banias . . . . 68 ins. A	Barnwell, mon. . . . 97 R i
Bahia Blanca . . . . 215 C f	Banjermassin, reg. . . . . 112 E d	Barroch
Bahia Blanca, bay . . . . . 215 C f	Banks Land, isl. . . . . . . 186 G a	Baroda . . . . 137 B d
Bahia del Almirante, bay . . . . 105 D e	Banks Strait . . . . 186 G a	Baros . . . . 112 C c
Bahia de Todos os Santos, bay 214 F d	Bann River. . . . . 49 C d	Barotse, people . . . 175 F f
Bahmanid Sultanate . . . . . . 92 H f	Bannocks, people . . . . 188 C a	Barquisimeto . . . . 105 C d
Bahrein, isl. . . .	Bañolas . . . . 82 C a	Barra do Rio Negro . . . 214 D c
Bahr el Ghazal, reg. . . . . 174 F d	Baños de Ledesma . . . . . 82 C a	Barra Island
Bahr el Ghazal, R. . . . . 174 F d	Bantam . . . . 112 D d	Barranquilla . . . 214 B a
Baiæ . . . . 31 ins. A	Bantia . . . . 31 F b	Barre, La . . . 192 C b
Baikal, lake	Bantry Bay . . . . . 127 G j	Barren Country, reg. . . . 212 C b
Baila Monos River	Banz, mon. . . . . 95 E a	Barrios, Puerto . . . 213 D c
Bailén . . . . 130 C f	Bauli . . . . 31 ins. A	Barrois mouvant, dist. . . . . 126 D b
Baindt, ab. . . . . 143 I j	Bapaume . . . . 117 A d	Barrow, Point . . . 186 D a
Baisan . . . . 68 ins. A	Baphyras River . . . . 11 D b	Barrow River . . . . 49 C e
Bajazet, Mosque of . . . . . . 93 G e(5)	Bar (Antivari) . . . 164 B c	Barrow Strait . . . . 186 J a
Bajocas or Bajocasses, see Bayeux	Bar, in Podolia . . . . 131 I d	Barrum, see Bar-le-Duc and Bar-sur-Aube
Baker City . . . . 210 B b	Bar-le-Duc . . . . 84 F e	Bartenstein, in Prussia . . . 155 K a
Baker Island . . . . 180 J h	Bar-sur-Aube . . . . 61 F b	Bartenstein, in Wurtemberg . . 143 I g
Bakkar	Bar-sur-Aube, cty. . . . . . 69 J f	Bartfeld . . . . 131 H d
Bakony Wald, mts. . . . . 159 I e	Bar-sur-Seine . . . . 69 J f	Barton, priory . . . 100 A b
Baktchiserai . . . . 93 D b	Bar, duchy, 14 cent. . . . . 76 F b	Barton-on-Humber, parl. bor. . .
Baku . . . . 139 G g	Bar, duchy, 15 cent. . . . 84 F e	Baruth . . . . 85 G d
Balabac Strait . . . . 171 M h	Bar, duchy, 17 and 18 cent. . . 126 D b	Bärwalde . . . . 123 H b
Balabo, mt. . . . . 30 E b	Bar, dist., 18 cent. . . . 134 C d	Basel. . . . . 91 P k
Balaklava . . . . 164 J f	Baranof Island . . . 212 ins.	Basel, bp. . . . 78 E e
Balasor	Baraque, La . . . 156 B a	Basel, canton . . . 91 P k
Balaton, lake. . . .	Barathrum, mt. . . . 23 D	Basel, imp. cy. . . . 78 E e
Balboa, route of . . . . 105 E e	Barataria Bay . . . 207 G e	Basel, univ. . . . 100 G e
Balbus, Crypta of . . . . 22 A	Barbados, isl. . . . 213 F c	Basentus (Busento) River . . 31 F c
Balbus, Theatre of . . . . . . 22 A	Barbary, reg. . . . 108 Q d	Bashan, reg. . . . 6 E c
Baldern . . . . 143 J h	Barbary States . . . . 118 D g	Bashkirs, people . . . 139 H e
Bâle, see Basel	Barbastro . . . 82 C a	Basilica Æmilia, bldg. . . . 24 B
Balearic Islands . . . . 2 E e	Barberton . . . 175 N l	Basilica Julia, bldg. . . . 24 B
Balearic Isles, Rom. prov. . . . 42 C f(7)	Barbuda, isl. . . . 213 F c	Basilica Porcia, bldg.
Balearic Sea . . . . 38 C e	Barca . . . 8 G e	Basilica Sempronia, bldg. . . . 24 A
Balesium . . . . 31 H b	Barca, reg. . . . 66 K g	Basilica Ulpia, bldg. . . . 24 B
Bali, isl. . . . . 112 E d	Barcaldine . . . 172 D c	Basilicata, dist. . . . 90 E d
Balingen . . . . 143 G g	Barcellos . . . 214 C c	Basilia, see Basel
Balize . . . . 191 H f	Barcelona, in Spain . . . 82 C a	Basingstoke . . . 127 X e
Balkan Mountains . . . . . . 2 G d	Barcelona, in Venezuela . . . 214 C b	Basingstoke, college . . . 100 A a(33)
Balkan Peninsula . . . . 2 G d	Barcelona, bp. . . . 94 C c	Basingstoke, deanery . . . . . 100 A a
Balkash, lake. . . .	Barcelona, cty . . . 82 C a	Basingstoke, hospital . . 100 A a(29)
Balkh	Barcelona, univ. . . . 100 F f	Basingstoke, parl. bor. . . .
Balkh, reg. . . . . 137 A a	Barcelonette . . . 126 E d	Basingwerk, mon. . . . 97 N h
Balla . . . . 11 D b	Barchin	Basle, see Basel
	Barchinona or Barcino (Barcelona) 38 C d	Basman . . . . 112 C c

Basques, people	57	C e
Basra	53	G c
Bas-Rhin, dept.	148	F e
Bassam, Grand	175	C d
Bassania	31	I a
Bassano	72	C b
Basse-Fontaine, mon.	94	C b (B. F.)
Bassein	112	A b
Basses-Alps, dept.	148	F f
Basses-Pyrénées, dept.	148	D f
Bassignano	130	Q j
Bassigny, dist.	126	D c
Bass Strait	172	D d
Bastarnæ, people	35	I c
Bastetani, people	38	B e
Basti	38	B e
Bastia	77	F d
Bastidas, route of	105	E d
Bastille, bldg.	149	B
Bastogne	117	D d
Batalha	83	J h
Batalha, mon.	94	A d
Batanæa, reg.	6	E c
Batanga, Gross		
Batangas	171	N g
Batava, Castra (Passau)	38	E c
Batavian Republic	151	H f
Batavians, people	38	C b
Batavodurum	39	H g
Bate	16	B a
Bateia		
Bath, in England		
Bath, in N. Carolina	193	F d
Bath, bp.	97	O j
Bath, parl. bor.	163	L f
Bathurst, in Gambia	174	B c
Bathurst, in N. S. Wales	172	D d
Bathurst, Cape	212	C a
Baticala	112	A b
Batinus River	27	I e
Batnæ	20	H d
Batoche	212	E c
Baton Rouge	191	G e
Battas, people		
Battersea	75	I i
Battery Wagner, fort.	208	E c
Battikalva	112	B c
Battle, mon.	97	R k
Battleford	212	E c
Baturin	131	J c
Baturite	214	F c
Bau	158	E a
Bauconia	39	J i
Baudemont	156	A a
Baugé, in Anjou	70	C c
Baugé, in Bresse	126	D c
Bauld, Cape	212	J c
Baume-les-Dames, mon.	95	D b
Baumgartenberg, mon.	95	E b
Bautzen	63	H c
Bautzen-Görlitz, dist.	85	D c
Bauzanum	27	F a
Bavaria, duchy, 10 cent.	63	G e
Bavaria, duchy, 13 cent.	72	C b
Bavaria, duchy, 16 cent.	115	G d
Bavaria, elect.	123	G d
Bavaria, Frank. prov., 8 cent.	53	O h
Bavaria, Frank. prov., 9 cent.	54	G d
Bavaria, km., 1806	151	L j
Bavaria, km., 1812	154	F d
Bavaria, km., 1815–1866	158	F d
Bavaria, km., since 1866	161	G d
Bavaria-Landshut, duchy	79	H d
Bavaria-Munich, duchy	79	G e
Bavaria-Straubing, duchy	79	H d
Bavarian East March (Ostmark)	63	H d
Bavarians, people	46	I d
Bawiti	150	A b
Bawtry	185	E d
Bayamon	199 ins. G
Bayeux	61	G d
Bayeux, bp.	94	B b
Baymen, people	136 ins. A
Bay of Chaleurs	212	I d
Bayona	82	A a
Bayonne	58	D e
Bayonne, bp.	94	B c
Bayou Pierre, R.	196	A d
Bayreuth	114	F d
Bayreuth, princ.	114	F d
Baza	82	B b
Bazadais, dist.	69	C d
Bazas	61	C d
Bazas, bp.	94	B c
Beachy Head	127	Z p
Bear River	198	C b
Béarn, gouv.	146	A c
Béarn, prov.	148	D f
Béarn, viscty.	76	C e
Bearroc Wood	49	F f
Beata, isl.	105	F c
Beaucaire	126	D e
Beauce, dist.	69	H f
Beau-Chêne	156	C c
Beaufort	193 ins. C
Beaugency	69	H g
Beaugency, mon.		
Beauharnais, Fort	191	G c
Beauharnois	212	H d
Beaujeu	76	F c
Beaujeu, seign.	69	F c
Beaulieu, ab.	100	A b
Beaulieu, castle	76	D c
Beaulieu, mon., near Tours	94	C b
Beaulieu, mon., near Tulle	94	C b
Beaumaris, parl. bor.	163	J d
Beaumont, in Anjou	76	C b
Beaumont, in Hainaut	157 ins.
Beaumont, in Normandy	65	G f
Beaumont, on the Oise	76	E b
Beaumont, cty., in Normandy	76	D b
Beauvais	61	E b
Beauvais, bp.	94	C b
Beauvais, cty.	61	E b
Beauvale, mon.	97	P h
Beaver	210	C c
Bebenhausen, mon.	143	H h
Bec	65	G f
Bec, mon.	94	C b
Bechuanaland, dist.	175	F g
Bechuanaland, prot., col.	175	F g
Beda	39	I i
Beddington	75	I i
Bedesis (Ronco) River	27	E d
Bedford, in England		
Bedford, in Virginia	195	B e
Bedford, cty.	127	Y n
Bedford, Fort	192	B c
Bedford, New	211	K b
Bedford, parl. bor.	163	N e
Bedlington		
Bedwyn, parl. bor.		
Beejapore	137	C e
Beerfelden	142	C a
Beer Alston, parl. bor.		
Beersheba	7	B f
Beeskow	85	H d
Beeston Castle	127	Wm
Behar	137	E c
Behar, reg.	137	D d
Beichlingen	85	F e
Beilan	164	F c
Beilstein	143	H g
Beinheim	142	B c
Beira	175	G f
Beira, Fort do Principe da	214	C d
Beirut	68	C c
Beja	82	A b
Beka, The, reg.	6	D a
Bekes	168	G c
Belbek River	164	J f
Belbina, isl.	15	D b
Belbuck, mon.	80	D d
Belecke, castle	62	E c
Beleigh, mon.	97	R j
Belem, in Brazil	214	E c
Belem, in Portugal	83	J h
Belem, mon.	94	A d
Belemina	14	C b
Belen	105	D e
Belesme	65	G f
Belfast	127	L g
Belfort, in the Sundgau	122	D e
Belfort, in Syria, castle	68 ins. A
Belgæ, people	51	O i
Belgard	63	H b
Belgern	63	G c
Belgian Congo, col.	175	F e
Belgica	39	I h
Belgica, Rom. prov.	38	D c (3)
Belgica I, Rom. prov.	42	D d (5)
Belgica II, Rom. prov.	42	C c (6)
Belgium, km.	158	C c
Belgrade	43	G e
Belgrade, bp.	95	G c
Belize	213	D c
Belkesheim, dist.	63	F b
Belknap, Fort, Ind. Res.	188	D a
Bell, route of	210	F c
Bellac	69	D c
Bellagio see Bellaggio	90	I h
Bellary	137	C e
Belle-Alliance, La, farm	156	C c
Bellecombe, mon.	94	C c
Belle Ile, isl.	69	B c
Belle Isle	148	A b
Belle Isle, Strait of	186	N c
Bellême, seign.	69	H f
Belleville, mon.	94	C b
Belley	69	F d
Belley, bp.	95	D b
Belli, people	38	B d
Bellinzona	91	R l
Bellona, Temple of	24	A
Bellovaci or Bellovacis, see Beauvais		
Bellovaci, people	38	C c
Belluno	63	G e
Belluno, bp.	95	E b
Bellunum	27	G a
Belmont	208	C b
Belrain	69	J f
Belt, Great, str.	88	D d
Belt, Little, str.	88	C d
Beltana	172	C d
Belts	59	I c
Belus River	6	C c
Belvoir, in Syria, castle	68 ins. A
Belvoir Castle, in England	127	Y n
Belzig	85	G d
Benacus (Garda), lake	26	E b
Benadir, reg.	175	H d
Benafrum, see Venafrum (Venafro)		
Benares	137	D c
Benavente	83	J g
Bencoolen		
Bender		
Bendigo	172	D d
Benediktbeuren, mon.	95	E b
Beneschau	135	H d
Benevento	46	I e
Benevento, abp.	95	E c
Benevento, duchy	54	G e
Benevento, princ.	64	B b
Beneventum (Benevento)	30	D a
Bengal, dist.		
Bengal, prov.	137	E d
Bengal, Bay of	112	B b
Benghazi	174	F a
Benguela	175	E f
Benguela, reg.	109	S i
Beni River	214	C d
Benin	174	D d
Benin, Bight of	174	D d
Benin, reg.	108	R g
Bénisson-Dieu, La, mon.	94	C b
Beni-Suef	150	B b
Benjamin, tribe	7 ins. D
Bennet, lake	212 ins.
Bennett's Plantation	193 ins. A (Benn.)
Ben Nevis, mt.	49	D c

Bennington . . . . 195 E b
Bentheim . . . . 62 D b
Bentheim, cty. . . . . 134 D b
Benton, Fort . . . . 198 C a
Bentonville . . . . 208 E b
Bent's Fort . . . . 198 E c
Benue River . . . . 174 D d
Berar, dist. . . . . 137 C d
Berar, prov. . . . . 170 I f
Berar, Rajah of, princ. . . . . .
Berat . . . . 165 A c
Berber . . . . 174 G c
Berbera . . . . 174 H c
Berbers, people . . . . 53 B-D c-d
Berchtesgaden . . . . 79 H e
Berchtesgaden, ab. . . . . . 79 H e
Berchtesgaden, mon. . . . . 72 C b
Berdera . . . . 175 H d
Berditchev . . . . 131 I d
Berea . . . . 7 C e
Bereïdah . . . . 170 F f
Berenice . . . . 34 H g
Beresina River . . . . 153 N g
Berezov . . . . 170 H b
Berg, cty. . . . . 78 E c
Berg, duchy . . . . 86 F c
Berg, gr. duchy . . . . 154 D c
Bergalei, people . . . . 26 D a
Berga . . . . 82 C a
Bergama . . . . 77 J e
Bergamo . . . . 90 I h
Bergamo, bp. . . . . 95 D b
Berge, in Macedonia . . . . . 11 E b
Berge, mon. near Magdeburg . 95 E a
Bergen, near Frankfort . . . . 134 E c
Bergen, in Netherlands . . . . 134 C b
Bergen, in New Jersey . . . . 189 ins. C
Bergen, in Norway . . . . . 166 F c
Bergen, on Rugen Island . . . 123 G a
Bergen, Hanse. for. off. . . . 98 D a
Bergen, mon., on Rugen I. . . . 80 C d
Bergen op Zoom . . . . . . 117 C c
Bergerac . . . . 69 D d
Bergerac, castle . . . . 76 D d
Bergomum (Bergamo) . . . . 26 D b
Bergues . . . . 126 C a
Bergula . . . .
Bergzabern . . . . 142 B b
Berhampur . . . . 171 J f
Bering Sea . . . . 179 I b
Bering Strait . . . . 186 C b
Beritini, people . . . . 26 A d
Berkeley, in California . . . . 210 A c
Berkeley, in England . . . . . 185 D f
Berkeley, in Virginia . . . . . 193 ins. A
Berkeley, castle . . . .
Berkeley County . . . . . . 193 ins. C
Berkhampstead . . . . 65 F e
Berkhampstead, parl. bor. 163
Berks, parl. dist. . . . . . . 163 M f
Berkshire, cty. . . . . 60 M i
Berlichingen . . . . 143 I g
Berlichingen, castle . . . . . 114 E d
Berlin . . . . 85 C b
Berlin, Hanse. cy. . . . . . . 99 ins. B
Bermejo River . . . . 215 C e
Bermius, mt. . . . . 10 C b
Bermondsey, mon. . . . . . 97 Q j
Bermuda, isl. . . . . 108 K d
Bermuda Hundred . . . . . . 191 J d
Bermudez, state . . . . 214 C b
Bermudez, route of . . . . . 108 K d
Bernalillo . . . . 190 D d
Bernardino River . . . . . .
Bernburg . . . . 154 F c
Berne . . . . 91 P l
Berne, canton . . . . 91 P l
Berne, New (Newbern) . . . . 193 F d
Berneck, castle . . . . 143 G h
Bernhardin Pass . . . . . . 150 E c
Bernicia, dist. . . . .
Bernicians, people . . . . . .
Bernina Pass . . . . 91 S l
Bornkastel . . . . 142 ins. A

Bernstein . . . . 85 D b
Berœa, in Macedonia . . . . . 10 D b
Berœa, in Syria . . . . 20 G d
Berœa, in Thrace . . . . . . 39 N l
Berones, people . . . . 38 B d
Berothai . . . . 6 D a
Berrhœa . . . . 10 D b
Berry, duchy . . . . 78 C e
Berry, gouv. . . . . 146 B b
Berry, prov. . . . . 148 E e
Berthold, Fort, Ind. Res. . . . 188 F a
Bertinoro, bp. . . . . 95 E c
Bertiscus, mt. . . . . 11 E b
Berwick, in England . . . . .
Berwick, in New Hampshire . . 189 C c
Berwick, cty. . . . .
Berwick on Tweed, parl. bor. . 163 M b
Berwick, South . . . . 189 C c (S. B.)
Berytus (Beirut) . . . . 6 D a
Besa . . . . 16 C b
Besalú, mon. . . . . 94 C c
Besançon . . . . 62 D e
Besançon, abp. . . . . 95 D b
Besançon, gen. . . . . 147 F b
Besançon, imp. cy. . . . . . . 78 E e
Besançon, univ. . . . . 100 G e
Beshicktash, quarter . . . . .
Besigheim . . . . 143 H g
Besika Bay . . . .
Besor River . . . . 7 B f
Bessapara . . . . 39 M l
Bessarabia, dist. in the Ottoman Empire . . . .
Bessarabia, dist. in Russia . . 139 C f
Bessi, people . . . . 39 M l
Bethany, in Georgia . . . . . 193 ins. C
Bethany, in Palestine . . . . . 7 C e
Bethar . . . . 7 B d
Betharbel . . . .
Beth-Aven . . . . 7 C e
Bethel, in Alaska . . . . . . 198 ins. A
Bethel, in Palestine . . . . . 7 C e
Bethelea . . . . 7 A e
Bethencourt, route of . . . . 108 O e
Bethesda, Pool of . . . . . . 6 ins. A
Beth-Haran . . . . 7 D e
Beth-Horon . . . . 7 C e
Beth-Jeshimoth . . . . 7 D e
Bethlehem, in Palestine . . . . 7 C e
Bethlehem, in Pennsylv. . . . 192 D c
Bethlen Gabor, route of . . . 121 F c
Beth-Markaboth . . . . 7 C f
Beth-Meon . . . . 7 D e
Beth-Nimrah . . . . 7 D e
Beth-Peor . . . . 7 D e
Bethsaida . . . . 6 D c
Bethshean . . . . 7 C d
Beth-Shemesh . . . . 7 B e
Bethso . . . . 6 ins. A
Bethulie . . . . 175 M m
Béthune . . . . 117 A d
Bethzur . . . . 7 C e
Betifulus . . . .
Betogabra . . . . 7 B e
Betonim . . . . 7 D e
Betriacum . . . . 26 E b
Beuil, Le, mon. . . . . 94 C b
Beutelsbach . . . . 143 H h
Beuthen . . . . 115 J c
Beveland, South, isl. . . . . . 117 B c
Beverley . . . . 127 Y m
Beverley, parl. bor. . . . . . 163 L e
Beverly Manor . . . . 194 K g
Bevern . . . . 134 E c
Beversrede, Fort . . . . 192 ins. A
Beverswyck . . . . 189 A c
Bewdley, parl. bor. . . . . . 163 L e
Bezabde . . . . 20 J d
Bézenas . . . . 126 C e
Bezetha . . . . 6 ins. A
Bezetha, Hill of . . . . 6 ins. A
Béziers . . . . 76 E e
Béziers, bp. . . . . 94 C c
Bhamo . . . . 171 K f

Bhartpur . . . .
Bhatkal . . . . 112 A b
Bhawalpore . . . . 137 B c
Bhawalpore, dist. . . . . . . 137 B c
Bhootan, Bhutan, princ. . . . 137 E c
Bhopal . . . . 137 C d
Bhotan, Bhutan, princ. . . . . 171 K f
Bhurtpore . . . .
Biafra, reg. . . . . 109 I g
Biafra, bight . . . . 175 D d
Bialystok . . . . 138 B e
Biana . . . .
Biandrate . . . . 72 B b
Biar . . . . 82 H f
Bias River . . . .
Biasca . . . . 91 Q l
Biberach . . . . 142 E d
Biberach, imp. cy. . . . . . . 143 I i
Bibracte . . . . 38 C c
Bibrax . . . . 38 C c
Bibrich . . . . 117 E e
Bibroci, people . . . .
Bicocca . . . . 90 I h
Bidar . . . .
Bidassoa River . . . . 130 C e
Biel . . . .
Bielefeld . . . . 154 E b
Bielefeld, Hanse. cy. . . . . . 99 ins. B
Bielgorod . . . . 139 E e
Bielgorod, gov. . . . . 131 K c
Bielitz . . . . 135 J d
Biella . . . . 90 I h
Bielosersk . . . . 138 E c
Bielsk . . . . 159 L b
Bienne . . . . 91 P k
Bierges . . . . 156 B a
Bieringen . . . . 143 G i
Big Mountain . . . . 212 ins.
Big River . . . . 212 H c
Big Black River . . . . 208 B c
Big Black River, battle . . . . 208 B c
Bigha . . . . 77 J d
Big Horn River . . . . 198 D b
Bigorre, cty. . . . . 76 C e
Bigorre, dist. . . . . 147 D c (Big.)
Bigorritis, lake . . . . 10 C e
Big Sioux River . . . . 198 F b
Bihacs . . . . 119 H e
Bijapur . . . . 137 C e
Bikaner . . . . 170 I f
Bikaner, dist. . . . . 137 B c
Bilbao . . . . 83 K g
Bilbilis . . . . 38 B d
Bilitio . . . . 26 C a
Billæus River . . . . 20 E b
Billingsgate, loc. in London . . 75 G g
Billungs, Lands of the . . . . 62 F b
Billungs, March of the . . . . 63 F b
Biloxi . . . . 191 H f
Bima . . . .
Bimlipatam . . . . 156 C e
Binche . . . . 117 A b
Binchester . . . .
Bingen . . . . 62 D d
Bingerville . . . . 174 C d
Bingium (Bingen) . . . . . . 39 I i
Binn . . . . 91 Q l
Binsdorf . . . . 143 G i
Bintang, isl. . . . .
Biobio River . . . . 215 B f
Birkenfeld . . . . 142 ins. A
Birkel-el-Kerun, lake . . . . .
Birket Israel . . . . 6 ins. A
Birmingham, in Alabama . . . 211 H d
Birmingham, in England . . . 127 X n
Birmingham, parl. bor. . . . . 163 M e
Birs River . . . . 91 P k
Birten . . . . 62 D c
Bisaltia . . . . 11 E b
Bisaltia, reg. . . . . 11 E b
Bisanthe . . . .
Biscay, Bay of . . . . 2 D d
Bisceglie . . . . 90 F d
Bischoflack . . . . 135 H e

Bischofsheim 142   E a
Bischofsheim, mon. 95   D b
Bischofswerda 155   H c
Bischofszell 142   D e
Biserta 58   F f
Bishbalk (Urumtsi) . . . .
Bishop - Auckland, mon. 97   P g
Bishop's Castle, parl. bor. . . .
Bishopsgate, loc. in London . . 75   G g
Bishops Stortford, parl. bor.163O f(Bish.St.)
Bisignano 98   G f
Biskra 174   D a
Bismarck 210   E a
Bismarck Archipelago 179   F h
Bissagos Islands 174   B c
Bistritz . . . .
Bitburg 117   E d
Biterræ, see Béziers
Bitervium, see Viterbo
Bithynia, dist. 20   D b
Bithynia, East Rom. prov. . . . 43 He(1.)
Bithynia, reg. 8   B a
Bithynia, Rom. prov. 35   K e
Bithynium 20   D b
Bitolia 164   C b
Bitonto 90   F d
Bitsch, fortress 154   D d
Bitter Lakes 174   K i
Bitterne 51   P i
Biturgia 27   F d
Bituriges or Biturigis, see Bourges
Bituriges, people 38   C c
Bivium . . . . 35 ins. B
Bizerta . . . .
Bizye 39   N l
Björneborg 120   J d
Blachernæ, palace 93   G e
Blackburn, parl. bor. 163   L d
Blackfeet, Ind. Res. 188   D a
Blackfeet, tribe 188   D a
Black Forest, mts. 62   D e
Black Friars, mon. in London . 75   G g
Blackheath 75   J i
Black Hills 210   E b
Black River 208   B b
Black Russia, reg. 139   C e
Black Sea 3   H d
Blacksnake Hills, fort 211   G b
Blackwall 75   J h
Blackwater River . . . .
Bladensburg 200   L i
Blagovestchensk . . . .
Blakeney, parl. bor. . . . . . .
Blamont . . . . 143 ins. F
Blamont, lordship . . . . 143 ins. F
Blanca Peak 187   I e
Blanche, lake 172   D c
Blanche Garde, castle . . . . . 68 ins. A
Blanchelande, mon. 65   F f
Blanchelande, mon. 94   B b
Blanco, Cape, in Guinea . . . 174   B b
Blanco, Cape, in Oregon . . . 210   A b
Blanco, Cape, in Peru 111   A b
Blanco, Cape, in Tunis 174   D a
Blanda, in Italy 30   E c
Blanda, in Spain 38   C d
Blandford, parl. bor. . . . . . .
Blankenberghe 117   B c
Blankenheim 117   E d
Blanmont 156   H d
Blariacum 39   H h
Blaubeuren 143   I i
Blaubeuren, mon. 95   D b
Blaye 76   C d
Bleiburg 115   H e
Bleichfeld 62   F d
Blekinge, dist. 88   C c
Bléneau 126   C c
Blenheim 129   F c
Blennerhasset's Island 196   C c
Blera, in Apulia 31   F b
Blera, in Etruria 27   G e
Blesum, see Blois
Bletchingley, parl. bor. . . . 163 N f (Blet.)

Blindheim 134   F d
Block Island 189   C d
Bloemfontein 175   M l
Blois 61   D c
Blois, cty. 61   D c
Blore Heath 84   B c
Bluefields 213   D c
Blue Horde, people . . . . . .
Blue Licks 196   C c
Blue Mountains 172   D d
Blue Nile River 174   G c
Blue Ridge, mts. . . . . . 193 C d — E b
Blumegg 142   B e
Blumenau, in Brazil 215   E e
Blumenau, in Hungary 159   I d
Blumenfeld 142   C e
Boactes River 26   D c
Bobbio 90   I h
Bobbio, bp. 95   D c
Bober River 63   H c
Bobium Castrum (Bobbio) . . . 26   D c
Böblingen 143   H h
Bobruisk 167   K e
Boca del Dragón, str. 105   H d
Boca del Sierpe. str. 105   H d
Boca del Toro, bay 213   D d
Bocca Tigris 171   M f
Bocchetta Pass, La 150   E d
Bochnia 123   K c
Bocholt 117   E c
Böckelheim, castle 62   D d
Bode River 85   F e
Boderiæ Æstuarium (Firth of Forth) 38 B a
Bodetia 26   D c
Bodfeld, castle 62   F c
Bödigheim 142   D b
Bodmann 62   E e
Bodmin, mon. 97   M k
Bodmin, parl. bor. 163   J g
Bodonitza 89   B c
Bodotria Æstuarium (Firth of Forth) 51 O g
Bœæ 15   D c
Bœæ, Bay of 15   D c
Bœbe 11   D c
Bœbeis, lake 11   D c
Bœotia, reg. 11   C d
Bœum 11   D d
Bogesund 88   E c
Bogotá 214   B b
Bohemia, duchy 63   H d
Bohemia, km. 72   C b
Bohemia, plain of 2   F d
Bohemia, reg. 54   G b
Bohemian March 55   R j
Bohemians, people . . . . . .
Bohio . . . .
Böhmer Wald, mts. 63   G d
Böhmisch - Brod 87   J c
Bohol, isl. . . . . 199 ins. H
Bohus, dist. 88   D b
Boii, people, in Italy 26   E c
Boii, people, in Pannonia . . . 38   F c
Bois Brulé River 191   N c
Boisé 210   B b
Boisé, Fort 198   B a
Bois Forte, Ind. Res. 188   H a
Bois - le - Duc 114   C c
Boissière, La, mon. 94   C b
Boïus, mt. 10   B b
Bojador, Cape 174   B a
Bojano, bp. . . . . 95 ins.
Bojeador, Cape . . . . . . 199 ins. H
Bojohæmum (Bohemia), reg . 38   E c
Bokhara . . . .
Bokhara, emir. . . . .
Bola . . . . 35 ins. B
Bolama 174   B c
Bolan Pass 170   H f
Bolar 99   N c
Bolbe, lake 11   E b
Bolghars, people . . . .
Boli 89   J f
Bolkhov 139   E e
Bolivia, country 214   C d

Bologna 90   C b
Bologna, bp. 95   E c
Bologna, univ. 100   H f
Bolsena, lake 90   L j
Bolsward 117   D c
Bolton, in England 127   W m
Bolton, in Mississippi 208   B c
Bolton, mon. 97   P h
Bolton, parl. bor. 163   L d
Bolton Abbey 127   X l
Bolton Castle 127   X l
Boma 175   E c
Bomarsund 131   H a
Bombay 137   B e
Bona 66   H f
Bona Dea, Temple of 22   A
Bonaire, isl. 214   C a
Bonavista 212   J d
Bonavista, Cape 194   J g
Bone 174   D a
Bonifacio 72   B c
Bonn 62   D c
Bonna (Bonn) 39   I h
Bonndorf 142   B e
Bonndorf, cty. 142   B e
Bonneval, mon. 94   C b
Bonnes Vaux, mon. 94   C b
Bonnevaux, mon. 95   D b
Bonneville, Fort 210   C b
Bönnigheim 143   H g
Bononia (Bologna) 27   F c
Bononia (Boulogne) 38   C b
Bontobrica 39   I h
Boonesboro 194   C c
Boone's Trail 194   C c
Boonville 211   G c
Boothia, Gulf of 186   K b
Boothia, isl. 186   J a
Boothia Felix, pen. 212   F a
Bopfingen, imp. cy. 143   J h
Boppard 62   D c
Bora, mt. 10   C a
Borbetomagus (Worms) . . . 39   J i
Borborus, lake 11   D b
Borculo 117   E b
Bordeaux 61   C d
Bordeaux, abp. 94   B b
Bordeaux, gen. 147   D c
Bordeaux, univ. 100   E f
Bordelais, dist. 76   C d
Bordesley, mon. 97   P i
Borgo San Donnino 90   J h
Borgo San Lorenzo 90   L j
Borgo San Sepolcro 90   M j
Borgo Sesia 130   Q l
Boriquen, isl. 105   G c
Borisov . . . .
Borkeloo 117   E b
Borku, reg. 174   E c
Borkum, isl. 117   E a
Bormio 90   J g
Borneo, isl. . . . .
Bornholm, isl. 88   F d
Bornhöved 72   C a
Bornu, reg. 174   E c
Borobodor . . . .
Borodino 131   K b
Boroughbridge 65   F c
Boroughbridge, parl. bor. . . 163   M c
Borovsk 153   P f
Borsippa 4   D e
Borysthenes (Dnieper) River . . 35   K d
Boscaudun, mon. 95   D c
Boshof 175   M l
Bosna River 159   J f
Bosnia, reg. . . . .
Bosnia, km. 93   A b
Bosnia, prov. in the Ottoman
    Empire 124   C b
Bosnia, prov. in Austria . . . 164   B b
Bosporus, Bosphorus, strait . . 2   G d
Bosporus, Kingdom of the
    Cimmerian 35   K e
Bosrah 6   F c

Bossiney, parl. bor.	163	J g
Boston, in England	127	Y m
Boston, Hanse. for. cy.	98 ins.	A
Boston, parl. bor.	163	O d
Boston, in Mass.	189 ins.	B
Boston Neck, pen.	195 ins.	A
Bostra	6	F c
Bostrenus River	6	C a
Bosworth	84	C c
Botany Bay	172	E d
Bothnia, Gulf of	2	G b
Bothwell		
Botroun	68	C c
Bottiæis, reg.	11	D b
Bottice, reg.	11	E b
Bottwar, Gross.	143	H h
Botzen	62	F e
Bouchain	117	B d
Bouches-du-Rhône, dept.	148	E f
Bouet, Port	175	C d
Bougainville, isl.	172	E a
Bougie	66	G f
Bouillon	117	D e
Bouillon, duchy	117	D e
Boulers	156	A a
Boulevard de la Reine, in Versailles	149	A
Boulevard du Roi, in Versailles	149	A
Boulogne	61	D a
Bounty Islands	179	I l
Bouras, mon.	94	C b
Bourbon	61	E c
Bourbon, cty.	61	E c
Bourbon, duchy	76	E c
Bourbon, isl.		
Bourbon, Palais, bldg. in Paris	149	B
Bourbon, seign.	69	E c
Bourbon-Lancy	69	I g
Bourbon-l'Archambault	76	E c
Bourbonnais, gouv.	146	B b
Bourbonnais, prov.	148	E e
Bourbonnais, seign.	69	E c
Bourbourg, mon.	148	B a
Bourg, in Bresse	126	D c
Bourg, in Saintonge	76	C d
Bourgachard, mon.	148	B b
Bourges	61	E c
Bourges, abp.	94	C b
Bourges, gen.	147	E b
Bourges, univ.	100	F e
Bourges, viscty.	69	D c
Bourgmont, route of	190	F d
Bourke	172	E d
Bourn, mon.	97	Q i
Bournet, mon.	94	B b
Boussac	69	D c
Bousval	156	A a
Bouvignes	117	C d
Bouvines	69	E a
Bouxières-aux-Dames, mon.	148	C b
Boves	81	M h
Bovianum Undecumanorum	30	D a
Bovianum vetus		
Bovillæ	35 ins.	B
Bovino, bp.	64	C b
Bovino, bp.	95	F c
Bow Church, in London	75	G g (5)
Bowling Green	208	C b
Boxberg	142	E b
Boxley, mon.	97	R j
Boxtel	117	D c
Boyacá, battle	214	B b
Boyen, fortress	159	K a
Boyne River	127	J h
Brà	90	H h
Braba	190	D d
Brabant, dist.	62	B c
Brabant, duchy, 12 cent.	72	A a
Brabant, duchy, 14 cent.	78	D c
Brabant, duchy, 16 cent.	117	C c
Bracara Augusta (Braga)	38	A d
Bracciano, lake	96	B a
Bracito	198	D d
Brackenheim	143	H g

Brackley, parl. bor.	163	M e
Bradanus (Bradano) River	31	F b
Braden Forest	49	E f
Bradenstoke, mon.	97	P j
Bradford, in Wiltshire		
Bradford, in Yorkshire	127	X m
Bradninch, parl. bor.		
Bradock Down	127	U p
Brady, Fort	211	H a
Braga	82	A a
Braga, abp.	94	A c
Braganza	82	A a
Brahe River	115	I b
Braila	93	C a
Braine-l'Alleud		
Braine-le-Château	156	A a
Braine-le-Comte	156	A a
Braintree	189	C c
Brake	158	E b
Bramber and Steyning, parl. bor.	163	N g
Branco, Cape	214	F c
Brandeis	123	H c
Brandenburg	63	G b
Brandenburg, bp.	79	H b
Brandenburg, castle	143	J i
Brandenburg, Hanse. cy.	99 ins.	B
Brandenburg, march	85	
Brandenburg, margr.	71	S j
Brandenburg, prov.	158	G b
Brandenburg, Neu	123	G b
Brandon, in Manitoba	212	F d
Brandon, in Virginia	193 ins.	A
Brandywine River	192 ins.	
Branford	189	B d
Brannkirka	88	G b
Branodunum (Brancaster)	51	Q h
Brant, route of	195	C c
Brantôme, mon.	94	C b
Braschimov		
Bratzlav	139	C f
Braunau, in Austria	135	G d
Braunau, in Bavaria	115	G d
Braunau, in Bohemia	123	I c
Bräunlingen	142	B e
Braunsberg	79	L a
Braunsberg, Hanse. cy.	99	H c
Brauron	15	D b
Brava	109	V g
Bray	69	I f
Brazen Gate	6 ins.	A
Brazil, col.	108	M i
Brazil, country	214	D d
Brazos River	191	F f
Brazos Santiago	201	F d
Brazza, isl.	90	F c
Brazzaville	175	E e
Breadalbane, dist.		
Bread Street, in London	75	G g
Breamore, priory	100	A b
Brechin, bp.	97	K c
Brecknock, cty.	127	V n
Brecknock, mon.	97	N i
Brecknock, parl. dist.	163	K e
Brecon, parl. bor.	163	K f
Breda	117	C c
Brede Fiord	166	A b
Breed's Hill	195 ins.	A
Brege River	142	B d
Bregenz	134	E e
Brehna, cty.	85	G e
Breisach	62	D e
Breisach, Alt (Old)	142	A d
Breisach, New	134	D e
Breisgau, dist.	142	B e
Breitenfeld	123	G c
Breitenwang	72	C b
Brema, see Bremen		
Bremberg	55	R j
Breme, mon.	95	D b
Bremen	62	E b
Bremen, abp.	95	D a
Bremen, duchy	134	E b
Bremen, Hanse. cy.	99 ins.	B
Bremen, imp. cy.	78	F b

Bremerhaven	158	E b
Bremetennacum, see Ribchester		
Brenner, pass	63	F e
Brenneville	69	H f
Brennus, mt.	26	E b
Brent River	75	I h
Brenta River	63	F f
Brentford	75	I i
Brentwood	75	J h
Brenz	143	J h
Brenz River	143	J h
Brescello	64	B b
Brescia	90	J h
Brescia, bp.	95	E b
Breslau	72	D a
Breslau, bp.	95	F a
Breslau, Hanse. cy.	99 ins.	B
Bresse, dist.	126	D c
Brest, in France	69	A b
Brest, in Poland		
Brest Litovsk		
Breteuil, near Amiens	69	I f
Breteuil, in Normandy	76	D b
Brétigny	76	D b
Breton, Cape	108	K c
Bretones, Tierra de los	108	L c
Bretones, people		
Bretten	142	C b
Breuckelen (Brooklyn)	189 ins.	C
Briançon	84	G g
Briansk	139	D e
Briantica, reg.		
Briar Creek	195	A g
Bridewell Palace, in London	75	G g
Bridgenorth	65	E d
Bridgeport	189	B d
Bridges, Fort	210	C b
Bridgetown	213	F c
Bridgnorth	127	W n
Bridgnorth, parl. bor.	163	L e
Bridgwater	84	B d
Bridgwater, parl. bor.	163	K f
Bridlington, mon.	97	J d
Bridport, parl. bor.	163	L g
Brie, dist.	69	I f
Brieg	79	J c
Brieg, princ.	79	J c
Briel	117	C c
Briel, Hanse. cy.	99 ins.	B
Brienne	76	F b
Brienz	91	P l
Brienz, lake	91	P l
Brig	91	Q l
Brigach River	142	B d
Brigæcium	38	A d
Brigantes, people, in England		
Brigantes, people, in Ireland	38	A b
Brigantinus, lake	39	J j
Brigantio	26	A c
Brigantium (Bregenz), in Rætia	39	J j
Brigantium (Corunna), in Spain	38	A d
Brigetio	38	F c
Brighton	127	Y p
Brighton, parl. bor.	163	N g
Brignais	81	M h
Brignolles	126	E e
Brilessus, mt.	15	D a
Brill	117	C c
Brindisi	90	G d
Brindisi, abp.	95	F c
Brinta River	27	F b
Brionne	76	D b
Brioude	76	E d
Brioude, mon.	148	B b
Brisbane	172	E c
Bristol, in England		
Bristol, in Rhode Island	189 ins.	A
Bristol, castle		
Bristol, parl. bor.	163	L f
Bristol Bay	198 ins.	C
Bristol Channel	49	D f
Bristol Coalfield	162	D f
Britain, West Rom. dioc.	42	B c
Britain, Rom. prov.	34	D c

Britain I, West Rom. prov. . . . 42 B c (3
Britain II, West Rom. prov. . . . 42 B c (4)
Britain, about 410 and 600 . . . 51
Britain, Lower, Rom. prov. . . 38 B b (2)
Britain, Upper, Rom. prov. . . . 38 B b (1)
Britannia, Rom. prov., see Britain 34 D c
Britannia I, II, Rom. prov. . . 38 B b
British Central Africa, see
  Nyasaland . . . . 175 G f
British Columbia, prov. . . . 212 C c
British East Africa, col. . . . . 175 G c
British Guiana, col. . . . . . . 214 D b
British Honduras, col. . . . . . 213 D c
British India, emp. . . . . 170 I f
British Isles . . . . 2 C c
British Kaffraria, dist. . . . . . 175 M m
British New Guinea, col. . . . 172 D a
British Somaliland, col. . . . . 174 H d
British South Africa Company 175 F f
Brito . . . . 213 D c
Britons, people
Brittany, cty. . . . . 61 B b
Brittany, duchy . . . . 76 B c
Brittany, gouv. . . . . 146 A b
Brittany, march . . . . 54 D d
Brittany, prov. . . . . 148 E d
Brittany, reg. . . . . 52 B b
Brivas, see Brioude
Brixellum . . . .
Brixen . . . . 63 F e
Brixen, bp. . . . . 79 G e
Brixham . . . . 127 V p
Brixia (Brescia) . . . . 26 E b
Broach . . . . 137 B d
Broad River . . . . 193 D d
Broad Way, street in Rome . . 22 A
Brocavium (Brougham) . . . . .
Brockville . . . . 212 H d
Brod, Böhmisch . . . . 87 I c
Brod, Deutsch . . . . 87 I d
Brode, mon. . . . . 80 C e
Brody . . . . 139 C e
Brogne, mon. . . . . 94 C a
Broken Hill . . . . 172 D d
Bromberg . . . . 79 J b
Bromberg Canal . . . . . 135 I b (Br. C.)
Bromiscus . . . . 11 E b
Bromley . . . . 75 J i
Brömsebro . . . . 120 I e
Bromsgrove, parl. bor. . . . . .
Bromyard, parl. bor. . . . . . .
Bronzell . . . . 158 E c
Brookfield, in Mass. . . . . . . 189 B c
Brookfield, in Ohio . . . . . . 206 ins.
Brooklyn . . . . 189 ins. C
Broome . . . . 172 B b
Broos . . . . 159 L f
Brou . . . . 69 H f
Brouage . . . . 126 A d
Brouwershaven . . . . 117 B c
Brown, mt., in Coast Range . . 212 ins.
Brown, mt., in Rocky Mts. . . 186 H c
Brown, Fort . . . . 201 F d
Brown's Hole, dist. . . . . . . 210 D b
Brownsville, Pa. . . . . 192 B c
Brownsville, Texas . . . . . . 201 F d
Bruanium . . . . 10 C a
Bruce, mt. . . . . 172 A c
Bruchium, quarter in Alexandria 34 ins. C
Bruchsal . . . . 142 C b
Bruck, on the Leitha R. . . . . 159 I d
Bruck, on the Mur R. . . . . . 87 J e
Bructeri, people . . . . 39 I h
Bruges . . . . 117 B c
Bruges, Hanse. for. off. . . . . 99 ins. B
Brugg . . . . 91 Q k
Brügge (Bruges) . . . . 117 B c
Brugnato, bp. . . . . 95 D c
Bruinsburg . . . . 208 B c
Bruja Point . . . .
Brundisium or Brundusium
  (Brindisi) . . . . 31 G b
Brundulum . . . . 27 G b
Brunei . . . .

Bruni Island . . . . 172 D e
Brünig Pass . . . . 91 Q l
Brunkeberg, mt . . . . 88 H b
Brünn . . . . 63 I d
Brunnen . . . . 91 Q l
Brunswick, in Germany . . . . 62 F b
Brunswick, in Georgia . . . . . 199 I d
Brunswick, in Maine . . . . . 189 C b
Brunswick, duchy, 14 cent. . . 79 G b
Brunswick, duchy, 18 cent. . . . 134 F c
Brunswick, duchy, 19 cent. . . . . 158 F c
Brunswick, Hanse. cy. . . . . . 99 ins. B
Brunswick-Grubenhagen, duchy 79 G c
Brunswick-Kalenberg, duchy . 86 G b
Brunswick-Lüneburg, duchy . 79 G b
Brunswick-Wolfenbüttel, duchy 114 F b
Brusa . . . . 77 J d
Brussels . . . . 117 C d
Bruton, mon. . . . . 97 O j
Bruttia and Lucania, West Rom.
  prov. . . . . 42 F f (6)
Bruttium, reg. . . . . 31 F d
Brüx . . . . 63 G c
Brye . . . . 156 B a
Bryges, people . . . . 17 B a
Bryseæ . . . . 14 C c
Bubastis or Bubastus (Tel Basta) 1 B b
Buca . . . . 27 I e
Bucaramanga . . . . 214 B b
Buccaneers, head quarters of the
Bucellarian Theme . . . . . . 59 K e
Bucephala . . . . 19 L d
Bucephala, prom. . . . . 15 D b
Buch, captalat . . . . 69 C d
Buch, mon. . . . . 95 E a
Buchan, dist. . . . .
Buchau, ab. . . . . 143 I i
Buchau, imp. cy. . . . . 143 I i
Buchau, mon. . . . . 95 D b
Buchegg, castle . . . . 91 P k
Buchen . . . . 142 D a
Buchenberg . . . . 122 E d
Buchetium . . . . 10 B c
Buchhorn, imp. cy. . . . . . . 143 I j
Buckfastleigh, mon. . . . . . . 97 N k
Buckingham . . . .
Buckingham, cty. . . . . 127 Y o
Buckingham, parl. bor. . . . . 163 N f
Buckland, mon. . . . . 97 M k
Bucks, cty. . . . . 163 N f
Bucoleon Palace . . . . 93 G e
Buda (Ofen) . . . . 66 J d
Buda, univ. . . . . 100 I e
Budamer . . . . 159 K d
Budapest . . . . 166 I f
Budatin . . . . 159 J d
Budini, people. . . . . 35 K c
Budorus River . . . . 11 E d
Budshaja (Bougie) . . . . 66 G f
Budua, bp. . . . . 95 F c
Budweis . . . . 79 I d
Budziak . . . . 131 I d
Buea . . . . 175 D d
Buena Guia, Rio de, R. . . . . 190 C e
Buenaventura . . . . 214 B b
Buena Vista, battle . . . . . . 201 E e
Buenos Ayres . . . . 215 D f
Buenos Ayres, audiencia . . . . 215 ins.
Buenos Ayres, viceroyalty . . . 215 ins.
Buffalo . . . . 196 D b
Buford, Fort . . . . 210 E a
Bug River, in Podolia . . . . . 139 D b
Bug River, in Poland . . . . . 99 H c
Bugey, dist. . . . . 126 D d
Bühl . . . . 142 B c
Buitrago, pass . . . . 82 B a
Bukarest . . . . 93 C b
Bukowina, dist. . . . . 139 C f
Bülach . . . . 91 Q k
Bulawayo . . . . 175 F g
Buleuterium . . . .
Bulgar . . . . 77 N b
Bulgaria, princ., about 1000 . . 59 I e
Bulgaria, km., 1203 . . . . . . 73 E b

Bulgaria, km., 1265 . . . . . . 89 B b
Bulgaria, km., 14 cent. . . . . 89 H f
Bulgaria, km., 1909 . . . . . . 164 C b
Bulgaria, prov., 15 cent. . . . 93 B b
Bulgaria, reg., 11 cent. . . . . 67 K e
Bulgarians, people, about 900 . 57 H e
Bulgarians, people, about 1190 71 K e
Bulgarians, people, 19 cent. . .
Bulgarians, Kama-, people . . . 71 P b
Bulis . . . . 11 D d
Bull, Fort . . . . 192 D b
Bulla . . . . 38 D e
Bulle . . . . 91 P l
Bull Run, battle . . . . 208 ins.
Bulotus River . . . . 31 F d
Bulun . . . . 171 N a
Bumodus River . . . . 20 J d
Bunarbashi . . . .
Bunarbashi Brook, canal . . . .
Bunbury . . . . 172 A d
Bundelcund, reg. . . . . 137 C d
Bundelkhand, reg. . . . . 137 C d
Bunker Hill, battle . . . . . . 195 ins. A
Bunzelwitz . . . . 135 I c
Bunzlau, in Bohemia . . . . . 63 H c
Bunzlau, in Silesia . . . . . . 155 H c
Buonconvento . . . . 72 C c
Buporthmus, prom. . . . . . . 15 D b
Buprasion . . . . 14 B a
Bura . . . . 14 C a
Büraburg . . . . 55 Q i
Buraicus River . . . . 14 C a
Burchana . . . . 38 D b
Burd . . . . 192 B c
Burdegala, Burdigala (Bordeaux) 38 B d
Büren, castle . . . . 62 E d
Burford . . . . 60 F e
Burford, parl. bor. . . . .
Burgau . . . . 143 J i
Burgau, margr. . . . . 79 G d
Burghas . . . .
Bürglen . . . . 91 Q l
Burgos . . . . 83 E a
Burgos, abp. . . . . 94 B c
Burgoyne, route of . . . . . . 195 E a
Burgrieden . . . . 143 I i
Burgsdorf . . . . 91 P k
Burgundarholm (Bornholm), isl. 38 E a
Burgundians, Kingdom of the . 50 D c
Burgundians, people . . . . . . 45 Hb,Ec
Burgundy, cty. . . . . 61 F c
Burgundy, duchy . . . . 58 E c
Burgundy, gouv. . . . . 146 B b
Burgundy, km. . . . . 58 F de
Burgundy, prov. . . . . 148 E e
Burgundy, Cisjurane (Arles) . . 56 CD cd
Burgundy, Free County of, 14 cent. 78 D e
Burgundy, Free County of, 17 cent. 126 D e
Burgundy, Lower, dist. . . . . 52 C f
Burgundy, Transjurane or Upper,
  km. . . . . 56 D c
Burgundy, Upper, dist.. . . . . 62 D e
Buri, people . . . . 34 H d
Burkersdorf . . . . 135 I c
Burlington, in Iowa . . . . . . 211 G b
Burlington, in New Jersey . . 192 D c
Burlington, in Vermont . . . . 211 K b
Burlyuk . . . . 164 J f
Burma, reg. . . . .
Burma, Lower, prov. . . . . . . 171 K g
Burma, Upper, prov. . . . . . 171 K f
Burnum . . . . 38 F c
Burriana . . . . 82 B b
Burrough, route of . . . . . . 109 W a
Bursfelde, mon. . . . . 95 D a
Burshena see Purchena . . . . 83 K b
Burton-on-Trent, mon. . . . . 97 P i
Bury, parl. bor. . . . . 163 L d
Bury Saint Edmunds.
Bury Saint Edmunds, mon.. . . .
Bury St. Edmunds, parl. bor. . 163 O e
Burzenland, dist. . . . . 80 I i
Busaco . . . . 130 B e
Busento River . . . . 50 G e

Bushire . . . . 170 G f
Bushwick . . . . 189 ins. C (Bush.)
Bushy Run, battle . . . . 194 K f
Busiris . . . . 1 B b
Busk . . . . 159 K c
Busselton . . . . 172 A d
Bussière, La, mon. . . . . . . 94 C b
Busuluk . . . . 139 H e
Bute, cty. . . . .
Bute, Fort . . . . 195 ins. B
Buthrotum (Butrinto) . . . . 10 B c
Butler, route of . . . . . . 195 C b
Butlers, The, fam. . . . . . .
Butley, mon. . . . . 97 S i
Buto . . . . 1 B b
Butonti . . . .
Bütow . . . . 115 I a
Butrinto . . . . 93 A c
Butte . . . . 210 C a
Buxar . . . . 137 D c
Buxentum . . . . 30 E b
Buxentum, prom. . . . . . . 30 E c
Buxentus River . . . . . . 30 E c
Buxtehude . . . . 62 E b
Buxtehude, Hanse. cy. . . . . 99 ins. B
Buzzards Bay . . . . 189 C d
Byblus . . . . 4 F c*
Byland, mon. . . . . 97 P g
Byllis . . . . 31 I b
Byrsa, citadel . . . . 34 ins. A (4)
Bytown (Ottawa) . . . . . . 212 H d
Byzacium, reg. . . . . . . 38 D e
Byzacium, West Rom. prov. . . 42 D g (1)
Byzantine Empire, about 814 54-55 F f
Byzantine Empire, about 1000 . 59 H-L f
Byzantine Empire, 12 cent. . . 71 K e
Byzantine Empire, in 1265 . . . 89
Byzantine Empire, in 1355 . . . 89
Byzantine Empire, in 1451 . . 93 C b
Byzantium (Constantinople) . .

Caacupe . . . . 215 D e
Cabalia, reg. . . . . 20 C d
Cabasa . . . . 43 I g
Cabellio or Cabellione, see Ca-
  vaillon
Cabes . . . .
Cabeza de Vaca, route of . . . 190 D f
Cabillonum or Cabilonum (Cha-
  lon) . . . . 39 H j
Cabira . . . . 20 G b
Cabo das Corrientes, cape . . . 109 U j
Cabot, John, route of . . . 108 O b, Q j
Cabot, Sebastian, route of . . 108 L k
Cabra . . . . 82 B b
Cabral, route of . . . . . . 108 O h, Q j
Cabrillo, route of . . . . . . 107 E d
Cabul (Kabul), in Afghanistan 53 I c
Cabul, in Palestine . . . . 6 C c
Cabura (Kabul in Afghanistan) 19 K d
Caburrum . . . . 26 B c
Cáceres . . . . 82 A b
Cache Valley, dist. . . . . . 210 C b
Cacyparis River . . . . . . 30 E e
Caddos, tribe . . . . 188 G d
Cadiz . . . . 82 A b
Cadiz, bp. . . . . 94 A d
Cadore . . . . 90 D a
Cadouin, mon. . . . . 94 C c
Cadurci or Cadurcis, see Ca-
  hors
Cadurci, people . . . . 38 C d
Cadusii (Cadusians), people . . 19 G c
Cæcina River . . . . 26 E d
Cæcinus River . . . . 30 E e
Cæcuban Territory . . . . . 30 C a
Cælemontane Gate . . . . . 23 D
Cælia, in Apulia . . . . . . 31 F a
Cælia, in Calabria . . . . . 31 G b
Cælian Mount . . . . 22 A
Cælian, quarter . . . . . . 96 A
Cælimontium, Aug. Reg. of
  Rome . . . . 22 A
Caen . . . . 69 C b

Caen, gen. . . . . 147 D b
Caen, mon. . . . . 94 B b
Caen, univ. . . . . 100 E e
Cænæ . . . . 20 J e
Cænepolis . . . . 14 C c
Cænia, mt. . . . . 26 A c
Cænys, prom. . . . . 31 E d
Cære . . . . 27 G e
Cærleon-upon-Usk . . . . . 42 B c
Cærwent . . . .
Cæsar, Statue of . . . . . . 24 B (12)
Cæsar, Gardens of . . . . . 22 A
Cæsaraugusta (Saragossa) . . . . 38 B d
Cæsarea, in Cappadocia
  (Kaisarieh) . . . . 20 F c
Cæsarea, in Mauretania . . . 38 C e
Cæsarea, in Samaria . . . . 6 B c
Cæsarea Philippi . . . . . 6 D b
Cæsarea, isl. (Jersey) . . . . 38 B c
Cæsarobriga (Talavera de la
  Reina) . . . . 38 B d
Cæsarodunum (Tours) . . . . 38 C c
Cæsaromagus, see Beauvais
Cæsar's Forum . . . . . . 24 B
Cæsena . . . . 27 G c
Cagli, bp. . . . . 95 E c (C.)
Cagliari . . . . 42 D f
Cagliari, abp. . . . . 95 D d
Caguas . . . . 199 ins. G
Cahokia . . . . 191 H d
Cahors . . . . 91 D d
Cahors, bp. . . . . 94 C c
Cahors, univ. . . . . 100 F f
Cahorsin, cty. . . . . 76 D d
Caiatia . . . . 30 D a
Caicos Islands . . . . 213 E b
Caicus River . . . .
Caieta (Gaëta) . . . . . . 30 C a
Caieta, bay . . . . 30 C a
Cailac . . . .
Cailloux, farm . . . .
Caimitillo River . . . .
Caino or Cainone, see Chinon
Cairns . . . . 172 D b
Cairo, in Egypt . . . . . . 67 M h
Cairo, in Illinois . . . . . . 199 H c
Cairo, in Italy . . . . . . 130 Q j
Cairo, calif. . . . .
Caithness, bp. . . . . 97 I a
Caithness, cty. . . . .
Caithness, dist. . . . .
Caius Cestius, Tomb of . . . 22 A
Cajamarca . . . . 111 B c
Cajon Pass . . . . 210 B d
Calabar . . . . 175 D d
Calabozo . . . . 214 C b
Calabria, dist., in Rom. times . 31 G b
Calabria, dist., 15 cent. . . . 90 F e
Calabria, duchy, 11 cent. . . 66 J f
Calabria, theme, 10 cent. . . 59 H f
Caladunum, see Châlons
Calaf . . . . 82 C a
Calagurris (Calahorra) . . . 38 B d
Calahorra . . . . 82 B a
Calahorra, bp. . . . . . . 94 B c
Calais, in France . . . . . 76 C a
Calais, in Maine . . . . . . 211 L a
Calama, in Algeria . . . . 42 D f
Calama, in Chile . . . . . . 215 C e
Calamar . . . . 214 B a
Calamine, dist. . . . . . . 10 B c
Calanicum . . . . 26 C c
Calatafimi . . . . 161 I i
Calatayud . . . . 82 B a
Calatha . . . . 38 D e
Calatia . . . . 30 D a
Calatrava . . . . 82 B b
Calatrava, mon. . . . . . . 94 B d
Calauria, isl. . . . . 15 D b
Calaurus, mt. . . . . 11 E b
Calcaria, see Tadcaster
Calchedon . . . .
Calchu . . . . 5 D b*
Calcutta . . . . 137 E d

Caldera . . . . 215 B e
Calderon . . . . 213 ins.
Caldiero . . . . 150 F d
Cale . . . . 191 I f
Cale, Portus (Oporto) . . . . . 38 A d
Caleacte . . . . 30 D e
Cale acte, Cape . . . . 15 E a
Caledonia (Scotland) . . . . . 38 B a
Caledonia, New, isl. . . . . . 172 F c
Caledonii, people . . . . . . 38 B a
Cales (Calvi), in Campania . . . 30 D a
Cales, in Umbria . . . . . . 27 G d
Caletes, people . . . .
Calgary . . . . 212 D c
Calhoun, Fort . . . . 210 F b
Cali . . . . 111 B a
Calicut . . . . 137 C f
Califate, emp. . . . .
Califate, reg. . . . . 71 O g
California, Gulf of . . . . . 187 H f
California, state . . . . . 202 A h
California, Lower, pen. . . . 187 H e-f
California, Lower, prov. . 107—108 F d e
California, Upper, prov. . . . 190 A B C
California Cut-off, route . . . 210 D c
California Trail . . . . . . 210 B b
California Valley . . . . . . 187 G e
Caligula, Palace of . . . . . 24 B
Calindœa . . . .
Call, parl. bor. . . . . . . 163 J g
Callao . . . . 214 B d
Callas River . . . . 11 E c
Callatis . . . . 39 N l
Calleva (Silchester) . . . . .
Callidromus, mt. . . . . . 11 D e
Callipolis, in Calabria . . . . 31 G b
Callipolis, in Thrace . . . . 39 N l
Callirrhoe . . . . 23 D
Callium . . . . 10 D d
Calliupolis . . . .
Callone . . . . 18 G d
Calmar . . . . 88 G c
Calmar, Hanse. for. cy. . . . 98 G b
Calne, parl. bor. . . . . . 163 L f
Calor River . . . . 30 D a
Calpe, in Bithynia . . . . . 20 D b
Calpe, in Spain . . . . . 12 B c
Calpulalpan . . . .
Caltanisetta . . . . 90 D f
Caluso . . . . 130 P i
Calvados, dept. . . . . . . 148 D e
Calverton . . . . 192 C d
Calvert Town . . . . 192 C d
Calvi, bp. . . . . 95 ins.
Calw . . . . 143 G h
Calw, cty. . . . . 143 G h
Calycadnus River . . . . . 20 E d
Calydon . . . . 10 C d
Calydon, Gulf of . . . . . 14 B a
Calymna, isl. . . . . 17 E c
Calynda . . . . 20 C d
Cam, Diogo, route of . . . . 108 R h
Camaldoli . . . . 90 L j
Camaldoli, mon. . . . . . . 95 E c
Camaracus, see Cambray
Camargo, in Bolivia . . . . 214 C e
Camargo, in Mexico . . . . 201 F d
Camarina . . . . 30 D e
Camarones River . . . . . 214 B d
Cambalec (Peking) . . . . .
Cambay . . . . 137 B d
Cambay, Gulf of . . . . . 137 B d
Cambete . . . . 39 I j
Cambodia, reg. . . . .
Cambodunum, in Britain . . . 51 P h
Cambodunum, in Rætia . . . 39 K j
Camboricum (Cambridge) . . . .
Cambray . . . .
Cambray, bp. . . . . 117 B d
Cambrésis, cty. . . . . . . 117 B d
Cambrian Mountains . . . . 49 E e
Cambridge, in England . . . .
Cambridge, in Mass. . . . . 189 ins. B
Cambridge, castle . . . . . 65 G d

Cambridge, cty.	127	Z n
Cambridge, mon.	97	R i
Cambridge, parl. bor.	163	O e
Cambridge, parl. dist.	163	O e
Cambridge, shire		
Cambridge, univ.	100	F d
Cambridge, univ., parl. bor.	163	O e
Cambunian Mountains	10	C c
Cambuskenneth	84	B a
Camden, in N. S. Wales		
Camden, in New Jersey	192	D d
Camden, in S. Carolina	195	A f
Camelford, parl. bor.	163	J g
Cameria	35 ins.	B
Camerino	90	D c
Camerino, bp.	95	E c
Camerino, march	64	B b
Camerinum	27	H d
Camerons, fam.	97	H c
Cameroons, see Kamerun		
Cameta	214	E c
Camexa		
Camillomagus	26	D b
Camirus	13	E c
Camisards, people	129	D d
Campagna, dist.	64 ins.	
Campanha	214	E e
Campania, dist.	30	D b
Campania, Rom. prov.	42	E e(1)
Campbell, route of	195	D f
Campbells, fam.	97	H c
Camp du Bois	199	H c
Campeche	213	C c
Campeche, state	213	C c
Campeche Bay	187	J f
Camperdown	153	E b
Camp Floyd	210	C b
Campidona, see Kempten		
Campi Raudii or Raudian Plain, dist.	26	C b
Campobasso	90	E d
Campos	214	E e
Campo Vitale	62	F f
Campsey Ash, mon.	97	S i
Campus Martius, loc. in Rome	22	A
Campus Sceleratus, loc. in Rome	23	B
Campylus River	10	C c
Camulodunum (Colchester)		
Camunni, people	26	E b
Camuy	199 ins.	G
Cana	6	C c
Cana River	7	B d
Canaan	207	L b
Canaan, reg.	4	F c
Canaanites, people	7 ins.	D
Canada, col.	194	Cb,Ea
Canada, Dominion of	212	H c
Canadian Pacific Railway	212	D c
Canadian River	190	F d
Canal du Midi	130	D e
Canal Zone, dist.		
Cananea, bay of	108	M j
Caña Quebrada, R.		
Canary Islands	174	B b
Canastræum, prom.	11	E c
Canatha	6	F c
Canaveral, Cape	191	I f
Canbury	55	R i
Cancellaria	96	A
Candahar	137	A b
Candavia	10	B a
Candavian Mountains	10	B a
Candelaria	215	C e
Canea	77	I e
Cangas de Onis	82	A a
Canigou, mon.	94	C c
Cannæ	31	F a
Cannanore	137	C f
Canne	64	C b
Canninefates, people	39	H g
Cannock Chase	49	E e
Cannon Gate	93	G e
Cannstadt	143	H h
Canonicut Island	189	C d
Canopic Gate	34 ins.	C
Canopus	1	B b
Canossa	64	B b
Canso	194	G a
Canso, strait of	212	J d
Cantabri, people	38	B d
Cantabria, reg.	82	B a
Cantabrian Mountains	2	D d
Cantal, dept.	148	E e
Canterbury, in Conn.	207	L b
Canterbury, in England		
Canterbury, abp.	97	N i
Canterbury, dist. in N. Zealand	172	G e
Canterbury, Hanse. for. cy.	98 ins.	A
Canterbury, parl. bor.	163	P f
Canterbury Bight	172	G e
Cantharus Port	16	D c
Cantii, people	51	Q i
Cantillana	82	A b
Canton	171	M f
Cantuaria, see Canterbury		
Canusium	31	F a
Cany	76	D b
Caononabo, chieftain	105	F c
Caorle, bp.	95	E b
Capara	38	A d
Capdenac	126	C d
Cape Ann	189	C c
Cape Coast Castle	175	C d
Cape Cod Bay	189	C d
Cape Colony, col.	175	F h
Cape Fear River	193	E d
Cape Haitien	213	E c
Capena	27	G e
Capena Gate, in Rome	23	B
Capena Gate, Aug. Reg., Rome	22	A
Cape of Good Hope, cape	175	F h
Cape of Good Hope, col.	175	F h
Cape of Storms	109	S k
Cape Porpoise	189	C c
Capernaum	6	D c
Cape Town	175	E h
Cape Verd	174	B c
Cape Verd Islands	174	A c
Cape York Peninsula	172	D b
Caphereus, prom.	15	E a
Caphyæ	14	C b
Capitanata, dist.	90	E d
Capitolias	6	D c
Capitoline, quarter	96	A
Capitoline Mount	24	A
Capo d'Istria		
Capo d'Istria, bp.	95	E b
Cappadocia, dist.	20	F c
Cappadocia, imp. prov.	35	L f
Cappadocia, prov.	18	D c
Cappadocia, reg.	8	B b
Cappadocia, satr.	8	H d
Cappadocia, theme	59	K f
Cappadocia I, East Rom. prov.	43	I f(6)
Cappadocia II, East Rom. prov.	43	I f(7)
Capraria, isl., near Corsica	26	D e
Capraria, isl., Balearic Is.	38	C e
Caprasia	31	F c
Capreæ (Capri), isl.	30	D b
Caprera, isl.	161	G g
Capri, bp.	95 ins.	
Capri, isl.	90	E d
Caprus	11	E b
Capsa	34	F g
Capua (ancient)	30	D a
Capua (modern)	90	E d
Capua, abp.	95	E c
Capua, princ.	64	B b
Capucines, The, ch.		
Caput Africæ	22	A
Caputvada	52	D c
Caqueta River	111	D c
Carabaros	105	D e
Carabobo, battle	214	C b
Caracalla, Baths of	22	A
Caracarum or Karakorum		
Caracas	214	C a
Caracas, cap. gen. and pres.	215 ins.	
Caraceni, people	27	I f
Caracuel	82	B b
Caradeña, mon.	94	B c
Caralis (Cagliari)	12	E c
Caramagna, mon.	95	D e
Caramoran River		
Carana	20	I c
Caranchuas, tribe	188	G e
Caraques, Bahia de, bay	111	A b
Caravaggio	90	B b
Caravellas	214	F d
Carbonera	82	B b
Carcaso, Carcasona or Carcasso (Carcassonne)	38	C d
Carcassonne	76	E e
Carcassonne, bp.	94	C c
Carchemish	4	C d
Carcinus River	31	F c
Cardamyle	14	C c
Cárdenas	213	D b
Cárdenas, route of	190	C d
Cardenas River		
Cardia		
Cardiff	65	E e
Cardiff, parl. bor.	163	K f
Cardigan, castle	74	C e
Cardigan, cty.	127	U n
Cardigan, parl. bor.	163	J e
Cardigan, parl. dist.	163	J e
Cardigan Bay		
Cardona	130	D e
Careiæ	35 ins.	B
Carentan	76	C b
Carentonus River, see Charente River		
Careta	105	E e
Carey, lake	172	B c
Caria, dist.	20	C d
Caria, East Rom. prov.	43	H f(3)
Caria, reg.	5	B b
Caria, satr.	18	N h
Cariæ	14	C b
Cariari	105	D d
Caribbean Sea	187	L k
Carical		
Carinæ	22	A
Carinthia, duchy, about 1000	63	H e
Carinthia, duchy, 14 cent.	79	I e
Carinthia, march	63	H e
Carinthia, reg.	54	G d
Carioli	35 ins.	B
Carisbrooke		
Carisbrooke, mon.	100	A b
Carisbrooke Castle	127	X p
Carisiacus, see Kiersy		
Carlat	76	E d
Carlat, viscty.	76	E d
Carlingford		
Carlisle, in England		
Carlisle, in Pa.	188	K b
Carlisle, bp.	97	O g
Carlisle, parl. bor.	163	L c
Carlos, Bahia de, bay	191	I f
Carlow		
Carlow, cty.	127	K i
Carlowitz	159	J f
Carlsbad	79	H c
Carlskrona	131	G b
Carlsruhe	142	B c
Carlstein, castle	79	H c
Carmagnola	130	P j
Carmalas River	20	F d
Carmana (Kirman)	19	I d
Carmania (Kirman), prov.	19	I e
Carmania, satr.	18	Q i
Carmanians, people	8	J e
Carmarthen, castle		
Carmarthen, cty.	127	U o
Carmarthen, mon.	97	M j
Carmarthen, parl. bor.	163	J f
Carmarthen, parl. dist.	163	J f
Carmel	7	C f
Carmel, mt.	6	C c
Carmelites, mon. in London	75	G g
Carmelites, The, mon. in Paris	149	B

Carmen	213	C c	
Carmen de Patagonés	215	C g	
Carmenta Gate	24	A	
Carmona, castle	82	A b	
Carnarvon, castle			
Carnarvon, cty.	127	U n	
Carnarvon, parl. bor.	163	J d	
Carnarvon, parl. dist.	163	J e	
Carnatic, reg.	112	A b	
Carni, people	27	H a	
Carnic Alps, mts.	27	G a	
Carnicum Julium	27	G a	
Carniola, duchy	79	I f	
Carniola, march	63	H f	
Carniola, reg.	56	E c	
Carnsore Point	127	K i	
Carnuntum	38	F c	
Carnus, isl.	10	B d	
Carnotes or Carnutes, see Chartres			
Carnutes, people	38	C c	
Carolina, col.	193	C f-E e	
Carolina, North, col.	193	E d	
Carolina, North, state	196	C c	
Carolina, South, col.	193	D d	
Carolina, South, state	196	C d	
Carolina Proprietors, Grants to the	190	ins.	
Caroline, Fort	191	I e	
Caroline Island	180	M h	
Caroline Islands	179	F g	
Caroline River	214	C b	
Carolingian Empire	54		
Carpathian Mountains	2	G d	
Carpathian Sea	17	E d	
Carpathos, isl.	4	C b	
Carpentaria, Gulf of	172	C b	
Carpentoracte, see Carpentras			
Carpentras, bp.	95	D c	
Carpetani, people	38	B d	
Carpi	131	F e	
Carpi, people	38	F i	
Carpis	46	I f	
Carrara, near Pisa	90	L i	
Carrara, near Venice	90	J h	
Carrara, dist.	79	G f	
Carrea Potentia	26	B c	
Carrhæ	20	H d	
Carrick, dist.			
Carrickfergus			
Carrión de los Condes	83	K g	
Carsioli	27	H e	
Carson	210	B c	
Carson City	206	A c	
Carsulæ	27	G e	
Cartagena, in Colombia	214	B a	
Cartagena, in Spain	82	B b	
Cártago, in Colombia	214	B b	
Cártago, in Costa Rica	213	D d	
Carteia	38	A e	
Cartenna	38	C e	
Carteret, Cape	193	ins. C	
Carthæa	15	E b	
Carthage (ancient)	38	E e	
Carthage, in Missouri	207	G c	
Carthage, New (Cartagena)	38	B e	
Carthage, plan of	34	ins. A	
Carthaginiensis, West Rom. prov.	42	B f(5)	
Carthago	12	E c	
Carthusian Priory of the Salutation	75	G g	
Carthusians, The, mon. in Paris	149	B	
Cartier, routes of	108	M b, O c	
Caruanca, mt.	27	I a	
Carus River, see Cher River			
Carystus, in Eubœa	15	E a	
Carystus, in Laconia	14	C b	
Casablanca	174	C a	
Casale	90	I h	
Cascadas, Las			
Cascade Mountains	186	G c	
Casco, in Maine	189	C c	
Casco, in Mexico	190	E f	
Casco Bay	189	C c	
Caserta	90	E d	
Caserta, bp.	95	ins.	
Cashel			
Cashel, abp.	97	C d	
Cashmere or Kashmir, reg.			
Casilinum	30	D a	
Casimir, Fort	192	ins.	
Casinum	30	C a	
Casmenæ	30	D e	
Caspe	83	L g	
Caspian Depression, plain	3	I d	
Caspian Gates, pass	19	H c	
Caspian Sea	3	I d	
Caspians, people	8	I d	
Cassander, Kingdom of	18		
Cassandrea	11	E b	
Cassano	134	E f	
Cassano, bp.	95	F d	
Cassel, in Flanders	117	A d	
Cassel, in Hesse	62	E c	
Cassian Way, road	27	F e	
Cassii, Forum	27	G e	
Cassim Pasha, quarter			
Cassinelle	130	Q j	
Cassiope	10	A c	
Cassiquiare River	214	C b	
Cassiterides Islands	34	C c	
Cassope	10	B c	
Cassopia, reg.	10	B c	
Casteldelfino	130	O j	
Castelfidardo	161	I f	
Casteljaloux	126	B d	
Castell	122	F d	
Castellammare	161	J g	
Castellaneta	90	F d	
Castello Branco	94	A d	
Castellón de la Plana	83	E a	
Castellum (Kastel)	39	J h	
Castellum Felicitatis, see Città di Castello			
Castellum Firmanum	27	H d	
Castellum Flevum	39	H g	
Castelnaudary	69	D e	
Castelnuovo	125	G d	
Castelsagrat	126	B d	
Castets	126	A d	
Casthanæa	11	D c	
Castiglione, in Calabria	90	F e	
Castiglione, near Florence	90	L j	
Castiglione, near Mantua	150	F d	
Castiglione dalla Pescaja	90	L j	
Castile, cty.	82	B a	
Castile, km., 11 cent.	83	E c	
Castile, km., 12 cent.	82	H e	
Castile, km., 15 cent.	83	K g	
Castilla del Oro, reg.	105	D e	
Castillon	76	C d	
Castine	189	D b	
Castle Acre, mon.	97	R i	
Castle Jacob	68	ins. A	
Castle of the Seven Towers	93	E c	
Castle Rising, parl. bor.	163	O e	
Castor, near Norwich	51	Q h	
Castor, Temple of			
Castor and Pollux, Temple of			
Castores, Ad	26	E b	
Castoria	59	I e	
Castra Batava (Passau)	38	E c	
Castra Hannibalis	31	F d	
Castra Sarræ	39	H i	
Castra Vetera	39	I h	
Castres	76	E e	
Castres, bp.	94	C c (Cast.)	
Castres, cty.	84	E h	
Castres, seign.	76	E e	
Castrimœnium	35	ins. B	
Castriota, Dominion of	93	A b	
Castro, bp.	95	E c	
Castrogiovanni	64	C c	
Castrovillari	90	F e	
Castrum Bobium (Bobbio)	26	D c	
Castrum Gordonis, see Sancerre			
Castrum Minervæ	31	H b	
Castrum Nantonis, see Château-Landon			
Castrum novum, in Etruria	27	F e	
Castrum novum, in Picenum	27	I e	
Castrum Peregrinorum	68	ins. A	
Castrum Truentinum	27	H e	
Castulo	38	B e	
Castulo, bp.	42	B f	
Castulonensis, Saltus, mts.	38	B e	
Casuentus (Basento) River	31	F b	
Casus, isl.	17	B d	
Caswell, Fort	208	E c	
Catacombs of Saint Callistus	96	A	
Cataláo	214	E d	
Catalauni or Catalaunis, see Châlons			
Catalaunian Fields	48	E c	
Catalonia, princ.	83	L g	
Catalonia, reg.	82	I e	
Catamarca	215	C e	
Catana	30	E e	
Catania	90	E f	
Catania, bp.	95	F d	
Catania, univ.	100	I g	
Catanzaro	90	F e	
Catanzaro, bp.	95	F d	
Cataractonium (Catterick)	51	P g	
Catawba River	195	A f	
Catawbas, tribe	188	J d	
Cateau-Cambrésis	117	B d	
Cathay (China), cty.	92	K d	
Catholic Hennersdorf	135	H c	
Catillus, mt.	35	ins. B	
Cat Island	105	E b	
Catoche, Cape	105	C b	
Catskill	192	E b	
Catskill Mountains	192	D b	
Cattaraugus, Ind. Res.	188	K b	
Cattaro	90	G c	
Cattaro, abp.	95	F c	
Caturiges	39	H i	
Caturiges, people	26	A c	
Catuvellauni, people			
Caub	154	D c	
Cauca	38	B d	
Cauca River	214	B b	
Caucasians, people	57	K e	
Caucasus Mountains	3	I d	
Cauci, people	38	A b	
Caudebec	126	B b	
Caudine Forks, passes, near Caudium			
Caudini, people	30	D a	
Caudium	30	D a	
Caughnawaga	212	H d	
Caulonia	31	F d	
Caunus	20	C d	
Caura River	214	C b	
Causannæ	51	P h	
Caux, dist.	69	H f	
Caux, Chef de, cape	81	L h	
Cava, La, mon.	95	ins.	
Cavaillon	76	F e	
Cavaillon, bp.	95	D c	
Cavan, cty.	127	J g	
Cavite	199	ins. H	
Cavore, mon.	95	D c	
Cavour	130	P j	
Cawnpur, Cawnpore	137	D c	
Caxamarca	111	B c	
Caxias	214	E c	
Cayambe	214	B b	
Cayenne	214	D b	
Cayay	199	ins. G	
Cayos, Los, isl.	105	E b	
Cayphas	68	ins. A	
Cayster River	13	E b	
Caystrupedium			
Cayuga Lake	192	C b	
Cayugas, tribe	188	K b	
Cazalla de la Sierra	82	A b	
Cazlona	46	F f	
Cé, Pont de	130	C g	
Ceará	214	F c	
Ceará, state	214	F c	
Ceba	26	C c	

ebenna Mountains 38   C d
ebrene . . . .
ebu 112   F b
ebu, isl. . . . . 110 D D f
ecryphalæ, isl. . . .
edar Creek, battle 208   E b
edar Keys 213   D b
edar Mountain, battle . . . 208   E b
edar River 211   G b
edron, Vale of . . . . 6 ins. A*
efalù 90   E e
efalù, bp. 95   E d
eiriadæ, deme 23   D
eladussæ, isl. 27   J d
elebes, isl. . . . .
elebes Sea 171   N h
eleia 27   J a
elenderis 15   D b
eletrum 10   C b
eligny 91   O l
ellæ 10   C b
ellu 79   G b
eltiberians, people 32   A c
eltic Gaul . . . . 38 ins.
eltici, people 38   A e
elts, people 5   A a *
emenelum 26   B d
empoalla 106   D a
enabum (Orléans) 38   C c
enæum, prom. 11   D d
enchreæ, near Argos 14   C b
enchreæ, near Corinth . . . 15   D b
eneda, bp. 95   E b
eneda 27   G b
enis, Mont, pass 26   A b
enis, people 188   G d
enomani or Cenomanis see
    Le Mans
enomani, people 26   E b
enterville . . . . 208 ins.
entral Africa, British, see Nyasaland 175 G f
entral America, reg. 213   D c
entral America, Cordillera of 213   D c
entral Asia, reg. . . . . . 170 G I d
entral Californians, tribes . . 188   B c
entral German Commercial
    Union 160   D c
entripæ 30   D e
entula or Centulum (Saint Ri-
    quier), mon. 94   C a
entumcellæ (Civitavecchia) . . 27   F e
entum Gradus 24   A
enturinum 26   D e
eos (Cea), isl. 15   E b
ephale 16   B b
ephalenia, theme 59   H f
ephallenia (Cephalonia), isl. . 10   B d
ephalonia, cty. 73   D c
ephalonia, isl. 89   H g
ephalonia, palat. 89   A c
ephalœdium 30   D d
ephisia 16   B a
ephisus River, in Attica . . 16   B a
ephisus River, in Bœotia . . 11   D d
eprano 72   C c
eramic Gulf 17   F c
eramicus, Inner, quarter . . 23   D
eramicus, Outer, quarter . . 23   D
eramon - agora 20   C c
erasus 20   H b
eraunii Mountains . . . . .
erbalus River 30   E a
ercamp, mon. 94   B a
ertetius, mt. 10   C c
ercina, isl. 38   E f
ercinitis, lake 11   E b
erdagne, reg. 83   F c
erdylium 11   E b
ereatæ 30   C a
eredigion, reg. . . . .
Ceres, Temple of 24   B
Ceresius (Lugano) lake 26   C a
Ceretani, people 38   C d
Cereus River 11   E d

Cerignola 90   E d
Cerigo, isl. 89   B c
Cerillæ 30   E c
Cerinthus 11   E d
Cérisy, mon. 94   B b
Cerlier, castle 91   P k
Cermalus, quarter . . . .
Cerne, Ilha do, isl. 109   W j
Cerne, mon. 97   O k
Cerro Columbia, hill . . . . .
Cerro Comboy, hill . . . .
Cerro Culebra, hill . . . . . .
Cerro de Cabras, hill . . . . .
Cerro de los Harmigueros, hill
Cerro de Pasco 214   B d
Cerro de San Juan, hill . . . . .
Cerro Gordo, battle 201   H g
Cerro Mitra, hill . . . .
Certosa, mon. 95   D b
Ceruglio 90   L j
Cervia 90   M i
Cervia, bp. 95   E c
Cerynia 14   C a
Cesena 90   D b
Cesena, bp. 95   E c
Cessetani, people 38   C d
Cestian Bridge 22   A
Cestrine, reg. 10   B c
Cestrus River 20   D d
Cettigne 166   I g
Ceuta . . . .
Ceutrones, people 26   A b
Ceva 90   I h
Ceylon, isl. 137   D g
Chablais, dist. 91   O l
Chaboras River 20   I e
Chacabuco, battle 215   B f
Chachapoyas 111   B c
Chacon, Cape . . . . 212 ins.
Chad, lake 174   E c
Chads Ford, battle 195   C c
Chæronea 11   D d
Chagatai, khan. . . . .
Chagos Islands 182   II h
Chagres . . . .
Chagres River . . . .
Chaibasa, reg. 137   E d
Chaillot 149   B
Chaise - Dieu, La, mon. . . . 94   C b
Chalæum 11   D d
Chalastra 11   D b
Chalcedon . . . .
Chalcidice, reg. 11   E b
Chalcis, in Ætolia 10   C d
Chalcis, in Epirus 10   C c
Chalcis, in Eubœa 11   E d
Chalcis, in Syria 6   D a
Chalco 106   B a
Chalco, lake 106   B a
Chaldæi, people 18   G d
Chaldea, reg. 5   D b
Chaldean Empire 8
Chaldeans, people . . . . . .
Chaldia, theme 59   L e
Chaldiran . . . .
Chales, mon. 94   C b
Chaleurs, Bay of 194   G a
Chalgrove 127   X o
Chalia 11   E d
Chalish (Karashar) . . . . . .
Chalivoy, mon. 94   C b
Chaloché, mon. 94   B b
Chalon 61   F c
Chalon, cty. 69   J f
Chalon, sur - Saône, bp. . . . 94   C b
Châlons 61   F b
Châlons, cty. 61   F b
Châlons, duchy 76   F b
Châlons, gen. 147   E b
Châlons - sur - Marne, bp. . . 94   C b
Chalus, castle 69   D d
Cham 63   G d
Chamavi, people 39   I g
Chambal River 137   C c

Chambersburg . . . . 208 ins.
Chambéry 130   N i
Chambly, Fort 189   B b
Chambord 126   B c
Champa . . . .
Champa, reg. . . . .
Champagne, cty. 11 cent. . . . 61   E b
Champagne, cty. 12 cent. . . . 69
Champagne, cty. 14 cent. . . . 211   F b
Champagne, prov. 148   E e
Champagne and Brie, gouv. . . 146   B b
Champ de Mars, loc. in Paris . 149   B
Champaubert 154   B d
Champion Hill 208   B c
Champlain, lake 189   B b
Champs Elysées, loc. in Paris . 149   B
Champtoceaux 81   L h
Chanar 187   D c
Chañaral 215   B e
Chancellade, mon. 94   C b
Chancellerie, Rue de la, street
    in Versailles 149   A
Chancellor, route of 109Ub,Va
Chancellorsville . . . . 208 E b (Chan.)
Chanda 137   C d
Chandarnagar 137   E d
Chandax 59   J f
Chanderi . . . .
Chandernagore 137   E d
Changanor . . . .
Chang - chau 171   M f
Chang - chau - fu . . . .
Chang - kia - chwang . . . . 170 ins. A
Chang - sha 171   M f
Channel Islands 49   E g
Chaoni, people . . . .
Chaonia, dist. 10   A b
Chapelle - Saint - Lambert . . .
Chapultepec, castle 201   H g
Charadra 10   B c
Charadrus 11   F b
Charadrus River 14   C b
Charcas, pres. . . . . 215 ins.
Chard 127   V p
Chard, parl. bor. . . . .
Chardjui . . . .
Charente, dept. 148   E e
Charente River 76   C d
Charente - Inférieure, dept. . . 148   D e
Charenton 126   C b
Charidemi, prom. 38   B e
Charikar . . . .
Charing Cross, loc. in London 75   G g
Charisius, gate 93   G e
Charité, La, near Nevers . . . 126   C c
Charité, La, in Paris 149   B
Charkov . . . .
Charlemont 126   D a
Charleroi 117   C d
Charles, Cape, in Labrador . . 186   N c
Charles, Cape, in Virginia . . 193 ins. A
Charles X., route of 121   D a
Charles City . . . . 193 ins. A
Charles City County . . . . 193 ins. A (Ch.)
Charlesfort 191   I e
Charles River . . . . 189 ins. B
Charleston, in S.C. 211   J d
Charleston, in W. Va. 211   I c
Charlestown, near Boston . . . 189 ins. B
Charles Town, in S. Carolina . 193 ins. A
Charleville 172   D c
Charlotiana, proposed col. in U.S. 194   A a
Charlotte 191   I d
Charlotte, Fort . . . . 195 ins. B
Charlotte Harbor 191   I f
Charlottenburg 135   G b
Charlottesville 193   E c
Charlottetown 212   I d
Charolais, cty. 126   D c
Charolais, dist. 81   M h
Charolles 76   F c
Charolles, cty. 114   C e
Charroux, mon. 94   C b
Charsianon, theme 59   K f

Charter House, bldg. in London	75	G g	Cheremissians, people	138	G d	Chiltern Hills	49	F	
Charters Towers	172	D b	Cheribon			Chimalhuacan			
Chartres	61	D b	Chernaia River	164	J f	Chimay	117	B	
Chartres, bp.	94	C b	Cherokee, Ind. Res.	188	G c	Chimborazo, mt.	214	A	
Chartres, Fort	191	G d	Cherokee, Ind. Res. 1834	188	I d	Chimbote	214	B	
Chartreuse, mon.	69	F d	Cherokees, tribe	188	J c	Chimerium	10	D	
Charudes, people	38	D a	Cherronesus, proposed state			Chimkent			
Chassaigne, La, mon.	95	D b (L. Ch.)	in U. S.			Chimu	111	B	
Chastel Blanc, castle	68	C bc	Cherry Valley	195	D b	China, country	171	L	
Chastel Rouge, castle	68	C c	Cherson, in the Crimea	43	I e	China Sea	112	E	
Châteaubriant, castle	76	C c	Cherson, on the Dnieper			Chinalaph River, see Cheliff River			
Château-Chalon, mon.	148	C b	Cherson, theme	59	K e	Chincha	111	B	
Château Chinon	76	F c	Chersonese, Thracian, pen.	13	E a	Chincha Islands	214	B	
Château Dauphin	126	E d	Chersonese, Tauric, pen.	35	K d	Chinchilla	82	B	
Château de Joux	126	E c	Chersonesus, prom.	11	F d	Chinese City, loc. in Peking	170 ins.	A	
Château d'If	126	D e	Chertsey	75	H i	Chinese Empire	171	J M	
Château d'Œx	91	P l	Chertsey mon.			Chinilla River			
Châteaudun	61	D b	Cherusci, people	38	J h	Chin-kiang	171	M	
Châteaudun, bp.	94	C b (Chât.)	Chesapeake Bay	193	F c	Chinon	69	H g	
Château Gaillard, castle	76	D b	Cheshire, cty.	127	W m	Chinon, castle	76	D	
Château-Landon	61	E b	Chester, in England			Chinooks, tribe	188	B	
Châteauneuf, in Angoumois	126	B d	Chester, in Illinois	207	H c	Chinsura	137	E	
Châteauneuf, in Perche	76	D b	Chester, in Pa.	192	D d	Chintabor			
Château-Porcien	69	F b	Chester, bp.	97	O h	Chiny			
Château-Renard	69	I g	Chester, castle			Chioggia	72	C b	
Châteauroux	76	D c	Chester, cty.	162	D d	Chioggia, bp.	95	E b	
Châteauroux, seign.	69	H g	Chester, cty. palat.			Chios, isl.	13	D b	
Château-Thierry	69	I f	Chester, parl. bor.	163	L d	Chipangu, empire (Japan)			
Châtelet, near Charleroi	117	C d	Chesterfield Inlet	212	F b	Chippawa, battle	200	D b	
Châtelet, loc. in Paris	149	B	Cheval-de-Bois			Chippenham			
Châtellerault	76	D c	Cheviot Hills	49	E d	Chippenham, parl. bor.	163	L f (Chipp.)	
Châtellerault, viscty.	76	D c	Chèvremont, castle	62	C c	Chippewa River	191	G c	
Chatelot	143 ins.	F	Cheyenne	210	E b	Chippewas, tribe	188	H	
Chatelot, lordship	143 ins.	F	Cheyenne River	198	E b	Chippewyan, Fort	212	D c	
Chatham, parl. bor.	163	O f	Cheyenne River, Ind. Res.	188	F a	Chipping Norton, parl. bor.			
Chatham Islands	172	H e	Cheyennes, tribe	188	D b	Chipping Wycombe, parl. bor.	163	N f	
Châtillon, on the Marne R.	69	I f	Chezal-Benoît, mon.	94	C b			(Ch. Wyc.)	
Châtillon, near Nevers	126	C c	Chiaha	191	I e	Chiquitos, tribe	214	C d	
Châtillon, in Savoy	91	P m	Chiapa	105	B c	Chira, Rio de la, river	111	A b	
Châtillon, on the Seine R.	76	F c	Chiapas, state	213	C c	Chiremai, mt.	112	D d	
Chattahoochee River	193	B e	Chiari	130	E d	Chiriqui Lagoon	105	D e	
Chattanooga	208	C b	Chiavari	90	I h	Chisey	76	C c	
Chatti, people	39	J h	Chiavenna	91	R l	Chiskiak or Chisklack	193 ins. A (Ch.)		
Chauci, people	38	D b	Chicaça	191	G e	Chiswell, Fort	193	D c	
Chaudière River	188	L a	Chicacoan	193	F c (Chi.)	Chita	171	M c	
Chaul			Chicago	211	H b	Chitral	170	I e	
Chaumont, in Champagne	76	F b	Chichagof Island	212 ins.		Chitral, reg.	137	B a	
Chaumont, in Vexin	76	E b	Chichester			Chittagong	137	F d	
Chauon	18	F c	Chichester, bp.	97	Q k	Chiusi	90	L j	
Chaussée, la	154	C d	Chichester, parl. bor.	163	N g	Chiusi, bp.	95	E c	
Chautauqua, lake	192	B b	Chichilticale	190	D e	Chivasso	130	P i	
Chauvigny	76	D c	Chiclayo	214	A c	Chlum	159	H c	
Chaves	82	A a	Chickamauga	208	D b	Chmielnik	92	C b	
Cheadle	127	X n	Chickasaw, Ind. Res.	188	G d	Choarene, reg.	19	H c	
Cheap, loc. in London	75	G g (35)	Chickasaw, Ind. Res. 1832	188	I d	Choaspes River	19	L c	
Cheat River	192	B d	Chickasaw Bluffs	191	H d	Choaspis River	19	G d	
Chef de Caux, Cape	81	L h	Chickasaws, tribe	188	I d	Cho-chau	170 ins. A		
Chehalis, Ind. Res.	188	B a	Chico River	215	B g	Choctaw, Ind. Res.	188	G d	
Chehalis, tribe	188	B a	Chidley, Cape	186	M b	Choctaw, Ind. Res. 1830	188	I d	
Che-kiang, prov.	171	M f	Chiemsee, bp.	95	E b	Choctawhatchee River	193	B f	
Cheliabinsk	170	H c	Chienti, bp.	95	F c	Choctaws, tribe	188	H d	
Chelidoniæ Islands	20	D d	Chieri	130	P i	Chœle-Chœl	215	C f	
Cheliff, or Sheliff, River	118	E f	Chiers River	62	C d	Chœrades Islands, in Eleusinian			
Chelmsford	127	Z o	Chieti	90	E c	Gulf	16	B a	
Chelmsford, parl. bor.			Chieti, bp.	95	E c	Chœrades Islands, in Gulf of			
Chelonatas Gulf	14	B b	Chièvres	117	B d	Tarentum	31	G b	
Chelonatas, prom.	14	B b	Chi-fu	171	N e	Choiseul, isl.	172	E a	
Chelsea	75	I i	Chihuahua	213	B b	Cholet	130	C d	
Cheltenham, parl. bor.	163	L f (Chelt.)	Chihuahua, prov.	190	D f	Cholm	159	L c	
Chemashevskœ	170	H b	Chihuahua, state	213	B b	Cholula	106	B a	
Cheminon, mon.	94	C b	Chilau			Choluteca	213	D c	
Chemmis	18	D e	Chile, capt. gen. and pres.	215 ins.		Chonos Archipelago	215	B g	
Chemnitz	85	G e	Chile, cty.	215	B g e	Chorasmii, people	19	I b	
Chemulpo	171	N e	Chilenfu			Chorazin	6	D c	
Chenab River	137	C b	Chilianwala	170	I e	Chorin, mon.	79	H b	
Cheng-tu-fu			Chilkat Pass	212 ins.		Chorsia(e)	11	D d	
Chen-si			Chilcoot	212 ins.		Chotin	131	I d	
Chepstow	127	W o	Chilcoot Pass	212 ins.		Chouteau's Landing	210	F c	
Chequamegon, Fort			Chillan	215	B f	Chotusitz	135	H d	
Cher, dept.	148	E e	Chillicothe, in Missouri	211	G c	Chowan River	193	F c	
Cher River	69	H g	Chillicothe, in Ohio	196 ins. B		Christanna, Fort	193	F c	
Cherasco	90	H h	Chillon, castle	91	O l	Christchurch, in New Zealand	172	G e	
Cheraw	195	B f	Chiloé Island	215	B g	Christchurch, parl. bor.	163	M g	
Cherbourg	76	C b	Chilpancingo	213	B c	Christchurch, priory	100	A b	

Christian IV., route of . . . . . 121 C b
Christiana . . . . 206 ins.
Christiania (Aggershuus) . . . .
Christiansand . . . . 166 G c
Christiansborg . . . .
Christina, Fort . . . . 192 ins.
Christmas I., Indian Ocean . . 179 B i
Christmas I., Pacific Ocean . . 180 L g
Christophsthal . . . . 143 F i
Chrobatia, reg. . . . . 59 I c
Chrysas River . . . . 30 D e
Chrysea, isl. . . . . 14 ins.
Chrysokeras (Golden Horn) str. 93 G e
Chrysopolis . . . .
Chrysorrhoas River . . . . 6 E a
Chrystler's Farm, battle . . . . 200 F a
Chubut . . . . 215 C g
Chubut River . . . . 215 C g
Chudes, people . . . . 138 B d
Chumbi . . . . 171 J f
Chundah . . . . 137 C e
Chung-kiang . . . . 171 L f
Chuquisaca . . . . 214 C d
Chur, see Coire
Church, States of the, 9 cent. . 56 E d
Church, States of the, 13 cent. 73 C b
Church, States of the, see also
    Papal States and Patrimony
    of Saint Peter
Churchill, Cape . . . . 186 J c
Churchill, Fort . . . . 212 F c
Churchill River . . . . 212 F c
Churubusco, battle . . . . 201 H g
Churwalchen . . . . 62 E e
Chusan, Islands . . . . 171 N e
Chuvashes, people . . . . 138 G d
Chylemath River . . . . 38 C e
Ciabrus River . . . . 39 M l
Ciando . . . .
Cibalis . . . .
Cibao, reg. . . . . 105 F c
Cibola, reg. . . . . 190 ·D d
Cibotus, Harbor of . . . . . 34 ins. C (4)
Cibyra . . . . 20 C d
Cibyrrhæots, Theme of the . . 59 K f
Cicero, House of . . . . 24 A
Cichyrus . . . . 10 B c
Cicuye . . . . 190 D d
Cicynethus, isl. . . . . 11 E c
Cidade do Salvador (Bahia) . . 214 F d
Ciechanow . . . . 155 K b
Cienfuegos . . . . 213 D b
Cierium . . . . 10 D c
Cilicia, imp. prov. . . . . . . 35 K f
Cilicia, Macedonian prov. . . 18 D c
Cilicia, reg. . . . . 4 F c*
Cilicia, Rom. prov. . . . .
Cilicia, satr. . . . . 18 O h
Cilicia, Strait of . . . . 20 E e
Cilicia, theme . . . . 59 L f
Cilicia I, E. Rom. prov. . . 43 I f (4)
Cilicia II, E. Rom. prov. . . 43 I f (13)
Cilli . . . . 72 D b
Cimarron River . . . . 190 F d
Cimbebas, people . . . . 109 S i
Cimbric Chersonese (Denmark) 38 D a
Ciminius, lake . . . . 27 C e
Cimmerian Bosporus, km. . . 33 L d
Cimolus (Kimolo), isl. . . . . . 15 E c
Cincinnati . . . . 211 I c
Cinga River . . . . 38 C d
Cingulum . . . . 27 H d
Cintra . . . . 82 A b
Cipango, emp. (Japan) . . . . .
Circæum, prom. . . . . 30 B a
Circars, reg. . . . . . . · . . 137 D e
Circassia, reg. . . . .
Circassian Mamelukes, Dom. of
    the . . . . 93 E c
Circassians, people . . . . . . 139 E g
Circei or Circeii (San Felice) . 30 C a
Circesium . . . . 30 I c
Circidius River . . . . 26 C e
Circle . . . . 198 ins. A

Circus Maximus, loc. in Rome 24 B
Circus Maximus, Aug. Reg., Rome 22 A
Cirencester . . . . 51 P i
Cirencester, mon. . . . . 97 O j
Cirencester, parl. bor. . . 163 M f (Cirenc.)
Cirphis, mt. . . . . 11 D d
Cirrha . . . . 11 D d
Cirta . . . . 38 D e
Cisa, La, pass . . . . 26 D c
Cisalpine Gaul, reg. . . . . . 38 ins.
Cisalpine Republic . . . . 151 H g
Cisjurane Burgundy, km. . . . . 56 C d
Cisoing, mon. . . . . 94 C a
Cispadane Gaul, reg. . . . . . 26 E c
Cispadane Gaul, Aug. Reg. . . 38 E d (8)
Cispius, mt. . . . . 22 A
Cisplatine Province . . . . . 215 D f
Cissia, prov. . . . . 19 G d
Cissus . . . . 11 E b
Cissus, mt. . . . . 11 E b
Cité, Paris . . . . 149 B
Citeaux, mon. . . . . 95 D b
Cithæron Mountains . . . . . 11 E d
Citium, in Cyprus . . . . . . 4 F c
Citium, in Macedonia . . . . . 10 D b
Citlaltepec . . . . 106 A a
Citlaltepetl, mt. . . . . 106 C a
Citracan (Astrakhan) . . . . . . 99 M d
Città di Castello . . . . 90 D c
Città di Castello, bp. . . . . . 95 E c
Cittanuova, bp. . . . . 95 E b
Cittavecchia, bp. . . . . 95 F c
City of Salt . . . . 7 C f
Ciudad Bolivar . . . . 214 C b
Ciudad de los Reyes . . . . . 111 B d
Ciudadela, bp. . . . . 94 C d
Ciudad Guzman . . . . 213 ins.
Ciudad Juarez (El Paso del Norte) 213 B a
Ciudad Porfirio Diaz . . . . . 213 B b
Ciudad Real . . . . 130 C f
Ciudad Rodrigo . . . . 82 G e
Ciudad Rodrigo, bp. . . . . . . 94 A c
Cius . . . .
Cius, Bay of . . . .
Cividale . . . . 90 D a
Cività Castellana . . . . 96 B a
Civitate . . . . 64 C b
Civitavecchia . . . . 64 ins.
Civitella . . . . 90 D c
Civray . . . . 126 B c
Clackmannan, cty. . . . .
Cladeus River . . . . 14 B b
Clagny, Parc de, loc. in Versailles 149 A
Claiborne, Fort . . . . 200 I f
Clairac . . . . 126 B d
Clairac, mon. . . . . 94 C c
Clairets, Les, mon. . . . . . . 94 C b
Clairlieu, mon. . . . . 95 D b
Clairvaux . . . . 69 J f
Clairvaux, mon. . . . . 94 C b
Clallams, people . . . . . . 188 B a
Clampetia . . . . 31 F c
Clanis (Chiana) River . . . . 27 G e
Clanius River . . . . 30 C b
Clare, cty. . . . . 127 H i
Clarendon . . . . 69 B a
Clarendon, castle . . . .
Clarendon, dist. . . . . . . 193 ins. C
Clark, Fort . . . . 210 E a
Clark, route of . . . 210 B a and D a
Clarke River . . . . 186 H d
Clarksville . . . . 210 F d
Clarus Mons, see Clermont-Ferrand
Clasis River . . . . 27 G d
Classes . . . . 27 G c
Clastidium . . . . 26 D c
Claterna . . . . 27 F c
Clatsop, Fort . . . . 210 A a
Clatsops, tribe . . . . 188 B a
Claudian Aqueduct . . . . . 35 ins. B
Claudian Augustan Way, road 27 G b
Claudian Valerian Way, road 27 H e
Claudiopolis . . . . 20 D b
Claudius, Arch of . . . . . 22 A

Clausentum (Bitterne) . . . . . . 51 P i
Clavenna (Chiavenna) . . . . . 26 D a
Claverack . . . . 189 B c
Clazomenæ . . . . 13 E b
Clear, Cape . . . . 49 B f
Cleeve, mon. . . . . 97 N j
Clemont . . . . 143 ins. F
Clemont, lordship . . . . . . 143 ins. F
Cleonæ, on Acte Pen. . . . . 11 F b
Cleonæ, in Argolis . . . . . . 15 C b
Clepsydra, Spring of . . . . . . 23 C (4)
Clerf . . . . 117 E d
Clerkenwell, loc. in London . . 75 G g
Clermont, in Auvergne . . . . 61 E d
Clermont-en-Beauvoisis . . . . 76 E b
Clermont, bp. . . . . 94 C b
Clermont, cty. . . . . 76 E b
Clermont-en-Argonne . . . . 126 D b
Clermont-Ferrand . . . . . . 134 B f
Clesis River . . . . 26 E b
Cleveland . . . . 196 ins. B
Cleves . . . . 78 E c
Cleves, cty. . . . . 78 E c
Cleves, duchy . . . . 114 D c
Clew Bay . . . . 127 H h
Clifton . . . . 127 W l
Clinch River . . . . 196 ins. A
Clinton . . . . 208 B c
Clinton, Fort, near Saratoga . 192 E b
Clinton, Fort, near West Point 195 D c
Clinton, route of . . . . . . 195 B g
Clipperton Island . . . . 180 ? f
Clisius River . . . . 26 B c
Clitæ, people . . . . 20 E d
Cliternia . . . . 30 E a
Clitor . . . . 14 C b
Clitumnus River . . . . . . 27 G e
Clivus Argentarius, loc. in Rome 24 A
Clivus Capitolinus, loc. in Rome 24 A
Clivus Scauri, loc. in Rome . . 22 A
Clivus Victoriæ, loc. in Rome. 24 A
Cloaca Maxima, loc. in Rome. 24 A
Clodiana . . . . 31 I a
Clodian Way, road . . . . . . 27 F e
Clodius, Port of . . . . . . 35 ins. B
Clodii, Forum, near L. Sabatinus 35 ins. B
Clodii, Forum, near Luca . . . 26 E d
Clogher, bp. . . . . 97 D b
Clomnacnoise, bp. . . . .
Clone, bp. . . . .
Clonfert, bp. . . . . 97 C c
Clonmel . . . .
Closter-Seven . . . .
Clota Æstuarium (Firth of Clyde) 38 A a
Cloyne, bp. . . . . 97 C e
Cluentus River . . . . 27 H d
Clugia, see Chioggia
Clunia, in Rætia . . . . . . 39 J j
Clunia, in Spain . . . . . . 38 B d
Cluny, mon. . . . . 94 C b
Clusium (Chiusi) . . . . . . 27 F d
Cluviæ . . . . 27 I f
Clyde, Firth of . . . . . . 49 D d
Clyde River . . . . 49 D e
Clydesdale, dist. . . . . . ·
Cnemides . . . . 11 D d
Cnemis, mt. . . . . 11 D d
Cnidus . . . . 12 I c
Cnossus . . . . 14 ins.
Coahuila, prov. . . . . . . 190 E f
Coahuila, state . . . . . . 213 B b
Coast District . . . . 171 O d
Coast Range, mts., California . 187 G d
Coast Range, mts., Canada . . 212 B b
Coatepec . . . . 106 B a
Coatzacoalco River . . . . . 105 B c
Coatzacoalcos . . . . 213 C c
Coban . . . . 213 C c
Cobar . . . . 172 D d
Cobija . . . . 214 B e
Coblenz . . . . 62 D c
Coburg . . . . 85 F e
Coburg, Pflege, dist. . . . . . 85 F e
Coburg Peninsula . . . . . . 172 C b

Coca 191   H e
Coca River 111   B b
Cocala 19   K e
Coccium (Ribchester) . . . . .
Cocconato . . . . 130 Q i (Co.)
Cochaba 6   E b
Cochabamba 214   C d
Cocheco 189   B c
Cochin 137   C g
Cochin-China, country 171   L g
Cockburn Land 186   K a
Cockermouth, parl. bor. 163   K c
Cockersand, mon. 97   O h
Coco River 213   D c
Cocos I., Pacific Ocean 214   A b
Cocos Is., Indian Ocean . . . 179   A i
Cocynthum, prom. 31   F d
Cocytus River 10   B c
Cod, Cape 186   M d
Codfish Land 108   L c
Cœle, Deme of . . . .
Cœle, reg. 14   B b
Cœel Syria, reg. . . . .
Cœletæ, people 39   N l
Cœnyra 11   F b
Cœur d'Alene, Ind. Res. . . . 188   C a
Coggeshall, mon. 97   R j
Cognac 76   C d
Cogolla, San Millan de la, mon. 94   B c
Cohœs 192   E b
Coiba, isl. 105   D e
Coimbatore 137   C f
Coimbra 82   G e
Coimbra, bp. 94   A c
Coimbra, univ. 100   D f
Coire 91   R l
Coire, bp. 78   F e
Colapis River 27   J b
Colatio 27   J a
Colberg . . . .
Colchester . . . .
Colchester, parl. bor. 163   O f
Colchis, reg. 20   J a
Colchis, satr. 8   I d
Cold Harbor, battle 208   E b
Col di Tenda Pass 130   P j
Coleman Street, in London . . . 75   G g
Colendonck . . . . 89 ins. C
Colenso 175   M l
Colesberg 175   M m
Colias, prom. 16   B b
Coligny 126   D c
Colima . . . . 213 ins.
Colima, vol. 187   I g
Collatia . . . . 35 ins. B
Colle 90   L j
Colle, La 200   G a
Colleton County . . . . 193 ins. C
Collier Bay 172   B b
Colline Gate 22   A
Collingwood 207   I b
Colmar . . . . 143 ins. D
Colmar, imp. city 78   E d
Colmenar de Oreja 82   H e
Cöln, see Cologne
Colnbrook 75   H i
Colne River 75   H h
Cologne (Cöln) 62   D c
Cologne, abp. 78   E c
Cologne, Hanse. cy. . . . . . . 99 ins. B
Cologne, imp. city 78   E c
Cologne, univ. 100   G d
Colombe, La, mon. 94   C b
Colombia, cty. 214   B b
Colombo 137   C g
Colón 214   A b
Colonea 59   L e
Colonea, theme 59   L f
Colonia Agrippina (Cologne) . 39   I h
Colonia Copia . . . . . . 31 F c (Col. Copia)
Colonia do Sacramento . . . .
Colonia Neptunia 31 G b (Col. Neptunia)
Colonia Traiana 39   I h
Colonides 14   B c

Colonna, Cape 64   C c
Colonna, Piazza 22   A
Colonus 16   B b
Colonus, Deme of . . . .
Colorado, ter. 203   Q h
Colorado, state 203   Q h
Colorado Chiquito, R. 190   C d
Colorado Plateau 187   H e
Colorado River, flowing into G.
   of Mexico 187   J e
Colorado River, flowing into G.
   of California 187   H e
Colorado River, in Arg. Rep. . 215   C f
Colorado River, Little 190   C d
Colorado River, Ind. Res. . . . 188   D d
Colorado Springs 210   E c
Colossæ 20   C d
Colosseum, bldg. in Rome . . . 24   B
Colquechaca 214   C d
Columbia, in Ohio . . . . . 196 ins. B
Columbia, in Pa. 211   J c
Columbia, in S. Carolina . . . 211   I d
Columbia, in Tennessee . . . 211   H c
Columbia, District of . . . . . 208 ins.
Columbia, mt. 186   H c
Columbia Plateau 187   H d
Columbia River 186   G d
Columbus, in Georgia 191   I e
Columbus, in Ohio 199   I c
Columbus, voyages of . . 105, 108 M N e f
Columna Rhegium 30   E d
Colville, Fort 198   B a
Colville, Ind. Res. 188   C a
Colville River 186   D b
Colvilles, tribe 188   C a
Comacchio 90   K h
Comacchio, bp. 95   E c
Comacenus, lake 26   D a
Comaclum, see Comacchio
Comana, in Çappadocia 20   G c
Comana, in Pontus 20   G b
Comanches, tribe 188   F d
Comayagua 213   D c
Combe, mon. 97   P i
Combermere, mon. 97   O i
Combrailles, cty. 76   E c
Comburg, castle 143   I g
Comfort, Point . . . . 193 ins. A
Cominges, cty. 76   D e
Comitium, loc. in Rome . . . 24   A
Commagene, reg. 20   G d
Commendah . . . .
Comminges, bp. 94   C c
Common Lands, dist. . . . . .
Communipaw . . . . 189 ins. C
Como 90   I h
Como, bp. 95   D b
Como, lake 90   I h
Comorin, Cape 137   C g
Comoro Islands 175   H f
Compendium, see Compiègne
Compiègne 126   C b
Compludo, mon. 94   A c
Complutum 38   B d
Compostella, Santiago de . . . .
Compostella, Santiago de, abp.
Compsa 30   E b
Compton, Little . . . . . . 189 ins. A
Comum (Como) 26   D b
Concepción, in Arg. Rep. . . . 215   D f
Concepción, in Chile 215   B f
Concepción, in Paraguay . . . 215   D e
Conception, Point 187   G e
Conception Island 108   P h
Conchos 190   D f
Conchos River 191   D f
Conciergerie, bldg. in Paris . . 149   B
Concord, Massachusetts . . . 189 ins. B
Concord, New Hampshire . . . 211   K b
Concord, Temple of . . . . . .
Concord River . . . . 195 ins. A
Concordia, in Arg. Rep. . . . 215   D f
Concordia, in Upper Germany 39   I i
Concordia, in Venetia 27   G b

Concordia, bp. 95   E b
Condé 126   C a
Condevincum or Condivincum
   (Nantes) 38   B e
Condom, bp. 94   C c
Condrusi, people 39   H h
Conedoquinet River . . . . . . 208 ins.
Conegliano 150   G c
Conembriga 38   A c
Conestoga 194   K b
Conewago Creek . . . .
Confederation of the Rhine . . 155 leg.
Conflans, cty. 69   E e
Conflans, dist. 126   C e
Confluens, see Münster
Confluentes or Confluentia
   (Coblenz) 39   I h
Congaree River 193   D e
Congo, reg. 109   S b
Congo, Belgian, col. 175   F e
Congo, French, col. 175   E d
Congo River 175   F d
Congo State 175   F e
Congress Lands . . . . 196 ins. B
Conii, people 38   A c
Connaught, prov. . . . .
Connecticut, col. 189   B d
Connecticut, state . . . . 211 K b (Conn.)
Connecticut River 189   B c
Connor, bp. 97   E b
Conococheague Creek . . . . . 208 ins.
Conope 10   C d
Conovium (Conway) 51   O h
Conques, mon., near Evreux . 94   C b
Conques, mon., near Rodez . . 94   C c
Conrad III., crusade of 70   I d
Consentia (Cosenza) 31   F c
Conserans, bp. 94   C c
Constance 62   E e
Constance, bp. 142   D e
Constance, imp. cy. 78   F e
Constantia (Constance) 39   J j
Constantia, see Coutances
Constantia, in Cyprus 43   I f
Constantina 82   A b
Constantine 70   H f
Constantine, Arch of 24   B
Constantine, Basilica of 24   B
Constantine, Baths of 22   A
Constantine, Burnt Column of 93 G e (4)
Constantine, Church of 23   D
Constantine, Statue of . . . . .
Constantine, Forum of 93   G e
Constantine, Wall of 93   G e
Constantinople 43   H e
Constantinople, patr. 52   L f
Constantinople, plan of 93   G e
Constantinople, Emp. of . . . 73   F b
Constanz (Constance), bp. . . . 95   D b
Constanza 164   D b
Constitución 215   B f
Contestani, people 38   B e
Contrebia 38   B d
Contreras, battle 201   H g
Conway . . . .
Conway, parl. bor. . . . . . .
Conz, bridge of 122   D d
Conza, abp. 95   F c
Cooch Behar, reg. 137   E c
Cook, mt., in Alaska . . . . . 212 ins.
Cook, mt., in New Zealand . . 172   F e
Cook Inlet . . . . 198 ins. A
Cook Islands 180   L i
Cook Strait 172   G e
Cooktown 172   D b
Coolgardie 172   B d
Cooper River, in Australia . . 172   D c
Cooper River, in S. Carolina . 193 ins. C
Coorg, reg. 137   C f
Coosa River 208   C c
Copæ 11   E d
Copais, lake 11   E d
Copan 105   C d
Copenhagen 77   G a

Copenhagen, Hanse. for. cy. . . . 98 F b
Copenhagen, univ. . . . . 100 H c
Cophen River . . . . 19 L d
Cophos Port . . . . 16 D c
Copia, col. . . . . 31 F c
Copiapó . . . . 215 B e
Coppermine River . . . . 212 D b
Coquimbo. . . . . 215 B f
Cora . . . . 35 ins. B
Coracesium . . . . 20 E d
Corah . . . . 137 D c
Coral Islands . . . . 110 FF g
Coral Sea . . . . 172 E b
Corax, mt. . . . . 11 D d
Corbais . . . . 156 B a
Corbeia, see Corbie
Corbeil . . . . 61 E b
Corbie, mon . . . . 55 P k
Corbridge . . . .
Corbridge, parl. bor. . . . .
Corcora River, in Noricum 27 I a
Corcora River, in Pannonia . 27 J b
Corcyra (Corfu), isl. . . . . . 10 A c
Corcyra Nigra . . . . 38 F d
Cordilleran Region. . . . . . 186 G c
Córdoba, in Arg. Rep . . . . . 215 C f
Córdoba, in Mexico . . . . 213 ins.
Cordova, in Spain . . . . 82 B b
Cordova, by. . . . . 94 B d
Cordova, calif. . . . . 58 C f
Cordova, emir. . . . . 54 D f
Cordova, km. . . . . . . 83 J h
Corduba (Cordova) . . . . . 38 A e
Corduëne, reg. . . . . . 20 J c
Corentine River . . . . . 214 D b
Coressus . . . . 15 E b
Corfe Castle . . . . . . 127 W p
Corfinium. . . . . 27 H e
Corfu, isl. . . . . 77 H e
Coria . . . . 82 A a
Coria, bp. . . . . 94 A d
Coria del Rio . . . . 82 A b
Corinium (Cirencester) . . . . 51 P i
Corinth, in Greece . . . . . . 15 C b
Corinth, in Mississippi . . . . 208 C c
Corinth, Gulf of . . . . . . 14 C a
Corinth, Isthmus of . . . . . 2 G e
Corinthian Gate. . . . . 6 ins. A
Coriovallum . . . . 39 H h
Coris . . . . 68 C b
Corisco Bay . . . . 175 D d
Coritani, people . . . . . . 51 P h
Cork . . . .
Cork, bp. . . . . 97 C e
Cork, cty. . . . . 127 I i
Corlær. . . . . 192 D b
Cormons . . . . 161 I e
Cornavii, people . . . .
Cornelimünster, mon. . . . . 95 D a
Corner Gate . . . . 6 ins. A
Corner Inlet . . . . 172 D d
Corneto . . . . 64 ins.
Corneto, bp. . . . . 95 E c
Corneville, mon. . . . . 94 E b (Cornev.)
Cornhill, in London . . . 75 G g
Corniculum. . . . . 35 ins. B
Corn Market, in London . . . 75 G g (34)
Cornouailles, cty. . . . . . . 69 C b
Cornwall, cty. . . . . 127 T p
Cornwall, reg. . . . .
Cornwallis, route of . . . 195 A g, B f, C f
Coro . . . . 105 G d
Corobilium, see Corbeil
Coromandel Coast . . . . . . 137 D f
Coron . . . . 14 B c
Corone, Cape . . . . 16 C b
Coronea, in Bœotia . . . . . 11 D d
Coronea, in Thessaly . . . . . 11 D c
Coronea, lake . . . . 11 E b
Corope . . . . 11 E c
Corozal . . . .
Corpus Christi. . . . . 201 F d

Correggio . . . . 90 J h
Corrèze, dept. . . . . 148 E e
Corrientes . . . . 215 D e
Corrientes, Cabo das, cape in
    Africa . . . . 109 U j
Corrientes, cape, in Arg. Rep. 215 D f
Corrientes, Cape, in Mexico . . 213 B b
Corsica, isl. . . . . 2 E d
Corsica, gen. . . . . 147 F c
Corsica, gouv. . . . . 146 C c
Corsica, French prov. . . . . . 148 F f
Corsica, W. Rom. prov. . . . . 42 D e (9)
Corsote . . . . 20 I e
Corso Umberto 1, street in Rome 22 A
Corstopitum (Corbridge) . . . 51 O g
Corte . . . . 146 C c
Cortemiglia . . . . 130 Q j
Cortenuova. . . . . 72 B b
Corte real, route of . . . . . . 108 L b
Cortez, routes of 105, 106
Cortil - Noirmont . . . . . 156 B a
Cortona . . . . 27 G d
Cortona, bp. . . . . 95 E c
Cortoriacus or Corturiacus, see
    Courtrai
Corumbá . . . . 214 D d
Corunna . . . . 82 G e
Corvey. . . . . 151 H f
Corvey, mon. . . . . 95 D a
Corycium, prom. . . . . . . 20 B c
Corydalus . . . . 16 B b
Corydalus, mt. . . . . 16 B b
Coryphasium, prom. . . . . . 14 B c
Cos . . . . 13 E c
Cos, isl. . . . . 13 E c
Cosa . . . . 27 F e
Cosa, route of . . . . 108 M g
Cosedia, see Coutances
Cosenza . . . . 90 F e
Cosenza, abp. . . . . 95 F d
Cosmidion, quarter . . . . . .
Cosmin . . . .
Cosmo y Damiano, Saints, mon. 94 A c
Cossium, see Bazas
Cosne . . . . 76 E c
Cossacks of the Don, people . 139 F f
Cossacks of the Terek, people . 139 G g
Cossacks, Uralian, people . . . 139 H e
Cossack, Zaporogian, people . . 139 D f
Cossæi, people . . . . 19 G d
Cosseans, people . . . . 8 I e
Cossonay . . . . 130 O h
Cossyra, isl. . . . . 38 E e
Costa Rica, reg. . . . . . . 105 C d
Costa Rica, country . . . . . 213 D c
Costnitz, (Constance), bp. . . 95 D b
Cotaxtla, river . . . . 106 D b
Côte - d'Or, dept. . . . . . . 148 E e
Côte - d'Or, mts. . . . . . . 148 E e
Cotentin, dist. . . . . 81 L h
Côtes - du - Nord, dept. . . . 148 D e
Cotini, people . . . . 38 F c
Cotopaxi. mt. . . . . 111 B b
Cotrone . . . . 90 F e
Cotrone, bp. . . . . 95 F d
Cotswold Hills . . . . 49 E f
Cottbus . . . . 155 H c
Cottian Alps, mts. . . . . . 26 B c
Cottian Alps, W. Rom. prov. . . 42 D e (5)
Cottius, Kingdom of . . . . . 26 A c
Cotyaëum . . . . 20 C c
Cotyora . . . . 20 G b
Coucou, le . . . . 156 C c
Coucy . . . . 76 E b
Coucy, seign. . . . . 69 I f
Coulommiers . . . . 126 C b
Council Bluffs . . . . 211 F b
Council House, bldg. in Jerusalem 6 ins. A
Courland, duchy . . . . . . 88 J c
Courland, reg. . . . . 138 B d
Courmayeur . . . . 91 O m
Couronne, La, mon. . . . . . 94 C b
Courtenay . . . . 69 I f
Courtrai . . . . 117 B d

Couserans, cty. . . . . 69 D e
Couserans, dist. . . . . . . 147 E c (Cous.)
Coutances . . . . 61 C b
Coutances, bp. . . . . 94 B b
Coutances, cty. . . . . 69 C b
Coutras . . . . 126 A d
Couvin. . . . . 117 C d
Covadonga, cave . . . . . . 82 A a
Covadonga, mon. . . . . . . 94 A c
Coventry . . . .
Coventry, bp. . . . . 97 P i
Coventry, parl. bor. . . . . . 163 M e
Coverham, mon. . . . . 97 P g
Cowpens, battle . . . . . . 195 A f
Coyohuacan . . . .
Cozumel, isl. . . . . 105 C b
Crac des Chevaliers, castle . . 68 C c
Cracow . . . . 70 J c
Cracow, bp. . . . . 95 F a
Cracow, Hanse. cy. . . . . . 98 G c
Cracow, rep. . . . . 159 J c
Cracow, univ. . . . . 100 I d
Cradle Mount . . . . 172 D e
Crailsheim . . . . 143 J g
Craiova . . . . 164 C b
Cranæa . . . . 10 B c
Cranganore . . . .
Crania, mt. . . . . 10 B c
Cranii . . . . 10 B d
Crannon . . . . 11 D c
Craon . . . . 76 C c
Craon, castle . . . . 69 C c
Craonne . . . . 154 B d
Craterus, route of . . . . . . 19 I d
Crathis, mt. . . . . 14 C a
Crathis River, in Achaia . . 14 C a
Crathis (Crati) River, in Bruttium 31 F c
Crato . . . . 83 J h
Craven County . . . . . 193 E e (Cra.)
Craven, Fort . . . . 192 D b
Crawford, Fort . . . . . . 211 G b
Crayford . . . . 75 J i
Crécy . . . . 76 D a
Crediton . . . .
Crediton, parl. bor. . . . . . .
Creek, Ind. Res. . . . . . . 188 G c
Creek, Ind. Res. 1832 . . . . 188 I d
Creeks, tribe . . . . 188 I d
Crefeld . . . . 117 E c
Creglingen . . . . 143 J g
Crema . . . . 90 I h
Cremera River . . . . 35 ins. B
Cremisa, see Krems
Cremona . . . . 26 E b
Cremona, bp. . . . . 95 E b
Crenæ . . . . 10 C d
Crenides . . . . 11 F a
Crépy, near Laon . . . . . 126 C b
Crépy, in Valois . . . . . . 69 I f
Crescentino . . . . 130 Q i (Cr.)
Crespy . . . . 114 B d
Crestonia, reg. . . . . 11 E b
Cretan Sea . . . . 15 D c
Crete, isl. . . . . 14 ins.
Crete, East Rom. prov. . . . 43 H f (2)
Crete, Rom. prov. . . . . . . 35 I g
Crete, theme . . . . 59 J g
Creuse, dept. . . . . 148 E e
Creuse River. . . . . 76 D c
Creusis . . . . 11 E d
Creussen, castle . . . . . . 63 F d
Crevacuore . . . . 130 Q i
Crévant . . . . 76 E c
Crèvecœur, Fort . . . . . . 191 H c
Crewe . . . . 162 D d
Crewkerne . . . . 127 W p
Crexa . . . . 27 I c
Crexi, isl. . . . . 27 I c
Cricklade, parl. bor. . . . 163 M f (Crick.)
Crillon, mt. . . . . 212 ins.
Crimea, Khan of the . . . . . .
Crimea, pen. . . . . 3 H d
Crimisa . . . . 31 G c
Crimisa, prom. . . . . 31 G c

Crimisius River . . . . 30 C e
Cripplegate, in London . . . . . 75 G g
Crisa or Crissa . . . . 11 D d
Crisa or Crissa (Salona), Gulf of 11 D d
Crisenon, mon. . . . . 94 C b
Crithote, prom. . . . . 10 B d
Criumetopon, prom. . . . . . . 14 ins.
Crius River . . . . 14 C a
Crixia . . . . 26 C c
Croatan Island . . . . 193 G d
Croatia, dist. . . . . 159 H f
Croatia, km. . . . . 59 H e
Croatia, reg. . . . . 54 H e
Croatian Military Frontier . . . 159 H f
Croats, people . . . . 53 P i
Croceæ . . . . 14 C c
Crocian Field . . . . 11 D c
Crocylia, isl. . . . . 10 B d
Cromarty, cty. . . . .
Crommyon . . . . 15 D b
Cronos Hill . . . .
Crooked Island . . . . 105 F b
Cropredy Bridge . . . . 127 X n
Cross, Cape . . . . 109 S k
Crossæa, reg. . . . . 11 E b
Cross Creek . . . . 195 B f
Cross Keys . . . . 208 E b (C. K.)
Crotalus River . . . . 31 F c
Croton . . . . 31 G c
Crow, Ind. Res. . . . . 188 E b
Crow Creek, Ind. Res. . . . . . . 188 G b
Crowland . . . .
Crown Point . . . . 192 E h
Crows, tribe . . . . 188 E a
Croxton, mon. . . . . 97 Q i
Croydon . . . . 75 I i
Croyland, mon. . . . .
Crozet Island . . . . 182 GG l
Crusade, fourth 73
Crusade of Conrad III. 70
Crusade of Frederick Barbarossa 70
Crusade of Frederick II. 73
Crusade of Louis VII. 70
Crusade of Louis IX. 73
Crusade of Philip II. (Augustus) 70
Crusade of Richard I. 70
Crusis, reg. . . . . 11 E b
Crustumerium . . . . 35 ins. B
Crustumium River . . . . 27 G d
Crutched Friars, mon. in London 75 G g
Cruzblanca . . . . 201 H g
Cruz del Marqués . . . . 106 A a
Csanad, bp. . . . . 95 G b
Csepel Island . . . . 159 J e
Csik-Sereda . . . . 159 M e
Csongrád . . . . 159 J e
Csorna . . . . 159 I e
Csucsa . . . . 159 L e
Ctesiphon . . . . 20 K f
Ctimene . . . . 10 D c
Cuarius River . . . . 11 D c
Cuba, Capt. Gen. of . . . . . . 213 C/F a/c
Cuba, isl. . . . . 105 E b
Cubagua, isl. . . . . 105 H d
Cuch Behar, reg. . . . . 137 E c
Cuco River . . . . 187 K g
Cudahy . . . . 198 ins. A
Cuddalore . . . .
Cuenca, in Ecuador . . . . 111 B b
Cuenca, in Spain . . . . 82 B a
Cuernavaca . . . . 106 A b
Cufitatchiqui . . . . 191 I e
Cugerni, people . . . . 39 H h
Cuitlahuac . . . . 106 B a
Cujavia, reg. . . . . 138 A e
Cularo (Grenoble) . . . . 38 D c
Culebra . . . .
Culebra, isl. . . . . 199 ins. G
Culenborg . . . . 117 D c
Culhuacan . . . .
Culiacan . . . . 213 B b
Cullera . . . . 82 B b
Culloden Moor . . . .
Cumæ . . . . 31 ins. A

Cumaná . . . . 105 H d
Cumaná, reg. . . . . 105 H e
Cumania, reg. . . . .
Cumans, people . . . . 71 L d
Cumberland . . . . 211 J c
Cumberland, cty. . . . .
Cumberland, Fort . . . . 192 B d
Cumberland District . . . 196 B c (C. D.)
Cumberland Gap, pass . . . . . . 194 C c
Cumberland House . . . . 212 E c
Cumberland Island . . . . 193 D f
Cumberland Mountains . . . . . 193 C c
Cumberland Peninsula . . . . . . 212 I b
Cumberland Plateau . . . . 187 K e
Cumberland River . . . . 191 H d
Cumberland Road, see legend. 210
Cumberland Sound . . . . 212 I b
Cumberland Valley . . . . 208 ins.
Cumbria, reg. . . . .
Cumbrian Mountains . . . . 49 E d
Cume . . . . 12 F b
Cumeoberg, mt. . . . . 54 H d
Cunaxa . . . . 20 J f
Cunene River . . . . 175 E f
Cuneo . . . . 90 H h
Cunerum, prom. . . . . 27 H d
Cuneus aureus . . . .
Cupra Maritima . . . . 27 H d
Curaçao, isl. . . . . 214 C a
Curalius River . . . . 10 C c
Curca . . . . 99 J f
Curetes, people . . . . 10 B d
Curia (Coire) . . . . 39 J j
Curia Hostilia . . . . 24 A
Curico . . . . 215 B f
Curicum . . . . 27 I b
Curitiba . . . . 215 E e
Curium . . . . 20 E e
Curles . . . . 193 ins. A (Cur.)
Currictæ, isl. . . . . 27 I b
Curta . . . . 99 J f
Curus . . . . 27 G e
Curzola, bp. . . . . 95 F c
Curzola, isl. . . . . 90 F c
Cusentia, see Consentia (Cosenza)
Cush, reg. . . . . 4 F e *
Customs-Union of Bavaria and
Wurtemberg . . . . 160 D c
Custoza . . . . 158 F f
Cutch, Gulf of . . . . 137 A d
Cutch, reg. . . . . 137 A d
Cutiliæ, Aquæ . . . . 27 G e
Cuttack . . . . 137 E d
Cuttiæ . . . . 26 C b
Cuttyhunk Island . . . . 189 C d
Cuxhaven . . . . 134 E b
Cuyabá . . . . 214 D d
Cuyahoga River . . . . 196 ins. B
Cuyk . . . . 117 D c
Cuyk, Land of . . . . 117 D c
Cuzco . . . . 111 C d
Cuzco, audiencia . . . . 215 ins.
Cyamosorus River . . . . 30 D e
Cyana, Shrine of . . . . 31 ins. B
Cyane River . . . . 31 ins. B
Cyathus River . . . . 10 C d
Cyclades, isl. . . . . 4 B b
Cycloborus River . . . . 23 D
Cydathenæum, deme . . . . 23 D
Cydnus (Tersus) River . . . . . . 20 F d
Cydonia . . . . 14 ins.
Cyllene . . . . 14 B b
Cyllene, gulf . . . . 14 B a
Cyllene, mt. . . . . 14 C b
Cyme, in Eubœa . . . . 11 F d
Cyme, in Italy . . . . 5 A a
Cymmer, mon. . . . . 97 N i
Cynætha . . . . 14 C a
Cynetes, people . . . . 38 A e
Cynkalan (Canton) . . . .
Cynkali . . . .
Cynosarges, loc. near Athens . 23 D
Cynoscephalæ, mts. . . . . 11 D c
Cynosura, prom. in Diacria .. 16 C a

Cynosura, prom. in Salamis .. 16 B b
Cyntia, lake . . . . 10 C d
Cynuria, dist. in Arcadia . . . . 14 B b
Cynuria, dist. in Argolis . . . . 14 C b
Cynus . . . . 11 E d
Cyparisseis River . . . . 14 B b
Cyparissia . . . . 15 C c
Cyparissiæ . . . . 14 B b
Cyparissian Gulf (Gulf of Ar-
cadia) . . . . 14 B b
Cyparissium, prom. . . . . 14 B b
Cyphanta . . . . 15 D c
Cyprus, isl. . . . . 20 E e
Cyprus, km. . . . . 71 M g
Cyprus, East Rom. prov. . . . . 43 I g (5)
Cyprus, Rom. prov. . . . . 35 K g
Cyprus, theme . . . . 59 K g
Cypsela . . . . 9 B c
Cyrene . . . . 12 H d
Cyrenaica, reg. . . . . 12 H d
Cyrenaica, Rom. prov. . . . . . . 35 I g
Cyreschata . . . . 19 K c
Cyretiæ . . . . 10 D c
Cyropolis . . . . 8 K e
Cyrrhus, in Macedonia . . . . . 11 D b
Cyrrhus, in Syria . . . . 20 G d
Cyrus River (Kur R.) . . . . . . 18 G b
Cythera . . . . 15 D c
Cythera (Cerigo), isl. . . . . . . 15 C c
Cythnus . . . . 15 E b
Cythnus (Termia), isl. . . . . . . 15 E b
Cytinium . . . . 11 D d
Cyzicus . . . .
Czaslau . . . . 135 H d
Czechs, people . . . . 56 E c
Czegléd . . . . 159 J e
Czenstochowa . . . . 79 K c
Czenstochowa, mon. . . . . 95 F a
Czernowitz . . . . 131 I d

Dabayba, reg. . . . . 105 E e
Dacca . . . . 137 F d
Dacia, Rom. prov. . . . . 35 I d
Dacia, East Rom. dioc. . . . . . 43 G e
Dacia Apulensis, Rom. prov. . . 39 M k
Dacia Maluensis, Rom. prov. . . 39 M l
Dacia mediterranea, East Rom.
prov. . . . . 43 G e (1)
Dacia ripensis, East Rom. prov. 50 H d
Daghestan, reg. . . . . 139 G g
Dagö, isl. . . . . 88 I b
Dagupan . . . . 171 N g
Dahæ, people . . . . 19 I c
Dahbul . . . . 112 A b
Dahlak Islands . . . . 170 F g
Dahomey, col. . . . . 174 D d
Daibul . . . .
Dakar . . . . 174 B c
Dakota, ter. 1861 . . . . 203 P f
Dakota, ter. 1863 . . . . 203 R f
Dakota, North, state . . . . 203 R f
Dakota, South, state . . . . 203 R g
Dakota River . . . . 198 F b
Dakotas, tribe . . . . 188 F a
Dalaminzians, people . . . . . . 63 G c
Dalecarlia, reg. . . . . 88 F a
Dalgety . . . . 172 D d
Dalhem . . . . 117 D d
Dalhousie . . . . 212 I d
Dalias . . . . 82 B b
Dalkeith . . . . 84 B b
Dalkey Island . . . . 127 K h
Dallas, in Georgia . . . . 208 D c
Dallas, in Texas . . . . 210 F d
Dalmatia, imp. prov. . . . . 34 H e
Dalmatia, reg. . . . . 56 F d
Dalmatia, theme . . . . 59 H e
Dalmatia, West Rom. prov. . . . 43 F e (11)
Dalny . . . . 171 N e
Dalon, mon. . . . . 94 C b
Dalriada, km. . . . .
Dal River . . . . 88 F a
Dalton . . . . 208 D c
Daly River . . . . 172 C b

Daman . . . . 137 B d
Damaraland, reg. . . . . 175 E g
Damariscotta . . . . 189 D b
Damascene, reg. . . . . 6 E b
Damascus . . . . 5 C b
Damascus, emir. . . . . 68 C c
Damgarten . . . . 154 G a
Damghan . . . .
Damietta . . . . 150 B a
Damm . . . . 123 H b
Dammartin . . . . 76 E b
Dammeshek (Damascus) . . . . . 6 E a
Damnii, people . . . . 38 B a
Dampier Archipelago . . . . . . 172 A b
Dampierre . . . . 143 ins. F
Damvillers . . . . 126 D b
Dan . . . . 6 D b
Dan River . . . . 193 E c
Dan, tribe . . . . 7 ins. D
Danbury . . . . 195 E c
Danelaw, The, reg. . . . .
Danes, people . . . . 46 H b
Danes, people, in England . . . 57 C c
Danewerk, wall . . . . 63 E a
Danish Kingdom . . . . 54 F b
Danish March . . . . 58 F c (D.M.)
Danish Mercia, reg. . . . .
Danish Northumbria, reg. . . . .
Dankov . . . . 139 E e
Dannenberg . . . . 79 G b
Dantzic . . . . 63 J a
Dantzic, Hanse. cy. . . . . 98 G c
Dantzic, rep. . . . . 155 J a
Danube River . . . . 2 F d
Danuvius (Danube) River . . . . 34 G d
Danville . . . . 195 B e
Daphne . . . . 4 ins. *
Daphnus . . . . 11 D d
Daphnus River . . . . 10 C d
Dara, in Dar-fur . . . . 174 F c
Dara, in Mesopotamia . . . . . . 20 I d
Darantasia . . . . 26 A b
Daras . . . . 52 M f
Dardanelles, str. . . . . 2 G e
Dardani, people . . . . 39 M l
Dardania, reg. . . . .
Dardania, East Rom. prov. . . . 43 G e (4)
Dardanus . . . .
Dar-es-Salaam . . . . 175 G e
Darent River . . . . 75 J i
Dar-fur, reg. . . . . 174 F c
Dargun, mon. . . . . 80 C e
Darien, Gulf of . . . . 105 E e
Darien, reg., in Colombia, see
    Urabá . . . . 105 E e
Darien, dist., in Georgia . . . . 193 ins. C
Darini, people . . . . 38 A b
Dariorigum, see Vannes
Darley, mon. . . . . 97 P i
Darling River . . . . 172 D d
Darlington . . . . 162 E c
Darmstadt . . . . 114 E d
Darnis . . . . 43 G g
Daroca . . . . 82 B a
Daron . . . . 68 ins. A
Dartford . . . . 75 J i
Dartfort, mon. . . . . 97 R j
Dartmoor . . . . 49 D f
Dartmouth, in England . . . . . 84 B d
Dartmouth, parl. bor. . . . . . . 163 K g
Dartmouth, in Mass. . . . . 189 C d (Dart.)
Darwin, mt. . . . . 215 B h
Dascon . . . . 31 ins. B
Dascylium . . . .
Dassaretæ, people . . . . 10 B b
Dassel . . . . 72 B a
Datis' fleet, route of . . . . . . 13 D c
Datum . . . . 11 F b
Daulatabad . . . .
Daulis . . . . 11 D d
Daunii, people . . . . 30 E a
Daunus River . . . . 30 E a
Dauphin, Fort . . . .
Dauphin, isl. . . . . 191 H e

Dauphin, Place du, Paris . . . . 149 B
Dauphiny, gouv. . . . . 146 C c
Dauphiny, prov. . . . . 148 F f
Davao . . . . 199 ins. H
Davenport . . . . 211 G b
Daventry . . . . 127 X n
Davey, Port . . . . 172 D e
David . . . . 214 A b
David, Street of . . . . 68 ins. B
David, Tomb(s) of . . . . 6 ins. A
David and Solomon, Wall of . . 6 ins. A
David Comnenus, Dom. of . . . 73 G b
David's Gate . . . . 68 ins. B
Davids house, Jerusalem . . . . 6 ins. A (3)
Davids Tower . . . . 68 ins. B
Davis Islands . . . . 108 L l
Davis, routes of . . . . 108 P b
Davis Strait . . . . 186 N b
Davos . . . . 91 R l
Dawson . . . . 212 B n
Dax . . . . 69 C e
Dax, bp. . . . . 94 B c
Dayton . . . . 200 A d
De Aar . . . . 175 L m
Dead Sea . . . . 7 C f
Dean, Forest of . . . . 49 E f
Dearborn, Fort (Chicago) . . . 199 H b
Dearborn, route of . . . . 200 C d
Death Valley . . . . 187 H e
Debeltum . . . . 43 H e
Debreczin . . . .
Decastadium . . . . 30 E e
Decatur . . . . 208 C c
Deccan, reg. . . . . 137 C f
Decelea . . . . 15 D a
Decempagi . . . . 39 I i
Deciates, people . . . . 26 A d
Decise . . . . 126 C c
Decius, Baths of . . . .
Decuman Gate . . . . 22 A
Deddington, parl. bor. . . .
Dedham . . . . 189 ins. B
Deer Creek, Ind. Res. . . . . . 188 H a
Deerfield, battle . . . . 189 B c
Deep River . . . . 195 B f
Dee River, in England . . . . .
Dee River, in Scotland . . . .
Dees . . . . 159 L e
Defiance . . . . 200 A c
Defiance, Fort . . . . 196 ins. B
Dego . . . . 150 E d
De Grey River . . . . 172 B c
Dcheubarth, reg. . . . .
Dei Consentes, Portico of the.
Deiotarus, Kingdom of . . . . 35 K e
Deira, reg. . . . .
Deirades . . . . 16 C b
Deirans, people . . . .
Dekapolis, dist. . . . . 7 D d
Delagoa Bay . . . . 175 G g
Delaware, state . . . . . . 199 J c (Del.)
Delaware Bay . . . . 192 D d
Delaware Counties, col. . . . . 192 D d
Delaware River . . . . 192 D c
Delawares, tribe . . . . 188 K c
Deleus . . . .
Delft . . . . 117 C b
Delftshaven . . . . 134 D b
Delfzyl . . . . 117 E a
Delgado, Cape . . . . 175 H f
Delhi . . . . 137 C c
Delhi, Empire of the Sultans of
Delian Amphictyony . . . . . . 8 P i
Delium . . . . 11 E d
Della Scala Dominions . . . . 79 G f
Delle . . . . 143 ins. F
Delminium . . . . 38 F d
Delos . . . . 15 F b
Delos, isl. . . . . 8 P i
Delphi (Kastri) . . . . 11 D d
Delphic Amphictyony . . . 8 O h legend
Delphini, Portus . . . . 26 D c
Demarcation Point, cape . . . . 198 ins. A

Demerara . . . . 214 D b
Demetæ, people . . . . 51 N i
Demeter, Temple of . . . . 31 ins. B (12)
Demetrias . . . . 11 E c
Demmin . . . . 63 G b
Demmin, Hanse. cy. . . . . 99 ins. B
Demonesi Islands . . . .
Demotika . . . . 131 I e
Denain . . . . 134 B c
Denain, mon. . . . . 148 B a
Denbigh, in Virginia . . . . . . 193 ins. A
Denbigh, cty. in Wales . . . . . 127 V m
Denbigh, parl. bor. . . . . 163 K d
Denbigh, parl. dist. . . . . 163 K d
Dendera . . . . 4 F d*
Dendermonde . . . . 117 C c
Denia . . . . 82 C b
Denkendorf . . . . 143 H h
Denmark, kingdom, about 1000 58 G b
Denmark, kingdom, 19 cent. . . 158 F a
Denmark and Norway, km. in 1812 155 ins.
Dennewitz . . . . 154 G c
Dennis, East . . . . 207 M b
Dentheletæ, people . . . . 39 M l
Dentheliatis, dist. . . . . 14 C c
Denver . . . . 210 E c
Deogir, reg. . . . .
Déols, reg. . . . . 61 D c
Déols, castle . . . . 76 D c
Déols, seign. . . . . 61 D c
Deorham . . . .
Deptford . . . . 75 I i
Dera Ghazi Khan . . . . 137 B b
Dera Ismail Khan . . . . 137 B b
Derbe . . . . 20 E d
Derbend . . . .
Derbiccans, people . . . . 8 J e
Derby . . . .
Derby, cty. . . . .
Derby, parl. bor. . . . . 163 M e
Derby, shire . . . .
Derg, Lough, lake . . . . 127 I h
Derindeh . . . . 124 G c
Derkos . . . . 165 F c
Dermbach . . . . 158 E c
Derrhis, prom . . . . 11 E c
Derry, bp. . . . . 97 D b
Dertona . . . . 26 C c
Dertosa (Tortosa) . . . . 38 C d
Desastre, Rio del, river . . . . 105 D d
Deseado, Cape . . . . 108 J l
Deseado River . . . . 215 C g
Deseret, see Utah . . . . 211 C b c
Des Moines . . . . 211 G b
Des Moines River . . . . 191 G c
Desna River . . . . 139 D e
Desplaines River . . . . 191 H c
Dessau . . . . 79 H c
Desterro . . . . 215 E e
Detmold . . . . 62 E c
Detroit, fort . . . . 191 I c
Detroit . . . . 199 I b
Dettingen . . . . 134 E c
Deulino . . . . 138 E d
Deuriopes, people . . . . 10 C a
Deutsch-Brod . . . . 87 J d
Deutsch-Krone . . . . 115 I b
Deutz . . . . 55 Q i
Deux Ponts (Zweibrücken) . . . 86 F d
Deux Ponts, princ. . . . . 134 D d
Deux-Sèvres, dept. . . . . 148 D e
Deva (Chester) . . . . 51 O h
Deva, in Transylvania . . . . . 159 L f
Deventer . . . . 117 E b
Deventer, Hanse. cy. . . . . . . 99 ins. B
Deventer, mon. . . . . 95 D a
Devil's Lake, Ind. Res. . . . . . 188 G a
Devizes . . . . 65 F e
Devizes, castle . . . .
Devizes, parl. bor. . . . . 163 M f
Devol . . . . 67 K e
Devon, cty. . . . .
Devon, shire . . . .
Devonport, parl. bor. . . . . . . 163 J g

De Vries, route of . . . .
Deynze . . . . 117 B d
Dhar . . . .
Dharwar. . . . . 137 C e
Dia, isl. . . . . 14 ins.
Diacira . . . . 20 J f
Diacria, dist. . . . . 16 B a
Diadochi, Kingdoms of the, about 200 B. C. 19
Diadochi, Kingdoms of the, 301 B. C. 18
Diagon River . . . . 14 B b
Dialas River . . . . 18 G c
Diamantina. . . . . 214 E d
Diamantine River . . . . . . 172 C c
Diamond, Cape . . . . 112 C c
Diana, Grove of . . . . 35 ins. B
Diana, Temple of . . . . 22 A
Dianium . . . . 38 C e
Dianium, isl. . . . . 26 F e
Diarbekir, reg.
Diarbekr . . . . 99 L f
Diaz, Bartholomew, route of . . 108 Q g
Diaz, Melchior, route of . . . . 190 C f
Dibio, see Dijon
Dibon . . . . 7 D f
Dicæa . . . . 13 J d
Dicæarchia . . . . 31 ins. A
Dickrich . . . . 117 E e
Dicte . . . . 4 C b
Dicte, mt. . . . . 14 ins.
Didyma, mt. . . . . 15 D b
Didyme, isl. . . . . 30 D d
Die . . . . 61 F d
Die, bp. . . . . 95 D c
Diedenhofen (Thionville) . . . . 62 C d
Diego, Fort . . . . 193 D f
Diego Garcia, isl . . . . 182 II h
Diego Rodriguez, isl. . . . . . 109 X i
Diego Suarez . . . . 175 H f
Diekirch . . . . 117 E e
Diepenow-Schanze, fort . . . . 123 H a
Diepholz . . . . 86 G b
Diepholz, cty. . . . . 86 G b
Dieppe . . . . 76 D a
Dieppe, Hanse. for. cy. . . . . 98 D d
Diessenhofen . . . . 142 C e
Diest . . . . 117 C d
Dieulacres, mon. . . . . 97 O h
Dieveren . . . . 117 E b
Digentia River . . . . 35 ins. B
Digne . . . . 69 G d
Digne, bp. . . . . 95 D c
Dijon . . . . 61 F c
Dijon, gen. . . . . 147 E b
Dillenburg . . . . 114 D c
Dillingen . . . . 114 F d
Dinan . . . . 76 B b
Dinant . . . . 117 C d
Dinant, Hanse. cy. . . . . . . 98 D d
Dinapur . . . . 137 E c
Dinaretium, prom. . . . . . . 20 F e
Dindigal, Dindigul, dist. . . . 137 C g
Dindymus, mt. near Cyzicus . .
Dindymus, mt. near Sardis . . 20 C c
Dine, isl. . . . . 15 C b
Dinerof . . . . 117 E e
Dingle Bay . . . . 127 G i
Dinia, see Digne
Diocæsarea . . . . 6 C c
Diochares Gate . . . . 23 D
Dioclea . . . . 59 H e
Diocletian, Baths of . . . . . 22 A
Diogenium . . . . 23 D
Diois, dist. . . . . 126 D d
Diomean Gate . . . . 23 D
Dion-le-Mont . . . . 156 B a
Dionysiades, isl. . . . . 14 ins.
Dionysius, Citadel of . . . . . 31 ins. B (4)
Dionysopolis . . . . 39 N l
Dionysus, Temple of . . . . . .
Dionysus, Theatre of . . . . . 23 C
Dioryctus . . . . 10 B d
Dioscurias . . . . 12 L b

Dioscurias, prom. . . . . 31 G d
Diospolis, in Bithynia . . . . . 20 D b
Diospolis, in Egypt . . . . . . 4 F d*
Diospolis, in Palestine . . . . 7 B e
Dipæa . . . . 14 C b
Diplokionion, quarter . . . . . 93 G e
Dipylum . . . . 23 D
Diribitorium, loc. in Rome . . . 24 B
Dirphys, mt. . . . . 11 E d
Dirschau . . . . 123 J a
Disentis, ab. . . . . 78 F e
Disentis, mon. . . . . 91 Q l
Disibodenberg, mon. . . . . 95 D b (Dis.)
Dismal Swamp . . . . 193 F c
District of Columbia . . . 211 J c (D. C.)
Dithmarschen (Ditmarsh) reg. . 62 E a
Dittani, people . . . . 38 B d
Diu . . . . 137 B d
Dium, in Chalcidice . . . . . 11 F b
Dium, in Eubœa . . . . 11 D d
Dium, in Macedonia . . . . . . 11 D b
Dium, in Syria . . . . 6 D c*
Divini, Portus . . . . 38 B e
Divione, see Dijon
Divirigi . . . . 99 K f
Divitia . . . . 39 I h
Divodurum (Metz) . . . . . . 39 I i
Divona, see Cahors
Divus Augustus, Temple of . . 24 B
Divus Claudius, Portico of. . . 22 A
Divus Claudius, Temple of . . 22 A
Divus Julius, Temple of . . . .
Divus Romulus, Temple of . .
Divus Trajanus, Temple of . . 24 B
Dixcove 175
Dixmuide . . . .
Dixmuyden . . . . 117 A c
Dixon Entrance . . . . 212 ins.
Dixon Sound . . . . 198 ins. A
Dmietrov . . . . 71 N b
Dnieper River . . . .
Dniester River . . . . 139 C f
Dobbs, Fort . . . . 193 D d
Doberan, mon. . . . . 80 B d
Doberus . . . . 17 E a
Dobrilugk . . . . 63 G c
Dobritch, Dobrudja, Dobrudsha, dist. . . . . 119 J e
Dobrzyn . . . . 79 K b
Dobuni, people . . . . 51 O i
Doclea . . . . 39 L l
Dudendorf . . . . 154 F b
Dodge, Fort . . . . 210 E c
Dodge City. . . . . 210 E c
Dodona . . . . 10 B c
Dœtinchem . . . . 117 E c
Doffingen . . . . 143 G h
Dohna . . . . 85 G e
Dohna, castle . . . . 63 G c
Dokkum . . . . 117 D a
Dol . . . . 61 C b
Dol, bp. . . . . 94 B b
Dolceacqua . . . . 130 P k
Dôle . . . . 114 C e
Dôle, univ. . . . . 100 G e
Doliche . . . . 10 D b
Doliche, isl. . . . . 10 C d
Dollart, The, bay . . . . 78 E b
Dolma Baghtcheh . . . .
Dolopes, people, in Scyrus . . 11 F d
Dolopes, people, in Thessaly . 8 N h
Dolopia, reg. . . . . 10 C c
Dolores Hidalgo . . . . 213 ins.
Dolyani, bp. . . . . 95 F c
Domana . . . . 20 H b
Dombes, gen. . . . . 147 F b
Domfront . . . . 69 C b
Domine quo vadis, loc. near Rome . . . . 96 A
Dominguez, route of . . . . . . 190 C d
Dominica, isl., Antilles . . . . 105 H c
Dominica, isl., Marquesas . . . 107 D h
Dominican Republic, country . 213 E c
Dominion of Canada . . . . . 211 C c

Domitian, Gardens of . . . . . 22 A
Domitian, Palace of . . . . . . 24 B
Domitian, Stadium of . . . . . 22 A
Dömitz . . . . 122 F b
Domo d'Ossola . . . . 90 I g
Domremy . . . . 81 N h
Domstadtl . . . . 135 I d
Doncaster. . . . .
Doncaster, parl. bor. . . . . . .
Donegal . . . . 127 J g
Donegal, cty. . . . . 127 J g
Donegal Bay . . . . 49 B d
Donelson, Fort . . . . 208 C b
Donetz River . . . . 139 F f
Dongola . . . . 174 F c
Donnington Castle . . . . . . 127 X o
Donnybrook, fair in Dublin . . 98 ins. A
Don River . . . . 139 F f
Donzy . . . . 76 E c
Dor, Dora . . . . 6 B c
Dora Baltea River . . . . . . 130 P i
Dora Ripaira River . . . . . . 130 O i
Dorat . . . . 126 B c
Dorchester, in Dorsetshire . . .
Dorchester, in Oxfordshire . . .
Dorchester, in Conn. . . . . . 189 B d
Dorchester, in Mass. . . . . . 189 ins. B
Dorchester, bp. . . . . 97 P j
Dorchester, parl. bor. . . . . . 163 L g
Dorchester Heights . . . . . . 195 ins. A
Dordogne, dept. . . . . 148 E e
Dordogne River . . . . 76 D d
Dordrecht . . . . 117 C c
Dordrecht, Hanse. cy. . . . . . 99 ins. B
Dorians, people . . . .
Doris, region, in Asia Minor . 8 Q i
Doris, state, in Greece . . . . 13 C b
Doriscus . . . .
Dorium . . . . 14 B b
Dorking . . . . 75 I i
Dormition, loc. in Jerusalem . 6 ins. A
Dornach, castle . . . . 91 P k
Dornhan . . . . 143 G i
Dornonia, see Dordogne
Dornstetten . . . . 143 G i
Dorocas, see Dreux
Dorogobusch . . . .
Dorogobuzh . . . . 153 O g
Dorostorium . . . . 43 H e
Dorpat . . . . 71 L b
Dorpat, Hanse. cy. . . . . . . 99 I b
Dorsætas, people . . . .
Dorset, cty. . . . .
Dorset, parl. dist. . . . . 163 L g
Dorset, shire . . . .
Dort . . . . 117 C c
Dortmund. . . . . 62 D c
Dortmund, Hanse. cy. . . . . . 99 ins. B
Dortmund, imp. city . . . . . 78 E c
Dorylæum . . . . 20 D c
Dörzbach . . . . 143 I g
Dossenbach . . . . 158 E e
Dothan . . . . 7 C d
Dotian Field . . . . 11 D c
Dotternhausen . . . . 143 G i
Douai . . . . 117 B d
Doubs River . . . . 62 D e
Doubs, dept. . . . . 148 F e
Douglas . . . . 212 ins.
Douglas, castle. . . . . 118 D b
Douglas, isl. . . . .
Douglas, fam. . . . .
Doullens . . . . 117 A d
Dour . . . . 157 ins.
Douro (Duero) River . . . . . 82 G e
Dover, in England . . . .
Dover, castle . . . . 65 G e
Dover, mon. . . . . 97 S j
Dover, parl. bor. . . . . 163 P f
Dover, in Delaware . . . . . . 192 D d
Dover, in New Hampshire . . 189 C c

ovre Field	166	G c	Dulcigno, bp.	95	F c	Düsseldorf	86	F c
owngate, in London	75	G g	Dulcis Portus, bay	10	B c	Dutch Guiana	214	D b
own, bp.	97	E b	Duluth	211	G a	Dutch Harbor	198	ins. A
own, cty.	127	K g	Dumah	7	B f	Duxbury, in England	185	D d
ownpatrick, bp.	97	F b	Dumbarton			Duxbury, in Mass.	189	C c
owns, North, dist.	49	G f	Dumbarton, cty.			Dwara-Samudra		
owns, South, dist.	49	F f	Dumbarton, dist.			Dwina, Gulf		
ownton, parl. bor.	163	M g	Dumbrek, R.			Dwina River		
rabescus	11	F a	Dumfries			Dyea	212	ins.
ragashan	164	C b	Dumfries, cty.			Dyle River	62	C c
ragon's Mouth, str.	105	H d	Dumfries, reg.			Dyne	14	B a
ragovitches, people	71	K c	Dumio, mon.	94	A c	Dynevwor		
raguignan	148	F f	Dummer, Fort	189	B c	Dyras River	16	E e
raheim	123	I b	Dumnonii, people	51	N i	Dyrrhachium (Durazzo)	31	I a
rake, route of	107	C e	Dünaburg	88	L c	Dyrrhachium, theme	59	H e
	108	M k	Düna River	138	C d	Dyrta	19	L c
	109	I j	Dunbar			Dyscus	11	F d
	110	II f	Dunblaine, bp.			Dysoron, mt.	11	E a
rake's Bay	107	E d	Duncansby Head					
rakenburg	114	E b	Dundalk			Eagle Pass	210	E e
rakensberg, mts.	175	M l	Dundalk Bay	127	K h	East, Dioc. of the	43	J g
ramburg	85	D b	Dundee			East, Pref. of the	43	I h
rangiana, prov.	19	J d	Dundra Head, cape			East Africa, British, col.		
rangiana, satr.	8	K e	Dunedin	172	G e	East Africa, German, col.		
rapsaca	19	K c	Dunfermline			East Africa, Portuguese, col.		
rave River	63	I f	Dung Gate, loc. in Jerusalem	6	ins. A	East Africa Company, German		
ravus (Drave) River	38	E c	Dunkeld			East Africa Company, Imperial		
red Scott „dicta", see legend 207			Dunkeld, bp.	97	J c	British		
reisam River	142	A c	Dunkeswell, mon.	97	N k	East Angles, people	51	S k
renthe, cty.	117	E b	Dunkirk	117	A c	East Anglia, km.		
repanum, in Asia Minor			Dunmow, Little, mon.	97	R j	East Anglia Heights	49	G e
repanum, in Sicily	30	B e	Dunnottar Castle			East Cape, in Asia	171	T b
repanum, prom.	14	B a	Dunois, cty.	84	D e	East Cape, in New Zealand	172	G d
resden	85	G e	Dunstable, castle			Eastcheap, in London	75	G g
reux	61	D b	Dunstable, mon.	97	Q j	East Cornwall, parl. dist.	163	J g
riesen	85	D b	Dunstable, parl. bor.			East Cumberland, parl. dist.	163	L c
rilon River	17	B a	Dunster, parl. bor.			East Dennis	207	M b
rina River	89	G f	Dunum, see Châteaudun			Easter Island	180	Q j
rinus River	39	L l	Dunwich			Eastern Euphrates River	20	H c
rissa	153	N f	Dunwich, parl. bor.	163	P e	Eastern Ghats, mts.	112	B b
riăti, bp.	95	F c	Düppel	158	E a	Eastern Rumelia, prov.	164	C b
robetæ	39	M l	Duquesne, Fort	192	A c	Eastern Sea	171	N f
rogheda			Dura in Assyria	20	J e	East Florida, col.	194	C de
	155	L b	Dura in Mesopotamia	20	I e	East Franconia, duchy	62	E d
roitwich, parl. bor.	163	L e	Durance River	69	F e	East Frankish Kingdom	56	C b
rokinsford, deanery	100	A b	Durango	213	B b	East Friesland, cty.	122	D b
rôme, dept.	148	F f	Durango, prov.	190	D f	East Friesland, dist.	86	F b
römling, dist.	62	F b	Durango, state	213	B b	East Friesland, princ.	134	D b
romore, bp.	97	E b	Duranius (Dordogne) River	38	C d	East Gloucester, parl. dist.	163	L f
romos, in Alexandria	34	ins. C	Durant's Neck, dist.	193	F c	East Göthland, reg.		
rübeck	122	F c	Durazzo	42	F e	East Goths, Kingdom of the	52	D b
ruentia (Durance) River	26	A c	Durazzo, abp.	95	F c	East Goths, people, in Asia		
rummondville	212	H d	Durban	175	N l	Minor, in 382		
rusi, Pons, bridge	27	F a	Durbuy	117	D d	East Goths, people, on the Dnie-		
rusus, Arch of	22	A	Durham			per, in 200	45	K c
rusus, Canal of	39	I h	Durham, battle	189	C c	East Goths, people, in Italy, in 493	45	G d
rymæa	11	D d	Durham, bp.	97	P g	East Goths, people, in Pannonia,		
ryopes, people	15	E a	Durham, castle	65	F c	in 454	45	H c
ry Tortugas, isl.	213	D b	Durham, cty.	127	X l	East Greenwich	189	ins. A
ubaunt Lake	186	I b	Durham, palat.			East Grinstead, parl. bor.	163	O f
üben	123	G c	Durham, shire			Eastham	189	D d
ubienka	139	B e	Duria Major (Dora Baltea) River	26	B b	Easthampton	189	B d
ubis (Doubs) River	39	I j	Duria Minor River	26	B b	East Indies, reg.	109, 110	X-DD, e-h
ubitza	131	G d	Dur-Ilu	5	D b	East Kent, parl. dist.	163	O f
ublin			Durius (Douro) River	38	A d	East London	175	M m
ublin, abp.	97	E d	Dur Kurigalzu	4	D e	East Looe, parl. bor.	163	J g
ublin, cty.	127	K h	Durlach	142	B c	East Main River	186	L c
ublin Bay	127	K h	Durnkrut	79	J d	East March, Bavarian	63	H d
ubra, see Dubræ			Durnomagus	39	I h	East March, in Scotland		
ubræ (Dover)	51	Q i	Durnovaria (Dorchester)	51	O i	East Marches, in Northumber-		
ubrovna	153	O g	Durobrivæ (Castor)	51	P h	land		
ubuque	199	G b	Durobrivæ (Rochester)	51	Q i	East New Jersey, col.	192	D c
ucal Saxony	85	G d	Durocasses, see Dreux			East Norfolk, parl. dist.	163	P e
uck Valley, Ind. Res.	188	C b	Durocatalaunum, see Châlons			Easton	192	D c
udeldorf	117	E d	Durocornovium, see Corinium			Eastphalia, dist.	62	F b
uderstadt	62	F c	(Cirencester)			Eastphalians, people	55	R i
udinskœ	171	J b	Durocortorum (Reims)	38	C c	East Prussia, prov.	159	K a
udley, parl. bor.	163	L e	Durolipons			East Prussia, reg.	135	K a
uero (Douro) River	82	A a	Durostorum (Silistria)	39	N l	East Retford, parl. bor.	163	N d
ufile	175	G d	Durotriges, people	51	O i	East Riding, dist.	162	F d
uisburg, in Belgium	50	D b	Durovernum (Canterbury)	51	Q i	East Riding, parl. dist.	162	N d
uisburg, in Germany	62	D c	Dürrenstein, castle	72	D b	East Roman Empire about 395	43	
uisburg, Hanse. cy.	99	ins. B	Dur-Samand, reg.			East Roman Empire in 486	50—51	
ukla	139	K d	Dur-Sharukin (Khorsabad)	5	D b	East Roman Empire, 6 cent.	52	

East Roman Empire, in 750 .. 53
East Saxons, people ..... 51 R k
East Somerset, parl. dist. .... 163 L f
East Suffolk, parl. dist. ... 163 P e
East Surrey, parl. dist. ... 163 N f (E.S.)
East Sussex, parl. dist. ... 163 O g
East Turkestan, reg. ...... 170 I e
East Voorne, isl. .... 117 B c
East Worcester, parl. dist. ... 163 L e
Eause (Eauze) .... 94 C c
Ebal, mt. .... 7 C d
Ebelsberg. .... 155 H d
Ebenezer, in Georgia ..... 193 ins. C
Ebenezer, in Judæa ..... 7 B e
Eberbach .... 142 C b
Eberbach, mon. .... 95 D a
Ebernburg, castle .... 114 D d
Ebersberg, castle .... 63 F d
Eberstein, castle .... 142 B c
Eberstein, cty. .... 142 B c
Ebgate, in London ...... 75 G g
Ebingen .... 143 H i
Eblana .... 34 C c
Eboracum or Eburacum (York
  in England) .... 51 P h
Ebrach, mon. .... 95 E b
Ebrodunum, see Embrun
Ebroicas, see Evreux
Ebro River .... 82 B a
Ebron .... 6 C c
Ebudae Islands (The Hebrides) 34 C b
Eburacum or Eboracum (York
  in England) .... 38 B b
Eburodunum (Embrun) ..... 26 A c
Eburodunum (Yverdon) ..... 39 I j
Eburones, people ...... 39 H h
Eburovices, see Evreux
Eburovices, people ..... 38 C c
Eburum .... 30 E b
Ebusus, isl. .... 38 C e
Ecbatana (Hamadan) ..... 5 D b
Ecdippa .... 6 C b
Ecetra .... 30 C a
Echallens .... 91 O l
Echedamia .... 11 D d
Echedorus River .... 11 D b
Echinades, isl. .... 10 B d
Echinus .... 11 D d
Echternach .... 117 E e
Echternach, mon. .... 95 D b
Écija .... 82 A b
Eckernförde .... 158 F a
Ecnomus, mt. .... 30 C e
Ecolesima, see Angoulême
Ecuador, country ...... 214 B c
Écuries, Grandes, in Versailles 149 A
Écuries, Petites, in Versailles 149 A
Écuries de la Reine, in Versailles 149 A
Edam .... 117 D b
Edenton .... 193 F c
Edessa, in Macedonia ... 10 D b
Edessa, in Mesopotamia ... 20 H d
Edessa, cty. .... 68 C b
Edgartown .... 189 C d
Edgecote .... 84 C c
Edge Hill .... 49 F e
Edge Hill, village .... 127 X n
Edinburgh
Edinburgh, cty. ....
Edisto, Fort .... 193 ins. C
Edisto River .... 193 D e
Edmonton .... 212 D c
Edom, reg. .... 5 C b
Edomites, people ...... 7 ins. D
Edones, people .... 11 E b
Edrei .... 6 E c
Edrisids, Dom. of the ... 83 E d
Edrum .... 26 E b
Edward, Fort .... 192 E b
Edward Augustus, Fort .... 194 B b
Edward Nyanza, lake ... 175 G d
Edwards Ferry .... 208 ins.
Eetionea .... 16 D c
Eferding .... 123 G d

Eger .... 72 C a
Egerland, dist. .... 79 ins.
Eger River .... 63 G c
Egersund .... 166 G d
Egg Harbor, Little .... 192 D d
Eggmühl .... 154 G d
Egham .... 75 H i
Eghezée .... 156 B a
Egisheim .... 62 D d
Eglaim .... 7 D f
Eglingen .... 143 H i
Eglingen, lordship ... 143 J h
Eglisau, castle ...... 91 Q k
Eglofs, cty. .... 143 I j
Eglon .... 7 B e
Egmond, castle .... 62 C b
Egmond, mon. .... 94 C a
Egnatia .... 31 G b
Egnatian Way ....
Egremont, parl. bor.
Egrigaia ....
Egypt, emp. 4
Egypt, Rom. prov. ... 35 J h
Egypt, East Rom. dioc. ... 43 H h
Egypt, East Rom. prov. ... 43 I g (4)
Egypt, prov. 12 cent. ... 71 M h
Egypt, state .... 174 F b
Egypt, Port of .... 18 ins. B
Ehingen .... 143 I i
Ehnheim, Ober- .... 122 D d
Ehrenberger Klause Pass .... 114 F e
Ehrenbreitstein ...... 122 D c
Eichsfeld, dist. ..... 114 F c
Eichstädt ....
Eichstädt, bp. ....
Eider River .... 62 E a
Eiham, mon. .... 94 C a
Eilenburg .... 85 G e
Einbeck .... 114 F c
Einbeck, Hanse. cy. ... 99 ins. B
Eindhoven .... 117 D c
Einsiedeln, mon. ..... 91 Q k
Eïon .... 11 E b
Eipel River .... 115 J d
Eisack River .... 62 F e
Eisenach .... 85 F e
Eisenberg .... 115 ins. B
Eisenburg .... 123 I e
Eiserntor Pass .... 159 L f
Eisleben .... 114 F c
Eislingen .... 143 I h
Ekaterinburg .... 138 J d
Ekaterinodar .... 167 M g
Ekaterinoslav .... 139 D f
Ekron (Akir) .... 7 B e
Elæa .... 10 B c
Elæatis, reg. .... 10 B c
Elæum, mt. .... 14 B b
Elæus, in Ætolia ..... 10 C d
Elæus, in Argolis .... 14 C b
Elæus, in Epirus ..... 10 B b
Elæus, in Thrace ....
Elæussa Island .... 16 B b
Elam, reg. .... 4 E e
Elandslaagte .... 175 N l
El Araish .... 118 C f
El Arish
Elatea, in Bœotia .... 11 D d
Elath .... 5 C c
Elatia .... 11 D c
Elatria .... 10 B c
Elatus, mt. .... 14 A b
Elaver (Allier) River .... 38 C c
Elba, isl. .... 90 L j
Elbassan ....
Elbe River .... 62 F b
Elberfeld .... 158 D b
Elbeuf .... 76 D b
Elbing .... 72 D a
Elbing, Hanse. cy. ... 98 G c
Elbrus, mt. .... 3 I d
Elburg .... 117 D b
Elburg, Hanse. cy. ... 99 ins. B
Elburz Mountains ...... 3 J e

Elcano, route of ...... 109 W
Elche .... 82 B
Elchingen, ab. .... 143 J
Elchingen, mon. ...... 143 J
Eldena, mon. .... 80 C
Elea .... 30 E
Elealah .... 7 D
Electoral Archchancellor, Ter.
  of the .... 151 H f (E.A.
Electoral Hesse, state ... 158 E
Electoral Saxony, state ... 85 G
Electorates, The Seven ... 78 leg
Elen .... 214 B
Eleon .... 11 E
Elephantine Island (Gezeret-
  Assuan) .... 1 C
Eleusinian Gulf ...... 16 B
Eleusis (Levsina) .... 15 D
Eleutheræ .... 15 D
Eleutherna .... 14 ins.
Eleutheropolis .... 7 B
Eleutherus River ..... 30 C
El Fasher .... 174 F
Elgin ....
Elgin, bp. .... 97 J b
Elgin, cty. ....
El Golea .... 174 D
El Gran Chaco, region ... 215 C
El Hasa, reg. ....
El Hejas, Hedjas, reg. ... 170 E
Elim .... 68 C
Elimea .... 10 C
Elimea, reg. .... 10 C
Elis .... 14 B
Elis, reg. .... 14 B
Elis, state .... 13 B
Elizabetgrad .... 167 L
Elizabeth .... 192 D
Elizabeth, Cape ...... 189 C
Elizabethtown .... 192 D
El Jesireh, reg. ..... 67 O
El Kantara .... 174 K
El Katif ....
Elk River .... 192 A
Elkton .... 195 C
El Kufa .... 73 I
Ellesmere .... 162 D
Ellesmere Land .... 186 K
Ellice Islands .... 172 G
Ellichpur .... 137 C
Ellingham, mon. ...... 100 A
Ellomenon .... 10 B
Ellwangen .... 143 J
Ellwangen, mon. ...... 95 E
Ellwangen, provostry ... 143 J
El-Mahdiya .... 73 C
Elmet, Forest of ..... 49 F
Elmet, dist. ....
Elmham ....
Elmina ....
Elmira .... 195 C
Elne, bp. .... 94 C
El Obeid .... 174 F
Elosa or Elusa, see Eause (Eauze)
El Pardo, castle ..... 130 C
El Paso .... 190 D
El Paso del Norte .... 213 B
Elphin, bp. .... 97 C
Elsfleth .... 122 E
Elsing Spital, bldg. in London . 75 G
Elster, Schwarze, river ... 85 G
Elster, Weisse, river ... 85 G
Elstow, mon. .... 97 Q
El Teb .... 174 G
Eltham .... 75 J
Eltville .... 78 F
Elusa, in France, see Eause (Eauze)
Elusa, in Palestine ... 7 B f
Elvas .... 82 A b
El Viejo .... 213 C
Elvira .... 42 B f
Ely, in England .....
Ely, in India ....
Ely, bp. .... 97 R i

Ely, Isle of, dist. . . . .
Ely, parl. bor. . . . .
El Yemamah
Elymæi, people . . . . 19 G d
Elymi, people . . . . 30 B e
Elymia . . . . 14 C b
Elymians, people . . . .
Ely Place, loc. in London . . 75 G g
Elz River . . . . 142 A d
Elzach . . . . 142 B d
Emathia, reg. . . . . 11 D b
Embrun . . . . . 69 G d
Embrun, abp. . . . 95 D c
Emden . . . . 78 E b
Emerita Augusta (Mérida) . . 38 A e
Emesa . . . 35 L g
Emilia, dist. . . . 90 C b
Emly, bp. . . . 97 C d
Emmaus . . . 7 B e
Emmendingen . . 142 A d
Emmerich, in Germany . . . . 122 D c
Emmerich, in Transylvania . . 119 I d
Emmetsburg . . . 208 ins.
Emona (Laibach) . . . 27 I a
Emperador
Empire, The . . . 81 H c
Empire of the French . . . . 155 ins.
Empire of the Sultans of Delhi
Emporiæ . . . 38 C d
Emporium, loc. in Rome . . . 22 A
Emporium, in Spain . . 12 D b
Empulum . . . 35 ins. B
Ems . . . 134 D b
Ems River . . . 62 D b
Enaghdune, bp.
Enchelei, people . . . . 31 I a
Encounter Bay . . . 172 C d
Endicott Range . . . 186 D b
Endidæ . . . 27 F a
Endor . . . 6 C c
En-Eglaim . . . 7 C e
Engadine, valley . . . 91 S l
Enganna . . . 7 D d
Engannim . . . 7 C d
Engaño, Cape . . . 171 N g
Engaño, Punta del, cape . . . 107 F e
Engeddi . . . 7 C f
Engelberg, mon. . . . 91 Q l
Engen . . . 142 C e
Enghien . . . 117 C d
England, km. . . . 66 F c
English, people
English Cl annel . . . 2 D d
English Grants in North America 190 ins.
English Kingdom, 9 cent. . . . 56 B b
English Marches, dist.
English Mercia, reg.
English Northumbria, km.
English Pale, The, dist.
English River . . . 212 F c
English Turn, loc. on Miss. R. 191 H f
Engstingen . . . 143 H i
Engyum . . . 30 D e
Enipeus River, in Elis. . . . 14 B b
Enipeus River, in Macedonia . 11 D b
Enipeus River, in Thessaly. . 11 D c
Enkhuizen . . . 117 D b
Enkhuizen, Hanse. cy. . . . 99 ins. B
Enna . . . 72 C d
En-Nasirah . . . 150 C a
Enniskillen . . . 127 J g
Enns . . . 115 H d
Enns River . . . 63 H e
Enos . . . 165 E c
Enschede . . . 117 E b
Ensisheim . . . 86 F e
Entella . . . 30 C e
Entre Minho e Douro, reg. . . 83 J g
Entre Rios, prov., in Argentina 215 D f
(E. R.)
Entre Tejo e Guadiana, reg. . . 83 J h
Enzberg, lordship . . . 143 G i
Enzheim . . . 122 D d
Enz River . . . 143 H h

Eordæa, reg. . . . 10 C b
Eordaïcus River . . . 10 B b
Eordi, people
Epamantodurum
Eperies . . . 159 K d
Épernay . . . 69 I f
Épernay, mon. . . . 94 C b
Ephesus . . . 17 E c
Ephraim, Gate of . . . 6 ins. A
Ephraim, mt. . . . 7 C d
Ephraim, tribe . . . 7 ins. D
Ephrata . . . 192 C c
Ephyra, in Elis . . . 14 B b
Ephyra, in Epirus . . . 10 B c
Ephyra, isl., near Melos . . . 15 E c
Ephyra, isl., near Argolis . . . 15 C b
Epidamnus (Durazzo) . . . 12 G b
Epidaurum . . . 38 F d
Epidaurus, in Argolis . . . 15 D b
Epidaurus Limera . . . 15 D c
Epidelium, prom. . . . 15 D c
Epila . . . 83 K g
Épinal . . . 78 E d
Épinal, mon. . . . 95 D b
Épineuil . . . 69 I g
Epiphania . . . 20 G e
Epipolæ, quarter in Syracuse . 31 ins. B
Epirus, country . . . 10 B b
Epirus, desp., 13 cent. . . . 73 E c
Epirus, desp., 15 cent. . . . 93 B c
Epirus, Rom. prov. . . . 35 I f
Epirus, state . . . 13 B b
Epirus nova, East Rom. prov. . 43 G e(5)
Epirus vetus, East Rom. prov. . 43 G f(4)
Epitalium . . . 14 B b
Epium . . . 14 B b
Epizephyrii, Locri . . . 31 F d
Epoissum . . . 39 H i
Epopeus, mt. . . . 30 C b
Eporedia (Ivrea) . . . 26 B b
Eppenstein, castle . . . 63 H e
Eppingen . . . 142 C b
Epping Forest . . . 49 F f
Epsom . . . 75 I i
Epternacus, see Echternach
Epworth, mon. . . . 97 Q h
Equatorial Provinces under
    Emin Pascha 1878—1889 . . . 174 F d
Equius
Erasinus River, in Arcadia . . 14 C b
Erasinus River, in Attica . . . 16 C b
Eratyra . . . 10 C b
Erbach, in Hesse . . . 142 C a
Erbach, in Wurtemberg . . . 143 I i
Erbstetten . . . 143 I i
Ercavica
Erchia . . . 16 B b
Ercte, mt. . . . 30 C d
Erechtheum
Eresburg, stronghold . . . 55 Q i
Eretria, in Eubœa . . . 11 E d
Eretria, in Thessaly . . . 11 D c
Eretum . . . 27 G e
Erfurt . . . 62 F c
Erfurt, mon. . . . 95 E a
Erfurt, univ. . . . 100 H d
Ergines River
Erginul, Erginur
Ergitium . . . 30 E a
Ericinium . . . 10 D c
Ericussa, isl. . . . 30 C b
Eridanus River, see Po River
Eridu (Abu Shahrein) . . . 4 E e
Erie . . . 199 I b
Erie, Fort . . . 200 D b
Erie, lake . . . 187 K d
Erie Canal . . . 211 J b
Eries, tribe . . . 188 J b
Erigon River . . . 10 C b
Erineus, in Achaia . . . 14 B a
Erineus, in Doris . . . 11 D d
Erith . . . 75 J i
Eritium . . . 10 D c
Eritrea, Italian col. . . . 174 G c

Erivan . . . .
Erivan, reg. . . . .
Erlach, castle . . . 91 P k
Erlangen . . . 122 F d
Erlau . . . 77 I c
Erlau, bp. . . . 95 G b
Ermeland, reg. . . . 87 M a
Ermeland, bp. . . . 115 K a
Ermes . . . 88 K c
Ermine Street, road . . . 51 P g
Erms River . . . 143 H h
Ernage . . . 156 B a
Erolzheim . . . 143 J i
Erpisfurt, see Erfurt
Er Riad
Er Rimmon . . . 7 B f
Erstein, castle . . . 62 D d
Eryces River . . . 30 D e
Erymanthus, mt. . . . 14 B b
Erymanthus River . . . 14 B b
Erythræ, in Ionia . . . 13 E b
Erythræ, in Locris . . . 10 D d
Eryx . . . 30 B d
Erzerum . . . 71 O f
Erzgebirge, mts., in Germany . 2 F c
Erz Gebirge, mts., in Hungary 159 J d
Erzinjan . . . 77 L e
Escalante, route of . . . 190 C d
Escambia River . . . 193 ins. B
Escaut River, see Scheldt River
Esch . . . 117 D e
Eschwege . . . 62 E c
Escondido, Rio . . . 105 D d
Escorial, San Lorenzo del, mon. 94 B c
Escurial, see Escorial
Esdrælon
Eshcol, vale . . . 7 C e
Esher . . . 75 I i
Eskishehr . . . 164 E c
Esmeraldas . . . 214 B b
Esmeraldas River . . . 111 A a
Esmûn, Temple of . . . 34 ins. A (5)
Esopus . . . 192 D c
Española, isl. . . . 105 F c
Esparza . . . 213 D d
Espinhaço, Serra do, mts. . . 214 E d
Espinosa . . . 130 C e
Espinosa, route of . . . 105 D e
Espirito Santo . . . 214 E e
Espirito Santo, state . . . 214 E d
Espiritu Santo, isl. . . . 172 F b
Espiritu Santo, Rio del (Mobile
    R.) . . . 107 I d
Esplechin . . . 81 M g
Esquiliæ, Aug. Reg. of Rome . 22 A
Esquiline, quarter . . . 96 A
Esquiline Gate . . . 22 A
Esquiline Mount . . . 22 A
Esquimalt . . . 212 C d
Es-Salihiyeh . . . 150 B a
Esseg . . . 158 D c
Essen . . . 158 D c
Essen, mon. . . . 95 D a
Essequibo River . . . 214 D b
Essex, cty.
Essex, km.
Essex, shire
Essington, Port . . . 212 ins.
Essling . . . 155 I d
Esslingen, imp. city . . . 143 H h
Este . . . 90 J h
Este, duchy . . . 90 C b
Estella . . . 82 H e
Esthonia, reg., 9 cent. . . . 55 I c
Esthonia, reg., 14 cent. . . . 88 K b
Esthonians, people . . . 59 I b
Estoy . . . 82 A b
Estremadura, reg. . . . 83 J h
Estrun, mon. . . . 94 C a
Etalle . . . 117 D e
Etam . . . 7 C e
Étampes . . . 76 E b
Etawah . . . 170 I f
Etchemins, tribe. . . . . 188 M a

Eteocretes, people	14 ins.		
Ether			
Ethiopia, reg., Egyptian emp.	4	F d	
Ethiopia, reg., Sudan	109	S U g	
Etna, mt.	36	E e	
Étoges	154	C d	
Étoile, L', mon.	94	C b	
Eton	75	H i	
Etropol	164	C b	
Etruria, Aug. Reg.	38	E d (7)	
Etruria, reg.	27	F d	
Etruscans, people			
Ettenheim	142	A d	
Ettenheimmünster, mon.	142	A d	
Ettlingen	142	B c	
Etymander River	19	J d	
Eu	61	D a	
Eu, cty.	76	D a	
Euboea (Negropont), isl.	4	B b	
Euboea, state	13	C b	
Euboic Gulf	11	E d	
Eudemia, isl.	11	F c	
Euenus River	10	C d	
Eufratensis, E. Rom. prov.	43	J f (9)	
Euganei, people	26	E b	
Eugubium, see Gubbio			
Euhydrium	11	D c	
Eumenes, Stoa of	23	C	
Eumenia	20	C c	
Eunostus, Portus	34 ins.	C	
Euonymus, isl.	30	E d	
Eupalium	10	C d	
Eupatoria, in Crimea	139	D f	
Eupatoria, in Pontus	33	U h	
Euphrates River	18	F d	
Eupilis, lake	26	D b	
Euporia	11	E b	
Eure, dept.	148	E e	
Eure-et-Loir, dept	148	E e	
Euripus, strait	11	E d	
Euroea	10	B c	
Europe, continent	2—3, 166—167		
Europe, E. Rom. prov.	43	H e (1)	
Europus, in Almopia	10	D b	
Europus, in Emathia	11	D a	
Europus, in Syria	52	L f	
Europus River	10	D c	
Eurotas (Iri) River	14	C b	
Euryalus	31 ins.	B	
Eurychorus	18 ins.	B	
Eurymedon River	20	D d	
Eurymenae	11	D c	
Eurytanes, people	10	C d	
Eutaea	14	C b	
Eutaw Springs, battle	195	A g	
Eutin	114	F a	
Eutresia, reg.	14	C b	
Evangelista, isl.	105	D b	
Evansville	208	C b	
Evaux	126	C c	
Everest, mt.	171	J f	
Everglades, The, swamp	191	I f	
Evesham	127	X n	
Evesham, mon.	97	P i	
Evesham, parl. bor.	163	M e	
Evora	82	A b	
Evora, abp.	94	A d	
Évreux	61	D b	
Évreux, bp.	94	C b	
Évreux, cty.	76	D b	
Evron, mon.	94	B b	
Ewell	75	I i	
Exarchate of Italy	53	D b	
Exeter, in England	127	V p	
Exeter, bp.	97	N k	
Exeter, castle	65	E e	
Exeter, parl. bor.	163	K g	
Exeter, in New Hampshire	189	C c	
Exeter, in Rhode Island	189 ins. A		
Exilles	126	E d	
Exmes	76	D b	
Exmoor	49	E f	
Eyach River	143	G i	
Bydtkuhnen	159	L a	

Eye, mon.	97	S i	
Eye, parl. bor.	163	P e	
Eyerland, isl.	117	C a	
Eylau	155	K a	
Eynesford	75	J i	
Eynsham, mon.	97	P j	
Eyoub, mosque			
Eyoub, quarter			
Eyre, lake	172	C c	
Eyre Peninsula	172	C d	
Eyre River	172	C c	
Ezion-Geber	5	C c *	
Fabrateria nova	30	C a	
Fabrician Bridge	22	A	
Faenza	90	J h	
Faenza, bp.	95	E c	
Faesulae (Fiesole)	27	F d	
Fagifulae	30	D a	
Fagundes, route of	108	L c	
Fagutal	22	A	
Fairfax	208 ins.		
Fairfield, in Conn.	192	E c	
Fairfield, in Pa.	208 ins.		
Fair Oaks, battle	208 E b (F. O.)		
Fairweather, mt.	212 ins.		
Faizabad	137	D c	
Fajardo	199 ins. G		
Faknur			
Falaise	65	F f	
Falempin, mon.	94 C a (Fal.)		
Falerii	27	G e	
Falerio	27	H d	
Falernian District	30	D a	
Falesia	26	E e	
Falkenstein, castle	62	E d	
Falkirk			
Falkland Islands	215	D h	
Fallen Timber, battle	196 ins. B		
Falling Creek	193	F c	
Falling Waters, falls	208 ins.		
Falls of the Ohio	193	B b	
Falmouth, in Maine	189	C c	
Falmouth, in Virginia	192	C d	
Falmouth, parl. bor.	163	J g	
Falster, isl.	114	F a	
Falsterbo, Hanse. for. cy.	98	F b	
Falun	88	F a	
Famagusta	68	B b	
Famine, La	192	C b	
Fanestris, Julia	27	H d	
Fang-shan	170 ins. A		
Fanning Island	180	L g	
Fano	90	M j	
Fano, bp.	95	E c	
Fansur			
Fanum or Fanum Fortunae (Fano)	27	H d	
Farah			
Farama	99	J g	
Farentia	27	F c	
Farewell, Cape	186	O c	
Farfa	64 ins.		
Farfa, mon.	96	B a	
Fargo	210	F a	
Farmington	192	E c	
Farnborough	75	J i	
Farnham, parl. bor.			
Farningham	75	J i	
Farnsburg, castle	91	P k	
Faro	82	A b	
Faroe Islands	2	D b	
Farquhar Island	182 GG i		
Fars, reg.			
Farsan Islands	170	F g	
Farther India, reg.			
Farther Pomerania, dist.	123	H b	
Farther Rhine River	91	R l	
Farther Spain, prov.	38 A e (3)		
Fasher, El-	174	F c	
Fashoda	174	G c	
Fatimite, dynasty, about 1097	67	M g	
Fatimites, Dom. of the, about 1000	58 D F f		
Faubourg du Temple, quarter in Paris	149	B	

Faubourg Montmartre, quarter in Paris	149	B	
Faubourg Saint Antoine, quarter in Paris	149	B	
Faubourg Saint Denis, quarter in Paris	149	B	
Faubourg Saint Germain, quarter in Paris	149	B	
Faubourg Saint Honore, quarter in Paris	149	B	
Faubourg Saint Honoré, Rue du, street in Paris	149	B	
Faubourg Saint Jacques, quarter in Paris	149	B	
Faubourg Saint Marcel, quarter in Paris	149	B	
Faubourg Saint Martin, quarter in Paris	149	B	
Faubourg Saint Michel, quarter in Paris	149	B	
Faubourg Saint Victor, quarter in Paris	149	B	
Faucigny	130	O h	
Fauresmith	175	L l	
Faustina, Temple of			
Faventia, see Faenza			
Faverney, mon.	95	D b	
Faversham, mon.	97	R j	
Faversham, parl. bor.			
Favianae	50	G c	
Faxa Fiord	166	A c	
Fayetteville, in N. Carolina	193	E d	
Fayetteville, in Pa.	208 ins.		
Fayum, reg.	1	B c	
Fear, Cape	191	J e	
Fécamp	65	G f	
Fécamp mon.	94	C b	
Fecht River	143 ins. D		
Feder, lake	143	I i	
Fehmarn, isl.	114	F a	
Fehrbellin	123	G b	
Feldkirch	78	F e	
Felicitas Julia	38	A e	
Felsina	27	F c	
Feltre, bp.	63	F e f	
Feltre, bp.	95	E b	
Feltria (Feltre)	27	F a	
Fenestrelle	126	E d	
Fenni, people	35	I a	
Fens, The, dist.	49	F e	
Feodosia	89	E b	
Ferdi, see Verden			
Fère-Champenoise	154	B j d	
Ferentini Grove	35 ins. B (4)		
Ferentino	72	C c	
Ferentinum, in Etruria	27	G e	
Ferentinum, in Latium	30	C a	
Ferghana, reg.			
Ferlech			
Fermanagh, cty.	127	J g	
Fermo	90	D c	
Fermo, bp.	95	E c	
Fernandina	208	D c	
Fernandina, isl.	105	F b	
Fernando Noronha Island	214	F c	
Fernando Po, isl.	175	D d	
Ferns, bp.	97	G e	
Feronia	27	G e	
Ferrara, bp.	90	J h	
Ferrara, bp.	95	E c	
Ferrara, duchy, 15 cent.	90	C b	
Ferrara, univ.	100	H f	
Ferraria, see Ferrara			
Ferrières, mon.	94	C b	
Ferro, Bay of	118	C e	
Ferryland	212	J d	
Ferté-sur-Grône, La, mon.	94	C b	
Fertur River	30	C a	
Feuillants, The, mon. in Paris	149	B	
Feurs	76	F d	
Fez	70	C g	
Fez, state	118	C g	
Fezensac, dist.	126	B e	
Fezenzac, cty.	69 D e (Fez)		

Fezzan, Oases of	2	F f	
Fezzan, reg.	174	E b	
Ficulea	35 ins. B		
Fidenæ	27	G f	
Fidentia	26	E c	
Field of Blood, loc. near Jerusalem	6 ins. A		
Fierbois	76	D c	
Fiesole	52	J e	
Fiesole, bp.	95	E c	
Fife, cty.			
Figeac	126	C d	
Figig	174	C a	
Fiji Islands	172	G b	
Filehne	155	I b	
Filles Saint Thomas, mon. in Paris	149	B	
Fillmore City	206	C c	
Fils River	143	I h	
Fines, near Divodurum	39	H i	
Fines, Ad-, near Florentia	27	F d	
Fingoland, reg.	175	M m	
Finisterre, Cape	83	J g	
Finistère, dept.	148	D e	
Finland, Gulf of	138	C d	
Finland, prov.	167	K c	
Finland, reg.	138	C c	
Finns, people	138	B c	
Finow Canal	123	G b	
Finsbury, parl. bor.	163	N f (Finsb.)	
Finstermünz	134	F e	
Fiorentino, castle	72	D c	
Firebr			
Fire Lands, dist.	196 ins. B		
Firenzuola	90	L i	
Firmanum, Castellum	27	H d	
Firmum (Fermo)	27	H d	
Firozabad	170	I f	
Fiscannum, see Fécamp			
Fischa River	63	I d e	
Fischbach	142	B d	
Fischhausen	80	F d	
Fischingen, mon.	91	Q k	
Fiscellus, mt.	27	H e	
Fisher, Fort	208	E c	
Fisher's Hill, battle	208	E b	
Fish Gate	6 ins. A		
Fish River. Great	175	M m	
Fitchburg	207	L b	
Fitero, mon.	94	B c	
Fitzgeralds, The, fam.			
Fitzroy River	172	B b	
Fiume	135	H f	
Five Forks, battle	208	E b	
Fivizzano	90	C b	
Fixtuinum, see Meaux, in France			
Fladungen	62	E c	
Flamborough			
Flamenco Island			
Fläming, mts.	80 ins.		
Flaminia and Picenum Annonarium, West. Rom. prov.	42	E e (4)	
Flaminian Circus	24	A	
Flaminian Circus, Aug. Reg. of Rome	22	A	
Flaminian Gate	22	A	
Flaminian Way, road	27	G e	
Flaminian Way, Old, road	27	G e	
Flanders, cty.	61	E a	
Flanders, duchy, about 1000	58	E c	
Flanders, prov.	148	E d	
Flanders and Artois, gen.	147	E a	
Flanders and Hainaut, gouv.	146	B a	
Flandrina			
Flanola, Gulf of	27	I c	
Flanona	27	I b	
Flarchheim	62	F c	
Flatbush	189 ins. C		
Flathead Post	210	C a	
Flatheads, tribe	188	C a	
Flatlands	189 ins. C		
Flattery, Cape	186	G d	
Flatow	79	J b	
Flavia Cæsariensis, West. Rom. prov.	42	B c (5)	

Flaviæ, Aræ	39	J i	
Flavian Amphitheatre	24	B	
Flavian Canal	27	G c	
Flavian Way, road	27	H b	
Flavigny, mon.	94	C b	
Flaviobriga	38	B d	
Fleet River, in London	75	G g	
Fleet Street, in London	75	G g	
Flensburg, Hanse. for. cy.			
Flensburg	86	G a	
Fleurus	156	B b	
Fleury, mon.	94	C b	
Flevo, lake (Zuider Zee)	39	H g	
Flinders Range	172	C d	
Flinders River	172	D b	
Flinders Island	172	D d	
Flint, cty.	127	V m	
Flint, parl. bor.	163	K d	
Flint, parl. dist.	163	K d	
Flint River	193	B f	
Flochberg, castle	72	C b	
Flodden	118	D b	
Flora, Temple of	23	B	
Florence, in Alabama	211	H d	
Florence, in Italy	64	B b	
Florence, abp.	95	E c	
Florence, rep.	90	M j	
Florence, univ.	100	H f (Fl.)	
Florentia (Florence, in Italy)	27	F d	
Florentiola	26	D c	
Flores	213	C c	
Flores, isl.	112	F d	
Flores Sea	172	B a	
Floriacus, see Fleury			
Florianopolis	215	E e	
Florida	215	D f	
Florida, Cape	191	I f	
Florida, pen.	187	K f	
Florida, col.	191	I e f	
Florida, state	211	I e	
Florida, Straits of	187	L f	
Florida, ter.	203	V d	
Florida, East, col.	194	C d e	
Florida, West, col.	194	B d	
Floyd, Camp	210	C b	
Fluela Pass	91	R l	
Flüelen	91	Q l	
Fluorn	123	F i	
Flushing, in Holland	117	B c	
Flushing, in New York	189 ins. C		
Flusor River	27	H d	
Fobbing	98 ins. A		
Fogaras	159	M f	
Foggia	90	E d	
Foggia Nuova	99	I f	
Foligno, bp.	95	E c	
Foix	61	D e	
Foix, cty.	76	D e	
Foix, gouv.	146	B c	
Foix, prov.	148	E f	
Fokchani	131	I d	
Fo-kien, prov.	171	M f	
Földvar	159	J e	
Foligno	90	D c	
Fond du Lac, Ind. Res.	188	H a	
Fondi	90	D d	
Fondi, bp.	95	E c	
Fontainebleau	126	C b	
Fontaine de Bèze, La, mon.	95	D b	
Fontaine Française	126	D c	
Fontanelle, mon.	94	C b (St. Van.)	
Fontenay, in Auxerrois	56	C c	
Fontenay, in Poitou	69	C c	
Fontenay, castle	76	C c	
Fontenay, mon.	94	B b (Font.)	
Fontenay-le-Comte	84	C f	
Fontenay, seign.	69	C c	
Fontenoy, near Tournay	134	B a	
Fontevrault	69	H g	
Fontevrault, mon.	94	B b	
Font-Marigny, mon.	94	C b	
Fontus, Gate of			
Foo-chau	92	M e	
Foot Hills	187	L e	

Forbach	142	B c	
Forcalquier	69	F e	
Forcalquier, cty.	69	F d	
Forchheim	55	R j	
Forchheim, mon.	95	E b	
Ford, mon.	97	O k	
Fordingbridge, deanery	100	A b	
Fordingbridge, hospital	100	A b	
Forentum	30	E b	
Forest Cantons, Three	91	S k	
Forez, cty.	61	F d	
Forfar, cty.			
Forli, in Romagna	90	C b	
Forli, bp., in Romagna	95	E c	
Forli, bp., in Venetia	95	E c	
Forlimpopoli, bp.	95	E c (F.)	
Formentera, isl.	83	L h	
Formiæ	30	C a	
Formigny	76	C b	
Formio River	27	H b	
Formosa, isl.	171	N f	
Formosa Bay	175	H e	
Fornix Fabianus	24	A	
Fornovo	90	B b	
Forest, routes of	172	leg.	
Fors Fortuna, Temple of	22	A	
Fort Adams, in Miss.	199	G d	
Fort Adams, in Ohio	196 ins. B		
Fort Albany	212	G c	
Fort Albuquerque	214	D d	
Fortaleza	214	F c	
Fort Amsterdam (New York)	189 ins. C		
Fort Anne	192	E b	
Fort Argyle	193 ins. C		
Fort Arkansas	191	G e	
Fort Armstrong, in Illinois	211	G b	
Fort Armstrong, in Pa.	195	B c	
Fort Atkinson	210	F b	
Fort Augusta, in Georgia	193	C e	
Fort Augusta, in Pa.	192	C c	
Fort Bard	150	D d	
Fort Beauharnais	191	G c	
Fort Bedford	192	B c	
Fort Belknap, Ind. Res.	188	D a	
Fort Benton	198	C a	
Fort Berthold, Ind. Res.	188	F a	
Fort Beversrede	192 ins.		
Fort Boisé	198	B a	
Fort Bonneville	210	C b	
Fort Brady	211	H a	
Fort Bridger	210	C b	
Fort Brown	201	F d	
Fort Buford	210	E a	
Fort Bull	192	D b	
Fort Bute	195 ins. B		
Fort Calhoun	210	F b	
Fort Caroline	191	I e	
Fort Casimir	192 ins.		
Fort Caswell	208	E c	
Fort Chambly	189	B b	
Fort Charlotte	195 ins. B		
Fort Chartres	191	G d	
Fort Chequamegon			
Fort Chippewyan	212	D c	
Fort Chiswell	193	D c	
Fort Christanna	193	F c	
Fort Christina	192 ins.		
Fort Churchill	212	F c	
Fort Claiborne	200	I f	
Fort Clark	210	E a	
Fort Clatsop	210	A a	
Fort Clinton, near Saratoga	192	E b	
Fort Clinton, near West Point	195	D c	
Fort Colville	198	B a	
Fort Craven	192	D b	
Fort Crawford	211	G b	
Fort Crèvecœur	191	H c	
Fort Cumberland	192	B d	
Fort Dauphin			
Fort Dearborn	199	H b	
Fort de la Présentation	192	D a	
Fort Defiance	196 ins. B		
Fort d'Huillier	191	G c	
Fort Diego	193	D f	

Fort Dobbs 193   D d
Fort Dodge 210   E c
Fort Donelson 208   C b
Fort do Principe da Beira . . 214   C d
Fort Dummer 189   B c
Fort Duquesne 192   A c
Fort Edisto . . . . 193 ins. C
Fort Edward 192   C b
Fort Edward Augustus 194   B b
Fort Erie 196   D b
Fort Fisher 208   E c
Fort Frédéric 192   E a
Fort Frederick 192   C d
Fort Frontenac 192   C a
Fort Gaines, in Alabama . . . 208   C c
Fort Gaines, in Minnesota . . 211   G a
Fort George, in Canada 200   D b
Fort George, in Maine . . . 189   D c
Fort George, in New York . . 192   E b
Fort Good Hope   212   C b
Fort Gibson 211   G c
Fort Granby 195   A g
Fort Granville 192   C c
Fort Gratiot 211   I b
Fort Greenville . . . . . . 196 ins. B
Fort Griswold 195   F c
Forth, Firth of   49   E c
Fort Hall 198   C b
Fort Hall, Ind. Res. 188   D b
Fort Halifax 189   D b
Fort Harmar . . . . 196 ins. B
Fort Hatteras 208   E b
Fort Henry 208   C b
Fort Herkimer 192   D b
Fort Howard 211   H b
Fort Independence 195   E a
Fort Jackson, in Louisiana . . 208   C d
Fort Jackson, in Mississippi . . 200   I f
Fort James . . . .
Fort Kaministiquia 191   G b
Fort Kearney 210   F b
Fort Kenai . . . . 198 ins. A
Fort King George 193   C f
Fort La Baye 191   H c
Fort Lac Pepin . . . .
Fort La Gallette 192   D a
Fort La Jonquière 190   C a
Fort Lamotte 189   B b
Fort Langley 210   A a
Fort Laramie 198   E b
Fort La Reine 190   F b
Fort L'Assomption 194   B c
Fort Leavenworth 198   F c
Fort Le Bœuf 192   A c
Fort Lee 195   D c
Fort Lévis 192   D a
Fort Liard 212   C b
Fort Ligonier 192   B c
Fort Lisa 210   F b
Fort Loudoun, in Pa. 192   B d
Fort Loudoun, in Tennessee . . 193   B d
Fort Louis 154   D d
Fort Lupton 210   E c
Fort Loyal 189   D c
Fort Mac Allister 208   D c
Fort Mac Henry 200   L h
Fort Mackinac 194   C a
Fort Mac Murray 212   D c
Fort Macon 208   E c
Fort Macpherson 212   B b
Fort Madison 199   G b
Fort Madison, Ind. Res. 188   B a
Fort Malden 200   B b
Fort Mandan 210   E a
Fort Manuel 210   D a
Fort Massac 192   B c
Fort Maurepas, in Mississippi . 191   H e
Fort Maurepas, on L. Winnipeg 191   F a
Fort Meigs 200   B c
Fort Mercer 195   D d
Fort Miami . . . . 196 ins. B
Fort Mifflin 195   D d
Fort Mims 200   I f
Fort Mitchell 211   H d

Fort Mohave 188   D c
Fort Moore . . . . 193 ins. C
Fort Morgan 208   C c
Fort Moritz 214   F d
Fort Moultrie 195   B g
Fort Nassau, in New Jersey . 191   K d
Fort Nassau, in New York . . . 192   E b
Fort Necessity 192   B d
Fort Nelson 212   C b
Fort New Elfsborg . . . . 192 ins.
Fort New Gothenburg . . . . . . 192 ins.
Fort New Korsholm . . . . . 192 ins.
Fort New Wasa . . . . 192 ins.
Fort Niagara 192   B b
Fort Nicholson 192   E b
Fort Nipigon 191   H b
Fort Nisqually 210   A a
Fort Norman 212   C b
Fort Okanagan 210   B a
Fort Ontario 192   C b
Fort Orange 192   D b
Fort Orleans 191   G d
Fortore River, see Frento River
Fort Osage 211   G c
Fort Oswegatchie 196   D b
Fort Oswego 192   C b
Fort Ouiatanon 191   H c
Fort Panmure 194   A d
Fort Peck, Ind. Res. 188   E a
Fort Pejepscort 189   C b
Fort Pentagöet 189   D b
Fort Pickens 208   C c
Fort Picolata 193   D g
Fort Pierre 210   E b
Fort Pillow 208   C b
Fort Pitt 212   E c
Fort Pontchartrain 191   I c
Fort Presqu'Isle 192   B b
Fort Prince George 193   C d
Fort Providence 212   D b
Fort Prudhomme 191   H d
Fort Pulaski 208   D c
Fort Rae 212   D b
Fort Recovery . . . . 196 ins. B
Fort Reliance 212   E b
Fort Resolution 212   D b
Fortress Monroe 208   E b
Fort Richelieu 189   B a
Fort Rosalie 191   G e
Fort Rouge . . . .
Fort Rouillé 192   B b
Fort Saint Andrew 193   D f
Fort Saint Charles, or Kaskaskia 191   G d
Fort Saint Charles, near Lake
   of the Woods 191   F b
Fort Saint David (Cuddalore) . 137   C f
Fort Saint Thérèse 189   B b
Fort Saint George, in Florida . 193   D f
Fort Saint George (Madras) . . 137   D f
Fort Saint John, in Brit. Colum-
   bia 212   C b
Fort Saint John, on Richelieu R. 189   B b
Fort Saint Joseph 191   H c
Fort Saint Louis, in Illinois
   Country 191   H c
Fort Saint Louis, in Texas . . 190   F f
Fort Saint Philip 200   I g
Fort Saint Pierre 191   G b
Fort Saint Vrein 210   E b
Fort Sandusky 194   C b
Fort San Mateo 191   I e
Fort Saratoga 192   E b
Fort Saskatchewan 212   D c
Fort Schuyler, near Montreal . 189   B b
Fort Schuyler (Oriskany) 195   D b
Fort Scott 211   G c
Fort Selkirk 212   B b
Fort Shirley 192   C c
Fort Simpson 212   C b
Fort Smith 211   G c
Fort Snelling 199   G b
Fort Stanwix 192   D b
Fort Stephenson 200   B c
Fort Steuben . . . . 196 ins. B

Fort Stoddert 196   B d
Fort Sumter 208   E c
Fort Tecumseh 210   E b
Fort Ticonderoga 192   E b
Fort Tombecbé 191   H e
Fort Toulouse 191   H e
Fort Trinity . . . . 192 ins.
Fortuna, Temple of 22   A
Fortuna, Fanum 27   H d
Fortunæ, Tres 23   B
Fort Union, in New Mexico . . 210   C b
Fort Union, in North Dakota . 210   E a
Fort Uintah 210   C b
Fort Vancouver 210   A a
Fort Venango 192   A c
Fort Vincennes 194   B c
Fort Walla Walla 198   B a
Fort Washington (Cincinnati) . 196 ins. B
Fort Washington, in Maryland . 200   L i
Fort Washington, near New York 195   D c
Fort Washita 210   F d
Fort Watson 195   A g
Fort Wayne 196   B b
Fort Western 189   D b
Fort William (Calcutta) 137   E d
Fort William, in Florida . . 193   D f
Fort William, in Ontario . . . 212   F d
Fort William (Portland, Ore.) . 210   A a
Fort William Henry 192   D b
Fort Williams 192   D b
Fort Winnebago 211   H b
Fort Wrangell . . . . 212 ins.
Forty-Niners, route of . . . . 210 legend
Fort York . . . .
Fort Yukon . . . . 198 ins. A
Foruli 27   H e
Forum, loc. in Carthage . . 34 ins. A (3)
Forum, loc. in Rome . . 24 A and B
Forum Aurelii 27   F e
Forum Boarium, loc. in Rome 24   A
Forum Cassii 27   G e
Forum Clodii, near L. Sabatinus 35 ins. B
Forum Clodii, near Luca . . . 26   E d
Forum Cornelii 27   F c
Forum Fulvii . . . .
Forum Gallorum 27   F c
Forum Germanorum 26   B c
Forum Holitorium, loc. in Rome 24   A
Forum Julii (Fréjus), in Gaul . 26   A d
Forum Julii (Cividale), in Venetia 27   H a
Forum Livii (Forli) 27   F c
Forum novum 26   E c
Forum Popilii (Forlimpopoli), in
   Cispadane Gaul 27   G c
Forum Popilii, in Lucania . . . 30   E b
Forum Sempronii 27   G d
Forum Vibii 26   B c
Forum Vulcani (Solfatara), vol. 31 ins. A
Fossæ Papirianæ 26   E d
Fossalta 72   C c
Fossano 150   D d
Fossanuova, mon. 96   C b
Fosse Way, road 51   P h
Fossombrone, bp. . . . . . . 95 E c (Fo.)
Fotheringhay 127   Y n
Fougères 69   C b
Fougères, castle 76   C b
Fountain City . . . . 206 ins.
Fountains, mon. 97   P g
Four Mile Tree . . . . 193 ins. A
Fowey 127   U p
Fowey, parl. bor. 163   J g
Fowler Bay 172   C d
Fox, Cape . . . . 212 ins.
Fox, Sauk and, Ind. Res. 188   H b
Fox Land 212   H b
Fox Channel 186   K b
Fox River 188   I b
Foxes, tribe 188   H b
Foyle, lake 127   J f
Fraga 82   C a
Francavilla 131   F f
France, km., 11 cent. 58   E d
France, km., 12 cent. 70   G d

France, km., 18 cent. 130 D d
France, rep. 166 F f
France, Plain of 2 E d
Franceville 175 E e
Franche Comté, gouv. 146 C b
Franche Comté, prov. 148 F e
Franche Comté, see also Free County of Burgundy
Francia, duchy, about 1000 58 E d
Francia, reg. 53 M h
Franconia, Frankish prov., 9 cent. 56 D b
Franconia, duchy, 12 cent. 71 R k
Franconia, E., duchy 62 E c d
Franconia, W., duchy 62 E c d
Franconofurt, see Frankfort-on-the-Main and Frankfurt-on-the-Oder
Frankenhausen 114 F c
Frankenthal 122 E d
Frankfort, in Kentucky 196 C c
Frankfort-on-the-Main 55 Q i
Frankfort-on-the-Oder 79 I b
Frankfort-on-the-Oder, Hanse. cy. 99 ins. B
Frankfort-on-the-Oder, univ. 100 H d
Frankfort, gr. duchy 154 E c
Frankfort, imp. cy. 78 F c
Fränkische Saale, river 158 E c
Franklin, in Kentucky 208 C b
Franklin, in Pa. 192 A c
Franklin, in Tennessee 208 C b
Franklin, dist. in Canada 212 E a
Franklin, proposed state in U.S. 196 ins. A
Franks, Kingdom of the, 486 50 D c
Franks, Kingdom of the, 526—600 52 C b
Franks, Kingdom of the, 6 cent. 52 I e
Franks, people in France, 486-496 45 E c
Franks, people in Italy, 774 45 G d
Franks, people, about 900 57 D E c
Franzensfeste 158 F e
Franzens Canal 159 J f
Frascati, see Tusculum 64 ins.
Frascati, bp. 96 B b
Fraser River 212 C c
Frasnes 156 A a
Frastanz 91 R k
Fraubrunnen 91 P k
Frauenalb, ab. 142 B c
Frauenburg 115 J a
Frauenburg, bp. 95 F a
Frauenfeld 91 Q k
Fraustadt 135 I c
Fraxinet or Fraxinetum (Garde-Frainet) 56 D d
Frazers, fam. 97 I b
Frédéric, Fort 192 E a
Frederica 193 D f
Fredericia 158 E a
Frederick 192 C d
Frederick, Fort 192 B d
Frederick Barbarossa, crusade of 70 I d
Fredericksburg 193 F b
Frederick William Canal 135 H b (Fr. W. C.)
Fredericton 212 I d
Frederikshamn
Frederiksholm, castle 120 H e
Free County of Burgundy, 14 cent. 78 D e
Free County of Burgundy, 17 cent. 126 D c
Freeman's Farm, battle 195 E b
Freeport 207 H b
Freetown 174 B d
Fregellæ 30 C a
Fregenæ 27 G f
Freiberg 85 G e
Freiburg, in Breisgau 78 E e
Freiburg, in Breisgau, univ. 100 G e
Freiburg, in Switzerland, see Fribourg 91 P l
Freiburg, canton, see Fribourg 91 P l
Freising 63 F d
Freising, bp. 79 G d
Freyburg, on the Unstrut R. 85 F e
Fréjus 69 G e
Fréjus, bp. 95 D c
Fremantle 172 A d
Fremington, parl. bor.
Fremont 210 F b
Frémont, routes of 210 leg.
Fremont Peak 187 I d
French, empire of the, 1806 151 K j
French, people, about 900
French Bay 105 ins.
French Broad River 196 ins. A
French Congo, col. 175 E e
French Frigate Island 180 J e
French Guiana, col. 214 D b
French Guinea, col. 174 B c
French Indo-China, col. 171 L g
French Mills 200 F a
French Republic 151 H g
French Somaliland, col. 174 H c (Fr. Somal.)
Frenchtown 200 B c
French West Africa, col. 174 C c
Frentani, people 27 I e
Frentanians, people
Frento (Fortore) River 30 E a
Fresnaye 76 D b
Fresnillo 213 B b
Fréteval 69 H g
Fretum Gallicum (Strait of Dover) 51 Q i
Freudenberg 142 D a
Freudenstadt 143 F i
Fribourg 91 P l
Fribourg, canton 91 P l
Frichemont
Friday Street, in London 75 G g
Friedberg, in Swabia 143 H j
Friedberg, on the Taunus 122 E c
Friedewald 114 E c
Friedland, in Bohemia 123 H c
Friedland, in Moravia 123 I d
Friedland, in Prussia 155 K a
Friedrichshafen, imp. city 143 I j
Friedrichstadt 158 E a
Friedrich Wilhelm Canal 123 H b
Friendly Islands 172 H c
Friesach 63 H e
Friesack 85 C b
Friesack, castle 72 C a
Friesians, people 38 D b
Friesland, reg., 9 cent. 56 C b
Friesland, reg., 13 cent. 72 B a
Friesland, reg., 14 cent. 78 E b
Friesland lordship, 16 cent. 117 D a
Friesland, East, reg. 86 F b
Friesland, West, dist. 117 C b
Frigidus River 27 H b
Frijoles
Friniates, people 26 E c
Frio, Cape, in Brazil 215 E e
Frio, Cape, in Africa 175 E f
Frisches Haff, bay 123 J a
Frisians, people, see Friesians
Frisinga, see Freising
Fritzlar 55 Q i
Fritzlar, mon. 95 D a
Friuli, March of 54 G d
Friuli, people 52 J e
Friuli, dist. 63 G e
Frobisher, route of 108 L b
Frobisher Bay 212 I b
Froburg, castle 91 P k
Frohse 63 F b
Frohsdorf 159 I e
Frome, lake 172 D d
Frome, parl. bor. 163 L f
Fronsac, castle 76 C d
Frontenac, Fort 192 C a
Fronteras 190 D e
Frontiacus, see Fronsac
Front Royal 208 E b (F. R.)
Frutigen, castle 91 P l
Fruttuaria, mon. 95 D b
Fucens, Alba 27 H e
Fu-chau
Fucino, lake 96 C a
Fucinus (Fucino) lake 27 H f
Fuego, Tierra del, isl. 215 C h
Fuego, volcano 187 J g
Fuenterrabia 83 K g
Fuentes de Oñoro 130 B e
Fuentidueña 82 B a
Fuerte 190 D f
Fugger, lordship 143 J i
Fugui
Fulda 72 B a
Fulda, ab. 78 F c
Fulda, bp. 122 E c
Fulda, mon. 55 Q i
Fulginium (Foligno)
Fulham
Fulvii, Forum 26 C c
Fundi 30 C a
Fundoukli, quarter 93 G e
Fundy, Bay of 186 M d
Fünfkirchen 72 D b
Fünfkirchen, bp. 95 F b
Fünfkirchen, univ. 100 I e
Fünen, isl.
Furculæ Caudinæ, passes, see Caudine Forks
Furka Pass 91 Q l
Furlo Pass 27 G d
Furnes 69 E a
Furness, mon. 97 N g
Furth, in Bavaria 123 G d
Fürth, in Ansbach 122 F d
Fürstenau, castle 91 R l
Fürstenberg 142 C e
Fürstenberg, cty. 122 E e
Fürstenberg, princ. 142 B e
Fürstenfeld, mon. 95 E b
Fürstenwalde 79 I b
Fürstenwalde, bp. 95 E a
Furtwangen 142 B d
Fusan 171 N e
Füssen 134 F e
Futa, la-, Pass 27 F c
Futa Jalon, reg. 174 B c
Fuzo
Fyriswall 59 H b
Fyzabad 137 D c

Gabales or Gabalis, see Javols
Gabara 6 C c
Gabardan, dist. 147 E c (Gab.)
Gabarret 76 D d
Gabel 159 H c
Gabes 174 D a
Gabes, Gulf of 174 E a
Gabii 27 G f
Gabun, reg. 175 D e
Gad, tribe 7 ins. D
Gadara
Gadda 7 E d
Gadebusch 134 F b
Gades (Cadiz) 38 A e
Gadsden Purchase, reg. 1853 198 C d
Gaëta 90 D d
Gaëta, bp. 95 E c
Gaëtulia, reg. 34 F g
Gaikwar, Dom. of the 137 B d
Gaildorf 143 I g
Gaillac, mon. 94 C c (Gaill.)
Gaillard, castle 76 D b
Gaillon 76 D b
Gainas, people
Gaines, Fort, in Alabama 208 C c
Gaines, Fort, in Minnesota 211 G a
Gaines' Mill, battle 208 E b (G.M.)
Gainsborough 127 Y m
Gairdner, lake 172 C d
Galaaditis, reg. 7 D d
Galapagos Islands 214 A b
Galata, dist. in Constantinople 93 G e
Galatia, E. Rom. prov. 43 I f (2)
Galatia, Rom. prov.
Galatia Salutaris, E. Rom. prov. 43 I e (5)
Galatz 131 I d
Galeazzo Visconti, Dom. of 90
Galena 211 G b

Galepsus, in Pieria 11 F b
Galepsus, in Sithonia 11 E b
Galera 118 D f
Galicia, cty. in Spain 82 A a
Galicia, dist. in Austria-Hungary 159 K d
Galicia, dist. in Poland 139 B f
Galicia, km. in Spain 83 J g
Galicia, W. Rom. prov. 42 A e (3)
Galilee, dist. 6 C c
Galilee, Sea of 6 D c
Galitch
Gallæci, people 38 A d
Gallæcia, reg. 34 C e
Gallette, La, Fort 192 D a
Gallia, see Gaul 34 E d
Gallia Belgica, see Belgica 38 D c (3)
Gallia Cisalpina, see Cispadane and Transpadane Gaul 26
Gallia Cispadana, see Cispadane Gaul 26 E c
Gallia Lugdunensis, see Lugdunensis 38 C c (4)
Gallia Narbonensis, see Narbonensis 38 D d (6)
Gallia Transalpina, see Gaul 34 E d
Gallia Transpadana, see Transpadane Gaul 26 C b
Gallienus, Arch of 22 A
Gallinas, Cape 187 L g
Gallinas, Punta, cape 214 B a
Gallipoli, in Italy 90 F d
Gallipoli, in Thrace 71 L e
Gallipolis, in Ohio 196 ins. B
Gallo, Isla del, isl. 111 B a
Galloway, bp. 97 I e
Galloway, dist.
Galtelli 72 B c
Galveston 199 G e
Galvez, route of 195 ins. B
Galway
Galway, cty. 127 H h
Galway Bay 49 B e
Gamala 6 D c
Gambia, col. 174 B c
Gambia River 108 P f
Gambier Islands 180 N j
Gambrium
Gams 91 R k
Gandamak 170 H e
Gandavum, see Ghent
Gander River 212 J d
Gandersheim, mon. 95 D a
Gandia
Gando 174 D c
Gangani, people 38 A b
Ganges River 137 E c
Gangra 20 E b
Ganjam 137 E e
Gänserndorf 159 I d
Gap 126 E d
Gap, bp. 95 D c
Gard, dept. 148 E f
Garda 90 J h
Garda, lake 90 J h
Garde-Frainet, see Fraxinet or Fraxinetum
Gardelegen 85 B b
Gardiner's Island 189 C d
Gard Meuble, loc. in Versailles 149 A
Garendon, mon. 97 P i
Garessio 130 Q j
Gargano, mt. 64 C b
Garganum. prom. 31 F a
Garganus (Gargano), mt. 30 E a
Gargara
Gargettus 16 B a
Garigliano River 90 D d
Garmantes, people 35 G h
Garonne, Haute, dept. 148 E f
Garonne River 61 D d
Garrapata 214 B b
Garsaura 20 F c
Gartach, Gross 142 D b
Garts 123 H b
Garumna (Garonne) River 38 B d
Garz 63 H b
Gascony, dist. 50 C d
Gascony, duchy 61 C e
Gascony, prov. 148 D f
Gascoyne River 172 A c
Gaspé Peninsula 186 M d
Gastein 158 G e
Gates, route of 195 A f
Gateshead, parl. bor. 163 M c
Gath 7 B e
Gath Rimmon 7 B e
Gatheæ 14 C b
Gâtinais, dist. 69 I f
Gatineau River 199 J a
Gattinara 118 F d
Gatton, parl. bor. 163 N f (Gat.)
Gatun
Gatun River
Gaudus, isl. 14 ins.
Gaugamela 20 J d
Gaul, reg. 12 D a
Gaul, W. Rom. dioc. 42 C d
Gaul, W. Rom. pref. 42
Gaul, Cisalpine, reg. 38 ins.
Gaul, Cispadane, reg. 27 E c
Gaul, Transalpine, reg. 34 E d (Gaul)
Gaul, Transpadane reg. 26 C b
Gaur 92 I e
Gaure, dist. 126 B e
Gaurium 15 E b
Gaurus, mt. 31 ins. A
Gaya 137 E d
Gaza
Gazaca 35 N f
Gazaria, reg.
Gaziura 20 G b
Geba 7 C d
Gebal 6 D a
Gebal, reg.
Gebu, isl. 199 ins. H
Gederoth 7 B e
Gedid 174 G c
Gedrosia, prov. 19 J e
Gedrosia, satr. 8 K f
Geelong 172 G d
Geertsbergen 117 B d
Gefle 88 G a
Geislingen 143 I h
Geismar 55 Q i
Gela 30 D e
Gelas River 30 D e
Geldern 78 E e
Gelderland, Upper, dist. 117 E c
Gelderland, duchy 117 D b
Gelduba 39 I h
Gelnhausen 72 B a
Gelnhausen, imp. cy. 78 F c
Gembloux 156 B a
Gembloux, mon. 94 C a
Gemelli Hills 30 C e
Gemeticum, see Jumièges
Geminiacum (Gembloux) 39 H h
Gemioncourt 156 A a
Gemmingen 142 D b
Gemmi Pass 91 P l
Genappe 156 A a
Genava (Geneva) 26 A a
Generality Lands, see Common Lands
Genesee River 192 C b
Geneva 91 O l
Geneva, bp. 95 D b
Geneva, cty. 69 G d
Geneva, dist. 91 O l
Geneva, lake 39 I j
Genèvre, Mont, pass 26 A c
Genf, see Geneva 91 O l
Genfer See, see L. Geneva 91 O l
Gengenbach 142 B d
Gennath Gate 6 ins. A
Gennesaret, Lake of 6 D c
Gennesaret, Plain of 6 D c
Genoa, in Italy 90 I h
Genoa, abp. 95 D c
Genoa, Gulf of 26 C d
Genoa, rep. 90 B b
Genoa, in Nebraska 188 G b
Gentinnes 156 B a
Genua (Genoa) 26 C c
Genusia 31 F b
Genusus River 10 B a
Geographe Bay 172 A d
Geographer's Line 196 ins. B
George, Fort, in Canada 200 D b
George, Fort, in Maine 189 D c
George, Fort, in New York 192 E b
George, lake 192 E b
Georgeana 189 D c
Georgenthal, mon. 95 E a (G.)
Georgetown, in Brit. Guiana 214 D b
Georgetown, in Pulo Penang 171 K h
Georgetown, in S. Carolina 193 E e
Georgia, col. 193 C e
Georgia, km. 73 I b
Georgia, prov. 139 F g
Georgia, reg. 67 O e
Georgia, state 199 I d
Georgian Bay 191 I b
Georgina River 172 C c
Gepidæ, people 35 I d
Gepids, people 50 H c
Gera 87 I c
Gera River 85 F e
Gerabronn 143 I g
Gerace 90 F e
Gerace, bp. 95 F d
Geræstus, prom. 15 E b
Geraldton 172 A c
Gerania, mt. 15 D a
Gerasa 7 D d
Gerata, mt.
Gerberoy, castle 69 H f
Gerenia
Gergesa 6 D c
Gergithes 9 C c
Gergovia 38 C c
Geringswalde, mon. 80 ins.
Gerizim, mt. 7 C d
Germalus, mt. 23 B
German Confederation 157 C b
German East Africa, col.
German East Africa Company
German Empire
German South-West Africa, col.
Germania reg., see Germany
Germania I, West Rom. prov. 42 D d (3)
Germania II, West Rom. prov. 42 D c (4)
Germania Inferior, Rom. prov., see Lower Germany
Germania Superior, Rom. prov., see Upper Germany
Germanic Peoples, about 900 57
Germanicopolis 20 E b
Germanna 193 F b
German Ocean
Germanorum, Forum 26 B c
Germantown 192 D c
Germany, country, see German Empire
Germany, reg. 34 G c
Germany, Greater, reg.
Germany, km. 70 I d
Germany, Lower, Rom. prov.
Germany, Upper, Rom. prov.
German Zollverein, customs-union 160 D c
Germersheim 78 F d
Gernsbach 142 B c
Gerstungen
Geroldseck, castle 154 D d
Geroldseck, cty. 158 E d
Gerolstein 117 E d
Gerona 82 C a
Gerona, bp. 94 C c
Gerona, duchy 83 L g
Gerónimo de Yuste, San, mon. 94 A c
Geronthræ 14 C c

Gerontia, isl.	11	F c	
Gerresheim, mon.	95	D a	
Gerrha	19	H e	
Gerrhæi, people	19	G e	
Gers, dept.	148	E f	
Gersau	91	Q k	
Gersoriacum, see Boulogne			
Gertruydenberg	117	C c	
Gerunium	30	E a	
Geshur, reg.	6	D c	
Gesoriacum	38	C b	
Getæ, people	18	B b	
Gethsemane, loc. near Jerusalem	6 ins. A		
Gettysburg	208 ins.		
Gévaudan, cty.	61	E d	
Gévaudan, dist.	84	E g	
Gex, dist.	130	N h	
Gezer	7	B e	
Ghadames	174	D b	
Ghara River	137	B b	
Ghassanids, Dom. of the	52	L f	
Ghazal, Bahr el, reg.	174	F d	
Ghazal, Bahr el, R.	174	F d	
Ghazni	170	H e	
Gheel	117	D c	
Ghent	117	B c	
Ghent, Hanse. for. cy.	99 ins. B		
Gherardesca	90	L j	
Ghilan, reg.	139	G h	
Gian Galeazzo Visconti, Dom. of	90		
Giangtse	171	K f	
Giants, Stoa of the			
Gibeah			
Gibellum	68	C b	
Gibeon	7	C e	
Gibilet	68	C c	
Gibraltar	82	A b	
Gibraltar, strait of	2	D e	
Gibson, Fort	211	G c	
Gibson's Desert	172	K c	
Giebichenstein, castle	63	F c	
Gien	76	E c	
Giengen, imp. cy.	79	G d	
Giessen	114	E c	
Giglio Island	90	L j	
Gigny, mon.	148	C b	
Gigonus	11	E b	
Gijón	82	A a	
Gila Bend, Ind. Res.	188	D d	
Gila River	187	H e	
Gila River, Ind. Res.	188	D d	
Gilbert Islands	179	I g	
Gilboa	7	C d	
Gilboa, mt.	6	C c	
Gilead, mts.	7	D d	
Gilead, dist.			
Giles, routes of	172 leg.		
Gilgal, near Jericho			
Gilgal, near Ramathaim			
Gilgal, in Samaria	7	B d	
Gilgit	170	I e	
Gilly	156	A b	
Gilolo, isl.	112	F c	
Gimoës, cty.	76 D e (Gim.)		
Gincea			
Giornico	91	Q l	
Giovanni Visconti, Dom. of	90	I h	
Giovi, pass	26	D c	
Giovinazzo	90	F d	
Girgeh	150	B b	
Girgenti	90	D f	
Girgenti, bp.	95	E d	
Girishk	170	H e	
Gironde, dept.	148	D f	
Gisborne	172	G d	
Giseh	150	B a	
Gishiga	171	R b	
Gislikon			
Gisors	69	H f	
Gitana	10	B c	
Gitschin	159	H c	
Gitta	7	C d	
Giurgevo	93	C b	
Givet	117	C d	

Gizeh			
Glabais	156	A a	
Glacier Bay	212 ins.		
Glamorgan, cty.	127	V o	
Glamorgan, parl. dist.	163	K f	
Glandève, bp.	95	D c	
Glaphyræ	11	D c	
Glarus	91	R k	
Glarus, canton	91	R l	
Glasgow			
Glasgow, abp.	97	G b	
Glasgow, univ.	100	E c	
Glastonbury	60	E e	
Glastonbury, mon.	97	O j	
Glastonbury, parl. bor.	163	L f	
Glatz	63	I c	
Glatz, cty.	87	K c	
Glaucus River, in Achaia	14	B a	
Glaucus River, in Armenia	20	I b	
Gleichen, castle	115 ins. B		
Glen Coe, in Scotland			
Glencoe, in Natal	175	N l	
Glengarry			
Glen Shiel			
Glevum (Gloucester)	51	O i	
Glisas	11	E d	
Globukoie			
Glogau	63	I c	
Glogau, princ.	79	I c	
Glom River	166	H c	
Glommen River	120	H d	
Gloucester, in England			
Gloucester, castle			
Gloucester, cty.			
Gloucester, mon.			
Gloucester, parl. bor.	163	L f	
Gloucester, shire			
Gloucester, in Mass.	189	D c	
Gloucester, in New Jersey	192	D d	
Gloucester, cty. in Virginia	193 Fc (G.)		
Glücksburg	158	E a	
Glückstadt	122	E b	
Glurns			
Glykys Limen, bay	10	B c	
Glympeis	15	C b	
Gmünd, imp. cy.	143	I h	
Gmunden	123	G e	
Gnadenhuetten	194	C b	
Gnatia	31	G b	
Gnesen			
Gnesen, abp.			
Gnevin	63	G c	
Goa	137	B e	
Goajíra Peninsula	214	B a	
Gobæum, prom.	38	A c	
Gobannium (Abergavenny)	51	O i	
Gobi, desert	92	K c	
Goch	117	E c	
Gochsheim	142	C b	
Godavari River	137	C e	
Godmundingham			
Gödöllö	159	J e	
Gods, Portico of the	24	B	
God's House, League of, dist.	91	R l	
Godstow, mon.	97	P j	
Godwin Austen, mt.	170	I e	
Gogana	19	H e	
Gogo, in Africa	174	D c	
Gogo, in India			
Gogo, reg.	108	R f	
Göhrde	154	F b	
Goito	161	H e	
Gök-tepe	170	G e	
Golan	6	D c	
Golan, reg.	6	D c	
Golconda	137	C e	
Goldberg	123	H c	
Gold Coast, col.	174	C d	
Golden Castile, reg.	105	D e	
Golden Gate, in Constantinople	93	G e	
Golden Gate, The, in Jerusalem	68 ins. B		
Golden Horde, khan. of the	77	M c	
Golden Horn, bay	93	G e	
Goldenkron, mon.	80	D g	

Golden Mile-stone, in Rome			
Goldsboro	208	E b	
Golea, El	174	D a	
Golfo Dulce	105	C c	
Golgatha, loc. near Jerusalem	6 ins. A*		
Goliad	198	F e	
Göllheim	78	E d	
Gollnow	135	H b	
Gollnow, Hanse. cy.	99 ins. B		
Golo, dept.	148	F f	
Golowczyn	131	I c	
Golymin	155	K b	
Gomaringen	143	H i	
Gomel	139	D e	
Gomera, isl.	108	P e	
Gomez, route of	108	J c	
Gommern	85	F d	
Gomphi	10	C c	
Gondar	174	G c	
Gonnus	11	D c	
Gonzaga, fam.	79	G f	
Gonzales de Avila, route of	105	C d	
Good Hope, Cape of	109	S k	
Good Hope, Fort	212	C b	
Goole	162	F d	
Goor	117	E b	
Goose Creek	208 ins.		
Gophna	7	C e	
Göppingen	143	I h	
Gora	155	K c	
Gordleum	20	D c	
Gordillo, route of	191	J e	
Gordons, fam.			
Gordonsville	208 E b (Gord.)		
Gorée			
Gorgiana	189	D c	
Gorgon, isl.	26	D d	
Gorgona			
Gorgona Island	111	B a	
Gorinchem	117	C c	
Goritza	165	B c	
Görlitz	63	H c	
Gortyna			
Gortys	14	C b	
Görz	72	C b	
Görz, cty.	79	H f	
Gorze, mon.	95	D b	
Gorzno	123	J b	
Goshen, reg.	4 ins. *		
Goslar	62	F c	
Goslar, Hanse. cy.	99 ins. B		
Goslar, imp. cy.	79	G c	
Gosnold, route of	191	L c	
Göss, mon.	80	D h	
Gosselies	156	A b	
Göteborg			
Gotha	85	F e	
Götha River			
Götheborg			
Gothenburg			
Gothia, dist.	46	I b	
Gothia, marq.	61	E e	
Gothland, dist.	66	I b	
Gothland, isl.			
Göthland, E., dist.			
Göthland, W., dist.			
Goths, people, in Dacia	47	K d	
Goths, people, in Scandia	38	E a	
Gotland, see Gothland and Göth-land			
Gottenburg	184	F a	
Gottesgab	115 ins. B		
Gotteshausbund, dist.	91	R l	
Gotthard, Sankt	131	G d	
Göttingen	78	F c	
Göttingen, Hanse. cy.	99 ins. B		
Gottlieben, castle	86	G e	
Gottorp, castle	114	E a	
Gottschee	80	D h	
Göttweig, mon.	80	D g	
Gough Island	181 A A l		
Goulas	4	B b	
Goulburn	172	K d	
Gourdon	76	D d	

Gournay. . . . . 126 B b
Govola River . . . . 26 D e
Goyana . . . . 214 F c
Goyaz . . . . 214 D d
Goyaz, state . . . . 214 E d
Gozo, isl. . . . . 131 F f
Graaf Reinet. . . . . 175 L m
Grabow . . . . 85 B b
Gracay . . . . 76 D c
Gracias á Dios, Cape . . . . . 105 D c
Grado . . . . 63 G f
Gradus Monetæ . . . . 24 A
Græcia, Magna, reg. . . . . . 29 E e
Græcostasis, in Rome . . . . .
Grafton . . . . 172 E c
Graham Harbor . . . . 105 ins.
Graia, Alpis, pass . . . . . . 26 A b
Graian Alps, mts . . . . 26 B b
Graïce, dist. . . . . 16 B a
Grain Coast, reg. . . . . 174 B d
Graioceli, people . . . . 26 A b
Grammont . . . . 117 B d
Grampian Mountains . . . . . 49 D c
Grampound, parl. bor . . . .
Gramzow, mon. . . . . 80 ins.
Gran . . . . 59 H d
Gran, abp. . . . . 95 F b
Gran River . . . . 63 J d
Granada, in Nicaragua . . . . 105 C d
Granada, in Spain . . . . . . 83 E d
Granada, abp. . . . . 94 B d
Granada, emir. . . . . 83 E d
Granada, km. . . . . 83 K h
Granby, Fort . . . . 195 A g
Gran Chaco, El, reg. . . . . . 215 C e
Grand Bassam . . . . 175 C d
Grand Canyon . . . . 187 H e
Grande Chartreuse, La, mon. . 95 D b
Grande Gete River . . . . . . 156 B a
Grande Ronde, Ind. Res. . . . 188 B b
Grandes Écuries, in Versailles 149 A
Grand Forks . . . . 210 F a
Grand Gulf . . . . 208 B c
Grand Junction . . . . 188 E c
Grand Portage . . . . 211 G a
Grand Portage, Ind. Res. . . . 188 I a
Grandpré, in France . . . . . .
Grand Pré, in Nova Scotia . . . 194 G b
Grand Rapids . . . . 211 H b
Grand River, in Missouri . . . 199 G b
Grand River, in Utah . . . . . 198 D c
Grand River, in S. Dakota . . . 198 E a
Grand Selve, mon. . . . . . . 94 C c
Grandson . . . . 91 O l
Grand Trianon, in Versailles . 149 A
Grandvilliers . . . . 76 E b
Granges . . . . 143 ins. F
Granges, lordship . . . . . . 143 ins. F
Granicus River . . . .
Granja . . . . 214 E c
Granja, La, castle . . . . . . 130 C e
Granson . . . . 130 O h
Grantham . . . . 127 Y n
Grantham, parl. bor. . . . . . 163 N e
Grant Land . . . . 186 L a
Granville . . . . 172 D a
Granville, Fort . . . . 192 C c
Grasburg, castle . . . . 91 P l
Grasse . . . . 126 E e
Grasse, bp. . . . . 95 D c
Gratianopolis, see Grenoble
Gratiot, Fort . . . . 211 I b
Gratz . . . . 72 D b
Graubünden (Grisons), dist. . 91 R l
Graudenz . . . . 115 J b
Gravelines . . . . 126 C a
Gravelle . . . . 76 C b
Grävenstein, castle . . . . . . 142 ins. B
Grävenstein, lordship . . . . 142 ins. B
Gravesend, in Kent . . . . . . 75 J i
Gravesend, in Long Island . . 189 ins. C
Graviscæ . . . . 27 F e
Great Armenia, reg. . . . . . 99 L e
Great Australian Bight . . . . 172 B d

Great Barrier Reef . . . . . . 172 D b
Great Barrington . . . . 196 E b
Great Basin . . . . 187 H d
Great Bear Lake . . . . 186 H b
Great Belt, str. . . . . 88 D d
Great Bend . . . . 190 F d
Great Bulgaria, reg. . . . . . 77 N b
Great Canal . . . .
Great Cayman, isl. . . . . . . 105 D c
Great Central Plain . . . . . . 186 I b
Great Desert . . . .
Greater Antilles, isl. . . . . . 187 L g
Greater Armenia, reg. . . . . 33 N e
Greater Germany, reg. . . . . .
Greater Phrygia, satr. . . . . 18 O h
Greater Syrtis, gulf . . . . . . 51 G f
Great Exuma, isl. . . . . 105 E b
Great Falls . . . . 210 C a
Great Fish River, in Canada . 186 I b
Great Fish River, in Cape Col. 175 M m
Great Grimsby, parl. bor. . . . 163 N d
Great Harbor . . . . 189 C d
Great Inagua, isl. . . . . 213 E b
Great Kanawha River . . . . . 193 D b
Great Kei River . . . . 175 M m
Great Khan, Empire of the . . .
Great Lakes, The . . . . 186 K d
Great Lowland Plain . . . . . 2 E c
Great Malvern, mon. . . . . . 97 O i
Great Marlow, parl. bor. . 163 N f (Gr. M.)
Great Meadows, battle . . . . 192 B d
Great Miami River . . . . . . 196 ins. B
Great Namaqualand, reg. . . . 175 E g
Great Northern Coalfields, Eng-
land . . . . 162 E b
Great Oasis . . . . 4 E d *
Great Ouse River . . . . 49 F e
Great Pedee River . . . . . . 193 E d
Great Poland, reg. . . . . . . 131 G c
Great Redan, Fort . . . . . . 164 L g
Great Russia, see Muscovy
Great Russians, people . . . . 139 E e
Great Saint Bernard Pass . . 91 P m
Great Salt Lake . . . . 190 C c
Great Sandy Desert . . . . . 172 B c
Great Sandy Island . . . . . . 172 E c
Great Siberian Plain . . . . . 3 K c
Great Slave Lake . . . . 186 H b
Great Slave River . . . . . . 212 D b
Great Smoky Range . . . . . 193 C d
Great South Wales Coalfield . 162 C f
Great Valley . . . . 187 K e
Great Victoria Desert . . . . . 172 B b
Great Wall . . . .
Great Wallachia, reg. . . . . . 89 C b
Great Wahle River . . . . . . 212 H c
Great Yarmouth, parl. bor. . . 163 P e
Grecian Peninsula . . . . . . 2 G e
Greece, km. . . . . 164 C c
Greece, reg. . . . . 4 B b
Greek Patriarchate . . . . . . 93 G e (8)
Greeks, people . . . . 165 leg.
Green Bay . . . . 191 H c
Green Bay, cy. . . . . 199 H b
Greenbrier River . . . . 192 A d
Greencastle . . . .
Greene, route of . . . . 195 B f
Greenland, isl. . . . . 186 O a
Green Mountains . . . . 192 E b
Green River, in Kentucky . . . 193 A c
Green River, in Utah . . . . . 190 D d
Greensboro . . . . 211 J c
Greenspring . . . . 193 ins. A (Gr.)
Greenville . . . . 196 ins. A
Greenville, Fort . . . . 196 ins. B
Greenway Court . . . . 192 B d
Greenwich, in Conn. . . . . . 192 E c
Greenwich, in England . . . . 75 I i
Greenwich, parl. bor. . . . . . 163 O f
Greenwich, E. . . . . 189 ins. A
Greetsiel . . . . 122 D b
Greifenhagen . . . . 123 H b
Greifensee, castle . . . . . . 91 Q k
Greifswald . . . . 80 C d

Greifswald, Hanse. cy. . . . . . 99 ins. B
Greifswald, univ. . . . . 100 B
Greiz . . . . 135 G
Grenade, isl. . . . . 213 F
Grenadines, isl. . . . . 213 F
Grenoble . . . . 61 F
Grenoble, bp. . . . . 95 D
Grenoble, gen. . . . . 147 F
Grenoble, univ. . . . . 100 C
Greutungs, people . . . . . . 50 I
Grève, Place de, Paris . . . . . 149 B
Grève, Quai de la, Paris . . . 149 B
Grevenmacher . . . . 117 E
Grey Friars, mon. in London . 75 G
Greytown . . . . 213 D
Grèzes . . . . 76 E
Gries Pass . . . . 91 Q
Grignan . . . . 126 D
Grijalva River . . . . 213 C
Grijalva, route of . . . . 105 B
Grimma . . . . 85 G
Grimsby, Hanse. for. cy. . . . 98 ins. A
Grinsel Pass . . . .
Grinnell . . . . 207 G
Gripsholm, castle . . . . . . 120 I
Griqualand East, dist. . . . . 175 M m
Griqualand, West, dist. . . . . 175 L
Grisons, dist. . . . . 91 R
Griswold, Fort . . . . 195 F
Grobe, mon. . . . . 80 D d
Grodno . . . . 138 B e
Groenlo . . . . 117 E b
Groitzsch . . . . 63 G c
Grol . . . . 117 E b
Grone, castle . . . . 62 E c
Groningen . . . . 117 E a
Groningen, Hanse. cy. . . . . 99 ins. B
Groningen, lordship . . . . . 117 E a
Gross Batanga . . . . 154 G b
Gross Beeren . . . . 143 H h
Gross Bottwar . . . . 85 G e
Grossenhain . . . . 90 L j
Grosseto . . . . 95 E c
Grosseto, bp. . . . .
Gross Friedrichsburg . . . . .
Gross Gartach . . . . 142 D b
Gross Görschen . . . . . 153 G c (Gr. G.)
Gross Jägersdorf . . . . 135 K a
Gross Mariazell, mon. . . . . 95 F b
Gross Sachsenheim . . . . . 143 H h
Gross Scheuern . . . . 159 M f
Groton, in Conn. . . . . 189 C d
Groton, in England . . . . . . 185 G e
Groton, in Mass. . . . . 189 C c
Grotzko . . . .
Grubenhagen, castle . . . . . 122 F c
Grulla . . . . 190 B e
Grumbach, castle . . . . . . 114 E d
Grumentum . . . . 30 E b
Grumum . . . . 31 F b
Grünberg . . . . 123 H c
Grünhain, mon. . . . . 80 ins.
Grünsfeld . . . . 142 E a
Grünwettersbach . . . . 143 G h
Grussenheim . . . . 143 ins. D
Gruyères . . . . 91 P l
Gryneum . . . . 17 E b
Guadalajara, in Spain . . . . 82 B e
Guadalajara, in Mexico . . . 213 ins.
Guadalajara, pres. . . . . . . 213 B b
Guadalquivir River . . . . . . 82 A b
Guadalupe . . . . 214 C e
Guadalupe, isl., Antilles . . . 105 H c
Guadalupe, isl. off Lower Cal. 187 H f
Guadalupe, mon. . . . . 94 A d
Guadalupe Hidalgo . . . . . 201 F f
Guadeloupe, isl. . . . . 105 H c
Guadiana River . . . . 82 A b
Guadix . . . . 82 B b
Guadix, bp. . . . . 94 B d
Guaira . . . . 108 L j
Guaira, La, see Guayra, La
Gualtieri . . . . 90 J h
Guam, isl. . . . . 179 F f

Guanahani, isl.	105	F b
Guanajuato	213 ins.	
Guanare	214	C b
Guangja, isl.	105	D c
Guano Islands	175	E g
Guapore River	214	C d
Guarda, bp.	94	A c
Guardafui, Cape	174	I c
Guardia, bp.	95	F c
Guarionex, chieftain	105	F c
Guastalla	90	C b
Guastalla, duchy	151	L k
Guatemala	105	B d
Guatemala, capt. gen. and pres.	213	D c
Guatemala, country	213	C c
Guatemala, reg.	105	B d
Guaviare River	214	B b
Guaxenduba	214	E c
Guaxule	191	I e
Guayabero River	214	B b
Guayama	199 ins. G	
Guayaquil	111	B b
Guayaquil, Gulf of	111	A b
Guaymas	213	A b
Guayra, La	214	C a
Gubbio	90	D c
Gubbio, bp.	95 -	E c
Guben	85	H e
Guelf Domains	71 ins.	
Guerande	76	B c
Guéret	69	E c
Guernsey, isl.	69	B b
Guerrero, state	213 ins.	
Guevara, route of	108	J j
Guevari	190	C e
Güglingen	143	G g
Guiana, British, col.	214	D b
Guiana, Dutch, col.	214	D b
Guiana, French, col.	214	D b
Guiana, reg.		
Guidi, fam.	90	L j
Guienne, dist.	84	C g
Guienne, duchy, 11 cent.	61	D d
Guienne, duchy, 14 cent.	76	D d
Guienne, prov.	148	D f
Guienne and Gascony, gouv.	146	A c
Guildford, in England	75	H i
Guildford, parl. bor.	163	N f (Guildf.)
Guildford, in W. Australia	172	A d
Guildhall, bldg. in London	75	G g
Guild of the Holy Ghost, college	100 A a (33)	
Guilfort, in Conn.	192	E c
Guilford Court House	195	B e
Guinea, Gulf of	175	D d
Guinea, reg.	108	Q g
Guinea, French, col.	174	B c
Guinea, Lower, reg.	175	E e
Guinea, Portuguese, col.	174	B c
Guinea, Upper, reg.	174	C d
Guinegate	114	B c
Guines	69	D a
Guines, cty.	69	D a
Guingamp, castle	76	B b
Guingamp, mon.	94	B b
Guipúzcoa, dist.	83	K g
Guise	76	E b
Guitres, mon.	94	B b
Gujarat, reg.	137	B d
Gujrat	170	I e
Gulf Plain	187	J f
Gumbinnen	159	L a
Gum Coast	108	P e
Gumush Maden	165	E d
Gundelfingen	143	H i
Gundelfingen, lordship	143	H i
Gundelsheim	143	H g
Güns	115	I e
Günsburg	154	F d
Günthersthal, mon.	142	A e
Guntia	39	K i
Guntoor, Guntur	137	D e
Güns River	143	J i
Gura	174	G c
Gurgures Mountains	27	G e
Guriev	139	H f
Gurk	80	D h
Gurk, bp.	95	E b
Gurupa	214	D c
Gustavus Adolphus, route of	121	D b
Güstrow	79	H b
Güstrow, princ.	79	H b
Gutenberg, castle		
Gutenstein	142	D d
Gutenstein, lordship	142	D d
Gutensell, ab.	143	J i
Guthrie	210	F c
Guthrum's Kingdom		
Gutones, people	38	F b
Guzerat, reg., see Gujarat		
Guzman, route of	107	G e
Gwalior	137	C c
Gwent, dist.		
Gwynedd, dist.		
Gyarus, isl.	15	E b
Gympie	172	E q
Gyöngyös	159	J e
Gyrton	11	D c
Gythium	14	C c
Gzhatsk	153	O f
Haarlem	117	C b
Habbard, mt.	212 ins.	
Habitancium (Risingham)		
Habsburg, see Hapsburg		
Habsburg (Hapsburg), castle	62	E e
Hackensack	189 ins. C	
Hacsány	131	G d
Hadad-Rimmon	6	C c
Haddeby	62	E a
Haddington, cty.	127 R i (HA.)	
Hadeln, Land, dist.	86	G b
Hadley	189	B c
Hadramut, Hadramaut, reg.	53	G e
Hadranus River	30	D e
Hadranum	30	D e
Hadria	27	I e
Hadrian, Mausoleum of	22	A
Hadrian, Wall of, in Athens	23	D
Hadrian, Wall of, in Britain	42	B c
Hadrian, Stoa of	23	D
Hadrianopolis, in Epirus	10	B c
Hadrianopolis, in Thrace	39	N l
Hadrian's Circus	22	A
Hadrian's Gate	23	D
Hadrian's Mole	96	A
Hadrian's Villa	35 ins. B (7)	
Hadrian's Wall	51	O g
Hadrumetum	38	E e
Haegsted, see Eichstädt		
Hæmimont, theme	59	J e
Hæmimontium, E. Rom. prov.	43 He (3)	
Hæmus Mons (Mountains)	39	M l
Haff, Kurisches, bay	155	K a
Haff, Stettiner, bay	155	H b
Hafsids, dynasty	77	F e
Hagelberg	154	B b
Hagenau	72	B b
Hagerstown	208 ins.	
Hague, de la, Cape, battle off		
Hague, The	117	C b
Haidarabad, in Deccan	137	C e
Haidarabad, in Sind	137	A c
Haigerloch	143	G i
Haïl	170	F f
Hain River		
Hai-nan, isl.		
Hainau	155	H c
Hainault Forest	49	G f
Hainaut, cty.	117	B d
Hainaut, dist.	62	B c
Hainaut and Cambresis, gen.	147	E a
Hainburg	63	I d
Haine River	156	A b
Haitl, isl.	187	L g
Haiti, rep.	213	E c
Hakodate	171	P d
Hal	156	A a
Halæ	11	E d
Halæ Araphenides	16	C b
Halæ Æxonides	16	B b
Halæsa	30	D d
Halberstadt	62	F c
Halberstadt, bp.	95	E a
Halberstadt, Hanse. cy.	99 ins. B	
Halberstadt, princ.	122	F c
Haldensleben	72	C a
Haldenstein, castle	91	R l
Hales, mon.	97	P i
Hales Owen, mon.	97	O i
Hales River	30	E b
Halex River	30	E e
Haliacmon River	10	D b
Haliartus	11	E d
Halica	15	D b
Halicarnassus	13	E c
Halicyæ	30	B e
Halicz	59	I d
Halicz, princ.	71	K d
Halidon Hill		
Halieis	15	D b
Halifax, in England	162	E d
Halifax, parl. bor.	163	M d
Halifax, in Nova Scotia	212	I d
Halifax, Fort	189	D b
Halil-Eli		
Halimus	16	B b
Halipedon, dist.	16	D c
Haliussa Island	15	D b
Hall, in Tyrol	154	F e
Hall, imp. cy., in Wurtemberg	143	I g
Hall, Fort	198	C b
Hall, Fort, Ind. Res.	188	D b
Hall Peninsula	212	I b
Halland, dist.	88	E c
Halle	63	G c
Halle, Hanse. cy.	99 ins. B	
Halles, loc. in Paris	149	B
Hallstadt		
Halmahera, isl.	112	F c
Halmstad	120	H e
Halonnesus, isl.	11	F c
Haluntium	30	D d
Halus	11	D c
Halycus River	30	C e
Halys River	20	F b
Ham	117	B e
Hamadan		
Hamah	68	C b
Hamar	131	F a
Hamath, on Lake of Gennesaret	6	D c
Hamath, on the Orontes R.	4	C d
Hamaxitos, road	23	D
Hambach	158	E d
Hamble, mon.	100	A b
Hamburg, in Germany	62	F b
Hamburg, Hanse. cy.	99 ins. B	
Hamburg, imp. cy.	78	F b
Hamburg, in S. Carolina	211	I d
Hamburg, in Virginia	193	E b
Hamdanids, Dom. of the	59	L f
Hameln	122	E b
Hameln, Hanse. cy.	99 ins. B	
Hami		
Hamid, reg.	89	J g
Hamilton, in Canada	212	G d
Hamilton, in Scotland		
Hamilton Inlet	212	J c
Hamilton River	212	I c
Hamiltons, fam.	97	I d
Hamme	156	B a
Hammerfest	167	J a
Hammerstein, castle	62	D c
Hammon	6	C b
Hamont	117	D c
Hampshire, cty.		
Hampstead, in England	75	I h
Hampstead, in Georgia	193 ins. C	
Hampton, in England	75	I i
Hampton, in N. Hampshire	189	C c
Hampton, in Virginia	193 ins. A	
Hampton Court, castle	75	I i

Hampton Roads, harbor	208	E b	
Hana	198	ins. B	
Hanau	122	E c	
Hang-chau-fu			
Hanging Rock, battle	195	A f	
Hangö, isl.	131	H b	
Hannibal	211	G c	
Hannibalis, Castra	31	F d	
Ha-noi	171	L f	
Hanolelet			
Hanover, in Germany	86	G b	
Hanover, Hanse. cy.	99	ins. B	
Hanover, elect.	134	E b	
Hanover, km.	158	E b	
Hanover, in Pa.	208	ins.	
Hanover, in Virginia	193	F c	
Hansi			
Hanwell	75	I h	
Hanworth	75	I i	
Haparanda	167	J b	
Happiness, Temple of	24	A	
Hapsburg, castle	91	Q k	
Haran	5	C b *	
Harar	174	H d	
Harbin	171	N d	
Harbour Grace	212	J d	
Harburg	134	E b	
Hardanger Field	166	G c	
Harderwyk	117	D b	
Harderwyk, Hanse. cy.	99	ins. B	
Hardheim	142	D a	
Hard Times	208	B c	
Harfleur	76	D b	
Harfleur, Hanse. for. cy.	98	D d	
Harlech, castle			
Harlingen	117	D a	
Harmakut, mts.			
Harmar, Fort	196	ins. B	
Harmene	20	F a	
Harmersbach	142	B d	
Harmony, New	206	ins.	
Harmozia	8	D c	
Harmozica	20	K b	
Harpers Ferry	208	ins.	
Harplea			
Harran	67	N f	
Harris, dist.	127	N g	
Harris, Fort	192	C c	
Harrisburg	196	D b	
Harris Ferry	192	C c	
Harrismith	175	M l	
Harrison, route of	200	C d	
Harrodsburg	191	I d	
Harrow-on-the-Hill	75	I h	
Harsany	164	B a	
Hartford, in Conn.	189	B d	
Hartford, in England	185	D d	
Hartland, mon.	97	M k	
Harvard	189	C c	
Harwich	127	A A o	
Harwich, parl. bor.	163	P f	
Harz, mts.	62	F c	
Harzburg, castle	62	F c	
Hasa, El, reg.			
Haslach	142	B d	
Haslemere, parl. bor.	163	N f	
Hasle Thal, valley	91	Q l	
Hasnon, mon.	94	C a	
Hasselt, in Liège	117	D d	
Hasselt, in Overyssel	117	E b	
Hasta, in Liguria	26	C c	
Hasta, in Spain	38	A e	
Hastenbeck	134	E b	
Hastings			
Hastings, parl. bor.	163	O g	
Hatera	11	D b	
Hatfield, in England			
Hatfield, in Mass.	189	B c	
Hatita	7	E d	
Hatra	20	J e	
Hatria, see Atria	27	G b	
Hatria, see Hadria	27	I e	
Hatteras, Cape	193	G d	
Hatteras, Fort	208	E b	
Hatteras Island	193	G d	
Hattin	68	ins. A	
Hatvan	159	J e	
Hauara	18	E e	
Hauenstein	142	B e	
Hauenstein, cty.	142	B e	
Hauran, reg.	6	E c	
Hauraki Gulf	172	G d	
Hausach	142	B d	
Hausbergen	72	B b	
Hausen, lordship	142	B d	
Haute-Crète, mon.	95	D b	
Hauteford, castle	76	D d	
Haute-Garonne, dept.	148	E f	
Haute-Loire, dept.	148	E e	
Haute-Marne, dept.	148	E e	
Hauterive, mon.	95	D b	
Hautes-Alps, dept.	148	F f	
Hautes-Saône, dept.	148	F e	
Hautes-Pyrénées, dept.	148	D f	
Haute-Vienne, dept.	148	E e	
Hauteville	65	F f	
Haut-Rhin, dept.	148	F e	
Hautvillers, mon.	94	Cb(Hv.)	
Havana	105	D b	
Havel River	63	G b	
Havelberg	63	G b	
Havelberg, bp.	95	E a	
Havelberg, Hanse. cy.	99	ins. B	
Haverford	192	ins.	
Haverfordwest, mon.	97	M j	
Haverfordwest, parl. bor.	163	I f	
Haverhill	189	C c	
Havering-atte-Bower	75	J h	
Havre	69	H f	
Havre de Grace, in France	126	B b	
Havre de Grace, in Maryland	200	L h	
Hawaii, isl.	198	ins. B	
Hawaii, ter.	198	ins. B	
Hawaiian Islands	198	ins. B	
Hawke Bay	172	G d	
Haye, la, farm			
Haye Sainte, la, farm			
Hayling, mon.	100	B b	
Haynes Bluff	208	B c	
Hazah, reg.	99	M f	
Hazor, near Asamon Mts.	6	C c	
Hazor, near Ashdod	7	B e	
Hazor, near waters of Merom	6	D b	
Heathfield			
Hebdomon, palace	93	G e	
Hebrides, The, isl.	49	C c	
Hebrides, New, isl.	172	F b	
Hebron	7	C e	
Hebrus River	39	N l	
Hebulae Islands (The Hebrides)	38	A a	
Hecate Strait	212	B c	
Hecatompylus	19	I c	
Hechingen	143	G i	
Hecla, mt.	166	B c	
Hedjaz, El Hejas, reg.			
Hedon, parl. bor.	163	N d	
Heemstede	189	B d	
Heggbach, ab.	143	I i	
Hegyes	159	J f	
Heide	114	E a	
Heidelberg	142	C b	
Heidelberg, univ.	100	G e	
Heidelsheim	142	C b	
Heidenheim	143	J h	
Heidenheim, lordship	143	J h	
Heidenheim, mon.	95	E b	
Height of Land, The	186	K c	
Heilbronn	72	B b	
Heilbronn, imp. cy.	143	H g	
Heiligenbeil	123	K a	
Heiligenberg	142	D e	
Heiligenberg, cty.	142	D e	
Heiligenhafen	122	F a	
Heiligenkreuz, mon.	80	E h	
Heiligerlee	117	E a	
Heiligkreuzthal, ab.	143	H i	
Heilsberg	80	G d	
Heimsheim	143	G h	
Heinrichau, mon.	95	F	
Heisterbach, mon.	95	D	
Heitersheim	142	A	
Hejas, El, Hedjaz, reg.			
Hela	115	J	
Hela, pen.	88	H	
Helbon	6	E	
Helder	117	C	
Heldua	6	C	
Helena, Baths of	22	A	
Helena, in Arkansas	208	B	
Helena, in France, see Elne			
Helena, in Montana	210	C	
Helena, isl.	15	E b	
Helenopontus, East Rom. prov.	43	J e (8	
Helfenstein, castle	114	E d	
Helfenstein, ruin	143	I b	
Helgoland, isl.	62	D	
Helice	14	C	
Helicon, mt.	11	D d	
Helicon River	11	D b	
Helicranum	10	B c	
Heliopolis, in Egypt	1	B l	
Heliopolis, in Syria	6	E a	
Heliopolis, ruins of	150	B a	
Helisson River	14	C b	
Hellas, seg.	8	A b	
Hellas, theme	59	I f	
Helleporus River	31	F d	
Hellespont (Dardanelles), strait			
Hellespontine Phrygia, satr.			
Hellespontus, dioc.	43	H f	
Hellopia, dist.	10	B c	
Helme River	85	F e	
Helmern, castle	62	E c	
Helmond	117	D c	
Helmstedt	114	F b	
Helmstedt, Hanse. cy.	99	ins. B	
Helorine Way	31	ins. B	
Helorus	30	E e	
Helorus River	30	D e	
Helos	15	C c	
Helsingborg	120	H e	
Helsingborg, Hanse. for. cy.	98	F b	
Helsingfors	119	J a	
Helsingör	120	H e	
Helsingör, Hanse. for. cy.	98	F b	
Helston, parl. bor.	163	I g	
Heluan	174	J j	
Helvetian Republic	151	H g	
Helvetii, people	38	D c	
Helvii, people	38	C d	
Helvillum	27	G d	
Helvinus River	27	I e	
Hemeroscopium	12	C c	
Hemesa	20	G e	
Hemmingstedt	86	G a	
Hempstead	189	B d	
Hengstburg	63	H e	
Heniochi, people	35	L e	
Henlopen, Cape	192	D d	
Henna	30	D e	
Henneberg, castle	85	F e	
Henneberg, cty.	114	F c	
Hennebont, castle	76	B c	
Hennegau, see Hainaut			
Hennepin, route of	191	G c	
Hennersdorf, Catholic	135	H c	
Henrichemont	126	C c	
Henrico	193	ins. A (Hen.)	
Henrico County	207	K c	
Henrietta Maria, Cape	212	G c	
Henry, Cape	193	ins. A	
Henry, Fort	208	C b	
Henry the Illustrious, Poss. of	85		
Henton, mon.	97	O j	
Hepha	6	B c	
Heppenheim	142	C a	
Heptastadium, loc. in Alexandria	34	ins. C	
Heraclea, in Acarnania	10	C d	
Heraclea, in Cappadocia	67	M f	
Heraclea, in Elis	14	B b	
Heraclea, in Epirus	10	C c	
Heraclea, in Lucania	31	F b	

Ieraclea, in Macedonia.....	10	C a
Ieraclea (Perinthus).......		
Ieraclea Chersonesus......	12	J b
Ieraclea Minoa..........	30	C e
Ieraclea Pontica........	20	D b
Ieraclea Trachinia........	11	D d
Ieracleopolis............	1	B c
Ieracleum, in Athens....	23	D
Ieracleum, in Syracuse....	31 ins.	B(10)
Ieracleum, cy. in Macedonia.	11	D b
Ieraclius, Wall of........	93	G e
Ieræa.............	14	B b
Ieræan Mountains........	30	D e
Ieræum, cy. in Thrace.....		
Ieræum, temple, in Olympia.		
Ieræum, prom.........	15	C a
Ierat...............		
Hérault, dept...........	148	E f
Herault River.........	148	E f
Herbertshöhe..........	172	E a
Herbita...........	30	D e
Herbrechtigen.........	122	F d
Herck.............	117	D d
Herculaneum..........	30	D b
Hercules. isl...........	18 ins.	B
Hercules, Pillars of, (Calpe, or Gibraltar, and Abila), promontories............	38	B e
Hercules, prom.......	31	F e
Hercules, Temple of......	24	A
Hercules Custor, Temple of ..		
Herculian Way........	30	E a
Herculis Monœci, Portus (Monaco).............	26	B d
Hercynian Forest, mts.....	38	E b
Herdoniæ...........	30	E a
Hereford...........		
Hereford, bp.........	97	O i
Hereford, castle.......	65	E d
Hereford, cty.........		
Hereford, parl. bor.......	163	L e
Hereford, parl. dist.......	163	L e
Hereford, shire........		
Herenthals..........	117	C c
Herford...........	122	E b
Herford, Hanse. cy........	99 ins.	B
Herford, mon........	95	D a
Héricourt...........	143 ins.	F
Héricourt, lordship.......	143 ins.	F
Heristal...........	53	N g
Herjedalen, dist.........	120	H d
Herkimer, Fort.......	192	D b
Hermanitz...........	123	H c
Hermannstadt........	80	I i
Herminius, mt.......	38	A d
Herminones, people.....	38	E b
Hermione...........	15	D b
Hermon, mts.........	6	D b
Hermopolis (Eshmun)......	18	D e
Hermosillo.........	213	A b
Hermunduri, people.....	38	E b
Hermus............	16	B a
Hermus River........	20	C c
Hernad River........	115	K d
Hernandez de Cordova, route of	105	C b
Hernici, people.......	27	H f
Hernösand...........	166	I c
Herod, Tomb of........	6 ins.	A
Herod Agrippa, Wall of	6 ins.	A
Herodes Atticus, Exedra of ..		
Herodes Atticus, Odeum of ..	23	C
Herodium...........	7	C e
Herod's Palace, in Jerusalem .	6 ins.	A
Heroopolis...........	4 ins.	*
Herrenalb, mon......	95	D b
Herrenberg..........	143	G h
Herrenbreitungen, mon.....	95	E a
Herrenhausen, castle......	134	E b
Herrero Land, reg......	175	E g
Herrstein...........	142 ins.	A
Herrstein, lordship.......	142 ins.	A
Hersfeld............	56	D b
Hersfeld, ab...........	78	F c
Hersfeld, mon.........	95	D a
Hersfeld, princ..........	122	E c
Hertford............		
Hertford, cty.........		
Hertford, parl. bor.......	163	O f
Hertford, parl. dist,......	163	N f
Hertford, shire........		
Herulians, people, in Denmark	38	E a
Herulians, people, in Hungary	50	G c
Hervey Bay..........	172	E c
Hervey Islands........	180	K i
Herzogenbuchsee......	91	P k
Herzogenrath.........	117	E d
Herzegovina, dist., 15 cent...	93	A b
Herzegovina, dist., 20 cent...	164	B b
Hesdin............	117	A d
Heshbon...........	7	D e
Hesperis...........	12	G d
Hesse, dist..........	62	E e
Hesse, gr. duchy, 1812....	154	E c
Hesse, gr. duchy, 1866....	158	E c
Hesse, landgr.......	78	F c
Hesse, people.......	55	Q i
Hesse, Electoral, state....	158	E c
Hesse-Cassel, landgr.......	122	E c
Hesse-Darmstadt, landgr....	122	E c
Hestia, Temple of.......	16	D c(2)
Histiæotis, dist..........		
Heubach...........	143	I h
Heubach, Klein.......	142	D a
Heusden...........	117	C c
Hevellians, people.....	63	G b
Hexamilion...........		
Hexapylum, loc. in Syracuse	31 ins.	B(11)
Hexham...........		
Hexham, mon.........		
Hexham, dist.........		
Heyst............	117	C c
Heystesbury, parl. bor....	163	L f (Heyt.)
Hezekiah, Pool of......	6 ins.	A(6)
Hezekiah, Wall of......	6 ins.	A
Hibernia (Ireland)......	34	C c
Hibernii, people.......	38	A b
Hiberus River, see Ebro River		
Hidalgo, state..........	213 ins.	
Hiera, isl., Ægates Island....	30	B e
Hiera, isl., Liparææ Island...	30	E d
Hierapolis, in Asia Minor ...		
Hierapolis, in Syria	20	G d
Hierapytna..........	14 ins.	
Hieromyces River.....	6	D c
Hieron Æsculapii......	15	D b
Hierosolyma (Jerusalem)...	35	L g
Higham Ferrers, parl. bor....	163	N e
Highlanders, people.....	184	C a
Highlands, reg........	49	D c
Highworth, parl. bor....		
Higuey, reg.........	105	G c
Hilara River........	39	J i
Hildburghausen.......	134	F c
Hildesheim.........	62	E b
Hildesheim, bp.......	95	D a
Hildesheim, Hanse. cy.....	99 ins.	B
Hilerda, see Lérida		
Hili............		
Hill of Evil Counsel.....	6 ins.	A
Hill of the Muses......	23	D
Hill of the Nymphs.....	23	D
Hillsboro...........	195	B e
Hilo.............	198 ins.	B
Hilsbach...........	142	C b
Hilton Head, cape......	193 ins.	C
Hilton Head, cy.......	208	D c
Himalaya Mountains......	170	I e
Himella River.......	27	H e
Himera...........	30	C e
Himera River, N.......	30	C e
Himera River, S.......	30	D e
Himmelpforte, mon......	80 ins.	
Himmelpforten.......	122	E b
Hims, see Homs.......	59	L g
Hindon...........	127	W o
Hindon, parl. bor......	163	L f (Hind.)
Hindukush, mts........		
Hindustan, reg........	137	B-E c
Hingham............	189 ins.	B
Hinnom, valley.........	6 ins.	A
Hinter-Rhein, see Farther Rhine River.............	91	R l
Hinterpommern, see Farther Pomerania.........	123	H b
Hiogo.............		
Hippicus Tower..........	6 ins.	A
Hippodamea.........	16	D c
Hippodrome, loc. in Rome...	24	B
Hippola...........	14	C c
Hipponiates, gulf........	31	F d
Hipponium (Vibo)......	31	F d
Hippo Regius........	38	D e
Hippo Zarytus........	38	D e
Hippus............	6	D c
Hiram's Grave.........	6	C b
Hirato, isl...........		
Hiroshima...........	171	O e
Hirpini, people.......	30	D b
Hirrlingen..........	143	G i
Hirsau, mon........	95	D b
Hirschberg..........	123	H c
Hisn Keifa, on the Euphrates.	68	C b
Hisn Keifa, on the Tigris .	71	O f
Hispalis (Seville).......	38	A e
Hispania, see Spain		
Hispania Bætica, prov.....	38	A e(3)
Hispania Lusitana, prov....	38	A d(2)
Hispania Tarraconensis, prov..	38	B d(1)
Hispaniola, isl........	105	F c
Hispellum...........	27	G c
Hissar, in India........	137	C c
Hissar, in Turkestan.......		
Hissarlik...........		
Histiæa...........	11	E d
Histiæotis, dist.......	11	E d
Histonium..........	27	I e
Histria, reg., see Istria.....	27	H b
Hither Pomerania, dist....	123	G a
Hither Rhine River......	91	R l
Hither Spain, prov......	38	B d(1)
Hittites, people......	4	F c
Hlidbeki, see Lübeck		
Hoang-ho, R........		
Hobart............	172	D e
Hobkirks Hill, battle....	195	A f
Hoboken, castle.......	189 ins.	C
Hochberg, castle.......	142	A d
Hochberg, margr.......	142	A d
Hochdorf...........	143	G h
Hochelaga..........	191	K b
Hochkirch..........	135	H c
Höchst, S. of Frankfort...	122	E c
Höchst, W. of Frankfort...	62	E c
Höchstädt...........	134	F d
Hodeida...........	170	F g
Hof..............	154	F c
Hogland, isl.........	131	I a
Hogue or Hougue, la, see Saint Vaast-de-la-Hougue		
Hoh, Ind. Res.........	188	B a
Hohen-Altheim.......	62	F d
Hohenasperg.........	143	H h
Hohenberg, ruin.......	143	G i
Hohenberg, Lower, cty.....	143	G i
Hohenberg, Upper, cty.....	143	G i
Hohenburg, in Alsace....	72	B b
Hohenburg, in Bavaria....	63	F d
Hohenems..........	72	B b
Hohenfriedeberg.......	135	I c
Hohengeroldseck, cty......	142	A d
Hohengeroldseck, mon.....	142	A d
Hohenhöwen, castle.....	142	C e
Hohenkarpfen, ruin.....	143	G i
Hohenlinden........	135	G c
Hohenlohe, princ.......	143	I g
Hohen-Mölsen........	63	G c
Hohenneuffen, ruin.....	143	H h
Hohenrechberg, ruin.....	143	I h
Hohenstaufen, castle....	114	E d
Hohenstaufen, ruin.......	143	I h
Hohenstaufen Domains	71	
Hohentwiel, castle.......	114	E c

Hohen Urach, ruin 143   H i
Hohenzollern, castle 154   G b
Hohenzollern, princ. 143   H i
Hohnstein. 122   F c
Hojeda, route of . . . . 105 G d, 108 M g
Hole Bourn, loc. near London. 75   G g
Holebourn Bridge 75   G g
Holkar, Dom. of. 137   C c
Hollabrunn 155   I d
Holland, cty. 117   C c
Holland, dist. . . . .
Holland, km., 1806 151   K i
Holland, km., 1831 158   C b
Höllental, valley 134   E e
Holly Springs 208   G c
Holmby House 127   X n
Holme Cultram, mon. 97   N g
Holmiæ, prom. 15   C a
Holstein, cty. 72   B a
Holstein, dist. 62   E a
Holstein, duchy, 15 cent. . . . 86   G b
Holstein, duchy, 19 cent. . . . 151   H f
Holston River . . . . 196 ins. A
Holwan . . . .
Holyoke 211   K b
Holy Rock, loc. in Jerusalem . 6 ins. A (1)
Holy Roman Empire about 1000 58, 59
Holy Roman Empire, 1138—1254 72
Holy Sepulchre, Church of the   6 ins. A
Holy Sepulchre, street of the . 68 ins. B
Holy Trinity the less, ch. in
   London. . . . . 75 G g (22)
Homberg 114   E c
Homblières, mon. . . . . . 94 C b (Hombl.)
Homburg, in Bavarian Palatinate 142 ins. B
Homburg, in Hesse 158   E c
Homolium 11   D c
Homs 68   C c
Ho-nan, prov. 171   M e
Honawar 137   B f
Hondo, isl. 171   O e
Honduras, Cape 105   C c
Honduras, country 213   D c
Honduras, reg. 105   C d
Honduras, Gulf of 105   C c
Hondschoote 134   B c
Honfleur 76   D b
Hongkong 171   M f
Honiton 127   V p
Honiton, parl. bor. 163   K g
Honolulu . . . . 198 ins. B
Honor, Temple of 22   A
Honore 137   B f
Honorias, E. Rom. prov. . . . 43 I e (4)
Hood, mt. 187   G d
Hoogly . . . .
Hoogly River . . . .
Hoogstraeten 72   B a
Hoogwoud 72   A a
Hoopa Valley, Ind. Res. 188   B b
Hoorn 117   D b
Hoorn, cty. 117   D c
Hope, Temple of . . . .
Hopedale 212   I c
Hopetown 175   L l
Hopi, Ind. Res. 188   D c
Hopton Heath 127   W n
Horace, Villa of. . . . . 35 ins. B
Horb 143   G i
Horburg . . . . 143 ins. D
Horburg, cty. . . . . 143 ins. D
Horgen 91   Q k
Horma . . . .
Horn 123   H d
Horn, Cape, in Iceland 166   A b
Horn, Cape, in S. America . . . 215   C h
Hornachos 82   A b
Hornbach, mon. 95   D b
Hornberg 142   B d
Horncastle . . . . 98 ins. A
Horneck 143   H g
Hornisgrinde, pass 134   E d
Horologium, in Athens 23   D
Horrea. 26   A d

Horrea, loc. in Rome 23   A
Horse Gate. . . . . 6 ins. A
Horseham, parl. bor. . . . . . .
Horsens 158   E a
Horseshoe Bend, battle 200   I f
Horsham, mon. 97   S i
Horta 27   G e
Ho-si-wu . . . . 170 ins. A
Hostilia 26   F b
Hôtel des Invalides, in Paris . 149   B
Hôtel de Ville, in Paris 149   B
Hôtel Dieu 149   B
Hôtel du Grand Maître in Ver-
   sailles 149   A
Hôtels, Rue des, street in Ver-
   sailles 149   A
Hot Springs 211   G d
Hottentots, people 109   S k
Houffalize 117   D d
Hougomont, castle . . . .
Hougue, La 130   C d
Hounslow 75   I i
Housatonic River 189   B c
House of Hope 189   B d
House of the Mighty Men, in
   Jerusalem . . . . 6 ins. A (4)
Houston 198   F d
Houtain 156   A a
Howard, Fort 211   H b
Howe, Cape 172   E d
Howe, route of Lord 195   F c
Howe, route of Sir William 105 F c, D e
Höwen, lordship 142   C e
Howland Island 180   J g
Höxter 55   Q i
Höxter, mon. 95   D a
Höxter, Hanse. cy. . . . . . . 99 ins. B
Hoya 78   F b
Hoya, cty. 78   F b
Hoyerswerda 155   H c
Hradisch, mon. 80   E g
Hsiang-ho . . . . 170 ins. A
Hsiang-yang . . . .
Hsiung . . . . 170 ins. A
Huacho 214   B d
Huallaga River 111   B c
Hualpai, Ind. Res. 188   D c
Huamachuco 111   B c
Huamanga 111   C d
Huancabamba 111   B c
Huancavelica 214   B d
Huanchaca 214   C e
Huanuco nuevo 111   B c
Huanuco viejo 111   B c
Huaqui 214   C d
Huaraz 111   B c
Huascan (Huascaran), mt. . . 214   B c
Huasco 215   B e
Hubbardton 195   E b
Hubermont, Farm . . . .
Hubermont, Woods of. . . . . .
Hubert, Saint 117   D d
Hubertusburg 135   G c
Huddersfield, parl. bor. . 163 M d (Hudd.)
Hude, mon. 95   D a
Hudson, route of . . . .
Hudson Bay 186   K b
Hudson River 189   B d
Hudson Strait 186   L b
Hudson's Bay Company. . . . .
Hué 171   L g
Huejotlipan. . . . .
Huejotzingo . . . .
Huelgas, mon. 94   B c
Huelva 82   A b
Huesca 82   B a
Huesca, bp. 94   B c
Huesca, univ. 100   E f
Huescar 82   H f
Huete 82   B a
Hughenden 172   D c
Hugli 137   E d
Hugli River 137   E d
Hühnerwasser 159   H c

Huillier, Fort d' 191   G c
Hull, in Canada 212   H d
Hull, in England 127   Y m
Hull, Hanse. for. cy. . . . . . 98 ins. A
Hull, parl. bor. 163   N d
Hull, in Massachus. . . . . . 189 ins. B
Hull, route of 200   C d
Hulst 117   C c
Hulwan 99   M g
Humacao . . . . 199 ins. G
Humaitá 215   D e
Humber River 49   G e
Humboldt River. 187   H d
Huna Floi 166   A b
Hu-nan, prov. 171   M f
Hundheim 158   E d
Hungarian Plain 2   F d
Hungarians, people, on the Dnie-
   ster 55   J d
Hungarians, people, on the Theiss 168   G c
Hungary, km., about 1000 . . 59 H-I d
Hungary, km., about 1190 . . 70   K d
Hungary, km., part of the Otto-
   man Empire. 119   H d
Hungary, km., about 1740 . . 131   H d
Hungary, km., 19 cent. . . . 159   J e
Hungerford 127   X o
Hun-ho, R. . . . . 170 ins. A
Hüningen 122   D e
Hunkiar Skelessi 164   D b
Hunnic (Attila's) Empire . . 48 F-L b
Huns, people, on the Volga R. .
Hunte River 114   E b
Huntingdon 127   Y n
Huntingdon, castle 65   F d
Huntingdon, cty. . . . .
Huntingdon, mon. 97   Q i
Huntingdon, parl. bor. . . . 163   N e
Huntingdon, parl. dist. . . . 163   N e
Huntingdon, shire . . . . . .
Huntington 192   E c
Huntsville 211   H d
Hu-pei, prov. 171   M e
Huriel 69   I g
Huron, lake 187   K d
Hurons, tribe 188   J b
Hurst Castle 127   X p
Hushi 131   I d
Hussinetz 79   H d
Huy 117   D d
Hwang-chau . . . .
Hwiccas, people. . . . .
Hyampolis 11   D d
Hybla Heræa 30   D e
Hybla Maior 30   D e
Hyblæus River 30   D e
Hyccara 30   C d
Hydaspes River 19   L d
Hyderabad, in Deccan . . . 137   C e
Hyderabad, in Sind 137   A c
Hydraotes River 19   L d
Hydrea (Hydra), isl. 15   D b
Hydruntum (Otranto) 31   H b
Hydrusa, isl. 16   B b
Hyeres, isl. 126   E e
Hilæthus River 11   D d
Hyle 11   E d
Hylias River 31   F c
Hylice, lake 11   E d
Hymettus, mt. 15   D b
Hypæpa 20   B c
Hypanis River (Bug R.) . . . 18   D a
Hypanis River (Kuban R.) . . . 18   E a
Hypata 10   D d
Hypatus, mt. 11   E d
Hyphasis River 19   D d
Hyphormus, Port of 16   B b
Hypsas River 30   B e
Hyrcania, reg. 19   H c
Hyrcania, satr. 8   J e
Hyria, lake 10   C d
Hyrmine 14   B a
Hyrminus River. 30   E d

Hyrtacina 14 ins.
Hysiæ 14 C b
Hythe
Hythe, parl. bor. 163 P f

Iaccetani, people 38 C d
Iader 27 J c
Ialysus 4 C b
Iamo 38 C e
Iamnia 7 B e
Iamnia maritima 7 B e
Iamzai
Ianiculum, mt. 22 A
Iapis River 16 A a
Iapydes, people 27 I b
Iapygians, people 29 E d
Iapygium, prom. 31 H c
Iardanus River, in Crete 14 ins.
Iardanus River, in Elis 14 B b
Iassus 13 E c
Iazyges Metanastæ, people 38 F c
Ibagué 214 B b
Ibebin
Iberia, reg. (Caucasia) 18 F b
Iberia, reg. (Spain) 12 B c
Iberian Peninsula 2 D d
Iberian Sea 38 B e
Iberus River, see Ebro River
Ibir-Sibir, reg. 102 G b
Iburg, mon. 95 D a
Ica, battle 214 B d
Iça River
Icaria 16 B a
Icaria, isl. 13 E c
Icaros, see Icaria 17 E c
Icauna or Icaunus River, see Yonne River
Ice Cape 170 I a
Iceland, isl. 166 B c
Iceni, people 51 Q h
I-chang 171 M e
I-chau 170 ins. A
Ichnæ 11 D b
Ichtershausen, mon. 95 E a
Ichthyophagi, people 19 J e
Ichthys, prom. 14 B b
Iciodurum, see Issoire
Icknield Way, road 51 P i
Icolmkill, isl.
Iconium (Konieh) 20 E d
Iconium, sultanate, 12 cent. 68 B b
Iconium, sultanate, 13 cent. 73 H c
Icorigium 39 I h
Icosium 12 D c
Iculisna, see Angoulême
Icus 11 E c
Icus (Khiliodromia), isl. 11 E c
Icy Cape 198 ins. A
Ida, mt., in Crete 14 ins.
Idaho, state 210 B a
Idaho, ter. 1863 203 P f
Idaho, ter. 1864 203 P g
Idaho, ter. 1868 203 O g
Ida Mountains, in Troas
Idanha 82 A b
Idar 142 ins. A
Idex River 27 F c
Idistaviso 39 J g
Idomene
Idrisids, dom. of the 54 E f
Idstedt 158 E a
Idubeda Mountains 38 B d
Idumæa, reg. 7 B f
Ieracia, isl.
Ierne (Ireland), isl. 38 A b
Igilgilis 38 D e
Igilium, isl. 26 E e
Iglau 79 I d
Igli 174 C a
Iglo 159 K d
Iguala 213 ins.
Iguassú, river and falls 215 D e
Iguvium 27 G d
Ilanz 91 R l
Ilchester, parl. bor. 163 L g
Ildijis Atabeks, people 71 P f
Ile du Palais, loc. in Paris 149 B
Ilei 15 D b
Ilerda (Lérida) 38 C d
Ilergetes, people 38 B d
Ilfeld, mon. 95 E a
Ilheos, cap. 108 M i
Ili River 92 H c
Ilici 38 B e
Ilipula Mountains 38 B e
Ilissus River 16 B b
Ilium (Troy)
Ilium, in Epirus 10 B c
Il-Khans of Persia, Dom. of the
Illampu, Mount 214 C d
Illapel 215 B f
Ille-et-Vilaine, dept. 148 D e
Iller River 62 F d
Illiberi or Illiberis (Elvira) in Spain 38 B e
Illiberis, in France, see Elne
Illimani, Mount 214 C d
Illinoia, proposed stale in U. S.
Illinois, tribe 188 H c
Illinois Country, reg. 191 G H c
Illinois, ter. 1809 202 G a
Illinois, state 203 T b
Illinois River 191 G d
Illiturgi 38 B e
Illkirch 122 D d
Illurgavonenses, people 38 C d
Illyria, reg. 12 G b
Illyria, km. 159 H e
Illyrian Provinces 155 G e
Illyrians, people 5 A a
Illyricum, reg., 1st cent. 34 H e
Illyricum, reg., 5 cent. 50 H d
Illyricum, E. Rom. pref. 43 G f
Illyrii, people 17 B a
Illyris, dist. 10 B b
Ilm River 85 F e
Ilmen, lake 59 K b
Iloilo 199 ins. H
Iluro, see Oloron
Ilus, Burial mound of
Ilva (Elba), isl. 26 E e
Imbros, isl.
Imil
Immenstadt 143 J j
Imola 90 J h
Imola, bp. 95 E c
Imperial Canal 171 M e
Inachus River, in Ænianía 10 D d
Inachus River, in Argolis 14 C b
Inachus River, in Epirus 10 C c
Inagua, isl. 105 F b
Incas, Dom. of the 108 J h K j
In Castello 27 F c
Incia River 26 E c
Inda, mon. 95 D a
Independence, in Missouri 211 G c
Independence, in Texas 210 F d
Independence, Fort, in Vermont 195 E a
India, emp. 137
India, reg. 112 A b
India Inferior, prov. 19 K e
India infra terram, reg. 99 M g
Indiana, ter. 1803 202 H b
Indiana, ter. 1809 202 H b
Indiana, state 203 U b
Indianapolis 199 H c
Indian Country, reg. 1819 203 R b
Indian Lake 212 F c
Indian Ocean 109 W-A A h
Indian Pueblo Grants 188 E c
India Superior, prov. 19 L d
Indian Territories, in Canada 212 C c
Indian Territory, in the U. S. 203 S c
Indians in the United States 188
Indigetes, people 38 C d
Indies, E., reg. 109, 110 X-D D e-h
Indies, The, reg. 107, 108, leg.
Indien, W., reg. 107, 108 E-O, a-l
Indo-China, French col. 171 L g
Indore 137 C d
Indragiri
Indre, dept. 148 E e
Indre-et-Loire, dept. 148 E e
Indus River, in Caria 20 C d
Indus River, in India 137 A c
Industria 26 C b
Inessa 30 D e
Infantado, duchy 83 K g
Infante, Rio del, R. 109 T k
Ingævones, people 38 D b
Ingauni, people 26 C c
Ingelfingen 143 I g
Ingelheim 62 D d
Ingerkingen 143 I i
Ingermanland, reg. 138 C d
Ingolstadt 79 G d
Ingolstadt, univ. 100 H e
Ingria, reg. 138 C d
Iniada 165 F c
Inkerman 164 J f
Inland India, reg. 99 M g
Inn River 63 G d
Innichen 54 G d
Innichen, mon. 80 C h
Inn Quarter, dist. 135 G d
Innsbruck 72 C b
Innviertel, dist. 157 C c
Inowraclaw (Hohensalza) 135 J b
In Portu 26 E d
Insala 174 D b
Insterburg 155 K a
Insubres, people 26 C b
Interamna or Interamne (Terni), in Umbria 27 G e
Interamna Lirenas (Termini), in Latium 30 C a
Interamnia, in Picenum 27 H e
Interamnium 31 F c
Interlaken 91 P l
Internal Provinces, New Spain 190 B F e f
Interocrium 27 H e
Interpromium 27 H e
Intimilii, people 26 B d
Inverary
Invercargill 172 F e
Inverloch
Inverness
Inverness, cty.
Inycum 30 C e
Iol 38 C e
Iolcus 11 D c
Ion River 10 C c
Iona, bp. 97 G c
Iona, isl. 49 C c
Ionia, reg. 8 Q h
Ionia, satr. 8 G e
Ionian Islands 164 B c
Ionians, people
Ionian Sea 5 A b
Ios 13 D c
Iovavum (Salzburg), see Iuvavum
Ioventio, pass 26 D c
Iowa City 211 G b
Iowa, Ind. Res. 188 G c
Iowa, ter. 1838 202 F f
Iowa, state 202 G g
Iowa River 211 G b
Iowa, tribe 188 H b
Ipni Promontorium 11 E c
Ipoly-Ságh 159 J d
Ipsus 20 D c
Ipswich, in England
Ipswich, Hanse. for. cy. 98 ins. A
Ipswich, parl. bor. 163 P e
Ipswich, in Mass. 189 D c
Ipswich, in Queensland 172 E c
Iquique 214 B e
Iquitos 214 B c
Ira 14 B b
Ira River 26 D c
Irak, reg.
Irak Ajemi, reg.
Irak Arabi, reg.

Iran, Plateau of . . . . 3 J f
Irawadi River . . . .
Irbil . . . . 71 O f
Ireland, isl. . . . .
Iria . . . . 26 C b
Irish, people, about 900 . . . . .
Irish Sea . . . . 49 D e
Iris River . . . . 20 G b
Irkutsk . . . . 171 L c
Iron . . . . 6 C b
Iron Bridge, over the Orontes R. 68 C b
Ironton . . . . 206 ins.
Iroquois, tribes . . . . 192 D a
Iroquois River . . . . 191 H
Irrhesia, isl. . . . . 11 F c
Irtish River . . . .
Is (Hit) . . . . 18 F d
Isabel, isl. . . . . 172 E a
Isabella . . . . 105 F c
Isabella, isl. . . . . 105 F b
Isar River . . . . 63 G d
Isara, see Pontoise
Isara River (Isère R.) . . . . . . 38 D c
Isara River (Oise R.) . . . . . 38 C c
Isarci, people . . . . 27 F a
Isarcus River . . . . 27 F a
Isaszeg . . . . 159 J e
Isatis (Yezd) . . . . 19 H d
Isaura . . . . 20 E d
Isauria, reg. . . . .
Isauria, E. Rom. prov. . . . . . 43 I f (14)
Isauria, Rom. prov. . . . . . .
Isca Dumnoniorum (Exeter) . . 51 O i
Isca Silurum (Caerleon-upon-
Usk) . . . . 51 O i
Ischia, bp. . . . . 95 ins.
Ischia, isl. . . . . 90 D d
Ischl . . . . 158 G e
Isel-Berg, mt. . . . . 154 F e
Isenburg, princ. . . . . 154 E c
Iser River . . . . 115 H c
Isère, dept. . . . . 148 F e
Isère River . . . . 84 F g
Isernia . . . . 161 J g
Isernia, bp. . . . . 95 E c
Iseum . . . . 22 A
Ishim River . . . .
Ishmaelites, people . . . . . . 7 ins. C
Isis, Temple of . . . . 22 A
Isis and Serapis, Aug. Reg. of
Rome . . . . 22 A
Isker . . . . 138 K d
Isker River . . . . 168 H e
Iskut River . . . . 212 ins.
Isla del Gallo, isl. . . . . . . 111 B a
Isla de Pinos, isl. . . . . . . 105 C c
Isla de Sacrificios, isl. . . . . 106 D a
Isla de Términos, isl. . . . . . 105 B c
Islamabad . . . . 137 C b
Island No. 10, fort . . . . . . 208 C b
Islands, Bay of . . . . 172 G d
Isla Santa, isl. . . . . 111 B c
Isla Santa, i. e. South America 105 F e
Islay, isl. . . . . 49 C d
Isle de France, isl. . . . . . . 175 I f
Isle of France, gouv. . . . . . 146 B b
Isle of France, prov. . . . . . 148 E e
Isle of Wight . . . . 100 A b
Isle of Wight, parl. dist. . . . . 163 M g
Isles, The, bp. . . . . 97 G c
Islington . . . . 75 I h
Islip Bridge . . . . 127 X o
Ismail . . . . 131 I d
Ismailia . . . . 174 K i
Ismenus River . . . . 11 E d
Ismid . . . . 77 K d
Ismilan . . . . 165 D c
Isnik . . . . 89 I f
Isny . . . . 114 F e
Isny, imp. city . . . . 143 J j
Isocum . . . . 38 C e
Isontus River, see Salzach River
Isonzo River . . . . 50 F c
Ispahan . . . . 53 H c

Israel, Kingdom of . . . . 6 ins. B
Issachar, tribe . . . . 7 ins. D
Issoire . . . . 126 C d
Issoudun . . . . 61 E c
Issoudun, castle . . . . 76 E c
Issoudun, seign. . . . . 61 D c
Issus . . . . 20 G d
Issus, Gulf of . . . . 20 F d
Issyk-kul, lake . . . .
Istævones, people . . . . 38 D b
Ister (Danube) River . . . . . 35 I e
Istib . . . .
Istone, mt. . . . . 10 A c
Istria, reg. . . . . 27 H b
Istria, march . . . . 63 G f
Istropolis . . . . 39 N l
Istrus . . . . 12 I b
Istvæones, see Istævones
Isurium (Aldborough) . . . . . 51 P g
Italia, dist. in Bruttium . . . . 30 E d
Italia, see Italy
Italians, people . . . .
Italian Peninsula . . . . 2 F d
Italian Republic . . . . 151 H g
Italian Somaliland, col. . . . . 174 H d
Italica . . . . 38 A e
Italy, reg. . . . . 12 F b
Italy, West. Rom. dioc. . . . . 42 E d
Italy, exarch. of . . . . 52 J e
Italy, km., 9 cent. . . . . . . 56 E d
Italy, km., 12 cent. . . . . . 70 I e
Italy, km., 19 cent. . . . . . 154 F f
Itanus . . . . 14 ins.
Itapirú, Fort . . . . 215 D e
Itapua . . . . 215 D e
Itasca, lake . . . . 186 J d
Itati . . . . 215 D e
Ithaca . . . . 10 B d
Ithaca, isl. . . . . 10 B d
Ithaca (Leucas), isl. . . . . . 10 B d
Ithome . . . . 10 C c
Ithome, mt. . . . . 14 B b
Ithoria . . . . 10 C d
Itil (Astrakhan) . . . . 99 M d
Itius, Portus, bay . . . . . . 38 C b
Itonus . . . . 11 D c
Ituna Æstuarium (Solway Firth) 51 O g
Iturea, dist. . . . . 6 D a
Ituzaingó, battle . . . . . . 215 D f
Ityke . . . . 12 F c
Itzehœ . . . . 55 Q i
Iuenna . . . . 27 I a
Iuka . . . . 208 C c
Iuliabriga . . . . 38 B d
Iuliacum (Jülich) . . . . . . 39 I h
Iulia Fanestris . . . . 27 H d
Iuliobona . . . . 38 B c
Iuliomagus (Angers) . . . . 38 B c
Iulis . . . . 15 E b
Iulius, Vicus . . . . 39 J i
Iulium Carnicum . . . . . . 27 G a
Iunonia Falisca . . . . . . 27 G e
Iuvanum . . . . 27 I f
Iuvavum (Salzburg) . . . . . 38 E c
Ivangorod, in Ingria . . . . . 138 C d
Ivangorod, in Poland . . . . 159 L c
Ivanitza . . . . 165 B b
Ivanovo Vosnessensk . . . . .
Iviza, bp. . . . . 94 C d
Iviza, isl. . . . . 82 C b
Ivois, castle . . . . 62 C d
Ivory Coast, French col. . . . 174 C d
Ivrea . . . . 90 A b
Ivrea, bp. . . . . 95 D b
Ivrea, marq. . . . . 64 A a
Ivry . . . . 76 D b
Ixtacamaxtitlan . . . .
Ixworth, mon. . . . . 97 R i
Izium . . . . 139 E f
Iznalloz . . . . 82 B b
Iztaban . . . . 105 B c
Iztaccihuatl, volcano of . . . . 106 B a
Iztapalapan . . . .
Iztaplatzinco . . . .

Jabalpur, Jubbulpore . . . . . . 137 C d
Jabbok River . . . . 7 D d
Jabesh-Gilead . . . .
Jablunkau . . . . 123 J d
Jabneel, in Galilee . . . . . . 6 D c
Jabneel, in Philistæa . . . . . 7 B e
Jaca . . . . 82 B a
Jackson, in Michigan . . . . . 207 I b
Jackson, in Mississippi . . . . 211 G d
Jackson, Fort, in Alabama . . . 200 I f
Jackson, Fort, in Louisiana . . 208 C d
Jackson, route of . . . . . . 200 I g
Jackson's Hole, dist. . . . . . 210 C b
Jacksonville . . . . 199 I d
Jacob, castle . . . . 68 ins. A
Jacobins, The, bldg. in Paris . 149 B
Jacobsdal . . . . 175 L l
Jadera . . . . 54 H e
Jaén, in Peru . . . . 214 B c
Jaén, in Spain . . . . 82 B b
Jaén, bp. . . . . 94 B d
Jaén, km. . . . . 83 K h
Jaffa . . . . 68 ins. A
Jafna . . . . 112 B c
Jafnapatam . . . . 112 B c
Jagannath . . . . 137 E e
Jägerndorf . . . . 115 I c
Jägerndorf, princ. . . . . . 115 I c
Jagersfontein . . . . 175 M l
Jagst River . . . . 143 J g
Jagstberg . . . . 143 I g
Jagstheim . . . . 143 H g
Jagstzell . . . . 143 I g
Jaguarão . . . . 215 D f
Jaguaribe River . . . . . . 214 F c
Jahna, castle . . . . 63 G c
Jaipur, in Madras . . . . . 170 J g
Jaipur, in Rajputana . . . . 170 I f
Jaipur, Jaypore, dist. . . . . 137 C c
Jaisalmer, dist. . . . . . . 137 B c
Jaitza . . . .
Jalalabad . . . . 137 B b
Jalapa . . . . 106 D a
Jalayrs, Dom. of the . . . . 77 N f
Jaligny . . . . 69 E c
Jalisco, state . . . . . . 213 ins.
Jamaica . . . . 189 ins. C
Jamaica, isl. . . . . 105 E c
Jamapa, R. . . . . 106 D a
Jamary River . . . . 214 C d
Jambi . . . .
James, Fort . . . . 132 J h
James Bay . . . . 186 K c
James River . . . . 188 K c
Jamestown . . . . 193 ins. A
Janiculan citadel . . . . . . 23 B
Janina . . . .
Janitza . . . . 165 C c
Janizary Quarter, Old, in Con-
stantinople . . . . 93 G e
Jankau . . . . 123 H d
Jan Mayen, isl. . . . . . . 166 D a
Janus, Temple of, in Rome . .
Janus quadrifrons, in Rome . 24 B
Japan, emp. . . . .
Japan Sea . . . .
Jargeau . . . . 76 E c
Jarmuth Ramoth . . . . . 7 C d
Jarnac . . . . 126 A d
Jaroslaw . . . . 159 L c
Jarrow . . . .
Jarrow, mon. . . . . 97 P g
Jassy . . . . 139 C f
Játiva . . . . 82 B b
Jauer . . . . 79 I c
Jauja . . . . 111 B d
Java, isl. . . . .
Javols, about forty miles north-
east of Rodez
Jaxartes River (Syr-Daria) . . . 19 J a
Jazer . . . . 7 D e
Jean-Loo . . . .
Jeba . . . . 6 B c
Jeblaam . . . . 7 C d

Jedburgh . . . .
Jefferson City . . . . 211 G c
Jehlam . . . . 137 B b
Jehol . . . . 171 M d
Jehoshaphat, gate, in Jerusalem 68 ins. B
Jehoshaphat, street . . . . 68 ins. B
Jehoshaphat, Tomb of . . . . . 6 ins. A
Jehoshaphat, Valley of . . . . 6 ins. A
Jelairs, people . . . .
Jemappas . . . . 134 B c
Jemes . . . . 190 D d
Jemmingen . . . . 114 D b
Jemtland, dist. . . . . 120 E d
Jena . . . . 114 F c
Jeni-Kivi . . . .
Jeni-Shehr . . . .
Jenkinson, route of . . . . . . 108 R a
Jequitinhonha River . . . . . . 214 E d
Jerba, isl. . . . . 73 C d
Jerez de la Frontera . . . . . . 82 G f
Jerez de los Caballeros . . . . 82 G f
Jericho . . . . 7 C e
Jerichow . . . . 85 C b
Jerichow, mon. . . . . 80 ins.
Jersey, isl. . . . . 69 B b
Jersey City . . . . 189 ins. C
Jerusalem . . . . 7 C e
Jerusalem, plan of ancient . . 6 ins. A
Jerusalem, plan of mediaeval . 68 ins. B
Jerusalem, km., 12 cent. . . . 68 C c
Jerusalem, km., 13 cent. . . . 73 G d
Jerusalem, patr. . . . . . . 52 L f
Jervaulx, mon. . . . . 97 P g
Jeshua . . . . 7 B f
Jesi . . . . 90 D c
Jesi, bp. . . . . 95 E c
Jesireh, El, see El Jesireh
Jesulmere, reg. . . . . 137 B c
Jever . . . . 114 D b
Jever, lordship . . . . 122 D b
Jeypore, Jaipur, dist. . . . . 137 C c
Jezreel . . . . 6 C c
Jezreel, Plain of . . . . . . 6 C c
Jhansi . . . . 137 C c
Jheelum . . . .
Jibuti . . . . 174 H c
Jicarilla, Ind. Res. . . . . . 188 E c
Jiddah . . . .
Jimena . . . . 82 A b
Jiphtha . . . . 6 C c
Jitomir . . . . 139 C e
Joachimsthal . . . . 115 G c
Joanna Springs . . . . 172 B b
Joazeiro . . . . 214 E c
Jocko, Ind. Res. . . . . . . 188 D a
Jodhpur . . . . 137 B c
Jodoigne . . . . 156 B a
Johann Georgenstadt . . . . 123 G c
Johannesburg . . . . 175 M l
John Cabot, route of . . . . . 108 O b M c
John of Pian de Carpine, route
of . . . .
Johnson, mt. . . . . 212 ins.
Johnson Hall . . . . 194 L f
Johnstones, fam. . . . . . . 97 J d
Johnston Islands . . . . . . 180 K f
Joigny . . . . 61 E c
Joinville, in Brazil . . . . . 215 E e
Joinville, in France . . . . . 76 D b
Joinville, seign. . . . . . . 69 J f
Jokneam . . . . 6 C c
Joli-Bois . . . .
Joliet . . . . 211 H b
Jolliet, route of . . . . . . 191 G c
Joló Archipelago . . . . . . 199 ins. H
Jomsburg . . . . 63 H e
Jonesboro . . . . 196 ins. A
Jönköping . . . . 120 H e
Joppa, in Maryland . . . . . 192 C d
Joppa, in Palestine . . . . . 7 B d
Joppe . . . . 7 B d
Jordan River . . . . 7 D d
Josefstadt . . . . 159 I c
José Monteiro . . . . 214 D c

Joug-Dieu, Le, mon. . . . . . 94 C b
Jouy, mon. . . . . 94 C b
Juana (Cuba), isl. . . . . . . 105 D b
Juan de Fuca, Strait of . . . . 198 A a
Juan Fernandez Island . . . . 107 I k
Juba River . . . . 175 H d
Jubbulpore, Jabalpur . . . . . 137 C d
Judæa, reg. . . . . 7 B e
Judah, Kingdom of . . . . . . 6 ins. B
Judah, tribe . . . . 7 ins. D
Judah, Mountains of . . . . . 7 C e
Judah, Wilderness of . . . . . 7 C e
Judenburg . . . . 123 H a
Judith, Point, cape . . . . . . 189 ins. A
Juggernaut . . . . 137 E e
Juist, isl. . . . . 117 E a
Jujuy . . . . 215 C e
Julian Alps, mts. . . . . . . 27 H a
Julian Aqueduct . . . . 22 A
Julian Augustan Way, road . . 26 B d
Julias . . . . 6 D c
Julica, Basilia, bldg. in Rome . 24 B
Jülich . . . . 62 D c
Jülich, duchy . . . . 78 E c
Jülich-Cleves-Berg, prov. . . 158 D c
Julier, pass . . . . 26 D a
Jumet . . . . 156 A b
Jumièges . . . . 65 G f
Jumièges, mon. . . . . 94 C b
Jumna River . . . .
Junction City . . . . 210 F c
Juneau . . . . 212 ins.
Jungaria, reg. . . . . 92 I c
Jung-Bunzlau . . . . 115 H c
Juniata River . . . . 192 C c
Junin, battle . . . . 214 B d
Junkseylon . . . . 112 C c
Juno Lucina, Temple of . . . 22 A
Juno Moneta, Temple of . . . 24 A
Juno Regina, Temple of . . . 22 A
Jupiter Capitolinus, Temple of 24 A
Jupiter Dolichenus, Temple of 22 A
Jupiter Latiaris, Temple of 35 ins. B (5)
Jupiter Stator, Temple of . . . 24 A
Jupiter Victor, Temple of . . . 24 A
Jura, dept. . . . . 148 F e
Jura Mountains . . . . 38 D c
Jurjan . . . . 102 F d
Juruá River . . . . 214 B c
Jussy . . . . 91 O l
Justingen . . . . 143 I i
Justingen, lordship . . . . . 143 I i
Justinian, Statue of . . . . . 93 G e (2)
Jüterbog . . . . 63 G c
Jutes, people, 5 cent. . . . . .
Jutes, people, about 900 . . . .
Jutigalpa . . . . 213 D c
Jutland, reg. . . . . 70 H b
Juttah . . . . 7 C f
Juturna, Lake of . . . .

Kaaden . . . . 79 H c
Kabarda, reg. . . . .
Kabinda . . . . 175 E e
Kabul . . . . 137 A b
Kadesh . . . . 4 C e
Kadesh Barnea . . . . 7 ins. C
Kadesh Naphtali . . . . . . 6 ins. B
Kadesia . . . . 53 G d
Kadiak, isl. . . . . 198 ins. A
Kadikeui . . . . 93 G e
Kafche-kué, reg. . . . .
Kaffa . . . . 73 H a
Kaffraria, reg. . . . . 175 M m
Kaffraria, British, dist. . . . . 175 M m
Kafiristan, reg. . . . . 137 B a
Kafr Embabeh . . . .
Kagoshima . . . . 171 O e
Kahlen Berg, mt. . . . . . . 123 I d
Kahoolawe, isl. . . . . 198 ins. B
Kai-fong-fu . . . .
Kail . . . .
Kailua . . . . 198 ins. B
Kaindu . . . .

Kairwan . . . . 53 C c
Kais, isl. . . . .
Kaisarieh . . . .
Kaisersberg . . . . 126 E b
Kaiserslautern . . . . 122 D d
Kaiserstuhl . . . . 142 B e
Kaiserswerth . . . . 62 D c
Kaiserswerth, mon. . . . . . 55 Q i
Kaiser Wilhelms Land, col. . . 179 F h
Kaisheim, mon. . . . . 95 E b
Kalahari Desert . . . . 175 F g
Kalamata . . . . 164 C c
Kalenberg, Brunswick-, duchy . 86 G b
Kalgan . . . . 171 M d
Kalhat . . . .
Kalifati . . . .
Kalinga, reg. . . . .
Kalisz, Kalisch . . . . 79 K c
Kallundborg, Hanse. for. cy. . . 98 F b
Kalmucks, people . . . . . . 139 F f
Kalocsa . . . . 168 F c
Kalocsa, abp. . . . . 95 F c
Kalpi . . . . 170 I f
Kaluga . . . . 139 E e
Kalw . . . . 62 E d
Kama-Bulgarians, people . . . 71 P b
Kama River . . . . 138 H d
Kamakura . . . .
Kamaran Island . . . . 170 F g
Kamba . . . . 62 E d
Kamburg . . . . 63 F c
Kamen . . . . 153 N f
Kamenz . . . . 80 ins.
Kamerun, Cameroons, German
col. . . . . 174 E d
Kaminlets Podolski . . . . . . 119 J d
Kaministiquia, Fort . . . . . 191 G b
Kamloops . . . . 212 C c
Kammin . . . . 72 J a
Kammin, bp. . . . . 79 J a
Kammin, Hanse. cy. . . . . . 99 ins. B
Kamp, mon. . . . . 95 D a
Kampen . . . . 117 D b
Kampen, Hanse. cy. . . . . . 99 ins. B
Kamrup, reg. . . . .
Kamtchatka, pen. . . . .
Kanah . . . . 6 C b
Kanara, reg. . . . . 137 B f
Kanata . . . . 6 E c
Kanauj . . . .
Kan-chau-fu . . . .
Kandahar . . . .
Kandalakskaya . . . . 167 L b
Kandern . . . . 142 A e
Kandy . . . . 137 D g
Kané . . . .
Kane Sea . . . . 186 L a
Kanem, reg. . . . . 174 E c
Kanesville . . . . 199 F c
Kangaroo Island . . . . 172 C d
Kanin Peninsula . . . . 167 N b
Kankakee River . . . . 191 H c
Kanklis, reg. . . . .
Kano . . . . 174 D c
Kansan . . . .
Kansas, tribe . . . . 188 F c
Kansas, state . . . . 203 S h
Kansas, ter. 1854 . . . . . . 202 E b
Kansas City . . . . 211 G c
Kansas Osage, Ind. Res. . . . 188 G c
Kansas Pacific Grant . . . . . 210 E c
Kansas River . . . . 198 F c
Kan-su, prov. . . . . 171 L e
Kantara, El . . . . 174 K i
Kaoli, reg. (Korea) . . . . . .
Kao-tai . . . .
Kapfenburg, castle . . . . . . 143 J h
Kaphar Saba . . . . 7 B d
Kapolns . . . . 159 K e
Kappel . . . . 91 Q k
Kappenberg, mon. . . . . . . 95 D a
Kapunda . . . . 172 C d
Karabunar . . . . 165 D b

Karachal, mts.		
Karachi	137	A c
Kara Dagh, mts.	99	M f
Karahissar	89	K f
Karajang		
Karajang, reg.		
Karakhitai, reg.	92	H c
Karakodja		
Karakoram (Karakorum) Mountains		
Karakorum, Caracarum	92	K c
Kara-Kuyunli, people	77	L e
Karaman	93	D c
Karaman, princ.	93	D c
Karaman, reg.	89	J g
Kara Sea	170	H a
Karashar		
Karasi, reg.	89	I g
Karatova	165	C b
Karchedon (Carthage)	5	A b*
Kardis		
Karelia, reg.	138	C c
Karikal	137	D f
Karlsburg, near Bremen	122	E b
Karlsburg, in Transylvania . . .	159	L e
Karlstadt	155	H f
Karnak	1	C e
Karnata, reg.		
Karnul	137	C e
Kars	67	O e
Kartha	6	B c
Kasbek, mt.	167	O g
Kaschau		
Kashan		
Kashgar		
Kashgil	174	F c
Kashmir, Cashmere, reg.		
Kaskaskia	191	H d
Kaskaskia River	191	H d
Kasr el Kebir	118	C g
Kassai River	175	E e
Kassites, people	4	E e
Kassogs, people	71	O e
Kastamuni	77	K d
Kastamuni, dist.	77	K d
Kastelberg, lordship	142	B d
Kastellaun	142 ins. A	
Kastoria	71	K e
Katcha River	164	J f
Kates Needle, mt.	212 ins.	
Kathiawar, Kattiwar, dist. . . .	137	B d
Katieh	150	B a
Katif, El		
Kattegat, str.	88	D c
Katwyk	117	C b
Katzbach River	155	I c
Kauai, isl.	198 ins. B	
Kaufbeuren, imp. city	79	G e
Kaula, isl.	198 ins. B	
Kavala	131	H e
Kaveri River.		
Kawar, oasis.	2	F g
Kay	135	H b
Kayalik		
Kayeli		
Kayes	174	B c
Kayna	72	C a
Kaysersberg	143 ins. D	
Kazan	138	G d
Kazan, khan.	139	G e
Kazerun		
Kazvin		
Kearney, Fort	210	F b
Kearney, route of	201 legend	
Kecskemét	159	J e
Kedah		
Kedesh Naphtali	6	D b
Keeling Islands	179	A i
Keewatin, dist.	212	F b
Kehl	142	A c
Keilah	7	B c
Kei River, Great	175	M m
Kekaughtan	193 ins. A	
Kelat	67	O f

Kelat, reg.	73	I c
Kehlheim	122	F d
Kells	127	K h
Kelso		
Kem	138	D c
Kemkemjuts, people		
Kempsey	172	E d
Kempten, ab.	79	G e
Kempten, mon.	95	E b
Kenai, Fort	198 ins. A	
Kenath	6	F c
Kendal	127	W l
Kendal, parl. bor.	163	L c
Kendal, reg.	84	B b
Keneh	150	B b
Kenesaw Mount, battle	208	D c
Kenia, mt.	175	G e
Kenilworth		
Kenilworth, castle		
Kenilworth, mon.	97	P i
Kenites, people	7 ins. D	
Kenmare Bay	127	G j
Kennebec River	189	D b
Kennedys, fam.		
Kensington, in Pa.	192 ins.	
Kensington, castle, in England	75	I h
Kent, cty.		
Kent, kingdom		
Kentishmen, people		
Kent Island	192	C d
Kenton	206 ins.	
Kentucky, dist.	196	B c
Kentucky, state	211	H c
Kentucky River	193	B c
Kenzingen	142	A d
Keraits, people		
Kerak	68 ins. A	
Kerbela	77	M f
Kerguelen Islands	182 H H l	
Kerith River	7	C c
Kerko Porta	93	G e
Kermadec Islands	172	H d
Kermian, reg.	89	I g
Kerry, cty.	127	H j
Kertch		
Kerulen River		
Kerun, Birket el, lake		
Kesho		
Kesmacoran, reg.		
Kessel, dist.	117	D c
Kesselsdorf	135	G c
Kessin	63	F a
Kesteven and Holland, parl. dist.	163	N d
Ketsch	142	C b
Kexholm	138	D c
Keynsham, mon.	97	O j
Key West	211	I f
Khabarovka	171	O d
Khaibar Pass	170	I e
Khair-ed-Din Barbarossa, Tomb of	93 G e (12)	
Khairpur	137	A c
Khalkas, people		
Khalman (Aleppo)	5	C b
Khamil		
Khanate of the Golden Horde		
Khanbalig (Peking)		
Khandesh, reg.	137	B d
Kharesm		
Kharesm, Khuwarizm, reg. . .		
Kharesmians, people	8	K d
Kharezmians, dynasty	73	I d
Kharkov	139	E e
Kharluks, people		
Khartum	174	G c
Khatanga River		
Khatangskoe	171	L a
Khatmandu.	171	J f
Khazars, people	55	K c
Khelat		
Kherson	139	D f
Khingan Mountains		
Khitans, people		
Khiva	170	G d

Khiva, khan.		
Khojent		
Khokand		
Kholm	131	J f
Kholmogory	138	F c
Khorasan, reg.	53	H c
Khorat	171	L g
Khoritza	139	D f
Khorsabad	5	D b
Khotan		
Khuram		
Khuwarizm, Kharesm, reg. . .		
Khuzistan, reg.		
Khyrpore	137	A c
Kiakhta		
Kiang-si, prov.	171	M g
Kiang-su, prov.	171	M g
Kiao-chau	171	N f
Kia-yu-kwan		
Kiburg, castle	62	E c
Ki-chau	170 ins. A	
Kickapoo, Ind. Res.	188	G c
Kickapoos, tribe	188	H b
Kichinev	139	C f
Kidderminster, parl. bor. . . .	163	L e (Kidderm.)
Kiel	79	G a
Kiel, Hanse. cy.	99 ins. B	
Kielce	159	K c
Kien-chang-fu		
Kiersy	56	C c
Kieselbronn	142	C c
Kiev	71	M c
Kiev, prov.	131	J c
Kiev, dist.	71	L c
Kievits Hoeck	189	B d
Kiffhausen, castle	72	C a
Kij Mekran, reg.		
Kikinda	159	K f
Kilburn	75	I b
Kildare, bp.	97	E c
Kildare, cty.	127	K h
Kilfenora, bp.	97	B d
Kilia	164	D a
Kilia, mouth of the Danube R.	164	D a
Kilimandjaro, mt.	175	G e
Kilkenny		
Kilkenny, bp.	97	D d
Kilkenny, cty.	127	J f
Killala, bp.	97	B b
Killaloe, bp.	97	C d
Killarney.	127	H i
Killiecrankie		
Kilmacduagh, bp.	97	C c
Kilmore, bp.	97	D c
Kilsyth		
Ki-lung	171	N f
Kilwa	109	U h
Kimberley, in Africa	175	L l
Kimberley, dist. in Australia .	172	B b
Kimberley Goldfield	172	B b
Kinburn	139	D f
Kincardine, cty.		
Kincardine, dist.		
Kinchat		
Kingdom of the Two Sicilies, 15 cent.	90	E e
King George, Fort	193	C f
King George Sound	172	A d
King Island	172	D e
King of Jerusalem, Palace of the	68 ins. B (7)	
King's County	127	J h
King's Garden, isl.	105	E b
Kings Lynn, parl. bor.	163	O e
Kings Mountain, battle	195	A f
King Sound	172	B b
Kingston, in Canada	200	E a
Kingston, in Georgia	208	D c
Kingston, in Jamaica	213	D c
Kingston, in New York	192	D c
Kingston, in S. Australia . . .	172	C d
Kingston, South, Rhode Island	189 ins. A	
Kingston-upon-Hull, mon. . . .	97	Q h

Kingston-upon-Thames . . . . . 75 I i
Kingswood, mon. . . . . 97 O j
King William Land . . . . . 212 F b
Kinklas, tribe . . . . 188 B b
Kinross, cty. . . . .
Kinross, dist. . . . .
Kinsai (Hang-chau-fu) . . . . .
Kinsale . . . .
Kinzig Pass . . . . 134 E e
Kinzig River . . . . 142 A d
Kiovia, dist. . . . . 139 C e
Kiowas, tribe, in Colorado . 188 E b
Kiowas, tribe, in Texas . . . 188 F d
Kipchak, khan.
Kirchberg, on the Hunsrück
    Mts. . . . . 142 ins. A
Kirchberg, on the Jagst R. . . 143 I g
Kirchheim . . . . 143 H h
Kirghiz, people, in Turkestan . 92 G c
Kirghiz, people, on the Yenisei R.
Kirghiz Steppe . . . . 3 J d
Kiriathaim . . . . 7 D e
Kirin . . . . 171 N d
Kirjath-Jearim . . . . 7 C e
Kirkcudbright . . . .
Kirkcudbright, cty. . . . .
Kirkcudbright, dist. . . . . . .
Kirkham, mon. . . . . 97 Q g
Kirkstall, mon. . . . . 97 P h
Kirkstead, mon. . . . . 97 Q h
Kirkwall, seat of bishopric . . 97 Ka leg.
Kirman . . . .
Kirman, reg. . . . . 53 H d
Kirn . . . . 142 ins. A
Kir of Moab . . . . 7 D f *
Kish . . . .
Kishm, isl. . . . .
Kishon River . . . . 6 C c
Kiskiminitas River . . . . . . 192 B c
Kissingen . . . . 158 F c
Kisslegg . . . . 143 I j
Kistna River . . . . 112 A b
Kittanning . . . . 194 K f
Kittery . . . . 189 C c (Ki.)
Kitzen . . . . 154 G c (Ki.)
Kitzingen . . . . 72 C b
Kitzingen, mon. . . . . . . 95 E b
Kiung-chau . . . . 171 M g
Kiushiu, isl. . . . .
Kiutayeh . . . . 164 D c
Kiverova Gora . . . . 138 C d
Kizil Irmak River . . . . . 93 D b
Kladrau . . . . 79 H d
Kladrau, mon. . . . . 95 E b
Klagenfurt . . . . 79 I e
Klamath, Ind. Res. . . . . . 188 B b
Klamath River . . . . 198 A b
Klamath River, Ind. Res. . . 188 B b
Klamaths, tribe . . . . 188 B b
Klar River . . . . 88 E a
Klause Pass . . . . 72 C b
Klausen Pass . . . . 91 Q l
Klausenburg . . . . 80 H h
Klein-Heubach . . . . 142 D a
Klein-Mariazell, mon. . . . . 95 F b
Klein-Schnellendorf . . . . . 135 I c
Klephts, people . . . . 164 C c
Klettgau, landgr. . . . . . . 142 B e
Klissow . . . .
Klikitats, tribe . . . . 188 B a
Klondike Region . . . . . . 212 B b
Klostergrab . . . . 123 G c
Klosterneuburg, mon. . . . . 80 E g
Knaered . . . . 120 H e
Knaresborough . . . . . . 127 X l
Knaresborough, parl. bor. . . 163 M d
Kniebis Pass . . . . 142 B d
Knights of Saint John, Dom.
    of the . . . . 89 I g
Knights of Saint John, Hospital
    of the . . . . 68 ins. B (2)
Knin . . . . 131 G e
Knin, bp. . . . . 95 F c
Knittelfeld . . . . 155 H e

Knittlingen . . . . 143 G g
Knocke . . . . 134 B c
Knoxville . . . . 196 ins. A
Kobdo . . . . 171 K d
Kobdo, Plateau of . . . . . . 3 N d
Kobe . . . . 171 O e
Kocher River . . . . 143 J g
Kodiak, isl. . . . . 186 D c
Koesfeld, Hanse. cy. . . . . . 99 ins. B
Koevorden . . . . 117 E b
Koevorden, lordship . . . . . 117 E b
Koil . . . .
Kojak Pass . . . . 170 H e
Kokel River . . . . 159 M e
Koko-nor, lake . . . .
Koksherev . . . . 71 P b
Kola . . . . 138 D b
Kola Peninsula . . . . 3 H b
Kolachel . . . .
Kolapore . . . .
Kolbatz, mon. . . . . 80 ins.
Kolberg . . . . 63 H a
Kolberg, Hanse. cy. . . . . . 99 ins. B
Kolberger Heide, dist. . . . . 122 F a
Kolding . . . . 154 E a
Kolditz . . . . 154 G c
Kolguiev, isl. . . . . 138 H b
Kolhapur . . . . 137 B e
Kolimsk, Nijne . . . .
Kolimsk, Sredne . . . . . . 171 Q b
Kolin . . . . 79 I c
Kölln, on the Spree . . . . . 85 C b
Kölln. Hanse. cy. . . . . . . 99 ins. B
Kolmar . . . . 62 D d
Köln, see Cologne
Koloa . . . . 198 ins. B
Kolomna . . . . 138 E d
Kolonos . . . . 16 E e
Komorn . . . . 159 J e
Konakry . . . . 174 B d
Kongsberg . . . . 88 C b
Konieh . . . .
Königgrätz . . . . 135 H c
Königinhof . . . . 159 H c
Königsberg, in Prussia . . . 79 L a
Königsberg, Hanse. cy. . . . 99 H c
Königsberg, imp. cy. in Franco-
    nia . . . . 114 F c
Königsbronn . . . . 122 F d
Königseck, castle . . . . . . 143 H j
Königseck, cty. . . . . 143 H j
Königsfelden, mon. . . . . . 91 Q k
Königshofen . . . . 142 E a
Königslutter, mon. . . . . . 95 E a
Königstein . . . . 123 H c
Königswartha . . . . 155 H c
Königs-Wusterhausen . . . . 135 G b
Konin . . . . 123 J b
Koningsveld, mon. . . . . . 94 C a
Konitz . . . . 135 I b
Konkan, reg. . . . .
Konkan-tana . . . .
Konstanz, see Constance
Konzenberg . . . . 142 C d
Kootenay, lake . . . . 198 B a
Kootenay River . . . . . . 198 B a
Köpenick . . . . 123 G b
Koporiye . . . .
Koppenstein, castle . . . . . 142 ins. A
Korb . . . . 143 H g
Kordofan, reg. . . . . 174 F c
Korea, Jap. prot. . . . . . . 171 N e
Korea, reg. . . . .
Körmend . . . . 155 I e
Körmöczbanya . . . .
Korneuburg . . . . 123 I d
Körös River . . . . 159 K e
Korsör . . . . 158 F a
Kortrijk . . . . 122 B c
Koschmin . . . . 159 I c
Kosel . . . . 123 J c
Köslin . . . . 123 I a
Koslov . . . . 139 F e
Kosseir . . . . 150 B b

Kossovopolje, valley . . . . . 93 B b
Kostnitz, see Constance
Kostroma . . . . 138 F d
Kotah. . . . . 170 I f
Kotah, reg. . . . . 137 C c
Kota Rajah . . . . 171 K h
Kotchak Bay . . . . 167 P f
Kottbus . . . . 72 C a
Köthen . . . . 154 F c
Kötzschenbroda . . . . . . 123 G c
Kovel . . . . 159 M c
Kovno . . . . 77 I a
Kovno, Hanse. for. cy. . . . 99 H b
Koweyt. . . . .
Kraich River . . . . 142 C b
Krainburg . . . . 123 H e
Krajova . . . .
Krasnoi . . . . 153 O g
Krasnoi-Yar . . . . 139 G f
Krasnovodsk . . . . 170 G d
Krasnoyarsk . . . . 171 K c
Krasny . . . . 71 M c
Krautheim . . . . 142 E b
Krementchug . . . .
Kremmen . . . . 85 C b
Kremnitz . . . . 80 F g
Krems . . . . 63 H d
Kremsier . . . .
Kremsmünster, mon. . . . . 80 D h
Kreuzberg, pass . . . . . . 27 G a
Kreuznach . . . . 122 D d
Kriechingen . . . . 134 D d
Kroia . . . .
Kroia, bp. . . . . 95 F c
Kroissenbrunn . . . . . . 72 D b
Kronstadt, in Russia . . . . 138 C c
Kronstadt, in Transylvania . . .
Kroonstad . . . . 175 M l
Krossen . . . . 63 H b
Krugersdorp . . . . 175 M l
Krumau . . . . 135 H d
Kuban, dist. . . . . 170 E d
Kuban, reg. . . . . 77 L c
Kuban River . . . . 73 H a
Kubango River . . . . . . 175 E f
Kuchar . . . .
Kuen-lun Mountains . . . .
Kufstein . . . . 115 G e
Kufra, oases . . . . 2 G f
Kughi . . . .
Kuinder . . . . 117 D b
Kuinre . . . . 117 D b
Kuka, Kukawa . . . . . . 174 E c
Kulbarga . . . . 92 H f
Kuldja . . . .
Kulevdcha . . . .
Kulikovo . . . . 92 D b
Kulm, in Bohemia . . . . . 72 C a
Kulm, in Prussia . . . . . 72 D a
Kulm, bp. . . . . 95 F a
Kulm, Hanse. cy. . . . . . 98 G c
Kulmbach . . . . 87 H c
Kulmerland, dist. . . . . . 72 D a
Kulmsee, seat of bishopric . . 95 F a
Kuma River . . . . 99 M e
Kumaon, reg. . . . . 170 I e
Kumassi . . . . 174 C d
Kum-Kale . . . .
Kum-Kioi . . . .
Kunde . . . . 174 E d
Kunduz . . . .
Kunersdorf . . . . 135 H b
Ku-ngan . . . . 170 ins. A
Künzelsau . . . . 143 I g
Kuopio . . . . 167 K c
Kupiansk . . . . 139 E f
Kupreanof Island . . . . . 212 ins.
Kur River . . . .
Kura River . . . .
Kurachee . . . . 137 A c
Kuraiyat . . . .
Kurdistan, reg. . . . . . . 67 O f
Kurdistan Highlands . . . . 3 I e
Kurds, people . . . .

Kuria Muria Islands . . . . . . 170 G g
Kurile Islands . . . . 171 P d
Kurisches Haff, bay . . . . . 155 K a
Kürnbach . . . . 142 C b
Kurnegalle . . . .
Kursk . . . . 139 E e
Kushk . . . . 170 H e
Kuskokwim River . . . . 186 C b
Küssnacht . . . . 91 Q k
Kustendji . . . .
Küstrin . . . . 79 I b
Kutais . . . . 167 N g
Kutchuk Kainardji . . . .
Kutha (Tel Ibrahim) . . . . . . 4 D e
Kuttenberg . . . . 79 I d
Kwang-chau-wan . . . . 171 M f
Kwang-si, prov. . . . . 171 L f
Kwang-tung, prov. . . . . . 171 M f
Kwei-chau, prov. . . . . 171 L f
Kwei-lin-fu . . . .
Kwei-yang . . . . 171 L f
Kyburg, castle . . . . 91 Q k
Kyle, dist. . . . .
Kymmene River . . . . 120 K d
Kyoto . . . . 171 O e
Kyritz, Hanse. cy. . . . . . . 99 ins. B

Láa . . . . 123 I d
Laach, mon. . . . . 95 D a
Laaland, isl. . . . . 114 F a
La Bahia . . . . 190 F f
La Baraque . . . . 156 B a
La Barre . . . . 192 C b
La Baye, Fort . . . . 191 H c
Labdalum . . . . 31 ins. B
Labeates Lake . . . . 39 L l
La Belle-Alliance, farm . . . .
La Bénisson-Dieu, mon. . . . 94 C b
Labiau . . . . 131 H c
Labican Way, road . . . . . . 35 ins. B
Labicum . . . . 35 ins. B
La Boca . . . .
La Bocchetta Pass . . . . . . 150 E d
La Boissière, mon. . . . . . . 94 C b
Labourd, dist. . . . . . . 147 D c (Lab.)
Labrador Peninsula . . . . . . 186 L c
Labrador Plateau . . . . 186 L c
Labranda . . . . 13 E c
Labuan . . . . 171 M h
La Bussière, mon. . . . . 94 C b
La Cava, mon. . . . . 95 ins.
Laccadive Islands . . . . . . 137 B f
Lac Court Oreille, Ind. Res. . 188 H a
Lac de Flambeau, Ind. Res. . 188 I a
Lacedæmon . . . . 14 C b
Lacedæmonia, state . . . . . 14 C b
Laceria . . . . 11 D c
La Chaise-Dieu, mon. . . . . 94 C b
La Charité, on the Loire R. . . 126 C c
La Charité, in Paris . . . . . 149 B
La Chassaigne, mon. . . 95 D b (L. Ch.)
La Chaussée . . . . 154 C d
La Chine, Lachine . . . . . . 191 K b
Lachine Rapids . . . . 189 A b
Lachish . . . . 7 B e
Lachlan River . . . . 172 D d
Laciadæ, deme . . . . 23 D
Lacinium, prom. . . . . 31 G c
La Cisa, Pass . . . . 26 D c
Lackawaxen River . . . . . . 192 D c
Lacmus, mt. . . . . 10 C c
La Colle . . . . 200 G a
La Colombe, mon. . . . . . . 94 C b
Laconia, reg. . . . . 14 C c
Laconia, gulf of . . . . 14 C c
La Couronne, mon. . . . . . . 94 C b
Lac Pepin, Fort . . . . G c
La Crosse . . . . 211 G b
Lac Seul, lake . . . . 212 F c
Lactarius, mt. . . . . 52 D b
Lactora, see Lectoure
Lacus Asphaltites (Dead Sea) . 7 C f
Lade, isl. . . . . 13 E c
Ladenburg . . . . 142 C b

Lado . . . . 174 G d
Ladoga . . . . 138 D c
Ladoga, lake . . . . 138 D c
Ladon River, in Arcadia . . . . 14 B b
Ladon River, in Elis . . . . . 14 B b
Ladrones, isl. . . . . 110 FF f
Ladysmith . . . . 175 M l
Laebactes . . . . 27 G a
Laevi, people . . . . 26 D b
La Famine . . . . 192 C b
Lafayette . . . . 206 ins.
La Ferté-Bernard . . . . 76 D b
La Ferté-sur-Grône, mon. . . 94 C b
La Flèche . . . . 126 A c
La Fontaine de Bèze, mon. . . 95 D b
La Force, bldg. in Paris . . . . 149 B
La Gallette, Fort . . . . 192 D a
Lagash . . . . 4 E e
Lagina River . . . . 39 J g
Lagny . . . . 76 E b
Lago Maggiore, lake . . . . . 90 I h
Lagos, in Nigeria . . . . 174 D d
Lagos, in Portugal . . . . . . 82 J h
Lagos, dist. . . . . 174 D d
La Grande Chartreuse, mon. . 95 D b
La Granja, castle . . . . 130 C e
La Guayra, La Guaira . . . . . 214 C a
Laguna . . . . 215 E e
Laguna das Patos, lake . . . . 215 D f
Lagussa, isl. . . . . 15 F c
La Hague, Cape de, battle off . 125 C c
Lahaina . . . . 198 ins. B
Lahari . . . .
La Harpe, route of . . . . . . 191 F e
La Haye, farm . . . . 156 C c
La Haye Sainte, farm . . . . .
Lahn River . . . . . : . . . . 62 D c
La Hogue or La Hougue, see
  Saint Vaast-de-la-Hougue
Lahore . . . . 137 B b
La Hougue . . . . 130 C d
Lahr . . . . 142 A d
La Huerta, isl. . . . . 105 D d
La Hulpe . . . . 156 A a
Laibach . . . . 63 H f
Laietani, people . . . . 38 C d
Laino . . . . 90 E e
Laish . . . . 6 D b
Lajazzo . . . . 99 K f
La Jonquière, Fort . . . . . . 190 C a
Lake Country . . . . 49 E d
Lake of the Woods . . . . . . 191 G b
Lake Region . . . . 2 G b
Laknaoti . . . .
La Levette, farm . . . .
La Lusern, mon. . . . . 94 B b
La Maison-du-Roi . . . . . . 156 C c
La Mancha, dist. . . . . 83 K h
La Marche or Marche, cty. . . 61 D c
La Marche or Marche, gouv. . 146 B c
La Marche or Marche, prov. . 148 E e
Lambach, mon. . . . . 80 C g
Lambaesis . . . . 38 D e
Lambayeque . . . . 111 B c
Lambeth . . . . 75 I i
Lambeth, parl. bor. . 163 N f (Lamb.)
Lambethmoor, dist. . . . . . . 75 G g
Lambrus River . . . . 26 D b
Lamego . . . . 82 A a
Lamego, bp. . . . . 94 A c
Lametus River . . . . 31 F d
Lamia . . . . 11 D d
Laminium . . . . 38 B e
Lamotte, Fort . . . . 189 B b
Lampsacus . . . . 5 B a
Lamptræ inferior . . . . 16 B b
Lamptræ superior . . . . 16 B b
Lanai, isl. . . . . 198 ins. B
Lanark 127
Lanark, cty. 127
Lanark, dist. . . . .
Lancashire, cty. . . . .
Lancaster, in England . . . . .
Lancaster, cty. palat. . . . . .

Lancaster, parl. bor. . . . 163 L c
Lancaster, in Mass. . . . . . . 189 C c
Lancaster, in Ohio . . . . . . 196 ins. B
Lancaster, in Pa. . . . . 192 C c
Lancaster Sound . . . . 186 K a
Lancastrian Estates 84
Lan-chau-fu . . . .
Lancia . . . . 38 A d
Lanciano . . . . 64 B b
Landau . . . . 114 E d
Landeck . . . . 79 G e
Landen . . . . 117 D d
Landes, dept. . . . . 148 D f
Landeshut, in Silesia . . . . . 135 H c
Landrecies . . . . 126 C a (Land.)
Landsberg, in Styria . . . . . 135 H e
Landsberg, on the Warthe . . 80 ins.
Landsberg, march . . . . 85 G e
Land's End, cape . . . . 49 C f
Landshut, in Bavaria . . . . . 115 G d
Landskrona . . . . 123 J d
Landstuhl . . . . 114 D d
Lanercost, mon. . . . .
Lang Bourn, in London . . . 75 G g
Langenargen . . . . 143 I j
Langenau . . . . 143 I b
Langenbnrg . . . . 143 I g
Langensalza . . . . 158 F c
Langley . . . . 75 H h
Langley, Fort . . . . 210 A a
Langport . . . . 127 W o
Langport, parl. bor. . . . . . .
Langres . . . . 61 F c
Langres, bp. . . . . 95 D b
Langres, cty. . . . . 61 F c
Langres, duchy . . . . 76 F c
Langside . . . . 118 D b
Langs Nek . . . .
Lang-soi . . . .
Languedoc, dist. . . . . 69 E e
Languedoc, gouv. . . . . 146 B c
Languedoc, prov. . . . . 148 E f
Lankavi Island . . . .
Lansdown . . . . 127 X o
L'Anse, Ind. Res. . . . . 188 I a
Lansing . . . . 211 H b
Lanuvium . . . . 35 ins. B
Laodicea, in Coele-Syria . . . 20 G e
Laodicea, in Lycaonia . . . . 20 E c
Laodicea, in Phrygia . . . . . 20 C d
Laodicea, in Syria . . . . . . 20 F e
Lao-kai . . . . 171 L f
Laon . . . . 61 E b
Laon, bp. . . . . 94 C b
Laon, cty. . . . . 61 E b
La Part-Dieu, mon. . . . . . . 91 O l
Lapathus . . . . 11 D c
La Paz, in Bolivia . . . . 214 C d
La Paz, in Lower Cal. . . . . . 213 A b
Lapis Niger, in Rome . . . . .
Lapithas, mt. . . . . 14 B b
Lapland, reg. . . . . 167 J b
La Plata, in the Arg. Rep. . . 215 D f
La Plata, in Bolivia . . . . . . 214 C d
La Plata, viceroyalty . . . . . 215 ins.
La Pointe, Ind. Res. . . . . . 188 H a
La Pointe du Saint Esprit . . . 191 G b
La Pola de Gordon . . . . . . 82 A a
Lappa . . . . 14 ins.
Lapps, people . . . . 138 B b
La Prairie . . . . 189 B b
La Pré-sur-Arnon, mon. . . . . 94 C b
Lapurdum, see Bayonne
La Rábida . . . . 184 B e
Laramie . . . . 210 D b
Laramie, Fort . . . . 198 D b
Laranda . . . . 71 M f
Laredo, in Spain . . . .
Laredo, in Texas . . . . 198 F e
La Reine, Fort . . . . 190 F c
La Réole, castle . . . . 76 D d
Larga . . . . 39 I j
Larino . . . . 64 B b
Larino, bp. . . . . 95 E c

Larinum . . . . 30 D a
Larisa, see Larissa
Larissa, in Assyria . . . . 20 J d
Larissa, in Thessaly . . . . . . 11 D c
Larissa Cremaste . . . . 11 D d
Larisus River . . . . 14 B a
Larius (Como), lake . . . . . 26 D a
Larix . . . . 27 H a
La Roche, in Burgundy . . . 143 ins. F
Laroche, in Luxemburg . . . 117 D d
La Roche, cty. . . . . 69 F a (L. R.)
La Rochelle . . . . 130 C d
La Rochelle, gen. . . . . 147 D b
Laron . . . . 76 D d
La Rothière . . . . 154 C d
Larsa or Larsam (Senkereh) . 4 G c*
Larymna . . . . 11 E d
Las . . . . 14 C c
Lasalle, in France . . . . . . 184 D d
Lasalle, in Illinois . . . . 211 H b
La Salle, routes of . . . 191 H d, I c, F d
Las Cascadas . . . .
Las Cruces . . . .
La Serena . . . . 215 B e
Lasion . . . . 14 B b
Las Navas de Tolosa . . . . . 83 K h
Lasne . . . .
Lasne River . . . . 156 A a
Las Palmas . . . . 174 -B b
Las Salinas . . . . 108 J i
Lassen Pass . . . . 214 B b
L'Assomption, Fort . . . . . . 194 B c
Las Tabbas . . . . 214 A b
Las Vegas . . . . 198 D c
Las Vigas . . . . 201 H g
Lateran, Palace . . . . 22 A
Laterani, Palace of the . . . . . 22 A
La Teste de Buch . . . . . 76 C d
Latham House . . . . 127 W m
Latin Empire . . . . 73 E c
Latin Gate . . . . 22 A
Latini or Latins, people . . . 30 B a
Latin Way, road . . . . . . 30 B a
Latis River . . . . 26 B c
Latium, reg. . . . . : 30 B a
Latium and Campania, Aug. Reg.
of Rome . . . . 38 E d (1)
Latomiæ, loc. in Syracuse . . 31 ins. B (7)
La Tour . . . . 69 E d
Latovici, people . . . . 27 I b
Latovicorum Prætorium . . . . . 27 I b
La Trappe . . . . 126 B b
La Trappe, mon. . . . . 94 C b
La Tremouille . . . . 81 M h
Lauag . . . . 199 ins. H
Lauban . . . . 80 ins.
Lauchert River . . . . 143 H i
Lauchheim . . . . 143 J h
Laudonnière, set. of . . . . . 191 I e
Lauenburg, on the Elbe . . . . 72 C a
Lauenburg, in Pomerania . . . 123 I a
Lauenburg, duchy . . . . . 87 H b
Lauffen . . . . 143 H g
Laumellum . . . . 26 C b
L'Aumône, mon. . . . . 94 C b
Launceston, in England . . . . 127 U p
Launceston, mon. . . . . . 97 M k
Launceston, parl. bor. . . . . . 163 J g
Launceston, in Tasmania . . 172 D e
Laund, mon. . . . . 97 Q j
Laupen . . . . 91 P l
Lanpheim . . . . 143 I i
Laurentian Highlands . . . . 186 L d
Laurentum . . . . 35 ins. B
Lauresham, see Lorch, mon.
Lauriacum, (Lorch, in Austria) 38 E c
Laurium, mt. . . . . . 16 C b
Laurvik . . . . 166 G d
Laus . . . . 30 E c
Laus, Pompeia . . . . 26 D b
Laus, bay . . . . 30 E c
Laus (Lao) River . . . . . . 30 E c
Lausanne . . . . 91 O l
Lausanne, bp. . . . . 95 D b

Lausitz, march . . . . 58 G c
Lausitz, margr. see Lusatia . . 79 I c
Lausitz, Nieder. margr. see Lu-
satia, Lower . . . . 87 I c
Lausitz, Ober, margr. see Lusatia,
Upper . . . . 87 I c
Lausonna, see Lausanne
Lautern . . . . 72 B b
Lautrec . . . . 76 E e
Lautulæ . . . . 30 C a
Lautumiæ . . . . 24 A
Lauzelle . . . . 156 B a
Laval . . . . 76 C b
Lavant . . . . 80 D h
Lavant, bp. . . . . 95 E b
Lavant River . . . . 63 H e
Lavatræ . . . .
Lavaur . . . . 76 D e
Lavaur, bp. . . . . 94 C c
La Vérendrye, route of . . . . 190 D c
Laverna, Gate of . . . . 23 B
Lavinium . . . . 30 B a
Lawrence . . . . 206 F c
Laxenburg, castle . . . .
Laybach, see Laibach
Laycock, mon. . . . . 97 O j
La Zarca . . . . 190 E f
Lea River . . . . 75 I h
Leadenhall Street, in London . 75 G g
Leadville . . . . 210 D c
League of God's House, dist. . 91 R l
League of Ten Jurisdictions,
dist. . . . . 91 R l
Leander, Tower of . . . . 93 G e
Leavenworth, Fort . . . . . . 198 F c
Leba . . . . 123 I a
Lebadea . . . . 11 D d
Lebanon, House of . . . . . 6 ins. A
Lebanon Mountains . . . . . . 6 D a
Lebarge, lake . . . . . 212 B b
Lebedos . . . . 13 E b
Le Beuil, mon. . . . . 94 C b
Lebinthus, isl. . . . . 17 E c
Le Boeuf, Fort . . . . 192 A c
Lebonah . . . . 7 C d
Lebú . . . . 215 B f
Lebus . . . . 63 H b
Lebus, bp. . . . . 79 I b
Lebus, dist. . . . . 85 D b
Lebusa, castle . . . . 63 G c
Lecce . . . . 90 G d
Lecco . . . . 150 E d
Lech River . . . . 62 F e
Lechæum . . . . 15 C b
Lechfeld, dist. . . . . 62 F d
Leck River . . . . 117 D c
Lecompton . . . . 206 F c
Le Coucou . . . .
Lectoure . . . . 76 D e
Lectoure, bp. . . . . 94 C c
Lectum, prom. . . . . 17 D b
Ledbury, parl. bor. . . . .
Ledesma . . . . 82 A a
Lee, Fort . . . . 195 D c
Lee River . . . . 127 H j
Leech Lake . . . . 199 G a
Leech Lake, Ind. Res. . . . . . 188 H a
Leeds, in Yorkshire . . . . . 127 X m
Leeds, mon. in Kent . . . . 97 R j
Leeds, parl. bor. . . . . 163 M d
Leesburg . . . . 208 ins.
Leeuwarden . . . . 117 D a
Leeuwin, Cape . . . . 172 A d
Leeward Islands . . . . 213 F c
Le Fleix . . . . 126 B d
Lefroy, lake . . . . 172 B d
Legæ, people . . . . 35 N e
Legedia, see Avranches
Leghorn . . . . 90 L j
Legnago . . . . 150 F d
Legnano . . . . 72 B b
Le Havre . . . . 126 B b
Lehigh River . . . . 192 D c
Lehnin, mon. . . . . 72 C a

Leicester . . . .
Leicester, cty. . . . .
Leicester, parl. bor. . . . . 163 M e
Leicester, shire . . . .
Leichardt River . . . . 172 C b
Leighlin, bp. . . . . 97 D d
Lein River . . . . 143 I h
Leine River . . . . 158 E b
Leiningen, princ. . . . . 142 D a
Leinster, prov. . . . .
Leinstetten . . . . 143 G i
Leipheim . . . . 143 J i
Leipnik . . . . 123 I d
Leipsic, Leipzig . . . .
Leipsic, Leipzig, univ. . . . . . .
Leiria . . . . 82 G f
Leisnig . . . . 85 G e
Leiston, mon. . . . . 97 S i
Leith . . . .
Leitha River . . . . 63 l e
Leitmeritz . . . . 63 H c
Leitomischl . . . . 63 H d
Leitrim, cty. . . . . 127 I g
Leitzkau . . . . 63 F b
Leitzkau, mon. . . . . 80 ins.
Leiva . . . . 214 B b
Le Jafs, farm . . . .
Le Joug-Dieu, mon. . . . . . . 94 C b
Lelantian Fields . . . . 11 E d
Lelantus River . . . . 11 E d
Le Maire, route of . . . .
Le Mans . . . . 61 C b
Le Mans, bp. . . . . 94 C b
Lemanus (Geneva), lake . . . . 26 A a
Lemanus Portus (Lymne) . . . 38 C b
Lemberg . . . . 139 B f
Le Mesnil . . . .
Lemgo, Hanse. cy. . . . . 99 ins. B
Lemhi, Ind. Res. . . . . 188 D a
Lemnos, isl. . . . . 13 D b
Lemovices or Lemovicis, see
Limoges
Lemovices, people . . . . 38 C c
Lemovii, people . . . . 38 F b
Lena River . . . . 171 N b
Lenczyca . . . . 135 J b
Lenni-Lenapes, tribe . . . . . 188 K c
Lennox, dist. . . . .
Lens . . . . 117 A d
Lenton, mon. . . . . 97 P i
Lenzen . . . . 63 F b
Lenzin . . . .
Leo IV, Wall of Pope . . . . . 96 A
Leoben . . . . 135 H e
Leodicum, see Liège
Leominster, mon. . . . . 97 O i
Leominster, parl. bor. . . . . . 163 L e
Léon, in France . . . . 61 B b
León, in Mexico . . . . 213 ins.
León, in Nicaragua . . . . . 105 C d
León, in Spain . . . . 82 A a
León, bp. . . . . 94 A c
León, dist. . . . . 81 L h
Léon, km. . . . . 82 A a, G e
Léon, viscty. . . . . 69 A b
Leonberg . . . . 143 H h
Leone . . . . 199 ins. D
Leonidæum . . . .
Leonine City, in Rome . . . . 96 A
Leontine Way . . . . 31 ins. B
Leontini . . . . 30 D e
Leontium . . . . 14 B a
Leontopolis . . . . 43 I g
Leopoldina . . . . 214 F d
Leopoldstadt . . . . 155 I d
Leopoldville . . . . 175 E e
Lepanto . . . . 89 H g
Le Paraclet, mon. . . . . 94 C b
Lepel . . . . 153 N g
Lepelletier . . . . 149 B
Lepidum, Regium . . . . . . 26 E c
Le Pin, mon. . . . . 94 C b
Lepontii, people . . . . 26 C a
Lepontine Alps, mts. . . . . . 90 B a

Lepreum . . . . 14 B b
Lepsydrium . . . . 16 B a
Leptis maior or magna . . . . . 34 G g
Leptis minor . . . . 38 E e
Le Puiset . . . . 69 H f
Le Puy . . . . 61 E d
Le Puy, bp. . . . . 94 C b
Le Quesnoy . . . . 117 B d
Lérida . . . . 82 C a
Lérida, bp. . . . . 94 C c
Lérida, univ. . . . . 100 F f
Lérins, mon. . . . . 95 D c
Lerma, lake . . . . 106 A a
Lerna . . . . 14 C b
Leros, isl. . . . . 16 B b
Le Roussart . . . .
Lerus . . . . 13 E c
Lerus, isl., Sporades . . . . . . 13 E c
Les Allemands . . . . 191 ins. B
Lesbos, isl. . . . . 13 D b
Lescar . . . . 61 C e
Lescar, bp. . . . . 94 B c
Les Clairets, mon. . . . . 94 C b
Lesina, bp. . . . . 95 F c
Lesina, isl. . . . . 90 F c
Lesje . . . . 130 E a
Lesna . . . . 131 J c
Lessa . . . . 15 D b
Lesser Antilles, isl. . . . . 213 F c
Lesser Armenia , reg. in Pon-
tus . . . . 33 M e
Lesser Armenia, reg. in Sy-
ria . . . . 99 J f
Lesser Scythia, reg. . . . . 39 N l
Lesser Syrtis, gulf . . . . 51 F f
Lete . . . . 11 D d
Lethæus River, in Crete . . . . 14 ins.
Lethæus River, in Thessaly . . 10 C c
Lethbridge . . . . 212 D d
Letoa, isl. . . . . 14 ins.
Letocetum . . . . 51 P h
L'Etoile, mon. . . . . 94 C b
Letrini . . . . 14 B b
Letts, people . . . . 57 H c
Leubus, mon. . . . . 80 E f
Leuca . . . . 31 H c
Leuca, mt. . . . . 14 ins.
Leucadia, isl. . . . . 89 H g
Leucæ Islands . . . . 14 ins.
Leucas . . . .
Leucas (Santa Maura), isl. . . .
Leucate, prom. . . . .
Leuce, isl. . . . . 18 D a
Leuce acte . . . . 15 E b
Leuceræ . . . . 26 D b
Leuchtenberg . . . . 63 G d
Leuci, see Toul
Leuci, people . . . . 38 D c
Leucimma, prom. . . . . 10 B c
Leucopetra, prom. . . . . 30 E d
Leuctra . . . . 11 E d
Leuctrum . . . . 14 C c
Leuk . . . . 91 P l
Leuthen . . . . 135 I c
Leutkirch, imp. cy. . . . . 143 J j
Leutkircher Heide, dist. . . . . 143 J j
Leutschau . . . .
Levadia, reg. . . . . 131 H f
Leventina, valley . . . . 91 Q l
Lévêque, cape . . . . 172 B b
Levette, la, farm . . . . 156 C c
Lévis, Fort . . . . 192 D a
Lewes, in England . . . .
Lewes, castle . . . .
Lewes, mon. . . . . 97 Q k
Lewes, parl. bor. . . . . 163 O g
Lewes, in Delaware . . . . 192 D a
Lewis, dist. . . . . 127 N f
Lewis River, in Canada . . . . 198 ins. A
Lewis River, in Idaho . . . . . 198 C b
Lewis and Clark, routes of . . 198, 199
Lewiston . . . . 200 D b
Lexington, in Kentucky . . . . 208 D b
Lexington, in Mass. . . . . . 195 ins. A

Lexington, in Missouri . . . . . 208 B h
Lexington, in Virginia . . . . . 207 K c
Lexovii or Lexoviis, see Lisieux
Leyden . . . . 117 C b
Leyre, mon. . . . . 94 B c
Leyte, isl. . . . . 199 ins. H
Lezat, mon. . . . . 94 C c
Lhasa . . . . 92 J d
Liamone, dept. . . . . 148 F f
Liang-hiang . . . . 170 ins. A
Liao-yang . . . . 171 N d
Liard, Fort . . . . 212 C b
Liard River . . . . 212 C c
Liau-ho, R. . . . .
Liau-tung, pen. . . . .
Libarna . . . . 26 C c
Libau . . . . 77 I a
Libau, Hanse. cy. . . . . 99 H b
Liberia, country . . . . 174 C d
Libici, people . . . . 26 C b
Libisonis, Turris . . . . 38 D d
Libreville . . . . 175 D d
Liburnia, reg. . . . . 27 I b
Libya, reg. . . . . 18 C d
Libyan Desert . . . . 2 G f
Lichades Islands . . . . 11 D d
Lichfield . . . . 65 F d
Lichfield, bp. . . . . 97 P i
Lichfield, parl. bor. . . . . 163 N e
Lichtenau . . . . 142 A c
Lichtenberg, princ. . . . . 158 D d
Lichtenstein, castle . . . . 143 H i
Lichtenthal, ab. . . . . 142 B c
Licking River . . . . 196 ins. B
Licus (Gail) River . . . . 27 H a
Licus (Lech) River . . . . 39 K j
Lidford, parl. bor. . . . .
Liebenwalde . . . . 85 C b
Liebenzell . . . . 143 G h
Liechtenstein . . . . 154 E e
Liechtenstein, princ. . . . . . . 150 E c
Liège . . . . 117 D d
Liège, bp. . . . . 117 D d
Liegnitz . . . . 63 I c
Liegnitz, princ. . . . . 79 J c
Lienz . . . . 115 G e
Lierre . . . . 117 C c
Lies, Field of . . . . 56 D c
Liestal . . . . 142 A e
Liger (Loire) River . . . . 38 C c
Ligny . . . . 156 B a
Ligonier, Fort . . . . 192 B c
Ligures Baebiani . . . . 30 D a
Liguria, Aug. Reg. . . . . 39 D d (9)
Liguria, reg. . . . . 26 B c
Liguria, French prov. . . . . . . 152 B e
Liguria, West Rom. prov. . . 42 D d (3)
Ligurian Alps, mts. . . . . 90 B b
Ligurian Republic . . . . 151 H h
Ligurian Sea . . . . 150 E e
Ligurians, people . . . . 12 E b
Lilæa . . . . 11 D d
Lilienfeld, mon. . . . . 95 F b
Lille . . . . 117 B d
Lilleshall, mon. . . . . 97 O i
Lillois . . . . 156 A a
Lilybæum . . . . 30 B e
Lima . . . . 214 B d
Lima, audiencia . . . . 215 ins.
Limal . . . . 156 B a
Limasol . . . . 68 B c
Limay River . . . . 215 C f
Limburg . . . . 117 E d
Limburg, castle in Lower Lor-
raine . . . . 62 D c
Limburg, castle in Swabia . . 62 E d
Limburg, castle in W. Fran-
conia . . . . 62 E c
Limburg, duchy . . . . 117 D d
Limburg, prov. . . . . 158 C c
Limburg-on-the-Hardt, mon. . 95 D b
Limburg-on-the-Lahn, mon. . 95 D a
Limelette . . . . 156 B a
Limerick . . . . 74 A e

Limerick, bp. . . . . 97 C d
Limerick, cty. . . . . 127 H i
Limes (Roman Wall) . . . . . . 38 D c
Limestone . . . . 196 ins. B
Limia, dist. . . . . 83 J g
Limmen Bight . . . . 172 C b
Limnæ, in Athens . . . . 23 D
Limnæ, in Messenia . . . . . . 14 C b
Limonum, see Poitiers
Limousin, prov. . . . . 148 E e
Limpurg, castle . . . . 143 I g
Limpurg, cty. . . . . 143 I h
Linares . . . . 215 B f
Lin-ching . . . .
Lincoln, in England . . . .
Lincoln, bp. . . . . 97 Q h
Lincoln, castle . . . . 65 F d
Lincoln, cty. . . . .
Lincoln, parl. bor. . . . . 163 N d
Lincoln, shire . . . .
Lincoln, in Nebraska . . . . . . 210 F b
Lincoln Heights . . . . 49 F e
Lincoln Wolds . . . . 49 F e
Lindau . . . . 62 E e
Lindau, imp. cy. . . . . 78 F e
Lindau, mon. . . . . 95 D b
Lindenfels . . . . 142 C a
Lindisfarne, mon. . . . . 97 P f
Lindisfarne Island . . . .
Lindiswaras, people . . . .
Lindsay, mt. . . . . 172 E c
Lindsey, parl. dist. . . . . 163 N d
Lindum (Lincoln) . . . . 51 P h
Lindus . . . . 13 F c
Lingayen . . . . 199 ins. H
Lingen . . . . 62 D b
Lingones, see Langres
Lingones, people, in Gaul . . . 38 D c
Lingones, people, in Italy . . . 27 F c
Linhares . . . . 214 F d
Linköping . . . . 46 J b
Linlithgow . . . .
Linlithgow, cty. . . . .
Linones, people . . . . 55 R i
Lindsays, fam. . . . . 97 K d
Linth River . . . . 150 E c
Linththal . . . . 91 R l
Lin-tsing-chau . . . .
Linz . . . . 63 H d
Lion Hill, village . . . .
Lipans, people . . . . 188 G e
Lipara . . . . 30 E d
Liparææ (Æolin or Lipari) Is-
lands . . . . 30 D d
Lipari Islands . . . . 90 E e
Lippe, cty. . . . . 114 C e
Lippe, princ. . . . . 134 E c
Lippe, reg. . . . . 86 G c
Lippe River . . . . 62 D c
Lippe-Detmold, princ. . . . 154 E b (L.D.)
Lippeham . . . . 55 Q i
Lippstadt . . . . 158 E c
Liptrap, Cape . . . . 172 D d
Liquentia River . . . . 27 G b
Liques, mon. . . . . 94 C a
Lircay . . . . 214 B d
Liria . . . . 82 B b
Liris (Gargliano) River . . . . 30 C a
Lisa, Fort . . . . 210 F b
Lisaine River . . . . 143 ins. F
Lisbon . . . . 82 A b
Lisbon, abp. . . . . 94 A d
Lisbon, univ. . . . . 100 D g
Lisburne, Cape . . . . 198 ins. A
Lisieux . . . . 69 D b
Lisieux, bp. . . . . 94 C b
Liskeard, parl. bor. . . . . 163 J g (Lisk.)
L'Isle . . . . 143 ins. A
L'Isle Jourdan . . . . 126 B e
Lismore, bp. in Ireland . . . . 97 C d
Lismore, bp. in Scotland . . . . 97 H c
Lissa . . . . 115 I c
Lissa, island, off Spalato . . . . 90 F c
Lissa, island, off Zara . . . . . 27 J c

Lissa Island	161	J f
Lissabon, see Lisbon		
Lissus	31	I a
Lissus, prom.	14 ins.	
Lita River		
Litani River		
Liternum	30	C b
Lithuania, gr. princ.	119	J c
Lithuania, reg., about 1190	71	K b
Lithuania, reg., about 1360	77	J b
Lithuanians, people	59	I b
Littanum	27	G a
Little Belt, strait	88	C d
Little Burgundy, duchy	69	G c
Little Cayman, isl.	105	D c
Little Colorado River	198	C c
Little Compton	189 ins.	A
Little Dunmow, mon.	97	R j
Little Egg Harbor	192	D d
Little Harbour	189	C c
Little Miami River	196 ins.	B
Little Missouri River	198	C c
Little Oasis	4	E d *
Little Poland, reg.	131	H c
Little Redan, fort	164	L g
Little Rock	211	G d
Little Russia, reg.	139	C e
Little Russians, people	139	C e
Little Saint Bernard Pass	130	O i
Little Slave Lake	186	H c
Littlestown	208 ins.	
Little Tatary, reg.	139	D f
Little Wallachia, reg.	131	H d
Little Yarmouth, parl. bor.		
Littorale, reg.	123	G f
Litus Saxonicum (Saxon Shore)	51	Q i
Liu-kiu Islands	171	N f
Liutizians, people	63	G b
Liverpool	127	V m
Liverpool, parl. bor.	163	K d
Liverpool Range	172	E d
Livia, Palace of	24	B
Livia, Portico of	22	A
Livno	164	B b
Livny	139	E e
Livonia, reg., 9—14 cent.	80	I c
Livonia, reg., 14—16 cent.	88	K c
Livonia, reg., 17—18 cent.	138	C d
Livonia, Polish, reg.	131	I b
Livonians, people	59	I b
Livorno, see Leghorn	90	L j
Livraimont, farm		
Lixus	38	A e
Lizard Head	127	T p
Llamas del Moro	82	A a
Llandaff		
Llandaff, bp.	97	N j
Llangollen	162	C e
Llano Estacado, plain	210	E d
Llanthony, mon.	97	N j
Llerena	82	A b
Loa River	214	B e
Loampo	110	D D e
Loanda, Saint Paul de	175	E e
Loana	130	Q j
Loango	175	E e
Löbau, in Lusatia	115	H c
Löbau, in Prussia	115	J b
Löbau, dist.	72	D a
Lobbes, mon.	94	C a
Lobetani, people	38	B e
Lobos, isl.	201	F e
Lobositz	135	G c
Locarno	91	Q l
Locca, see Loches		
Loccum, mon.	95	D a
Locedia, mon.	95	D b
Lochau	115 ins.	B
Loches	61	D c
Lochias	34 ins.	C
Lochleven	118	D b
Locoritum	39	J h
Locras River	26	C f
Locris Epicnemidia, dist.	11	D d
Locris Epizephyrii, dist.	31	F d
Locris Opuntia, dist.	11	E d
Locris Ozolis, dist.	10	D d
Lod	7	B e
Lodève	76	E e
Lodève, bp.	94	C c
Lodi	90	I h
Lodi, bp.	95	D b
Lodz	159	J c
Lofoten Islands	2	E b
Logan, mt.	186	F b
Logroño	82	B a
Logstown	192	A c
Loidis		
Loir River	76	C c
Loire, dept.	148	E e
Loire River	61	C c
Loire-Inférieure, dept.	148	D e
Loiret, dept.	148	E e
Loir-et-Cher, dept.	148	E e
Loja, in Ecuador	214	B c
Loja, in Spain	82	H f
Lomagne, dist.	126	B e
Lomas de Ahorca Lagarto, hills		
Lomas de Palenquillo, hills		
Lombards, Kingdom of the	53	O i
Lombards, people	45	F b, G d
Lombard Street, in London	75	G g
Lombardy, Plain of	2	F d
Lombardy, prov.	158	E f
Lombardy, reg.	58	F d
Lombardy, theme	59	H e
Lombez, bp.	94	C c
Lombok, isl.	172	A a
Lome	174	D d
Lomellina, dist.	161	G e
Lomello	90	I h
Lomond, loch, lake	49	D c
Lomzha		
Lonato	150	F d
Londinium (London)	51	P i
London, in Canada	212	G d
London, in England		
London, plan, about 1300	75	G g
London, bp.	97	Q j
London, Hanse. for. off.	98 ins.	A
London, parl. bor.	163	O f
London, New.	189	B d
London Bridge	75	G g
London Compagny, Grants to the	190 ins.	
Londonderry, in Ireland	127	J f
Londonderry, in N. Hampshire	189	C c
Londonderry, cty.	127	J g
Londonderry, Cape	172	B b
Long, route of	210	E b
Longaticum	27	I b
Longford, cty.	127	J h
Long Island, in the Bahamas	105	F b
Long Island, off New York	189	B d
Long Island Sound	189	B d
Longjumeau	126	C b
Long's Peak	210	D b
Longueville	76	D b
Longula	30	B a
Longvilliers, mon.	94	C a
Longwy	114	C d
Lonicum	27	H a
Lons-le-Saunier	69	J f
Lons-le-Saunier, mon.	148	C b
Loo, mon.	94	C a
Lookout, Cape	193	F d
Lookout, Fort	210	F b
Lookout Mountain, battle	203	C c
Looz	117	D d
Lop		
Lopadusa	34	G f
Lopez de Sequeira, route of	109	Y g
Lop-nor, lake	92	I c
Lopodunum	39	J i
Lora del Rio	82	A b
Lorca	82	B b
Lorch, in Austria	42	E d
Lorch, in Wurtemberg	143	I h
Lorch, mon.	95	D b
Lord Fairfax's Line	194	K g
Lord Howe, route of	195	F c
Lord Howe Island	172	F d
Lorenzo Marques		
L'Orient	130	C d
Lorne, dist.		
Lorne, Firth of	49	C c
Lörrach	142	A e
Lorraine, duchy	126	E b
Lorraine, gouv.	146	C b
Lorraine, prov.	148	F e
Lorraine, Lower, duchy	62	C c
Lorraine, Upper, duchy	62	D d
Lorraine and Barrois, gen.	147	F b
Lorris	98	D d
Lorsch, mon.	95	D b
Los Angeles	190	B e
Losantiville (Cincinnati)	196 ins.	B
Los Cayos, isl.	105	E b
Los Corazones	190	C f
Losoncz	159	J d
Lostwithiel	127	U p
Lostwithiel, parl. bor.	163	J g
Lot, dept.	148	E f
Lot River	76	E d
Lota	215	B f
Lot-et-Garonne, dept.	148	E f
Lotharingia, duchy	56	D b
Lothbury	75	G g
Lothian, dist.		
Lothian		
Loudoun, Fort, in Pa.	192	B d
Loudoun, Fort, in Tennessee	193	B d
Loudun, in France	61	D c
Lough Corrib, lake	127	H h
Lough Derg, lake	127	I h
Lough Erne, lake	127	J g
Lough Mask, lake	127	H h
Lough Neagh, lake	127	K g
Lough Ree, lake		
Louis VII., crusade of	70	H d
Louis, Fort	191	H e
Louisbourg	212	J d
Louisiade Archipelago	172	E b
Louisiana, dist.	202	G c
Louisiana, reg.	190	D b — H e
Louisiana, state	203	T d
Louisiana, ter.	202	G c
Louisville	199	H c
Loup Fork, R.	198	E b
Louroux, mon.	94	C b
Lousonna (Lausanne)	26	A a
Louth, cty. in Ireland	127	K h
Louth, parl. bor. in England.		
Louvain	117	C d
Louvain, univ.	100	F d
Louvier, Ile	149	B
Louviers	126	B b
Louvre, The, palace, in Paris	149	B
Louvre, Quai du, in Paris	149	B
Lovat River	88	N c
Lovejoy	208	D c
Low Archipelago	180	N i
Lowell	211	K b
Löwen, see Louvain		
Löwenstein	143	H g
Löwenstein, cty.	143	H g
Löwenstein-Wertheim, cty.	142	D a
Lower Argen River	143	I j
Lower Bavaria, dist.	123	G d
Lower Britain, prov.	38	B b (2)
Lower Brule, Ind. Res.	188	F b
Lower Burgundy, dist.	62	C f
Lower Burma, reg.	171	K g
Lower California, pen.	187	H e
Lower California, reg.	190	C f
Lower California, ter.	213	A b
Lower Canada, reg.	212	H d
Lower Dacia, prov.	39	N k (1 b)
Lower Egypt, reg.		
Lower Germany, prov.		
Lower Gihon, well	6 ins.	A
Lower Guinea, reg.	175	E c

Lower Libya, East Rom. prov. 43 H g (2)
Lower Lorraine, duchy . . . . 62 C c
Lower Lusatia, dist. . . . . . 85 H e
Lower Lusatia, margr. . . . . 87 J c
Lower Moesia, prov. . . . . . 35 J e
Lower Pannonia, prov. . . . . 34 H d
Lower Peru, reg. . . . . 214 B c
Lower Rhenish Province . . . . 158 D c
Lower Silesia, dist. . . . . . . 72 D a
Lower Tunguska River . . . .
Lowlands, reg. . . . . 49 D d
Loyalty Islands . . . . 172 F c
Lo-yang . . . .
Loyola . . . . 94 B c
Lozère, dept. . . . . 148 E f
Loznitza . . . . 165 A a
Lübbecke . . . . 55 Q i
Lübben . . . . 115 G c
Lübeck . . . . 62 F b
Lübeck, bp. . . . . 95 E a
Lübeck, Hanse. cy. . . . . . . 99 ins. B
Lübeck, imp. cy. . . . . 79 G b
Lublin . . . . 139 B e
Luca (Lucca) . . . . 26 E d
Lucania, reg. . . . . 30 E b
Lucania and Bruttium, Aug.
    Reg. . . . . 38 F e (3)
Lucca . . . . 90 L j
Lucca, bp. . . . . 95 E c
Lucca, duchy . . . . 161 G f
Lucca, princ. . . . . 151 K j
Lucca, rep. . . . . 150 F e
Lucena . . . . 82 B b
Lucens . . . . 91 O l
Lucentum . . . . 38 B e
Lucera . . . . 64 C b
Luceria . . . . 30 E a
Luceria, bp. . . . . 95 F c
Lucerne . . . . 91 Q k
Lucerne, canton . . . . 91 Q k
Lucerne, Lake of . . . . 91 Q l
Lucignano . . . . 118 G e
Lucka . . . . 79 H c
Luckau . . . . 85 C c
Lucknow, see Luknow
Luçon . . . . 76 C c
Luçon, bp. . . . . 94 B b
Lucretilis, mt. . . . . 35 ins. B
Lucrinus Lake . . . . 31 ins. A
Lucullus, Gardens of . . . . . 23 B
Lucus. Augusti (Luc-en-Die) 38 D d
Lucus Augusti (Lugo) . . . . 38 A d
Lüderitz Bay . . . . 175 E g
Lüderitzbucht, see Lüderitz Bay
Ludgate, loc. in London . . . . 75 G g
Ludgershall, parl. bor.
Ludias River . . . . 11 D b
Ludlow . . . . 127 W n
Ludlow, parl. bor. . . . . . . 163 L e
Ludomeria, dist.
Ludwigsburg . . . . 143 H h
Lueg, pass . . . . 154 G e
Lugano . . . . 91 Q l
Lugano, lake . . . . 91 Q m
Lugansk . . . . 167 M f
Lugdunensis, Rom. prov. . . 38 C c (4)
Lugdunensis, West Rom. prov. 42 C d (2)
Lugdunum (Bagnères de Luchon) 38 C d
Lugdunum, see Laon
Lügenfeld (Field of Lies) . . . . 56 D c
Lugeus, lake . . . . 27 I b
Lugii, people . . . . 38 F c
Lugo . . . . 82 A a
Lugo, bp. . . . . 94 A c
Lugos . . . . 131 H d
Lugudunensis, prov. . . . . . 34 D d
Lugudunum (Lyons) . . . . . 38 C c
Lugudunum Batavorum (Leyden) 38 C b
Luguvallium (Carlisle) . . . . . 51 O g
Luith . . . .
Lu-kiang, R. . . . . 171 K f
Lukmanier Pass . . . . 91 Q l
Luknow, Lucknow . . . . . . 137 D c
Lule River . . . . 166 I b

Luleå . . . . 167 J b
Lummi, Ind. Res. . . . . 188 B a
Luna . . . . 26 E c
Lunæ Portus (Gulf of Spezia) 26 D d
Lund . . . . 46 I b
Lund, abp. . . . . 95 D a
Lundenburg . . . . 168 E b
Lundy's Lane, battle . . . . . 200 D b
Lüneburg . . . . 62 F b
Lüneburg, duchy . . . . 122 E b
Lüneburg, Hanse. cy. . . . . . 99 ins. B
Lunéville . . . . 62 D d
Lung-chau . . . . 171 L f
Luni . . . . 64 B b
Luni River . . . . 137 B c
Lnpercal, grotto . . . . 24 A
Lupfen, ruin . . . . 143 G i
Lupia (Lippe) River . . . . . 39 I h
Lupiæ . . . . 31 H b
Lupton, Fort . . . . 210 E c
Lure, mon. . . . . 148 C b
Lurgan . . . . 127 K g
Luristan, reg. . . . . 99 M g
Lusatia, march . . . . 62 H c
Lusatia, margr . . . . 76 C a
Lusatia, Lower, margr. . . . . 87 J c
Lusatia, Upper, margr. . . . . 87 J c
Lusatians, people . . . . 63 G c
Lusern, La, mon. . . . . 94 B b
Lusheim, Alt . . . . 142 C b
Lustenau . . . . 143 J g
Lu-tai . . . . 170 ins. A
Lutetia (Paris) . . . . 38 C c
Luteva, see Lodève
Lutter am Barenberge . . . . . 122 F c
Lutterberg . . . . 134 E c
Lutterworth, about thirtheen
    miles north-east of Coventry 97 P i
Lüttich, see Liège
Lützelburg . . . . 62 C d
Lützen . . . . 123 G c
Lutzk . . . . 139 C e
Luxembourg, palace . . . . . 149 B
Luxemburg . . . . 117 D e
Luxemburg, duchy . . . . . . 78 D d
Luxemburg, gr. duchy . . . . 158 C d
Luxeuil, mon. . . . . 95 D b
Luxor . . . . 1 C e
Luxovium (Luxeuil) . . . . . . 39 I j
Luzern, see Lucerne
Luzon, isl. . . . . 199 ins. H
Luzy . . . . 69 I g
Lycabettus, mt. . . . . 23 D
Lycæus, mt. . . . . 14 B b
Lycaonia, East Rom. prov. 43 I f (5)
Lycaonia, Macedonian prov. . . 18 D c
Lycaonia, Rom. prov. . . . . .
Lycandos, theme . . . . 59 L f
Lyceum, quarter . . . . 23 D
Lychnidus . . . . 10 B a
Lychnites, lake, in Epirus . . . 10 B a
Lychnitis, lake, in Armenia . . 20 K b
Lycia, East Rom. prov. . . 43 H f (4)
Lycia, Macedonian prov. . . . . 18 C c
Lycia, reg. . . . . 8 A b
Lycia, Rom. prov. . . . . . . 20 C d
Lycia, satr. . . . . 18 N h
Lyck . . . . 155 L b
Lycosura . . . . 14 C b
Lycus River, in Phœnicia . . 6 D a
Lycus River, in Pontus . . . 20 H b
Lycus, The, river, in Constanti-
    nople . . . . 93 G e
Lydda . . . . 7 B e
Lydia, East Rom. prov. . . . 43 H f (2)

Lydia, Macedon. prov. . . . . 18 C c
Lydia, reg. . . . . 8 A b
Lydia, Rom. prov. . . . . . . 20 C c
Lydia, satr. . . . . 18 N h
Lydian Kingdom . . . . 5 B b
Lyme Regis . . . . 127 W p
Lyme Regis, parl. bor. . . . . 163 L g
Lymington, parl. bor. . . . . 163 M g
Lyncestis, dist. . . . . 10 C a
Lynchburg . . . . 208 E b
Lyncus, mt. . . . . 10 C c
Lynn, in England . . . . 65 G d
Lynn, Hanse. for. cy. . . . . . 98 ins. A
Lynn, in Mass. . . . . 189 ins. B
Lynn Canal . . . . 212 ins.
Lyonnais, cty. . . . . 69 F d
Lyonnais, gouv. . . . . 146 B b
Lyonnais, prov. . . . . 148 E e
Lyons . . . . 70 G d
Lyons, abp. . . . . 94 C b
Lyons, gen. . . . . 147 E b
Lyons, Gulf of . . . . 38 C d
Lyrcea . . . . 14 C b
Lys River . . . . 117 A d
Lysikrates, Monument of . . . .
Lysimachia, in Ætolia . . . . 10 C d
Lysimachia, on the Propontis .
Lysimachus, Kingdom of 18
Lysimelian Marsh . . . . 31 ins. B
Lystra . . . . 20 E d
Lyttus . . . . 14 ins.

Maacha, reg. . . . . 6 D b
Ma'bar, reg. . . . . 102 H f
McAllister, Fort . . . . 208 D c
Macao . . . . 110 CC e
Macapá . . . . 214 D b
Macara . . . . 30 C c
Macaria, dist. . . . . 14 C b
Macassar . . . .
Macassar, Strait of . . . . . . 171 M h
Macclesfield . . . . 127 W m
Macclesfield, parl. bor. . . . . 163 L d
McClintock Channel . . . . . 212 E a
Macdonald, lake . . . . 172 B c
Macdonalds, fam. . . . .
McDonnell Range . . . . . . 172 C c
McDowell . . . . 208 E b
Macedonia, East Rom. dioc. . . 43 G e
Macedonia, East Rom. prov. 43 Ge(1.)
Macedonia, reg. . . . . 10 C b
Macedonia, Rom. imp. prov. 39 Ml(4.)
Macedonia, Rom. sen. prov. . 35 I e
Macedonia, state . . . . 18 B b
Macedonia, theme . . . . . . 59 J e
Macedonia Salutaris, East Rom.
    prov. . . . . 43 Ge (6.)
Macedonian Empire, The 18, 19
Maceió . . . . 214 F c
Macellum Liviae, in Rome . . . 22 A
Macellum magnum, in Rome . . 22 A
Macerata . . . . 90 D c
Macerata, bp. . . . . 95 E c
Macestus River . . . .
Maceta, Cape . . . . 19 I e
McGillivray's Town . . . . . . 196 B d
Machadodorp . . . . 175 N e
Machærus . . . . 7 D e
McHenry, Fort . . . . 200 L h
Machias . . . . 189 E b
Macijowice . . . .
MacIntoshes, fam. . . . .
Macintyre River . . . . 172 D c
Macistus . . . . 14 B b
Macistus, mt. . . . . 11 E d
Mackay . . . . 172 D c
MacKays, fam. . . . .
Mackenzie, dist. . . . . 212 C b
MacKenzies, fam. . . . .
Mackenzie Bay . . . . 212 B b
Mackenzie River . . . . 186 G b
Mackinac . . . . 211 H a
Mackinac, Fort . . . . 194 C a
McKinley, mt. . . . . 186 D b

MacLeans, fam.
Macleod 212 D d
MacLeods, fam.
McMurray, Fort 212 D c
Macomades 46 H f
Mâcon, in France 61 F c
Mâcon, bp. 94 C b
Macon, in Georgia 208 D c
Macon, Fort, in N. Carolina 208 E c
MacPhersons, fam.
Macpherson, Fort 212 B b
Macquarie Harbor 172 D e
Macra River 26 D c
Mactan, isl. 110 D Dg
Macynia 10 C d
Madagascar, isl. 175 H g
Madaura 38 D e
Madeira Islands 174 B a
Madeira River 214 C c
Madeket 189 C d
Madeleine, The, church, in Paris 149 B
Mâdion, mon. 94 B b
Madison 211 H b
Madison, Fort 199 G b
Madison, Fort, Ind. Res. 188 B a
Madrak, Ras 170 G g
Madras 137 D f
Madre de Dios River 214 C d
Madrid 83 K g
Madura 137 C g
Madytus
Mæander (Mendere) River 20 C d
Mæcenas, Gardens of 22 A
Mædi, people 39 M l
Mæetae, people 35 L d
Mænalus 14 C b
Mænalus, mt. 14 C b
Mænan, mon. 97 N h
Mæotis, lake (Sea of Azov) 12 K a
Maeseyck 117 D c
Maestricht 117 D d
Mafeking 175 F g
Mafia, isl. 175 H e
Magadaburg, see Magdeburg
Magadoxo 175 H d
Magalhães (Magellan) Strait 108 K l
Magalhães, route of, see Magellan 107—110 leg.
Magalia, quarter in Carthage 34 ins. A
Magdala, in Abyssinia 174 G c
Magdala, in Palestine 6 D c
Magdalen, Postern of the 68 ins. B
Magdalena 213 A a
Magdalena, isl. 107 D j
Magdalena Bay 111 B a
Magdalena River 214 B b
Magdeburg 63 F b
Magdeburg, abp. 95 E a
Magdeburg, duchy 122 F b
Magdeburg, Hanse. cy. 99 ins. B
Magdiel 6 B c
Magdolum 4 ins. *
Magellan, route of 107 Ah, 108 Ng, 110 DDg
Magellan, Straits of 215 B h
Magenta 158 E f
Mägerkingen 143 H i
Magersfontein 175 L l
Magetobriga 39 H j
Maggia 91 Q l
Maggiore, Lake 91 Q m
Magia 39 J j
Magna Charta Island 75 H i
Magna Græcia, reg. 29 E e
Magna Mater, Temple of 24 A
Magnano 150 F d
Magnesia (Manissa) 93 C c
Magnesia, reg. 11 D c
Magnetic Pole, Northern 186 J a
Mago 38 C e
Magoras River 6 D a
Magrib, reg. 98 C g
Maguelonne, bp. 94 C c
Magyars, people, 800
Magyars, people, about 900
Mahanadi River 137 E d
Mahanaim 7 D d
Mahanuddy River 137 E d
Mahé 137 C f
Mahedia 70 I f
Mahlberg 142 A d
Mahlberg, lordship 142 A d
Mahmoud Bridge 93 Ge (10.)
Maholm 88 L b
Mahon 83 L h
Mahra, reg. 53 H e
Mahratta Confederacy 137 B d
Mahukona 198 ins. B
Maidstone, in England 127 Z o
Maidstone, parl. bor. 163 O f
Maidstone (Easthampton), in New York 189 C d
Maienfeld 91 R k
Mail, Plaine du, Versailles 149 A
Mailand, see Milan
Mailapur
Mailberg 63 H d
Maillezais, bp. 94 B b
Mailly 69 I g
Maimatchin 171 L d
Mainau, isl. 142 D e
Maine, cty., in France 61 D b
Maine, gouv., in France 146 A b
Maine, prov., in France 148 D e
Maine, col., in U. S. 189 C c
Maine, dist., in U. S. 196 F b
Maine, state, in U. S. 203 Y a
Maine-et-Loire, dept. 148 D e
Mainots, people 164 C c
Main River 62 F c
Main River, East 186 L c
Maintenon 126 B b
Maintenon, castle 130 D d
Mainz, see Mayence
Maior (Majorca), isl. 38 C e
Maipo, battle 215 B f
Maison-du-Roi, la 156 C c
Maitland 172 E d
Majapahit 112 E d
Majar 99 L e
Majella, Mount, mon. 95 E c
Majorca, bp. 94 C d
Majorca, isl. 82 C b
Majorca and Roussillon, km. 83 L g
Majuba Hill, mt. 175 M l
Majumas 7 A e
Makah, Ind. Res. 188 A a
Makalla 170 F g
Makarska, bp. 95 F c
Makhlaf 170 F g
Makri 99 I f
Makua River 175 F d
Malabar, reg. 137 C f
Malabar Coast 137 B e
Malaca (Málaga) 38 B e
Malacca 112 D c
Malacca, pen. 112 D c
Málaga 82 B b
Málaga, bp. 94 B d
Malakoff, Fort 164 L g
Mälar, lake 119 H b
Malaspina, fam. 90 L i
Malaspina Glacier 212 A c
Malatia 99 K f
Malatieh
Malay Peninsula 171 L h
Malborn 142 ins. A
Malden 189 ins. B
Malden, Fort 200 B b
Malden Island 180 L h
Maldive Islands 112 A c
Maldon 65 G e
Maldon, parl. bor. 163 O f
Maldonado 215 D f
Malea, prom. in Laconia 15 D c
Malea, prom. in Lesbos
Malécites, mission 189 E a
Malian Gulf 11 D d
Malian Plain 16 E e
Malindi 175 H e
Malines, abp. 148 B a
Malin Head 127 J f
Malis, dist. 11 D d
Mallets, route of the 190 E d
Malli, people 19 L d
Mallianum, bp. 96 B a
Malling, mon. 97 R j
Malmedy 117 E d
Malmedy, mon. 95 D a
Malmesbury
Malmesbury, mon
Malmesbury, parl. bor. 163 L f (Malm.)
Malmö 88 E d
Malmö, Hanse. for. cy. 98 F b
Mallœa 10 D c
Maloja Pass 91 R l
Maloyaroslavets 153 P g
Malpelo Island 214 A b
Malplaquet 134 B c
Malta, isl. 50 F e
Malton, parl. bor. 163 N c
Maluentum 30 D a
Maluinas (Falkland), isl. 215 D h
Malvasia 124 D c
Malvern, Great, mon. 97 O i
Malvern Hill, in Virginia 208 E b
Malvern Hills, in England 49 E e
Malwa, reg. 137 C c
Mamanguape 214 F c
Mamei
Mamelukes, Dom. of the 73 H d
Mameluke Sultanates 77 I e
Mamertium 31 F d
Mamistra 68 C b
Mamoré River 214 C d
Man, Isle of 49 D d
Manado
Managua 213 D c
Manahiki Islands 180 L i
Manaos 214 D c
Manar, Gulf of 137 C g
Manassas Junction 208 ins.
Manasseh, tribe 7 ins. D
Manbij 68 C b
Mancha, La, dist. 83 K h
Manchac 191 G e
Manche, dept. 148 D e
Manchester, in England 127 W m
Manchester, parl. bor. 163 L d
Manchester, in New Hampshire 211 K b
Manchester, in Ohio 196 ins. B
Manchu City, in Peking 170 ins. A
Manchuria, reg. 171 N c d
Manchus, people
Mancunium (Manchester)
Mandalay 171 K f
Mandans, tribe 188 D a
Mandan, Fort 210 E a
Manderscheid 117 E d
Mandeure 143 ins. F
Mandingo River
Mandræ
Mandu 112 A a
Mandubii, people 38 C c
Manduessedum
Manduria 31 G b
Manfredonia (Siponto) 90 F d
Mangalore 137 B f
Mangarewa Island 180 O j
Mangaseya
Manhardsberg, mt. 54 H d
Manhattan 189 ins. C
Manhattan Island 189 ins. C
Manila 171 N g
Manila Bay 171 N g
Manipur 171 K f
Manissa (Magnesia) 93 C c
Manitoba, lake 186 I c
Manitoba, prov. 212 F c
Mannheim 142 B a
Manosque 126 D c

Manosque, mon. ..... 148 C c (Man.)
Manresa
Mans, Le ..... 61 C b
Mans, Le, bp. ..... 94 C b
Mansfeld ..... 62 F c
Mansfeld, cty. ..... 114 F c
Mansfeld, Ernest of, route ... 121 C c
Mansfield Island ..... 212 G b
Mansura, in Egypt ..... 174 J i
Mansurah, in India ..... 53 I d
Mantes ..... 69 H f
Manthyrea ..... 14 C b
Mantinea nova ..... 14 C b
Mantinea vetus ..... 14 C b
Mantinum ..... 26 D e
Mantua ..... 26 E b
Mantua, bp. ..... 95 E b
Mantua, duchy ..... 150 F d
Mantua, marq. ..... 90 C b
Manua Islands ..... 199 ins. D
Manuel, Fort ..... 210 D a
Manukau Harbor ..... 172 G d
Manytch River ..... 164 G a
Manzanillo ..... 213 B c
Manzanillo, Bay of
Manzi, reg. ..... 92 L e
Manzikert ..... 67 O f
Maon ..... 7 C f
Maqueda ..... 82 B a
Mar, dist.
Maracaibo ..... 214 B a
Maracaibo Lake ..... 105 F e
Maracanda ..... 19 K c
Maragha ..... 73 J c
Marajo Island ..... 214 E c
Marakesh (Morocco) ..... 174 C a
Maranguape ..... 214 F c
Maranham ..... 214 E c
Maranhão, state ..... 214 E c
Marañon River ..... 214 B c
Marans ..... 126 A c
Maransart
Marash ..... 68 C b
Marash, reg. ..... 124 G c
Marathon ..... 15 D a
Marathon, Plain of ..... 16 B a
Marbach ..... 143 H h
Marbais ..... 156 B a
Marbella ..... 82 B b
Marblehead ..... 189 ins. B
Marburg ..... 123 H e
Marcellus, Theatre of ..... 22 A
March River ..... 63 I d
Marche, or La Marche, cty. ..... 61 D c
Marche, or La Marche, gouv. ..... 146 B b
Marche, or La Marche, prov. ..... 148 E e
Marches, The, dist. ..... 90 D c
Marchfeld, dist. ..... 79 J d
Marchienne ..... 156 A b
Marchthal, ab. ..... 143 I i
Marchthal, mon. ..... 143 I i
Marcian Aqueduct ..... 35 ins. B
Marcianopolis ..... 39 N l
Marcinelle ..... 156 A b
Marcodurum ..... 39 I h
Marcomagus ..... 39 I h
Marcomanni, people ..... 38 E c
Marco Polo, route of .....
Marcus Aurelius, Arch of ... 22 A
Marcus Aurelius, Column of .. 22 A
Marcus Aurelius, Temple of .. 22 A
Marcus Hook ..... 192 ins.
Mar del Norte (Caribbean Sea) 108 J f
Mar del Plata ..... 215 D f
Mar del Sur (South Sea or
   Pacific Ocean) ..... 107 F H g
Mardin ..... 68 C b
Mardocho ..... 6 F c
Mardonius' Fleet, route of ... 13 D b
Mardyck ..... 122 B c
Marengo ..... 150 E d
Mareotis, lake ..... 4 ins.
Margalæ ..... 14 B b
Margam, mon. ..... 97 N j

Margarita, isl. ..... 105 H d
Margat ..... 68 C b
Marghilan ..... 170 I e
Margiana, prov. ..... 19 J c
Margus River (Morava R.) ... 39 M l
Margus River (Murgab R.) .. 19 J c
Maria Galante, isl. ..... 105 H c
Mariamne ..... 6 ins. A
Mariampol ..... 155 L a
Mariana ..... 26 D e
Marianne Islands ..... 110 F F f
Marias River ..... 210 C a
Maria Theresiopel ..... 159 J e
Maria van Diemen, Cape .. 172 G d
Mariazell, Gross, mon. .. 95 F b
Mariazell, Klein, mon. .. 95 F b
Marici, people ..... 26 D b
Maridunum (Carmarthen) .. 51 N i
Marie Galante, isl. ..... 213 F c
Marienbourg ..... 117 C d
Marienburg ..... 79 K b
Marienburg, Hanse. cy. ..... 98 G c
Marienstern, mon. ..... 95 E a
Marienthal, mon.. ..... 95 E a
Marienwalde, mon. ..... 80 ins.
Marienwerder ..... 72 D a
Marienwerder, bp. ..... 95 F a
Marietta ..... 196 ins. B
Marignano ..... 90 I h
Mariguana, isl. ..... 105 F b
Marinids, dynasty ..... 77 C f
Mario, Monte ..... 96 A
Mariposa ..... 201 B b
Maritima, isl. ..... 30 A e
Maritime Alps, mts. ..... 26 B c
Maritime Alps, West Rom. prov. 42 D e (7)
Maritza River ..... 89 C b
Mariua ..... 214 C c
Mariupol ..... 139 E f
Mark, cty. ..... 78 E c
Mark, see Brandenburg
Market Harborough ..... 98 ins. A
Markgröningen ..... 143 H h
Markovo ..... 171 S b
Marlborough, in England ... 127 X o
Marlborough, parl. bor. 163 M f (Marlb.)
Marlborough, route of ..... 129 leg.
Marlborough, in Tasmania .. 172 D e
Marle ..... 69 I f
Marmande ..... 126 B d
Marmarica, dist. ..... 35 I g
Marmarium ..... 15 E a
Marmora, Sea of ..... 3 H d
Marmoutier, mon. ..... 94 C b
Marne, dept. ..... 148 E e
Marne River ..... 69 I f
Maroneus, mt. ..... 30 D e
Maronia ..... 13 D a
Maroni River ..... 214 D b
Maros River ..... 73 E a
Maros-Vasarhely ..... 159 M e
Marpessa, mt. ..... 15 F b
Marquesas de Mendoza, isl. ... 107 D h
Marquesas Islands ..... 180 M h
Marquette, route of ..... 191 H c
Marra ..... 68 C b
Marrucini, people ..... 27 I e
Marruvium ..... 27 H f
Mars, Temple of ..... 22 A
Mars the Avenger, Temple of 24 B
Marsala ..... 90 D f
Marsalquivir ..... 130 C f
Marsan, dist. ..... 147 D c
Marsan, viscty. ..... 84 C g
Marsdiep, strait ..... 117 C b
Marseilles ..... 61 F e
Marseilles, bp. ..... 95 D c
Marshall ..... 211 G d
Marshall Islands ..... 179 I f
Mars' Hill, (Areopagus) in
   Athens
Mars Hill, mt. in Maine ... 199 L a
Marsi, people, in Germany .. 39 I h
Marsi, Marsians, people, in Italy

Marsico, bp. ..... 95 F c
Marston Moor ..... 127 X m
Martaban
Marta River ..... 27 F e
Martel ..... 76 D d
Martha's Vineyard, isl. .. 189 C d
Martigny ..... 91 P b
Martin Garcia, Island of .. 215 D f (M.)
Martinino (Martinique), isl. .. 105 H d
Martinique, isl. ..... 213 F c
Martinsbruck ..... 150 F e
Martinsburg ..... 193 F b
Martin's Hundred ... 193 ins. A (Mart.)
Martinstein ..... 142 ins. A
Martinstein, lordship ..... 142 ins. A
Martinswand ..... 87 H e
Martirano ..... 72 D d
Marton, mon. ..... 97 Q g
Martyropolis ..... 52 M f
Marusium ..... 31 I b
Marus River (March R.) .. 38 F c
Marvejols ..... 126 C d
Marwar, dist. ..... 137 B c
Marwell, college ..... 100 A b
Maryborough ..... 172 E c
Maryland, col. ..... 192 C d
Maryland, state ..... 211 J c
Mary-le-bone, parl. bor.
Marysville ..... 210 A c
Masada ..... 7 C f
Masampo, Masampho ..... 171 N e
Masbate, isl. ..... 199 ins. H
Mascara ..... 130 D f
Mascarenhas, isl. ..... 109 W i
Mascoutins, tribe ..... 188 H b
Masefau ..... 199 ins. D
Maserfield (Oswestry) .....
Mases ..... 15 D b
Mashonaland, dist. ..... 175 G f
Masis, mt. ..... 18 F c
Masius Mountains ..... 20 I d
Maskat ..... 170 G f
Mason and Dixon's Line ... 194 K g
Mason and Gorges' Claim .. 189 C c
Masovia, dist. ..... 138 B e
Massa ..... 90 L j
Massa, bp. ..... 95 E c
Massa Marittima ..... 90 L j
Massa Veternensis ..... 26 E d
Massac, Fort ..... 194 B c
Massaca ..... 19 L d
Massachusetts, state, till 1820 . 202 K b
Massachusetts, state, since 1820 203 X b
Massachusetts Bay ..... 189 C c
Massachusetts Bay, col. .... 189 C c
Massagetæ, Massagetans,
   people ..... 19 J b
Massanutting ..... 193 E b
Massaua or Massawa, see Masso-
   wah
Masserano ..... 130 Q i
Massicus, mt. ..... 30 C a
Massilia (Marseilles) ..... 38 D a
Massowah ..... 174 G c
Massylii, people ..... 38 D e
Mastanli ..... 165 D c
Masulipatam ..... 137 D e
Matabeleland, reg. ..... 175 F f
Matachin
Matagorda Bay ..... 190 F f
Matamoros ..... 201 F d
Matanzas ..... 213 D b
Matanzas Island ..... 191 I f
Matapan, Cape ..... 167 J h
Matape ..... 190 D f
Matatane ..... 109 V j
Matelots, Allée des, Versailles 149
Matera ..... 64 C b
Matera, abp. ..... 95 F c
Maternum ..... 27 F e
Mathia, mt. ..... 14 B c
Mathis River ..... 31 I a
Mathraval
Matianus, lake ..... 18 G c

Matifu, Cape . . . . 118　E f
Matilica . . . . 27　H d
Matinum . . . . 31　F a
Matisco or Matiscone (Mâcon, in France) . . . . 39　H j
Matrega, Matriga . . . . 73　H b
Matrinum . . . . 27　I e
Matrona, Mount (Mt. Genèvre), pass . . . . 26　A c
Matrona (Marne) River . . . . 38　C c
Mattagami River . . . . 211　D d
Mattium . . . . 39　J h
Matto Grosso (Villa Bella) . . . 214　D d
Matto Grosso, state . . . . . . 214　D d
Mattox . . . . 193　F b (Ma.)
Mauzi, isl. . . . . 198 ins. B
Maubeuge . . . . 117　B d
Maubeuge, mon. . . . . 148　B a
Maugio . . . . 76　F e
Maulbronn, ab. . . . . 143　G h
Maulbronn, mon. . . . . 143　G g
Maule River . . . . 215　B f
Mauléon . . . . 126　A e
Maullin . . . . 215　B g
Maultasch, castle . . . . 79　G e
Maumee River . . . . 200　A c
Mauna Kea, mt. . . . . . . 198 ins. B
Mauna Loa, mt. . . . . . . 198 ins. B
Maupertuis . . . . 81　M h
Maurepas, lake . . . . . 191　G e (L. M.)
Maurepas, Fort (Biloxi) . . . . 191　H e
Maurepas, Fort (on Winnipeg L.) 191　H e
Mauretania, reg. . . . . 46　F g
Mauretania Cæsariensis, prov. . . 34　D g
Mauretania Cæsariensis, West Rom. prov. . . . . 42 C f (5.)
Mauretania Sitifensis, West Rom. prov. . . . . 42 C f (4.)
Mauretania Tingitana, imp. prov. 34　C g
Mauretania Tingitana, West Rom. prov. . . . . 42 B g (6.)
Mauretanians, people . . . . . 51　C f
Mauriac . . . . 126　C d
Maurici, Portus . . . . 26　C d
Maurienne, bp. . . . . 95　D b
Mauritius, isl. . . . . 175　I f
Mauritsstad . . . .
Maursmünster, mon. . . . . . 95　D b
Mauvezin . . . . 126　B e
Mauze, castle . . . . 69　C c
Mavila . . . . 191　H e
Maxen . . . . 135　G c
Maxima Cæsariensis, West Rom. prov. . . . . 42 B c (1.)
Maxima Sequanorum, West Rom. prov. . . . . 42 D d (9.)
Maximianopolis . . . . 6　C c
May, Cape . . . . 192　D d
May, River of . . . . 191　D d
Maya . . . . 82　B a
Mayaguana, isl. . . . . 105　F b
Mayaguez . . . . 199 ins. G
Mayas, people . . . . 105　C c
Mayence . . . . 62　E d
Mayence, abp. . . . . 95　D b
Mayence, univ. . . . . 100　G d
Mayenne . . . . 76　C b
Mayenne, dept. . . . . 148　D e
Mayo, bp. . . . . 97　H d
Mayo, cty. . . . . 127　H h
Mayotte Island . . . . 175　H f
Maysi, Cape . . . . 105　F c
Maysville . . . . 211　I c
Mayumba . . . . 175　D e
Mazaca (Kaisarieh) . . . . . . 20　F c
Mazagan . . . . 108　P d
Mazamet . . . . 126　C e
Mazan, mon. . . . . 94　C c
Mazanderan, reg. . . . . 139　H h
Mazara . . . . 30　B e
Mazatlan . . . . 213　B b
Mazovia, reg. . . . . 59　I c
Mazzara . . . . 90　D f
Mazzara, bp. . . . . 95　E d

Mazzo . . . . 91　S l
McCarthys, The, fam. . . . . .
McGuires, The, fam. . . . . .
McMahons, The, fam. . . . . .
McMurroughs, The, fam. . . . .
Meadville . . . . 206 ins.
Meara . . . . 6　D a
Mearns, dist. . . . .
Meath, bp. . . . . 97　E c
Meath, cty. . . . . 127　K h
Meath, dist. . . . .
Meat Market, in London . . 75 G g (33.)
Meauléon . . . . 76　C e
Meaux, in France . . . . . . 61　E b
Meaux, bp. . . . . 94　C b
Meaux, mon., in England . . . . 97　Q h
Mecca . . . .
Mechanicstown . . . . . . 208 ins.
Mechlin . . . . 76　F b
Mechlin, abp. . . . . 148　B a
Mechlin, lordship . . . . . . 117　C d
Mecklenburg . . . . 55　R i
Mecklenburg, castle . . . . . 63　F b
Mecklenburg, dist. . . . . . . 79　G b
Mecklenburg, duchy . . . . . 87　H b
Mecklenburg Court House . . . 195　A f
Mecklenburg-Güstrow, duchy . 123　G b
Mecklenburg-Schwerin, duchy . 122　F b
Mecklenburg-Schwerin, gr.duchy 158　F b
Mecklenburg-Strelitz, duchy . 135　G b
Mecklenburg-Strelitz, gr. duchy 158　G b
Mecyberna . . . . 11　E b
Medama . . . . 12　G c
Medeba . . . .
Medellin, in Columbia . . . . 214　B b
Medellin, in Mexico . . . . . 106　D a
Medellin, in Spain . . . . . . 82　A b
Medemblik . . . . 117　D b
Medeon . . . . 10　C d
Medes, people . . . . 5　D b
Medeshamstead . . . . . . 189 ins. B
Medford . . . .
Medgyes . . . . 159　M e
Media, prov. . . . . 19　G c
Media, reg. . . . . 8　C b
Media, satr. . . . . 8　I e
Media Atropatene, reg. . . . . 35　N f
Media Atropatene, satr. . . . . 18　P h
Media Magna, satr. . . . . . . 18　P h
Median Empire 8
Median Wall . . . . 18　F d
Mediasch . . . . 159　M e
Medicine Hat . . . . 212　D d
Medina . . . .
Medinaceli . . . . 82　B a
Medina del Campo . . . . . . 83　K g
Medina de Pomar . . . . . . 82　B a
Medina de Rioseco . . . . . .
Medina Sidonia . . . . 82　A b
Medinet el Fayum . . . . . . 174　J j
Mediolanium, Mediolanum (Milan) 26　D b
Mediolanum, see Evreux
Mediolanum, see Saintes
Mediomatrici, see Metz
Mediomatrici, people . . . . . 38　D c
Mediterranean Sea . . . . . . 2　E e
Medjidie . . . . 165　F a
Medma . . . . 30　E d
Medma River . . . . 31　F d
Medrano . . . . 215　C f
Meduacus (Brenta) River . . . 27　F b
Medulli, people . . . . 26　A b
Medullia . . . . 35 ins. B
Meenen . . . .
Meersberg . . . . 142　D e
Meerut . . . . 137　C c
Meewocs, tribe . . . . 188　B c
Megalopolis . . . . 14　C b
Megara, in Greece . . . . . . 15　D a
Megara, quarter in Carthage . 34 ins. A
Megara Hyblæa . . . . 30　E e
Megaris, dist. . . . . 15　D a
Megaris, isl. . . . . 31 ins. A
Megiddo . . . . 6　C c

Mehadia . . . . 159　L f
Mehaigne River . . . . 156　B a
Meia Ponte . . . . 214　E d
Meigs, Fort . . . . 200　B c
Meiningen . . . . 154　F c
Meiringen . . . . 91　Q l
Meisenheim . . . . 158　D d
Meissen . . . . 63　G c
Meissen, bp. . . . . 95　E a
Meissen, march . . . . 85　G e
Me-Jarkon . . . . 7　B d
Mejillones . . . . 215　B e
Mekong River . . . .
Mekran, reg. . . . . 170　H f
Melænæ . . . . 16　B a
Melæneæ . . . . 14　B b
Melas, gulf . . . .
Melas River . . . . 16　E e
Melbourne . . . . 172　D d
Melcart, Island of . . . . . . 18 ins. B
Melchior Diaz, route of . . . . 190　C f
Melchthal . . . . 91　Q l
Melcombe Regis, parl. bor. . . 163　L g
Meldæ or Meldis, see Meaux
Meldorf . . . . 62　E a
Meleda, isl. . . . . 90　F c
Meledunum, see Melodunum
Melencze . . . . 159　K f
Melfi . . . . 90　E d
Melfi, bp. . . . . 95　F c
Melgueil, cty. . . . . 69　E e
Melibocus Mountains . . . . . 39　K h
Melibœa . . . . 11　D c
Melilla . . . . 118　D f
Melinde . . . .
Melita (Malta), isl. . . . . . . 34　G f
Melita (Meleda), isl. . . . . . 38　F d
Melitæa . . . . 11　D c
Melite, deme of . . . . 23　D
Melite, lake . . . . 10　C d
Melitean Gate . . . . 23　D
Melitene (Malatieh) . . . . . 20　H c
Melk . . . . 63　H d
Melk, mon. . . . . 95　F b
Mella River . . . . 26　E b
Melli . . . . 108　Q f
Mellrichstadt . . . . 62　F a
Melnik . . . . 63　H c
Melno, lake . . . . 88　H e
Melodunum (Melun) . . . . . 38　C c
Melon, mon. . . . . 94　A c
Meloria, isl. . . . . 72　C c
Melos . . . . 15　E c
Melos (Milo), isl. . . . . . . 15　E c
Melpes River . . . . 30　E c
Melrose . . . .
Melton Mowbray, parl. bor. . . .
Melun . . . . 76　E b
Mellville Island, off Australian coast . . . . 172　B b
Melville Island, Parry Is. . . . 186　H a
Melville Peninsula . . . . . . 212　G b
Melville Sound . . . . 186　H a
Memel . . . . 80　G d
Memleben . . . . 63　F c
Memleben, mon. . . . . 95　F c
Memmingen . . . . 79　G d
Memphis, in Egypt . . . . . . 1　B c
Memphis, in Tennessee . . . . 199　H c
Menæum . . . . 30　D e
Menam River . . . . 171　K g
Menapii, people . . . . 39　H h
Menat, mon. . . . . 94　C b
Menawaski . . . . 174　F c
Mendana, route of . . . . . . 110 H H h
Mende, in Chalcidice . . . . . 11　E c
Mende, in France . . . . . . 61　E d
Mande, bp. . . . . 94　C c
Mendere River (Scamander R.)
Mendere River (Mæander R.)
Mendes . . . . 1　B b
Mendip Hills . . . . 49　E f
Mendocino, Cape . . . . . . 187　G d
Mendon . . . . 189　C c

Mendoza 215   C f
Mendoza, route of 107   G f
Mendrisio 91   Q m
Menendez, set. of 191   J e
Mengen 143   H i
Meng-tsze . . . .
Menin 117   B d
Meninx 34   G d
Men-nofer (Memphis) 4   F d *
Menominee, Ind. Res. 188   I a
Menominee River 191   H b
Menominees, tribe 188   I a
Mentana 161   I f
Menteith, dist. . . . .
Mentesa 82   H f
Mentesha, reg. 89   I g
Mentone 130   P k
Mentorides, isl. 27   I c
Mentz, see Mayence
Menzaleh, lake . . . .
Meonwara, people . . . . . .
Meppel 117   E b
Meppen 122   D b
Meppen, mon. 95   D a
Mequinenza 82   C a
Meran 114   F e
Meran, mon. 95   E b
Merash . . . .
Merbe Braine . . . .
Mercer, Fort 195   D d
Merchant's Hope . . . . . . 193 ins. A
Mercia, Kingdom . . . .
Mercia, Danish, reg. . . . . .
Mercia, English, reg. . . . . .
Mercians, people 51   R k
Mercoeur, castle 69   E d
Mercurii, prom. 38   E e
Mercury, Temple of 22   A
Mercy, Cape 212   I b
Mere, parl. bor. . . . .
Merena, isl. 172   F b
Merevale, mon. 97   P i
Mergens, Pitinum 27   G d
Mergentheim 143   I g
Mergen 112   A b
Mérida, in Spain 82   A b
Mérida in Venezuela 214   B b
Mérida, in Yucatan 213   D b
Meridian 208   C c
Mérindol 126   D e
Mering 62   F d
Merinum 31   F a
Merioneth, cty. 74   D e
Merioneth, parl. dist. 163   K e
Merkits, people . . . .
Merom 6   C c
Merom, Waters of 6   D b
Merrimac River 189   C c
Merry Mount, in Mass. 189   C c
Merry Mount, in Virginia . . . 193 ins. A
Merse, dist. . . . .
Merseburg 63   G c
Merseburg, bp. 95   E a
Merseburg, Hanse. cy. . . . . 99 ins. B
Merseburg, march 63   G c
Mersen 55   Q i
Mersey River 127   W m
Merthyr Tydfil, parl. bor. . . . 163   K f
Merry Mount, village 189   C c
Mertola 82   A b
Merton 75   I i
Merton, mon. 97   Q j
Merv 53   I c
Méry 45   E c
Mesambria, on the Ægean Sea 17   D a
Mesambria, Mesembria, on the
    Black Sea 12   I b
Mescalero Apache, Ind. Res. . 188   E d
Meseritz 155   H b
Meseritz, mon. 95   F a
Meshed . . . .
Meshed-Ali 99   L g
Mesogæa, dist. 15   D b
Mesopotamia, Rom. prov. . . . 35   M f

Mesopotamia, East Rom. prov 43 J f (12.)
Mesopotamia, reg. 3   K f
Mesopotamia, satr. 18   P h
Mesopotamia, theme 59   L f
Mesopotamia Plains 3   I e
Messa 14   C c
Messana (Messina) 30   E d
Messapii, Messapians, people . 31   G b
Messene 14   B b
Messenia, Gulf of 14   C c
Messenia,, state 14   B b
Messina 90   E e
Messina, abp. 95   E d
Messina, Strait of 30   E d
Messkirch 142   D d
Messkirch, lordship 142   D d
Meta River 214   B b
Metammeh 174   G c
Metanastæ, Jazyges, people . . 38   F c
Metapontum, Metapontium . . 31   F a
Metaris Æstuarium (The Wash) 51   Q h
Meta sudans, in Rome 24   B
Metauro River 90   M j
Metaurus River, in Bruttium . . 30   E d
Metaurus River, in Umbria . . 27   G d
Methana 15   D b
Methone, in Macedonia 11   D b
Methone, in Magnesia 11   E c
Methone (Modoni), in Messenia 14   B c
Methydrium 14   E b
Methymna . . . .
Metis River 199   L a
Metropolis, in Acarnania . . . 10   C d
Metropolis, in Epirus 10   C d
Metropolis, in Pelasgiotis . . . 11   D c
Metropolis, in Thessaliotis . . 10   C c
Metropotamia, proposed state in
   U. S. . . . .
Metroum . . . .
Metrovian Gate 22   A
Metsovo . . . .
Mettis (Metz) 39   I i
Metulum 27   J b
Metz 62   D d
Metz, bp. 78   E d
Metz, imp. cy. 78   E d
Metz and Verdun, gouv. . . . 146   C b
Metzingen 143   H h
Meulant, castle 76   D b
Meung 76   D c
Meurs 117   E c
Meurthe, dept. 148   F e
Meuse, dept. 148   F e
Meuse River 62   C c
Mevania 27   G e
Mevaniola 27   F c
Mewar, dist. 137   B d
Mexicaltzinco . . . .
Mexican Plain 187   I f
Mexico 106   A a
Mexico, audiencia 213   C c
Mexico, viceroyalty, see New Spain
Mexico, country . . . . . . A — D a — c
Mexico, Gulf of 187   J f
Mexico, New, ter. 203   Q h
Meymac, mon. 94   C b
Mezen 167   N b
Mézières 69   J f
Miami 213   D b
Miami, Fort . . . .
Miami River 191   I d
Miamis, tribe 188   I b
Miana . . . .
Miani 170   H f
Miantonomo . . . . 189 ins. A
Michael, parl. bor. . . . . . .
Michaelovsk . . . .
Michigan, lake 187   K d
Michigan, state 202   H f
Michigan, ter. 1805 202   H b
Michigan, ter. 1818 203   T a
Michigan, ter. 1834 203   S a
Michigania, proposed state in
   U. S. . . . .

Michillimackinac, or
Michillimackinac 191   I
Michipicoten . . . .
Michipicoten River 188   J
Michmash 7   C
Michoacan, state 213   ins.
Mickleham, mon. 97   R
Micmacs, tribe 188   M
Middleburg, in Holland 117   D
Middelburg, Hanse. cv. . . . . 99 ins.
Middelburg, in Transvaal 175   M
Middelfart 88   C
Middle Angles, people 51   R
Middleborough . . . . . . 189 C d (Mid
Middle District, New South
   Wales 172   leg
Middle Empire, see Chagatai .
Middle March, dist. . . . .
Middle Plantation . . . . . . 193 ins.
Middle Saxons, people . . . . .
Middlesbrough 162   E
Middlesex, cty. . . . .
Middlesex, dist. . . . .
Mindlesex, parl. dist. . . . . .
Middletown 189   B
Midea 15   C
Midhurst, parl. bor. 163   N
Midi, Canal du 130   D
Midia 165   F
Midian, dist. 4   F
Midianites, people . . . . . . 7 ins.
Midnapur 137   E
Midway Islands 180   J
Midwout . . . . 189 ins.
Mien . . . .
Mien, reg. 109   A A
Mies 87   I
Mifflin, Fort 195   D
Migdol 4   ins.
Milan 90   B
Milan, abp. 95   D
Milan, duchy, 1395 78   F
Milan, duchy, 1494 90   B
Milan, duchy, 1796. 150   E
Milanese, The, dist., 1339–1402
           90   H-K g-h
Milassa (Miletus) . . . .
Milazzo 161   J
Milborne Post, parl. bor.
Mile End Meadow 75   I
Miletopolis . . . .
Miletus 20   B
Mileve 42   D
Milford, in Conn. 192   E
Milford, in New Jersey 192   D
Milford, in Wales 70   E
Milford Haven 84   A
Milhaud 76   E
Milhaud, viscty. 69   E
Milid (Maladieh) 5   C
Military boundary, 1806 109   G
Military Bounty Lands . . . . 196 ins. B
Military Frontier, Croatian, Sla-
   vonian and Banat . . . . . 159 H-L
Milk River 210   D
Milledgeville 208   D
Mille Lac, Ind. Res. 188   H
Millen 208   D
Millesimo 130   Q
Millikens Bend, point on Miss. R. 208   B
Mill Springs, battle 208   D
Miloslaw 159   I b
Miltenberg 142   D
Milton Abbas, mon. 97   O
Milvian Bridge 96   A
Milwaukee 199   H b
Milyana 73   A
Milyas, dist. 20   D
Milzienians, people 63   H
Mimate, see Mende
Mimigerniford, see Münster
Mims, Fort 200   I
Minagara 18   R
Minas 215   D

nas Geraes, state	214	E d
nas Novas	214	E d
nch, The, strait	49	C c
ncio River	150	F d
ncius (Mincio) River	26	E b
nda, see Minden		
ndanao, isl.	199 ins.	H
ndel River	143	J i
nden	62	E b
nden, bp.	95	D a
nden, Hanse, cy.	99 ins.	B
nden, princ.	122	E b
ndi		
ndoro, isl.	199 ins.	H
nehead, parl. bor.	163	K f
nerva, Temple of, on the Aventine Mt.	22	A
nerva, Temple of, in the Forum	24	B
nerva, Temple of, on Sunium Promontory	16	C b
nerva, prom.	30	D b
nerva Archegetis	23	D
nervæ, Castrum	31	H b
nervia, see Scolacium (Squillace)		
ngio	103	M e
ngrelia, reg.	164	G b
nhla	171	K g
ninho River	82	A a
ninibar, reg.		
ninieh	150	B b
ninio River	27	F e
ninius (Minho) River	38	A d
ninneapolis	199	G a
ninnesota, state	203	S f
ninnesota, ter.	202	F f
ninnesota River	198	F b
ninnith	7	D e
ninnodunum	39	I j
ninoa, in Laconia	15	D c
ninoa, on Siphnus I.		
ninoa, isl.		
ninor (Minorca), isl.	38	C d
ninorca, bp.	94	C d
ninorca, isl.	82	C b
ninsk	138	C e
ninthe, mt.	14	B b
ninturnæ	30	C a
ninucian Portico	22	A
ninyæ, people	11	D d
niquelon, isl.	212	J d
nirabel, in France	69	D d
nirabel, castle in Palestine	68 ins.	A
niraflores, in Panamá		
niraflores, in Perú	214	B d
niramichi Bay	212	I d
niranda	214	D e
niranda de Corvo	82	G e
niranda do Douro	83	J g
niranda de Ebro	82	B a
nirande, in France	126	B e
nirandola	90	J h
niravet	82	C a
nirbat	170	G g
nirebeau	69	H g
nirebeau, castle	76	D c
nirepoix	76	D e
nirepoix, bp.	94	C c
nirepoix, seign.	76	D e
nirim, lake	215	D f
niriquidi, mts.	63	G c
niró, District of	196 B c (C. D.)	
niscus River		
nisenum, harbor of	31 ins.	A
nisenum, prom.	30	C b
nishawum	189 ins.	A
nisiones, dist.	215	D e
niskolcz	159	K d
niso River	27	H d
nisquamicut	189 ins.	A
nissanabie River		
nissema	6	E b
nissenden, mon.	97	Q j

Missinnippi River	186	I c
Mission Indian Reservation	188	C d
Missionary Ridge, battle	208	C c
Mississippi, state	203	U d
Mississippi, ter.	202	H d
Mississippi River	191	G e
Mississippi River, Delta of the	187	J f
Mississippi Valley	187	J d
Missolonghi	164	C c
Missouri, state	203	F c
Missouri, ter. 1812	203	Q a
Missouri, ter. 1819	203	Q b
Missouri Plateau	186	I d
Missouri River	187	J d
Missouri River, Little	198	E a
Missouria, Ind. Res.	188	G c
Missouris, tribe	188	G c
Missunde	158	E a
Mistassini, lake	212	H c
Mistra	89	B c
Mistra, desp.	93	B c
Mitau	88	J c
Mitchell, Fort	211	H d
Mitchell, mt.	187	K e
Mitchell, parl. bor.	163	I g
Mitchell River	172	N b
Mithradates VI., Kingdom of	33	leg.
Mitla	213	C c
Mitrovitza, in Slavonia	9	
Mitrovitza, in Turkey		
Mittelmark, dist.	85	C b
Mitys River	11	D b
Mizpah, N. of Jerusalem	7	C e
Mizpah, W. of Jerusalem	7	B e
Mizpah, mt.		
Mizpah, Valley of	6	D a
Mizquiz		
Mława	155	K b
Moab, dist.	7	D f
Moabites, people	7 ins.	D
Moapa River, Ind. Res.	188	C c
Mobar, reg.		
Mobile	191	H e
Mobile Bay	191	H e
Mocha	174	H c
Möckern, near Leipsic	154	G c
Möckern, near Magdeburg	154	G b
Möckmühl	143	H g
Mocsa	159	J e
Modbury, parl. bor.		
Modder River	175	M l
Modena	90	J h
Modena, bp.	95	E c
Modena, duchy	90	C b
Modicia	26	D b
Modigliana	90	L i
Modin	7	C e
Modlin	155	K b
Modocs, tribe	188	B b
Modon		
Modrush, bp.		
Möen, isl.	115	G a
Mœnus (Main) River	38	D b
Mœris, lake	4 ins.	*
Mœsia, reg.	47	K e
Mœsia, Lower, imp. prov.	35	J e
Mœsia, Upper, imp. prov.	35	I e
Mœsia I, East Roman prov.	43	F e (2.)
Mœsia II, East Roman prov.	43	H e (5.)
Mogadisho	175	H d
Mogador	174	B a
Mogaung		
Möggingen	142	D e
Moghan, plain	99	M f
Moghilev		
Mogul Empire in 1700	137	leg.
Mogontia or Mogontiacum (Mayence)	39	J i
Mohammed Artin, Dom. of	77	L e
Mohammed II., mosque	93	G e
Mohammedans	67 ins., leg.	
Mohave, Mojave	210	B d
Mohave, Fort	188	D c
Mohaves, Mojaves, tribe	188	C d

Mohawk River	192	D b
Mohawks, tribe	188	L b
Mohegans, tribe	188	L b
Mohi	92	C c
Möhra	114	F c
Möhringen	143	H h
Mohrungen	155	J b
Moidart		
Moissac, mon.	94	C c
Mola	90	F d
Moldau River	63	H d
Moldavia, dist. 19 cent.	164	D a
Moldavia, princ. 16 cent.	119	J d
Moldavia, reg., 14 cent.	77	J c
Moldavia, reg., 18 cent.	131	I d
Mole River	75	I i
Molesme, mon.	94	C b
Molina	83	K g
Molina, barony	83	K g
Molino del Rey, battle	201	H g
Molinos, R.	106	B b
Molise, dist.	90	E d
Mollendo	214	B d
Mollwitz	135	I c
Molodechno	153	N g
Molokai, isl.	198 ins.	B
Molopo River	175	E g
Molossi, people		
Molossis, dist.	10	B c
Moluccas, isl.	112	F d
Molycria	10	C d
Mombasa	175	H e
Momemphis	8	B b*
Mömpelgard	143 ins.	F
Mömpelgard, cty., see Montbéliard	86	F e
Mömpelgard, princ. cty.	143 ins.	F
Mompos	214	B b
Mona (Anglesey), isl.	51	N h
Mona, isl., West Indies	105	G c
Monaco	90	A c
Monaco, princ.	161	F f
Mona Passage, str.	213	F c
Monaghan, cty.	127	K g
Monapia (Isle of Man)	51	N g
Monastir	164	C b
Moncalieri	130	P j
Monchique	83	J h
Monclova	213	B b
Moncontour	76	D c
Moncton	212	I d
Mondego River	82	G e
Mondoñedo	82	A a
Mondoñedo, bp.	94	A c
Mondovi	90	H h
Mandovi, bp.	95	D c
Mondsee, mon.	95	E b
Monemvasia	89	B c
Monflanquin	126	B d
Monforte, mon.	94	A c
Monghyr, Mongheer	137	E c
Mongolia, reg.	92	K c
Mongols, Khanate of the		
Mongols, people		
Monhegan Island	189	D c
Monilia	26	D c
Monk-Bretton, mon.	97	P h
Monkey Hill, village	216	
Monk Sherborne, mon.	100	A a
Monks Corner	195	B g
Monkton Farleigh, mon.	97	O j
Monmouth, in England		
Monmouth, cty.	127	W o
Monmouth, parl. bor.	163	L f
Monmouth, parl. dist.	163	K f
Monmouth, in New Jersey	195	D c
Monnikendam	117	D b
Monocacy River	208 ins.	
Monœcus (Monaco)	26	B d
Monongahela River	192	A d
Monopoli	90	F d
Monos, tribe	188	C c
Mon Plaisir, farm		
Monreale, abp.	95	E d

Monroe, Fortress . . . . 208 E b
Monrovia . . . . 174 B d
Mons, in Hainaut . . . . . . 117 C d
Mons Brisiacus (Breisach) . . . 39 I i
Mons Casinus, see Monte Cassino
Monserrate, isl. . . . . 105 H c
Mons Ferrandus, castle . . . . 68 C c
Mons Gaudii, mt. . . . . 96 A
Mons Regalis, see Montreal, in
  Syria . . . . 68 C c
Montacute, parl. bor. . . . .
Montafon Valley . . . . 91 R k
Montaigu . . . . 69 C c
Montaigu, seign. . . . . 69 C c
Montalcino, bp. . . . . . 95 E c (Mo.)
Montana, ter. 1864 . . . . . . 203 P f
Montana, state . . . . 203 P f
Montaperto . . . . 90 L j
Montargis . . . . 69 I f
Montauban . . . . 76 D d
Montauban bp. . . . . 94 C c
Montauban, gen. . . . . 147 E c
Montbard . . . . 69 J f
Montbéliard, cty. . . . . . . 143 ins. F
Montbéliard, cty. . . . . 86 F e
Montbéliard, princ.-cty. . . . 143 ins. F
Mont Blanc, mt. . . . . 2 E d
Montbrison . . . . 69 E d
Mont Cenis Pass . . . . 130 O i
Montcontour . . . . 118 D d
Mont-de-Marsan . . . . 148 D f
Montdidier . . . . 126 C b
Montebello . . . . 150 E d
Montebourg, mon. . . . . 94 B b
Montecarlo, near Pisa . . . . 90 L j
Monte Cassino . . . . 64 B b
Monte Cassino, bp. . . . . . . 95 E c
Monte Cassino, mon. . . . . . 95 E c
Montechiaro, near Asti . . . . 130 Q f
Montechiaro, near Brescia . . 90 J h
Montefeltro . . . . 64 B b
Monteleone . . . . 161 K h
Montélimart . . . . 126 D d
Monte Mario . . . . 96 A
Montemór, near Coimbra . . . 82 A a
Montemór, near Evora . . . 83 J h
Montendre . . . . 126 A d
Montenegro, princ. . . . . . . 164 B b
Montenegro, reg. . . . . 93 A b
Montenotte . . . . 150 E d
Monte Nuovo, mt. . . . . . . 31 ins. A
Montepulciano . . . . 90 L j
Montereau . . . . 154 B d
Monterey, in California . . . 198 A c
Monterey, in Mexico . . . . . 201 E d
Monterey, in Pa. . . . . . . 208 ins.
Monte Rosa, mt. . . . . 2 E d
Monte Santo, town . . . . . . 214 F d
Montesha, reg. . . . . 77 J e
Montes Serrorum (Transylvanian
  Alps) . . . . 39 M k
Monte Testaccio . . . . 22 A
Montevideo . . . . 215 D f
Montfaucon, mon. . . . . 95 D b
Montferrat, marq. . . . . . . 90 B b
Montfort, in France . . . . .
Montfort, in Syria . . . . . 68 ins. A
Montfort, castle, in France . . 69 H f
Montfort, castle, in Vorarlberg 78 F e
Montfort, cty., in France . . 76 D b
Montfort, cty., in Swabia . . 143 I j
Mont Genèvre Pass . . . . . . 130 O j
Montgomery, in Alabama . . . 211 H d
Montgomery, in Wales . . . . 127 V n
Montgomery, castle . . . . . .
Montgomery, cty. . . . . 127 V n
Montgomery, parl. bor. . . . . 163 K e
Montgomery, parl. dist. . . . 163 K e
Montiel . . . . 83 K h
Montigny, mon. . . . . 148 C b
Montlaur . . . . 76 E d
Montlhéry . . . . 76 E b
Montlucon . . . . 69 I g
Montluel . . . . 130 N i

Montmartre, Faubourg, quarter
  in Paris . . . . 149 B
Montmartre, mt. . . . . 62 B d
Montmédy . . . . 126 D b
Montmirail, in Champagne . . . 154 B d
Montmirail, in Perche . . . . . 76 D b
Montmorency . . . . 69 I f (Montm.)
Montmorency, Falls of . . . . . 191 K b
Montpelier . . . . 211 K b
Montpellier . . . . 76 E e
Montpellier, gen. . . . . 147 E c
Montpellier, univ. . . . . . . 100 F f
Montpensier . . . . 76 E c
Montreal, in Canada . . . . . 189 B b
Montreal, in Syria . . . . . . 68 C c
Montreuil . . . . 61 D a
Montreuillon . . . . 69 I g
Montriond . . . . 62 D e
Montrose . . . .
Mont-Saint-Guibert . . . . . . 156 B a
Mont-Saint-Jean, farm . . . . .
Mont-Saint-Jean, village . . . .
Mont-Saint-Michel, mon. . . . 94 B b
Montserrat, isl. . . . . 213 F c
Montserrat, mon. . . . . 94 C c
Monza . . . . 90 I h
Mook . . . . 117 D c
Mooltan . . . . 137 B b
Moon, Gate of the, in Alexan-
  dria . . . . 34 ins. C
Moon, Temple of the, in Rome 24 B
Moore, Fort . . . . 193 ins. C
Moore, lake . . . . 172 A c
Moorfields, in London . . . . 75 G g
Moorgate, in London . . . . . 75 G g
Moorish States, in Spain . . . 82 B a
Moors, people, in Spain . . . 57 C f
Moorshedabad . . . . 137 E d
Moose Factory . . . . 212 G c
Moose Jaw, post . . . . 212 E c
Moose River . . . . 212 G c
Mopsium . . . . 11 D c
Mopsuestia, Mopsuhestia . . . 20 F d
Moquegua . . . . 214 B d
Moqui, Ind. Res. . . . . 188 D c
Moquis, tribe . . . . 188 D c
Mor . . . . 159 J e
Mora . . . . 88 F a
Moradabad . . . . 137 C c
Morat . . . . 91 P l
Morava River . . . . 119 I e
Moravia, march, about 1000 . . 59 H d
Moravia, march, 12 cent. . . . 72 D b
Moravian Kingdom, 9 cent. . . 56 F c
Moravians, people, about 900 . 57 G d
Moray, bp. . . . . 97 I b
Moray, dist. . . . .
Moray Firth . . . . 49 E c
Morbegno . . . . 91 R l
Morbihan, dept. . . . . 148 D e
Mordvins, people . . . . 139 G e
Morea Peninsula . . . . 2 G c
Morecambe Bay . . . . 127 V m
Morelia . . . . 213 ins.
Morella . . . . 82 B a
Morelos, state . . . . 213 ins.
Moresby Island . . . . 172 E b
Moreton . . . . 172 D b
Moreton Bay . . . . 172 K c
Moreton Bay District . . . . 172 leg.
Morgan, Fort . . . . 208 C c
Morgan, route of . . . . 195 A f
Morgantina . . . . 30 D b
Morgantown . . . . 206 ins.
Morgarten . . . . 91 Q k
Moriah, mt. . . . . 68 ins. B
Moril . . . . 91 Q l
Morimont, mon. . . . . 148 C b
Morini, see Thérouanne
Morini, people . . . . 38 C b
Moritz, Fort . . . . 214 F d
Mornington Island . . . . . . 172 C b
Morocco . . . . 174 C a
Morocco, reg., 14 cent. . . . . 77 C f

Morocco, state, 16 cent. . . . . 118 C
Morocco, state, 20 cent. . . . 174 C
Morón . . . . 82 A
Morontobara . . . . 19 K
Morpeth, parl. bor. . . . . . 163 M
Morristown . . . . 195 D
Mortagne . . . . 61 D
Mortain . . . . 69 C
Mortain, cty. . . . . 69 C
Mortara . . . . 130 Q
Mortemer, mon. . . . . . . 94 C b (Mor
Mortes River . . . . 214 D
Mortimers Cross . . . . 84 B
Mosa (Meuse) River . . . . . . 38 D
Mosbach . . . . 142 D
Mosbach, Palatine, princ. . . . 87 H
Moschi, people . . . . 35 M
Moscow 138
Moscow, princ. . . . . 77 L
Moscow, gov. . . . . 131 K
Mosella (Moselle) River . . . . 38 F
Moselle, dept. . . . . 148 F
Moselle River . . . . 62 D
Moskva River . . . . 153 P
Mosomagus . . . . 39 H
Mosquito Coast . . . . 213 D
Moss . . . . 131 F
Mossámedes . . . . 175 E
Mostar . . . . 93 A
Mosul . . . . 67 O
Mosul, Dominion of . . . . . . 67 O
Mosyr . . . . 167 K
Motola . . . . 90 F
Motrone . . . . 90 L
Mottisfont, priory . . . . . . 100 E
Motupe . . . . 111 B
Motyca . . . . 30 D
Motye . . . . 30 B
Moulins . . . . 76 E
Moulins, gen. . . . . 147 E
Moulmein . . . . 171 K
Moultrie, Fort . . . . 195 B
Mount Desert Island . . . . . 189 D
Mount Gambier, town . . . . . 172 C
Mount Grace, mon. . . . . 97 P
Mount Hope, town . . . . . 189 ins. A
Mount Majella, mon. . . . . . . 95 E
Mount of Offense . . . . . . 6 ins. A
Mount of Olives . . . . 6 ins. A
Mount Sinai, mon. of . . . . . 150 B
Mount Vernon, town . . . . . . 193 D
Mount Wollaston, village . . . 189 C
Mount Zion, Street of . . . . 68 ins. B
Moura . . . . 83 J
Moureille, mon. . . . . 94 B
Mouse River, see Souris River
Moutier-Ramey, mon. . . . . 94 C b (M. R
Moutiers . . . . 130 O
Mouzon . . . . 76 F
Mouzon, mon. . . . . 95 D
Moyobamba . . . . 214 B
Moys . . . . 135 H
Mozambique . . . . 175 H
Mozambique, see Portuguese
  East Africa
Mozambique Channel . . . . . . 175 H
Mozhaisk . . . . 138 E
Mozufferpore . . . . 137 D
Mpapwa . . . . 175 G
Muchelney, mon. . . . . 97 O
Much Wenloch, parl. bor. . . . 163 L
Muckleshoot, Ind. Res. . . . . 188 B
Mudki . . . . 170 I
Mugonian Gate . . . . 24 A
Mühlberg . . . . 115 G
Mühldorf . . . . 79 H
Mühlenbach . . . . 159 L
Mühlhausen, in Thuringia . . . 62 F
Mühlhausen, in Thuringia, imp.
  cy. . . . . 79 G
Mühlheim, on the Danube R . . 143 G
Muiden . . . . 117 D
Muir Glacier . . . . 212 B

Mukden . . . . 171 N d
Mukdishu . . . . 175 H d
Mula . . . . 82 B b
Mulde River . . . . 85 G e
Mülhausen, in Alsace, imp. cy. 78 E f
Mul-Java (Malacca), pen. . . . .
Mull, isl. . . . .
Multan . . . . 137 B b
Mulucha River . . . . 38 B e
Müncheberg . . . . 80 ins.
München, see Munich
Münchengrätz . . . . 159 H c
Müdnen . . . . 134 E c
Munderkingen . . . . 143 I i
Munich . . . . 72 C b
Munkacs . . . . 131 H d
Münsingen . . . . 143 I i
Munster, in Ireland, prov. . . .
Münster, in Alsace . . . . . . 126 E b
Münster, in Bp. of Basel . . . . 91 P k
Münster, in Westphalia . . . . 62 D c
Münster, bp. . . . . 78 E c
Münster, Hanse. cy. . . . . . 99 ins. B
Münsterberg . . . . 79 J c
Münsterberg, princ. . . . . . . 79 J c
Münster Thal, valley . . . . . 91 S l
Munychia, dist. . . . . 16 D c
Munychia Port . . . . 16 D c
Muota Tal, valley . . . . 150 E c
Mur River . . . . 63 I e
Muranum . . . . 31 F c
Murat, viscty. . . . . 69 E d
Murbach, ab. . . . . 78 E e
Murbach, mon. . . . . 95 D b
Murbogi, people . . . . 38 B d
Murchison River . . . . 172 A c
Murcia . . . . 82 B b
Murcia, bp. . . . . 94 B d
Murcia, Km. . . . . 83 K h
Muret . . . . 76 D e
Murfreesboro . . . . 208 C b
Murg River . . . . 142 B c
Murshidabad . . . . 137 E d
Muri, mon. . . . . 91 Q k
Murom . . . . '. 138 F d
Murr River . . . . 143 H d
Murray River . . . . 172 D d
Murrays, fam. . . . . 97 I c
Murrhardt . . . . 143 I h
Murrumbidgee River . . . . . 172 D d
Mursa . . . . 42 F d
Murten . . . . 91 P l
Murus (Mur) River . . . . . . 38 E c
Murviedro . . . . 82 B b
Musarna . . . . 19 J d
Muscat . . . .
Musciacus, see Moissac
Muscle Shoals . . . . 196 B d
Muscovite Dominions, 16 cent. 119 K b
Muscovy, reg. . . . . 109 U b
Musgrave Range . . . . 172 C c
Musha Islands . . . . 174 H c
Mushki, people . . . . 5 C b
Muskingum River . . . . . . 196 ins. B
Muskingum, tribe . . . . . . 188 J c
Muspa, Punta de, cape . . . . 191 I f
Mussidan . . . . 126 B d
Mussumba . . . . 175 F e
Musulami, people . . . . . . 38 D e
Mutapili . . . .
Muthul River . . . . 38 D e
Mutilum . . . . 27 G c
Mutina (Modena) . . . . . . 26 E c
Muttra . . . . 170 I f
Muwahhids, Dom of the . . . . 73 C d
Muzaffarpur . . . . 137 D c
Muzon, Cape . . . . 212 ins.
Mweru, lake . . . . 175 F e
Mycale, mt. . . . . 13 E c
Mycalessus . . . . 11 E d
Mycenæ . . . . 15 C b
Mycenean Greece . . . . . . 4 B b
Mygdonia, dist., in Macedonia 11 D b
Mygdonia, dist., in Mesopotamia 20 I d

Mykonos . . . . 13 D c
Mylæ, in Sicily . . . . 30 E d
Mylæ, in Thessaly . . . . . . 10 D c
Mylasa . . . . 17 E c
Myndus . . . . 17 E c
Mynyw (Saint Davids) . . . . 60 D e
Myonia . . . . 11 D d
Myonnesus . . . . 20 B b
Myra . . . . 20 D d
Myrcinus . . . . 11 E b
Myriandrus . . . . 18 E c
Myrina . . . . 17 E b
Myrmex . . . . 34 ins. C
Myrrhinus . . . . 16 B b
Myrtea . . . . 9 D c
Myrto, isl. . . . . 15 E b
Myrtoum Sea . . . . 15 D b
Myrtuntium . . . . 14 B b
Myrtuntium, lake . . . . . . 10 B d
Mysia, Macedonian prov. . . . 18 C c
Mysia, Rom. prov. . . . . . 20 B c
Mysia, reg. . . . . 8 G e
Mysore . . . . 137 C f
Mysore, reg. . . . . 137 C f
Mystic . . . . 189 C d
Mystic River . . . . 189 ins. B
Mytilene . . . .
Mytilene, isl. . . . .
Myus . . . . 13 E c

Naarath . . . . 7 C e
Naarden . . . . 117 D b
Naas . . . . 127 K h
Naauw Poort . . . . 175 L m
Nab River . . . . 63 G d
Nabatæi, people . . . . . . 35 L h
Nabburg . . . . 63 G d
Nablus, see Neapolis . . . . 68 ins. A
Nachod . . . . 159 C c
Nacogdoches . . . . 191 G e
Nadjivan . . . . 99 M f
Nævian Gate . . . . 23 B
Näfels . . . . 91 R k
Nagasaki . . . . 171 N e
Nagold . . . . 143 G h
Nagold River . . . . 143 G h
Nagpur, Nagpore . . . . . 137 C d
Nagpur, state . . . . 170 I f
Nagy-Kanizsa . . . . 159 I e
Nagy Sallo . . . . 159 J d
Nahe River . . . . 62 D d
Naimans, people . . . . . .
Nain, in Galilee . . . . . . 6 C c
Nain, in Labrador . . . . . 212 I c
Nairi, people . . . .
Nairn, cty. . . . .
Naissus . . . . 39 M l
Nájera . . . . 82 B a
Nakel . . . . 63 I b
Namaqualand, Great, dist. . . 175 E g
Namnetes, see Nantes
Namnetes, people . . . . . 38 B c
Namnetum, isl. . . . . . . 38 B c
Namnetum, Portus (Nantes) . 38 B c
Namoi River . . . . 172 D d
Namugum, see Namur
Namur . . . . 117 C d
Namur, cty. . . . . 117 C d
Nan-chan-fu . . . .
Nancy . . . . 84 G e
Nandurbar . . . .
Nangis . . . . 154 B d
Nanipacna . . . . 191 H e
Nanking . . . .
Nanrantsouck Mission . . . . 189 D b
Nansemond River . . . . . 193 ins. A
Nantasket . . . . 189 ins. B
Nantes . . . . 61 C c
Nantes, bp. . . . . 94 B b
Nantes, cty. . . . . 69 C c
Nantes, univ. . . . . 100 E e
Nanteuil, mon. . . . . . . 94 B b
Nanticoke River . . . . . 192 D d
Nanticokes, tribe . . . . . 188 K b

Nantuates, people . . . . . . 26 A a
Nantucket, isl. . . . . 189 D d
Nantwich . . . . 127 W m
Napata (Jebel Barkal) . . . . 4 F e'
Naphtali, Mountains of . . . . 6 C c
Naphtali, tribe . . . . 7 ins. D*
Napier . . . . 172 G e
Naples . . . . 90 E d
Naples, abp. . . . . 95 E c
Naples, Bay of . . . . 30 D b
Naples, km., 14 cent. . . . . 81 I d
Naples, km., 16 cent. . . . . 119 H e
Naples, km., 1812 . . . . . . 152 E c
Naples, theme . . . . 58 G e
Naples, univ. . . . . 100 H f
Napo River . . . . 111 B b
Napoca . . . . 35 I d
Napoleonshöhe, castle . . 154 E c (N.)
Nar River . . . . 27 H e
Naragarra . . . . 38 C c
Narbada River . . . . 137 C d
Narbata . . . . 6 B c
Narbo Martius (Narbonne) . . . 38 C d
Narbonensis, Rom. prov. . . 38 D d (6)
Narbonne . . . . 61 E e
Narbonne, abp. . . . . 94 C c
Narbonne, viscty. . . . . . . 76 E e
Narbonnensis I, West Rom.
    prov. . . . . 42 C e (13)
Narbonnensis II, West Rom.
    prov. . . . . 42 D e (14)
Narew River . . . . 87 M b
Narni . . . . 90 D c
Narnia . . . . 27 G e
Narona . . . . 38 F d
Narova River . . . . 88 L b
Narragansett Bay . . . . . . 189 ins. A
Narragansetts, tribe . . . . . 189 ins. A
Narthacius, mt. . . . . 11 D c
Narva . . . . 88 M b
Narva, Hanse. cy. . . . . . . 99 I b
Narvaez, route of . . . . . . 191 I f
Naseby . . . . 127 Y n
Nashboro . . . . 194 B c
Nashua . . . . 211 K b
Nashville . . . . 199 H c
Nasium . . . . 39 H i
Nasos, quarter in Syracuse . . 31 ins. B
Nass River . . . . 212 ins.
Nassau, Bahama Is. . . . . . 213 E b
Nassau, in Germany . . . . . 72 B a
Nassau, cty. . . . . 78 F c
Nassau, duchy . . . . 154 E c
Nassau, princ. . . . . 122 E c
Nassau, Fort, in New York . . 192 E b
Nassau, Fort in Pa. . . . . . 192 ins.
Natal . . . . 214 F c
Natal, col. . . . . 175 N l
Natchez . . . . 208 D c
Natchez, tribe . . . . 188 H d
Natchitoches . . . . 191 G e
Natick . . . . 189 C d
Natiso River . . . . 27 H b
Natuna, isl. . . . .
Nauen . . . . 85 C b
Naugard . . . . 155 H b
Naukratis . . . . 1 B b
Naulinco . . . . 106 C a
Naulochus . . . . 30 E d
Naumachia of Augustus . . . . 22 A
Naumburg . . . . 63 F c
Naumburg, bp. . . . . 95 E a
Naumkeag . . . . 189 ins. B
Naupactus . . . . 10 C d
Nauplia . . . . 15 C b
Nauportus . . . . 27 I b
Nautaca . . . . 19 K c
Nauvoo . . . . 211 G b
Nava River . . . . 39 I i
Navajo, Ind. Res. . . . . . . 188 E c
Navajos, tribe . . . . 188 E c
Navalia (shipyards in Rome) . . 22 A
Navalia River . . . . 39 I g
Navari, people . . . . 35 J d

Navarre, dist. . . . . 56 B d
Navarre, km. . . . . 82 H e
Navarre and Béarn, km. . . . 126 A e
Navarrete . . . . 83 K g
Navas de Tolosa, Las . . . . 83 K h
Navidad . . . . 105 F c
Navigator Islands . . . . . . 180 K i
Nawsett . . . . 189 D d
Naxos . . . . 13 D c
Naxos, duchy . . . . 89 C c
Naxos, isl. . . . . 13 D c
Naxua . . . . 99 M f
Naxus
Nay . . . . 126 A e
Nazareth, in Palestine . . . . 6 C c
Nazareth, abp. in Italy . . 95 F c
Nazas, Rio de, R. . . . . 213 B b
Nazianzus . . . . 20 F c
Nazli . . . . 165 F d
Neæ, isl. . . . .
Neæthus (Neto) River . . . . 31 F c
Neagh, lough, lake . . . . 49 C d
Neapel, see Naples
Neapolis, in Africa . . . . . 38 E e
Neapolis, in Apulia . . . . 31 G a
Neapolis, in Campania (Naples) 30 D b
Neapolis, in Chalcidice . . . 11 E b
Neapolis, in Istria . . . . . 27 H b
Neapolis, in Macedonia . . . . 11 F b
Neapolis, in Palestine . . . . 7 C d
Neapolis, in Sardinia . . . . . 38 D e
Neapolis, quarter in Syracuse . 31 ins. B
Nearchus, route of . . . . . . 19 H e
Neath, mon. . . . . 97 N j
Nebbio . . . . 148 C c
Nebelhöhle . . . . 143 H i
Nebo, mt. . . . . 7 D e
Nebouzan, reg. . . . . 146 B f
Nebraska City . . . . . . 206 F b
Nebraska, state . . . . . . 203 R g
Nebraska, ter. 1854 . . . . . 202 C f
Nebraska, ter. 1861 . . . . . 203 Q g
Nebraska, ter. 1863 . . . . . 203 R g
Nebrodes Mountains . . . . 30 D e
Necessity, Fort . . . . . . 192 B d
Neckar River . . . . 62 E d
Neckar-Bischofsheim . . . . 142 C b
Neckargemünd . . . . . . 142 C b
Neckarsulm . . . . 143 H g
Necropolis, dist. . . . . . 16 D c
Nectansmere . . . .
Neda River . . . . . . 14 B b
Nedad River . . . . . . 50 G c
Nedjed, reg. . . . . . .
Nedjef . . . .
Nedon River . . . . . . 14 C b
Neerwinden . . . . 122 C c
Neetum . . . . 30 E e
Negapatam . . . . . . 137 D f
Nègrepelisse . . . . . . 126 B d
Negro, Cabo, cape . . . . 108 R i
Negropont, isl. . . . . . . 89 H g
Negros, isl. . . . . . . 199 ins. H
Neidenburg . . . . 115 K b
Neïus, mt. . . . . 10 B d
Neipperg . . . . 143 H g
Neisse . . . . 115 I c
Neisse River, Glatzer. . . . . 63 I c
Neisse River, Görlitzer . . . 63 H c
Neiva . . . . 214 B b
Nelea . . . . 11 E c
Neleus River . . . . . . 11 E d
Nellenburg, castle . . . . 142 C e
Nellenburg, landgr. . . . . . 142 C e
Nellore . . . . 137 D f
Nelson, in Alberta . . . . 212 D d
Nelson, in New Zealand . . . . 172 G e
Nelson, Fort . . . . 212 C c
Nelson River . . . . . . 186 J c
Nemara . . . . 6 F c
Nemausus (Nimes) . . . . . 38 C d
Nemea . . . . 15 C b
Nemetacus, see Arras
Nemetes, see Spires

Nemetes, people . . . . 39 I i
Nemorensis, lake . . . . . . 35 ins. B
Nemossus . . . . 38 C c
Nemours . . . . 69 I f
Nemours, duchy . . . . . . 84 E e
Nen River . . . . 127 Y n
Neocæsarea . . . . 20 G b
Neosho River . . . . 198 F c
Nepal, Nepaul, state . . . . . 171 J f
Nepete . . . . 27 G e
Nepi, bp. . . . . 95 E c
Nepomuk, mon. . . . . 95 E b
Neponset River . . . . . . 189 ins. B
Nepos, Dom. of emperor . . . 50 G d
Neptune, Basilica of . . . . 22 A
Neptune, Mts. of . . . . . . 30 E d
Neptune, Temple of . . . . . 34 ins. C (8)
Neptunia, Colonia (Taranto) . . 31 G b
Nequinum . . . . 27 G e
Nérac . . . . 126 B d
Nerbudda River . . . . . . 137 C d
Neresheim . . . . 143 J h
Neresheim, ab. . . . . . . 143 J h
Neretum . . . . 31 G b
Neris . . . . 14 C b
Néritus, mt. . . . . 10 B d
Nerium, prom. . . . . . . 38 A d
Nero, Aqueduct of. . . . . . 22 A
Nero, Baths of . . . . 22 A
Nero, Circus of . . . . . . 22 A
Nero, Colossus of . . . . . 24 B
Nero, Villa of . . . . . . 22 A
Neronian Meadows . . . . . 96 A
Nerós house, in Olympia . . . .
Nertchinsk . . . .
Nertobriga . . . . 38 B d
Nerulum . . . . 31 F c
Nerva, Forum of . . . . . . 24 B
Nervii, people . . . . . . 38 C b
Nesactium . . . . 27 H c
Nesis, isl. . . . . 31 ins. A
Nesle . . . . 69 I f
Ness, loch, lake . . . . . . 49 D c
Nesselwang . . . . 114 F e
Nessonis, lake . . . . . . 11 D c
Nestorians, sect . . . . . 67 X m
Nestus River . . . . . . 11 F b
Netherlands, Austrian, prov. . . 134 B c
Netherlands, Kingdom of the . 158 C c
Netherlands, Spanish, prov. . . 122 B c
Netherlands, The, reg. . . . 117
Netherlands, United, country . 122 C b
Netley, ab. . . . . 100 A b
Netolitz . . . . 63 G d
Netze District . . . . 135 I b
Netze River . . . . 63 I b
Neu-Brandenburg . . . . . . 123 G b
Neubreisach . . . . 154 D e
Neuburg . . . . 62 F d
Neuburg, palat. . . . . . . 122 F d
Neuburg, princ. . . . . . 134 F d
Neuchâtel . . . . 91 O l
Neuchâtel, dist. . . . . . . 91 O l
Neuchâtel, lake . . . . . . 91 O l
Neuchâtel, princ. . . . . . 151 K j
Neudenau . . . . 142 D b
Neuenburg, in Baden . . . . 142 A e
Neuenburg, in Switzerland . . 91 O l
Neuenburg, (Neuchâtel) princ. . 134 D e
Neuenstadt . . . . 143 H g
Neuenstein . . . . 143 I g
Neufchâteau . . . . 117 D e
Neuffen . . . . 143 H h
Neufra . . . . 143 H i
Neuhaldensleben . . . . . . 122 F b
Neuhaus . . . . 154 F b
Neuhäusel . . . . 131 G d
Neukamp . . . . 123 G a
Neumark, dist. . . . . . . 85 D b
Neumarkt, in Bavaria . . . . 154 F d
Neumarkt, in Galicia . . . . 135 K d
Neumarkt, in Styria . . . . . 135 H e
Neumünster . . . . 72 B a
Neuquen . . . . 215 C f

Neu-Ravensburg . . . . 143 I j
Neu-Ruppin . . . . 158 G b
Neu-Sandec . . . . 159 K d
Neusatz . . . . 159 J f
Neuse River . . . . . . 193 F d
Neusohl . . . . 159 J d
Neuss . . . . 62 D c
Neuss, Hanse. cy. . . . . . 99 ins. B
Neustadt, in the Black Forest . 142 B e
Neustadt, on the Hardt . . . 142 B b
Neustadt, in Moravia . . . . . 135 I d
Neustadt, on the Orla . . . . 114 F c
Neustadtl . . . . 123 H f
Neu-Stettin . . . . 123 I b
Neu-Strelitz . . . . 123 G b
Neustria, reg. . . . . . . 54 E d
Neutra . . . . 72 D b
Neutra, bp. . . . . 95 F b
Neutra River . . . . . . 159 J d
Neuzelle, mon. . . . . . . 80 ins.
Neva, lake . . . . 71 M a
Nevada, state . . . . . . 203 O h
Nevada, ter. . . . . . . 203 O g
Nevada, Sierra, mts. . . . . 187 H e
Nevado de Tolima, mt. . . . 214 C c
Neve . . . . 6 E c
Nevers . . . . 61 E c
Nevers, bp. . . . . 94 C b
Nevers, cty. . . . . 61 E c
Nevilles Cross . . . .
Nevirnum, see Nevers
Nevis, isl. . . . . 213 F c
New Albany . . . . 211 H c
New Abbey of Saint Mary of
Grace Cisterciana . . . . . 75 G g
New Amstel . . . . 192 ins.
New Amsterdam, in Dutch Gui-
ana . . . . 214 D b
New Amsterdam (New York) . 189 ins. C
New Amsterdam Island . . . . 182 II k
New Andalusia, reg. . . . . . 105 E e
Newark, in England . . . . 74 E e
Newark, parl. bor. . . . . . 163 N d
Newark, in New Jersey . . . . 192 D c
New Athens . . . . 23 D
New Aurelian Gate . . . . 22 A
New Bedford . . . . . . 211 K b
New Berne, Newbern . . . .
New Biscay, prov. . . . . . 190 D f
Newborough, parl. bor. . . .
New Breisach . . . . 134 D e
New Brunswick, in New Jersey 192 D c
New Brunswick, col. . . . . 212 I d
Newburgh, in New York . . . 195 D c
Newburgh, mon. in England . . 97 P g
Newburn . . . . 127 X k
Newbury, in England . . . . 127 X o
Newbury, parl. bor. . . . .
Newbury, in Mass. . . . . . 189 C c
New Caledonia, isl. . . . . . 172 F c
New Caledonia, reg. . . . . 212 C c
New Carthage (Cartagena) . . . 38 B e
New Castle, (Newcastle), in De-
laware . . . . 192 D d
Newcastle, New South Wales . 172 E d
Newcastle-on-Tyne . . . . . 65 F c
Newcastle, parl. bor. . . . . 163 M b
Newcastle - under - Lyme, parl.
bor. . . . . 163 L d
New Castile, km., in Spain . . 83 K h
New Castile (Peru), reg. . . . .
New Claudian Way . . . . 27 H e
New East Prussia, dist. . . . 138 K e
New Elfsborg, Fort . . . . . 192 ins.
New England Colonies, The . . 189
New England Confederation,
see . . . . 189 leg.
New England Range . . . . 172 E d
Newenham, mon. in Bedford . 97 Q i
Newenham, mon. in Devon . . 97 N k
New Estremadura (Chile), reg. 108 J k
New Estremadura, prov. in
Mexico . . . . 190 E f
New Forest, The . . . . . . 49 F i

Newfoundland, col. . . . . . . 212 I c
New France, reg. . . . . . 191 I c K b
New Galicia, prov. . . . .
Newgate, loc. in London . . . 75 G g
New Gothenburg, Fort . . . . 192 ins.
New Granada, reg. . . . . . . 108 J g
New Granada, viceroyalty . . 215 ins.
New Guinea, isl. . . . . . . 110 F F h
New Hampshire, col. . . . . 189 C c
New Hampshire, state . . . . 199 K b
New Harmony . . . . 206 ins.
New Haven, in Conn. . . . . 189 B d
Newhaven, in England . . . 185 G g
New Haven, col. . . . . . . 189 B d
New Hebrides, isl. . . . . . 172 F b
New Inverness . . . . 193 ins. C
New Jersey, col. . . . . . . 192 D c
New Jersey, East, col. . . . . 192 D c
New Jersey, West, col. . . . 192 D d
New Jersey, state . . . . . . 199 K c
New Korsholm, Fort . . . . . 192 ins.
New León, prov. . . . . . . 190 E f
New London . . . . 189 B d
New Madrid . . . . 208 C b
Newmarket . . . . 127 Z n
New Mecklenburg, isl. . . . . 179 G h
New Mexico, prov. . . . . . 190 D e
New Mexico, ter. 1850 . . . . 202 C h
New Mexico, ter. 1863 . . . . 203 Q h
Newminster, mon. . . . . . . 97 P f
New Netherland, col. . . . . 192 D c
New Norcia . . . . 172 A d
New Norfolk . . . . 172 D e
New Orleans . . . . 191 G f
New Park, dist. . . . . 210 D b
New Philippines, prov. . . . . 190 F e
New Plymouth, col. . . . . . 189 C d
New Plymouth, in New Zealand 172 G d
New Pomerania, isl. . . . . . 172 E a
Newport, parl. bor. in Cornwall 163 J g
Newport, in I. of Wight . . . 127 X p
Newport, parl. bor., I. of Wight 163 E g
Newport, in Rhode Island . . . 189 ins. A
Newport News . . . . 193 ins. A
New Providence . . . . . . 213 E b
New Romney, parl. bor. . . . . 163 P g
Newry . . . . 127 K g
New Santander, prov. . . . . 190 F f
New Seraglio, loc. in Constanti-
nople . . . . 93 G e
New Seraglio, Wall of the . . 93 G e
Newsham, mon. . . . . 97 Q h
New Shops, loc. in Rome . . .
New Shoreham, parl. bor. . . . 163 N g
New Shoreham, parl. dist. . . 163 N g
New Silesia, dist. . . . . . . 135 J c
New Siberia Islands . . . . . 171 O a
New Spain, viceroyalty . . . . 213 leg.
New South Wales, col. . . . . 172 leg.
New South Wales, state . . . . 172 D d
Newstead, mon. . . . . 97 P h
New Sweden, col. . . . . . . 192 ins.
New Toggenburg, castle . . . . 91 R k
Newton, parl. bor. . . . . . . 163 L d
Newton Abbot . . . . 127 V p
Newtown, in Conn. . . . . . 189 B d
Newtown, in Mass. . . . . . 189 ins. B
Newtown, in New York . . . . 195 C b
Newtown, in Wales . . . . . 162 C e
Newtown, parl. bor., I. of Wight 163 M g
New Utrecht . . . . 189 ins. C
New Wasa, Fort . . . . 192 ins.
New White Russia, reg. . . . . 138 C d
New Windsor, in Maryland . . 208 ins.
New Windsor, parl. bor. in Eng-
land . . . . 163 N f
New Woodstock, parl. bor. . . . 163 M f
(New. Wood.)
New York . . . . 189 ins. C
New York, col. . . . . 192 D b
New York, state . . . . 199 J b
New York Bay . . . . 189 ins. C
New Zealand, col. . . . . . .
Nez Percés, tribe . . . . . . 188 C a

Ngan-hwei, prov. . . . . 171 M e
Nganking . . . .
Niagara, Fort . . . . 192 B b
Niagara Falls . . . . 192 B b
Niagara River . . . . 200 D b
Nicæa, in Bithynia . . . . . . 20 C b
Nicæa, in India . . . . 19 L d
Nicæa (Nice), in Liguria . . . 26 B d
Nicæa, in Locris . . . . 16 F e
Nicæa, Empire of . . . . . . 73 G c
Nicaragua, lake . . . . 105 C d
Nicaragua, country . . . . . . 213 D c
Nicaragua, reg. . . . . 105 C d
Nice . . . . 61 G e
Nice, bp. . . . . 95 C c
Nicephorium . . . . 20 H e
Nicer (Neckar) River . . . . . 39 J i
Nicholson, Fort . . . . 192 E b
Nickajacks, tribe . . . . . . 188 I d
Nicobar Islands . . . .
Nicomedia . . . . 20 C b
Nicopolis, in Epirus . . . . . 10 B c
Nicopolis, in Mœsia . . . . . 39 N l
Nicopolis, in Palestine . . . . 7 B e
Nicopolis, in Pontus . . . . . 20 H b
Nicopolis, on the Danube . . .
Nicopolis, theme . . . . . . 59 I f
Nicosia . . . . 68 B b
Nicotera . . . . 30 E d
Nicoya . . . . 213 D c
Nicoya, Gulf of . . . . 105 D e
Nictheroy . . . . 215 E e
Nida . . . . 39 J h
Nidum (Neath) . . . .
Niebla . . . . 82 A b
Nieder Schopfheim . . . . . . 142 A d
Niederstetten . . . . 143 I g
Niemîtsch . . . . 63 H c
Niemen River . . . . 138 B e
Nienburg, on the Saale . . . . 63 F c
Nienburg, on the Weser . . . . 134 E b
Nienburg, mon. . . . . 95 E a
Nieuport . . . . 117 A c
Nieuwstad . . . . 117 D c
Nièvre, dept. . . . . 148 E e
Niezhin . . . . 167 L e
Niger River . . . . 174 D c
Nigeria, col. . . . . 174 D d
Nigritia, reg. . . . . 108 Q f
Niigata . . . . 171 O e
Niihau, isl. . . . . 198 ins. B
Nijne Kolimsk . . . .
Nijni Novgorod . . . . 138 F d
Nike, Temple of . . . . 23 C (7)
Niklashausen . . . . 86 G d
Nikolaiev . . . . 139 D f
Nikolaievsk . . . . 171 O c
Nikolaistad . . . . 138 B c
Nikolsburg . . . . 159 I d
Nikolskaya . . . . 171 O d
Nikopol . . . .
Nile, Delta of the . . . . . . 4 ins. *
Nile River . . . . 174 G b
Nile River, Blue . . . . 174 G c
Nile River, White . . . . . . 174 G c
Nil-Saint-Vincent . . . . . . 156 B a
Nimbschen, mon. . . . . . . 80 ins.
Nimburg . . . . 63 H c
Nimeguen, see Nimwegen
Nimes . . . . 76 F e
Nimes, bp. . . . . 94 C c
Nimptsch . . . . 63 I c
Nimwegen . . . . 117 D c
Nimwegen, Hanse. cy. . . . . 99 ins. B
Ninety Six . . . . 195 A f
Nineveh . . . . 4 D d
Ning.hia . . . .
Ning-ho . . . . 170 ins. A
Ning-po . . . . 171 N f
Ningus River . . . . 27 H b
Ninus . . . . 20 J d
Niobrara, Ind. Res. . . . . . 188 G b
Niobrara River . . . . 198 E b
Niort . . . . 69 C c

Nipigon, Fort . . . . 191 H b
Nipigon, lake . . . . 191 H a
Nipissing, lake . . . . 191 I b
Nippon (Japan), empire . . . .
Nippur (Niffer) . . . . 4 E e
Nisæa . . . . 15 D b
Nisæa, dist. . . . . 18 R h
Nisæan Plain . . . . 19 G c
Nish . . . . 93 B b
Nishapur . . . .
Nisibin . . . .
Nisibis . . . . 4 D d
Nisqually, Fort . . . . 210 A a
Nisqually, Ind. Res. . . . . . 188 B a
Nissa (Nish) . . . . 59 I e
Nisyrus, isl. . . . . 17 E c
Nithsdale, dist. . . . .
Nitiobroges, people . . . . . 38 C d
Niuche, people . . . . 103 M c
Niu-chwang . . . . 171 N d
Niumaga, see Nimwegen
Nivelles . . . . 117 C d
Nivelles, mon. . . . . 94 C a
Nivernais, gouv. . . . . 146 B b
Nivernais, prov. . . . . 148 E e
Nivernis, see Nevers
Nizam, Dom. of the . . . . . 137 C e
Nizib . . . . 164 F c
Nizza, see Nice
Nizza della Paglia . . . . . . 130 Q j
Noas Island 216
Noce River . . . . 91 S l
Nocera . . . . 90 E d
Nocera, bp. in Campania . . . 95 ins.
Nocera, bp. in Umbria . . . . 95 E c
Nogaians, people . . . . . . 139 E f
Nogales . . . . 213 A a
Nogays, people . . . . 77 L c
Nogent . . . . 69 I f
Nogent-le-Rotrou . . . . . . 69 H f
Noirmoutier, isl. . . . . 69 B c
Noisy, Allée de, in Versailles . 149 A
Nola . . . . 30 D b
Nola, bp. . . . . 95 ins.
Noli, bp. . . . . 95 D c
Nollendorf . . . . 155 H c
Nombre de Dios . . . . 105 E e
Nome . . . . 198 ins. A
Nomentan Gate . . . . 22 A
Nomentan Way, road . . . . . 35 ins. B
Nomentum . . . . 27 G e
Nomia, mt. . . . . 14 B b
Nona, bp. . . . . 95 F c
Nonacris . . . . 14 C a
Nonantola . . . . 64 B b
Nonantola, mon. . . . . . . 95 E c
Nonnenweier . . . . 142 A d
Nonsuch, castle . . . . 75 I i
Nora, in Cappadocia . . . . . 18 O h
Nora, in Sardinia . . . . . . 38 D e
Norba . . . . 35 ins. B
Norba Cæsarea . . . . 38 A e
Norbona, see Narbo Martius
(Narbonne)
Narcia, New . . . . 172 A d
Nord, dept. . . . . 148 E d
Nordalbingia, dist. . . . . . 55 Q i
Norddeutscher Bund, see North
German Federation
Norden . . . . 62 D b
Nordgau, dist. . . . . 55 R j
Nordgau, margr. . . . . . . 63 F d
Nordhausen . . . . 62 F c
Nordhausen, imp. cy. . . . . 79 G c
Nordheim, mon. . . . . . . 95 E a
Nördlingen . . . . 62 F d
Nördlingen, imp. cy. . . . . . 79 G d
Nordmark, march . . . . . . 63 G b
Noreia . . . . 38 E c
Norfolk, in Virginia . . . . . 193 ins. A
Norfolk, cty. in England . . . .
Norfolk, shire . . . .
Norfolk Island . . . . 172 F c
Norfolk, New . . . . 172 D e

Norham . . . .
Noricum, Rom. prov. . . . . . . 38 E c
Noricum mediterraneum, West Rom. prov. . . . . 42 E d (12)
Noricum ripense, West Rom. prov. . . . . 42 E d (13)
Norman, Fort . . . . 212 C b
Norman Principalities . . . . . 66 I f
Normandy, duchy . . . . 61 D b
Normandy, gouv. . . . . 146 A b
Normandy, prox. . . . . 148 D e
Normanton . . . . 172 D b
Normans, people, in England . 45 D b
Normans, people, in France . 45 D c
Normans, people, in Italy . . 45 H e
Norridgewock . . . . 189 C b
Norrköping . . . . 131 G b
Northallerton . . . . 65 F c
North Allerton, parl. bor. . . .
Northam, in N. Hampshire . . 189 C c
Northam, in W. Australia . . 172 A d
North America, continent . . 186 187
Northampton, in England . . .
Northampton, cty. . . . .
Northampton, mon. . . . . . . 97 Q i
Northampton, parl. bor. . . . 163 N e
Nordhamptan, shire . . . . . .
Northampton, in Mass. . . . 189 B c
North Australia, reg. . . . . . .
North Borneo, col. . . . . . . 171 M h
North Cape, in Europe . . 2 G a
North Cape, in New Zealand . 172 G d
North Channel . . . . 49 C d
North Carolina, col. . . . . . 193 E d
North Carolina, state . . . . . 199 I c
North Castle . . . . 195 E c
North Chester, parl. dist. . . . 163 L d
North Dakota, state . . . . . 203 R f
North Derby, parl. dist. . . . 163 M d
North Devon, isl. . . . . 186 K a
North Devon, parl. dist. . . . 163 J g
Nord Downs, dist. . . . . 49 G f
North Durham, parl. dist. . . 163 M c
Northeim . . . . 62 E c
Northern Californians, tribes . 188 B b
Northern Cheyenne, Ind. Res. . 188 E a
Northern District, Queensland . 172 leg.
Northern Dwina River . . . . . 3 I b
Northern Ghats, mts. . . . . . 112 A a
Northern Pacific Grant . . . 210 D a
Northern Plain, The . . . . . 186 J c
Northern Territory, S. Australia 172 C b
North Essex, parl. dist. . . . 163 O f
Northfield . . . . 189 B c
Northfleet . . . . 75 J i
North Folk (Angles), people . 51 S k
North Fort, Sevastopol . . . 164 L g
North Gate, in Olympia . . . .
North German Federation . . 161 D c
North Hants, parl. dist. . . . 163 M f
North Humbrians, people . . .
North Isles (Hebrides) . . . .
North Island, New Zealand . . 172 G d
North Lancaster, parl. dist. . . 163 L c
North Leicester, parl. dist. . . 163 M e
North March, dist. . . . . . . 58 G c
Northmen, people, in Scandinavia . . . . 45 F a
Northmen, people, in Russia . 45 K b
North Northampton, parl. dist. 163 N e
North Northumberland, parl. dist. . . . . 163 L b
North Nottingham, parl. dist. . 163 M d
North Platte River . . . . . . 190 E c
North Point, in Maryland . . 200 L h
North Potomac River. . . . . 192 B d
North Riding, parl. dist. . . . 163 M c
North (Hudson) River. . . . . 189 B d
North Salop, parl. bor. . . . 163 L e
North Saskatchewan River . . 186 H c
North Sea . . . . 2 E c
North Somerset, isl. . . . . . 212 F a
North Sporades, isl. . . . . . .
North Stafford, parl. dist. . . . 163 L e

Northumberland, cty., in England
Northumberland County, in Virginia . . . . 193 F b (N.)
Northumberland, shire . . . .
Northumbria, km. . . . . .
Northumbria, Danish, reg. . . .
Northumbria, English, km. . .
North Wales, town in Pa. . . . 192 D c
North Wales, dist. . . . . . .
North Warwick, parl. dist. . . 163 M e
North West Cape, Australia . . 172 A c
North West Territories, Canada
Northwest Territory, in U. S., 1787 . . . . 196 B b
Northwest Territory, in U. S., 1800—1802 . . . . 196 C b
Northwich . . . . 162 D d
North Wilts, parl. dist. . . . . 163 L f
Norton, mon. . . . . 97 O h
Norton Folgate . . . . 75 G g
Norton Sound . . . . 186 C b
Norwalk . . . . 189 B d
Norway, km., about 1000 . . . 58 F a
Norway, km. 1910 . . . . . . 166 G d—I b
Norwegians, people . . . . . . 46 H a
Norwich, in Conn. . . . . . . 189 B d (Nor.)
Norwich, in England . . . . . 84 D c
Norwich, bp. . . . . 97 S i
Norwich, castle . . . . 65 G d
Norwich, Hanse. for. cy. . . . 98 ins. A
Norwich, parl. bor. . . . . . . 163 P e
Nossen . . . . 85 G e
Nossi Bé, isl. . . . .
Nostell, mon. . . . . 97 P h
Noteborg . . . . 119 K b
Notium . . . . 17 E c
Notium, prom. . . . . 38 A b
Notre Dame, church, Paris . . 149 B
Notre Dame, bridge, Paris. . 149 B
Notre Dame, church, Versailles 149 A
Notre Dame Bay . . . . 212 J c
Notre-Dame-de-la-Grasse, mon. 94 C c
Nottingham . . . .
Nottingham, castle . . . . . . 65 F d
Nottingham, cty. . . . .
Nottingham, parl. bor. . . . . 163 M e
Nottingham, shire . . . .
Nottoway River . . . . 193 F c
Noumea . . . . 172 F c
Nouvion, le . . . . 117 B e
Nova Coimbra . . . . 214 D d
Novæ . . . . 39 N l
Novæsium . . . . 39 I h
Nova Friburgo. . . . . 215 E e
Novantæ, people . . . . 38 B a
Novara . . . . 90 I h
Novara, bp. . . . . 95 D b
Novaria . . . . 26 C b
Novas, Ad, on the Clanis R. . 27 F d
Novas, Ad, on L. Sabatinus . . 35 ins. B
Nova Scotia, prov. . . . . . . 212 I d
Nova Scotia Peninsula . . . 186 M d
Novaya Zemlya (Nova Zembla) islands . . . . 170 G a
Novempopulana . . . . . . 42 B e (12)
Novgorod . . . . 57 J b
Novgorod, gov. . . . . 131 J b
Novgorod, Hanse. for. off.. . . 99 J b
Novgorod, reg. . . . . 138 D d
Novgorod, rep. . . . . 92 D b
Novgorod, ter. . . . . 71 N a
Novgorod Sieversk . . . . . . 77 K b
Novi, in Bosnia . . . .
Novi, in Italy . . . . 90 I h
Novi Bazar . . . . 119 I e
Noviodunum, in Aquitana . . 38 C c
Noviodunum, in Lugdunensis . 38 B c
Noviodunum, in Mœsia . . . . . 39 N k
Noviodunum, in Pannonia . . .
Noviomagus, see Lisieux
Noviomagus (Neufchâteau), on the Meuse . . . . 39 H i
Noviomagus (Neumagen), near the Moselle . . . . 39 I i

Noviomagus (Nimwegen), on the Waal . . . . 39 H b
Noviomagus, see Noyon
Noviomagus (Spires), on the Rhine . . . . 39 J i
Noviomum, see Noyon
Novo-Georgievsk . . . . 155 K b
Novogrudek . . . . 119 J c
Novo-Tscherkask . . . .
Novum Castrum . . . . 29 D c
Noyers . . . . 126 D c
Noyon . . . . 61 E b
Noyon, bp. . . . . 94 C b
Noyon, cty. . . . . 61 E b
Nubia, reg. . . . . 174 G c
Nubian Desert. . . . . 3 H f
Nuceria Alfaterna . . . . 30 D b
Nuceria Camellaria . . . . . . 27 G d
Nudionnum, see Sées
Nueces River . . . . 190 F f
Nuevitas . . . . 213 E b
Nuevo León, state . . . . . . 213 B b
Numana . . . . 27 H d
Numantia . . . . 38 B d
Numicus River . . . . 35 ins. B
Numidia, reg. . . . . 38 D e
Numidia, Rom. prov. . . . . . 34 F f
Numidia, West Rom. prov. . . 42 D f (2)
Numistro . . . . 30 E b
Nun, Cape . . . . 174 B b
Nunivak, isl. . . . . 198 ins. A
Nur . . . . 159 L b
Nure River . . . . 26 D c
Nuremberg . . . . 62 F d
Nuremberg, burgraviate . . . 79 G d
Nuremberg, imp. cy. . . . . . 79 G d
Nursia . . . . 27 H e
Nürtingen . . . . 143 H h
Nusco, bp. . . . . 95 F c
Nussbaum . . . . 142 C c
Nutmeg Islands . . . .
Nyasa, lake . . . . 175 G f
Nyasaland, col. . . . . 175 G f
Nykerk . . . . 117 D b
Nyköping . . . . 131 G b
Nymphæum, loc. in Rome . . 22 A
Nymphæum, prom. . . . . . . 11 F b
Nymphenburg, castle . . . . . 134 F d
Nysa . . . . 17 F c
Nyssa . . . . 20 F c
Nystad . . . . 138 B c

Oahu, isl. . . . . 198 ins. B
Oajaca . . . . 213 C c
Oajaca, state . . . . 213 C c
Oakala . . . . 198 ins. A
Oak forest, near Mizpah . . . 7 B e
Oakland . . . . 210 A c
Oaracta, isl. . . . . 19 I e
Oatlands, castle . . . . 75 I i
Oaxas . . . .
Oaxes River . . . . 14 ins.
Obdorsk . . . . 170 H b
O Becse . . . . 159 K f
Obeid, El . . . . 174 F c
Oberalp Pass . . . . 91 Q l
Ober-Ehnheim . . . . 122 D d
Oberlahnstein . . . . 78 E c
Oberlin . . . . 206 ins.
Oberndorf . . . . 143 G i
Oberried, mon. . . . . 142 A e
Oberried, provostry . . . . . . 142 A e
Ober-Sontheim . . . . 143 I g
Oberstenfeld . . . . 143 H g
Obi, Gulf of . . . . 138 L b
Obi River . . . .
Obilinnum . . . . 26 A b
Obispo . . . .
Obok . . . . 174 H c
O'Brennans, The, fam. . . . .
O'Briens, The, fam. . . . . .
Observatory Inlet . . . . 212 ins.
Ocaña, in Colombia . . . . . . 214 B b
Ocaña, in Spain . . . . 82 H f

Oceanus Britannicus (English Channel) . . . . 51 O i
Oceanus Germanicus (North Sea) . . . . 51 Q g
Oceanus Hibernicus (Irish Sea) 51 N h
Ocelum . . . . 26 B b
Ocha, mt. . . . . 15 E a
Ochrida . . . .
Ochsenfurt . . . . 62 F d
Ochsenfurt, mon. . . . . . . 95 E b
Ochsenhausen, ab. . . . . . . 143 I i
Ochus River . . . . 19 J c
Ockley . . . .
Ocklockonee River . . . . . . 193 B f
Ocmulgee River . . . . 193 C e
Oconee River . . . . 193 C e
O'Connels, The, fam. . . . . .
O'Connors, The, fam. . . . . .
Ocra, mt. . . . . 27 I b
Ocriculum . . . . 27 G e
Octavia, Portico of . . . . . . 24 B
Octovius, Portico of . . . . . 22 A
Octodurus . . . . 26 B a
Octagesa . . . . 38 C d
Octogon, in Olympia . . . . .
Ocumare . . . . 214 C a
O'Dempseys, The, fam. . . . .
Ödenburg (Sopron) . . . . . . 63 I e
Odenheim, mon. . . . . 142 C b
Odenheim, princ. . . . . 142 C b
Odense . . . . 154 F a
Odéon, bldg. in Paris . . . . . 149 B
Oderberg . . . . 115 J d
Oder River . . . . 63 H b
Odessa . . . . 139 D f
Odessus . . . . 39 N l
Odeum vetustissimum, bldg. in Athens . . . . 23 D
Odeypore . . . . 137 B d
Odiham, parl. bor. . . . . . .
Odoacer, Kingdom of . . . . . 50 F d
Odomanti, people . . . . 11 E a
O'Donnells, The, fam. . . . .
O'Donoghues, The, fam. . . . . .
O'Doughertys, The, fam. . . . .
Odrysæ, people . . . . 39 N l
O'Dwyers, The, fam. . . . . .
Oea . . . . 34 G g
Oeanthea . . . . 11 D d
Oechalia, in Ætolia . . . . . . 10 C d
Oechalia, in Messenia . . . . . 14 B b
Oedenburg, see Ödenburg
Oee . . . . 16 B a
Oeiras . . . . 214 E c
Oeneon . . . . 10 C d
Oeniadæ . . . . 10 C d
Oenoë, in Argolis . . . . . . 14 C b
Oenoë, near Cythæron Mts. . . 16 A a
Oenoë, in Elis . . . . 14 B b
Oenoë, on the Isthmus of Corinth 15 D a
Oenoë, near Marathon . . . . . 16 B a
Oenophyta . . . . 11 E d
Oenotrians, people . . . . . . 29 D e
Oenus (Inn) River . . . . . . 14 C b
Oenussæ Island . . . . 14 B c
Oëroë River . . . . 11 E d
Oescus . . . . 39 M l
Oescus River (Isker R.) . . . . 39 M l
Oesyme . . . . 11 F b
Oeta, mt. . . . . 11 D d
Oetæa, dist. . . . . 10 D d
Oetylus . . . . 14 C c
Oeum . . . .
O'Farrells, The, fam. . . . . .
Ofen (Buda) . . . . 63 J e
Ofen (Buda) univ. . . . . . . 100 I e
Ofen Pass . . . . 91 S l
Offa's Dike . . . .
Offenburg . . . . 142 A d
Ofingen . . . . 142 C e
O'Flahertys, The, fam. . . . . .
Ofu, isl. . . . . 199 ins. D
Ogden . . . . 210 C b
Ogdensburg . . . . 192 D a

Ogeechee River . . . . 193 C e
Oglasa, isl. . . . . 26 E e
Oglio River . . . . 90 J h
Ogowe River . . . . 175 E e
Ohain . . . .
Ohain, Woods of . . . .
Ohain River . . . .
O'Hanlons, The, fam. . . . . .
O'Haras, The, fam. . . . . .
Ohiv Company . . . . 196 ins. B
Ohio, Falls of the . . . . . . 196 B c
Ohio, state . . . . 202 I b
Ohio, ter. . . . . 196 C b
Ohio River . . . . 187 K e
Ohrdruf, mon. . . . . 95 E a
Ohre River . . . . 85 F d
Öhringen . . . . 143 H g
Oil River, dist. . . . . 174 D d
Oil Spring, Ind. Res. . . . . . 188 K b
Oise dept. . . . . 148 E e
Oise River . . . . 126 C b
Ojibwas, Chippewas, tribe . . . 188 H a
Okanagan, Fort . . . . 210 B a
Oka River . . . . 139 E e
Okechobee, lake . . . . 191 I f
Okehampton, parl. bor. . . . . 163 J g
O'Kellys, The, fam. . . . . .
Okhotsk . . . . 171 P c
Okhotsk, Sea of . . . . 171 P c
Oklahoma . . . . 210 F c
Oklahoma, state . . . . 203 S h
Oklahoma, ter. . . . . 203 S h
Olana River . . . . 27 F c
Öland, isl. . . . . 77 H a
Olbia, in Gaul . . . . 12 E b
Olbia, in Sardinia . . . . . . 38 D d
Olbia, in Sarmatia . . . . . . 35 K d
Old Appian Way, road . . . . 35 ins. B
Old Basing . . . . 127 X o
Old Castile, km. . . . . 83 K g
Old Celtic Church, area under influence of . . . . 46 E c
Olp Charles Town . . . . . . 193 ins. C
Old Dean's Lane, in London 75 G g (32)
Oldenburg, in Holstein . . . . 62 F a
Oldenburg, in Oldenburg . . . 72 B a
Oldenburg, cty. . . . . 78 F b
Oldenburg, duchy . . . . . . 134 E b
Oldenburg, gr. duchy . . . . . 158 E b
Oldenesche . . . . 72 B a
Oldesloe . . . . 72 C a
Old Fish Street, in London . . 75 G g
Old Flaminian Way, road . . . 27 G e
Old Gate, in Jerusalem . . . 6 ins. A
Oldham, parl. bor. . . . . . . 163 L d
Old Park, dist. . . . . 210 D c
Old Sarum . . . .
Old Sarum, parl. bor. 163 M f (Old S.)
Old Seraglio, loc. i. Constantinople 93 G e
Old Shops, loc. in Rome . . .
Old Toggenburg, castle . . . . 91 R k
Old Tyre . . . . 18 ins. B
Old Versailles . . . . 149 A
Olenus . . . . 14 B a
Oléron, isl. . . . . 76 C d
Oliarus (Antiparos), isl. . . . . 15 F b
Olid, route of . . . . 105 D c
Olifants River . . . . 175 N k
Oligyrtus, mt. . . . . 14 C b
Olinda . . . . 214 F c
Olisipo (Lisbon) . . . . 38 A e
Olite . . . . 83 K g
Oliva, mon. . . . . 95 F a
Olivença, in Brazil . . . . . . 214 C c
Olivenza, in Portugal . . . . . 83 J h
Olives, Mount of . . . . 68 ins. B
Olizon . . . . 11 E c
Ollius River . . . . 26 E b
Ölmedo . . . . 83 K g
Olmütz . . . . 63 I d
Olmütz, bp. . . . . 95 F b
Olocáu . . . . 82 B b
Oloosson . . . . 10 D c
Olophyxus . . . . 11 F b

Oloron . . . . 76 C e
Oloron, bp. . . . . 94 B c
Olorone, see Oloron
Olpæ . . . . 10 C d
Öls . . . . 79 J c
Öls, princ. . . . . 79 J c
Oltenitza . . . . 164 D b
Oltis (Lot) River . . . . 38 C d
Olubria River . . . . 26 C c
Olusiga, isl. . . . . 199 ins. D
Olympia, in Elis . . . . 14 B b
Olympia, Plan of 9
Olympia, in Washington . . . 210 A a
Olympieum, in Athens . . . . 23 D
Olympieum, in Syracuse . . . 31 ins. B
Olympus, mt., in Attica . . . . 16 B b
Olympus, mt., in Cyprus . . . . 20 E e
Olympus, mt., in Macedonia . . 11 D b
Olympus Mysius, mt. . . . . .
Olynthus . . . . 11 E b
Omagh . . . . 127 J g
Omaha . . . . 198 F b
Omaha, Ind. Res. . . . . . . 188 G b
Omahas, tribe . . . . 188 G b
O'Malleys, The, fam. . . . . .
Oman, Gulf of . . . .
Oman, reg. . . . .
Oman, Sea of . . . .
Ombrone River . . . . 90 L j
Omdurman . . . . 174 G c
Omekonsk . . . . 171 P b
Omercote . . . . 137 A c
Ommiad Emirate of Cordova . 54 C e
Omoa . . . . 213 D c
Omont . . . . 61 F b
O'Mores, The, fam. . . . . .
Omphalium . . . . 10 B b
Omsk . . . . 170 I c
On . . . . 4 F d *
Oñate, routes of . . . . . 190 C e, D e
Onchesmus . . . . 10 B c
Onchestus River . . . . 11 D c
Onea, mt. . . . . 15 C b
Onchonus River . . . . 10 D c
Onega, Gulf of . . . . 167 M c
Onega, lake . . . . 138 E c
Oneglia . . . . 130 Q k
Oneida Ind. Res. . . . . . 188 I b, K b
Oneida Lake . . . . 192 D b
Oneidas, tribe . . . . 188 L b
O'Neills, The, fam. . . . . .
Onis, Cangas de . . . . 82 A a
Ono . . . . 7 B d
Onochonus River . . . . 10 D c
Onondaga, battle . . . . 192 C b
Onondaga, Ind. Res. . . . . . 188 K b
Onondagas, tribe . . . . 188 K b
Onon River . . . .
Ontario, Fort . . . . 192 C b
Ontario, lake . . . . 187 L d
Ontario, prov. . . . . 212 G d
Ontonagon, Ind. Res. . . . . . 188 I a
Onugnathos, prom. . . . . . . 15 C c
Oodnadatta . . . . 172 C c
Oostburg . . . . 117 B c
Opelousas . . . . 211 G d
Opequan Creek . . . . 208 E b (O. Cr.)
Opequon Court . . . . 192 B d
Opequon River . . . . 192 B d
Ophel . . . . 6 ins. A
Ophiones, people . . . . 10 C d
Ophis River . . . . 14 C b
Ophiussa, isl. . . . . 38 C e
Ophrah . . . . 7 C c
Ophrynium . . . .
Opis . . . . 20 K f
Opisthomarathus . . . . 11 D d
Opitergium . . . . 27 G b
Oporto . . . . 82 A a
Oporto, bisp. . . . . 94 A c
Oppeln . . . . 79 K c
Oppeln, princ. . . . . 79 K c
Oppenau . . . . 142 B d
Oppenheim . . . . 62 E d
Oppius, mt. . . . . 22 A

Opsician Theme . . . . 59 J f
Opslo . . . . 88 D b
Optimaton, Theme of the. . . . 59 K e
Opus . . . . 11 E d
Opus, prom. . . . . 11 D d
Oraculum Fauni, loc. near Rome 35 ins. B
Oräfa Jökul, mt. . . . . . . 166 B c
Oran, in Algeria . . . . . . 174 C a
Orán, in Arg. Rep. . . . . . 215 C e
Orange . . . . 61 F d
Orange, bp. . . . . 94 C c
Orange, Cape . . . . 214 D b
Orange, Fort. . . . . 192 D b
Orange, princ. . . . . . . 114 ins. A
Orange, univ. . . . . 100 F f
Orangeburg . . . . 195 A g
Orange Free State, rep. . . . . 175 M l
Orangerie, Rue de l', street in
    Versailles. . . . . 149 A
Orange River . . . . 175 E g
Orange River Colony . . . . . 175 F g
Orbais, mon. . . . . 94 C b
Orbe. . . . . 91 O l
Orbelus, mt. . . . . 11 F a
Orbetello . . . . 90 L j
Orcades Islands (Orkneys) . . 34 D b
Orchard Knob, battle . . . . . 208 C b
Orchies . . . . 117 B d
Orchimont . . . . 117 C e
Orchoë . . . . 18 G d
Orchomenus, in Arcadia . . . . 14 C b
Orchomenus, in Bœotia . . . . 11 D d
Ordessus River . . . . 39 N l
Ordovices, people . . . .
Örebro . . . . 88 F b
Oregon Country, The . . . . . 198 A a
Oregon, state . . . . 203 N g
Oregon, ter. 1848 . . . . 202 A f
Oregon, ter. 1853 . . . . 202 A g
Oregon Trail, route . . . . . . 210 B b
O'Reillys, The, fam. . . . . . .
Orel . . . . 139 E e
Orellana, route of . . . . . . 214 B c
Orenburg . . . . 139 I e
Orense . . . . 82 A a
Orense, bp. . . . . 94 A c
Oreshek . . . .
Oresticum . . . . 10 C b
Orestis, dist. . . . . 10 C b
Oretani, people . . . . 38 B e
Oretum . . . . 38 B e
Oreus . . . . 11 E d
Orfani . . . . 165 D c
Orford, parl. bor. . . . . 165 P e
Orgellis, see Urgel
Orgus River . . . . 26 B b
Oria . . . . 90 F d
Oricum . . . . 31 I b
Orient, L' . . . . 130 C d
Origny, mon. . . . . 94 C b
Orihuela . . . . 82 B b
Orinoco River . . . . 214 C b
Oriskany, battle . . . . 195 D b
Orissa, reg. . . . . 137 D d
Oristano, abp. . . . . 95 D d
Oritæ, people . . . . 19 K e
Orizaba . . . . 106 C b
Orizaba, vol. . . . . 106 C b
Orkhon River . . . .
Orkney, bp. . . . . 97 J a
Orkney Islands . . . . 49 E b
Orlamünde . . . . 85 F e
Orléanais, gouv. . . . . 146 B b
Orléanais, prov. . . . . 148 E e
Orléans . . . . 61 E c
Orléans, bp. . . . . 94 C b
Orléans, duchy . . . . 84 D f
Orléans, gen. . . . . 147 E b
Orléans, univ. . . . . 100 F e
Orleans, ter. . . . . 202 G d
Orleans, Fort . . . . 191 G d
Orleans, Island of, Mississippi R. 194 A e
Orleans, Island of, St. Lawrence
    R. . . . . 191 K b

Orlov, Cape . . . . 167 N b
Ormea . . . . 130 P j
Ormenium . . . .
Ormskirk . . . . 98 ins. A
Ormuz, isl. . . . .
Ormuz, km. . . . .
Ornas . . . .
Orne, dept. . . . . 148 D e
Orne River, in Belgium . . . . 156 B a
Orne River, in France. . . . . 148 D e
Orneæ . . . . 14 C b
Orneau River . . . . 156 B a
Oro, Rio de, dist. . . . . . . 174 B b
Orobiæ . . . . 11 E d
Orolaunum . . . . 39 H i
Orontes River . . . . 68 C b
Oropus . . . . 15 D a
Oropus River . . . . 10 B c
O'Rorkes, The, fam. . . . . . .
Oroya . . . . 214 B d
Orsha . . . . 153 O g
Orsini, fam. . . . . 90 L j
Orsk . . . . 139 I e
Orsovo . . . . 71 K e
Orte, bp. . . . . 95 E c
Ortegal, Cape . . . . 166 D g
Ortenau, dist. . . . . 142 A c
Ortez de Retes, route of . . . .
Orthez . . . . 126 A e
Orthokids, people . . . . 75 I c
Orthospana (Kabul). , ... 19 K d
Ortona . . . . 27 I e
Ortopla . . . . 27 I c
Ortospana, see Orthospana
Ortygia, quarter in Syracuse . . 31 ins. B
Orumbovii, people . . . . . . 26 D b
Oruro . . . . 214 C d
Orval . . . . 69 I g
Orval, mon. . . . . 95 D b
Orvieto . . . . 90 M j
Orvieto, bp. . . . . 95 E c
Oryxis, mt. . . . . 14 C b
Osage, Fort . . . . 211 G c
Osage River . . . . 191 G d
Osages, tribe . . . . 188 F b
Osaka . . . . 171 O e
Osawatomie . . . . 206 F c
Osca (Huesca) . . . . 38 B d
Oscela . . . . 26 C a
Öschelbronn . . . . 142 C c
Ösel, isl. . . . . 138 B d
Osenay, mon. . . . . 97 P j
Osette, Ind. Res. . . . . 188 A a
O'Shaugnessys, The, fam. . . . .
Oshmiany . . . . 153 N g
Osi, people . . . . 38 F c
Osimii, people . . . . 38 B c
Osimo . . . . 90 D c
Osma . . . . 82 B a
Osma, bp. . . . . 94 B c
Osmanli (Ottoman Turks), Dom.
    of the . . . . 89 I g
Osnabrück . . . . 62 D b
Osnabrück, bp. . . . . 78 F b
Osnabrück, Hanse. cy. . . . . 99 ins. B
Osoppo . . . . 158 G e
Osopus . . . . 27 H a
Osorno . . . . 215 B g
Osrhoëne, dist. . . . . 20 H d
Osrhoëne, prov. . . . . 43 J f(11)
Ossa, mt. . . . . 11 D c
Ossawatomie, see Osawatomie
Osse . . . . , . . 126 A e
Osseg, in Bohemia . . . . . . 123 G c
Osseg, on the Vistula R. . . . .
Osseg, mon. . . . . 80 ins.
Ossero, bp. . . . . 95 E c
Ossola, val d', valley . . . . . 91 Q l
Ossory, bp. . . . . 97 D d
Ostend . . . . 117 A c
Ostend, mon. . . . . 94 C a
Osteodes, isl. . . . . 30 C d
Osterburken . . . . 142 D b
Osterland, margr. . . . . . . 79 H c

Osterland, dist. . . . . 85 G e
Osterode . . . . 155 K b
Ostia . . . . 27 G f
Ostia, bp. . . . . 96 B b
Ostiaks, people . . . .
Ostian Gate . . . . 22 A
Ostian Way, road . . . . . . 35 ins. B
Ostmark (Austria), march . . . 63 H d
Ostmark, march. in Brandenburg 63 G c
Ostrach . . . . 134 E e
Ostrog . . . . 119 J c
Ostrogoths, Dom. of the . . . 50 G c
Ostrolenka . . . . 155 K b
Ostrov . . . . 138 C d
Ostrovno . . . . 153 N f
Ostrowo . . . . 135 I c
O'Sullivans, The, fam. . . . . .
Osuna . . . . 82 A b
Oswegatchie, Fort . . . . . . 196 D b
Oswego . . . . 196 D b
Oswego, Fort . . . . 192 C b
Oswego River . . . . 192 C b
Oswestry . . . . 127 V n
Otago, prov. . . . . 172 F e
Otaheite, isl. . . . . 136 ins. B
Otalini, people . . . . 38 B a
Otavalo . . . . 214 B b
Otchakov . . . . 139 D f
Otford . . . .
Othrys, mt. . . . . 11 D c
Otochatz, bp. . . . .
O'Tooles, The, fam. . . . . . .
Otranto . . . . 90 G d
Otranto, abp. . . . . 95 F c
Otrar . . . .
Otryne . . . . 16 C a
Ottawa . . . . 212 H d
Ottawa River . . . . 199 J a
Ottawas, tribe . . . . 188 I b
Ottenbourg . . . . 156 B a
Ottensen . . . . 154 E b
Ottignies . . . . 156 B a
Otilienberg, mon. . . . . . . 95 D b
Ötting, Alt . . . . 123 G d
Öttingen . . . . 122 F d
Öttingen, princ. . . . . 143 J h
Ottobeuren, mon. . . . . . . 95 E b
Ottocar of Bohemia, Dom. of . 79 ins.
Ottoman (Turkish) Empire, 1451
    —1481 93
Ottoman (Turkish) Empire, 1481
    —1683 124
Ottoman (Turkish) Empire,
    since 1683 164
Ottoman Turks, Dom. of the,
    14 cent. . . . . 89 I g
Ottoman Turks, Dom. of the,
    early 15 cent. . . . . 92 C d
Otumba . . . . 106 B a
Otway, Cape . . . . 172 D d
Oudenarde . . . . 117 B d
Oudh, Oude, reg. . . . . . . 137 D c
Ouiatanon, Fort . . . . 191 H c
Ourique . . . . 82 G f
Ouro Prereto . . . . 214 E e
Ourthe River . . . . 117 D d
Ouse River, R. . . . . 49 F e
Ouse River, Great . . . . . . 49 F e
Ovalle . . . . 215 B f
Oven Tower, loc. in Jerusalem 6 ins. A
Översee . . . . 158 E a
Overton, parl. bor. . . . . . .
Overyssel, Lordship of . . . . 117 E b
Oviedo . . . . 82 A a
Oviedo, bp. . . . . 94 A c
Ovilava . . . . 38 C c
Ovile (Sæpta) . . . . 23 B
Owen . . . . 143 H h
Öwisheim, Unter . . . . . . 142 C b
Owston, mon. . . . . 97 Q i
Oxford, in England . . . . . 127 X o
Oxford, castle . . . . 94 E f
Oxford, cty. . . . . 127 X o
Oxford, mon. . . . . 97 P j

Oxford, parl. bor. . . . . 163 M f
xford, parl. dist. . . . . 163 M f
xford, univ. . . . . 100 E d
xford University, parl. bor. . . 163 M f
xford, in Maryland . . . . . . 192 C d
xford, in Mass. . . . . . . 189 C c
xford, in Miss. . . . . . 208 C c
xford Town . . . . 192 C d
xus (Amu - Daria) River . . . . 92 G d
xybii, people . . . . 26 A d
xynia . . . . 10 C c
xyrhynchus . . . . *
yapock River . . . . 214 D b
Oyster Bay, town in New York 189 B d
yster Bay . . . . 172 G e
zark Mountains . . . . 211 G c
zark Plateau . . . . 187 J e
zora . . . . 159 J e

aanpack . . . . 192 E b
aardeberg, mt. . . . . 175 M l
acaha, reg. . . . . 191 G d
acaraima Mountains . . . . . . 214 C b
acasmayo . . . . 111 B c
achacamac . . . . 111 B d
a - chau . . . . 170 ins. A
achuca . . . . 213 ins.
achynus, prom. . . . . . 30 E e
acific Ocean . . . . 179 — 180
acific Slope . . . . 186 G c
acocha . . . . 214 B d
actolus River . . . . . . 20 B c
actyans, people . . . . . 8 E b
actye . . . .
Paderborn . . . . 62 E c
Paderborn, bp. . . . . . . 95 D a
Paderborn, Hanse. cy. . . . . . 99 ins. B
adrabrunna, see Paderborn
Padrão, Rio do, river . . . . . 108 R h
Padrón . . . . 82 A a
Padua . . . . 90 J h
Padua, bp. . . . . 95 E b
Padua, univ. . . . . 100 H e (Pa.)
Paducah . . . . 208 C b
adum, Ad . . . . 27 G c
Padus River, see Po River
Padusa River . . . . . . 27 F c
Pæania . . . . 16 B b
Pædagogium, loc. in Rome . . 24 B
Pæligni, people . . . . . 27 H e
Pæmani, people . . . . . 39 H h
Pæonia, dist. . . . . . . 17 B a
Pæonidæ . . . . 16 B a
Pæstum . . . . 30 D b
Pæstum, Bay of . . . . . . 30 D b
Pagæ . . . . 15 D a
Pagan
Pagasæ . . . . 11 D c
Pagasæan Gulf . . . . . . 11 D c
Pageh Islands . . . .
Pago Pago . . . . 199 ins. D
Pagus Ianiculensis, dist. in Rome 22 A
Pahala . . . . 198 ins. B
Paia . . . . 198 ins. B
Paiutes, Piutes, tribe . . . 188 C b
Paja River . . . .
Pajajaran . . . . 112 D d
Pajeau . . . .
Pak - hoi . . . . 171 L f
Paks . . . . 159 J e
Palachwe . . . . 175 M k
Palæbyblus . . . . 6 D a
Palæo - Kastro . . . .
Palæopolis . . . . 31 ins. A
Polærus . . . . 10 B d
Palæstra . . . .
Palætyrus . . . . 6 C b
Palais Bourbon, bldg. in Paris . 149 B
Palais Royal, bldg. in Paris . 149 B
Palam . . . .
Palatinate, see Rhenish Bavaria 158 D d
Palatinate, Bavarian, dist. . . . 142 C b
Palatinate, Upper, dist. . . . 79 G d
Palatinate of the Rhine, elect. . 78 F d

Palatinate - Saxony . . . . 85 F e
Palatine, quarter in Rome . . . 96 A
Palatine, Aug. Reg. of Rome . 22 A
Palatine Library, bldg. in Rome 24 B
Palatine Mosbach, princ. . . . . 87 H d
Palatine Mount . . . . . . 24 A
Palatine Simmern, princ. . . . . 86 F d
Palatine Zweibrücken, princ. . . 86 F d
Palau Islands . . . . . . 179 E g
Palawan, isl. . . . . 112 E c
Palazzo Borghese, bldg. in Rome 96 A
Palazzo Colonna, bldg. in Rome 96 A
Palazzo di Venezia, bldg. in
  Rome . . . . 96 A
Palazzo Farnese, bldg. in Rome 96 A
Palazzo Massimi, bldg. in Rome 96 A
Palazzo Orsini Savelli, bldg. in
  Rome . . . . 96 A
Pale . . . . 10 B d
Pale, The English, dist. . . . . .
Palea . . . . 14 B a
Palembang
Palencia . . . . 82 B a
Palencia, bp. . . . . . . 94 B c
Palencia, univ. . . . . . . 100 E f
Palenque . . . . 105 B c
Palermo . . . . 90 D e
Palermo, abp. . . . . . . 95 E d
Palestine, reg. . . . . . . 6 — 7
Palestine I, East Rom. prov. . . 43 I g (1)
Palestine II, East Rom. prov. . 43 J g (6)
Palestine (Salutaris), East Rom.
  prov. . . . . 43 I h (7)
Palestrina . . . . 64 ins.
Palestrina, bp. . . . . . . 96 B b
Palice . . . . 30 D e
Pa - li - kioa . . . . 170 ins. A
Palinurus, prom. . . . . . 30 E c
Pallacopas Canal . . . . . 18 G d
Pallantia . . . . 38 B d
Pallantium . . . . 14 C b
Pallanum . . . . 27 I e
Pallanza . . . . 90 I h
Pallas, Gardens of . . . . . 22 A
Pallene, in Attica . . . . . 16 B a
Pallene, pen. . . . . . . 11 E b
Pallia River . . . . 27 F e
Palma . . . . 38 C e
Palma, bp. . . . . 94 C d
Palma, univ. . . . . . . 100 F g
Palmanova . . . . 158 G f
Palmaria, isl. . . . . . . 30 B b
Palmas, Cape . . . . . . 175 C d
Palmas, Las . . . . . . 174 B b
Palmerston . . . . 172 C b
Palmyra . . . . 20 H e
Palmyra Island . . . . . 180 K g
Palo Alto, battle . . . . . .
Paloos, tribe . . . . . . 188 C a
Palos . . . . 83 J h
Pambotis, lake . . . . . . 10 B c
Pamiers . . . . 126 B e
Pamiers, bp. . . . . . . 94 C c
Pamier, plateau . . . . . 3 L e
Pamir, reg. . . . . . . 170 I e
Pamisus River, in Messenia . 14 B b
Pamisus River, in Thessaly . 10 C c
Pamlico River . . . . . . 193 F d
Pamlico Sound . . . . . 193 F d
Pamodus . . . . 27 I c
Pampeluna, see Pamplona
Pamphia . . . . 10 C d
Pamphylia, Macedonian prov. . 18 D b
Pamphylia, Rom. prov. . . 35 K f
Pamphylia, East Rom. prov. . . 43 I f (1)
Pamphylia, reg. . . . . . 20 D d
Pamphylia, satr. . . . . . 8 H e
Pamphylians, people . . . . . 5 C b
Pamplona . . . . 82 B a
Pamplona, bp. . . . . . . 94 B c
Pamunkey River . . . . . 193 F c
Pan, Cave of . . . . 23 C
Panachaicus, mt. . . . . . 14 B a
Panactum . . . . 16 B a

Panætolius, mt. . . . . 10 C d
Panamá . . . .
Panamá, Bay of . . . .
Panamá, Gulf of . . . . . . 213 E d
Panamá, country . . . . . . 214 A b
Panay, isl. . . . . 199 ins. H
Pancalieri . . . . 130 P j
Pancsova . . . . 159 K f
Pandarani . . . .
Pandateria, isl. . . . . . . 30 C b
Pandosia, in Epirus . . . . 10 B c
Pandosia, in Lucania . . . . 31 F b
Paneas . . . . 6 D b
Pangæus, mt. . . . . . . 11 E b
Panhandle, The, reg. . . . . . 210 E c
Panionium . . . . 13 E c
Panipat, Paniput . . . . . 137 C c
Panixer Pass . . . . . . 150 E c
Panjdeh . . . . 170 F c
Panmure, Fort . . . . . . 194 A d
Pannonia, reg. . . . . . . 38 F c
Pannonia I, West Rom. prov. . 42 F d (10)
Pannonia II, West Rom. prov. . 42 F d (8)
Pannonia, Lower, Rom. prov. . 34 H d
Pannonia, Upper, Rom. prov. . 34 H d
Pannonian March . . . . . . 54 H d
Panopeus . . . . 11 D d
Panopolis (Chemmis) . . . . . 18 D e
Panormus, in Peparethus . . . . 11 E c
Panormus (Palermo), in Sicily 30 C d
Panormus, port, in Epirus . . 10 A b
Pantanus, lake. . . . . . . 30 E a
Pantelleria Island . . . . . 161 H i
Pantheon, bldg. in Rome . . . . 22 A
Panticapæum (Kertch). . . . . . 12 K a
Pánuco River . . . . . . 201 F e
Paons, Allée des, Versailles . 149 A
Pao - ting . . . . 170 ins. A
Papago, Ind. Res. . . . . . 188 D d
Papal States . . . . . . 131 F e
Papelotte, farm . . . .
Paphlagonia, Macedonian prov. 18 D b
Paphlagonia, reg. . . . . . 8 B a
Paphlagonia, Rom. prov. . . 20 E b
Paphlagonia, East Rom. prov. . 43 I e (3)
Paphlagonia, satr. . . . . . 18 O g
Paphlagonia, theme . . . . 59 K e
Paphos . . . . 20 E e
Papia (Pavia) . . . . . . 26 D b
Papirianæ, Fossæ . . . . . 26 E d
Pappua, mt. . . . . 52 C c
Papua, col., see British New
  Guinea
Papua Gulf . . . . 172 D a
Pará . . . . 214 E c
Pará, state . . . . 214 D c
Paracatú . . . . 214 E d
Paraclet, Le, mon. . . . . . 94 C b
Paradies, mon. . . . . . . 95 F a
Parætacene, reg. . . . . . 19 K c
Parætaceni, people . . . . . 19 H d
Parætonium . . . . 18 C d
Paragua, isl. . . . . 199 ins. H
Paraguay, country . . . . . 215 D e
Paraguay River . . . . . . 21 D d
Parahyba . . . . 214 F c
Parahyba, state . . . . . 214 F c
Parahyba River . . . . . 214 E e
Paraiso 216
Paralia, dist. . . . . 15 D b
Paramanga . . . . 111 B d
Paramaribo . . . . 214 D b
Paraná . . . . 215 C f
Paraná, state . . . . . . 215 D e
Paraná River . . . . . . 214 D e
Paranaguá . . . . 215 D e
Paranapema River . . . . . 215 D e
Parapanisadæ, people . . . . 19 K d
Parapanisus Mountains . . . 19 K c
Parapotamii . . . . 11 D d
Parauæa, dist. . . . . . . 10 B b
Parchim . . . . 158 F b
Pardiac, cty. . . . . . . 69 D e (P. \)
Pardo, El, castle . . . . . . 130 C c

Pardubitz . . . . 159 H d
Parentium (Parenzo) . . . . . . 27 H b
Parenzo . . . . 90 D b
Parenzo, bp. . . . . 95 E b
Parga . . . . 93 B c
Paria, Gulf of . . . . . . 105 H d
Paria, reg. . . . . 105 H d
Paricanii, Paricanians, people . 19 K e
Pariña, Punta, cape . . . . 111 A b
Paris . . . . 61 E b
Paris in 1789, plan of . . . . . 149 B
Paris, bp. . . . . 94 C b
Paris, gen. . . . . . . 147 E b
Paris, univ. . . . . 100 F e
Parisii or Parisius, see Paris
Parisii, people . . . . 38 C c
Parita, reg. . . . . 105 D e
Parium . . . .
Parkersburg . . . . 206 ins.
Parma . . . . 26 E c
Parma, bp. . . . . 95 E c
Parma, duchy . . . . 150 E d
Parma River . . . . 26 E c
Parnahyba . . . . 214 E c
Parnahyba River . . . . . . 214 E c
Parnassus, mt. . . . . 11 D d
Parnes Mountains . . . . . . 15 D a
Parnon Mountains . . . . . . 14 C b
Paroisse, Rue de la, street in
Versailles . . . . . 149 A
Paros . . . . 15 F b
Paros, isl. . . . . 15 F b
Parramatta . . . . 172 E d
Parrhasia, reg. . . . . . . 14 B b
Parrtown . . . . 212 I d
Parry Islands . . . . . . 186 H a
Parsdorf . . . . 134 F d
Part-Dieu, La, mon. . . . . . . 91 O l
Partenkirchen . . . . 72 C b
Partenkirchen, mon. . . . . 95 E b
Parthanum . . . . 38 E c
Parthenay . . . . 69 C c
Parthenius, mt. . . . . . 14 C b
Parthenius River . . . . . . 20 E b
Parthenon, bldg. in Athens . . . 23 C
Parthenopæan Republic . . . . . 151 I h
Parthenope (Naples) . . . . 5 A a
Parthia, prov. . . . . . . 19 I c
Parthia, reg. . . . . . . 8 D b
Parthia, satr. . . . . . . 18 Q h
Parthians, Empire of the . . . . 35 N g
Paru River . . . . 214 D b
Paryadres Mountains . . . . . . 20 H b
Pasado, Cape . . . . 111 A b
Pasargadæ . . . . . . 19 H d, H e
Pasargadæ, people . . . . . 8 D c
Pas-de-Calais, dept. . . . . . 148 E d
Paseir . . . . 112 C c
Pasewalk . . . . 85 C b
Pashat . . . .
Pasitigris River . . . . . 19 G d
Passaic River . . . . 189 ins. C
Passarge River . . . . . . 155 J a
Passaro, Cape . . . . . . 131 G f
Passaron . . . . 10 B c
Passarowitz . . . .
Passau . . . . 63 G d
Passau, bp. . . . . 95 E b
Passavant, castle . . . . . 143 ins. F
Passavant, lordship . . . . . 143 ins. F
Passeier Tal, valley . . . . . 154 F e (Pa.)
Pastaza River . . . . 111 B b
Pasto . . . . 214 B c
Patagonia, reg. . . . . . 215 C g
Patani . . . .
Patapsco River . . . . . . 200 L h
Patara . . . . 20 C d
Patavia, see Passau
Patavium (Padua) . . . . . . 26 F b
Patay . . . . 76 D b
Paterno . . . . 64 ins.
Paternum . . . . 31 G c
Patiala . . . . 137 C b
Patillas . . . . 199 ins. G

Patmos, isl. . . . . 13 E c
Patna . . . . 137 D c
Patos, Laguna dos . . . . 215 D f
Patræ . . . . 14 B a
Patras . . . . 89 H g
Patras, desp. . . . . 93 B c
Patriarchates, 593—600. 52
Patrimony of Saint Peter (States
of the Church), 9 cent.
Patrimony of Saint Peter (States
of the Church), 12 cent. . . . 70 I e
Patrimony of Saint Peter (States
of the Church), 15 cent. . . . 90 C c
Patroclus, Burial mound of . .
Patroclus Island . . . . 15 D b
Pattala . . . . 19 K e
Pattan Somnath . . . .
Patti, bp. . . . . 95 E d
Patuca River . . . . 105 D c
Patuxent River . . . . 192 C d
Patzinaks or Petchenegs, people
Pátzcuaro . . . . 213 ins.
Pau . . . . 69 C e
Pau and Bayonne, gen. . . . . 147 D c
Paul, journeys of the Apostle 46, 47 leg.
Paulinzella, mon. . . . . . 95 E a
Paulus Hoeck . . . . 189 ins. C
Paumotu, isl. . . . . . . 180 M i
Paus . . . . 14 B b
Pausilypum . . . . 31 ins. A
Pausulæ . . . . 27 H d
Pau-ti . . . . 170 ins. A
Pavia . . . . 90 I h
Pavia, bp. . . . . 95 D b
Pavia, univ. . . . . . . 100 G e
Pavonia . . . . 189 ins. C
Pawnees, tribe . . . . . . 188 F b
Pawtucket . . . . 189 ins. A
Pawtuxed . . . . 189 ins. A
Pax Iulia . . . . 38 A c
Paxo, isl. . . . . 157 D e
Paxus, isl. . . . . 10 B c
Payerne . . . . 91 O l
Payne Lake . . . . 212 H c
Paysandú . . . . 215 D f
Payta . . . . 111 A c
Paz, La . . . . 214 C d
Peace, Altar of . . . . . . 22 A
Peace, Temple of. . . . . . 24 B
Peace River . . . . . . 186 H c
Peakland, dist. . . . . . .
Pea Ridge, mts. . . . . . . 208 B b
Pearl Coast . . . . 105 G d
Pearl River . . . . 191 H e
Pe-chi-li, gulf. . . . . . . 171 M e
Pe-chi-li, prov. . . . . . 171 M e
Pechora, River . . . . . . 3 J b
Peck, Fort, Ind. Res. . . . . 188 E a
Pecos . . . . 190 E d
Pecos River . . . . 190 E e
Pedasus (Methoni) . . . . . 14 B c
Pedee River, Great . . . . 193 E d
Pediæus River . . . . . 20 E e
Pedias, dist. . . . . . . 15 D a
Pedion, dist. . . . . . 16 B b
Pedir . . . . 112 C c
Pedo . . . . 26 B c
Pedroche . . . . 82 B b
Pedro Miguel 216
Pedum . . . . 35 ins. B
Peebles, cty. . . . .
Peebles, dist. . . . .
Peekskill . . . . 195 E c
Peene River . . . . . . 63 G b
Peenemünder Schanze, fort . . 123 G a
Peer . . . . 117 D c
Pegau, mon. . . . . 80 ins.
Pegu . . . .
Pegu, reg. . . . .
Pei-ho, R. . . . . 170 ins. A
Peipus, lake . . . . . . 88 L b
Peishwa, Doms. of the . . . 137 B e
Pei-tang . . . . 170 ins. A
Pei-tsang . . . . 170 ins. A

Pejepscot, Fort . . . . 189 C
Peking . . . .
Pelagonia . . . . 10 C
Pelagonia, dist. . . . . . . 17 B
Pelasgiotis, dist. . . . . . 11 C
Pelendones, people . . . . 38 E
Pelew Islands . . . . . . 179 E
Pelican Point, cape . . . . 108 R
Pelinnæum . . . . 10 C
Pelion, mt. . . . . 11 E
Pelisipia, proposed state in U.S.
Pelium . . . . 10 B
Pella, in Gilead . . . . 7 D
Pella, in Macedonia . . . . . 11 D
Pellana . . . . 14 C
Pellene . . . . 14 C
Pelly River . . . . 212 B
Pelopium . . . .
Peloponnesus, Byzantine prov. 89 B
Peloponnesus, pen. . . . . . 13 C
Peloponnesus, theme . . . 59 I
Pelorus, prom. . . . . . 30 E
Pelotas . . . . . . 215 D
Pelplin, mon. . . . . . 95 F
Peltuinum . . . . . . 27 H
Pelusium . . . . . . 1 C
Pelusium, ruins of . . . 150 B
Pemaquid . . . . . 189 D
Pemba, isl. . . . . . 175 H
Pembroke . . . . . . 84 A c
Pembroke, castle . . .
Pembroke, cty. . . . . . 127 U c
Pembroke, parl. bor. . . . 163 J
Pembroke, parl. dist. . . . 163 J
Peña Blanca . . . . . 215 B
Penas (Peñas) Gulf of . . . . . 215 B
Penay . . . . 91 N
Pendennis Castle . . . . 127 T
Penedo . . . . . . 214 F
Peneus River, in Elis . . . . . 14 B
Peneus River, in Thessaly . . . 11 D
Peñiscola . . . . . . 82 C
Penjhir . . . . . .
Pennar River . . . .
Penneloci . . . . . 26 A
Pennine Alps, mts. . . . 26 B
Pennine Chain, mts. . . . 49 E
Pennine Valley . . . . . . 26 B
Pennine and Graian Alps, West
Rom. prov. . . . . 42 D d (8)
Pennsylvania, col. . . . . . . 192 C c
Pennsylvania, state . . . 199 J b
Penobscot . . . . . 189 D b
Penobscot Bay . . . . . 189 D b
Penobscot River . . . . 189 D b
Peñon de Velez . . . . . 130 C f
Penrhyn Islands . . . . 180 L i
Penryn and Falmouth, parl. bor. 163 I g
Penrith . . . . . 127 W l
Pensacola . . . . . . 191 H c
Pensacola Bay . . . . . 193 ins. B
Pentagöet, Fort . . . . . . 189 D b
Pentapolis, dist., in Cyrenaica. 43 G g
Pentapolis, dist., in Italy . . . 64 B b
Pentapylum . . . . 31 ins. B (5)
Pentele . . . . . 16 B a
Pentelicus, mt. . . . 16 B a
Penthièvre, cty. . . . . 69 B b
Pentney, mon. . . . . 97 R i
Pentri, people . . . 30 D
Penuel . . . . . . 7 D d
Penza . . . . . . 139 G e
Peoria . . . . . . 212 G b
Peparethus, isl. . . . . 11 E c
Pephnos . . . . . 14 C c
Pequots, tribe . . . 189 C d
Pera . . . . . . 93 G c
Peræa, dist., in Palestine . . . 7 D e
Peræa, dist., in Greece . . 15 C a
Perche, cty. . . . . . 76 H f
Perche-Gouet, dist. . . . 76 D b (P.G.)
Percote . . . . . .
Perdido River . . . . . . 193 ins. B
Pered . . . . 159 I f

Perekop . . . . 139 D f
Perekop, Isthmus of . . . . . . 3 H d
Pereslawl . . . . 138 E d
Pergamum . . . .
Pergamum, km. . . . . 33 C b
Pergamus . . . . 11 F b
Perge . . . . 43 I f
Périgord, cty. . . . . 61 D d
Périgueux . . . . 61 D d
Périgueux, bp. . . . . 94 C b
Perim Island . . . . 174 H c
Perinthus . . . .
Peristhlava . . . . 59 J e
Perlas, Isla de, isl. . . . . 105 E e
Perlasz . . . . 159 K f
Perleberg . . . . 154 G b
Perm . . . . 138 I d
Permians, people . . . . 138 H d
Pernambuco or Recife . . . . 214 F c
Pernambuco, state . . . . 214 F c
Pernau . . . . 88 K b
Pernau, Hanse. cy. . . . . 99 H b
Péronne . . . . 76 E b
Perosa . . . . 130 P j
Perote . . . . 106 C a
Perote, Cofre de, mt. . . . . . 106 C a
Perovsk . . . . 170 H d
Perpignan . . . . 61 E e
Perpignan, gen. . . . . 147 E c
Perpignan, univ. . . . . 100 F f
Perrhæbi, people . . . . 10 C c
Perrhæbia, dist. . . . . 10 C c
Perryville . . . . 208 C b
Persante River . . . . 159 I b
Perseigne, mon. . . . . 94 C b
Persephone, Temple of . . . 31 ins.B (12)
Persepolis . . . . 8 J f
Pershore, mon . . . . 97 O i
Pershore, parl. bor. . . . .
Persia, country . . . . 170 G e
Persia, khan. . . . .
Persia, reg. . . . .
Persian Empire, about 500 B. C. 8
Persian Gulf . . . . 3 I f
Persis, prov. . . . . 19 H e
Persis, reg. . . . . 8 D b
Persis, satr. . . . . 8 J f
Perth, in Australia . . . . 172 A d
Perth, in Scotland . . . .
Perth, cty. . . . .
Perth, dist. . . . .
Perth Amboy . . . . 192 D c
Peru, Conquest of 111
Peru, reg. . . . . 111 B c
Peru, rep. . . . . 214 B c
Peru, viceroyalty . . . . 215 ins.
Peru, Lower, reg. . . . . 214 B c
Peru, Upper, reg. . . . . 214 C d
Perugia . . . . 90 D c
Perugia, bp. . . . . 95 E c
Perugia, univ. . . . . 100 H f
Perusia (Perugia) . . . . 27 G d
Perwez . . . . 156 B a
Pesaro . . . . 90 D c
Pesaro, bp. . . . . 95 E c
Pescado River . . . .
Pescadores, isl. . . . . 171 M f
Pescara . . . . 90 E c
Peschiera . . . . 90 C b
Peshawar, Peshawur . . . . . . 137 B b
Pessinus . . . . 20 D c
Petaliæ Islands . . . . 15 E b
Petchenegs or Patzinaks, people
Petchora River . . . .
Petelia . . . . 31 G c
Peten, isl. . . . . 105 B c
Petenisca . . . . 39 I j
Peterborough . . . .
Peterborough, mon. . . . .
Peterborough, parl. bor. . . . . 163 N e
Peterborough, soke and abbey of
Peterhead . . . .
Peterhof . . . . 131 I b
Peterlingen, mon. . . . . 95 D b

Petermann's Peak . . . . 186 P a
Petersberg, mon. . . . . 85 G e
Petersburg, in Virginia . . . . . 193 F c
Petersburg, Saint, in Russia . 138 D c
Petersburgh, in S. Australia . . 172 C d
Petersfield, parl. bor. 163 M g (Petersf.)
Petersham . . . . 196 E b
Petershausen, ab. . . . . 142 D e
Peterwardein . . . . 159 K f
Petitarus River . . . . 10 C d
Petites Écuries, loc. in Versailles 149 A
Petite Venise, loc. in Versailles 149 A
Petite Venise, Allée de la, in
    Versailles . . . . 149 A
Petit Rœulx . . . . 156 A a
Petit Trianon, loc. in Versailles 149 A
Petra, in Arabia . . . . 18 E d
Petra, in Macedonia . . . . . . 11 D b
Petra, in Sicily . . . . 30 D e
Petracoris, see Périgueux
Petræantheatre . . . . 16 D c (3)
Petro-Alexandrovsk . . . . 170 H d
Petrocorii, see Périgueux
Petronell . . . . 54 H d
Petropavlovsk . . . . 171 Q c
Petropolis . . . . 215 E e
Petrovsk . . . . 167 O g
Petrozavodsk . . . . 138 D c
Pettau . . . . 54 H d
Petten . . . . 117 C b
Petty Armenian States . . . . 67 N f
Peuce Island . . . . 18 C a
Peucelaotis . . . . 19 L d
Peucetii, people . . . . 31 F b
Pevensey . . . .
Pfaffenhofen . . . . 134 F d
Pfalzburg . . . . 158 D d
Pfävers, mon. . . . . 91 R l
Pfeddersheim . . . . 142 B a
Pfinz River . . . . 142 C c
Pflege Coburg, dist. . . . . . . 85 F e
Pforta, mon. . . . . 95 E a
Pforzheim . . . . 142 C c
Pfullendorf . . . . 142 D e
Pfullingen . . . . 143 H i
Phacium . . . . 10 D c
Phæca . . . . 10 C c
Phæna . . . . 6 E b
Phæstus, in Crete . . . . 14 ins.
Phæstus, in Locris . . . . 11 D d
Phæstus, in Thessaly . . . . . 10 D c
Phagres . . . . 11 E b
Phalacrum, prom. in Corcyra . 10 A c
Phalacrum, prom. in Sicily . . 30 E d
Phalæsiæ . . . . 14 C b
Phalanna . . . . 11 D c
Phalara . . . . 11 D d
Phalasia, prom. . . . . 11 E d
Phalerum . . . . 15 D b
Phaliga . . . . 20 I e
Phaloria . . . . 10 C c
Phanagoria . . . . 12 K a
Phanariote Quarter, in Constan-
    tinople . . . . 93 G e
Phanote . . . . 10 A b
Phara . . . . 10 B d
Pharæ, in Achaia . . . . 14 B a
Pharæ, in Messenia . . . . . . 14 C b
Pharcadon . . . . 10 C c
Pharis . . . . 14 C b
Pharmacussa, isl. . . . . 16 B b
Pharnacia . . . . 20 H b
Pharpar River . . . . 6 E b
Pharos, isl. . . . . 12 G b
Pharos, lighthouse . . . . 34 ins.C
Pharsalus (Pharsala) . . . . . . 11 D c
Pharus, isl. . . . . 38 F d
Phaura, isl. . . . .
Phasael . . . . 6 ins.A
Phasaëlis . . . . 7 C d
Phaselis . . . . 20 D d
Phasis . . . . 12 L b
Phasis River . . . . 20 J a
Phea . . . . 14 B b

Pheasants, Isle of . . . . 126 A e
Pheneus . . . . 14 C b
Pheræ . . . . 11 D c
Phigæa . . . . 16 B b
Phigalia . . . . 14 B b
Phila . . . . 11 D c
Philadelphia, in Asia Minor . . 20 C c
Philadelphia, in Brazil . . 214 E d (Phil.)
Philadelphia, in Pa. . . . . . . 192 D c
Philadelphia, in Syria . . . . . 7 D e
Philæ Island . . . . 4 F d
Philiphaugh . . . .
Philippeum, in Olympia . . . .
Philippeville . . . . 117 C d
Philippi . . . . 11 F a
Philippine Islands . . . . 199 ins. H
Philippopolis, in Syria . . . . . 6 F c
Philippopolis, in Thrace . . . . 39 M l
Philippopolis, in Bulgaria . . 167 J g
Philippsburg . . . . 142 B b
Philippus, Portico of . . . . . . 22 A
Philistæa, dist. . . . . 7 A f
Philistines, people . . . . 7 ins. D
Philomelium . . . . 67 M f
Philopappus, Monument of. . . 23 D
Phinopolis . . . .
Phintias . . . . 30 C e
Phlegra, pen. . . . . 11 E c
Phlegræan Fields . . . . 31 ins.A
Phlius . . . . 14 C b
Phlya . . . . 16 B a
Phlygonium . . . . 11 D d
Phocæa . . . . 12 I c
Phocian Wall . . . . 16 F e
Phocis, state . . . . 11 D d
Phœnice . . . . 10 B c
Phœnicia, country . . . . 6 C c
Phœnicia, East Rom. prov. . . 43 J g(2)
Phœnicia, reg. . . . . 4 F c
Phœnicia Libani, East Rom. prov. 43 J g(8)
Phœnicians, people . . . . 7 ins.D
Phœnicus, in Cythera . . . . . 15 D c
Phœnicus Port, in Messenia . . 14 B c
Phœnicussa, isl. . . . . 30 D d
Phœnix . . . . 210 C d
Phœnix Islands . . . . 180 J h
Phœnix River, in Achaia . . . . 14 B a
Phœnix River, in Malis . . . . 16 F e
Pholegandrus, isl. . . . . 15 E c
Pholoë, mt. . . . . 14 B b
Phorbantia, isl. . . . . 30 B d
Phoron, Port of . . . . 16 B b
Photice . . . . 10 B c
Phra . . . . 19 J d
Phrixa . . . . 14 B b
Phrygia, reg. . . . . 20 D c
Phrygia, Macedonian prov. . . . 18 D c
Phrygia Pacatiana, East Rom.
    prov. . . . . 43 H f(7)
Phrygia Salutaris, East Rom.
    prov. . . . . 43 I f(8)
Phrygians, people . . . . 5 C b
Phthiotis, reg. . . . . 11 D c
Phylacæ, in Macedonia . . . . . 10 D b
Phylace, in Epirus . . . . 10 B c
Phylace, in Thessaly . . . . . . 11 D c
Phyle . . . . 15 D a
Phyllus . . . . 10 D c
Phytia . . . . 10 C d
Piacenza . . . . 90 I h
Piacenza, bp. . . . . 95 D c
Piacenza, univ. . . . . 100 G f
Pialia . . . . 10 C c
Pian de Carpine, John of, route
    of . . . .
Piankishaws, tribe . . . . 188 I c
Piauhy, state . . . . 214 E c
Piave River . . . . 90 D b
Picardy, gouv. . . . . 146 B b
Picardy, prov. . . . . 148 E d
Picentes, Picentians, people . .
Picentia . . . . 30 D b
Picentini, people . . . . 30 D b
Picenum, dist. . . . . 27 H d

Picenum Suburbicarium, West
  Rom. prov. . . . . 42 E e (3)
Pichincha, battle . . . . 214 B c
Pickawillany . . . . 194 C b
Pickens, Fort . . . . 208 C c
Pickering, parl. bor. . . . . . .
Picolata, Fort . . . . 193 D g
Pictavi, see Poitiers
Pictavi, people . . . . 38 B c
Pictland (Scotland), reg. . . . .
Picton . . . . 172 G e
Picts, people, 5 cent. . . . . . 50 C a
Picts, people, 9 cent. . . . . . 54 D b
Piedmont, dist. . . . . 90 A b
Piedmont, princ. . . . . 150 D d
Piedmont Hills . . . . 187 K e
Piedra, mon. . . . . 94 B c
Piedras Negras . . . . 213 B b
Pieria, dist., on the Strymonic Gulf 11 F b
Pieria, dist., on the Thermaic Gulf 11 D b
Pierre . . . . 210 F b
Pierre, Fort . . . . 210 E b
Pierre's Hole, dist. . . . . . . 210 C b
Pierus, mt. . . . . 10 D b
Pierus River . . . . 14 B a
Pietas Iulia, col. . . . . 27 H c
Pietermaritzburg . . . . 175 N e
Piéton River . . . . 156 A a
Pietramala . . . . 90 L i
Pietra Santa . . . . 90 C c
Pigeon Creek . . . . 105 ins.
Pike, route of . . . . . . 198 F c, 199 G b
Pike's Peak . . . . 198 E c
Pilar . . . . 191 G e
Pilate, House of . . . . . . 68 ins. B (16)
Pilcomayo River . . . . 214 C e
Pilica River . . . . 87 M c
Pillars of Hercules (Calpe, or
  Gibraltar, and Abila), prom. . 12 B c
Pillau . . . . 115 J a
Pillnitz, castle . . . . 135 G c
Pillow, Fort . . . . 208 C b
Pilsen . . . . 63 G d
Pilten . . . . 88 I c
Pimas, tribe . . . . 188 D d
Pimería, Upper, dist. . . . . . 190 C e
Pin, Le, mon. . . . . 94 C b
Pinacotheca, bldg. in Athens . 23 C
Pinar del Rio . . . . 213 D b
Pinciacus, see Poissy
Pincian, quarter in Rome . . . . 96 A
Pincian Gate . . . . 22 A
Pincian Mount . . . . 22 A
Pincian Way . . . . 22 A
Pinczow . . . . 123 K c
Pindus . . . . 11 D d
Pindus Mountains . . . . . . 10 C c
Pine Creek . . . . 172 C e
Pineda, route of . . . . 191 G f
Pine Ridge, Ind. Res. . . . . . 188 F b
Pinerolo . . . . 90 A b
Pines, Isle of . . . . 105 D b
Ping-yang, in China . . . . . .
Ping-yang, in Corea . . . . . . 171 N e
Pinhel . . . . 94 A c
Pinkie . . . . 118 D b
Pinna . . . . 27 H e
Pinos Puente . . . . 184 C e
Pinsk . . . . 139 C e
Pinto, route of . . . .
Pinzgau, valley . . . . 115 G e
Pinzon, route of, 1499 . . . . . 108 N g
Pinzon, route of, 1508 . . . . . 105 D c
Piombino . . . . 90 L j
Piombino, princ. . . . . 151 L k
Piotrkow . . . . 159 J c
Pipe Creek, stream . . . . . . 208 ins.
Pipewell, mon. . . . . 97 Q i
Piqua . . . . 200 A c
Piquentum . . . . 27 H b
Piræus, The . . . . 16 B b
Piræus, harbor of the . . . . . 16 D c
Piraic Gate . . . . 23 D
Piranhas . . . . 214 F c

Piranum . . . . 27 H b
Piratininga . . . . 215 E e (P.)
Piresiæ . . . . 10 D c
Pirmasens . . . . 134 D d
Pirna . . . . 115 G c
Pirot . . . . 164 C b
Pirus River . . . . 14 B a
Pisa, ruins, in Elis . . . . . . 14 B b
Pisa, in Italy . . . . 90 L j
Pisa, abp. . . . . 95 E c
Pisa, univ. . . . . 100 H f
Pisæ (Pisa, in Italy) . . . . . 26 E d
Pisanus, Portus . . . . . : . . 26 E d
Pisatis, dist. . . . . 14 B b
Pisaurum (Pesaro) . . . . . . 27 G d
Pisaurus River . . . . 27 G d
Piscataqua . . . . 189 C c
Piscina Publica, in Rome . . . . 23 B
Piscina Publica, Aug. Reg. of
  Rome . . . . 22 A
Pisco . . . . 214 B d
Pisek . . . . 79 H d
Pisgah, mt. . . . . 7 D e
Pishin . . . . 170 H e
Pisidia, E. Rom. prov. . . . . 43 I f (6)
Pisidia, Macedonian prov. . . . 18 D c
Pisidia, reg. . . . . 20 D d
Pisino, bp. . . . . 95 E b
Pisistratus, Aqueduct of . . . . 23 D
Piski . . . . 159 L f
Pistoja . . . .
Pistoriæ (Pistoja) . . . . . . 26 E d
Pistum . . . . 31 I a
Pistyrus . . . . 11 F b
Pisura, Punta, cape . . . . . . 111 A c
Pitcairn Island . . . . 180 O j
Pithecussæ, isl. . . . . 30 C b
Pithom . . . . 1 C b
Pitinum Mergens . . . . 27 G d
Pitinum Pisaurense . . . . . . 27 G d
Pitt, Fort, in Canada . . . . . 212 A c
Pitt, Fort, in Pa. . . . . 192 A c
Pittsburgh . . . . 195 B c
Pittsburg Landing . . . . . . 208 C b
Pityus . . . . 12 L b
Pityusæ, isl. . . . . 38 C e
Pityussa, isl. . . . . 15 D b
Piura . . . . 111 A c
Piura River . . . . 111 A c
Pizarro, route of 111
Place d'Armes, in Versailles . . 149 A
Place de Grève, in Paris . . . . 149 B
Place de Louis XV., in Paris . 149 B
Place des Victoires, in Paris . 149 B
Place du Carrousel, in Paris . 149 B
Place du Dauphin, in Paris . . 149 B
Place Vendôme, in Paris . . . . 149 B
Placentia (Piacenza), in Italy . 26 D b
Placentia. in Newfoundland . . 212 J d
Placentia Bay . . . . 212 J d
Placilla . . . . 215 C e
Plaine de la Ménagerie, loc. in
  Versailles . . . . 149 A
Plaine de Trianon, loc. in Ver-
  sailles . . . . 149 A
Plaine du Mail, loc. in Versailles 149 A
Plaine Saint Antoine, loc. in
  Versailles. . . . . 149 A
Plaine-Selve, mon. . . . . . . 94 B b
Planasia, isl. . . . . 26 E e
Planchenoit . . . .
Plantations across the Water . 193 ins. A
                 (Plan.)
Plasencia . . . . 83 J g
Plasencia, bp. . . . . 94 A c
Plassey . . . . 137 E d
Plata, La, in the Arg. Rep. . . 215 D f
Plata, La, in Bolivia . . . . . . 214 C d
Plata, La, viceroyalty . . . . . 215 ins.
Plataeæ . . . . 11 E d
Platamodes, prom. . . . . . . 14 B b
Platanistus, prom. . . . . . . 15 C c
Platte River . . . . 190 F c
Platte River, North . . . . . . 190 E c

Platte River, South . . . . . . 190 E c
Plattsburg . . . . 200 G a
Plattsmouth . . . . 210 F b
Plaue . . . . 85 C b
Plauen . . . . 85 G e
Plauer Canal . . . . 135 G b
Plavis (Piave) River . . . . . . 85 G e
Pleissnerland, dist. . . . . . . 85 G e
Plemmyrium, dist. . . . . . . 31 ins. B
Plemmyrium, prom. . . . . . 30 E e
Plenty, Bay of . . . . 172 G d
Pleskau . . . . 88 M c
Pless . . . . 135 J d
Plessis-les-Tours . . . . 126 B c
Plestinus, lake . . . . 27 G d
Pleuron . . . . 10 C d
Plevlie . . . . 164 B d
Plevna . . . . 164 C b
Plistus River . . . . 11 D d
Plock . . . . 115 J b
Plock, bp. . . . . 95 F a
Ploërmel . . . . 76 B c
Ploesti . . . . 165 D a
Plökenpass . . . . 27 G a
Plombières-les-Bains . . . . . 158 D e
Plothia . . . . 16 B a
Plymouth, in England . . . . .
Plymouth, parl. bor. . . . . . 163 J g
Plymouth, in Mass. . . . . . . 189 C d
Plymouth, in N. Carolina . . . 208 E b
Plymouth, New, col. in Mass. . 189 C d
Plymouth, New, New Zealand . 172 G d
Plymouth Company, Grants to the 190 ins.
Plympton, mon. . . . . 97 M k
Plympton, parl. bor. . . . . . 163 K g
Pnom-Penh . . . . 171 L g
Pnyx, loc. in Athens . . . . . 23 D
Poblet, mon. . . . . 94 C c
Pocasset . . . . 189 ins. A
Pocatello . . . . 210 C b
Pöchlarn . . . . 63 H d
Podandus . . . . 59 K f
Podgoritza . . . . 164 B b
Podiebrad . . . . 87 J c
Podlesia, dist. . . . . 139 C e
Podolia, dist. . . . . 139 C f
Podolsk . . . . 153 P f
Pœcilus, mt. . . . . 16 B a
Pœdiculi, people . . . . 31 F a
Pœessa . . . . 15 E b
Poel, isl. . . . . 122 F a
Pœnina, Alpis, pass . . . . . . 26 B b
Pœtovio . . . . 42 F d
Pöhlde . . . . 62 F c
Point au Baril . . . . 192 D a
Point au Fer . . . . 196 E b
Point Comfort, cape . . . . . 193 ins. A
Pointe Coupée . . . . 191 G e
Point de Galle, cape . . . . . 112 B c
Point Pleasant, battle . . . . . 194 C c
Poischwitz . . . . 155 H c
Poissy . . . . 76 E b
Poitiers . . . . 61 D c
Poitiers, bp. . . . . 94 C b
Poitiers, gen. . . . . 147 D b
Poitiers, univ. . . . . 100 F e
Poitou, cty. . . . . 61 C c
Poitou, gouv. . . . . 146 A b
Poitou, prov. . . . . 148 D e
Pojang Lake . . . .
Pola . . . . 27 H c
Pola, bp. . . . . 95 E c
Pola de Gordon, La . . . . . . 82 A a
Polabians, people . . . . 62 F b
Poland, duchy . . . . 59 H c
Poland, km., 11 cent. . . . . . 63 I c
Poland, km., 12 cent. . . . . . 70 J c
Poland, km., 16 cent. . . . . . 119 I c
Poland, km., 18 cent. . . . . . 131 J c
Poland, km., 19 cent. . . . . . 159 J b
Poland, Great, dist. . . . . . . 139 A e
Poland, Little, dist. . . . . . . 139 B e
Polati, bp. . . . . 95 F c
Polaticum, prom. . . . . 27 H c

Polden Hills . . . . 49 E f
Poles, people . . . . 57 H c
Polesina, dist. . . . . 90 C b
Policastro . . . . 90 E e
Policastro, bp. . . . . 95 F c
Polichne, quarter in Syracuse . 31 ins. B
Poligny . . . . 126 D c
Polillo, isl. . . . . 171 N g
Polish Livonia, dist. . . . . . . 131 I b
Pollentia, Balearic Is. . . . . . 38 C e
Pollentia, in Liguria . . . . . 26 B c
Pollenza . . . . 50 E d
Polling . . . . 62 F e
Polling-places, loc. in Rome . 24 B
Polo, Marco, route of . . . . .
Polotsk . . . . 71 L b
Polotsk, princ. . . . . 71 L b
Polovzians, people . . . . . . 71 N d
Poltava . . . . 139 D f
Polyægus, isl. . . . . 15 E c
Polypotamia, proposed state in
  U.S. . . . .
Polyrrhenia . . . . 14 ins.
Polytimetus River . . . . 19 K b
Pombia . . . . 62 E f
Pomerania, dist. . . . . 59 H c
Pomerania, Farther, dist. . . . 123 H b
Pomerania, Hither, dist. . . . 123 G b
Pomerania, duchy, 12 cent. . . 72 D a
Pomerania, duchy, 15 cent. . . 87 J b
Pomerania, prov. . . . . 159 H b
Pomerania, Swedish, dist. . . . 154 G a
Pomeranians, Bp. of the . . . . 95 E a
Pomeranians, people . . . . . . 46 J c
Pomerelia, dist. . . . . 72 D a
Pomoria, dist. . . . . 138 D b
Pomos, tribe . . . . 188 B c
Pompadour . . . . 126 B d
Pompælo (Pamplona) . . . . . 38 B d
Pompeii . . . . 30 D b
Pompeiopolis, in Cilicia . . . . 20 F d
Pompeiopolis, in Paphlagonia . 20 F b
Pompey, Gardens of . . . . . 23 B
Pompey, Portico of . . . . . . 22 A
Pompey, Senate-house of . . . 22 A
Pompey, Theatre of . . . . . . 22 A
Pompey's Pillar . . . . 34 ins. C (7)
Pomptine Marshes . . . . 30 B a
Ponca, Ind. Res. . . . . 188 G c
Poncas, tribe . . . . 188 G b
Ponce . . . . 199 ins. G
Ponce de León, Bahia de, bay 191 I f
Ponce de León, landing-place of 191 I e
Pondicherry . . . . 137 C f
Pondoland, dist. . . . . 175 M m
Pons, castle . . . . 76 C d
Pons Ælii (Newcastle) . . . . .
Pons Aureoli . . . . 26 D b
Pons Drusi . . . . 27 F a
Pons Ferri (Iron Bridge) . . . . 68 C b
Pons Saravi . . . . 39 I i
Ponta Grossa . . . .
Pontafel Pass . . . . 135 G e
Pontarlier . . . . 122 D e
Pont au Change, loc. in Paris. 149 B
Pont Audemer . . . . 76 D b
Pontchartrain, Fort . . . . . . 191 I c
Pontchartrain, lake . . . . . . 208 B c
Pont de Cé . . . . 126 A c
Pont de l'Arche . . . . 76 D b
Ponteamas . . . .
Pontecorvo . . . . 90 D d
Pontecorvo, princ. . . . . . . 151 L k
Pontefract . . . . 65 F d
Pontefract, mon. . . . . 97 P h
Pontefract, parl. bor. . . . . . 163 M d
Ponte Molle, loc. in Rome. . . 96 A
Ponte Sant' Angelo, loc. in Rome 96 A
Ponthieu, cty. . . . . 76 D a
Pontiac . . . . 211 I b
Pontiæ, isl. . . . . 30 B b
Pontiæ Islands . . . . 30 C b
Pontica, reg. . . . . 50 J d
Ponticus, lake . . . . 19 J d

Pontifex Maximus, House of the 24 A
Pontigny . . . . 69 I g
Pontigny, mon. . . . . 94 C b
Pont Notre Dame, loc. in Paris 149 B
Pont Neuf, loc. in Paris . . . . 149 B
Pontoise . . . . 126 C b
Pontremoli . . . . 90 I h
Pontresina . . . . 91 R l
Pont Royal, loc. in Paris . . . . 149 B
Pont Saint Michel, loc. in Paris 149 B
Pontus, East Rom. dioc. . . . . 43 J f
Pontus, reg. . . . .
Pontus, Rom. prov. . . . .
Pontus Euxinus (Black Sea) . . 12 J b
Pontus Polemoniacus, East Rom.
  prov. . . . . 43 J e(9)
Pony Express, route of the . 210 F b
Ponzone . . . . 130 Q j
Pool of the Aqueduct . . . . . 6 ins. A(5)
Poole . . . . 127 X p
Poole, parl. bor. . . . . 163 L g
Poona . . . . 137 B e
Popayan . . . . 111 B a
Poperinghe . . . . 117 A d
Popilian Way, road . . . 27 G c, 31 F d
Popocatepetl, vol. . . . . . . 106 B a
Popotlan . . . .
Poppi . . . . 90 L j
Populoniæ, Aquæ . . . . 26 E d
Populonium . . . . 26 E e
Po River . . . . 90 J h
Porchester . . . .
Porcien, cty. . . . . 69 J f
Porcobera River . . . . 26 C c
Porcupine River . . . . 212 A b
Porfirio Diaz, Ciudad . . . . . 213 B b
Porhoët, castle . . . . 76 B b
Porhoët, cty. . . . . 76 B b
Porman . . . . 82 B b
Porphyrion . . . . 6 C a
Porpoise, Cape . . . . 189 C c
Porta Appia, loc. in Rome . . . 96 A
Porta aurea, loc. in Jerusalem . 68 ins. B
Portæ Caspiæ, pass, see Caspian
  Gates . . . . 19 H c
Portæ Caucasiæ, pass, see Cau-
  casian Gates . . . . 18 F b
Porta Flaminia, loc. in Rome . 96 A
Portage la Prairie . . . . 212 F c
Porta Latina, loc. in Rome . . 96 A
Portalegre . . . . 94 A d
Porta Pia, loc. in Rome. . . . . 96 A
Port Arthur, in Canada . . . . 212 F d
Port Arthur, in Asia . . . . . . 171 N e
Porta Salaria, loc. in Rome . 96 A
Porta San Pancrazio, loc. in Rome 96 A
Porta San Paolo, loc. in Rome 96 A
Porta Tiburtina, loc. in Rome . 96 A
Port Augusta, S. Australia . . 172 C d
Port Augusta, W. Australia . . 172 A d
Port au Prince . . . . 213 E c
Port Bouet . . . . 175 C d
Port Clarence . . . . 198 ins. A
Port Darwin . . . . 172 B b
Port Davey . . . . 172 D e
Port Elizabeth . . . . 175 M m
Porte Saint Denis, loc. in Paris 149 B
Porte Saint Martin, loc. in Paris 149 B
Portese, Porta, loc. in Rome . . 22 A
Port Essington, in Australia . . 172 C b
Port Essington, in Canada . . . 212 ins. A
Port Eyre . . . . 172 C d
Port Gibson . . . . 208 B c
Port Hamilton . . . . 171 N e
Porthmus . . . . 11 F d
Port Hope . . . . 198 ins. A
Port Hudson . . . . 208 B c
Portico of the Gods, loc. in Rome 24 B
Port Jackson . . . . 172 E d
Portland, in Australia . . . . . 172 D d
Portland, in England . . . . . 127 W p
Portland, in Maine . . . . . . 179 K b
Portland, in Oregon . . . . . . 198 A a
Portland Canal . . . . 212 ins.

Port Lincoln . . . . 172 C d
Port Louis . . . . 175 I g
Port Macquarie . . . . 172 E d
Port Natal . . . . 175 N l
Port Nicholson . . . . 172 G e
Porto, bp. . . . . 96 B b
Porto Alegre . . . . 215 D e
Porto Bello . . . . 105 E e
Porto Cabello, see Puerto Cabello
Porto Calvo . . . . 214 F c
Port of Spain . . . . 214 C a
Porto Maurizio . . . . 90 B c
Porto Novo . . . . 174 D d
Porto Rico, col. . . . .
Porto Rico, isl. . . . . 199 ins. G
Porto Santo . . . . 108 P d
Porto Seguro . . . . 214 F d
Porto Viejo . . . .
Port Phillip . . . . 172 G d
Port Phillip District . . . . . . 172 leg.
Port Republic . . . . 208 E b (P.R.)
Port Royal, in Jamaica . . . . .
Port Royal, in Nova Scotia . . 212 I d
Port Royal, loc. in Paris . . . . 149 B
Port Royal, near Paris . . . . 126 B b
Port Royal, in S. C. . . . . . 193 ins. C
Port Said . . . . 174 K i
Port Simpson . . . . 212 ins.
Portsmouth, in England . . . . 69 C a
Portsmouth, parl. bor. . . . . .
Portsmouth, hospital . . . . . . 100 A b
Portsmouth, in N. Hampshire . 189 C c
Portsmouth, in Ohio . . . . . . 206 ins.
Portsmouth, in Rhode Island . 189 ins. A
Portsmouth, in Virginia . . . . 207 K c
Portsmouth Harbor . . . . . . 51 P i
Port Stanley . . . . 206 ins.
Port Sudan . . . . 174 G b
Portugal, cty. . . . . 83 D c
Portugal, km., 12 cent. . . . . 82 G e
Portugal, km., 15 cent. . . . . 83 J g
Portuguese, people . . . .
Portuguese East Africa, col. . . 175 G g
Portuguese Guinea, col. . . . . 174 B c
Portuguese West Africa, col. . 175 E f
Portunata, isl. . . . . 27 I c
Portunus, Temple of . . . . . . 24 A
Portus, bp. . . . . 96 B b
Portus Ædro . . . . 27 G b
Portus Augusti . . . . 27 G f
Portus Cale (Oporto) . . . . . 38 A d
Portus Delphini . . . . 26 D c
Portus Divini . . . . 38 B e
Portus Eunostus . . . . 34 ins. C
Portus Herculis Monœci (Mo-
  naco) . . . . 26 B d
Portus Itius . . . . 38 C b
Portus Lemanus (Lymne) . . . . 38 C b
Portus Magnus (Portsmouth
  Harbor) . . . .
Portus Maurici (Porto Maurizio) 26 C d
Portus Namnetum (Nantes) . . . 38 B c
Portus Pisanus . . . . 26 E d
Portus Traianus . . . . 26 E e
Portus Veneris . . . . 26 D e
Port Way, road . . . . 35 ins. A
Poschiavo . . . . 91 S l
Posen . . . . 63 I b
Posen, bp. . . . . 95 F a
Posen, prov. . . . . 159 I b
Posidium, near Alexandria . . . 34 ins. C
Posidium, near Corinth . . . . 15 D b
Posidium, prom., Acanthian Gulf 11 E b
Posidium, prom., Bay of Pæstum 30 D b
Posidium, prom., Phthiotis . . . 11 E c
Posidium, prom., Propontis . . .
Posidium, prom., Thermaic Gulf 11 E c
Posidonia . . . . 12 F b
Posilipo, mt. . . . . 31 ins. A
Pospol, farm . . . .
Postern, loc. in London . . . . 75 G g
Postumian Way, in Liguria, road 26 C c
Postumian Way, in Venetia, road 27 G b
Poswol . . . . 131 H b

Potaïssa . . . . 35 I d
Potamii . . . . 16 C b
Potchefstroom . . . . 175 M l
Potentia, in Lucania . . . . . . 30 E b
Potentia, in Picenum . . . . . . 27 H d
Potenza . . . . 90 E d
Poti . . . . 99 L e
Potidæa . . . . 11 E b
Potomac River . . . . 187 L e
Potosí . . . . 214 C d
Potsdam . . . . 123 G b
Pottawatomi, Ind. Res.. . . . . . 188 G c
Pottawatomi of Huron, Ind. Res. 188 I b
Pottawatomies, tribe . . . . 188 I b
Poultry, loc. in London . . . . 75 G g (36)
Pourré, route of . . . . 195 ins. B
Poussay, mon. . . . . 148 C b
Pouzo Alegre . . . . 214 D d
Poverty Bay . . . . 172 G d
Powder River . . . . 198 D b
Powell River . . . . 196 ins. A
Powhatans, tribes . . . . 188 J c
Pozhega . . . . 159 I f
Pozzuoli . . . . 46 I e
Pozzuoli, bp. . . . . 95 ins.
Præneste . . . . 27 G f
Præneste, bp. . . . . 96 B b
Prænestine Gate . . . . 22 A
Prænestine Way, road . . . . 35 ins. B
Prætorian Camp, loc. in Rome . 22 A
Prætorian Gate . . . . 22 A
Prætorian Latovicorum . . . . 27 I b
Prætuttii, people . . . . 27 H e
Prævalitana, prov. . . . . 43 F e (3)
Praga . . . . 115 K b
Pragel Pass . . . . 150 E c
Prague . . . . 63 H c
Prague, abp. . . . . 95 E b
Prague, univ. . . . . 100 H d
Prairie, La, battle . . . . 189 B b
Prairie du Chien . . . . 211 G b
Prasiæ, in Attica . . . . 16 C b
Prasiæ, in Laconia . . . . 15 C b
Prata Quinctia, loc. in Rome . 22 A
Prato, near Florence . . . . . . 90 L j
Prattigau, valley . . . . 91 R l
Pratzen . . . . 155 I d
Právia . . . . 82 A a
Pré - sur - Arnon, La, mon. . . . 94 C b
Préaux, mon. . . . . 94 C b
Prechthal . . . . 142 B d
Pregel River . . . . 87 M a
Prela . . . . 130 P k
Prémontré . . . . 69 l f (Prém.)
Prémontré, mon. . . . . 94 C b
Prenzlau . . . . 79 H b
Prenzlau, Hanse. cy . . . . . . 99 ins. B
Preobrazhensk . . . . 138 E d
Prepesinthus, isl. . . . . 15 E c
Presburg . . . . 63 I d
Presburg, univ. . . . . 100 I e
Prescott . . . . 210 C d
Présentation, Fort de la . . . . 194 D b
Presidio del Norte . . . . 190 E f
Presidio, State of the . . . . . 151 I h
Presqu'Isle, Fort . . . . 192 B b
Presteign, parl. bor. . . . .
Preston . . . . : . . . . 127 V m
Preston, parl. bor. . . . . 163 L d
Prestonpans . . . .
Pretoria . . . . 175 M l
Preussisch - Eylau . . . . 153 I b
Prevesa . . . . 93 B c
Priapus . . . .
Pribilof Islands . . . . 180 K b
Priene . . . . 13 L c
Prignitz, dist. . . . . 85 B b
Prilip . . . . 89 B b
Prilius, lake . . . . 26 E e
Prince Albert, town . . . . . . 212 E c
Prince Albert Land . . . . . . 186 H a
Prince Edward Island, Canada 186 M d
Prince Edward Island, Ind. Oc. 182 E E l
Prince George, Fort . . . . . . 193 C d

Prince of Wales, Cape . . . . . 186 C b
Prince of Wales Island, Arctic
  Ocean . . . . 186 J a
Prince of Wales Island, Pacific
  Ocean . . . . 212 ins.
Prince of Wales Land . . . . 212 F a
Prince of Wales Strait . . . . 212 D a
Prince Patrick, isl. . . . . 186 G a
Prince Regent Inlet . . . . . . 212 F a
Prince Rupert, town . . . . . . 212 ins.
Prince's Island . . . . 175 D d
Princeton . . . . 192 D c
Principati, dist. . . . . 90 E d
Principe da Beira, Fort do . . 214 C d
Printzdorp . . . . 192 ins.
Printzhof . . . . 192 ins.
Pripet, Marshes of the . . . . 2 G c
Pripet River . . . . 139 C e
Prishtina . . . . 89 B b
Prison Gate, in Jerusalem . . . 6 ins. A
Prisrend . . . . 77 I d
Prittlewell, mon. . . . . 97 R j
Pritzwalk, Hanse. cy. . . . . . 99 ins. B
Privas . . . . 126 D d
Privernum . . . . 30 C a
Prizlawa . . . . 63 G b
Probalinthus . . . . 16 B a
Probus, Bridge of . . . . 22 A
Prochyta, isl. . . . . 30 C b
Procida, isl. . . . . 90 D d
Proclamation Line of 1763 . 194 C d, E a
Proconnesus . . . .
Proconnesus, isl. . . . .
Proconsular Africa, Rom. prov. 34 F f
Proërna . . . . 11 D c
Progreso . . . . 213 D b
Prome . . . .
Promontorium pulchrum, cape. 15 E a
Pronni . . . . 10 B d
Pronsk . . . . 71 N c
Propaxus, isl. . . . . 10 B c
Prophthasia . . . . 19 J d
Propylæa, bldg. in Athens . . 23 C (6)
Propylæum, bldg. in Olympia .
Propontis (Sea of Marmora) . .
Proschium . . . . 10 C d
Propopis . . . . 4 ins. *
Prospalta . . . . 16 B b
Prote, isl. . . . . 14 B b
Provence, cty., 11 cent. . . . . 61 F e
Provence, cty., 12 cent. . . . . 69 G e
Provence, cty., 15 cent. . . . . 84 F h
Provence, gouv. . . . . 146 C c
Provence, marq. . . . . 69 F d
Provence, prov. . . . . 148 F f
Providence, in Rhode Island . 189 ins. A
Providence, in Maryland . . . 192 D c
Providence, Fort . . . . 212 D b
Providence Islands . . . .
Provins . . . . 76 E b
Prudhomme, Fort . . . . 191 H d
Prüm . . . . 117 E d
Prüm, mon. . . . . 95 D a
Pruntrut . . . .
Prusa . . . . 77 I b
Prussia, dist. . . . . 88 I d
Prussia, duchy . . . . 88 l d
Prussia, km., 1701 . . . . 135 K a
Prussia, km., 1812 . . . . 155 J a
Prussia, km., 1815—1866 . . . 158—159
Prussia, km., 1910 . . . . . . 161 B-E b
Prussian Customs - Union . . . 160 D c
Prussian Hessian Customs-Union 160 D c
Prussians, people, about 1000 . 59 I c
Pruth River . . . . 59 J d
Pruvinum, see Provins
Prytaneum, bldg. in Athens . . 23 D
Prytaneum, bldg. in Olympia .
Przemyśl . . . . 159 L d
Psacum, prom. . . . . 15 D d
Psamathus Port . . . . 14 C c
Psaphara . . . . 11 E b
Psaphis . . . . 15 D a
Psephinus Tower, in Jerusalem 6 ins. A

Pskov . . . . 88 M c
Pskov, Hanse. for. cy. . . . . . 99 I b
Psophis . . . . 14 B b
Psyra, isl. . . . . 13 D b
Psyttalea, isl. . . . . 16 B b
Pteleum . . . . 11 D c
Ptolemaïs, in Cyrenaica . . . . 35 I g
Ptolemaïs, in Egypt . . . . . . 47 M k
Ptolemaïs (Acre), in Phœnicia . 6 C c
Ptolemies, Kingdom of the . . 19 U l
Ptolemy, Kingdom of . . . . . 18 Pi, leg.
Ptoon, mt. . . . . 11 E d
Ptychia, isl. . . . . 10 A c
Pucinum . . . . 27 H b
Puebla de los Ángeles (Puebla) 106 B a
Pueblo . . . . 198 E c
Pueblo Indians, tribe . . . . . 188 E c
Puerto Barrios . . . . 213 D c
Puerto Bello, see Porto Bello . 214 B b
Puerto Cabello . . . . 214 C a
Puerto de Bastimentos . . . . 105 E e
Puerto de Caballos . . . . . . 105 C c
Puerto de Luna . . . . 190 E e
Puerto de Retrete . . . . 105 E e
Puerto de Santa Gloria . . . . 105 C c
Puerto Limon . . . . 213 D c
Puerto Mexico, see Coatzacoalcos
Puerto Montt . . . . 215 B g
Puerto Principe . . . . 213 E b
Puerto Plata . . . . 213 E c
Puerto viejo . . . . 111 A b
Puget Sound . . . . 198 A a
Puig . . . . 82 B b
Puigcerda . . . . 82 C a
Puiset, Le . . . . 69 H f
Pukapuka, isl. . . . . 107 D i
Pulaski, Fort . . . . 208 D c
Pulicat . . . .
Pullaria . . . . 27 H c
Pulo Condore, isl. . . . .
Pulo Penang, isl. . . . . 171 K h
Pultusk . . . . 87 M b
Puna, see Poona
Puna Island . . . . 111 A b
Punakha . . . . 171 K f
Punicum . . . . 27 F e
Punitz . . . . 135 I c
Punjab, Punjaub, reg. . . . . . 137 B b
Puno . . . . 214 B d
Punta Arenas, in Chile . . . . 215 B h
Punta Arenas, in Costa Rica . 213 D d
Punta Bernal . . . . 106 D a
Puntarenas, see Punta Arenas, in
  Costa Rica
Pura . . . . 19 J e
Purchena . . . . 83 K h
Puri . . . . 137 E e
Purísima Concepción, in Cali-
  fornia . . . . 190 C e
Purísima Concepción, in Texas 190 F f
Purus River . . . . 214 C c
Purysbourg . . . . 193 ins. C
Pustertal, valley . . . . 115 G e
Pustozersk . . . . 138 H b
Puteoli . . . . 31 ins. A
Put - in - Bay . . . . 200 B c
Putlam . . . .
Putlitz . . . . 85 C b
Putney . . . . 75 I i
Putten, isl. . . . . 117 C c
Puttiala . . . . 137 C b
Putzig . . . . 123 J a
Puy, Le . . . . 61 E d
Puy, Le, bp. . . . . 94 C b
Puy - de - Dôme, dept. . . . . . 148 E e
Puyallup, Ind. Res. . . . . . . 188 A a
Puylaurens . . . . 126 C e
Pydna . . . . 11 D b
Pydna vetus . . . . 11 D b
Pylæ Caucasiæ, pass, see Cau-
  casian Gates . . . . 18 F b
Pylene . . . . 10 C d
Pylos or Pylus, in Messenia . 14 B c
Pylus, in Elis . . . .

Pyramid Lake, Ind. Res. 188   C b
Pyramids, in Egypt. 174   J j
Pyramus River 20   F d
Pyrasus 11   D c
Pyrenæum, prom. 38   C d
Pyrenees Mountains 38   B d
Pyrénées, Hautes, dept. . . . 148   D f
Pyrénées Orientales, dept. . . 148   E f
Pyrgi, in Greece . . . .
Pyrgi, in Italy . . . .
Pyritz 63   H b
Pyrmont 158   E b
Pyrrha . . . .
Pyrrha, prom. 11   D c
Pyrrhichus 14   C c
Pythium, in Athens 23   D
Pythium, in Thessaly 11   D b
Pyxus 30   E b
Pyxus River 30   E c

Quadi, people 38   F c
Quadratæ 26   C b
Quai de la Grève, loc. in Paris 149   B
Quai du Louvre, loc. in Paris. 149   B
Quakenbrück 122   E b
Qualla, Ind. Res. 188   J c
Qu'Appelle 212   E c
Quarr, ab. 100   A b
Quathlamba, mts. 175   M m
Quatres Bras. 156   A a
Quatre Vallées, dist. . . 147 E c (Q. V.)
Quatre Vallées, viscty 76   D e
Quauhtitlan. . . . . ?   A a
Quebec 191   K b
Quebec, prov. 1763. 194   E a
Quebec, prov. 1774. 194   E a
Quebec, prov. 1910. 212   H d
Quebrancha River . . . .
Quedlinburg 62   F c
Quedlinburg, mon. 95   E a
Queenborough, parl. bor. . . . 163   O f
Queen Charlotte Islands, near
    British Columbia 186   F c
Queen Charlotte Islands (Santa
    Cruz Island) north east of
    Queensland 172   F b
Queen Charlotte Sound 212   C c
Queenhithe, loc. in London . . 75   G g
Queen's County 127   J i
Queen's Garden, isl. 105   E b
Queensland, state. 172   D c
Queenston Heights, battle . . . 200   D b
Queenstown 127   I j
Queis River 85   H e
Quelpart, isl. 171   N e
Quengian . . . .
Quercy, cty. 61   D d
Querétaro . . . . 213 ins.
Querquetulan Gate 23   B
Querquetulum . . . . 35 ins. B
Quesada. 82   B b
Quesnoy, le 117   B d
Quetta. 170   H e
Quezaltenango. 105   B d
Quiaca 214   C e
Quibdo 214   B b
Quiberon 130   C d
Quiberon Bay 132   B c
Quierzy, see Kiersy
Quilimane 175   G f
Quillota 215   B f
Quiloa 109   U h
Quilon . . . .
Quimper 76   A b
Quimper, bp. 94   B b
Quimperlé 76   B d
Quimperlé, mon. 94   B b
Quinaielt, Ind. Res. 188   B a
Quincy 211   G c
Quinsai (Hang-chau-fu) . . . .
Quirinal, palace 96   A
Quirinal Gate 23   B
Quirinal Hill 22   A
Quirinus, Temple of 22   A

Quiros, discoveries of . . . . .
Quito 111   B b
Quito, pres. . . . . 215 ins.
Quito, reg. 111   C b
Quitzow 85   B b
Quivira, reg. 190   F d

Raab 9
Raab, bp. 95   F b
Raab River 159   I e
Raba River, see Raab River
Rabat 174   C a
Rabba 99   K g
Rabbath Ammon 7   D e
Rabbath Moab 7   D f
Rabida, La 184   B e
Racca . . . .
Radkersburg 135   I e
Radnor, in Pa. . . . . 192 ins.
Radnor, in Wales 163   K e
Radnor, cty. 127   V n
Radnor, parl. bor. 163   K e
Radnor, parl. dist. 163   K e
Radolfzell. 142   C e
Radom. 87   M c
Radstadt 123   G e
Radusculan Gate 23   B
Radziejewo . . . .
Radzin 131   H c
Rae, Fort 212   D b
Raetia, dist. 62   E e
Rætia, prov. 38   D c
Rætia I, prov. . . . . 42 E d (6)
Rætia II, prov. . . . . 42 E d (7)
Rætian Alps, mts. 26   D a
Ragaba 7   D d
Ragaz 91   R k
Raglan Castle 127   W o
Ragusa, in Dalmatia 73   D b
Ragusa, abp. 95   F c
Ragusa, rep. 131   G e
Ragusa, in Sicily 90   E f
Ragy . . . .
Rahin River . . . . 143 ins. F
Rahmanieh or Rahmaniyeh . . 174   J i
Rai . . . .
Rain 122   F d
Rainham 75   J h
Rainier, mt. 186   G d
Rainy Lake 191   G b
Raipur. 137   D d
Rais, dist. 81   L h
Rais, seign. 69   C c
Raisin River 200   B c
Rajamahendri 112   B b
Rajpootana or Rajputana, dist. . 137   B c
Rajputs, people 92   H e
Rakka 99   K f
Rakosfeld, dist. 159   J e
Raleigh 211   J c
Raleigh's col. 191   J d
Rama, dist. 72   D c
Ramadan, reg. . . . .
Ramah, in Galilee 6   C c
Ramah, in Judæa 7   C e
Rahmah, in Labrador 212   I c
Ramah, in Phœnicia 6   C b
Ramathaim 7   C d
Rambacia 19   K e
Ramillies 134   C c
Ramleh . . . . 68 ins. A
Ramoth-gilead 6   E c
Ramsay's Mills 195   B f
Ramsey, mon. 97   Q i
Rancagua 215   B f
Rangoon 171   K g
Rankokus Kill, stream . . . . 192 ins.
Ransbecke . . . .
Rapallo 130   R j
Rapidan River 192   B d
Raphia 7   A f
Raphoe, bp. 97   D b
Rappahannock River . . . . 193 F c (Rap.)
Rapperswyl, castle 91   Q k

Rappoltsweiler . . . . 143 ins. D
Rara . . . . 62 E d, F c
Raritan River 192   D c
Raron 91   P l
Rasa . . . .
Ras Madrak 170   G g
Rastatt. 142   B c
Ratæ (Leicester) 51   P h
Ratanpura . . . .
Rathenow 85   C b
Rathlure, bp. 97   D b
Ratiaria 39   M l
Ratibor 79   K c
Ratibor, princ. 79   K c
Ratisbon 63   G d
Ratisbon, bp. 79   H d
Ratisbon, imp. cy. 79   G d
Ratkau 154   F a
Rat Portage 212   F d
Ratzeburg 62   F b
Ratzeburg, bp. 79   G b
Raudii, or Raudian Plain, Campi,
    dist. 26   C b
Raurici, people 39   I j
Rauricorum, Augusta (Augst) . 39   I j
Ravendal . . . .
Ravenna. 27   G c
Ravenna, abp. 95   E c
Ravensburg 72   B b
Ravensburg, cty. 86   G b
Ravensburg, imp. cy. 143   I j
Ravensburg, Neu 143   I j
Ravenspur 84   D c
Ravenstein 117   D c
Rawa 135   K c
Rawalpindi 137   B b
Rawdon, route of 195   A g
Rawicz . . . .
Rawka 135   J c
Rawson 215   C g
Rawulpindee, see Rawalpindi
Raymond 208   B c
Raystown 192   B c
Razlawice 135   K c
Räzüns 91   R l
Ré, isl. 76   C c
Reading, in England . . . . . .
Reading, mon. 97   Q j
Reading, parl. bor. . . . . . 163 N f (Read.)
Reading, in Mass. . . . . 189 ins. B
Reading, in Pa. 196   D b
Reate 27   G e
Rechberg, Hohen, ruin 143   I h
Rechberg, lordship 143   I h
Recife, or Pernambuco 214   F c
Reckheim 117   D d
Recknitz River 63   G a
Recovery, Fort . . . . 196 ins. B
Reculver . . . .
Red Lake. 211   F a
Red Lake, Ind. Res. 188   G a
Red River, in southern U. S. . 211   G d
Red River, in Tongking . . . 171   L g
Red River of the North, in U. S.
    and Canada 210   F a
Redan, Great and Little, forts 164   L g
Redarians, people 63   G b
Red Cedar River 199   G b
Red Cliff, Ind. Res. 188   H a
Redesdale, dist. . . . .
Redonis, see Rennes
Redones, people 38   B c
Red Russia, reg. 139   B e
Red Sea 3   H f
Redstone, Old, Fort . . . . . 195 ins. B
Reepsholt, mon. 95   D a
Reganesburg, see Ratisbon
Regen River 63   G d
Regensburg, see Ratisbon
Reggio, in Calabria 90   E e
Reggio, abp. 95   F d
Reggio, in Emilia 90   J h
Reggio, bp. 95   E c
Reggio, univ. 100   H f

Regia, in Rome . . . .
Regia, quarter in Alexandria . 34 ins. C
Regillus, lake . . . . 35 ins. B
Regina, in Saskatchewan . . . . 212 E c
Regina castra (Ratisbon) . . . 38 E c
Regium (Reggio in Emilia). . . 26 E c
Regium, see Riez
Regni, people . . . . 51 P i
Regnitz River . . . . 62 F d
Regnum (Chichester) . . . . . . 51 P i
Regulbium (Reculver) . . . . . . 51 Q i
Rehoboth, in Mass.. . . . . . . 189 ins. A
Rehoboth, in Palestine . . . . . 7 B f
Reichenau, ab. . . . . 142 D e
Reichenau, mon. . . . . 95 D b
Reichenbach . . . . 135 I c
Reichenbach, mon. . . . . 143 F h
Reichenberg . . . . 135 H c
Reichenweier . . . . 143 ins. D
Reichenweier, lordship . . . . 143 ins. D
Reichersberg, mon.. . . . . . . 95 E b
Reigate . . . . 75 I i
Reigate, parl. bor. . . . . 163 N f
Reims . . . . 61 F b
Reims, abp. . . . . 94 C b
Reims, cty. . . . . 61 F b
Reims, duchy . . . . 76 F b
Rein, mon. . . . . 95 F b
Reindeer Lake 212
Reinhardsbrunn, mon . . . . . . 95 E a
Rejaf . . . . 175 G d
Rejang . . . . 112 D d
Reliance, Fort. . . . . 212 E b
Remesiana . . . . 43 G e
Remi or Remis, see Reims
Remi, people . . . . 38 C c
Remich . . . . 117 E e
Remiremont, mon. . . . . 148 C b
Rems River . . . . 143 I h
Remuria, in Rome . . . . 23 B
Renaix . . . . 117 B d
Rench River . . . . 142 B d
Rendsburg . . . . 78 F a
Renfrew, cty. . . . .
Rennes . . . . 61 C c
Rennes, bp. . . . . 94 B b
Rennes, cty. . . . . 69 C b
Rennes, gen. . . . . 147 D b
Rennsteig, road . . . . 62 F c
Reno. . . . . 210 B c
Reno River . . . . 150 F d
Rense . . . . 78 E c
Rensselærswyck, dist. . . . . . . 192 D b
Renus (Reno) River . . . . . . 27 F c
Rephaim, Valley of . . . . 6 ins. A
Republican River. . . . . 198 E c
Resaca, battle . . . . 208 D c
Resaca de la Palma, battle. . . 201 F d
Resaina . . . . 20 H d
Reschen-Scheideck Pass . . . . 91 S l
Resengo . . . . 6 ins. C
Reseph . . . . 6 ins. C
Réservoirs, Rue des, street in
  Versailles . . . . 149 A
Resht . . . . 170 F e
Resolution, Fort . . . . 212 D b
Resolution Island . . . . 212 I b
Rest, House of, in Jerusalem 68 ins. B (15)
Restigouche River . . . . 199 L a
Retford, parl. bor. . . . . 163 N d
Rethel . . . . 69 J f
Rethel, cty.. . . . . 76 F b
Retimo . . . . 164 C c
Retovium . . . . 26 D c
Retz, duchy . . . . 126 A c
Retz, seign. . . . . 76 C c
Reuben, tribe . . . . 7 ins. D
Reunion, isl. . . . . 175 I g
Reuss, cty. 114
Reuss River . . . . 91 Q l
Reutlingen, imp. cy. . . . . 78 F d
Reval . . . . 88 K b
Reval, Hanse. cy. . . . . 99 H b
Revesby, mon. . . . . 97 R h

Revilla Gigedo Island, Alaska 212 ins.
Revilla Gigedo Islands, to
  Mexico . . . . 213 A c
Revin . . . . 117 C e
Rewa . . . . 170 J f
Rewa, dist.. . . . . 137 D d
Rewley, mon. . . . . 97 P j
Reyes, Ciudad de los (Lima) . 111 B d
Reykjavik. . . . .
Rha (Volga) River . . . . 35 N d
Rhætian Wall . . . . 39 K i
Rhagæ. . . . . 8 D b
Rhakotis, quarter in Alexandria 34 ins. C
Rhamnus . . . . 15 E a
Rheba . . . .
Rhegium (Reggio in Calabria). 30 E d
Rhein River, see Rhine River
Rheinau . . . . 142 A d
Rheinau, mon.. . . . . 91 Q k
Rheinberg. . . . . 117 E c
Rheinbund, see Confederation
  of the Rhine
Rheinfelden . . . . 91 P k
Rheinfelden, lordship . . . . . 142 A e
Rheinsberg . . . . 135 G b
Rheinwald, valley . . . . 91 R l
Rheitoi, lake . . . . 16 B a
Rheneia, isl. . . . . 15 F b
Rhenish Prussia, prov. . . . . . 158 D c
Rhense, see Rense
Rhenus (Rhine) River . . . . . 34 F c
Rhesus River . . . .
Rhetra . . . . 63 G b
Rhin, Bas, dept.. . . . . 148 F e
Rhin, Haut, dept. . . . . 148 F e
Rhine River . . . . 2 E c
Rhinocolura . . . . 47 M g
Rhion . . . . 14 B c
Rhium, prom., in Corsica. . . . 26 C e
Rhium, prom., in Greece . . . 14 B a
Rhizus, in Magnesia . . . . . . 11 D c
Rhizus, in Pontus . . . . 20 I b
Rhitymna . . . . 14 ins.
Rhoda or Rhodæ, in Spain . . 38 C d
Rhodanus River, see Rhône
  River
Rhode, in Belgium . . . . 156 A a
Rhode Island, col. . . . . 189 C d
Rhode Island, isl.. . . . . 189 ins. A
Rhode Island, state. . . . . . 199 K b (K I)
Rhodes, state. . . . . 33 C b
Rhodes, isl. . . . . 5 B b
Rhodes, Knights of . . . . 77 J e
Rhodesia, prot.. . . . . 175 F f
Rhodius River. . . . .
Rhodope, mt. . . . . 39 M l
Rhodope, Rom. prov. . . . . . 43 H e (4)
Rhodt . . . . 142 B b
Rhodus . . . . 43 H f
Rhœdias River . . . . 10 D b
Rhœteum . . . .
Rhœteum, prom. . . . .
Rhône, dept. . . . . 148 E e
Rhône River . . . . 61 F d
Rhotanus River . . . . 26 D e
Rhyndacus River . . . .
Rhypes . . . . 14 C a
Riade . . . . 62 F c, 63 G c
Riadh . . . .
Riazan . . . . 139 E e
Ribagorza, dist.. . . . . 83 F c
Ribaut, set. by . . . . 191 J e
Ribble River . . . . 127 V m
Ribchester . . . .
Ribe . . . . 158 E a
Ribemont . . . . 56 C c
Riblah . . . . 6 ins. C
Ribnitz . . . . 123 G a
Ricciacum . . . . 39 I i
Richelieu, in France . . . . . . 126 B c
Richelieu, Fort, in Canada 189 B a
Richelieu River . . . . 189 B b
Richelieu, Rue de, street in
  Paris . . . . 149 B

Richmond, in England . . . .
Richmond, parl. bor.. . . . . . 163 M c
Richmond, in Indiana . . . . . 211 H b
Richmond, in Virginia. . . . . 193 F c
Richmond, castle, near London 75 I i
Richmond Island . . . . . 189 C c (Rich.)
Ricina . . . . 27 H d
Ricomagus, see Riom
Riddagshausen, mon.. . . . . . 95 E a
Riding Rocks, cape . . . . 105 ins.
Ried . . . . 135 G d
Riedlingen . . . . 143 H i
Rienzi, so-called House of . . 96 A
Riesa . . . . 135 G c
Riesa, mon. . . . . 95 E a
Riesenberg, castle . . . . 87 I d
Rieti . . . . 161 I f
Rieti, bp. . . . . 95 E c
Riet Spruit . . . . 175 M l
Rieux, bp. . . . . 94 C c
Riez, bp. . . . . 95 D c
Riffins, isl. . . . . 112 G c
Riga . . . . 138 B d
Riga, abp. . . . . 95 F a
Riga, Hanse. cy. . . . . 99 H b
Riga, Gulf of . . . . 80 H c
Rigomagus, on the Po R. . . . 26 C b
Rigomagus (Remagen), on the
  Rhine R. . . . . 39 I h
Rigodulum . . . . 39 I i
Rijnsburg . . . . 62 B b
Rimac River . . . . 111 B d
Rimini . . . . 90 M i
Rimini, bp.. . . . . 95 E c
Rimmon, in Galilee . . . . . . 6 C e
Rimmon, in Judæa . . . . 7 C e
Rimouski River . . . . 199 L a
Rinteln . . . . 122 E b
Riobamba . . . . 111 B b
Rio Blanco, in Mexico . . . . . 106 D b
Rio Branco, in Brazil . . . . . 214 C b
Rio Colorado Chiquito, R. . . . 190 C d
Rio das Boas Sinaes, R. . . . 108 U i
Rio de Janeiro . . . . 215 E e
Rio de Janeiro, state . . . . . . 215 E e
Rio de la Antigua, R. . . . . . 106 D a
Rio de la Buena Guia, R. . . . 190 C e
Rio de la Chira, R. . . . . . . 111 A b
Rio de la Plata, R. . . . . . . 215 D f
Rio de las Balsas, R. . . . . . 213 ins.
Rio de Natas, R. . . . . 213 B b
Rio de Oro, dist. . . . . 175 B b
Rio Dulce (delta of the Orinoco
  R.) . . . . 105 H e
Rio Florido . . . . 190 D f
Rio Grande, cty. in Brazil . . . 215 D f
Rio Grande, river, in south
  central Brazil . . . . 214 D d
Rio Grande, river, in south-
  eastern Brazil . . . . 214 E e
Rio Grande, river, between Mexi-
  co and U. S. . . . . 187 I f
Rio Grande, river, in Panamá 216
Rio Grande de Santiago, river,
  in Mexico . . . . 213 B b
Rio Grande do Norte, state . . 214 F c
Rio Grande do Sul, state. . . . 215 D e
Riohacha . . . . 214 B a
Rioja . . . . 215 C e
Rioja, dist. . . . . 82 B a
Riom. . . . . 76 E d
Riom, gen. . . . . 147 E b
Riomum, see Riom
Rio Muni, dist. . . . . 175 D d
Rio Negro, river, in Arg. Rep. 215 C f
Rio Negro, river, in Brazil . . 214 C d
Rions, castle . . . . 70 C d
Rio Real, R. . . . . 214 F d
Rio Salado, river, northern Arg.
  Rep. . . . . 215 C e
Rio Salado, river, southern Arg.
  Rep. . . . . 215 C f
Ripa, Alta . . . . 39 J i
Ripaille, mon. . . . . 86 F e

Ripley . . . . 206 ins.
Ripoll, mon. . . . . 94 C c
Ripon . . . . 65 F c
Ripon, mon. . . . . 97 P g
Ripon, parl. bor. . . . . 163 M c
Rippoldsau, mon. . . . . 142 B d
Ripuarians, people . . . . . . 50 E c
Risano, bp. . . . . 95 F c
Risingham . . . .
Risinum . . . . 38 F d
Riss River . . . . 143 I i
Ritzebüttel . . . . 114 E b
Riu - kiu (Liu - kiu) Islands . . . 171 N f
Riva . . . . 134 F f
Rivaulx, mon. . . . . 97 Q g
Rivera . . . . 215 D f
River Gate . . . .
Rivières du Sud, dist. . . . . . 174 B c
Rivoli, near Turin . . . . 130 P i
Rivoli, near Verona . . . . . . 150 F d
Roanne . . . . 76 E c
Roanoke Island . . . . 193 G d
Roanoke River . . . . 193 F c
Robertsbridge, mon. . . . . . . 97 R k
Robertsons, fam. . . . .
Robertson's Trail, route. . . . . 194 B c
Roberval . . . . 184 D c
Rocca San Casciano . . . . . . 90 L i
Roccasecca . . . . 90 D d
Rochdale, parl. bor. . . . . . . 163 L d
Roche, mon., in England . . . 97 P h
Roche, la, in Belgium . . . . . 76 F a
Roche, la, in France . . . . . . 143 ins. F
Roche, la, cty. . . . . 69 F a
Rochedale Hundred . . 193 ins. A (Roch.)
Rochefort, in Belgium . . . . . 117 D d
Rochefort, in France. . . . . . 84 C g
Rochelle, La . . . . 76 C c
Rochelle, La, gen. . . . . 147 D b
Rochester, in England . . . . . 127 Z o
Rochester, bp. . . . . 97 R j
Rochester, castle and mon. . . 74 F f
Rochester, Hanse. for. cy. . . .
Rochester, parl. bor. . . . . . . 163 O f
Rochester, in New York . . . . 211 J b
Rochlitz . . . . 115 G c
Rock Island . . . . 211 G b
Rock River . . . . 191 H c
Rockhampton . . . . 172 E d
Rockingham . . . . 65 F d
Rocky Mountains, The . . . . 186 H c
Rocoux . . . . 134 C c
Rocroy . . . . 157 ins.
Rodalben . . . . 142 ins. B
Rodez . . . . 76 E d
Rodez, bp. . . . . 94 C c
Roding River . . . . 75 J h
Rodomum, see Rouen
Rodosto . . . . 93 C b
Rodriguez Island . . . . 182 H H i
Roebourne . . . . 172 A c
Roer River . . . . 117 E d
Roermond . . . . 117 E c
Roermond, Hanse. cy. . . . . . 99 ins. B
Roeskilde . . . . 58 G b
Roeskilde, Hanse. for. cy. . . . 58 G b
Rœulx . . . . 156 A a
Rogalin . . . . 159 I b
Rogel, Well of . . . . 6 ins. A
Rohan . . . . 69 B c
Rohilcund, Rohilkhand, dist. . . 137 C c
Roidomna, see Roanne
Rojas . . . . 215 C f
Roma, Temple of . . . .
Roma, in Queensland . . . . . . 172 D c
Roma quadrata, loc. in Rome,
Italy . . . . 23 B
Romagna, dist. . . . . 90 D b
Roman Empire about 395 . . . . 42, 43
Roman Empire of the German
Nation about 1000 . . . . . . 58, 59
Roman Empire of the German
Nation, 1138—1254 72

Roman Empire, Holy, about 1000 58, 59
Roman Empire, Holy, 1138—1254 72
Roman Forum, The . . . . . . 24 B
Roman Forum, Aug. Reg. of
Rome . . . . 22 A
Roman Gate, in Olympia . . . .
Romania, desp. . . . . 93 A c
Romania, emp. . . . . 73 F b
Romano, Cape . . . . 191 I f
Roman Republic, 1803 . . . . . 151 I h
Romans . . . . 126 D d
Romanula Gate . . . . 24 A
Roman Wall, in England . . . .
Roman Wall, in Hungary. . . . 159 J f
Romanzof, Cape . . . . 198 ins. A
Rome, in Georgia . . . . 208 C c
Rome, in Italy . . . . 27 G f
Rome, abp. . . . . 95 E c
Rome, ancient imperial, plan of 22 A
Rome, ancient republican, plan of 23 B
Rome, medieval, plan of . . . . 96 A
Rome, modern, plan of . . . . . 22 A
Rome, patr. . . . . 52 J f
Rome, territorial expansion of 34, 35
Rome, univ. . . . . 100 H f
Rome, vicinity of ancient. . . . 35 ins. B
Rome, in New York . . . . . . 192 D b
Rome, Temple of . . . . 24 B
Rome, City of, Rom. dioc. . . . 42 E e
Romford . . . . 75 J h
Romney . . . .
Romont, castle . . . . 91 O l
Romorantin . . . . 126 B c
Romorantin, castle . . . . 76 D c
Romsey, ab. . . . . 100 A b
Romulus, Grave of . . . .
Romulus, Hut of . . . . 24 A
Roncaglia . . . . 72 B c
Roncesvalles . . . . 82 B a
Roncesvalles, mon. . . . . 94 B c
Ronda . . . . 82 A b
Ronnenberg . . . . 52 C a
Ronsse . . . . 117 B d
Roosbeke . . . .
Roosendaal . . . . 117 C c
Roper River . . . . 172 C b
Ropicum . . . . 26 C e
Roraima, mt. . . . . 214 C b
Rorkes Drift . . . . 175 N l
Rorschach . . . . 142 F c
Rosalie, Fort . . . . 191 G e
Rosario, in Arg. Rep. . . . . . 215 C f
Rosario, in Mexico . . . . 213 B b
Rosasna . . . . 153 O g
Roscianum . . . . 31 F c
Roscommon, bp. . . . . 97 C c
Roscommon, cty. . . . . 127 I h
Rosebud, Ind. Res. . . . . 188 F b
Roselle . . . . 64 B b
Rosenfeld . . . . 143 G i
Rosemarkie, bp. . . . .
Rosetta . . . . 174 J i
Rosheim . . . . 126 E b
Rosières . . . . 156 B a
Ross, bp., in Ireland . . . . . . 97 B e
Ross, bp., in Scotland . . . . . 97 H b
Ross, cty. . . . .
Ross, parl. bor. . . . .
Ross, dist. . . . .
Rossano . . . . 64 C c
Rossano, abp. . . . . 95 F d
Rossbach . . . . 134 F c
Rossbühl Pass . . . . 134 E d
Rossieny . . . . 159 L a
Rossland . . . . 212 D d
Rosslau . . . . 123 C c
Rossomme, farm . . . . 156 C c
Rossstall . . . . 62 F d
Rostock, mt. . . . . 150 E c
Rostock, Hanse. cy. . . . . . . 99 ins. B
Rostock, univ. . . . . 100 H d
Rostov, on the Don R. . . . . . 71 N d
Rostov, north - east of Moscow 138 E d
Rostra, loc. in Rome . . . . . . 24 A (6)

Rostra Julia, loc. in Rome . . . 24 B (15)
Rostro Hermoso . . . . 108 N h
Röteln, lordship . . . . 142 A e
Rotenturm Pass . . . . 159 M f
Roth, ab. . . . . 143 J j
Roth River, flowing into Danube
R. . . . . 143 I i
Roth River, flowing into Kocher
River . . . . 143 J g
Rothenburg, imp. cy. on the
Tauber . . . . 143 J g
Rothenfels, ruin . . . . 143 J j
Rotherham . . . . 162 E d
Rotherhithe . . . . 75 I i
Rothesay . . . .
Rothière, La . . . . 154 C d
Rotomagus (Rouen) . . . . . . 38 C c
Rottenburg . . . . 143 G i
Rottenmünster, ab. . . . . 143 G i
Rotterdam . . . . 117 C c
Rottumeroog, isl. . . . . 117 E a
Rottweil, imp. cy. . . . . 143 G i
Roucy . . . . 69 I f
Roucy, cty. . . . . 69 I f
Rouen . . . . 61 D b
Rouen, abp. . . . . 94 B b
Rouen, gen. . . . . 147 E b
Rouergue, cty. . . . . 61 E d
Rouge, Fort . . . .
Rouillé, Fort . . . . 192 B b
Roulers . . . . 117 B d
Roum, sultanate . . . . 67 M f
Round Valley . . . . 188 B c
Rouse's Point . . . . 199 K b
Roussart, Le . . . . 156 C c
Rousselaere . . . . 117 B d
Roussillon . . . . 126 D d
Roussillon, cty. . . . . 61 E e
Roussillon, gouv. . . . . 146 B c
Roussillon, prov. . . . . 148 E f
Roussy . . . . 69 J f
Rouvray . . . . 76 E b
Rovereto . . . . 114 F f
Rovigno . . . . 90 D b
Rovigo . . . . 90 J h
Rovuma River . . . . 175 G f
Roxburgh . . . .
Roxbury . . . . 189 ins. B
Roxolani or Roxolans, people . 35 L d
Royal Canal . . . . 126 B e
Royal Castle, in Athens . . . . 23 D
Royal Niger Company . . . . . 174 D c
Royan . . . . 76 C d
Rubi . . . . 31 F a
Rubicon River . . . . 27 G c
Rubruck or Rubruquis, William
of, route of . . . .
Rudau . . . . 79 L a
Ruden, isl. . . . . 123 G a
Rudiæ . . . . 31 H b
Rudnia . . . . 153 O f
Rudolf, lake . . . . 175 G d
Rudolstadt . . . . 62 F c
Rueda . . . . 82 A a
Rue de la Chancellerie, street
in Versailles . . . . 149 A
Rue de la Paroisse, street in
Versailles . . . . 149 A
Rue de la Surintendance, street
in Versailles . . . . 149 A
Rue de l'Orangerie, street in
Versailles . . . . 149 A
Rue de Richelieu, street in Paris 149 B
Rue des Hôtels, street in Ver-
sailles . . . . 149 A
Rue des Réservoirs, street in
Versailles . . . . 149 A
Rue de Faubourg Saint Honoré,
street in Paris . . . . 149 B
Rue du Temple, street in Paris 149 B
Rue Saint Antoine, street in Paris 149 B
Rue Saint Denis, street in Paris 149 B
Rue Saint Honoré, street in Paris 149 B
Rue Saint Jacques, street in Paris 149 B

Rue Saint Martin, street in Paris 149 B
Rue Saint Martin, street in Ver-
sailles . . . . 149 A
Rue Vivienne, street in Paris . 149 B
Rufford, mon. . . . . 97 P h
Rugeley . . . . 162 D e
Rügen, isl. . . . . 63 G a
Rügen, princ. . . . . 79 I a
Rügenwalde . . . . 135 I a
Rügenwalde, Hanse. cy. . . . . . 98 G c
Rugia (Rugen), isl. . . . . 38 E b
Rugians or Rugii, people . . .
Ruginium (Rovigno) . . . . . . 27 H b
Ruha . . . . 77 L e
Ruhr River . . . . 62 D c
Ruith . . . . 142 C b
Rûm, sultanate, see Roum
Rumania, km. . . . . 164 D b
Rumania, princ. . . . . 164 D b
Rumanians, people . . . . 165 leg.
Rum Cay, isl. . . . . 105 F b
Rumelia, dist. . . . . 93 B b
Rumelia, Eastern, prov. . . . . . 164 C b
Rumigny . . . . 69 J f
Runnymede . . . . 75 H i
Runsiens, people . . . . 188 B c
Rupert River . . . . 212 H c
Rupert's Land . . . .
Ruppin . . . . 79 H b
Ruppin, cty. . . . . 87 I b
Rura (Ruhr) River . . . . 39 I h
Rusa . . . . 138 E d
Rusaddir . . . . 38 B e
Rusellæ . . . . 27 F e
Rusicade . . . . 38 D e
Ruspæ or Ruspe . . . . 12 F c
Ruspina . . . . 38 E e
Russell . . . . 172 G d
Russia, reg., about 1000 . . . . 59 J L c
Russia, reg., about 1190 . . . . 71 L c
Russian Empire, about 1740 . . 131 J b
Russian Empire, 14—18 cent. . . 138/139
Russian Empire, 1910 . . . . . . 170 F/O c
Russians, people . . . . 47 L c
Russian States, 14 cent. . . . . . 77 K a
Russo . . . . 71 M b
Rustchuk . . . .
Rustdorp . . . . 189 ins. C
Rustenburg . . . . 175 M l
Ruteni or Rutenis, see Rodez
Ruteni, people . . . . 38 C d
Ruthenians, people . . . . 168 leg.
Rutland, cty. . . . . 127 Y n
Rutland, parl. dist. . . . . 163 N e
Rütli . . . . 91 Q l
Rutuba River . . . . 26 B d
Rutuli, people . . . . 35 ins. B
Rutupiæ (Richborough) . . . . . 51 Q i
Ruvo . . . . 90 F d
Rybinsk . . . . 167 M d
Rye . . . . 189 D c
Rye, parl. bor. . . . . 163 O g
Rypin . . . . 159 J b
Ryswick . . . . 122 C b
Rzhev . . . . 138 D d

Saale River, flowing into Elbe R. 63 F c
Saale River, flowing into Main R. 62 E c
Saalfeld . . . . 63 F c
Saalkreis, dist. . . . . 122 F c
Saanen . . . . 91 P l
Saane River . . . . 150 D c
Saarbrücken . . . . 62 D d
Saarlouis . . . . 122 D d
Saar River . . . . 114 D d
Saarwerden . . . . 114 D d
Saavedra, route of . . . 107 B f, 110 F F g
Saaz . . . . 63 G c
Sabará . . . . 214 D c
Sabaria . . . . 42 F d
Sabate . . . . 27 G e
Sabatia, Vada . . . . 26 C c
Sabatinus, lake . . . . 27 G e
Sabatus River, in Bruttium . . . 31 F c

Sabatus River, in Samnium . . 30 D b
Sabatum, Ad . . . . 31 F c
Sabellians, people . . . . 39 C c
Sabina, bp. . . . . 96 B a
Sabina, dist. . . . . 90 D c
Sabine River . . . . 211 G d
Sabini, people, west of L. Benacus 26 E b
Sabines, or Sabini, north-east
of Rome . . . . 27 G e
Sabino . . . . 189 D c
Sabis River . . . . 39 H h
Sablé . . . . 76 C c
Sable, Cape, in Florida . . . . . 187 K f
Sable, Cape, in Nova Scotia . . 186 M d
Sable Island . . . . 212 J d
Sabrata . . . . 12 F d
Sabrina (Severn) River . . . . . 38 B b
Sabrina Æstuarium (Bristol
Channel) . . . . 51 O i
Sabutum . . . . 27 F a
Sacæ, Sacans, people . . . . . . 18 S h *
Sacaraucæ, people . . . . 19 H b
Sacasene, dist. . . . . 35 N e
Sacaseni, people . . . . 18 G b
Sacer River . . . . 26 D e
Sachion 103
Sachsenburg, in Carinthia . . . 135 G e
Sachsenburg, castle in Thuringia 115 ins. B
Sachsenhausen . . . . 78 F c
Sachsenheim, Gross . . . . . . 143 H h
Sachsenklemme, pass . . . . . . 154 F e
Sacile . . . . 154 G f
Sacketts Harbor . . . . 200 E b
Säckingen . . . . 142 A e
Säckingen, mon. . . . . 95 D b
Saco . . . . 189 C c
Saco River . . . . 189 C b
Sacramento, in Cal. . . . . 210 A c
Sacramento, in Mexico . . . . . 193 D e
Sacramento River . . . . 210 A c
Sacra Urbs, Temple of . . . . . 24 B
Sacred Mount . . . . 35 ins. B
Sacred Gate . . . . 23 D
Sacred Way, street in Athen . . 23 C
Sacred Way, street in Rome . . 24 A,B
Sacrificios, Isla de, isl. . . . . . 106 D a
Sacriportus . . . . 35 ins. B
Sacrum, prom., in Corsica . . . 26 D d
Sacrum, prom., in Portugal . . 38 B b
Sadowa . . . . 159 H c
Sæpinum . . . . 30 D a
Sæpta Julia, loc. in Rome . . . 24 B
Sætabis . . . . 38 B e
Sævo, mt. . . . . 34 F a
Safed . . . . 68 ins. A
Sagadahoc . . . . 191 L c
Sagadahoc River . . . . 189 D b
Sagan . . . . 85 H e
Sagan, duchy . . . . 115 H c
Sagar . . . . 137 C d
Sagartians, people . . . . 8 D b
Sagartii . . . . 19 I d
Sagii, see Sées
Saginaw . . . . 211 I b
Saginaw Bay . . . . 211 I b
Saginaws, tribe . . . . 188 I b
Sagis River . . . . 27 G c
Sagone . . . . 148 C c
Sagra River . . . . 31 F d
Sagres . . . . 82 A b
Sagrus (Sangro) River . . . . . 27 I e
Saguenay River . . . . 212 H d
Saguntum . . . . 38 C e
Sahagun . . . . 82 B a
Sahagun, mon. . . . . 94 A c
Sahara, desert . . . . 175 C b
Saigon . . . . 171 L g
Saint, see also Sankt
Saint-Affrique see Saint-Frique 126 C e
Saint Alban, church in London 75 G g (10)
Saint Albans, in England . . . .
Saint Albans, mon. . . . .
Saint Albans, parl. bor. . . . . . 163 N f
Saint Albans, in Vermont . . . . 207 L b

Saint-Amand . . . . 156 B a
Saint-Amand-la-Haye . . . . . 156 B a
Saint Andrew, church in London,
near Holebourn Bridge . . . 75 G g
Saint Andrew, church in London,
on Leadenhall Street . . . . . 75 G g (13)
Saint Andrew, Fort, in Georgia 193 D f
Saint Andrews, in Scotland . .
Saint Andrews, abp. . . . . . . 97 I b
Saint Andrews, univ. . . . . . . 100 E c
Saint Anne, in Mackenzie Ter. 212 D b
Saint Anne, church in Jerusalem 68 ins. B(14)
Saint Anthony, Falls of . . . . . 191 G a
Saint-Antoine, near Paris . . . 122 B d
Saint-Antoine, Faubourg, quar-
ter in Paris . . . . 149 B
Saint-Antoine, mon. . . . . . . 148 C b
Saint-Antoine, Plaine, loc. in
Versailles . . . . 149 A
Saint-Antoine, Rue, street in
Paris . . . . 149 B
Saint Asaph, bp. . . . . 97 N h
Saint Augustine, in Florida . . 193 D g
Saint Augustine, church in Lon-
don . . . . 75 G g (4)
Saint-Avit, mon. . . . . 94 C b
Saint Barthélemy, isl., in West
India . . . . 213 F c
Saint Bartholomew, priory in
London . . . . 75 G g
Saint Bartholomew's Spital, in
London . . . . 75 G g
Saint Benets-at-Hulme, mon. . .
Saint-Benoit-sur-Loire, mon. . 94 C b
Saint-Bernard, mon. . . . . . . 95 D b (S. B.)
Saint Bernard, Great, pass . . 26 B b
Saint Bernard, Little, pass . . . 26 A b
Saint Bernardino, pass . . . . . 26 D a
Saint Blaise, ab. . . . . 142 B e
Saint Blaise, mon. . . . . 142 B e
Saint Botolph, church near Ald-
gate, in London . . . . 75 G g
Saint Botolph, church near Bi-
shopsgate, in London . . . . . 75 G g
Saint Botolph, church near Lon-
don Bridge, in London . . 75 G g (28)
Saint Bride, church in London 75 G g (2)
Saint-Brieuc . . . . 61 B b
Saint-Brieuc, bp. . . . . 94 B b
Saint-Bris . . . . 126 A d
Saint Callistus, Catacombs of . 96 A
Saint Catharines . . . . 207 I b
Saint Charles, in Missouri . . . 199 C c
Saint Charles, Fort, in Illinois 191 G d
Saint Charles, Fort, in Manitoba 191 F b
Saint-Chef, mon. . . . . 148 C c
Saint Christopher (St. Kitts), isl. 213 F c
Saint Clair, lake. . . . . 200 B b
Saint Clairsville . . . . 206 ins.
Saint Clare, abbey in London . 75 G g
Saint-Claude . . . . 126 D c
Saint-Claude, mon. . . . . . . 148 C b
Saint Clement's Danes, church
in London . . . . 75 G g
Saint Clement's Well, loc. in
London . . . . 75 G g
Saint-Cloud . . . . 114 B d
Saint-Cloud, Avenue de, in
Versailles . . . . 149 A
Saint Croix, isl. . . . . 105 H c
Saint Croix River, between
Minnesota and Wisconsin . . 191 G b
Saint Croix River, eastern boun-
dary of Maine . . . . 191 L b
Saint Cross, mon. . . . . 100 A b
Saint Cyril . . . . 138 E d
Saint David, Fort (Cuddalore) . 137 C f
Saint Davids (Mynyw) . . . . . .
Saint Davids, bp. . . . . 97 L j
Saint Demetrius, loc. near an-
cient Troy . . . .
Saint Denis, in Illinois . . . . . 191 H d
Saint-Denis, near Paris . . . . 76 E b
Saint-Denis, mon. . . . . 94 C b

Saint Denis, on Réunion I. . . 175   I g
Saint-Denis, Faubourg, quarter
   in Paris. 149   B
Saint-Denis, Porte, loc. in Paris 149   B
Saint-Denis, route of 190   E e
Saint-Denis, Rue, street in Paris 149   B
Saint-Dié, mon. 95   D b
Sainc Dimitri, quarter in Con-
   stantinople. 93   G e
Saint-Dizier . . . . : 134   C d
Saint Domingue, col. . . . . . .
Saint Dunstan, in the East,
   church in London . . . . . . 75 G g (29)
Saint Dunstan, in the West,
   church in London 75   G g
Saint Edmund the King, church
   in London . . . . 75 G g (16)
Sainte-Foy. 126   B d
Sainte-Geneviève. 191   G d
Sainte-Geneviève, church in
   Paris. 149   B
Saint Elias, mt. 186   E b
Saint Elias Range . . . . . . 212 ins.
Sainte-Marguerite, isl. 126   E e
Sainte-Marie. 191   I c
Sainte-Marie, isl. 175   I f
Sainte-Menehould 134   C d
Saintes 76   C d
Saintes, bp. 94   B b
Saint Ethelburga, church in
   London 75   G g
Sainte-Thérèse, Fort 189   B b
Saint-Étienne 76   F d
Saint-Étienne-de-Vaux, mon. 94   B b
Saint-Eustache, Saint Eustatius,
   isl. 213   F c
Saint Fagans 127   V o
Saint-Flour 76   E d
Saint-Flour, bp. 94   C b
Saint Francis River 189   B b
Saint-François-de-Sales 189   C a
Saint-Frique. 126   C e
Saint-Fuscien, mon. 94   C b
Saint Gall 56   D c
Saint Gall, mon. . . . . : 95   D b
Sainte-Geneviève, church in
   Paris 149   B
Saint George, Fort, in Florida 193   D f
Saint George, Fort (Madras) . . 137   D f
Saint George Mouth, Danube R. 164   D b
Saint Georges, in Maine . . . 189   D c
Saint George's Bay. 215   C g
Saint George's Channel 49   C f
Saint-Germain-en-Laye 126   C b
Saint-Germain, Faubourg, quar-
   ter in Paris 149   B
Saint-Germain-des-Prés, church
   in Paris. 149   B
Saint Germans, mon. 97   M k
Saint Germans, parl. bor. . . . 163   J g
Saint-Gildas-de-Ruis, mon. . . 94   B b
Saint-Gildas-de-Bois, mon. . . 94   B b
Saint Giles, church in Jeru-
   salem . . . . 68 ins. B (5)
Saint-Gilles, mon. 94   C c
Saint Gotthard Pass 91   Q l
Saint Helena, isl., in the Atlantic
   Ocean. 108   Q i
Saint Helena Island, off S. C. 193 ins. C
Saint Helens, mon. 100   A b
Saint Helen's Priory, in London 75   G g
Saint-Hippolyte. . . . . 143 ins. F
Saint-Honorat, isl. 126   E e
Saint-Honoré, Faubourg, quar-
   ter in Paris 149   B
Saint-Honoré, Rue, street in
   Paris 149   B
Saint-Honoré, Rue du Faubourg,
   street in Paris. 149   B
Saint-Hubert 117   D d
Saint-Hubert, ab. of 117   D e
Saint-Hubert, mon. 95   D a
Saint-Ignace, in Canada . . . 191   J c
Saint-Ignace, in Michigan . . . 191   H b

Saint Inigoes. 192   C d
Saint Ives. . . . . 98 ins. A
Saint Ives, parl. bor. 163   I g
Saint-Jaques, Faubourg, quar-
   ter in Paris 149   B
Saint-Jaques, Rue, street in Paris 149   B
Saint James, church, in London 75 Gg(23)
Saint James the Elder, church, in
   Jerusalem . . . . 68 ins. B (11)
Saint James the Less, chapel,
   in Jerusalem . . . . 68 ins. B (6)
Saint-Jean-d'Acre . . . . 68 ins. A
Saint-Jean-d'Angély 76   C c
Saint-Jean-d'Angély, mon. . . . 94   B b
Saint-Jean-de-Losne 69   J g
Saint-Jean-de-Maurienne . . . 130   O i
Saint-Jean-Pied-de-Port . . . 126   A e
Saint John, in Quebec 194   E a
Saint John, in New Brunswick 212   I d
Saint John, Fort, on Peace R. 212   C c
Saint John, Fort, on Richelieu R. 189   B b
Saint John, Knights of 73   F c
Saint John, lake 212   H d
Saint John, priory in London . 75   G g
Saint John River 211   L a
Saint John Lateran, ch. 96   A
Saint John the Baptist, ch. . . 68 ins. B (4)
Saint Johns, in Newfoundland 212   J d
Saint Johns-at-Colchester, mon. 97   R j
Saint-John's Field 75   I h
Saint John's Island (Prince
   Edward Island) 212   I d
Saint Johns River 211   I e
Saint Joseph, in Missouri . . . 211   G c
Saint Joseph, in Michigan . . . 211   H b
Saint Joseph, Fort . . . .
Saint Joseph River 191   H c
Saint-Josse 76   D a
Saint-Jouin-de-Marnes, mon. . 94   B b
Saint Julian, Port. 108   K l
Saint Katherine, hospital in Lon-
   don 75   G g
Saint Katherine Cree, bldg. in
   London . . . . 75 G g (14)
Saint Kitts (St. Christopher), isl. 213   F c
Saint Ladre, postern, gate in
   Jerusalem . . . . 68 ins. B
Saint-Laurent, mon. 94   C b
Saint Laurentius Island 109   V j
Saint Lawrence, church in Lon-
   don . . . . 75 G g (11)
Saint Lawrence, Gulf of 186   M d
Saint Lawrence Basin . . . . . 187 K-L d
Saint Lawrence Island 180   J a
Saint Lawrence River 186   L d
Saint-Lazare, ch. 149   B
Saint Lazarus Islands 212   F b
Saint Leger, route of 195   D a
Saint-Lô 76   C b
Saint-Lô, mon. 94   B b
Saint-Lomer-le-Moutier, mon. 94   C b
Saint Louis, in Canada . . . 191   I c
Saint Louis, in Missouri . . . 191   G d
Saint Louis, in Senegal 174   B c
Saint Louis, Fort, in Illinois
   Country. 191   H c
Saint Louis, Fort, in Texas . . 190   F f
Saint-Louis, Ile, isl. 149   B
Saint Louis River 188   H a
Saint Louis and San Francisco
   Grant 210   D c
Saint Lucia, isl. 213   F c
Saint Magnus, church in London 75 Gg(27)
Saint-Maixent 126   A c
Saint-Maixent, mon. 94   B b
Saint-Malo 76   B b
Saint-Malo, bp. 94   B b
Saint-Marcel, Faubourg, quar-
   ter in Paris 149   B
Saint-Marcel, mon. 94   C c
Saint Margarets Church, London 75   G g
Saint Marks 193   B f
Saint-Martin, near Ligny. . . . 156   B b
Saint Martin, ch. . . . . . . 68 ins. B (10)

Saint-Martin, Faubourg, quar-
   ter in Paris 149   B
Saint Martin, isl. 213   F c
Saint-Martin, Porte, loc. in Paris 149   B
Saint-Martin, Rue, street in
   Paris 149   B
Saint-Martin, Rue, street in Ver-
   sailles 149   A
Saint Martin le Grand, church
   in London 75   G g
Saint Martin of Tours, mon. . . 94   C b
Saint Martin Outwich, church
   in London . . . . 75 G g (12)
Saint Mary Aldermary, church
   in London . . . . 75 G g (19)
Saint Mary Bothaw, church in
   London . . . . 75 G g (25)
Saint Mary Magdalen, church in
   Jerusalem . . . . 68 ins. B (13)
Saint Mary Magdalene, church
   in London, east of St. Pauls 75 G g (7)
Saint Mary Magdalene, church
   in London, south of St. Pauls 75 G g (20)
Saint Mary of Grace, abbey in
   London 75   G g
Saint Mary of the Germans,
   hospital . . . . 68 ins. B (9)
Saint Mary of the Latins, ch. 68 ins. B (3)
Saint Mary Overey's Priory, in
   London 75   G g
Saint Mary Spital, bldg. in Lon-
   don 75   G g
Saint Mary's-at-York, mon. . 97   Q h
Saint Mary's, in Maryland . . . 192   C d
Saint Mary Somerset, church in
   London . . . . 75 G g (21)
Saint Mary's River 193   D f
Saint-Maur-des-Fossées, mon. 94   C b
Saint-Maur-sur-Loire, mon. . 94   B b
Saint-Maurice, mon. 91   O l
Saint Maurice River 212   H d
Saint Mawes, parl. bor. 163   J g
Saint Maximin, mon. 95   D b
Saint Michael, in Alaska . . . . 198 ins. A
Saint Michael, church in Lon-
   don . . . . 75 G g (15)
Saint Michael le Querne, church
   in London . . . . 75 G g (9)
Saint Michael Paternoster, church
   in London . . . . 75 G g (24)
Saint-Michel, Faubourg, quarter
   in Paris 149   B
Saint-Michel, Pont, loc. in Paris 149   B
Saint-Mihiel 184   E c
Saint Neots, mon. 97   Q i
Saint Nicolas 117   C c
Saint Olave, church in London 75   G g
Saint-Omer 76   E a
Saint-Omer, mon. 94   C a
Saintonge, cty. 61   C d
Saintonge, prov. 148   D e
Saintonge and Angumois, gouv. 146   A b
Saint-Papoul 94   C c
Saint-Paul, near Nice 126   E e
Saint Paul, in Minnesota 199   G b
Saint-Paul, bp., near Orange . 94   C c
Saint Paul Island 182   II k
Saint Paul de Loanda 175   E e
Saint Paul's, church in London 75   G g
Saint Paul's Bakehouse, in Lon-
   don . . . . 75 G g (31)
Saint Paul's Cross, in London 75   G g (3)
Saint Peter in Gallicantem,
   church in Jerusalem . . . . 68 ins. B
Saint Peter, church in Cheapside,
   London . . . . 75 G g (8)
Saint Peter, church in Cornhill,
   London 75   G g
Saint Peter, church in Jerusalem 68 ins. B (12)
Saint Peter, Patrimony of (States
   of the Church) . . . . 64 ins.
Saint Peter's, church in Rome 22 A, 96 A
Saint Petersburg 138   D c
Saint Peters' Yard, Hanse. for.
   off. 88   N b

Saint Philip, Fort........ 200 I g
Saint-Pierre, Fort....... 191 G b
Saint-Pierre, isl..... 212 J d (St. P.)
Saint-Pol............. 76 E a
Saint-Pol-de-Leon ..... 76 A b
Saint-Pol-de-Leon, bp.... . 94 B b
Saint-Pons, bp........ 94 C c
Saint-Pourçain, mon. .... 94 C b
Saint-Quentin......... 61 E b
Saint-Rambert, mon...... 95 D b
Saint Regis............ 200 F a
Saint Regis, Ind. Res..... 188 L b
Saint-Riquier, mon..... . 94 C a
Saint-Roch, church in Paris . 149 B
Saint Romanus, Late of ....
Saint-Sacrement, lake..... 192 E b
Saint-Sauveur........... 69 I g
Saint-Seine, mon. .... 95 C b
Saint-Seurin, mon...... 94 B c
Saint-Sever, castle...... 76 C e
Saint-Sever, mon...... 94 C c
Saint Simeon .... 68 C b
Saint Simon Island ..... 193 D f
Saint Sophia, church in Con-
 stantinople......... 93 G e (1)
Saint Stephen, church in London 75 G e (17)
Saint Stephen, gate ..... 68 ins. B
Saint Stephen, street..... 68 ins. B
Saint-Sulpice, mon. ..... 95 D b
Saint Swithin, church in London 75 G g (18)
Saint-Thierry, mon. ..... 94 C b (S.T.)
Saint Thomas, isl., Gulf of
 Guinea............ 175 D e
Saint Thomas, isl., West Indies 213 F c
Saint Thomas of Acon, church
 in London........... 75 G g (6)
Saint-Trond .... 117 C d
Saint-Trond, mon. ..... 95 D a
Saint Trudpert, mon. .... 95 D b
Saint-Urbain, mon., in France . 94 D b
Saint Urban, mon., in Switzer-
 land .... 91 P k
Saint-Vaast, mon., near Arras . 94 C a
Saint-Vaast-de-la-Hougue . . 126 A b
Saint-Valery, mon........ 94 C a
Saint-Vandrille, mon. .. 94 C b (St. Van.)
Saint-Victor, Faubourg, quarter
 in Paris............ 149 B
Saint Vincent, cape ..... 83 J h
Saint Vincent, isl....... 213 F c
Saint Vincent Gulf ...... 172 C d
Saint-Vrain, Fort....... 210 E b
Saint Xavier........ 191 H c
Saint-Wandrille, mon. see Saint-
 Vandrille
Saint-Yrieux........... 126 B d
Sairam............
Sais .... 1 B b
Sajama, volcano........ 214 C d
Sajo River .... 115 K d
Sakaria River .... 93 C b
Sakhalin, isl. .... 171 P c
Sala (Saale) River ...... 38 E b
Saladin, Dom. of ...... 71 M g
Salamanca .... 82 A a
Salamanca, bp......... 94 A c
Salamanca, univ. ...... 100 D f
Salamis, in Attica ..... 16 B b
Salamis, on Cyprus I..... 47 M f
Salamis, isl. .... 15 D b
Salapia .... 31 F a
Salapia, lake .... 31 F a
Salarian Gate .... 22 A
Salarian Way, road..... 27 H e
Salassi, people .... 26 B b
Saldæ .... 38 C e
Saldaña .... 82 B a
Salem, in Mass......... 189 ins. B
Salem, in New Jersey ..... 192 D d
Salem, in Ohio .... 207 I b
Salem, in Oregon ...... 198 A b
Salem, in Palestine..... 7 C d
Salem Creek ..... 192 ins.
Salemi .... 161 I i

Saleph River........... 67 M f
Salerno .... 90 E d
Salerno, abp. .... 95 F e
Salerno, princ. .... 64 C b
Salerno, univ........ 100 H f
Salernum (Salerno) ... 30 D b
Saletio .... 39 J i
Salford .... 162 D d
Salford, parl. bor..... 163 L d (Salf.)
Salians, people .... 50 D b
Salihiyeh .... 174 J i
Salina Cruz .... 213 C c
Salinæ (Castellane).... 26 A d
Salins .... 69 J f
Salinus (Saline) River .... 27 I e
Salisbury, in England ....
Salisbury, bp. .... 97 P j
Salisbury, parl. bor. ... 163 M f (Salisb.)
Salisbury, in Mass.... 189 C c (Salisb.)
Salisbury, in N. Carolina ... 195 A f
Salisbury, in Rhodesia..... 175 G f
Salisbury Plain ...... 49 F f
Salkhat .... 6 F c
Sallentini........... 31 G b
Sallentinum, prom. .... 31 H c
Sallust, Gardens of .... 22 A
Salm, in the Ardennes ... 62 C c
Salm, in the Vosges .... 126 E b
Salm, cty. in the Vosges .... 134 D d
Salm, cty., in Westphalia ... 151 H f
Salmansweiler, ab..... 142 D e
Salmantica (Salamanca)..... 38 A d
Salmon Falls, town ..... 189 C c
Salmon River .... 198 B a
Salmydessus .... 39 N l
Salò .... 150 F d
Salobreña .... 82 B b
Salodurum (Solothurn) ... 39 I j
Salofo, reg.......... 108 P f
Salona, in Dalmatia .... 42 F e
Salona, in Greece ..... 89 B c
Salonæ (Salona, in Dalmatia) . 38 F d
Salonica or Saloniki..... 59 I e
Salsette Island...... 137 B e (S.)
Salt River, Ind. Res.. .... 188 D d
Salta .... 215 C e
Saltanovka ...... 153 O g
Saltillo....... 201 E d
Salt Lake City ...... 198 C b
Salto .... 215 D f
Saltus Castulonensis, mts. ... 38 B e
Saluda River....... 193 C d
Salurnis .... 27 F a
Salus, Gate of...... 23 B
Salus, Temple of ..... 22 A
Saluzzo .... 90 H h
Saluzzo, marq....... 126 E d
Salvador, country..... 213 D c
Salvatierra .... 213 ins.
Salwin River.......
Salz .... 55 R i
Salza........ 72 C a
Salzach River ..... 63 G e
Salzburg .... 63 G e
Salzburg, abp. ..... 95 E b
Salzburg, elect. ..... 157 I g
Salzungen ..... 62 E c
Salzungen, mon. .... 95 E a
Salzwedel...... 62 F b
Salzwedel, Hanse. cy. .... 99 ins. B
Sama River ...... 214 B d
Samag....... 99 M e
Samalanga ...... 112 C c
Samana, cape ..... 105 G c
Samana, isl. ...... 105 F b
Samar, isl........ 199 ins. H
Samara .... 139 H e
Samara River, see Sambre River
 and Somme River
Samaria....... 7 C d
Samaria, dist...... 7 C d
Samarcand or Samarkand.... 92 G d
Samarobriva (Amiens)...... 38 C c
Samaron .... 99 M e

Samarovskoe........ 170 H b
Sambalpur .... 137 D d
Sambhal....
Sambhal, reg.....
Sambor....
Sambracitan Gulf .... 26 A d
Sambre River ..... 62 C c
Sambreffe ...... 156 B a
Same....... 10 B d
Samicum ..... 14 B b
Samme River ..... 156 A a
Samnites, people ....
Samnium, reg..... 30 D a
Samnium, Rom. prov.... 42 E e (7)
Samoa Islands ..... 199 ins. D
Samogitia, reg. .... 88 J d
Samonium, prom.... 14 ins.
Samos ...... 13 E c
Samos, isl. ..... 13 E c
Samos, theme .... 59 J f
Samosata ..... 20 H d
Samothrace, isl.....
Samsun .... 89 K f
Samoyedes, people ....
San River ...... 159 L d
Sana....
Sanabria, dist..... 83 J g
San Agostinho, Cabo, cape .
San Antonio ...... 210 F e
San Antonio, Cape .... 105 D b
San Antonio River .... 190 F f
San Antonio de Béjar ... 190 F f
San Bernardino, pass, see Saint
 Bernardino
San Bernardino Mountains... 187 H e
San Bernardino Strait..... 199 ins. H
San Bernardo, isl..... 107 A h
San Blas ...... 213 B b
San Buenaventura .... 190 B e
San Carlos de Ancud ... 215 B g
San Carlos de Monterey .... 190 A d
Sancerre ...... 76 E c
Sancerre, cty. ..... 76 E c
San Cesareo, ch. .... 96 A
San Clemente, ch. .... 96 A
San Crisogono, ch..... 96 A
San Cristóbal ..... 213 C c
San Cristóbal, isl. .... 110 HH i
Sanctus Ægidius, see Saint-
 Gilles
Sanctus Dionysius, see Saint-
 Denis
Sanctus Gallus, see Saint Gall
Sancus, Gate of .... 23 B
Sand........ 154 F e
Sandal Castle ...... 127 X m
Sandalwood Island .... 172 A b
Sandau ...... 154 G b
Sandía...... 214 C d
San Diego...... 190 B e
Sandomierz ...... 87 M c
Sandrocotta, Kingdom of.... 18 S h
Sandu....
Sandusky...... 200 B c
Sandusky, Fort .... 194 C b
Sandusky Bay .... 200 B c
Sandwich, in Canada .... 200 B b
Sandwich, in England ....
Sandwich, parl. bor. .... 163 P f
Sandwich, in Mass. .... 189 C d
Sandy Cape ...... 172 E c
Sandy Desert, Great ... 172 B c
Sandy Hook, cape .... 192 E c
Sandy Island, Great ... 172 E c
Sandy Sea, desert ....
Sane, in Acte ..... 11 E b
Sane, in Pallene ..... 11 E b
San Estéban ......
Sanf, reg.....
San Felipe ...... 215 B f
San Fernando ..... 214 C b
San Francisco, in California. 190 A d
San Francisco, in Florida . 193 D g
San Francisco, Cape .... 111 A a

San Francisco Bay 187   G e
San Francisco Mountains 187   H e
San Francisco de la Espada . . 190   F f
San Francisco de los Nechas . 191   F e
San Francisco de los Tejas . . 191   F e
Sanga River 175   E d
San Gabriel 190   B e
Sangala 19   L d
Sangarius (Sakaria) River . . . 20   D b
San Germano 72   C c
San Gerónimo de Yuste, mon. 94   A c
San Gimignano 90   L j
San Giovanni, Porta, gate . . . 22   A
San Giovanni in Fiori, mon. . 95   F d
            (S. G. i. F.)
San Giusto, mon. 95   D b
Sangpo River . . . .
San Gregorio Magno, mon. . . 96   A
San Ildefonso 184   C d
San Ildefonso, castle 130   C e
Sanitium, see Senez
San Javier del Bac 190   C e
San Joaquin River 198   C c
San Jorge, Gulf of 215   C g
San Jorge da Mina . . . .
San Jorge da Minha, see San
    Jorge da Mina
San José, in California 190   A d
San José, in Costa Rica . . . 213   D d
San José, in Guatemala . . . 213   C c
San José, in Uruguay 215   D f
San José, pen. 215   C g
San José de Cúcuta 214   B b
San Juan, in Arg. Rep. 215   C f
San Juan, in Porto Rico . . . 199 ins. G
San Juan Island 198   A a
San Juan River, in Ecuador . 111   B a
San Juan River, in New Mexico 198   D c
San Juan River, in Nicaragua . 213   D c
San Juan Bautista, in Mexico . 213   C c
San Juan Bautista (Porto Rico),
    isl. 105   G c
San Juan Capistrano, in Cali-
    fornia 190   B e
San Juan Capistrano, in Texas 190   F f
San Juan de la Peña, mon. . . 94   B c
San Juan del Norte 213   D c
San Juan de los Caballeros . 190   D d
San Juan de Ulúa, Fort 106   D a
Sankt-Blasien, see Saint Blaise
Sankt-Florian, mon. 95   E b
Sankt-Gallen, see Saint Gall
Sankt-Georgen 142   B d
Sankt-Goar 62   D c
Sankt-Goar, mon. 95   D a
Sankt-Gotthard Pass 91   Q l
Sankt-Gotthard, in Hungary . 123   I e
Sankt-Jacob 91   P k
Sankt-Lambrecht, mon. 80   D h
Sankt-Leonhardt 154   F e
Sankt-Luziensteig, pass 150   E c
Sankt-Märgen, mon. 142   B d
Sankt-Maximin, mon. 95   D b
Sankt-Peter, ab. 142   B d
Sankt-Pölten 63   H d
Sankt-Pölten, mon. 80   D g
Sankt-Trudpert, ab. 142   A e
Sankt-Trudpert, mon. 95   D b
Sankt-Urban, mon. 91   P k
Sankt-Vith 117   E d
Sankt-Wendel 154   D d
San Leo 64   B b
San Leo, bp. 95   E c
San Lorenzo del Escorial, mon. 94   B c
San Lorenzo in Damaso, ch. . . 96   A
San Lorenzo in Lucina, ch. . . 96   A
San Lorenzo fuori le Mura, ch. 96   A
San Lucar de Barrameda 83   J h
San Lucas, Cape 187   H f
San Luis, in Arg. Rep. 215   C f
San Luis Amarillas 190   F e
San Luis Obispo 190   A d
San Luis Potosí 201   E e
San Luis Potosi, state 213   B b

San Marco, in Calabria 90   F e
San Marco, bp. 95   F d
San Marco, church in Rome . . 96   A
San Marino, rep. 90   D c
San Martin, isl. 105   H c
San Martin, mon. 94   C d
San Mateo, Bahia de, bay . . . 111   B a
San Mateo, Fort 191   I e
San Mateo River 191   I e
San Matias, Gulf of 215   C g
San Michele 64   C b
San Michele, mon. 95   F c
San Miguel, in California 190   A d
San Miguel (Piura) 111   A c
San Miguel, in Salvador 213   D c
San Miguel (Tangarara) 111   A b
San Miguel Allende . . . . 213 ins.
San Miguel de Cuellar 191   G e
San Miguel de Gualdape 191   J e
San Miguel, Cape 105   F c
San Miguel, Gulf of 105   E e
San Miguel River 214   C d
San Millan de la Cogolla, mon. 94   B c
San Miniato al Tedesco 90   L j
San-mun Bay . . . .
San Pablo 216
San Pablo, isl. 107   D i
San Pancrazio, ch. 96   A,
San Pancrazio, Porta, gate . . . 22   A
San Paola, Porta, gate 22   A
San Paolo fuori le Mura, ch. . 96   A
San Pedro 191   I e
San Pedro, Rio, R. 190   C e
San Pedro y San Pablo, Rio de
    (Arkansas R.) 190   E d
San Pietro, Piazza di, loc. in Rome 22   A
San Pietro in Vincoli, ch. 96   A
San Remo 130   P k
San Roman, Cape 105   F d
San Roque, Cape . . . .
San Sabá 190   F e
San Salvador, in Angola 175   E e
San Salvador (Bahia) . . . . . .
San Salvador, in Salvador . . . 105   C d
San Salvador, isl. 105   F b
San Sebastian, in Columbia . . 105   E e
San Sebastian, in Spain 82   H e
San Sebastiano, ch. 96   A
San Sebastiano, Porta, gate . . 22   A
San Sebastiano, Via di Porta,
    street 22   A
San Severino 90   E d
San Severo 90   E d
San Silvestro, mon. 95   E c
San Silvestro in Capite, ch. . . 96   A
San Sisto, ch. 96   A
San Stefano, near Constantinople 164   D b
San Stefano Rotondo, ch. 96   A
Santa Anna (Goyaz) 214   D d
Santa Balbina, ch. 96   A
Santa Bárbara, in California . . 190   B e
Santa Bárbara, in Mexico . . . 190   D f
Santa Bárbara Islands 187   H e
Santa Catalina Island 108   M j
Santa Catharina, state 215   E e
Santa Catharina Island 215   E e
Santa Cecilia in Trastevere, ch. 96   A
Santa Clara, in California . . . 190   A d
Santa Clara, in Cuba 213   D b
Santa Clara Island 111   A b
Santa Croce in Gerusalemme, ch. 96   A
Santa Cruz, in Brazil 214   F d
Santa Cruz de la Sierra 214   C d
Santa Cruz de Teneriffe 174   B c
Santa Cruz Quiché 105   B c
Santa Cruz, Cape 105   E c
Santa Cruz, Rio, R. 190   C e
Santa Cruz, Terra de (Brazil) . 108   M i
Santa Cruz, isl., Atlantic Ocean 105   H c
Santa Cruz Islands, Pacific Ocean 172   F b
Santa Cruz River, in Patagonia 215   C g
Santa Elena, Punta, cape . . . 111   A b
Santa Fé, in Arg. Rep. 215   C f
Santa Fé, in New Mexico . . . 190   D d

Santa Fé, in Spain 184   C e
Santa Fé, audiencia . . . . 215 ins.
Santa Fé, mon. in Spain 94   B d
Santa Fé Trail, route 210   E c
Sant' Agata in Suburra, ch. . . . 96   A
Sant' Agata, bp. . . . . 95 ins.
Santa Gloria, Puerto de. 105   E c
Sant' Agnese fuori le Mura, ch. 96   A
Sant' Agostino, ch. 96   A
Santa Isabel 214   E c
Santa Isabel de la Estrella, isl. 110 G G h
Sant' Alessio 96   A
Santa Lucia, in Italy 161   H e
Santa Lucia, in Florida 191   I f
Santa Lucia Bay 175   N l
Santa Maria, in Arg. Rep. . . . 215   C e
Santa Maria, in Brazil 214   E c
Santa Maria Aventinese, ch. . . 96   A
Santa Maria de la Concepción,
    isl. 105   F b
Santa Maria della Pace, ch. . . 96   A
Santa Maria in Cosmedin, ch. . 96   A
Santa Maria in Domnica, ch. . 96   A
Santa Maria in Trastevere, ch. 96   A
Santa Maria la Antigua del
    Darien 105   E e
Santa Maria Maggiore, ch. . . . 96   A
Santa Maria Rotonda, ch. 22   A
Santa Marta 105   F d
Santander 82   B a
Santander, bp. 94   B c
Sant' Andrea, mon. 96   A
Sant' Angelo, castle 96   A
Sant' Apollinare in Classe, mon. 95   E c
Santa Prassede, ch. 96   A
Santa Prisca, ch. 96   A
Santa Pudenziana, ch. 96   A
Santarem, in Brazil 214   D c
Santarem, in Portugal 82   A b
Santa Rosalia 213   B b
Santa Sabina, ch. 96   A
Santas Creus, mon. 94   C c
Santa Severina, in Calabria . . 90   F e
Santa Severina, abp. 95   F d
Santa Susanna, ch. 96   A
Santee River 193   E e
San Teodore, ch. 96   A
Santhià 130   Q i
San Thomé 112   B b
San Thomé, Cape . . . .
Santiago, in Chile 215   B f
Santiago de Compostella . . . .
Santiago de Compostella, abp. .
Santiago de Cuba 213   E c
Santiago del Estero 215   C e
Santiago, isl. (Jamaica) 105   E c
Santiago River 111   B a
Santi Apostoli, ch. 96   A
Santi Cosma e Damiano, ch. . . 96   A
Santi Giovanni e Paolo, ch. . . 96   A
Santillana 82   B a
Santi Quattro Coronati, ch. . . 96   A
Santistéban 82   B b
Santo Colmado, mon. 94   A c
Santo Domingo 105   G c
Santo Domingo, rep. 213   E c
Santo Domingo, Audiencia of. 213   E b
Santones, see Saintes
Santones, people 38   B c
Sant' Onofrio, ch. 22   A
Santos, city in Brazil 215   E e
Santos Cosmoy Damiano, mon. 94   A c
Santo Spirito, mon. 95   E c
Santo Stefano 164   D b
Santo Tomas, in Guatemala . . 213   D c
Santo Tomas, in Lower Cal. . . 190   B e
San Vicente Ferrer 190   B e
San Vitale, ch. 96   A
San Zoilo, mon. 94   B c
Sanzumata
São Christovão 214   F d
São Francisco River 214   E d
São João, in Minas Geraes . . 214   E e
São João da Barra 214   E e

São Jorge dos Ilheos . . . . . . 214 F d
São José, in Amazonas . . . . . 214 C b
São Leopoldo . . . . 215 D e
São Luiz de Maranhão . . . . . 214 E c
Saona, isl. . . . . 105 G c
Saône River . . . . 62 C e
Saône, Haute, dept. . . . . . 148 F e
Saône-et-Loire, dept. . . . . . 148 E e
São Paulo . . . . 215 E e
São Paulo, state . . . . 214 D e
São Pedro (Rio Grande) . . . . 215 D f
São Salvador . . . . 214 F e
São Sebastião . . . . 215 E e
São Sebastião Island . . . . . . 215 E e
São Thomé, cape, see San Thomé
São Thomé, isl. . . . . 108 R h
São Vicente, in Brazil . . . . . 215 E e
São Vicente, mon., in Portugal . 94 A d
Sapera . . . . .
Sapis River . . . . 27 F d
Sapphe . . . . 20 J d
Saracano . . . . 99 N d
Saracenic poss. . . . . 58 D F f
Saracens, people, see Arabs . 45 leg.
Saragossa . . . . 82 B a
Saragossa, abp. . . . . 94 B c
Saragossa, emir. . . . . 83 E c
Saragossa, univ. . . . . 100 E f
Sarai . . . . 92 E c
Saraitchikovsk . . . .
Sarakhs . . . .
Sarandi . . . . 215 D f
Sarangians, people . . . . . 8 E b*
Saransk . . . . 139 G e
Saratoga . . . . 194 L f
Saratoga, proposed state in U.S.
Saratoga, Fort . . . . 192 E b
Saratov . . . . 139 G e
Saravus (Saar) River . . . . . 39 I i
Sarawak, col. . . . . . , . . . 171 M h
Sardica . . . . 39 M l
Sardinia, isl. . . . . 2 E d
Sardinia, km., 16 cent. . . . . 118 E e
Sardinia, km., 18 cent. . . . . 130 E e
Sardinia, km., 19 cent. . . . . 161 F e
Sardinia, Rom. prov. . . . . 34 F e
Sardinia, W. Rom. prov. . . . 42 D e (8)
Sardis . . . . 13 F b
Sared River . . . . 7 D f
Sarepta . . . . 6 C b
Sari . . . .
Sarius (Serio) River . . . . . . 26 D b
Sarlat . . . . 76 C c
Sarlat, mon. . . . . 94 C c
Sarmatæ, people . . . . 18 F a
Sarmatia, reg. . . . . 35 J c
Sarmizegetusa . . . . 39 M k
Sarnen . . . . 91 Q l
Sarni . . . . 26 F b
Sarnia, isl. . . . . 38 B c
Sarnius (Atrek) River . . . 19 II c
Sarno, bp. . . . . 95 ins.
Sarnus (Sarno) River . . . . 30 D b
Saronic Gulf . . . . . 15 D b
Sarpedon, prom. . . . . . 33 D b
Sarsina . . . . 27 G d
Sarsina, bp. . . . . 95 E c
Sarta River, see Sarthe River
Sartaba, mt. . . . . . . 7 C d
Sarthe, dept. . . . . . . 148 D e
Sarthe River . . . . 69 C c
Sarukhan, reg. . . . . 89 I g
Sarum, Old . . . . 60 F e
Sarus River . . . . 20 F d
Sarzana . . . . 90 L i
Sarzana, bp. . . . . 95 D c
Sasbach, near Achern . . . . 142 B c
Sasbach, near Alt-Breisach . 142 A d
Sashiversk . . . . 171 P b
Saskatchewan, Fort . . . . . . 212 D c
Saskatchewan, prov. . . . . . 212 E c
Saskatchewan River . . . . . 186 I c
Saskatchewan River, North... 186 I c
Saskatchewan River, South... 186 I c

Sason . . . . 31 I b
Saspeirans, people . . . . . 8 I d
Sassanids, Dom. of the . . . . 43 K g
Sassari . . . . 77 F d
Sassula . . . . 35 ins. B
Saszvaros . . . . 159 L f
Satara . . . . 137 B e
Saternus (Santerno) River . . . 27 F c
Satganw . . . .
Saticula . . . . 30 D a
Satilla River . . . . 193 C f
Satpura Mountains . . . . . 137 C d
Satricum . . . . 30 B a
Sattagydans, people . . . . . 8 K e
Saturn, Temple of
Saturnia . . . . 27 F e
Saucourt . . . . 56 C b
Sauer River . . . . 117 E e
Saufeld . . . . 62 F c
Saugona River, see Saône River
Saugus River . . . . 189 ins. B
Sauk and Fox, Ind. Res. . . . 188 H b
Sauks and Foxes, tribes . . . . 188 H b
Saulgau . . . . 143 H i
Sault Sainte Marie, in Michigan 191 I b
Sault Sainte Marie, in Ontario . 212 G d
Saumur . . . . 76 C c
Saumurois, gouv. . . . . . . 146 B b
Sausenberg, landgr. . . . . . 142 A e
Sauvenière . . . . 156 B a
Savah . . . .
Savaii, isl. . . . . 172 H b
Savannah . . . . 193 ins. C
Savannah River . . . . 193 D e
Savaria . . . . 38 F c
Save River . . . . 87 J e
Savia, West Rom. prov. . . . . 42 F d (9)
Savigliano, mon. . . . . . . 95 D c
Savigny, mon. . . . . 94 B b
Savo . . . . 26 C c
Savo River . . . . 30 C a
Savona . . . . 90 I h
Savona, bp. . . . . 95 D c
Savoy, cty. . . . . 69 G d
Savoy, duchy . . . . 86 F f
Savoy, growth of, 1418—1748 . 130 ins.
Savoy, neutral dist. . . . . . 161 F e
Savoy, The, bldg. in London . 75 G g
Savus (Save) River . . . . . . 38 F c
Saxa Rubra . . . . 35 ins. B
Saxon March . . . . 58 G c (Sax. M.)
Saxons, people, before fifth cent. 38 D b
Saxons, people, in Britain . . 51 R k
Saxons, people, in Germany . . 45 F b
Saxon Shore, dist. . . . . . 51 Q i
Saxony, Frankish prov., 9 cent. 56 D b
Saxony, duchy, 10 cent. . . . 62 E b
Saxony, duchy, 13 cent. . . . 72 B a
Saxony, elect., 14 cent. . . . 79 H c
Saxony, elect., 16 cent. . . . 115 G c
Saxony, elect., 17—18 cent... 123 G c
Saxony, km., 1812. . . . . . 154 G c
Saxony, km., 1815. . . . . . 158 G c
Saxony, prov. of Prussia . . . 158 F c
Saxony-Lauenburg, dist. . . . 79 G b
Sayansk Mountains . . . . . 171 K c
Saybrook . . . . 189 B d
Scalæ Caci, loc. in Rome . . 24 A
Scalæ Gemoniæ, loc. in Rome.
Scala Santa, loc. in Rome . . 96 A
Scaldis (Scheldt) River . . . . 38 C b
Scallabis . . . . 38 A e
Scamander River
Scambonidæ, deme . . . . . 23 D
Scampa . . . . 10 B a
Scandea . . . . 15 D c
Scandia (Scandinavia), reg... 38 E a
Scandile, isl. . . . . . . 11 F c
Scandinavian Highlands . . . . 2 E b
Scandinavian Peninsula . . . 2 F c
Scania, dist. . . . . 88 E c
Scapsa . . . . 11 D b
Scara . . . .
Scarbantia (Ödenburg) . . . . . . 38 F c

Scarborough . . . . 60 J g
Scarborough, parl. bor. . . . . 163 N c
Scardona . . . . 38 F d
Scardona, bp. . . . . 95 F c
Scardus, mt. . . . . 39 M k
Scarphea . . . . 11 D d
Scarpona . . . . 39 H i
Scepsis . . . .
Schächen Tal, valley . . . . . 150 E c
Schaffhausen . . . . 91 Q k
Schaffhausen, canton . . . . . 91 Q k
Schaffhausen, imp. cy. . . . . 78 F e
Schaftersheim . . . . 122 F d
Schalksburg . . . . 62 E b
Schärding . . . . 79 H d
Scharnitz, fort . . . . 154 F e
Scharnitz Pass . . . . 134 F e
Schässburg . . . . 159 M e
Schauenburg, castle . . . . . 142 B b
Schaumburg, castle . . . . . 72 B a
Schaumburg-Lippe, princ. 155 E b (S. L.)
Scheer . . . . 143 H i
Scheer, princ. cty. . . . . . 143 H i
Scheidungen . . . . 63 F c
Scheldt River . . . . 117 B d
Schelklingen . . . . 143 I i
Schemnitz . . . . 155 J d
Schenectady . . . . 192 D b
Schenkenschanz . . . . 122 D c
Schesel . . . . 55 R i
Scheyern, castle . . . . 62 F d
Schiermonnikoog, isl. . . . . . 117 D a
Schillingsfürst, castle . . . . . 143 J g
Schiltach . . . . 142 B d
Schivelbein . . . . 85 D b
Schladming . . . . 115 G e
Schlawe . . . . 85 E a
Schlei, inlet . . . . 62 E a
Schleiden . . . . 117 E d
Schleiz . . . . 154 E e
Schleswig . . . . 62 E a
Schleswig, bp. . . . . 95 D a
Schleswig, duchy . . . . . . 158 E a
Schleswig, march . . . . . . 62 E a
Schleswig-Holstein, prov. . . . 161 B b
Schlettstadt . . . . 126 E b
Schlettstadt, imp. cy. . . . . . 78 E d
Schliengen . . . . 142 A e
Schluchtern . . . . 142 D b
Schlüsselburg . . . . 138 D d
Schmalkalden . . . . 114 F c
Schneidemühl . . . . 159 I b
Schœnus . . . . 15 D b
Schoharie . . . . 195 D b
Schokland, isl. . . . . 117 D b
Schönau . . . . 142 A e
Schönbrunn, castle . . . . . . 135 I d
Schönbuch, dist. . . . . 143 H h
Schonen, dist., see Scania
Schönhausen . . . . 158 F b
Schönthal, ab. . . . . 143 H g
Schopfheim . . . . 142 A e
Schopfheim, Nieder . . . . . 142 A d
Schorndorf . . . . 143 I h
Schouten, route of . . . . . .
Schouwen, isl. . . . . 117 B c
Schramberg . . . . 143 B c
Schroda . . . . 159 I b
Schussen River . . . . 143 I j
Schussenried, ab. . . . . 143 I i
Schütt Island . . . . 159 I e
Schuyler, Fort . . . . 189 B b
Schuylkill River . . . . 195 D c
Schwabach . . . . 114 F c
Schwaigern . . . . 143 H g
Schwarzach, in Bavaria . . . . 114 F d
Schwarzach, mon. in Baden . . 142 D c
Schwarzburg, castle . . . . . 79 G c
Schwarzburg, principalities... 154 Fc(S.)
Schwarze Elster, R. . . . . . 85 G e
Schwarzenburg, in Switzerland. 91 P l
Schwarzenberg, lordship in Baden . . . . 142 A d
Schwaz . . . . 154 F e

Schwechat	159	I d	Sebenico, bp.	95	**F c**	Selymbria		
Schwedt	85	D b	Sebennytos	1	B b	Selz	142	B c
Schweidnitz	63	I c	Sebinus (Iseo), lake	26	E b	Selz, mon.	95	D b
Schweinfurt	62	F c	Sebzewar	92	F d	Semana (Thuringian) Forest	39	K h
Schweinfurt, imp. cy.	79	G c	Secia (Secchia) River	26	E c	Semendria	93	B b
Schweinschädel			Seckau	80	D h	Semenud	150	B a
Schwerin, in Mecklenburg	62	F b	Seckau, bp.	95	E b	Semgallia, dist.		
Schwerin, on the Warthe R.	79	I b	Seckenheim	142	C b	Seminara	90	E e
Schwerin, bp.	95	E a	Secondee			Seminole, Ind. Res.	118	G c
Schwerin, duchy	79	G b	Secunderabad	137	C e	Seminoles, tribe	188	J e
Schwetz	87	L b	Sedan	126	D b	Semipalatinsk	170	J c
Schwetzingen	142	C b	Sedetani, people	38	B d	Semlin		
Schwiebus	115	H b	Sedge Moor, dist.	49	E f	Semlov	153	O f
Schwyz	91	Q k	Sedgemoor	127	W o	Semmering Pass	135	H e
Schwyz, canton	91	Q k	Seduni, people	26	B a	Semnones, people	38	E b
Schyl River	168	H d	Sedunum (Sion)	26	B a	Semo Sancus, Temple of	23	B
Sciathus	11	E c	Seehausen, Hanse. cy.	99	ins. B	Sempronii, Forum	27	G d
Sciathus, isl.	11	E c	Seekonk	189	ins. A	Sempach	91	Q k
Scidrus	30	E b	Sées	76	D b	Sempronia Basilica, bldg. in		
Scillus	14	B b	Sées, bp.	94	C b	Rome	24	A
Scilly Islands	130	B d	Segeberg	72	C a	Senaculum, bldg. in Rome		
Scingomagus	26	A b	Segeberg, mon.	95	D a	Sena Gallica (Sinigaglia)	27	H d
Scione	11	E c	Segedunum	38	B a	Sena Iulia	27	F d
Scioto Company, grant	196	ins. B	Segesta, in Liguria	26	D c	Sena (Cesano) River	27	H d
Scioto River	196	ins. B	Segesta, in Sicily	30	B e	Senate House, in Rome	24	B
Scipios, Tomb of the	22	A	Segni	64	ins.	Seneca Creek	208	ins.
Scipio's camp	34	ins. A	Segni, bp.	96	C b	Seneca Lake	192	C b
Scipio's mole	34	ins. A	Segobodium	39	H j	Senecas, tribe	188	K b
Sciri, people			Segobriga			Senécu	190	D e
Sciritis, dist.	14	C b	Segodunum, see Rodez			Seneffe	156	A a
Scituate	189	ins. B	Segontia (Sigüenza)	38	B e	Senegal, col.	174	B a
Scodra (Scutari in Albania)	39	L l	Segontium (Carnarvon)	51	N h	Senegal River	174	B c
Scolacium (Squillace)	31	F d	Segor	68	ins. A	Senez, bp.	95	D c
Scollis, mt.	14	B b	Segorbe	82	H f	Senger River	215	C g
Scolus, in Bœotia	11	E d	Segorbe, bp.	94	B d	Senia	27	I c
Scolus, in Chalcidice	11	E b	Segovia	38	B d	Senigallia, see Sinigaglia	90	M j
Scomius, mt.	39	M l	Segovia, bp.	94	B c	Senlis	61	E b
Scone			Segovia River	213	D c	Senlis, bp.	94	C b
Scopia (Uskub)	73	E b	Segura, near Murcia	82	B b	Senlac	65	F G e
Scordisci, people	39	L k	Segura, near Saragossa	82	B a	Sennabrin		
Scotch, people			Segura de la Frontera	106	C b	Sennar, dist.	174	G c
Scotland, km.	58	D b	Seguro, captaincy	108	M i	Senne River	156	A a
Scotland Yard, in London	75	G g	Segusio (Susa)	26	A b	Sennette River	156	A a
Scots, people	54	C c	Segustero or Segusterone, see			Senones (Sens)	38	C c
Scots, people in Ireland			Sisteron			Senones, people, in Gaul	38	C c
Scott, Fort	211	G c	Sehwan			Senones, people, in Italy	27	G d
Scott, route of	201	leg.	Seine-et-Marne, dept.	148	E e	Sens	61	E b
Scott, fam.			Seine-et-Oise, dept.	148	E e	Sens, abp.	94	C b
Scotussa	11	D c	Seine-Inférieure, dept.	148	E e	Sens, cty.	69	I f
Scrooby	185	E d	Seine River	61	D b	Sentinum	27	G d
Scultenna (Panaro) River	27	F c	Seistan, reg.			Seoul	171	N e
Scupi (Uskub)	39	M l	Selas River	14	B b	Seph	6	C c
Scutari in Albania	93	A b	Selborne, priory	100	B a	Sepharvaim, see Sippar		
Scutari, on the Bosporus	93	G e	Selby	127	X m	Sepias, prom.	11	E c
Scutari, bp.	95	F c	Selby, mon.	97	P h	Sepphoris	6	C c
Scylla	90	E e	Selefke	93	D c	Sepsi-Szent-György	159	M e
Scylacium (Squillace)	31	F d	Selenga River			Septem peda	27	H d
Scylacium, gulf	31	F d	Seleucia, in Babylonia	18	P h	Septimania, reg.	53	M i
Scyllæum	30	E d	Seleucia, in Cilicia	20	E d	Septimian Gate	22	A
Scyllæum, prom., in Greece	15	D b	Seleucia, in Syria	20	F d	Septimius Severus, Arch of		
Scyllæum, prom., in Italy	30	E d	Seleucia, theme	59	K f	Septimius Severus, Palace of	24	B
Scylletium (Squillace)	31	F d	Seleucids, Kingdom of the	19	W k	Septizonium, loc. in Rome	22	A
Scyrians, people	50	F c	Seleucus, Kingdom of	18	P i	Septs-Fonts, mon.	94	C b
Scyrus	11	F d	Selge	20	D d	Sepulcretum, loc. in Rome	24	A
Scyrus (Skyros), isl.	11	F d	Selgovæ, people	38	B a	Sepulveda	94	B c
Scythia, East Rom. prov.	43	H e (6)	Seligenstadt, mon.	95	D a	Sequana (Seine) River	38	C c
Scythia, Lesser, reg.	39	N l	Selinus, in Cilicia	20	E d	Sequani, people	38	D c
Scythians, people, in Asia	8	J d, L e	Selinus, in Laconia	14	C b	Seraglio, New and Old, in Con-		
Scythians, people, in continent			Selinus, in Sicily	30	B e	stantinople	93	G e
of Europe	18	D a	Selinus River	14	C a	Seraglio Point	93	G e
Scythopolis	7	C d	Seljuk Turks, Dom. of the	67	O f	Serai	77	N c
Seaford, parl. bor.	163	O g	Seljuk Turks, people	77	K e	Serajevo	119	H e
Sea of the Indies (Arabian Sea)			Selkirk			Serapeum, loc. in Alexandria	34	ins. C (7)
Seattle	210	A a	Selkirk, cty.			Serapeum, loc. in Rome	22	A
Sea View, mt.	172	E d	Selkirk, dist.			Serapis, Temple of	22	A
Sebago, lake	189	C c	Selkirk, Fort	212	B b	Serbs, people	57	G e
Sebaste, in Palestine	7	C d	Selkirk Forest	49	F d	Serena, La	215	B e
Sebaste, in Pontus	43	J f	Sella	98	G h	Seres	93	B b
Sebastea, theme	59	L f	Sellasia	14	C b	Sergievski	138	E d
Sebastea, theme	59	L f	Selleis River	14	B b	Sergipe, state	214	F d
Sebastia	20	G b	Selles	69	H g	Seringapatam	137	C f
Sebastian Cabot, route of	108	L k	Selma	208	C c	Seriphus (Serpho)	15	E b
Seben	62	F e	Selsey			Seriphus (Sériphos), isl.	15	E b
Sebenico	90	E c	Selwood	49	E f			

Sermyle	11	E b
Serpa	38	A e
Serpent Column, in Constantinople	93	G e (3)
Serpent Pool, in Jerusalem	6 ins.	A
Serpent's Mouth, str.	105	H e
Serra do Espinhaço, mts.	214	E d
Serra do Mar, mts.	215	E e
Serra dos Aimores, mts.	214	E d
Serra Geral, mts.	215	D e
Serran	111	B c
Serra parda, Cabo, cape	108	R j
Serravalle	90	K h
Serrhæ	11	E a
Serrhium, prom.		
Serrorum Montes (Transylvanian Alps), mts.	39	M k
Servia, reg.	54	H e
Servia, km., 13 cent.	89	B b
Servia, km., 14 cent.	89	H f
Servia, km., 15 cent.	93	B b
Servia, km., 19 cent.	164	C b
Servia, princ., 19 cent.	164	C b
Servia, prov. of Ottoman Empire		
Servian Principalities, 14 cent.	77	I d
Servians, people		
Servian Wall	23	B
Sesamus	20	E b
Sesia River	130	Q i
Sesites River	26	C b
Sessa	90	E d
Sessa, bp.	95 ins.	
Sessorium	22	A
Sestinum	27	G d
Sestus		
Setauket	189	B d
Setia	30	C a
Setif	70	H f
Setons, fam.	97	J d
Setu, isl.		
Setúbal	83	J h
Seul, see Seoul	171	N e
Seurre	126	D c
Sevastopol, in the Crimea	164	E b
Sevastopol, plan of	164	L g
Sevastopoli, in Abkhasia	99	L e
Seven Basilicas, churches	96	A
Seven Lakes	27	F c
Sevenoaks, battle	75	J i
Seven Ranges, The, dist.	196 ins.	B
Seven Towers, Castle of the	93	G e
Severia, dist.	139	D e
Severians, people	71	M c
Severian Way, road	35 ins.	B
Severin	77	I d
Severin, banat	89	B b
Severn River, in England	49	E e
Severn River, in Canada	212	G c
Severus, wall of	34	E b
Sevier, lake	210	C c
Sevier River	198	C c
Seville	82	A b
Seville, abp.	94	A d
Seville, emir.	83	J d
Seville, km.	83	J h
Seville, univ.	100	D g
Sevre River	148	B b
Sewan-hacky (Long Island)	189	B d
Sexi	38	B e
Sextum, Ad	27	F d
Seybothenreuth	158	F d
Seychelles Islands	175	I e
Sfax	73	C d
Sha-chau		
Shackamaxon	192 ins.	
Shaftesbury		
Shaftesbury, mon.		
Shaftesbury, parl. bor.	163	L g
Shahr Zor	67	P f
Shahrzur, reg.		
Shah-Armen, Dom. of	71	O f
Shaliyat		
Shanghai	171	N e
Shangtu		
Shan-hai-kwan	171	M d
Shannon River	49	B e
Shan-si, prov.	171	M e
Shan-tung, prov.	171	M e
Shap, mon.	97	O g
Shari River	174	E c
Shark Bay	172	A c
Shark's Island	107	C i
Sharmakhi	99	M e
Sharon, Plain of	7	B d
Sharpness	162	D f
Sharpsburg	208 ins.	
Shasta, mt.	210	A b
Shau-hsien	171	N f
Shavly	131	H b
Shaw	127	X o
Shawmut	189 ins.	B
Shawnee Mission	206	F c
Shawnees, tribe	188	J c
Shawneetown	211	H c
Shawomet	189 ins.	A
Shechem	7	C d
Sheen, mon.	97	Q j
Sheep Gate, in Jerusalem	6 ins.	A
Sheffield	162	E d
Sheffield, parl. bor.	163	M d
Sheik-ul-Islam, loc. in Constantinople	93	G e
Shelburne	212	I d
Sheliff River	125	D e
Shelter Island	192	E c
Shelton	127	W n
Shenandoah	193	E b
Shenandoah River	193	E b
Shen-si, prov.	171	L e
Shephela, Plain of	7	B e
Shepherdstown	208 ins.	
Sheppey, isl.		
Sherborne	65	E e
Sherborne, mon.	97	O k
Sherborne, parl. bor.	163	L g (Sherb.)
Sherboro, Island	174	B d
Sherbrooke	212	H d
Sheriffmuir		
s'Hertogenbosch	117	D c
Sherwood Forest	49	F e
Shetland Islands	49	F a
Shigansk	171	N b
Shikoku, isl.	171	O e
Shilka River		
Shiloh, in Palestine	7	C d
Shiloh, in Tennessee	208	C b
Shimoda	171	O e
Shimonoseki	171	O e
Ship Island	208	C c
Shipka Pass	164	C b
Shipyards, loc. in Rome	22	A
Shiraz		
Shirley	193 ins.	A
Shirley, Fort	192	C c
Shirpurla	4	G c
Shirvan, reg.		
Shoa, dist.	174	G d
Shoalwater, Ind. Res.	188	B a
Shoebury		
Shomron	7	C d
Shoreditch	75	I h
Shoreditch, street in London	75	G g
Shoreham		
Shoshones, tribe	188	C c
Shreveport	208	B c
Shrewsbury, in England		
Shrewsbury, castle		
Shrewsbury, mon.	97	O i
Shrewsbury, parl. bor.	163	L e
Shrewsbury, in New Jersey	192	E c
Shropshire, cty.		
Shropshire, shire		
Shtiplie	164	C b
Shubra Kheit		
Shumagin Islands	198 ins.	A
Shumla	131	I e
Shunem	6	C c
Shun-i	170 ins.	A
Shuri, isl.	171	N f
Shuster		
Sialkot	137	B b
Siam, km.	171	L g
Siam, Gulf of	171	L h
Siam, reg.		
Siberia, khan. of	138	J d
Siberia, reg.	171	J-R b
Sibir		
Sibir, khan.	92	H b
Sibir, reg.	109	X b
Sibota Islands	10	B c
Sibton, mon.	97	S i
Sicani or Sicanians, people	30	C e
Sicca	42	D f
Sicels, people		
Sicilia, see Sicily		
Sicilian Sea	34	H f
Sicilies, Kingdom of the Two	72	C d
Sicily, Rom. prov.	30	C d
Sicily, isl.	2	F e
Sicily, km.	77	G d
Sicily, West Rom. prov.	42	Ef(4)
Sicinus (Sikinos), isl.	15	F c
Sickingen, castle	114	E d
Sicoris River	38	C d
Siculi, people	30	D e
Sicyon	14	C b
Side, in Laconia	15	D c
Side, in Pamphylia	18	D c
Sidicinum, Teanum	30	D a
Sidodone	19	H e
Sidon	6	C a
Sidon, Port of, in Tyre	18 ins.	B
Sidra, Gulf of	174	E a
Sidus	15	D b
Siedlce	155	L b
Siegburg, mon.	95	D a
Siegen	158	E c
Siena	90	L j
Siena, abp.	95	E c
Siena, univ.	100	H f
Sierra de Piña, mts.		
Sierra Leone, col.	174	B d
Sierra Madre, mts. in Mexico	187	I f
Sierra Madre, mts. in New Mexico	190	D d
Sierra Mindi, mts.		
Sierra Morena, mts.	2	D e
Sierra Nevada, mts. in Spain	2	D e
Sierra Nevada, mts. in California	190	A d
Sierra Nevada de Santa Marta, mts.	187	L g
Sierra Quebrancha, mts.		
Sievershausen	114	F b
Siga	38	B e
Sigeum	9	A a
Sigeum, prom.	9	A a
Sigiburg	55	Q i
Sigmaringen	143	H i
Sigmaringen, castle	62	E d
Signau, castle	91	P l
Signia	35 ins.	B
Signia, bp.	96	C b
Signy, mon.	94	C b
Sigtuna	46	J b
Sigüenza	83	K g
Sigüenza, bp.	94	B c
Sigüenza, univ.	100	E f
Sihuatan, Puerto	107	G f
Sihut	170	G g
Sikanderabad		
Sikhim		
Sikh States		
Si-kiang, R.		
Sila Mountains	31	F d
Silarus River, in Æmilia	27	F c
Silarus River, in Campania	30	D b
Silberberg, fortress	155	I c
Silesia, dist.	59	H c
Silesia, duchy	72	D a
Silesia, Austrian, dist.	159	I c
Silesia, Lower, dist.	72	D a

Silesia, Prussian, prov.	159	I c
Silesia, Upper, dist.	72	D a
Siletz, Ind. Res.	188	B b
Silingæ, people	38	F b
Silis River	19	K b
Silistria	73	F b
Siloam, Pool of	6 ins.	A
Silures, people	51	O i
Silves	82	A b
Silves, bp.	94	A d
Silvium	31	F b
Simancas	82	B a
Simbach	135	G d
Simbirsk	139	G e
Simeon, tribe	7 ins.	D
Simferopol	139	D g
Simla	170	I e
Simmern	86	F d
Simmern, princ.	86	F d
Simœis River (Dumbrek R.)		
Simplon Pass	91	Q l
Simpson, Fort	212	C b
Simpson, Port	212	ins.
Sinaes, Rio das boas, R.	108	U i
Sinai, mt.	3	H f
Sinai Peninsula	150	B b
Sinaloa	190	D f
Sinaloa, prov.	190	D f
Sinaloa, state	213	B b
Sinclairs, fam.		
Sind, reg. in 8 cent.	53	I c
Sind, reg. in 18 cent.	137	A c
Sindelfingen	114	E d
Sindi, people	35	L e
Sindia, Dom. of	137	C c
Sindomana	19	K e
Sindringen	143	H g
Sindus	11	D b
Si-ngan-fu		
Singapore		
Singara	20	I d
Singidunum (Belgrade)	50	H d
Singitic Gulf (Gulf of Monte Santo)	11	E b
Sing-ngan	171	L e
Singus	11	E b
Sinigaglia	90	M j
Sinigaglia, bp.	95	E c
Si-ning-fu		
Sinjar		
Sin-kiang, prov.	171	J d
Sinnius River	27	F c
Sinonia, isl.	30	E b
Sinope (Sinub)	20	F a
Sinsheim	142	C b
Sinteozesavia, see Reichenau		
Sinuessa (Mondragone)	30	C a
Sion	91	P l
Sion, bp.	95	D b
Sion, mon.	75	I i
Sioux, tribe	188	F c, G a
Sioux City	210	F b
Sioux Falls, town	210	F b
Sioux River, Big	198	F b
Siphæ	11	E d
Siphnus	15	E c
Siphnus (Siphnos), isl.	15	E c
Siponto	64	C b
Siponto, abp.	95	F c
Sipontum (Manfredonia)	30	C a
Sippar (Abu Habba)	4	D e
Sippara	20	J f
Sipylus, mt.	20	B c
Siraca	19	J c
Siracæ, people	35	M e
Siraf		
Sirgune River	72	D a
Siris, in Lucania	31	F b
Siris, in Macedonia	11	E a
Siris River	31	F b
Sirmio (Sermione)	26	E b
Sirmium (Mitrovitza)	38	F d
Sirt	98	G g
Sis	73	H c

Sisal	213	C b
Sisapon	38	A e
Siscia	38	F c
Sisia	68	C b
Sissek	54	H d
Sisteron	126	D d
Sisteron, bp.	95	D c
Sistova	93	C b
Sit River	92	D b
Sitacus River	19	H e
Sithiu, see Saint-Omer		
Sithonia, pen.	11	E b
Sitifis	38	D e
Sitka	198	ins. A
Sitomagus		
Sitones, people	34	G a
Sittace	20	K f
Sitten, see, Sion	91	P l
Siugui		
Siut	174	G b
Sivas	89	E c
Siwah Oasis		
Six Nations, tribes	192	D b
Sixt, mon.	95	D b
Skaga Fiord	166	B b
Skager Rak, str.	88	C c
Skagway	198	ins. A
Skalitz	159	I c
Skåne, dist.	88	E d
Skanör, Hanse. for. cy.	98	F b
Skeena River	212	C c
Skenesborough	195	E b
Skidaway	193	ins. C
Skipton	127	V m
Skopia (Uskub), see Scopia		
Skye, isl.	49	C c
Slamat, mt.		
Slankamen	131	H d
Slatoust	167	Q d
Slave Coast, reg.	174	D d
Slaviansk	167	M f
Slavic Peoples about 900	57	leg.
Slavinia, reg.	58	G c
Slavonia, reg.	70	J d
Slavonian Military Frontier	159	I f
Sligo	127	I g
Sligo, cty.	127	I g
Sligo Bay	49	B d
Sliven	165	E b
Slivnitza	164	E b
Sloboneva	153	O f
Slonim	139	C e
Slovaks, people	168	leg.
Slovenes, people, about 900		
Slovenes, people, 1910		
Sluys	117	B c
Sluys, Hanse. for. cy.	99	ins. B
Smaland, dist.	88	F c
Smederevo	93	B b
Smenus River	14	C c
Smith, Fort, town	211	G c
Smith, routes of	210	B c
Smithfield, loc. near London	75	G g
Smith Island	193	ins. A
Smohain		
Smoky Range, Great	193	C d
Smolensk	153	O g
Smolensk, gov.	131	J b
Smoothfield (Smithfield), loc. near London	75	G g
Smyrna	20	B c
Smyrna vetus	20	B c
Snake River	198	C b
Snakes, tribe	188	C b
Snelling, Fort	199	G b
Snowdon, mt.	49	E e
Soana	64	ins.
Soana, bp.	95	E c
Sobat River	174	G d
Sobernheim	142	ins. A
Sobral	214	C b
Sobràon	170	I e
Sobrarbe, dist.	83	E c
Society Islands	180	L i

Socoh, in Idumæa	7	B f
Socoh, in Judæa	7	B e
Soconusco, reg.	105	B c
Socorro, in Colombia	214	B b
Socorro, in New Mexico	190	D e
Socorro Island	213	A c
Socotra, isl., see Sokotra		
Socrates, Prison of, in Athens	23	D
Söderhamn	166	I c
Söderköping	88	G b
Soest	62	E c
Soest, Hanse. cy.	99	ins. B
Sofia	93	B b
Soflingen	143	I i
Soflingen, ab.	143	I i
Sogamoso	214	B b
Sogd, reg.		
Sogdiana, prov.	19	K c
Sogdiana, satr.	18	R h
Sogne Fiord	166	G c
Sohar	170	G f
Soignes, Forest of	156	A a
Soignies	117	C d
Soissons	61	E b
Soissons, bp.	94	C b
Soissons, gen.	147	E b
Sokoto	174	D c
Sokotra, isl.	174	I c
Solander Island	172	F e
Soldaia (Sudak)	99	K e
Soldau	123	K b
Soledad	190	A d
Solent, str.	49	F f
Solfatara, vol.	31	ins. A
Solferino	158	F f
Solignac, mon.	94	C b
Solikamsk	138	I d
Solimariaca	39	H i
Solis, route of	105	D d
Solis River (Rio de la Plata)	108	L k
Solitaria, isl.	107	A i
Sollium	10	B d
Solmona	64	B b
Solomon, Palace of, in ancient Jerusalem	6	ins. A
Solomon, Palace of, in medieval Jerusalem	68	ins. B (7)
Solomon Islands	172	E a
Solomon's Pool, in ancient Jerusalem	6	ins. A (2)
Solona	27	F c
Solothurn	91	P k
Solothurn, canton	91	P k
Solovets	138	E c
Solsona	82	C a
Solsona, bp.	94	C c
Soluntum, or Solus	30	C d
Solway Firth		
Solway Moor	118	D c
Solway Moss		
Solygea	15	D b
Somah	165	E d
Somaliland, British, col	174	H d
Somaliland, Italian, col	174	H d
Somborne, deanery	100	A a
Somberete	213	B b
Sombrero, isl.	213	F c
Somena River, see Somme River		
Somersætas, people		
Somerset, in Maryland	194	K g
Somerset, in Queensland	172	D b
Somerset, cty. in England		
Somerset, shire		
Somerset House, in London	75	G g
Somme, dept.	148	E e
Somme River	76	E b
Sommerschenburg	85	B b
Sommerschenburg, castle	72	C a
Sommières	126	D e
Somnath, Pattan		
Somosierra	130	C e
Sonderburg	88	C d
Sondershausen	134	F c
Sondrio	91	R l

Songhar . . . .
Song-ka River . . . .
Sonoma 201   A b
Sonora 190   C f
Sonora, prov. 190   C e
Sonora, Rio de, R. 190   C f
Sonora, state 213   A b
Son-tai 171   L f
Sontheim, Ober 143   I g
Sontius (Isonzo) River 27   H b
Soor 135   H c
Sophene, reg. 20   H c
Sophia . . . .
Sopianæ 38   F c
Sopron (Ödenburg) 63   I e
Sora 30   C a
Sora, bp. 95   E c
Soracte, mon. 95   E c
Soracte, mt. 27   G e
Sorata, mt. 214   C d
Sorau 79   I c
Sorbian March 55   R i
Sorbiodunum (Old Sarum) . . .
Sorbiodurum (Straubing) . . . 38   E c
Sorbonne, bldg. in Paris . . . 149   B
Sorbs, people 53   O g
Sorek River 7   B e
Sorel 189   B b
Soria 82   H e
Sorocaba 215   E e
Soros 16   B a
Sorrento 90   E d
Sorrento, abp. 95   E c
Soto, route of . . . . 191 H e, I e
Soubise, near La Rochelle . . . 126   A d
Soubise, loc. in Paris 149   B
Soule, dist. 147   C e
Soule, viscty. 76   C e
Souna, dist. 63   H e
Sound, The, strait 88   E d
Souris River 198   E a
South Africa Company, British 175   F f
South African Republic 175   M k
South America, continent . . . 214,   115
Southampton, in England . . . .
Southampton, deanery 100   A b
Southampton, hospitals 100   A b
Southampton, mon. 100   A b
Southampton, parl. bor. 163   M g
Southampton, on Long Island . 189   B d
Southampton, Cape, in Canada 212   G b
Southampton County, in Virginia 207   K c
Southampton Hundred 193 ins. A (South.)
Southampton Island 212   G b
South Angles, people . . . . . .
South Australia, state 172   C c
South (Delaware) Bay 192   D d
South Bend, tower 211   H b
South Berwick . . . . 189 C c (S. B.)
South Beveland, isl. 117   B c
South Cape, Tasmania 172   D e
South Carolina, col. 193   D e
South Carolina, state 199   I d
South Carolina Yazoo Company 196   A d
South Chester, parl. dist. . . . 163   L d
South Dakota, state 210   E b
South Derby, parl. dist. 163   M d
South Devon, parl. dist. 163   K g
South Downs, dist. 49   F f
South Durham, parl. dist. . . . 163   M c
Southern Californians, tribes . 188   C d
Southern District, Victoria . . 172   leg.
Southern Pacific Grant 210   C d
Southern Uplands, Scotland . . 49   E d
South Essex, parl. dist. 163   O f
South Folk (Angles), people . .
South Hants, parl. dist. 163   M g
South Island, New Zealand . . 172   G e
South Isles, Scotland . . . . . .
South Kingston . . . . 189 ins. A
South Lancaster, parl. dist. . . 163   L d
South Leicester, parl. dist. . . 163   M e
South Molton, parl. bor. 163
South Northampton, parl. dist. 163   N e

South Northumberland, parl.
   dist. 163   L b
South Nottingham, parl. dist. . 163   N d
Southold 189   B d
South Pass 210   D b
South Platte River 210   E b
South Potomac River 192   B d
South Prussia, dist. 135   I c
South (Delaware) River 192   D d
South Salop, parl. dist. 163   L e
South Saskatchewan River . . . 186   H c
South Saxons, people 51   R k
South Sea (Pacific Ocean) . . . 107   F h
South Shields, parl. bor. 163   M c
South Sporades, isl. 164   D c
South Stafford, parl. dist. . . . 163   L e
South Stafford Coalfield 162   D e
South Voorne, isl. 117   C c
South Wales Coalfield, Great . 162   C f
Southwark, suburb of London . 75   G g
Southwark, parl. bor. . 163 N f (Southw.)
South Warwick, parl. dist. . . . 163   M e
South West Africa, German, col.
South West Cape, Tasmania . . 172   D e
Southwest Gate, in Olympia . .
Southwick, priory 100   A b
South Wilts, parl. dist. 163   L f
Söul, see Seoul 171   N e
Souvigny, mon. 94   C b
Sox, castle 91   R k
Sozopolis, in Asia Minor 71   M f
Sozopolis, in Bulgaria 73   F b
Spaichingen 143   G i
Spain, country, 910—1492 . . 82, 83
Spain, km., about 1560 . . . 118   D e
Spain, km., about 1740 130   C f
Spain, reg., in Roman times . . 34   C c
Spain, Rom. dioc. 42   B e
Spalato 90   F c
Spalato, abp. 95   F c
Spalauthræ 11   E c
Spalding, mon. 97   Q i
Spalding, parl. bor. . . . .
Spalt 114   F d
Spandau 85   C b
Spanish Algarve, dist. 83   J h
Spanish March, 8 cent. 53   L i
Spanish March, 9 cent. 56   C d
Spanish Netherlands, prov. . . . 122   B c
Spanish Peaks 198   D d
Spanish Plateau 2   D d
Spanish Town 213   E c
Spanish Trail, route 210   B d
Sparnacus, see Épernay
Sparta 14   C b
Spartel, Cape 2   D e
Spartolus 11   E b
Speen . . . .
Spencer Gulf 172   C d
Spercheus River 10   D d
Spes Vetus, Temple of 22   A
Speyer, see Spires
Spey River . . . .
Spezia 90   B b
Spezzia, isl. 164   C c
Sphacteria, isl. 14   B c
Sphagia, isl. 14   B c
Sphendale 16   B a
Sphettus 16   B b
Spice Islands 112   F d
Spielberg, castle 159   I d
Spier 62   F c
Spina 27   G c
Spinæ (Speen)
Spineticum Ostium, mouth of
   Po R. 27   G c
Spion Kop, mt. 175   M l
Spiræum, prom. 15   D b
Spira (Spires) 39   J i
Spires 62   E d
Spires, bp. 78   F d
Spires, imp. cy. 78   F d
Splügen 91   R l
Splügen Pass 91   R l

Spokane, or Spokane House . 210   B a
Spokane, Ind. Res. 188   C a
Spokanes, tribe 188   C a
Spoletium (Spoleto) 27   G e
Spoleto 90   D c
Spoleto, bp. 95   E c
Spoleto, duchy 54   G e
Sponheim, castle . . . . 142 ins. A
Sponheim, cty. 114   D d
Sponheim, mon. 95   D b
Sporades, isl. 13   E c
Spree River 85   G d
Spremberg 85   H e
Sprimont 117   D d
Springfield, in Illinois 211   H c
Springfield, in Mass. 189   B c
Springfield, in Missouri 211   G c
Springfield, in Ohio 211   I c
Sprinfontein 175   M m
Squillace 90   F e
Squillace, bp. 95   F d
Sredne Kolimsk 171   Q b
Stabiæ 30   D b
Stabulaus, see Stavelot
Stadaconá (Quebec) 191   K b
Stade 62   E b
Stade, Hanse. cy. . . . . 99 ins. B
Stadion, castle and town . . . 143   I i
Stadtlohn 122   D b
Staffarda 130   P j
Staffis 91   O l
Stafford, in England 127   W m
Stafford, in Virginia 193   F b
Stafford, cty. 127   W n
Stafford, parl. bor. 163   L l
Staggia 90   L j
Stagira, or Stagirus 11   E b
Stagno, bp. 95   F c
Stagnum Tuneticum (Bay of
   Tunis) . . . . 34 ins. A
Stahremberg, castle . . . . . .
Staines 75   H i
Stainforth 162   F d
Staked Plain 210   E d
Stalida, isl. 16   D c
Stamford, in Connecticut . . . 189   B d
Stamford, in England 127   Y n
Stamford, castle 65   F d
Stamford, parl. bor. 163   N e
Stamford Bridge 65   F d
Stampæ, see Étampes
Standing Rock, Ind. Res. 188   F a
Standish 185   D d
Stanislau 168   I b
Stanislawow 159   M d
Stanley, mon. 97   O j
Stanley Falls 175   F d
Stanley Pool, lake 175   E e
Stanleyville 175   F d
Stanovoi Mountains 171   Q b
Stanwix, Fort 192   D b
Stanz 91   Q l
Starbuck Island 180   L h
Star Fort 164   L g
Stargard, in Mecklenburg . . . 79   H b
Stargard, duchy 79   H b
Stargard, in Pomerania 79   I b
Stargard, Hanse cy. . . . . . . 99 ins.
Starkenburg, castle, in Hesse . 142   C a
Starkenburg, castle, on the Mo-
   selle R. . . . . 142 ins. A
Starodub 139   D e
Staten Island, South America . 215   C h
Staten Island, U. S. . . . . . 189 ins. C
States of the Church, 9 cent. . 56   E d
States of the Church, 13 cent. 73   C b
States of the Church, see also
   Papal States and Patrimony
   of St. Peter
State Treasury, in Rome . . . .
Statilii, Tomb of the 22   A
Statonia 27   F e
Statuas, Ad . . . . 35 ins. B
Staufen, in Baden 142   A e

Staufen, lordship . . . . 142 A e
Staufen or Hohenstaufen, castle
  in Wurtemberg . . . . 62 E d
Staufenberg, castle . . . . . . 142 B d
Staufenberg, lordship . . . . . 142 B d
Staunton . . . . 193 E b
Staunton River . . . . 193 E c
Stavanger . . . . 88 A b
Stavelot . . . . 117 D d
Stavelot, ab. . . . . 117 D d
Stavelot, mon. . . . . 95 D a
Stavoren . . . . 117 D b
Stavoren, Hanse. cy. . . . . . 99 ins. B
Stavropol . . . . 139 F f
Steckelberg, castle . . . . . . 86 G c
Stecknitz Canal . . . . 79 G b
Stedingen, dist. . . . . 72 B a
Steelyard, The, loc. in London 98 ins. A
Steenbergen . . . . 117 C c
Steenkerque . . . . 122 C c
Steenwyk . . . . 117 E b
Steep Point, cape. . . . . 172 A c
Stegeborg . . . . 119 H b
Steier, castle . . . . 63 H d
Stein . . . . 91 Q k
Steinamanger . . . . 135 I e
Steinau . . . . 123 I c
Steinfeld . . . . 142 E a
Steinfurt . . . . 122 D b
Steinhuder Lake . . . . 39 J g
Stelvio Pass . . . . 91 S l
Stenay . . . . 126 D b
Stendal . . . . 72 C a
Stendal, Hanse. cy. . . . . . . 99 ins. B
Stenimakhos . . . . 165 D c
Stenyclarus . . . . 14 B b
Stephenson, Fort . . . . 200 B c
Sternberg, dist. . . . . 85 D b
Sterzing . . . . 154 F e
Steterburg . . . . 62 F b
Steterburg, mon. . . . . . . 95 Ea (St.)
Stetten . . . . 142 D d
Stetten, lordship . . . . 142 D d
Stettenfels, castle . . . . 143 H g
Stettenfels, lordship . . . . . . 143 H g
Stettin . . . . 63 H b
Stettin, duchy, 14 cent. . . . . 79 I b
Stettin, duchy, 16 cent. . . . . 115 I a
Stettin, Hanse. cy. . . . . 99 ins. B
Stettin, Neu . . . . 123 I b
Steuben, Fort . . . . 196 ins. B
Steuerverein (Tax-Union) . . . 160 I f
Steusslingen . . . . 143 I i
Stewart Island . . . . 172 F e
Stewarts, fam. . . . .
Steyning, parl. bor. . . . . . . 163 N g
Steyr, in Austria . . . . 135 H e
Stikine River . . . . 212 ins.
Stiklestad . . . . 64 F d
Stilfser Joch, pass . . . . 26 E a
Stiria . . . . 16 C b
Stiris . . . . 11 D d
Stirling . . . .
Stirling, cty. . . . .
Stobi . . . . 39 M l
Stockach . . . . 142 D e
Stockbridge, Ind. Res. . . . . 188 I a
Stockelsdorf . . . . 88 D e
Stockholm . . . . 77 H a
Stockholm, Hanse. for. cy. . . 98 G b
Stockport . . . . 127 W m
Stockport, parl. bor. . . . . . . 163 L d
Stocks Market, in London . . 75 G g (37)
Stockton . . . . 162 E c
Stoddert, Fort . . . . 200 I f
Stœni, people . . . . 26 E b
Stoke-upon-Trent, parl. bor. . 163 L d
Stoke-Courcy, parl. bor. . . . .
Stolbovo. . . . . 138 D d
Stollhofen . . . . 134 D d
Stollhofen Lines, military dist. 129 E c
Stolp . . . . 123 I a
Stolp, Hanse. cy. . . . . 98 G c
Stolpen . . . . 115 H c

Stoneleigh, mon. . . . . 97 P i
Stonington . . . . 189 C d
Stony Point, on Hudson R. . . 195 D c
Stork Tower, in Jerusalem . . 6 ins. A *
Storkyro . . . . 131 H a
Stormarn, dist. . . . . 62 E b
Storm Bay . . . . 172 D e
Stormberg Junction. . . . . . . 175 M m
Storms, Cape of . . . . 109 S k
Stoss, Pass . . . . 91 R k
Stotzingen . . . . 143 J h
Stour River . . . . 49 G e
Stourbridge. . . . . 98 ins. A
Stourport . . . . 162 D e
Stow-on-the-Wold . . . . 127 X o
Stradella . . . . 130 R i
Straits Settlements, col. . . . . 171 L h
Stralsund . . . . 79 H a
Stralsund, Hanse. cy. . . . . . . 99 ins. B
Strand, street in London . . . . 75 G g
Strasburg, in Alsace . . . . . . 62 D d
Strasburg, bp. . . . . 78 E d
Strasburg, imp. cy. . . . . 78 E d
Strasburg, in Virginia . . . . . 193 E b
Strata Florida, mon. . . . . . . 97 N i
Stratford, near London . . . . 75 J h
Stratford, in Connecticut . . . 189 B d
Stratford Langthorne, mon. . . 97 R j
Strathclyde, km. . . . .
Strathcona . . . . 212 D c
Strathearn, dist. . . . .
Strathnaver, dist. . . . .
Stratonicea . . . . 11 E b
Straton's Tower in Jerusalem. 6 B d
Strättligen, castle . . . . 91 P l
Stratton . . . . 127 U p
Stratus . . . . 10 C d
Straubing . . . . 79 H d
Strausberg . . . . 85 D b
Strawberry Bank, village . . . 189 D c
Strehla . . . . 63 G c
Strehlen . . . . 135 I c
Strengnäs . . . . 119 H b
Stresow . . . . 135 G a
Stretensk . . . . 171 M c
Streu River . . . . 86 F c
Stridon . . . . 42 F e
Striegau . . . . 135 I c
Strivali Islands . . . . 157 E e
Strogonov, Colony of . . . . . .
Strongyle, isl. . . . . 30 E d
Strood . . . . 98 ins. A
Strophades Islands . . . . 14 B b
Stroud, parl. bor. . . . . 163 L f
Stryme . . . .
Strymon River . . . . 11 E a
Strymonic Gulf . . . . 11 F b
Stuart, routes of . . . . 172 leg.
Stuart Town . . . . 193 ins. C
Studzianka . . . . 153 N g
Stühlingen . . . . 142 B e
Stühlingen, landgr. . . . . 142 B e
Stuhlweissenburg . . . . 159 J e
Stuhmsdorf . . . . 123 J b
Stura River (Stura di Demonte) 26 B c
Stura River (Stura di Lanzo) . 26 B b
Sturni . . . . 31 G b
Stuttgart . . . . 143 H h
Styberra . . . . 10 C a
Stymphalus . . . . 14 C b
Styra . . . . 15 E a
Styria, duchy, 12 cent. . . . . . 72 D b
Styria, duchy, 14 cent. . . . . . 79 I e
Styria, march, 11 cent. . . . . 63 H e
Styx River . . . . 14 C b
Suakin . . . . 174 C c
Suana . . . . 27 F e
Suanetes, people . . . . 26 D a
Subiaco . . . . 64 ins.
Subiaco, mon. . . . . 96 C b
Subig . . . . 199 ins. H
Sublaqueum (Subiaco) . . . . 27 H f
Sublavio (Seben) . . . . 27 F a
Sublette's Cut-off, route . . . 210 C b

Sublician Bridge, Rome . . . . 24 A
Sublime Porte, loc. in Constan-
  tinople . . . . 93 G e
Subura, quarter in Rome . . . 22 A
Succoth . . . . 7 D d
Succur . . . .
Su-chau, in Kan-su . . . . . . 171 K e
Su-chau, in Kiang-su . . . . . 171 N e
Suchester . . . .
Sucré . . . . 214 C d
Sucro River (Júcar R.) . . . . 38 B e
Suczawa . . . . 168 J c
Sudak . . . . 99 K e
Sudan, reg. . . . . 174 C c
Sudan, Anglo-Egyptian, reg. . 174 F c
Sudbury, in England . . . . . . 163 O e
Sudbury, parl. bor. . . . . 163 O e
Sudbury, in Mass. . . . . 189 C c (Sudb.)
Sudbury, in Ontario . . . . . . 212 G d
Sudermania, dist. . . . . 119 H b
Sudetes, mts. . . . . 166 I e
Sudeti Mountains . . . . 38 E b
Sueones, people . . . . 38 E a
Suessa Aurunca or Suessa (Sessa) 30 C a
Suessa Pometia . . . . 30 B a
Suessiones or Suessionis, see
  Soissons
Suessiones, people . . . . 38 C c
Suessula (Torre di Sessola) . . 30 D a
Sueves, people, in Germany . . 45 G b
Sueves, people, in Spain 45 C d, 50 B d, 52 H e
Suez . . . . 174 K i
Suez, Gulf of . . . . 174 K j
Suez, Isthmus of . . . . 3 H e
Suez Canal . . . . 174 K i
Sufes . . . . 42 D f
Suffolk, cty. . . . . 127 Z n
Sugambri, people . . . . 39 I h
Suhar . . . .
Suhl . . . . 154 F c
Suhlingen . . . . 154 E b
Sui-chau-fu . . . .
Suindinum, see Le Mans
Suipacha . . . . 214 C e
Sukadana . . . . 112 E d
Sukhona River . . . . 167 N c
Sukhum Kaleh . . . . 164 G b
Sulby, mon. . . . . 97 Q l
Sulci . . . . 38 D e
Suleïman. mosque . . . . 93 G e
Sulina . . . . 165 F a
Sulina Mouth of Danube . . . 164 D a
Suliots, people . . . . 164 C c
Sully . . . . 126 C c
Sulmo . . . . 27 H e
Sulmone . . . . 90 E c
Sultaniyeh . . . . 99 M f
Sultan's Pool . . . . 6 ins. A
Sultan Valideh, mosque . . . . 93 G e (6)
Sulu, isl. . . . . 110 D D g
Suluan, isl. . . . . 110 D D g
Sulu Archipelago . . . . 199 ins. H
Sulu Sea . . . . 199 ins. H
Sulz . . . . 143 G i
Sulzbach, in Bavaria . . . . . . 79 G d
Sulzbach, in Wurtemberg . . . 143 I g
Sulzbach, palat. . . . . 123 G d
Sumatium . . . .
Sumatra, isl. . . . . 112 C c
Sumba, isl. . . . . 172 A b
Sumbal . . . .
Sumbal, reg. . . . .
Sumbawa, isl. . . . .
Sumelocenna . . . . 39 J i
Sumer, reg. . . . . 5 D b
Sumiswald, castle . . . . 91 P k
Summo lacu . . . . 26 D a
Summus Pœninus, see Great
  Saint Bernard
Sumter, Fort . . . . 208 E c
Sun, Gate of the, in Alexandria 34 ins. C
Sunarganw . . . .
Sunderland, parl. bor. . . . . . 163 M c
Sundgau, dist. . . . . 114 D e

Sundhofen . . . . 143 ins. D
Sun Dial, in Rome . . . . 22 A
Sundswall . . . . 166 I c
Sungari River . . . .
Sumian Gate, in Athens . . . .
Suntar . . . . 171 M b
Süntel, mts. . . . . 55 Q i
Supe . . . . 214 B d
Superior, lake . . . . 186 K d
Suppai, Ind. Res. . . . . 188 D c
Süpplingenburg, castle . . . . . . 62 F b
Sura, Baths of . . . .
Surabaja . . . . 172 A a
Surat . . . . 137 B d
Surgut . . . . 170 I b
Surinam, col. . . . . 214 D b
Surintendance, Rue de la, street
 in Versailles . . . . 149 A
Surrentum (Sorrento) . . . . . . 30 D b
Surrey, cty. . . . . 127 Y o
Surreymen, people . . . .
Sursee . . . . 91 Q k
Surt . . . .
Susa, in Italy . . . . 90 A b
Susa, marq. . . . . 64 A a
Susa, in Persia . . . . 19 G d
Susia . . . . 19 I c
Susiana, prov. . . . . 19 G d
Susiana, reg. . . . . 8 C b *
Susiana, satr. . . . . 18 P h
Susquehanna River . . . . 192 C c
Susquehannocks, tribe . . . . 188 K b
Sussex, cty. . . . . 127 Y p
Sussex, km. . . . .
Sutherland, cty. . . . .
Sutherland, dist. . . . .
Sutherlands, fam. . . . . 97 I a
Sutley River . . . . 137 B a
Sutri . . . . 64 ins.
Sutri, bp. . . . . 95 E c
Sutrium (Sutri) . . . . 27 G e
Sutter's Fort (Sacramento) . . . 198 A c
Sutter's Mill . . . . 210 A c
Suva . . . . 172 G b
Suwali . . . .
Suwanee River . . . . 193 C f
Suya . . . . 190 C e
Suzdal . . . . 138 F d
Sveaborg, fortress . . . . 131 H a
Svendborg . . . . 88 D d
Svendborg, Hanse. for. cy. . . 98 E b
Svenigrod . . . . 71 L d
Sventziany . . . . 153 N f
Svir River . . . . 107 L c
Swaanendael see Zwaanendael. 191 J d
Swabia, Frank. prov., 9 cent. . 56 D c
Swabia, duchy, about 1000 . . 58 F d
Swabia, duchy, 11 cent. . . . . 62 E e
Swabia, duchy, 12 cent. . . . 72 B b
Swabia, Lower, "landvogtei" . . 143 I j
Swabia, Upper, "landvogtei" . 143 I j
Swabians, people . . . . 57 E d
Swakopmund . . . . 175 E g
Swale River . . . . 127 X l
Swan Hill, town . . . . 172 D d
Swan River . . . . 172 A d
Swanscombe . . . . 75 J i
Swansea . . . . 189 ins. A
Swansea, parl. bor. . . . . 163 J f
Swaziland, reg. . . . . 175 N l
Sweet Waters, Valley of the, loc.
 in Constantinople . . . . . 93 G e
Sweden, km., about 1000 . . 59 H b
Sweden, km., about 1097 . . . 66 J b
Sweden, km., about 1190 . . . 70 J a
Sweden, km., about 1569 . . 119 I a
Sweden, km., about 1658 . . 120 leg.
Sweden, km., about 1740 . . 131 H a
Sweden, km., about 1812 . . 155 ins.
Sweden, km., 1910 . . . . . . 166 H d
Swedes, people . . . . 46 I b
Swedish Pomerania, dist. . . . . 154 G a
Swift Current, town . . . . 212 E d
Swinemünde . . . . 135 H b

Swineshead, mon. . . . . 97 Q i
Swinomish, Ind. Res. . . . . 188 B a
Swiss Confederation, 14—18 cent. 91
Syagrius, km. of . . . . 33 M h
Sybaris . . . . 31 F c
Sybaris River . . . . 31 F c
Sycæ . . . . 93 G e
Sycaminon . . . . 6 B c
Sycurium . . . . 11 D c
Sydney, on Cape Breton I. . . . 212 J d
Sydney, in New South Wales . 172 E d
Sydney District . . . . 172 leg.
Syene (Assuan) . . . . 4 F d *
Sylhet . . . . 137 F c
Sylt, isl. . . . . 114 E a
Sylvania, proposed state in U. S.
Symæthus River . . . . 30 D e
Syme, isl. . . . . 13 E c
Symmes Purchase, dist. . . . . 196 ins. B
Synnada . . . . 20 D c
Sypalettus . . . . 16 B a
Syracusæ, see Syracuse, in Sicily
Syracuse, in New York . . . . . 196 D b
Syracuse, in Sicily . . . . 30 E e
Syracuse, bp. . . . . 95 F d
Syracuse, plan of . . . . 31 ins. B
Syra Orda . . . .
Syrastrene, reg. . . . . 19 L f
Syr Daria, River . . . .
Syria, km. . . . . 33 E b
Syria, Macedon. prov. . . . . . 18 E d
Syria, reg. . . . . 67 N g
Syria, Rom. prov. . . . . 35 L g
Syria, satr. . . . . 18 O h
Syria I, E. Rom. prov. . . . . 43 J f (3)
Syrian Desert . . . . 3 H e
Syria Salutaris, Rom. prov. . . 43 J f (10)
Syrias, prom. . . . . 20 F a
Syros, isl. . . . . 15 E b
Syrtis, Greater, gulf . . . . . 174 E a
Syrtis, Lesser, gulf . . . . . . 174 E a
Syrtis Maior (Greater Syrtis), gulf 34 H g
Syrtis Minor (Lesser Syrtis), gulf 34 G g
Sys River, in Achaia . . . . . 14 C b
Sys River, in Macedonia . . . . 11 D c
Sythas River . . . . 14 C b
Szamos Rirer . . . . 159 L e
Szamos-Ujvar . . . . 159 M e
Szasz-Regen . . . . 159 M e
Szathmar . . . .
Sze-chwan, prov. . . . . 171 L e
Szentes . . . . 159 K e
Szent Imre . . . . 119 I d
Szent Tamas . . . . 159 J f
Szolnok . . . . 159 K e
Szöreg . . . . 159 K e

Taanach . . . . 6 C c
Tabæ, in Asia Minor . . . . . 47 L f
Tabæ, in Palestine . . . . . 6 D c
Tabæ, in Persia . . . . 19 I d
Tabard, The, inn, near London 75 G g
Tabasco . . . . 107 H f
Tabasco, reg. . . . . 105 B c
Tabasco River . . . . 105 B c
Tabasco, state . . . . 213 C c
Tabatinga . . . . 214 C c
Tabbas, Las . . . . 214 A b
Tabernæ (Zabern) . . . . . . 39 I i
Tabernæ (Rheinzabern) . . . . 39 J i
Taberna frigida . . . . . . 26 E d
Tabernas . . . . 82 B b
Tabernilla . . . .
Tabor, in Bohemia . . . . . 87 J d
Tabor, in Iowa . . . . 206 F b
Tabor, mt. . . . . 6 C c
Tabora . . . . 175 G e
Tabriz . . . . 139 G H
Tabularium (Record Office) in
 Rome . . . . 24 A
Taburi, people . . . . 19 H c
Tacape . . . . 12 F d
Tacna . . . . 214 B d
Tacoma . . . . 210 A a

Tacubaya . . . . 106 A a
Tadcaster . . . . 127 X m
Tadmor . . . . 20 H e
Tadousac . . . . 212 H d
Tænarum . . . . 14 C c
Tænarum, prom. (Cape Matapan) 14 C c
Tænia . . . . 34 ins. A
Tæzalorum, prom. . . . . 38 B a
Taff River . . . .
Tafilet . . . . 98 C g
Taganrog . . . . 139 E f
Tagaste . . . . 42 D f
Tagernauseo, see Tegernsee
Taghaza . . . . 108 Q e
Taginæ . . . . 52 D b
Tagliacozzo . . . . 72 C c
Tagliamento River . . . . 135 G e
Tagong . . . .
Tagus River . . . . 82 A b
Tahiti, isl. . . . . 180 M i
Tahlequah . . . . 211 G c
Tahoe, lake . . . . 210 B c
Taido (Peking) . . . .
Taillebourg . . . . 69 C d
Taillebourg, castle . . . . 76 C d
Taimur Peninsula . . . . 171 K a
Tai-wan . . . . 171 N f
Tai-yuen-fu . . . .
Taiza . . . . 105 C c
Ta-ku . . . . 170 ins. A
Taku River . . . . 212 ins.
Talabriga . . . . 38 A b
Talamone . . . . 72 C c
Talas . . . .
Talavera de la Reina . . . . . 82 A a
Talay River . . . .
Talca . . . . 215 B f
Talcahuano . . . . 212 B f
Ta-lien-wan . . . . 171 N e
Ta-li-fu . . . .
Tallahassee . . . . 211 I d
Tallapoosa River . . . . 193 B c
Talley, mon. . . . . 97 N j
Talmont . . . . 69 C c
Talmont, seign. . . . . 69 C c
Taltal . . . . 215 B e
Talva, see Tarbes
Taman . . . . 93 E a
Tamar . . . . 7 C f
Tamar River, in Cornwall . .
Tamar River, in Tasmania . . . 172 D e
Tamara . . . . 83 E c
Tamarus River . . . . 30 D a
Tamatave . . . . 175 H f
Tamaulipas, state . . . . . . 213 C b
Tambo, near Cuzco . . . . . 111 C d
Tambo, near Mollendo . . . . 214 B d
Tambov . . . . 139 F e
Tamesa (Thames) River . . . . 38 C b
Tampico . . . . 201 F e
Tammerfors . . . . 131 H a
Tampa . . . . 211 I e
Tampa Bay . . . . 211 I e
Tampico . . . . 107 H f
Tamworth . . . . 127 X n
Tamworth, parl. bor. . . . . . 163 M e
Tamynæ . . . . 11 F d
Tamyras River . . . . 6 C a
Tana (Azov) . . . . 77 M c
Tanager River . . . . 30 E b
Tanagra . . . . 11 E d
Tanaïs . . . . 35 L b
Tanaïs (Don) River . . . . . 35 M d
Tanana River . . . . 212 A b
Tanarus (Tanaro) River . . . 26 C c
Tanatis Island . . . . 38 C b
Tancred's Tower, in Jerusalem 68 ins. B
Tanegashima Island . . . . . 110 E E e
Taneytown . . . . 208 ins.
Tangarara . . . . 111 A b
Tanganyika, lake . . . . . . 175 F e
Tangermünde . . . . 85 B b
Tangermünde, Hanse. cy. . . . 99 ins. B
Tangier . . . . 174 C a

Tang-shan . . . . 170 ins. **A**
Tangut, reg. . . . .
Tanis 1   **B b**
Tanjore 137   **C f**
Tannenberg 87   **L b**
Tanners, Postern of the, loc. in
  Jerusalem . . . . 68 ins. **B**
Tannetum 26   **E c**
Tan-sui 171   **N f**
Tanta 150   **B a**
Tantalam Island 171   **L h**
Tanus River 14   **C b**
Taormina 90   **E f**
Taos 190   **D d**
Tapajos River 214   **D c**
Tophiæ Islands 10   **B d**
Taphus, isl. 10   **B d**
Tappahannock 193   **F c**
Tappan 192   **D c**
Tapti River 137   **C d**
Taranaki, prov. 172   **G d**
Taranto 90   **F d**
Taranto, abp. 95   **F c**
Tarapacá 214   **C d**
Taras (Taranto) 31   **G b**
Tarascon, in Foix 69   **D e**
Tarascon, in Provence 72   **A c**
Tarasp 122   **F e**
Tarazona 82   **B a**
Tarazona, bp. 94   **B c**
Tarbes 61   **C e**
Tarbes, bp. 94   **C c**
Tarentaise 61   **G d**
Tarentaise, abp. 95   **D b**
Tarentum (Taranto) 31   **G b**
Tarentum, dist. in Rome 23   **B**
Tarentum, Gulf of 31   **G c**
Targovitza 131   **J d**
Tarifa 82   **A b**
Tarifa, Cape 166   **D h**
Tarija 214   **C e**
Tarim River . . . .
Tarleton, raid of 195   **B e**
Tarleton, route of 195   **A f**
Tarma 111   **B d**
Tarn, dept. 148   **E f**
Tarn River 76   **E d**
Tarn-et-Garonne, dept. 148   **E f**
Tarnaiæ 26   **A a**
Tarnis River, see Tarn River
Tarnopol 139   **C f**
Tarnow 87   **M c**
Taro River 150   **E d**
Tarphe 16   **F e**
Tarquinii 27   **F e**
Tarracina (Terracina) 30   **C a**
Tarraco (Tarragona) 38   **C d**
Tarraconensis, Rom. prov. . . . 38 B d (1)
Tarraconensis, West Rom. prov. . 42 B e (4)
Tarragona 82   **C a**
Tarragona, abp. 94   **C c**
Tarrant, mon. 97   **O k**
Tarrytown 195   **E c**
Tarsatica 27   **I b**
Tarshish, reg. 12   **B c**
Tarsi, people . . . .
Tarsius River . . . .
Tarsus 20   **F d**
Tartars or Tatars, people, north
  of Black Sea 93   **D a**
Tartars or Tatars, people in
  eastern Asia . . . .
Tartars or Tatars, people in
  eastern Russia 138   **H d**
Tartarus River 27   **F b**
Tartary or Tatary, reg. . . 109 W-BB c
Tartary or Tatary, Little, reg. . 139   **D f**
Tartas 76   **C e**
Tarua 8   **D c***
Taruana or Taruenna, see Thé-
  rouanne
Tarus (Taro) River 26   **E c**
Tarvis 135   **G e**
Tarvisium (Treviso) 27   **G b**

Tashkent . . . .
Tasman, route of . . . .
Tasman Peninsula 172   **D e**
Tasmania, state 172   **D e**
Tatars, see Tartars
Tatary, reg., see Tartary
Tatra, mts. 166   **I f**
Tatta 137   **A d**
Tatta, lake 20   **E c**
Tau . . . . 199 ins. **D**
Tau, isl. . . . . 199 ins. **D**
Tauber River 114   **E d**
Tauberbischofsheim 158   **E d**
Taulantii, people 10   **A b**
Taungu . . . .
Taungu, reg. . . . .
Taunton, in England 127   **V p**
Taunton, mon. 97   **N k**
Taunton, parl. bor. 163   **K f**
Taunton, in Mass. . . . . . . 189 ins. **A**
Taunus Mountains 39   **J h**
Taupo, lake 172   **G d**
Taurasia (Turin) 26   **B b**
Tauresium 52   **K e**
Taurianum, prov. 30   **E d**
Tauric Chersonese (Crimea) . . 35   **K d**
Taurida, reg. 139   **D f**
Taurini, people 26   **B c**
Taurinum, see Turin
Taurisci, people 38   **E c**
Tauroggen 131   **H b**
Tauromenium 30   **E e**
Taurus Mountains 3   **H e**
Taurus, prom. 30   **E e**
Taus 87   **I d**
Tavan 119   **K d**
Tavastehus 119   **I a**
Tavira 82   **A b**
Tavoy . . . .
Tavoy, reg. . . . .
Tavistock, mon. 97   **M k**
Tavistock, parl. bor. 163   **J g**
Tavium 20   **F c**
Tawali, isl. 112   **F d**
Tawalisi, people . . . .
Tawi-Tawi, isl. 112   **F c**
Taxila 19   **L d**
Taxis, castle 143   **J h**
Taxis, princ. 143   **J h**
Tay River 49   **D c**
Taygetus Mountains 14   **C b**
Taylor, route of . . . . 201 leg.
Tcheragan Palace 92
Tcherkasy 139   **D f**
Tchernigov 139   **D e**
Tchernoi-Yar 139   **G f**
Tchesme 164   **D c**
Tchigrin 139   **D f**
Tchirmen 93   **C b**
Tchorgun 164   **J f**
Tchuds, people 71   **K b**
Tchuguiev 139   **E f**
Teano, bp. . . . . 95 ins.
Teanum Apulum 30   **E a**
Teanum Sidicinum 30   **D a**
Teate, Apulum 30   **E a**
Teate, Marrucinum (Chieti) . . 27   **I e**
Teb, El 174   **G c**
Tebuk 99   **K h**
Teck, duchy 143   **H h**
Teck, ruin 143   **H h**
Tecklenburg 78   **E b**
Tecklenburg, cty. 78   **E b**
Tecmon 10   **B c**
Tecumseh, Fort 210   **E b**
Tees River 49   **F d**
Tegea 14   **C b**
Tegernsee, mon. 95   **E b**
Tegesta 191   **I f**
Tegianum 30   **E b**
Tegucigalpa 213   **D c**
Tehachapi Pass 210   **B c**
Teheran 170   **G e**
Tehuacan . . . . 213 ins.

Tehuacanas, tribe 188   **G d**
Tehuantepec 105   **A c**
Tehuantepec, Gulf of 213   **C c**
Tehuantepec, Isthmus of . . . 213   **C c**
Teixeira, route of 214   **C c**
Tejada 46   **F f**
Tejas, tribe 188   **G d**
Tejuco 214   **E d**
Tekfour Serai, loc. in Constan-
  tinople 93   **G e**
Tekka, reg. 89   **J g**
Tekoa 7   **C e**
Tela 20   **H d**
Telamon 27   **F e**
Telesia 30   **E a**
Telethrius, mt. 11   **E d**
Telium 26   **E a**
Tell, The, reg. 2   **E e**
Tellicherri 137   **C f**
Tellena . . . .
Tellus, Temple of, Rome . . . 22   **A**
Telmessus, Telmissus 20   **C d**
Telo Martius (Toulon) 38   **D d**
Telshi 125   **H a**
Telus 13   **E c**
Tembuland, reg. 175   **M m**
Temenites . . . . 31 ins. **B**
Temenium 15   **C b**
Temes River 159   **K f**
Tempe, valley 11   **D c**
Templars, House of the, Jeru-
  salem . . . . 68 ins. **B (8)**
Temple, Faubourg du, quarter
  in Paris 149   **B**
Temple, Rue du, street in Paris 149   **B**
Temple, Inner, Middle and
  Outer, loc. in London . . . 75   **G g**
Temple, The, in Jerusalem . . 68 ins. **B**
Temple, Rue du, street in Paris 149   **B**
Temple, Street of the, Jerusalem 68 ins. **B**
Temple, The, bldg. in Paris . . 149   **B**
Temple, Vieille, Rue du, street
  in Paris 149   **B**
Temple Church, in London . . 75 G g (1)
Temple of Peace, Aug. Reg. of
  Rome 22   **A**
Tempsa 31   **F c**
Temrink 119   **L d**
Temuco 215   **B f**
Tenancingo 106   **A a**
Tenasserim . . . .
Tenasserim, prov. 171   **K g**
Tenby 65   **D e**
Tencteri, people 38   **D b**
Tenda 130   **P j**
Tenda, Col di, pass 150   **D d**
Tenduc, people . . . .
Tenea 15   **C b**
Tenebrium, prom. 38   **C e**
Tenedos 13   **E b**
Tenedos, isl. 13   **E b**
Teneriffe, isl. 108   **P e**
Teneriffe, Santa Cruz de . . . 174   **B b**
Tenes 66   **G f**
Tenimber Islands 172   **C a**
Ten Jurisdictions, League of,
  dist. 91   **R l**
Tenneberg 85   **F e**
Tennessee, state 202   **H c**
Tennessee River 211   **H d**
Tennessee Yazoo Company . . 196   **A d**
Tennis Court, loc. in Versailles 149   **A**
Tenochtitlan 106   **A a**
Tenos 15   **F b**
Tenos, isl. 15   **F b**
Tentura or Tentyris (Dendera) . 4   **F d**
Teodosia 124   **G b**
Teos 13   **E b**
Teotihuacan 106   **B a**
Tepeaca 106   **C b**
Tepexacac . . . .
Tepfenhardt 142   **D e**
Tepic 213   **B b**

Tepic, ter.	213	B b
Tepl, mon.	95	E a
Teplitz	154	G c
Tepotzotlan	106	A a
Tepulaw Aqueduct	22	A
Teramo	90	D c
Teramo, bp.	95	E c
Teredon	19	G d
Terek River	139	G g
Terek, Cossacks of the, people	139	G g
Tergeste (Trieste)	27	H b
Tergeste, Gulf of	27	H b
Tergovist	77	J c
Terina	31	F d
Terjan	93	E c
Ter la Haye		
Termes	38	B d
Termini	90	D f
Termoli	90	E c
Termoli, bp.	95	E c
Termonde	117	C c
Ternate, isl.	112	F c
Terni	90	D c
Terni, bp.	95	E c
Ternodurum, see Tonnerre		
Terracina	90	D d
Terracina, bp.	95	E c
Terranova, in Calabria	90	F e
Terranova, in Sicily	90	E f
Terre Haute	211	H c
Terrenate	190	C e
Terrington, parl. bor.		
Terschelling, isl.	117	D a
Teruel	82	H e
Terventum		
Teschen	79	K d
Teschen, princ.	79	K d
Teslin, lake	212	B b
Tessin (Ticino) River	78	F f
Tessin, dist., see Ticino	91	Q l
Testaccio, Monte, Rome	22	A
Teste de Buch, la	76	C d
Testry	55	P j
Tetrica, mt.	27	H e
Tetschen	123	H c
Tettnang	143	I j
Tetuan	70	E f
Teufelsbrücke, bridge	150	E c
Teumessus	11	E d
Teurnia	27	H a
Teuthrania, dist.		
Teuthrone	14	C c
Teutoburger Forest, Teutobur-		
giensis Saltus, mts.	39	J g
Teutones, people	34	F c
Teutonic Order, Dom. of the,		
14 cent.	77	H b
Teutonic Order, Dom. of the,		
16 cent.	119	J b
Teviotdale, dist.		
Tewkesbury	84	B d
Tewkesbury, mon.	97	O b
Tewkesbury, parl. bor. 163 L f (Tewkesb.)		
Texas, prov.	190	F e
Texas, state	202	E i
Texas Prairies, reg.	187	J f
Texel, isl.	117	C a
Textricum, see Testry		
Texuandri, people	39	H h
Tezcuco		
Tezcuco, lake		
Thabraca	46	H f
Thagines River	31	F c
Thala	38	D e
Thamatha	7	D e
Thame, mon.	97	Q j
Thames River, in Canada	200	B b
Thames River, in Connecticut 189 B d (Th.R.)		
Thames River, in England	49	F f
Thames, Battle of the	200	C b
Thamesis Æsturianum (Thames		
River)	51	Q i
Thana		
Thanet, island of	51	S k
Thann	154	G d
Thannheim	143	J i
Thantia	7	E d
Thapsacus	20	H e
Thapsus, in Algeria	12	E c
Thapsus, in Sicily	30	E e
Thapsus, in Tunis	38	E e
Thara	19	H c
Thasos	11	F b
Thasos, isl.	11	F b
Thaumaci	11	D c
Thaya River	63	I d
Theanum, see Teano		
Thebæ Phthiotides	11	D c
Thebais, Rom. prov.	43	I h (3)
Thebes, in Bœotia	11	E d
Thebes, in Egypt	1	C e
Thebez, in Samaria	7	C d
The Close, loc. in London	75	G g
The Danelaw, reg.		
The Downs, roadstead	185	H f
The Filder, dist.	143	H h
The Free Land, reg.	117	A c
Theganussa, isl.	14	B c
The Hague	117	C b
The Isles, bp.	97	G c
Theiss River	73	D a
Thelepte	34	F g
Thelpusa	14	B b
Theniscyra	20	G b
Themistocles, Grave of	16	D c
Themistocles, Wall of	23	D
Thenæ	34	G g
The Naze, cape	166	G d
Thengen	142	C e
Thengen, cty.	142	C e
Theocoleum		
Theodonis Villa, see Thionville		
Theodosia	12	K a
Theodosiopolis (Erzerum)	20	I c
Theodosius II., Wall of, Con-		
stantinople	93	G e
Theophilo	214	E d (Phil.)
Theotmelli, see Detmold		
Thera	13	D c
Thera, isl.	13	D c
Therambus	11	E c
Therapne	14	C b
Theres, castle	62	F c
Therezina	214	E c
Therma (Salonika)	11	D b
Thermæ Himeræ	30	C e
Thermæ Selinuntiæ	30	C e
Thermaic Gulf	11	D b
Therme		
Thermessa, isl.	30	E d
Thermodon River	20	G b
Thermopylæ, pass	11	D d
Thermopylæ, plan of	16	
Thermum, in Ætolia	10	C d
Thérouanne, bp.	94	C a
Thervings, people	50	I d
Theseum, loc. in Athens	23	D c
Theseum, loc. in the Pyræus	16	D c
Thespiæ	11	E d
Thesprotia, dist.	10	B c
Thesprotian Gulf	10	B c
Thessaliotis, dist.	10	D c
Thessalonica (Salonika)	11	D b
Thessalonica, km.	73	E b
Thessalonica, theme	59	I e
Thessaly, Rom. prov.	43	G f (3)
Thessaly, Turkish prov.	164	C c
Thessaly, reg.	10	C c
Thessaly, Wallachian, princ.	89	B c
Thestium	10	C d
Thetford		
Thetford, castle	65	G d
Thetford, mon.	97	R i
Thetford, parl. bor.	163	O e
Theudoria	10	C c
Theveste	38	D e
Thiengen, near Freiburg in		
Breisgau	142	A e
Thiengen, near Waldshut in		
Baden	142	B e
Thiers	69	E d
Thiers, mon.	94	C b
Thierstein, castle	91	P k
Thieves Islands	110	GG
Thilabus	20	J e
Thimnathah		
Thines	156	A a
Thines River	156	A a
Thionville, or Diedenhofen	62	C d
Thirsk, parl. bor.	163	M c
This	4	F d
Thisbæ		
Thisoa	14	C b
Thoire	76	F c
Tholen	117	C c
Tholey	157	ins.
Thoræ	15	D b
Thoricus	15	E b
Thorigny	76	C b
Thorn, in the Netherlands	117	D c
Thorn, in Prussia	72	D a
Thorn, Hanse. cy.	98	G c
Thorney, mon.	97	R i
Thornton-upon-Humber, mon.	97	Q h
Thospitis, lake	20	J c
Thouars	61	C c
Thouars, viscty.	76	C c
Thourout, mon.	94	C a
Thrace, East Rom. prov.	43	G e (a)
Thrace, reg.	8	A a
Thrace, Rom. dioc.	43	H e
Thrace, Rom. prov.	35	I e
Thrace, theme	59	J e
Thracesian Theme	59	J f
Thracian Bosporus, str.		
Thracian Chersonese, pen.	17	E a
Thracian Sea	17	C b
Three Bishoprics, gen.	147	F b
Three Kings Islands	172	G d
Three Points, cape		
Three Rivers, town	191	K b
Thremhall, mon.	97	R j
Thria	16	B a
Thriasian Plain	16	B a
Thronium	11	D d
Thuin	117	C d
Thun	150	D c
Thun, lake of	91	P l
Thun, stronghold	91	P l
Thurgarton, mon.	97	Q h
Thurgau, dist.	62	C c
Thurii	31	F c
Thüringer Wald (Thuringian		
Forest), mts.	62	F c
Thuringia, dist.	62	F c
Thuringia, landgr.	85	F e
Thuringia, march	63	G c
Thuringians, people	45	F b
Thurrock	75	J i
Thursday Island	172	D b
Thyamis (Kalamas) River	10	B c
Thyamus, mt.	10	C d
Thyatira	20	C c
Thyle River	156	B a
Thymbra		
Thymbrius River		
Thymœtadæ	16	B b
Thynias, prom.	20	C b
Thyreum	10	C d
Thyrides, prom.	14	C c
Thyssagetæ, people	19	G a
Thyssus	11	F b
Tian-shan Mountains		
Tiber River	64	B b
Tiber Island	22	A
Tiberias	6	D c
Tiberine Way, road	35	ins. B
Tiberinum	27	G d
Tiberis River, see Tiber River		
Tiberius, Arch of, on the Cam-		
pus Martius	22	A
Tiberius, Arch of, in the Forum		

Tiberius, Palace of 24   B
Tibestl, reg. 174   E b
Tibet, reg. . . . .
Tibiscus River 39   M k
Tibur (Tivoli) 27   G f
Tiburon, Cape 105   F c
Tiburones, Isla de los, isl. . . . 107   C h
Tiburtian Way, road . . . . . . 35 ins. B
Tiburtine Gate 22   A
Ticino, dist. 91   Q l
Ticino River 130   Q i
Ticinum (Pavia) 26   D b
Ticinus (Ticino) River 26   C a
Tickhill, parl. bor. . . . .
Ticonderoga 196   E b
Ticonderoga, Fort 192   E b
Tidore, isl. 112   F c
Tiel 117   D c
Tie-ling, see Tie Pass 171   N d
Tienen 117   C d
Tien-tsin . . . . 170 ins. A
Tie Pass 171   N d
Tierra del Fuego, isl. 215   C h
Tierra de los Bacallaos, reg.. 108   L c
Tierra de los Bretones, reg. . . 108   L c
Tierra Firme, reg. 105   G e
Tieté River 214   D e
Tifata, mt. 30   D a
Tifernum 27   G d
Tifernus, mt. 30   D a
Tifernus (Biferno) River 27   I f
Tiflis 67   O e
Tiger Hill, village 216
Tigisis, in Mauretania 42   C f
Tigisis, in Numidia 46   H f
Tigranocerta . . . .
Tigre, dist. 174   G c
Tigris River 5   D b
Tiguex, reg. 190   D e
Ti-hwa (Urumtsi) 171   J d
Tilburg 117   D c
Tilburg, castle 75   J i
Tilingana . . . .
Tiliventus (Tagliamento) River 27   G a
Tilleda 62   F c
Tilly 156   B a
Tilox, prom. 26   D e
Tilsit 88   I d
Tilty, mon. 97   R j
Timan Mountains 3   I b
Timavus (Timavo) River 27   H b
Timbuktu 174   C c
Timnah 7   B e
Timonium . . . . 34 ins. C (3)
Timor, isl. 112   F d
Timor Sea 172   B b
Timorlaut, isl. 172   C e
Timsah, lake 174   K i
Timur, Dom. of . . . .
Tinchebrai 65   F f
Tinetio 26   D a
Tingis (Tangier) 38   A e
Tinia River 27   G d
Tinnicum Island . . . . 192 ins.
Tinna River 27   H d
Tinnevelli . . . .
Tinnogasta 215   C e
Tintern, mon. 97   O j
Tiphsach . . . . 6 ins. C
Tippecanoe, battle 211   H b
Tipperah, dist. 137   F d
Tipperary, cty.. 127   I i
Tippermuir . . . .
Tippoo, Dominions of 137   C f
Tirano 91   S l
Tirhut, reg.. . . . .
Tirlemont 117   C d
Tirmidh . . . .
Tirnova 59   J e
Tiron, mon. 94   C b
Tiryns 15   C b
Tirzah 7   C d
Tisaeus, mt. 11   E c
Tisia (Theiss) River 35   I d

Tisné, route of 190   F d
Tisza, River, see Theiss River 43   G d.
Tisza-Füred 159   K e
Titane 14   C b
Titanus, mt. 10   D c
Titaresius River 10   D c
Titarius, mt. 10   D b
Titchfield, ab. 100   A b
Titel 159   K f
Tithe Lands, dist. 39   J i
Tithorea 11   D d
Tithronium 11   D d
Titicaca, lake 214   C d
Titulcia 38   B d
Titus, Arch of 24   B
Titus, Baths of 22   A
Tium 20   E b
Tiumen 138   K d
Tiveden, dist. 88   F b
Tiverton 189   C d
Tiverton, parl. bor. 163   K g
Tivoli, bp. 96   B b
Tivoli, bp. 95   E c
Tizón, Rio del, R. 190   C e
Tlacopan . . . .
Tlalmanalco 106   B a
Tlalpan 201   H g
Tlascala, Tlaxcala 106   B a
Tlemsen. 66   F g
Tlemsen, dist. 118   D g
t'Loo 117   D b
Tmolus, mt. 20   C c
Toarcis, see Thouars
Tobago, isl. 105   H d
Tobitschau 159   I d
Tobol River . . . .
Tobolsk 170   H c
Tocaima 214   B b
Tocantins River. 214   E c
Tocci, Dom. of the 93   C
Tocobaga 191   I f
Tocopilla 214   B e
Tocuyo 214   C b
Todi . . . . 64 ins.
Todi, bp. 95   E c
Todos os Santos, Bahia de, bay 214   F d
Todtnau. 142   A e
Toggenburg, dist. 91   R k
Toggenburg, New, castle . . . 91   R. k
Toggenburg, Old, castle 91   R k
Togoland, German col. . . . . .
Tokay 159   K d
Tokelau Islands 172   H a
Tokyo 171   O e
Tolbiacum 39   I h
Toledo, in Ohio 211   I b
Toledo, in Spain 82   B b
Toledo, abp. 94   A c
Toledo, emir. 83   E d
Tolentino 151   I h
Tolenus (Turano) River. 27   G e
Toleria . . . . 35 ins. B
Tolerus (Sacco) River 30   C a
Toletum (Toledo) 38   B e
Tolima, Nevada de, mt.. 214   B b
Tolna 159   J e
Tolone, see Toulon
Tolophon 10   D d
Tolosa (Toulouse) 38   C d
Toluca 106   A a
Tomarus, mt. in Epirus 10   B c
Tomarus, mt. in Illyris 10   B b
Tombecbé, Fort 191   H e
Tombigbee River 191   H e
Tombs of the kings, in Jerusalem 6 ins. A
Tombstone 210   C d
Tomebamba. 111   B b
Tomi 39   N l
Tomis 35   J e
Tömös Pass 159   M f
Tomsk 171   J c
Tonala 213   C c
Tonawanda, Ind. Res. 188   K b
Tondern 80   A d

Tonga Islands 180   J i
Tongaland, dist. 175   N l
Tongatabu, isl. 172   H c
Tongking, reg. 92   K e
Tongres 117   D d
Tongrinne 156   B a
Tonk 137   C c
Tonkawas, Ind. Res. 188   G c
Tonnerre 61   E c
Tonnerre, cty. 76   F c
Tönning 134   E a
Toongabuddra River 137   C e
Topeka 198   F c
Tophane, quarter in Constan-
tinople 93   G e
Tor, mon.. 97   N k
Tor Bay 127   V p
Torcello, bp. 95   E b
Tordesillas . . . .
Torgau 115   G c
Torinna, see Turenne
Torksey, castle 65   F d
Torne River 167   J b
Torneå 167   J b
Tornodorum, see Tonnerre
Toro 82   A a
Toron . . . . 68 ins. A
Toronaic Gulf. 11   E b
Torone 11   E b
Toronto 199   J b
Toropetz 71   M b
Torre di Faro 161   J h
Torrens, lake 172   C d
Torreon 213   B b
Torres, abp. 95   D c
Torres Strait 172   D a
Torres Vedras 130   B f
Torrington 127   U p
Torris 72   B c
Tortona 90   I h
Tortona, bp. 95   D c
Tortosa, in Spain 82   C a
Tortosa, bp. 94   C c
Tortosa, in Syria 68   C c
Tortuga, isl., near Haiti 105   F b
Tortuga, isl., near Venezuela . 105   G d
Toryne 10   B c
Törzburger Pass 159   M f
Torzhok 99   J b
Toskih . . . .
Totnes 127   V p
Tottenham 75   I h
Toul 62   C d
Toul, bp. 95   D b
Toul, gouv. 146   C b
Toul, imp. cy. 78   D d
Toulon 69   F e
Toulon, bp. 95   D c
Toulouse, in France 61   D e
Toulouse, abp. 148   B c
Toulouse, cty. about 1000 . . . 58   E e
Toulouse, cty. 12 cent. 69   E e
Toulouse, cty. 15 cent. 84   D b
Toulouse, gen. 147   E c
Toulouse, univ. 100   F f
Toulouse, Fort, in Alabama . . 191   H e
Touques 146   G e
Touraine, cty. 69   H g
Touraine, duchy 78   B e
Touraine, gouv. 146   B b
Touraine, prov. 148   B e
Tourcoing 134   B c
Tourinnes 156   B a
Tournai 117   B d
Tournai, bp. 94   C a
Tournai, cty. 61   E a
Tourneppe 156   A a
Tournon 76   F d
Tours 61   D c
Tours, abp. 94   B b
Tours, cty. 69   H g
Tours, gen. 147   D b
Tovar, route of 190   C d
Tovin 73   I b

Tower, in London . . . . 75 G g
Tower of Leander, in Constan-
tinople . . . . 93 G e
Tower of the Winds, in Athens 23 D
Tower Hamlets, parl. bor. . . . 163 O f
Tower Street, in London . . . . 75 G g
Townsend, mt. . . . . 172 D d
Townsville . . . . 172 D b
Towton . . . . 84 C c
Toxandria, dist. . . . . 62 C c
Tozan, people . . . .
Trachea, dist. . . . . 33 L e
Trachenberg . . . . 154 I c
Trachinia . . . . 11 D d
Trachinian Cliffs . . . . 16 F e
Trachis . . . . 16 E e
Trachonitis, dist. . . . . 6 E c
Trachselwald, castle . . . . . . 91 P l
Trafalgar, Cape . . . . 130 B f
Tragia, isl. . . . . 20 B d
Traiana, Colonia . . . . 39 I h
Traianopolis, in Cilicia . . . . . 20 E d
Traianopolis, in Thrace . . . . 39 N l
Traianus, Portus . . . . 26 E e
Traiectum (Utrecht, in the Ne-
therlands) . . . . 39 H g
Traiectus, see Maestricht
Traietto . . . . 90 D d
Trais River . . . . 31 F c
Traisen River . . . . 63 H d e
Trajan, Caths of . . . . 22 A
Trajan, Port of . . . . 35 ins. B
Trajan, Statue of . . . . 24 B
Trajan's Aqueduct . . . . 35 ins. B (6)
Trajan's Column . . . . 22 A (14)
Trajan's Forum . . . . 24 B
Trajan's Way, road . . . . . . 30 E a
Traktir . . . . 164 J f
Tralles . . . . 17 E c
Tramin . . . . 150 F c
Trancoso . . . . 83 J g
Trani . . . . 90 F d
Trani, abp. . . . . 65 F c
Transalpine Gaul, reg. . . . . 34 E d (Gaul)
Trans Baikal Province . . . . . 171 M c
Transcaspian District . . . . . 170 G e
Transjurane Burgundy, km. . . 56 D c
Transkei, reg. . . . . 175 M m
Transpadane Gaul, reg. . . . . 26 B b
Trans Siberian Railway . . . . 170 G c
Trans Tiberim, Aug.Reg of Rome 22 A
Transvaal Colony . . . .
Transvaal, rep. . . . . 175 M l
Transylvania, gr. prim. in Hun-
gary . . . . 131 H d
Transylvania, princ. . . . . . . 119 I d
Transylvania, reg. . . . . 59 I d
Transylvania, proposed col. in
U. S. . . . . 194 B c
Transylvanian Alps, mts . . . . 39 M l
Trapani . . . . 90 D f
Trapezus, in Arcadia . . . . . . 14 C b
Trapezus, in Pontus (Trebizond) 20 H b
Trappe, La, mon. . . . . 94 C b
Trarbach . . . . 134 D d
Trasimenus (Trasimeno), lake . 27 G d
Trastamare, cty. . . . . 83 J g
Trastevere, quarter . . . . . . 96 A
Trasyllus, Monument of . . . . 23 C (9)
Traú, bp. . . . . 95 F c
Trauchburg, ruin . . . . 143 J j
Traungau, dist. . . . . 63 G e
Trausnitz, castle . . . . 79 H d
Trautenau . . . . 135 H c
Travancore, reg. . . . . 137 C g
Travendal, castle . . . . 134 F b
Travemünde . . . . 154 E a
Traz os Montes, dist. . . . . . 83 J g
Trea . . . . 27 H d
Treba . . . . 27 H f
Trebia . . . . 27 G e
Trebia (Trebbia) River . . . . . 26 D c
Trebizond. . . . . 67 N e
Trebizond, empire, 13 cent. . . 73 H b

Trebizond, empire, 14 cent. . . 89 K l
Trebizond, empire, 15 cent. . . 93 E b
Trebnitz, mon. . . . . 80 E f
Trebujena. . . . . 82 A b
Trebula, in Samnium . . . . . . 30 D a
Trebula Mutuesca . . . . 27 G e
Trecas, see Troyes
Tre Fontane, mon. . . . . 96 B b
Tregony, parl. bor. . . . . 163 J g
Tréguier . . . . 61 B b
Tréguier, bp. . . . . 94 B b
Trémoins . . . . 143 ins. F
Tremouille, La . . . . 81 M h
Trencsin . . . .
Trent . . . . 62 F e
Trent, bp. . . . . 79 G e
Trent River . . . . 49 F e
Trenton . . . . 192 D c
Tréport, mon. . . . . 94 C a
Trerus River, see Tolerus R. . 30 C a
Tres Pinos . . . . 210 A c
Treuenbrietzen . . . . 85 C b
Treveri or Treveris, see Trèves
Treveri, people . . . . 38 D c
Trèves. . . . . 62 D d
Trèves, abp. . . . . 95 D b
Trèves, univ. . . . . 100 G d
Treviso . . . . 90 K h
Treviso, bp. . . . . 95 E b
Treviso, univ . . . . 100 H e
Trévoux . . . . 147 F b
Triaditza . . . . 59 I e
Triana . . . . 82 A b
Trianon, Avenue de, in Versailles 149 A
Trianon, Grand, loc. in Versailles 149 A
Trianon, Petit, loc. in Versailles 149 A
Trianon, Plaine de, loc. in Ver-
sailles . . . . 149 A
Triballi, people . . . . 39 M l
Triberg . . . . 142 B d
Triberg, lordship . . . . 142 B d
Triboci, people . . . . 39 I i
Tribulation, Cape . . . . 172 D b
Tribur . . . . 62 E d
Tricameron . . . . 52 C c
Tricasses, see Troyes
Tricca (Trikala) . . . . 10 C c
Trichinopoly . . . . 137 C f
Trichonis, lake . . . . 10 C d
Trichonium . . . . 10 C d
Tricorythus . . . . 16 C a
Tricrana, isl. . . . . 15 D b
Tridentine Alps . . . . 27 F a
Tridentini, people . . . . 27 F a
Tridentum (Trent) . . . . 27 F a
Trient, see Trent
Trier, see Trèves
Trieste . . . . 63 G f
Trieste, bp. . . . . 95 E b
Trifanum . . . . 30 C a
Trifels, castle . . . . 62 D d
Trigemina Gate . . . . 23 B
Trikala . . . . 89 B c
Trileucum, prom. . . . . 38 A d
Trim, bp. . . . . 97 E c
Trimenia . . . . 16 B a
Trinacria, km. . . . . 77 C g
Trincomalee . . . . 137 D g
Trinidad, in Bolivia . . . . . . 214 C d
Trinidad, in Cuba . . . . 213 E b
Trinidad, isl. . . . . 105 H d
Trinidad River . . . .
Trinity, Fort . . . . 192 ins.
Trinity River . . . . 191 G e
Trinius River . . . . 27 I f
Trinkomali . . . .
Trino . . . . 130 Q i
Trinobantes, people . . . .
Triopium, prom. . . . . 20 B d
Triparadisus . . . . 18 O h
Triphylia, dist., in Elis . . . . 14 B b
Triphylia, dist., in Epirus . . . 10 B c
Tripodiscus . . . . 15 D a
Tripoli, in Africa. . . . . 53 D c

Tripoli, reg. . . . . 77 G i
Tripoli, vilayet . . . . 174 E a
Tripoli, in Syria . . . . 68 C c
Tripoli, cty. . . . . 68 C b
Tripolis, in Phœnicia . . . . . 20 F e
Tripolis, in Pontus . . . . . . 20 H b
Tripolis, dist., in Thessaly . . . 10 D b
Tripolis, reg., in Africa . . . . 34 G g
Tripolitana, W. Rom. prov. . . 42 E g (3)
Tripolitza . . . . 131 H f
Tristan da Cunha, isl. . . . . . 108 P k
Tritæa, in Achaia . . . .
Tritæa, in Locris . . . . 11 D d
Triumphal Way, road . . . . . 35 ins. B
Trivandrum. . . . . 137 C g
Trivento, bp. . . . . 95 E c
Troarn . . . . 76 C b
Troarn, mon. . . . . 94 B b (Tr.)
Troas, reg. . . . . 9 B d
Trochtelfingen . . . . 143 H i
Trœsmis. . . . . 39 N l
Trœzen . . . . 15 D b
Trogen . . . . 91 R k
Trogilus Port . . . . 31 ins. B
Troglodytes, people . . . . . . 4 F d
Troian Plain . . . .
Trois Fontaines, mon. . . . . . 94 C b
Troitsa. . . . . 138 E d
Troitski . . . . 171 J b
Troitzkoi, mon. . . . . 131 K b
Troja, in Asia Minor, see Ilium
Troja, in Italy . . . . 90 E d
Troja, bp. . . . . 95 F c
Trombetas River . . . . 214 D c
Tromsoe. . . . . 166 I b
Tropea, bp. . . . . 95 F d
Troppau . . . . 79 J d
Troppau, princ. . . . . 79 J d
Troy, in Asia Minor . . . .
Troy, in New York . . . . . . 192 E b
Troyes . . . . 61 E b
Troyes, bp. . . . . 94 C b
Troyes, cty. . . . . 61 E b
Troyland, reg. . . . .
Trubchevsk. . . . . 131 J b
Truentus (Tronto) River . . . 27 I f
Trujillo, in Honduras . . . . . 213 D b
Trujillo, in Peru . . . . 111 B f
Trujillo, in Spain . . . . 82 A b
Trujillo, in Venezuela . . . . . 214 B a
Trumplini, people . . . . 26 E b
Truro . . . . 127 T l
Truxillo (Trujillo, in Honduras) 105 C j
Tsanpu River . . . . 171 J f
Tshiblak. . . . .
Tsi-nan . . . . 171 M e
Tsi-ning-chau . . . .
Tsitsihar . . . . 171 N c
Tsuen-chau-fu . . . . 103 L g
Tuam, abp. . . . . 97 C a
Tuamotu, isl. . . . . 180 N h
Tuat, oasis . . . . 2 D c
Tubac . . . . 190 C e
Tubantes, people . . . . 39 I g
Tubariyeh . . . .
Tübingen . . . . 143 H i
Tübingen, palat. . . . . 143 H i
Tübingen, univ. . . . . 100 G d
Tublinum . . . . 26 E b
Tubuai Islands . . . . 180 M h
Tucacas. . . . . 214 B a
Tucci . . . . 42 B g
Tuchcov . . . . 131 I b
Tucson . . . . 190 C e
Tucumán . . . . 215 C f
Tuder . . . . 27 G d
Tugela River . . . . 175 N l
Tuileries, The, loc. in Paris . . 149 B
Tula . . . . 139 E d
Tulalip, Ind. Res. . . . . 188 B a
Tulare, lake . . . . 210 C c
Tularenos, tribe . . . . 188 C c
Tule River, Ind. Res. . . . . . 188 C c
Tullahoma . . . . 208 C e

Tulle	84	D g
Tulle, bp.	94	C b
Tullear	175	H g
Tullianum	24	A (3)
Tulln	63	I d
Tullum (Toul)	39	H i
Tultcha	164	D a
Tumbez	111	A b
Tumuc Humac Mountains	214	D b
Tumut		
Tunbridge, parl. bor.		
Tunes (Tunis)	38	E e
Tungabhadra River	137	C e
Tung-chang	171	M e
Tung-chau	170 ins.	A
Tungri, people	39	H h
Tung-tahu	170 ins.	A
Tunguses, people		
Tunguska River, Lower		
Tunguska River, Upper		
Tunis	53	D c
Tunis, bay of	34 ins.	A
Tunis, French dependency	174	D a
Tunis, reg.	54	F f
Tunis, state	77	F e
Tunjá	214	B h
Tunsberg	58	F b
Tupiza	214	C e
Turan, khan.	92	G b
Turcilingians, people		
Turcomans, people	170	G e
Turdetani, or Turdetanians, people	38	A e
Turduli, people	38	B e
Turenne	61	D d
Turenne, castle	76	D d
Turenne, viscty.	78	B f
Turenum (Trani)	31	F a
Turfan		
Turholz, mon.	94	C a
Turicum (Zurich)	39	J j
Turin	90	H h
Turin, univ.	100	G e
Türkheim	126	E b
Türkheim, imp. cy.	122	D d
Turkestan, reg.	170	H d
Turkestan, E., reg.	170	I e
Turkish (Ottoman) Empire, 1451—1481	93	
Turkish (Ottoman) Empire, 1481—1683	124	
Turkish (Ottoman) Empire, since 1683	164	
Turkmanchai	170	F e
Turkomans, people	77	L e
Turks, people	165 leg.	
Turks Islands	213	E b
Turner's Falls, village	189	B c
Turnhout	117	C c
Turones, see Tours		
Turones, people, in Gaul	38	C c
Turones, people, in Germany	38	E c
Turoqua	38	A d
Turriff		
Turris Libisonis	38	D d
Tursan, viscty.	69	C e
Turtle Mountain, Ind. Res.	188	G a
Turukhansk	171	J b
Tusayan, reg.	190	C d
Tuscaloosa	211	H d
Tuscan Presidios, dist.	118	G e
Tuscan Street, in Rome	24	A
Tuscana	27	F e
Tuscany, gr. duchy	161	H f
Tuscany, dist.	64	B b
Tuscany and Umbria, West Rom. prov.	42	E e (2)
Tuscarawas River	188	J b
Tuscarora, Ind. Res.	188	J b
Tuscaroras	193	F d
Tuscaroras, tribe	188	J c
Tuscia, dist.	27	F d
Tusculum	35 ins.	B
Tusculum. bp.	96	B b

Tuskegee	207	H d
Tutbury	118	D c
Tutbury, mon.	97	P i
Tutela, see Tudela		
Tutikorin	170	I h
Tuttlingen	143	G j
Tutuila, isl.	199 ins.	D
Tuxtla	213	C c
Tuy	82	A a
Tuy, bp.	94	A c
Tver	138	E d
Twann	91	P k
Twat, reg.	53	B d
Tweed River	49	E d
Tweeddale, dist.		
Twickenham	75	I i
Twiel, castle	62	E e
Twillingate, isl.	212	J d
Two Sicilies, km., 12 cent.	72	C d
Two Sicilies, km., 15 cent.	90	E e
Tyana	20	F d
Tybee Island	193 ins.	C
Tyburn	75	I h
Tycha, quarter in Syracuse	31 ins.	B
Tykocin	159	L b
Tylus Island	19	H e
Tymphæa, dist.	10	C b
Tymphe, mt.	10	C b
Tymphrestus, mt.	10	C d
Tyndale, dist.		
Tyndaris	30	E d
Tyne River	49	E d
Tynemouth, mon.	97	P f
Tynemouth, parl. bor.	163	M b
Typhrestus, mt.	10	C d
Tyra	35	K d
Tyras River	35	J d
Tyrconnel, cty.	127	I g
Tyre	6	C b
Tyre, Ladder of, cape	6	C b
Tyre, plan of	18 ins.	B
Tyrissa	10	C b
Tyrnau	115	I d
Tyrol, castle	72	C b
Tyrol, cty.	79	G e
Tyrol, princ. cty.	150	F c
Tyrone, cty.	127	J g
Tyropœon Valley	6 ins.	A
Tyrrhenian Sea	27	B d
Tyrus (Tyre), in Phœnicia	6	C b
Tyrus, in Laconia	15	C b
Tyrus, in Perœa	7	D c
Tzaritzyn	139	F f
Uaupes River	214	C b
Ubangi River	175	E d
Úbeda	82	B b
Uberaba	214	E d
Uberi, people	26	B a
Überlingen, imp. cy.	142	D e
Ubii, people	39	I h
Ubulla	99	M g
Ucaca	99	M c
Ucayali River	111	C c
Uceda	83	E c
Ucetium, see Uzès		
Uclés	82	B b
Udaipur	137	B d
Udine	90	D a
Udine, bp.	95	E b
Ufa	139	I e
Uffnau, isl.	91	Q k
Uganda, prot.	175	G d
Ugernum, see Beaucaire		
Uglitch		
Ugrians, people		
Uigurs, people		
Uintah, Fort	210	C b
Uintah, Ind. Res.	188	D b
Uirats, people		
Ujjain		
Ukak	99	M c
Uker River	154	G b
Ukermark, dist	85	C b

Ukraine, reg.	139	D f
Ukrians, people	63	G b
Ulatha, dist.	6	D b
Uleåborg	138	C c
Uliarus (Oléron), isl.	38	B c
Uliassutai		
Ulloa, route of, 1537	107	F e
Ulm	62	E d
Ulm, imp. cy.	143	I h
Ulpia (Sardica)	39	M l
Ulpia, Basilica, bldg. in Rome	24	B
Ulpia Traiana	39	M k
Ulpiana	39	M l
Ulrichen	91	Q l
Ulster, prov.		
Ulu-kem River		
Ulwar	137	C c
Ülzen, Hanse. cy.	99 ins.	B
Umachiri	214	B d
Uman	139	D f
Uman, reg.		
Umarkot	137	A c
Umatas	198 ins.	C
Umatilla, Ind. Res.	188	C a
Umballa	137	C b
Umber, lake	27	G d
Umbilicus, loc. in Rome		
Umbria, Aug. Reg.	27	G e
Umbria, dist., 15 cent.	90	D c
Umbrians, people	29	C c
Umbro (Ombrone) River	27	F e
Umeå	166	I c
Umpquas, tribe	188	B b
Umtata River	175	M m
Unalaska, isl.	198 ins.	A
Uncompahgre Mountains	198	D c
Uncompahgre, Ind. Res.	188	E c
Unestrudis River, see Unstrut River		
Ungarisch Altenburg	155	I e
Ungava, dist.	212	H c
Ungava Bay	212	I c
Unghvar	168	H b
Unimak, isl.	198 ins.	A
Union, Fort, in New Mexico	210	D c
Union, Fort, in N. Dakota	210	E a
Union Islands	172	H a
Union Pacific Grant	210	D b
Uniontown	206 ins.	
United Netherlands, country	122	C b
United States, 1783	196	
United States, 1910	198, 199	
Unna River	155	I f
Unstrut River	62	F c
Unter-Öwisheim	142	C b
Unterwalden, canton	91	Q l
Upi	5	D b
Upland (Chester, in Pa.)	192 ins.	
Upminster	75	J h
Upolu, isl.	172	H b
Upper Alsace, landgr.	114	D e
Upper Argen River	143	I j
Upper Bavaria, dist.	122	F e
Upper Britain, prov.	38	B b (1)
Upper Burgundy, dist.	62	C e
Upper Burgundy, km.	56	C c
Upper Burma, prov.	171	K f
Upper California, prov.	190	B d
Upper Canada, prov.	190	
Upper Dacia, prov.	39	M k (1 a)
Upper Egypt, reg.		
Upper Gelderland	117	E c
Upper Germany, prov.		
Upper Gihon, well	6 ins.	A
Upper Guinea, reg.	174	C d
Upper Libya, East Rom. prov.	43	G g (1)
Upper Lorraine, duchy	62	C c
Upper Lusatia, dist.	80 ins.	
Upper Lusatia, margr.	87	J c
Upper Mœsia, prov.	39	M l (2 a)
Upper Palatinate, dist.	79	G d
Upper Pannonia, prov.	34	H d
Upper Peru, reg.	214	C d
Upper Pimería, dist.	190	C e

Upper Silesia, dist. . . . . 72 D a
Upper Tunguska River . . . . .
Upsala . . . . 88 G b
Upsala, univ. . . . . 100 I c
Ur (Mugheir) . . . . 4 E e
Urabá, Gulf of . . . . 105 E e
Urabá, reg. . . . . 105 E e
Urach . . . . 143 H h
Urach, castle . . . . 62 E d
Urach, cty. . . . . 143 H i
Urach, Hohen, ruin . . . . 143 H i
Ural Mountains . . . . 138 I c
Ural River . . . . 139 H e
Uralian Cossacks, people . . . . 139 H e
Uralsk . . . . 139 H e
Urba (Orbe) . . . . 39 I j
Urban VIII, Wall of Pope . . . 96 A
Urbevetum, see Orvieto
Urbino . . . . 90 M j
Urbino, bp. . . . . 95 E c
Urbinum (Urbino) . . . . 27 G d
Urbs Salvia . . . . 27 H d
Urci . . . .
Urcinium . . . . 26 C e
Urés . . . . 213 B b
Urga . . . . 171 L d
Urgel . . . . 82 C a
Urgel, bp. . . . . 94 C c
Urgenj . . . .
Urgo, isl. . . . . 26 D d
Uri, canton . . . . 91 Q l
Uri, dist. . . . . 71 R k
Uria . . . . 31 G b
Uria, lake . . . . 10 C d
Urias Bay . . . . 30 E a
Uriconium (Wroxeter) . . . . . . 51 O h
Urium . . . . 30 E a
Urk, isl. . . . . 117 D b
Ursberg, mon. . . . . 95 E b
Urseren . . . . 91 Q l
Urspring, mon. . . . . 143 I i
Urubamba . . . . 214 B d
Urubamba River . . . . 111 C d
Uruguay, country . . . . 215 D f
Uruguay River . . . . 215 D e
Uruguayana . . . . 215 D e
Uruk (Warka) . . . . 4 E e
Urumiah . . . .
Urumiah, lake . . . .
Urumtsi . . . .
Uscosium . . . . 27 I f
Usedom . . . . 63 G b
Usellis . . . . 38 D e
Usb . . . .
Ushuaia . . . . 215 C h
Usipetes, people . . . . 38 D b
Usk River . . . .
Uskub . . . . 77 I d
Uspallata Pass . . . . 215 C f
Ussuri River . . . .
Ustica, isl. . . . . 30 C d
Ustrina . . . . 22 A
Ust Maiskaya . . . . 171 O b
Ust Sysolsk . . . . 167 P c
Ust-Urt, reg. . . . . 139 H g
Ust Yansk . . . . 171 O a
Ust Zylma . . . . 138 H b
Usuguaya . . . . 215 C h
Utah, state . . . . 210 C c
Utah, ter. 1850 . . . . 202 D c
Utah, ter. 1861 . . . . 203 P g
Utah Lake . . . . 190 C c
Ute, Ind. Res. . . . . 188 E c
Utelle . . . . 150 D e
Utes, tribe . . . . 188 C b
Utians, people . . . . 8 J f
Utica, in Afrika . . . . 38 D e
Utica, in New York . . . . . . 207 K b
Utii, people . . . . 35 N e
Utinum, see Udine
Utis River . . . . 27 F c
Utrecht, in the Netherlands . . 117 D b
Utrecht, bp. . . . . 95 D a
Utrecht, lordship . . . . 114 C b

Utrecht, in Transvaal . . . . . 175 N l
Utrecht, New, in New York . . 189 ins. C
Uxbridge . . . . 75 I h
Uxellodunum . . . .
Uxentis, isl. . . . . 38 A c
Üxküll . . . . 80 I c
Uyuni . . . . 214 C e
Uzentum . . . . 31 H c
Uzès . . . . 76 F d
Uzès, bp. . . . . 94 C c
Uzgent . . . .
Uzi, people . . . .
Uznach, castle . . . . 91 Q k

Vaal River . . . . 175 M l
Vabres, bp. . . . . 94 C c
Vacalus River . . . . 39 H h
Vacapa . . . . 190 C f
Vaccæi, people . . . . 38 B d
Vaccanæ . . . . 35 ins. B
Vada Sabatia . . . . 26 C c
Vada Volaterrana . . . . 26 E d
Vadimonis, lake . . . . 27 G e
Vaduz . . . . 134 E e
Vaduz, castle . . . . 91 R k
Vaga . . . . 46 H f
Vaigatch, isl. . . . . 138 J a
Vaihingen . . . . 143 G h
Vaison, bp. . . . . 95 D c
Valais, dist. . . . . 91 P l
Valais, rep. . . . . 151 H g
Valangin, castle . . . . 91 O k
Valcour . . . . 157 ins.
Valdai . . . . 131 J b
Valdai Hills . . . . 167 L d
Val de Grâce, church in Paris 149 B
Valdivia . . . . 215 B f
Val d'Ossola . . . . 91 Q l
Valence . . . . 61 F d
Valence, bp. . . . . 94 C c
Valence, univ. . . . . 100 F f
Valencia, in Spain . . . . . . 82 B b
Valencia, abp. . . . . 94 B d
Valencia, emir. . . . . 83 E d
Valencia, km. . . . . 83 K h
Valencia, univ. . . . . 100 E g
Valencia, in Venezuela . . . . 214 C a
Valencia de Don Juan . . . . . 82 A a
Valenciennes . . . . 117 B d
Valens, Aqueduct of . . . . . . 93 G e
Valentia, see Vibo
Valentia (Valence, in France) . 38 D c
Valentia (Valencia, in Spain) . 38 B e
Valentia, Rom. prov., in southern
    Scotland . . . . 38 B a (3)
Valentia (Wales), Rom. prov. . . 42 B c (2)
Valentia Island . . . . 166 C e
Valentianæ, see Valenciennes
Valentinois, cty. . . . . 76 F d
Valentinois, dist. . . . . . . 126 D d
Valenza . . . . 90 I h
Vale of the Camenæ (Muses),
    loc. in Rome . . . . 22 A
Valera de Abajo . . . . 82 B b
Valeria, Rom. prov. . . . . . . 42 E e (10)
Valeria ripensis, Rom. prov. . . 42 F d (14)
Valeria Way, in Italy, road . . 27 H e
Valerian Way, in Sicily, road . 30 D d
Valerius Asiaticus, Gardens of . 22 A
Vale Royal, mon. . . . . 97 O h
Val-ès-Dunes . . . . 65 F f
Valetium . . . . 31 H b
Valideh Bridge . . . . 93 G e (11)
Valkenburg . . . . 117 D d
Valladolid, in Michoacan, Mexico 213 ins.
Valladolid, in New Mexico . . . 190 D d
Valladolid, in Spain . . . . . 82 H e
Valladolid, bp. . . . . 94 B c
Valladolid, univ. . . . . 100 E f
Valladolid, in Yucatan, Mexico 213 D b
Vallæ . . . . 11 D b
Valle Crucis, mon. . . . . . . 97 N h
Val Leventina, valley . . . . . 91 Q l
Valley . . . . 72 C b

Valley Forge . . . . 195 C c
Valley Gate . . . . 6 ins. A
Valley of the Sweet Waters . .
Vallombrosa . . . . 64 B b
Vallombrosa, mon. . . . . 95 E c
Valmont, mon. . . . . 94 C b
Valmy . . . . 134 C d
Valognes . . . . 76 C b
Valois, cty. . . . . 76 E b
Valois, duchy . . . . 84 E e
Valona, bp. . . . . 95 F c
Valparaiso . . . . 215 B f
Valromey . . . . 126 D d
Val Sainte, mon. . . . . 91 P l
Val-Secret, mon. . . . . 94 C b (V.S.)
Valsers, mon. . . . . 94 C b (Val.)
Valtellina, dist. . . . . 91 R l
Valvata . . . . 26 C f
Van . . . . 20 J c
Van, lake . . . . 99 L f
Van Buren . . . . 211 G c
Vancouver . . . . 212 C d
Vancouver, Fort. . . . . 198 A a
Vancouver, isl. . . . . 186 G d
Vandalia . . . . 211 H c
Vandalia, proposed col. in U. S. 194 C c
Vandals, kingdom of the, 5 cent. 50 E e
Vandals, kingdom of the, 6 cent. 52 C c
Vandals, people . . . . . 45 H b, C e, F e
Van Diemen Gulf . . . . 172 C b
Van Diemen's Land, isl. . . . . 172 D e
Vandili, people . . . . 38 E e
Vangrones, people . . . . 39 J i
Vannes . . . . 61 B c
Vannes, bp. . . . . 94 B b
Van Reenen's Pass . . . . 175 M l
Vanua Levu, isl. . . . . 172 H b
Vapincum, see Gap
Var, dept. . . . . 148 F f
Var (Vara) River . . . . 130 O k
Varallo . . . . 130 Q i
Varanger Fiord . . . . 167 L a
Varangians, people . . . . . . 45 J d
Varangians, route of the . . . 59 I b
Vararis Æstuarium (Moray Firth) 38 B a
Varaville . . . . 65 F f
Varch Bosna . . . . 72 D c
Vardar River . . . . 119 I e
Varduli, people . . . . 38 B d
Varennes . . . . 134 C d
Varese . . . . 161 G e
Varia . . . .
Varini, people . . . . 38 E b
Varkenskill . . . . 192 D d
Varna . . . . 59 J e
Varnitza . . . . 131 I d
Varus (Var) River . . . . 26 A d
Vasa . . . . 138 B c
Vasates, see Bazas
Vasco da Gama, route of . . . . 108 Q i
    . . . . 109 W g
Vascones, people . . . . 38 B d
Vasio or Vasione, see Vaison
Vassy . . . . 114 C d
Vasvar . . . . 123 I e
Vatican, palace in Rome . . . . 22 A
Vatican Bridge . . . . 96 A
Vatrenus (Santerno) River . . . 27 F c
Vaucelles . . . . 118 D d
Vauclair, mon. . . . . 94 C b
Vaucluse, dept. . . . . 148 F f
Vaucouleurs . . . . 69 J f
Vaud, dist. . . . . 91 O l
Vaudemont . . . . 86 E d
Vauluisant, mon. . . . . 94 C b
Vauxchamps . . . . 154 B d
Vazerol . . . . 91 R l
Veamini, people . . . . 26 A c
Vecht River . . . . 117 E b
Vectilii, Palace of the . . . . 22 A
Vectis, isl. (I. of Wight) . . . 51 P i
Vediantii, people . . . . 26 A d
Vegia . . . . 27 J c
Veglia, bp. . . . . 95 E b

Veii . . . . 27 G e
Veile . . . . 158 E a
Vela, Cape de la . . . . 105 F d
Velabrum, quarter in Rome . . 24 A
Velay, cty. . . . . 61 E d
Veldenz . . . . 122 D d
Veldidena . . . . 38 E c
Veleia . . . . 26 D c
Veleiates, people . . . . 26 D c
Velencze . . . . 159 J e
Vélez . . . . 214 B b
Velez, Peñon de . . . . 130 C f
Veleze . . . . 165 B c
Vélez Málaga . . . . 82 B b
Velia, in Lucania . . . . 30 D b
Velia, quarter in Rome . . . . . 24 A
Veliki Luki . . . . 138 D d
Velinus, lake . . . . 27 G e
Velitræ (Velletri) . . . . 35 ins. B
Velitræ, bp. . . . . 96 B b
Vellberg . . . . 143 I g
Velletri . . . . 90 D d
Velletry, bp. . . . . 96 B b
Vellinghausen . . . . 134 D c
Vellore . . . . 137 C f
Veltæ, people . . . . 38 G b
Veltlin, dist., see Valtellina . . 91 R l
Venafri, bp. . . . . 95 ins.
Venafrum (Venafro) . . . . 30 D a
Venaissin, cty. . . . . 69 F d
Venaissin, prov. . . . . 148 F f
Venango, Fort . . . . 192 A c
Vence, mon. . . . . 148 C c
Vendée, dept. . . . . 148 D e
Vendée, dist. . . . . 130 C d
Vendôme . . . . 69 H g
Vendôme, cty. . . . . 69 H g
Vendôme, Place, loc. in Paris . 149 B
Venedæ, people . . . . 38 F b
Venedic Bay . . . . 38 F b
Venelli, people . . . . 38 B c
Veneris, Portus . . . . 26 D c
Venetes or Venetis, see Vannes
Veneti, people, in Brittany . . . 38 B c
Veneti or Venetians, people, in
   Italy . . . . 27 F b
Venetia, see Venice
Venetia, dist. in Roman times . 27 F b
Venetia, prov., 19 cent. . . . . . 158 F f
Venetia and Istria, prov. . . . . 42 E d (1)
Venetia and Istria, reg. . . . . . 38 E c (10)
Venetian Alps, mts. . . . . 27 H a
Venetian Republic, 11 cent. . . 64 B a
Venetian Republic, 14 cent. . . 79 H f
Venetian Republic, 15 cent. . . 90 C b
Venetian Republic, 16 cent. . . 118 G d
Venetian Republic, 18 cent. . . 131 F d
Venetus, lake . . . . 39 J j
Venezia, Piazza, loc. in Rome . 22 A
Venezuela, Gulf of . . . . 105 F d
Venezuela, reg. . . . . 105 F d
Venezuela, rep. . . . . 214 C b
Venice . . . . 56 E c
Venice, abp. . . . . 95 E b
Venice, duchy . . . . 63 G f
Venise, Petite, loc. in Versailles 149 A
Venlo . . . . 117 E c
Venlo, Hanse. cy. . . . . 99 ins. B
Venonæ . . . . 51 P h
Venonetes, people . . . . 26 D a
Venosa . . . . 90 E d
Venostes, Venostæ, people . . . 26 E a
Venta Belgarum (Winchester) . 51 P i
Ventadour . . . . 69 E d
Ventadour, castle . . . . 76 E d
Ventadour, cty. . . . . 78 C f
Venta Icenorum (Castor near
   Norwich) . . . .
Venta Silurum (Cærwent) . . . . 51 O i
Ventersdorp . . . . 175 M l
Ventimiglia . . . . 90 A c
Ventimiglia, bp. . . . . 95 D e
Venus, Temple of, on Mt. Ægaleos 16 B a
Venus and Rome, Temple of . 24 B

Venus Cloacina, Temple of . . 24 A (9)
Venus Erycina, Temple of . . . 22 A
Venus Genetrix, Temple of . 24 B (11)
Venus Victrix, Temple of . . 22 A
Venusia . . . . 30 E b
Veprik . . . . 131 J c
Vera . . . . 82 B b
Vera Cruz, modern site of . . . 106 D a
Vera Cruz, Villa Rica de la . . 106 D a
Vera Cruz, la Antigua . . . . . 106 D a
Vera Cruz, state . . . . 213 ins.
Veragri, people . . . . 26 B a
Veragua, reg. . . . . 105 D e
Veramin . . . .
Verbanus (Maggiore), lake . . . 26 C a
Vercellæ (Vercelli) . . . . 26 C b
Vercelli . . . . 90 I h
Vercelli, bp. . . . . 95 D b
Vercelli, univ. . . . . 100 G e
Vercheres . . . . 189 B b
Verd, Cape . . . . 174 B c
Verden . . . . 62 E b
Verden, bp. . . . . 95 D a
Verden, princ. . . . . 122 E b
Verdun . . . . 62 C d
Verdun, bp. . . . . 78 D d
Verelå . . . . 131 I a
Veretum . . . . 31 H c
Vereya . . . . 153 P f
Vergil's Grave . . . . 31 ins. A
Veria . . . . 165 C c
Veringen . . . . 143 H i
Verkhoyansk . . . . 171 O b
Vermandois, cty. . . . . 61 E b
Vermilion Lake, Ind. Res. . . . 188 H a
Vermont, dist. . . . . 189 B c
Vermont, state . . . . 199 K b
Verneuil . . . . 69 H f
Verneuil, castle . . . . 76 D b
Verni . . . . 170 I d
Vernio . . . . 90 L i
Vernon, in British Columbia . . 212 D c
Vernon, in France . . . . 69 H f
Vernon, Mount, town in Virginia 193 F b
Verodunum, see Verdun
Veroli, bp. . . . . 95 E c
Verona . . . . 26 F b
Verona, bp. . . . . 93 E b
Verona, march . . . . 72 C b
Verona and Aquileia, march. . . 64 B a
Verrazano, route of . . . . 108 M d
Versailles . . . . 126 C b
Versailles, in 1789, plan . . . . . 149 A
Versailles, Old . . . . 149 A
Versecz . . . . 168 G d
Verteræ . . . . 51 O g
Vertus . . . . 76 F b
Veruela, mon. . . . . 94 B c
Verulæ . . . . 30 C a
Verulam (Ferryland) . . . . 212 J d
Verulamium (Saint Albans, in
   England) . . . . 51 P i
Vervins . . . . 114 B d
Vesontio, see Visontio
Vesoul . . . . 122 D e
Vespasian, Forum of . . . . . . 24 B
Vespasian, Temple of . . . . . . 24 A
Vespucci, route of . . . 105 G d, 108 L k
Vesta, Grove of . . . . 24 A
Vesta, Temple of . . . . 24 A
Vestals, House of the . . . . . . 24 A
Vestini, people . . . . 27 H e
Vesubia River . . . . 26 B d
Vesulus, mt. . . . . 26 A c
Vesunna (Périgueux) . . . . . . 38 C c
Vesuvius, mt. . . . . 30 D b
Veszprim . . . .
Veszprim, bp. . . . .
Vettona . . . . 27 G d
Vettones, people . . . . 38 A d
Vetulonium . . . . 26 E e
Veurne (Furnes) . . . .
Vexin, dist. . . . . 69 H f
Vézelay . . . . 69 I g

Vézelay, mon. . . . . 94 C b
Via Æmilia (Æmilian Way), road 26 E c
Via Æmilia Scauri (Æmilian
   Way of Scaurus), road . . . . 26 D c
Via Antiana (Antian Way), road 35 ins. B
Via Appia (Appian Way), road 31 F b
Via Appia vetus (Old Appian
   Way), road . . . . 35 ins. B
Via Aurelia (Aurelian Way), road 26 E d
Via Cassia (Cassian Way), road 27 F e
Via Claudia Augusta (Claudian
   Augustan Way), road . . . . 27 G b
Via Claudia Valeria (Claudian
   Valerian Way), road . . . . . . 27 H e
Via Clodia (Clodian Way), road 27 F e
Via di Ripetta, street in Rome 22 A
Via Dolorosa, in Jerusalem . . 68 ins. B
Viadua (Oder) River . . . . . . 38 F b
Via Flaminia (Flaminian Way),
   road . . . . 27 G e
Via Flaminia vetus (Old Flami-
   nian Way), road . . . . 27 G e
Via Flavia (Flavian Way), road 27 H b
Via Julia Augusta (Julian Au-
   gustan Way), road . . . . . . 26 B d
Via Labicana (Labican Way), road 35 ins. B
Via Lata, Aug. Reg. of Rome . 22 A
Via lata (Broad Way), street in
   Rome . . . . 22 A
Via Latina (Latin Way), road . 30 B a
Viale Aventino, street in Rome 22 A
Viale Giulio Cesare, street in
   Rome . . . . 22 A
Via mala, pass . . . . 150 E c
Via Merulana, street in Rome . 22 A
Viana . . . . 214 E c
Via Nomentana (Nomentan
   Way), road . . . . 35 ins. B
Via Ostiensis (Ostian Way), road 35 ins. B
Via Popilia (Popilian Way), road 31 F d
Via Portuensis (Port Way), road 35 ins. B
Via Postumia (Postumian Way,
   in Liguria), road . . . . 26 C c
Via Postumia (Postumian Way,
   in Venetia), road . . . . 27 G b
Via Prænestina (Prænestine
   Way), road . . . . 35 ins. B
Via Sacra (Sacred Way), street
   in Rome . . . . 23 A, B
Via Salaria (Salarian Way), road 27 H e
Via Severiana (Severian Way),
   road . . . . 35 ins. B
Viasma or Vyasma . . . . 138 D d
Via Tiberina (Tiberine Way),
   road . . . . 35 ins. B
Via Tiburtina (Tiburtian Way),
   road . . . . 35 ins. B
Viatka or Vyatka . . . . 138 G d
Viatka, dist. . . . . 71 P b
Via Traiana (Trajan's Way), road 30 E a
Via Triumphalis (Triumphal
   Way), road . . . . 35 ins. B
Via Valeria (Valerian Way, in
   Italy), road . . . . 27 H e
Via Valeria (Valerian Way, in
   Sicily), road . . . . 30 D d
Vibii, Forum . . . . 26 B c
Vibinum . . . . 30 E a
Vibo, Gulf of . . . . 31 F d
Vibo Valentia . . . . 31 F d
Viborg, in Denmark . . . . 88 C c
Viborg, in Finland . . . . 138 C c
Vic . . . . 76 E d
Vicenza . . . . 90 J h
Vicenza, univ. . . . . 100 H e (Vic.)
Vicetia (Vicenza) . . . . 26 F b
Vich . . . . 82 C a
Vich, bp. . . . . 94 C c
Vicinonia River, see Vilaine River
Vicksburg . . . . 208 B c
Vico, lake . . . . 96 B a
Victoria, in Alberta . . . . 212 D c
Victoria, in Brazil . . . . 214 F e
Victoria, in Vancouver . . . . . 198 A a

Victoria, state . . . . 172 D d
Victoria Desert, Great . . . . . 172 B c
Victoria Falls . . . . 175 F f
Victoria Land . . . . 186 I a
Victoria Nyanza, lake . . . . . 175 G e
Victoria River . . . . 172 B b
Victoria Strait . . . . 212 E b
Victoriæ, Clivus, loc. in Rome 24 A
Victrix Julia Tarraconensis(Tarragona) . . . . 38 C d
Victumulæ . . . . 26 C b
Vicus Augustanus . . . . 35 ins. B
Vicus Aurelii . . . . 39 J i
Vicus Iulius . . . . 39 J i
Vicus Jugarius, street in Rome 24 A
Vicus Tuscus, street in Rome 24 A
Vidin . . . . 164 C b
Vidrus (Vecht) River . . . . 39 I g
Viejo, el . . . . 213 D c
Vielsalm . . . . 117 D d
Vienna (Vienne), in France . 38 C c
Vienna . . . . 63 I e
Vienna, univ. . . . . 100 I e
Vienne, in France . . . . . . 69 F d
Vienne, abp. . . . . 95 D b
Vienne, dept. . . . . 148 E e
Vienne River . . . . 69 D c
Viennensis, Rom. prov. . . . 42 D e (1)
Viennois, Dauphiny of, dist. . 76 F d
Viennois, dist. . . . . 126 D d
Vieques, isl. . . . . 199 ins. G
Viersen . . . . 117 E o
Vierwaldstätter See, see Lucerne, lake . . . . 91 Q l
Vierzon . . . . 69 I g
Vieux - Amis . . . .
Vigan . . . . 199 ins. H
Vigas, las . . . . 201 H g
Vigenna, see Vienne
Vigevano . . . . 90 B b
Vigo . . . . 130 B e
Vijayanagar, Kingdom of . . . 112 A b
Viktring, mon. . . . . 95 E b
Vilaine River . . . . 148 D e
Vilcobamba . . . . 214 B d
Vilija River . . . . 159 M a
Vilini River . . . .
Vilkomir . . . . 159 M a
Villa Albani, loc. in Rome . . 96 A
Villa Bella . . . . 214 D d
Villa Borghese, loc. in Rome . 96 A
Villach . . . . 63 G e
Villa Encarnación . . . . . 215 D e
Villa Farnesina, loc. in Rome . 96 A
Villafranca . . . . 158 F f
Villagos . . . .
Villa Ludovisi, loc. in Rome . 96 A
Villa Madama, loc. in Rome . . 96 A
Villa Nova, in Santa Catharina 215 E e
Villa Nueva, in Arg. Rep. . 215 C f
Villa Publica, loc. in Rome . . 24 A
Villa Rica, in Paraguay . . . . 215 D e
Villa Rica de la Vera Cruz . .
Villa rica la Vieja . . . .
Villars, in Provence . . . . . 126 E e
Villars - sur - Ecot . . . . . 143 ins. F
Villa Umberto I, loc. in Rome 22 A
Villaviciosa, in Asturias . . . 83 J g
Villaviciosa, in Castile . . . . 130 C e
Villa Viçoza, in Brazil . . . . 108 N i
Villefranche . . . . 76 E d
Villegaignon Island . . . . . 108 M j
Villemur . . . . 76 D e
Villena, marq. . . . . 83 K h
Villeneuve . . . . 126 B d
Villingen . . . . 142 B d
Vilna . . . . 138 C e
Vilvorde . . . . 117 C d
Vimeiro . . . . 130 B f
Viminacium . . . . 39 M l
Viminal, quarter in Rome . . 96 A
Viminal Gate . . . . 22 A
Viminal Hill . . . . 22 A
Vincennes . . . .

Vinciacus, see Vinchy
Vinchy . . . . 55 P i
Vindava, see Windau
Vindelicia, dist. . . . . 38 E c
Vindhya Mountains . . . . . . 137 C d
Vindilis, isl. . . . . 38 B c
Vindobona (Vienna in Austria) 38 F c
Vindocinum, see Vendôme
Vindogladia . . . .
Vindonissa (Windisch) . . . . 39 J j
Vinegar Hill . . . . 127 K i
Vinnitsa . . . . 139 C f
Vinovia (Binchester) . . . . 51 P g
Vintium . . . . 26 B d
Vintodurnum, see Winterthur
Vipsanian Portico . . . . . . 22 A
Virballen . . . . 159 L a
Virère, Woods of . . . .
Virgin Aqueduct . . . . . . 35 ins. B (2)
Virginia City . . . . 210 B c
Virginia, col. . . . . 193 E c
Virginia, reg. . . . .
Virginia, state, 1788 . . . . . 202 I c
Virginia, state, 1863 . . . . . 203 V h
Virginia Military Lands . . . . 196 ins. B
Virginia, West, state . . . . 203 V h
Virginia Yazoo Company . . . 196 A d
Virgin Islands . . . . 105 H c
Virgin River . . . . 210 C c
Virgin's Well . . . . 6 ins. A
Viriballum, prom. . . . . . 26 C e
Virneburg . . . . 122 D c
Viroconium (Wroxeter) . . . .
Virodunum (Verdun) . . . . . 39 H i
Viromandis, see Saint - Quentin
Virtoa . . . . 117 D e
Virtue, Temple of . . . . . 22 A
Viru . . . . 111 B c
Virunum . . . . 39 E c
Visa . . . . 165 E c
Visconti, Dom. of the . . . . 78 F f
Visconti, Milanese under the . 90
Visé . . . . 117 D d
Visentium . . . . 27 F e
Visontio (Besançon) . . . . 39 H j
Visp . . . . 91 P l
Vistula River . . . . 159 J b
Visurgis (Weser) River . . . 38 D b
Vita . . . . 42 E f
Vitebsk . . . . 138 D d
Viterbo . . . . 90 D c
Viterbo, bp. . . . . 95 E c
Vith, Sankt . . . . 117 E d
Viti Levu, isl. . . . . 172 G b
Vitim River . . . .
Vitodurum . . . . 39 J j
Vitoria . . . . 83 B a
Vitricium . . . . 26 B b
Vitry . . . .
Vittorio Emanuele, Corso, street in Rome . . . . 22 A
Vittorio Emanuele, Piazza, loc. in Rome . . . . 22 A
Vivarais, dist. . . . . 76 F d
Vivarium, see Viviers
Vivienne, Rue, street in Paris . 149 B
Viviers . . . . 78 D f
Viviers, bp. . . . . 94 C c
Viviers, cty. . . . . 69 F d
Viviscus . . . . 26 A a
Vizagapatam . . . . 137 D e
Vizakna . . . . 159 L f
Vizcaya, dist., see also Biscay . 83 K g
Vizéu . . . . 82 A a
Vizéu, bp. . . . . 94 A c
Vizianagram . . . . 137 D e
Vlaardingen . . . . 62 C c
Vladikavkas . . . . 167 O g
Vladimir . . . . 138 F d
Vladimir Volynsk . . . . . . 139 B e
Vladivostok . . . . 171 O d
Vlieland, isl. . . . . 117 C a
Vlissingen (Flushing), in Holland . . . . 117 B c

Vlissingen (Flushing), in New York . . . . 189 ins. C
Vöcklabruck . . . . 123 G d
Voclade, see Vouillé
Vocontii, people . . . . . . 38 D d
Vogtland, dist. . . . . 85 G e
Vogules, people . . . .
Volane River . . . . 27 F c
Volaterræ . . . . 26 E d
Volcæ Arecomici, people . . . 38 C d
Volcæ Tectosages, people . . 38 C d
Volcei . . . . 30 E b
Volcera . . . . 27 I b
Volci . . . . 27 F e
Volerius River . . . . 26 D e
Volga River . . . . 139 G f
Volhynia, dist. . . . . 139 C e
Volkerode, mon. . . . . . . 95 E a
Volkhov River . . . . 88 N b
Volkovisk . . . . 155 M h
Vollenhove . . . . 117 D b
Vollmaringen . . . . 143 G h
Volo . . . . 164 C c
Vologda . . . . 138 E d
Vologesia . . . . 20 K f
Volsci, people . . . . 30 C a
Volsiniensis, lake . . . . . 27 F e
Volsinii novi . . . . 27 G e
Volsinii veteres . . . . . . 27 G e
Volta . . . . 161 H e
Volta River . . . . 128 ins. D
Volterra . . . . 90 L j
Volterra, bp. . . . . 95 E c
Voltri . . . . 150 E d
Volturara, bp. . . . . 95 F c
Volturnum . . . . 30 C b
Volturnus (Volturno) River . . 30 D a
Vomanus River . . . . . . 27 I e
Von der Leyen, princ. . . . . 154 E d
Vonitsa . . . . 131 H f
Voorne, East, isl. . . . . . 117 B c
Voorne, South, isl. . . . . . 117 C c
Voorne, West, isl. . . . . . 117 B c
Vorarlberg, dist. . . . . . . 114 E e
Vorder - Rhein, see Hither Rhine River . . . . 91 R l
Voronezh . . . . 139 E e
Voronezh, gov. . . . . . . 131 K c
Voronov . . . . 153 P f
Vorsfelde . . . . 85 B b
Vorskla River . . . . 92 D c
Vosges, dept. . . . . 148 F e
Vosges Mountains . . . . . 38 D c
Vosolvia . . . . 39 I h
Vossem . . . . 122 C c
Votyaks, people . . . . . . 138 H d
Vouillé . . . . 50 D c
Voullon . . . . 50 D c
Vratza . . . . 165 C b
Vredeland . . . . 189 ins. C
Vriesendael . . . . 192 D c
Vryburg . . . . 175 F g
Vryheid . . . . 175 N l
Vuelta, Cabo de la, cape . . . . 111 A b
Vulcan Island . . . . 30 E d
Vulcaniæ (Æolian, Lipari) Islands 30 E d
Vultur, mt. . . . . 30 E b
Vyasma or Viasma . . . . . 138 D d
Vyatka or Viatka . . . . . 138 G d
Vychegda River . . . .

Waadt, dist., see Vaud . . . 91 O l
Waag River . . . . 63 J d
Waal River . . . . 117 D c
Wabash River . . . . 191 H d
Wacos, tribe . . . . 188 D d
Wadai, sultanate . . . . . . 174 E c
Wadan . . . . 174 B b
Wadelai . . . . 175 D d
Wadi Natrun, reg. . . . . . 150 B a
Wadstena . . . . 88 F b
Wady Halfa . . . .
Wagadugu . . . . 174 C c
Waghäusel . . . . 158 E d

Wagnelée	156	A a	
Wagner, Battery, fort	208	E c	
Wagram	155	I d	
Wagrians, people	62	F a	
Wahlstatt	155	I c	
Wahlstadt, mon.	72	D a	
Wahlwies	62	E e	
Waialua	198 ins. B		
Waiblingen	143	H h	
Waibstadt	142	C b	
Waidhofen	115	H e	
Waikato River	172	G d	
Wailuku	198 ins. B		
Waimanalo	198 ins. B		
Waimea	198 ins. B		
Wain	143	J i	
Wain, lordship	143	J i	
Wainganga River	137	C d	
Waitangi	172	H e	
Waitara	172	G d	
Waitzen	159	J e	
Waitzen, bp.	95	F b	
Wakefield, in England	127	X m	
Wakefield, parl. bor.	163	M d	
Wakefield, in Miss.	196	B d	
Wake Island	179	H f	
Walata	174	C c	
Walbeck	62	F b	
Walcheren, isl.	117	B c	
Walck	131	I b	
Waldangeloch	143	G g	
Waldburg	143	I j	
Waldburg, cty.	143	I j	
Waldeck, cty.	114	E c	
Waldeck, dist.	86	G c	
Waldeck, princ.	134	E c	
Walden, mon.	97	R i	
Waldenburg	143	I g	
Waldkirch	142	A d	
Waldsassen, mon.	95	E b	
Waldsee	143	I j	
Waldshut	142	B e	
Waldstein, castle	123	H c	
Waldstetten	143	I h	
Wales, dist.			
Wales, march			
Wales, princ. about 1300			
Wales, princ. 17 cent.	127	V n	
Wales, North, dist.			
Wales, West, dist.			
Walfisch Bay	175	E g	
Walhain	156	B a	
Walkenried	122	F c	
Walkenried, mon.	95	E a	
Walker Pass	210	B c	
Walker River, Ind. Res.	188	C c	
Walkers	196	B c	
Wallachia, dist.	77	I d	
Wallachia, princ.	119	I e	
Wallachia, Great, dist.	89	C b	
Wallachia, Little, dist.	89	B b	
Wallachian Plain	2	G d	
Wallachian Thessaly, princ.	89	B c	
Walla Walla, Fort	198	B a	
Walla, Wallas, tribe	188	C a	
Wall Brook, in London	75	G g	
Wallenstein, route of	121	D c	
Wallerstein	143	J h	
Wallhausen	63	F c	
Wallingford			
Wallingford, castle			
Wallingford, parl. bor.	163	M f (Wall.)	
Wallis, dist., see Valais	91	P l	
Walloons, people	184	D b	
Wallnut Hills, village	208	B c	
Walnut Hills, Fort	196	A d	
Walsall, parl. bor.	163	M e	
Walsingham, Cape	212	I b	
Walsingham, mon.	97	S i	
Walsleben	63	F b	
Waltham, mon.	97	R j	
Waltham Abbey	75	J h	
Walton	75	I i	
Wampanoags, tribe	189	C d	

Wandewash or Wandiwash	137	C f	
Wanganui	172	G d	
Wangen, imp. cy.	143	I j	
Wangenies	156	B b	
Wantage			
Wappingers, tribe	188	L b	
Warangal			
Warasdin	159	I e	
Warberg, in Sweden	88	E c	
Warberg, Hanse. for. cy.	98	F b	
Warburg, Hanse. cy. in Germany	99 ins. B		
Warden, mon.	97	Q i	
Wardour Castle	127	W o	
Warego River	172	D c	
Wareham, in England	127	W p	
Wareham, castle	65	E e	
Wareham, barl. bor.	163	L g	
Wareham, in Mass.	207	L b	
Warekauri Islands	172	H e	
Waren	79	H b	
Waren, princ.	79	H b	
Wargla, oasis	2	E e	
Warka	159	K c	
Warley	75	J h	
Warm Spring, Ind. Res.	188	B b	
Warnabians, people	63	F b	
Warneton	117	A d	
Warns, people	50	F b	
Warnstedt	62	F c	
Warren	189 ins. A		
Warrenton	208	B c	
Warrington	127	W m	
Warrington, parl. bor.	163	L d (Warr.)	
Warsaw	79	L b	
Warsaw, duchy	155	K b	
Warsaw, gr. duchy	152	D c	
Warta River, see Warthe River			
Wartau, castle	91	R k	
Wartburg, castle	62	F c	
Wartenberg, in Silesia	123	I c	
Wartenburg, in Saxony	154	G c	
Warthausen	143	I i	
Warthe	63	I c	
Warthe River	63	I b	
Warwick, in England	127	X n	
Warwick, castle	65	F d	
Warwick, cty.			
Warwick, parl. bor.	163	M e	
Warwick, shire			
Warwick, in Rhode Island	189 ins. A		
Warwick Lane, street in London	75 G g (32)		
Wasatch Mountains	187	H e	
Wash, The, bay	49	G e	
Washington, in District of Columbia	208 ins.		
Washington, in Miss.	196	A d	
Washington, in Pa.	211	I b	
Washington, Fort, in Maryland	200	L i	
Washington, Fort, in New York	195	D c	
Washington, Fort, in Ohio	196 ins. B		
Washington, route of			
Washington, proposed state			
Washington, state	210	A a	
Washington, ter. 1853	202	A f	
Washington, ter. 1859	203	O f	
Washington, ter. 1863	203	N f	
Washita, River	199	G d	
Washita Fort	210	F d	
Wasit	99	M g	
Wassenberg	72	B a	
Wasseralfingen	143	J h	
Watauga	191	I d	
Watauga Association	194	C c	
Watauga River	196 ins. A		
Watauga Settlements	196 ins. A		
Watchet, parl. bor.			
Waterford, in Ireland			
Waterford, bp.	97	D d	
Waterford, cty.	127	J i	
Waterford, in Pa.	192	A c	
Water Gate	6 ins. A		

Waterloo			
Watertown	189 ins. B		
Watling's Island	105 ins.		
Watling Street, road in England	51	P h	
Watling Street, in London	75	G g	
Watson, Fort	195	A g	
Wattignies	134	B c	
Waverley, mon.	97	Q j	
Wavre	156	B a	
Waxhaw Creek	195	A f	
Wayne, Fort	196	B b	
Wayne's Treaty Line	196 ins. B		
Ways.	156	A a	
Weald, The, forest	49	F f	
Weare, parl. bor.			
Wearmouth			
Wearmouth, mon.	97	P g	
Wedmore			
Weehawken	192	D c	
Wehlau	123	K a	
Weibertreu, ruin	143	H g	
Weichsel River, see Vistula River			
Weiden	123	G d	
Wei-hai-wei	171	N e	
Weikersheim	143	I f	
Weilburg	114	E c	
Weilburg, castle	62	E c	
Weil der Stadt, imp. cy.	143	G h	
Weiler	143	H g	
Weilheim	143	I h	
Weiltingen	143	J g	
Weimar	85	F e	
Weinfelden	142	D e	
Weingarten, ab.	143	I j	
Weingarten, mon.	95	D b	
Weinheim	142	C a	
Weinsberg	143	H g	
Weinsberg, lordship	143	H g	
Weisse Elster River	63	G c	
Weissenau, ab.	143	I j	
Weissenburg, imp. cy., in Alsace	78	E d	
Weissenburg, mon.	95	D b	
Weissenburg, imp. cy., in Bavaria	79	G d	
Weissenburg, castle, in Switzerland	91	P l	
Weissenburg, in Transylvania			
Weissenfels	135	G c	
Weissenhorn	143	J i	
Weissenstein	143	I h	
Weisser Berg, mt.	123	H c	
Weisses Meer, see Kara Sea	170	H a	
Weisskirchen	159	K f	
Weisweil	142	A d	
Welbeck, mon.	97	P h	
Weldon	208	E b	
Weld Springs, village	172	B c	
Welehrad, mon.	95	F b	
Welfesholz	63	F c	
Welland River	127	Y n	
Well Gate	6 ins. A		
Wellington	172	G e	
Wellington Island	215	B g	
Wells, in England			
Wells, bp.	97	O j	
Wells, parl. bor.	163	L f	
Wells, in New Hampshire	189	C c	
Wels, in Austria	63	G d	
Welsh, people			
Wels Mountains			
Welzheim	143	I h	
Welzheim, lordship	143	I h	
Wen-chau	171	N f	
Wenden	88	K c	
Wendish March, dist.	77	I f	
Wendover, parl. bor.	163	N f (We.)	
Wends, people, in Austria	54	G d	
Wends, people, in Germany	46	I c	
Wener, lake	88	E b	
Wenersborg	88	F b	
Wennington	75	J h	
Weobley, parl. bor.	163	L e	

Werben	63	F b
Werden, mon.	95	D a
Werdenberg, castle	91	R k
Werl	62	D c
Werla, castle	62	F b
Werra River	79	G c
Werschitz	159	K f
Wertheim	142	D a
Werwick	117	A d
Wesel	114	D c
Wesel, Hanse. cy.	99 ins.	B
Wesen	91	R k
Weser River	62	E b
Wessagussett	189 ins.	B
Wessex, km.		
Wessobrunn, mon.	95	E b
Westacre, mon.	97	R i
West Africa, French, col.	174	C c
West Africa, Portuguese, col.	175	E f
West Bromwich	162	D e
Westbury, parl. bor.	163	L f
Westchester	189 ins.	C
West Cornwall, parl. dist.	163	I g
West Cumberland, parl. dist.	163	K c
West Dereham, mon.	97	R i
Westerås	88	G b
Westerham	75	J i
Westerly	189 ins.	A
Western, Fort	189	D b
Western Australia, state	172	C c
Western Ghats, mts.	112	A b
Western Plain	187	I d
Western Reserve of Connecticut, dist.	196 ins.	B
West Fiord	166	H b
West Florida, col.	194	B d
West Frankish Kingdom	56	B c
West Franconia, duchy	62	E d
West Friesland, dist.	117	C b
West Galicia, dist.	139	B e
West Gloucester , parl. dist.	163	L f
West Göthland, dist.		
West Goths, Kingdom of the, 486	50	D d
West Goths, Kingdom of the, 6 cent.	52	
West Goths, people	45	I c, D d
West Indies, reg.	107, 108	E-O, a-l
West Indies, isl.	187	L f
West Kent, parl. dist.	163	O f
Westland, dist.	172	F e
West Love, parl. bor.	163	J g
West Marches, dist., in England		
West March, dist., in Scotland		
West Meath, cty.	127	J h
Westminster, in England	65	F e
Westminster, mon.	97	Q j
Westminster, parl. dist.	163	N f (Westm.)
Westminster, in Maryland	208	ins.
Westminster, New, in British Columbia	212	C d
Westminster Hall, in London	75	G g
Westmoreland, cty.		
Westmoreland, parl. dist.		
Westmoreland, shire		
West New Jersey, col.	192	D d
West Norfolk, parl. dist.	163	O e
Westover	193 ins.	A
Westphalia, dist.	62	D b c
Westphalia, duchy	78	F c
Westphalia, km.	154	E c
Westphalia, prov.	158	E c
Westphalians, people	55	Q i
West Point	195	D c
Westport	210	F c
West Prussia, dist.	135	I b
West Prussia, prov.	159	I b
West Riding, parl. dist.	163	M d
West Roman Empire	42	A-F e
West Saxons, people		
West Somerset, parl. dist.	163	K f
West Suffolk, parl. dist.	163	O e
West Surrey, parl. dist.	163	N f
West Sussex, parl. dist.	163	N g

Westsylvania, proposed state in U. S.	195	A d
West Turkistan, Plains of	3	K d
West Virginia, state	211	I c
West Voorne, isl.	117	B c
West Wales, dist.		
West Worcester, parl. dist.	163	L e
Wethersfield, in Connecticut	189	B d
Wethersfield, in England	185	G f
Wetter, lake	88	F b
Wettin, castle	63	F c
Wettin, cty.	85	F e
Wettin Lands	85	
Wettingen, mon.	95	D b
Wetzlar	62	E c
Wetzlar, imp. cy.	78	F c
Wexford		
Wexford, cty.	127	K i
Weybridge	75	I i
Weymouth, in England	84	B d
Weymouth, parl. bor.	163	L g
Weymouth, in Mass.	189 ins.	B
Wey River, in Hereford	127	W n
Wey River, in Surrey	75	H i
Wezet	117	D d
Whalley, mon.	97	O h
Wheeling	196	C b
Wherwell, ab.	100	A a
Whitby		
Whitby, mon.	97	Q g
Whitby, parl. bor.	163	N c
Whitchurch, parl. bor.	163	M f
White Chapel, loc. near. London	75	I h
White Earth, Ind. Res.	188	G a
White Friars, mon.	75	G g
Whitehall, loc. in London	75	G g
Whitehall, in New York	195	E b
Whitehaven, parl. bor.	163	K c
White Horde, people		
White Horse, village	212	ins.
White Mountain, in Bohemia	123	H c
White Mountain, Ind. Res.	188	D d
White Mountains, in N. Hampshire	189	C b
White Nile River	174	G c
White Pass	212	ins.
White Plains, town	195	D c
White River, in Arkansas	191	G d
White River, in Indiana	208	C b
White River, in S. Dakota	198	E b
White Russia, reg.	138	C e
White Russians, people	138	C e
White Sea	138	E b
Whithorn, bp.	97	I e
Whitney, mt.	210	B c
Whorekill (Lewes, in Delaware)	192	D d
Whydah	174	D d
Wiblingen, ab. in Wurtemberg	143	I i
Wiblingen, mon.	143	J i
Wichita	210	F c
Wichitas, tribe	188	G d
Wicklow	127	K i
Wicklow, cty.	127	K i
Widdern	143	H g
Widin, see Vidin		
Wieblingen, in Baden	142	C b
Wieliczka	115	I d
Wielun		
Wien, see Vienna in Austria		
Wiener Neustadt	115	H e
Wieprz River	159	L c
Wieringen, isl.	117	D b
Wieselburg	159	I e
Wiesensteig	143	I h
Wiesensteig, lordship	143	I h
Wiese River	142	A e
Wiesloch	142	C b
Wigan	127	W m
Wigan, parl. bor.	163	L d
Wight, Isle of	49	F f
Wight, Isle of, parl. dist.	163	M g
Wigmore, mon.	97	O i
Wigtown		
Wigtown, cty.		

Wigtown, dist.		
Wi-ju	171	N e
Wildbad	143	G h
Wildberg, in Wurtemberg	143	G h
Wildberg, castle, in Austria	79	I d
Wildenstein	143	J g
Wilderness, battle	208	E b (Wil.)
Wildeshausen	62	E b
Wildhaus	91	R k
Wilhelmshaven	158	D b
Wilhelmstein, Fort	134	E b
Wilhelmsthal	134	E c
Wilkesbarre	195	D c
Wilkinson, route of	200	C d
Willamette River	198	A b
William, Fort (Calcutta)	137	E d
William, Fort, in Florida	193	D f
William, Fort (Portland)	210	A a
William, Fort, in Ontario	212	F d
William Henry, Fort	192	D b
William of Rubruck, route of		
Williams, Fort, in New York	192	D b
Williamsburg	193 ins.	A
Williamsport	208	ins.
Willoughby, route of	108	R a
Willow Brook	6 ins.	B
Wills Creek, Fort	192	B d
Wilmington, in Delaware	192	D d
Wilmington, in N. Carolina	193	F d
Wilsaetas, people		
Wilsnack	87	H b
Wilson's Creek, battle	208	B b
Wilson's Promontory	172	D d
Wilten	63	F e
Wilton		
Wilton, mon.	97	O j
Wilton, parl. bor.	163	M f
Wiltshire, cty.		
Wiltwyck	192	D c
Wiltz	117	D e
Wilzi or Wilzians, people	63	G b
Wimbledon	75	I i
Wimmera River	172	D d
Wimmis, castle	91	P l
Wimpfen	62	E d
Wimpfen, imp. cy.	142	D b
Winburg	175	M l
Wincanton	127	W o
Winceby	127	Y m
Winchcombe, mon.	97	P j
Winchelsea, parl. bor.	163	O g
Winchester, in England		
Winchester, bp.	97	P j
Winchester, castle	65	F e
Winchester, college	100	A a
Winchester, deanery	100	A a
Winchester, hospitals	100	A a
Winchester, mon.	100	A a
Winchester, parl. bor.	163	M f (Winch.)
Winchester, in Virginia	193	E b
Windau, Hanse. cy.	99	H b
Windhoek, or Windhuk	175	E g
Wind River	210	D b
Wind River, Ind. Res.	188	E b
Windsheim	114	E c
Windsor, in Canada	212	G d
Windsor, in Connecticut	189	B d
Windsor, in England	75	H i
Windsor, castle		
Windsor, New, in Maryland	208	ins.
Windward Channel	213	E c
Windward Islands	213	F c
Winibigoshish, Ind. Res.	188	H a
Winnebago, Fort	211	H b
Winnebago, Ind. Res.	188	G b
Winnebagos, tribe	188	I b
Winnenden	143	H h
Winnepesaukee, lake	189	C c
Winnington Bridge	127	W m
Winnipeg	212	F d
Winnipeg, lake	212	F c
Winnipegosis, lake	186	A c
Winnsboro	195	A f
Winschoten	117	E a

Winterburg . . . 142 ins. A
Winterstetten . . . 143 I i
Winterthur . . . 91 Q k
Wintney, priory . . . 100 B a
Winton . . . 172 D c
Winwaedsfield . . .
Wirtemberg, ruin . . . 143 H h
Wirzaburg, see Würzburg
Wisbech, parl. bor. . . . 163 O e
Wisby . . . 88 H c
Wisby, Hanse. cy. . . . 98 G b
Wischehrad . . .
Wisconsin, state . . . 211 G b
Wisconsin, ter. 1836 . . . 202 F f
Wisconsin, ter. 1838 . . . 202 G f
Wisconsin River . . . 199 H b
Wisera River, see Weser River
Wismar . . . 80 B e
Wismar, Hanse. cy. . . . 99 ins. B
Witham, mon. . . . 97 O j
Wittelsbach, castle . . . 72 C b
Wittenberg . . . 72 C a
Wittenberg, univ. . . . 100 H d
Wittstock . . . 123 G b
Witu . . . 175 H e
Witwaters Rand, mts. . . . 175 M l
Wloclawek . . . 159 J b
Wloclawek, bp. . . . 95 F a
Wlodawa . . . 155 L c
Woburn . . . 189 ins. B
Woburn, mon. . . . 97 Q j
Wogastisburg . . . 55 R j
Wohlau . . . 115 I c
Wohlau, princ. . . . 115 I c
Woiwodina, dist. . . . 159 J f
Wola . . . 135 K b
Wolfach . . . 142 B d
Wolfegg . . . 143 I j
Wolfenbüttel . . . 79 G b
Wolfenbüttel, duchy . . . 122 E c
Wolfsegg . . . 123 G d
Wolgast . . . 63 G a
Wolgast, duchy . . . 115 G b
Wolgast, Hanse. cy. . . . 99 ins. B
Wollaston, Mount, village . . . 189 C c
Wollaston Lake . . . 186 I c
Wollaston Land . . . 212 D b
Wollin . . . 63 H b
Wolmirstedt . . . 85 B b
Wolvega . . . 117 D b
Wolverhampton, parl. bor. 163 L e (Wolv.)
Women's Tower, loc. in Jerusalem . . . 6 ins. A
Won-san . . . 171 N e
Woods, Lake of the . . . 191 G b
Wood Street, in London . . . 75 G g
Woodstock . . . 127 X o
Woodstock, New 163 M f (New Wood.)
Woolwich . . . 75 J i
Wootton Bassett, parl. bor. 163 M f (W. B.)
Worcester, in England . . .
Worcester, bp. . . . 97 O i
Worcester, cty. . . .
Worcester, parl. bor. . . . 163 L e (Worc.)
Worcester, shire . . .
Worcester, in Mass. . . . 189 C c
Wörgl . . . 154 G e
Worksop, mon. . . . 97 P h
Workum . . . 117 D b
Wormatia, see Worms, on the Rhine River
Worms, on the Rhine River . . 62 E d
Worms, bp. . . . 95 D b
Worms, imp. cy. . . . 78 F d
Worms (Bormio), on the Adda. 122 F e
Worndorf . . . 142 C e
Wörnitz River . . . 143 J g
Worringen . . . 78 E c
Wrangell . . . 198 ins. A
Wrangell, Fort . . . 212 ins.
Wrangell, mt. . . . 186 E b
Wreschen . . . 159 I b
Wrexham parl. bor. . . . 163 K d

Wrightstown . . . 192 D c
Wrightsville . . . 208 ins.
Wroxeter . . . 51 O h
Wu-chau . . . 171 M f
Wu-hu . . . 171 M e
Wurm River . . . 143 G h
Wurtemberg, castle . . . 62 E d
Wurtemberg, cty. . . . 78 F d
Wurtemberg, elect. . . . 151 H g
Wurtemberg, km. . . . 151 K j
Wurzach . . . 143 I j
Würzburg . . . 62 E d
Würzburg, bp. . . . 95 D b
Würzburg, gr. duchy . . . 154 E d
Würzburg, elect. . . . 151 K j
Würzburg, univ. . . . 100 G e
Wurzen . . . 85 G e
Wu-sing . . . 170 ins. A
Wutach River . . . 142 B g
Wyandots, tribe . . . 188 J b
Wychwood . . . 49 F f
Wye River . . . 49 E e
Wyk, in Holland . . . 117 C b
Wyk by Duurstede . . . 117 D b
Wymondham, mon. . . . 97 S i
Wyoming . . . 196 D b
Wyoming, state . . . 210 D b
Wyoming, ter. . . . 203 Q g
Wyoming Valley . . . 195 C c
Wyre, Forest of . . . 49 E e
Wyschehrad, castle . . .

Xaltocan . . . 106 A a
Xaltocan, lake . . . 106 B a
Xanten . . . 62 D c
Xanthus . . . 20 C d
Xanthus River . . . 20 C d
Xaragua, reg. . . . 105 F c
Xauxa (Jauja) . . . 111 B d
Xerxes Canal . . . 11 E b
Xerxes, route of fleet of . . . 13 D a
Xico . . . 106 B a
Xingu River . . . 214 D c
Xions . . . 159 I b
Xochicalco . . . 106 A b
Xochimilco . . . 106 A a
Xuala . . . 191 I d
Xyniæ . . . 11 D c
Xynias, lake . . . 11 D c
Xypete . . . 16 B b
Xystus . . . 6 ins. A *

Yablonoi Mountains . . . 171 M c
Yacki . . .
Yadkin River . . . 195 A e
Yakima, Ind. Res. . . . 188 B a
Yakutat Bay . . . 198 ins. A
Yakutsk . . . 171 N b
Yalta . . . 164 K f
Ya-lu River . . . 171 N d
Yama . . . 119 J b
Yamasees, tribe . . . 188 J d
Yamburg . . . 119 K b
Yanaon . . . 137 D e
Yandabo . . .
Yang-tse-kiang, R. . . .
Yang-tun . . .
Yangui . . .
Yankton, Ind. Res. . . . 188 G b
Yap, isl. . . . 179 E g
Yapura River . . . 214 C c
Yaqui, Rio, R. . . . 190 C f
Yaquimi . . . 190 D f
Yarkand . . .
Yarm, parl. bor. . . .
Yarmouth, in England . . . 65 G d
Yarmouth, Hanse. for. cy. . . . 98 ins. A
Yarmouth, parl. bor. . . . 163 M g
Yarmouth, in Mass. . . . 189 C d
Yarmouth, in Nova Scotia . . . 212 I d
Yarmouth River . . . 6 D c
Yaroslavl . . . 138 E d
Yarrawonga . . . 172 D d
Yass . . . 172 D d

Yatwegs, people . . . 71 K c
Yauco . . . 199 ins. G
Yautepec, R. . . . 106 B b
Yazoo Company . . . 196 A d
Yazoo River . . . 208 B c
Yedi Kouleh, castle . . . 93 G e
Yedisan, reg. . . . 139 C f
Yedo . . . 171 P e
Yeletz . . . 139 E e
Yellow Sea . . . 171 N e
Yellowstone National Park . . . 210 C b
Yellowstone River . . . 210 D a
Yelnia . . . 153 O g
Yemamah, el . . .
Yemen, reg. . . . 170 F g
Yenikale . . . 164 F a
Yenisei River . . .
Yeniseisk . . . 171 K c
Yeni Shehr, quarter in Constantinople . . . 93 G e
Yeovil . . . 127 W p
Yeu, isl. . . . 84 B f
Yezd . . .
Yezo, isl. . . . 171 P d
Yildiz Kiosk . . . 93 G e
Ylst . . . 117 D b
Yokohama . . . 171 P e
Yola . . . 174 E d
Yonkers . . . 192 E c
Yonne, dept. . . . 148 E e
Yonne River . . . 62 B e
York (Toronto), in Canada . . . 194 D b
York, in England . . .
York, abp. . . . 97 N g
York, castle . . . 65 F d
York, cty. . . .
York, Hanse. for. cy. . . . 98 ins. A
York, in New Hampshire . . . 189 C c
York, in Pa. . . . 208 ins.
York, in Western Australia . . . 172 A d
York, Cape . . . 172 D b
York, Fort, in Sumatra . . . 136 O e
York, Vale of . . . 49 F d
York County . . . 193 ins. A
York Factory, post . . . 212 F c
York River . . . 193 ins. A
York Town (Yorktown) . . . 193 ins. A
York Wolds, dist. . . . 49 F d
Yorkist estates . . . 84
Yorkshire Coalfield . . . 162 E d
Yosemite Valley . . . 210 A c
Yoshino . . .
Youghal . . .
Youghiogheny River . . . 192 B c
Ypres . . . 117 A d
Ypres, Hanse. for. cy. . . . 99 ins. B
Yssel River . . . 117 E b
Ysselstein . . . 117 C b
Yucatan, pen. . . . 105 C c
Yucatan, state . . . 213 D b
Yucatan Strait . . . 187 K f
Yukon, ter. . . . 212 B b
Yukon River . . . 186 D b
Yuma . . . 210 C d
Yuma, Ind. Res. . . . 188 C d
Yumas, tribe . . . 188 D d
Yü-mon-kwan, pass . . . 92 J f
Yun-nan, prov. . . . 171 K f
Yun-nan, reg. . . . 92 J e
Yun-nan-fu . . . 171 L f
Yungay . . . 214 B c
Yung-ning, in Kwang-si . . . 171 M f
Yung-ning-fu, in Yun-nan . . .
Yung-ting . . . 170 ins. A
Yuste, mon., see San Gerónimo de Yuste
Yverdon . . . 91 O l
Yvetot . . . 126 B b
Yvoix . . . 117 D e

Zaandam . . . 122 C b
Zabatus River . . . 20 J d
Zabeda . . . 6 E a
Zabern . . . 114 D d

Zabern, castle 62   D d
Zacatecas 213   B b
Zacatecas, state 213   B b
Zacatula . . . . 213 ins.
Zacharias, Tomb of . . . . . . 68 ins. B
Zacynthus, in Greece 14   A b
Zacynthus, isl. 14   A b
Zacynthus, in Spain 12   C c
Zadracarta 19   H c
Zafa, reg. . . . .
Zafra 82   A b
Zagazig 174   J i
Zagrab . . . .
Zahara 83   J h
Zähringen, castle 142   A d
Zaitun (Tsuen-chau-fu) . . . . .
Zalaca 82   A b
Zalmon Mountains 6   F c
Zama regia 38   D e
Zamboanga . . . . 199 ins. H
Zambesi River 175   G f
Zamora, in Mexico . . . . . . 213 ins.
Zamora, in Spain 82   A a
Zamora, bp. 94   A c
Zamosc 139   B e
Zampa, reg. . . . . K   I
Zancle (Messina) 30   E d
Zandvliet 117   C c
Zane's Trace, road . . . . . . 196 ins. B
Zanesville 196   C c
Zante, isl. 89   H g
Zanzibar 175   H e
Zanzibar, isl. 175   H e
Zaporogian Cossacks 139   D f
Zara 90   E b
Zara, abp. 95   E c
Zaradrus River 19   L d
Zarax 15   D c
Zarax, mt. 15   D c
Zardandan, reg. . . . . 10 ,
Zarephath (Sarepta) 6   C b
Zaretra 11   F d
Zariaspa 19   K c
Zarnow 123   K c
Zea Port 16   D c
Zealand Island 154   F a
Zealand, New, col. 172   F d
Zebid . . . .
Zebulon, Plain of 6   C c
Zebulon, tribe . . . . 7 ins. D
Zeeland, cty. 117   B c
Zeeland, dist. 78   C c
Zehdenick, mon. . . . . 80 ins.
Zehngerichtebund (League of
   Ten Jurisdictions), dist. . . . 91   R I

Zeil, castle 143   I j
Zeila 109   V g
Zeirids, people 66   H f
Zeithain 135   G c
Zeitz 63   G c
Zeitz, march 63   G c
Zela 20   F b
Zelea . . . .
Zell, on the Harmersbach,
   imp. cy. 142   B d
Zell, on the Moselle R. . . . . 142 ins. A
Zell, on the Wiese R. 142   A e
Zell, on the Ziller R. 154   G e
Zemaun Shah, Dom. of . . . .
Zengg 72   D c
Zengg, bp. 95   F b
Zengid Atabeks, people 71   O f
Zenobia 20   H e
Zenta 131   G d
Zephyrium, prom. 31   F d
Zerbst 63   G c
Zerdan 68   C b
Zerenj . . . .
Zermatt 91   P l
Zeugitana, reg. 38   D e
Zeugma 20   G d
Zeus, Altar of . . . .
Zeus, Temple of . . . .
Zeus Soter, Temple of . . . . . 16 D c (1)
Zevenaar 117   E c
Zhagubitza . . . .
Zianids, dynasty 77   E e
Zichi, or Zichians, people . . . 35   L e
Zichia, reg. 99   K e
Zidon 6   C a
Zierikzee 78   C c
Zierikzee, Hanse. cy. . . . . . 99 ins. B
Zigana 20   H b
Zilis 12   B c
Ziller Tal, valley in Tyrol . . . 114   F e
Zillerthal, in Silesia 159   H c
Zinder 174   D c
Zinjar . . . .
Zinna, mon. . . . . 80 ins.
Zion, cy., see Jerusalem
Zion, Gate of . . . . 68 ins. B
Zion, mt. . . . . 68 ins. B
Zion, quarter in Jerusalem . . . 6 ins. A
Ziph 7   C f
Zips, dist. 80   G g
Ziskaberg, mt. 87   J c
Zitácuaro . . . . 213 ins.
Zittau, in Bohemia 79   I c
Zittau, in Lusatia 115   H c
Zituni 89   H g

Znaym 3   A d
Zoar 7   C f
Zollern, castle 62   E d
Zollern, cty. 86   G d
Zollverein, German, (Customs-
   Union) 160   D c
Zolyom . . . .
Zombor 159   J f
Zor (Tyre) 6   C b
Zorah 7   B e
Zorndorf 135   H b
Zoroa 6   E c
Zoster, prom. 15   D b
Zschillen, mon. . . . . 80 ins.
Zsibo 159   L e
Zsibo Pass 129   H c
Zug 91   Q k
Zug, canton 91   Q k
Zug, lake 91   Q k
Zuider Zee, bay 117   D b
Züllichau 123   H b
Zülpich 62   D c
Zultepec 106   B a
Zululand, reg. 175   N l
Zumpango 106   A a
Zumpango, lake of 106   A a
Zungaria, reg. . . . .
Zungeru 174   D d
Zuñi 190   D d
Zuñis, tribe 188   E c
Zurich 91   Q k
Zurich, canton 91   Q k
Zurich, lake of 91   Q k
Zurich, mon. 95   D b
Zurichgau, dist. 62   E e
Zurita 82   H e
Zusmarshausen 122   F d
Zutfen, Hanse. cy. . . . . . . 99 ins. B
Zutphen 117   E b
Zutphen, cty. 117   E b
Zwaanendael 192   D d
Zweibrücken 86   F d
Zweibrücken, princ. 134   D d
Zwettl, mon. 95   F b
Zwickau 85   G e
Zwiefalten, ab. 143   H e
Zwiefalten, mon. 143   H e
Zwingenberg 142   C a
Zwinguri, Fort 91   Q l
Zwittau 168   E b
Zwolle 117   E b
Zwolle, Hanse. cy. . . . . . . 99 ins. B
Zwornik 119   H e

INDEX-SUPPLEMENT

Aalst (Alost) . . . . 86 D c
Aarhus . . . . 88 D c
Abadeh . . . . 168 K F c
Abash, reg. . . . . 1C4 B D f
Abbadan, isl. . . . . 168 K E d
Abdon . . . . 6 C b
Abel ha Sittim . . . . 7 D e
Abel Mehola . . . . 7 D d
Abercorn, bp. . . . . 60 C b
Aberdeen . . . . 128 F c
Aberdeen, cty. . . . . 128 F c
Aberffraw . . . . 60 G c
Abergavenny . . . . 74 J h
Aherystwith . . . . 74 J g
Abitibi, lake . . . . 191 I i
Abitibi River . . . . 191 I a
Abitibis, Fort des . . . . . . 191 J b
Abkhasia, auton. rep. . . . 168 G M/N g
Abrettene, reg. . . . . . . 9 F e
Abrittus . . . . 39 N l
Abrushum, R. . . . . . . 168 K G b
Abulliond Geul . . . . . . 168 J A a
Abus Aestuarium . . . . . . 51 Q h
Abusir, Pyramids of . . . . . 1 B c
Abydus . . . . 9 D d
Academy of Science, bldg.
     in Athens . . . . 23 D
Academy Street, in Athens. 23 D
Acarnanians, people . . . . 8 N h
Accra . . . . 128 C ins. D
Achaeans (Achaians), people 8 N h
Achaia, Proconsulate of . . 43 G f
Achilles, Burial mound of . 9 A b
Achilleum . . . . 9 A b
Achonry . . . . 74 B a
Acilius, Compitum of . . . . 24 D
Acre . . . . 168 J C
Acton Burnell . . . . 74 K g
Adabazar . . . . 168 J B b
Adalia, Gulf of . . . . . . 168 J B b
Adam's Peak. . . . . 137 D g
Addis Ababa . . . . 174 G d
Aden . . . . 104 B E f
Ad Fines, near Florencia . 27 F d
Ad Fines, near Volaterrae . 26 E d
Adida . . . . 7 B e
Adonis River . . . . 6 D a
Adramyttium . . . . 9 D e
Adramyttium, Gulf of . . . 9 D e
Adranos River . . . . . . 168 J A b
Adyge Cherkises, auton.
     area . . . . 168 F leg.
Advge Cherkises, people. 168 J C a
Aegaei Mountains . . . . 14 ins.
Aegospotami River . . . . . 9 D d
Aegusae Islands . . . . . . 30 B d
Aena . . . . 7 D g
Aenianians, people . . . . 8 N h
Aenus . . . . 9 D d
Aeolians, people . . . . 14 leg.
Aerarium, bldg. in Rome . 24 A (15)
Aesepus River . . . . . . 9 E e
Aethiopia, reg., Egyptian emp. 4 F d
Aetolians, people . . . . . 8 N h
Aghan Dominions . . . . . 137 A b
Afiun Karahissar . . . . . 164 E c
Afrau . . . . 174 Q n
Africa, Proconsulate of . . 42 D f
African Sea . . . . 29 B f
Afso . . . . 174 Q n
Agdir, reg. . . . . 45 F a

Agora (Lysimachia) . . . . 9 D d
Agrae Hills . . . . 23 D
Agreda . . . . 83 K g
Agrianes River . . . . . . 9 D c
Aguas Blancas . . . . . . 216 ins.
Aguatulco . . . . 107 E d
Agylla . . . . 27 G f
Ahaggar, reg. . . . . . . 174 D b
Ahaus . . . . 78 E b
Ahram . . . . 168 K F d
Aianteum . . . . 9 B a
Aigues-Mortes . . . . . . 102 G g
Ain-Aicha . . . . 174 P n
Ain-Defali . . . . 174 P n
Ain-Tab . . . . 168 J C b
Airds Moss . . . . 128 D e
Aire River, in France . . 104 A C c
Airobol . . . . 165 E c
Aisma . . . . 168 L D c
Ajax, Burial mound of . . 9 B b
Ajdir . . . . 174 Q n
Ajlun . . . . 168 J C c
Ajudia . . . . 128 C N e
Akershuus (Christiania) . . 88 D b
Akhsi . . . . 104 B H c
Ak Mechet . . . . 168 G N f
Akrabatta . . . . 7 C d
Akshi-Kioi . . . . 9 B b
Ak-su . . . . 104 B I c
Ala . . . . 154 F f
Ala Kul . . . . 104 B I c
Alans, people in Russia . 45 M d
Alashia (Cyprus) . . . . 4 B d
Alba Julia (Karlsburg) . . 159 L d
Albanians, people, about 900 57 G-H
Albanians, people, in 1929 168 H G c
Albarracin Mountains . . 82 B a
Albreda . . . . 136 I d (A)
Alcacer-el-Kebir . . . . . 174 O n
Alcimus, prom. . . . . . 16 D c
Alclyde . . . . 60 B b
Alcoraz . . . . 82 H e
Aldan River . . . . 104 C M b
Aldborough (Isurium) . . 51 P g
Aleppo (Haleb) . . . . . 68 C b
Alesund . . . . 181 B D a
Alexander's Port . . . . 19 K f
Alexandria Troas . . . . . 9 D e
Alexandropol (Leninakan). 168 J D a
Alexandrovsk (Caspian sea) 168 G D a
Alford . . . . 128 F c
Alhucemas Bay . . . . . 174 Q n
Aller . . . . 60 H d
Alma Ata (Verni) . . . . 170 I d
Almenara . . . . 83 K h
Almonacid . . . . 153 D c
Almoravids, Dom. of the . 66 E g
Alnwick . . . . 74 L d
Alopeconnesus . . . . . 9 D d
Alpis Iulia . . . . 9 I b
Altai Mountains . . . . 104 B I c
Altenberg (in Saxony) . . 87 I c
Altendorf (Stará Ves) . . 79 L d
Altis, loc. in Olympia . . 9 H f
Altkirch . . . . 91 P k
Alto Adige, reg. . . . . 168 H ins.
Altsohl (Svolen) . . . . 79 K d
Alt-Zella, mon. . . . . . 85 G e
Alula . . . . 182 G G f
Amadia . . . . 168 J D b
Amalion, bldg. in Athens . 23 D

Amance . . . . 104 A D c
Amara . . . . 168 K E c
Amardus (Kizil Uzen) River 44 G c
Ambly . . . . 104 A C b
Amboina, isl. . . . . . . 128 C ins. C.
Ambrones . . . . 38 D a
Amecameca . . . . . . 106 B a
Amerongen . . . . . . 168 D B c
Amjhera . . . . 104 B R i
Ammon, dist. . . . . . 7 D e
Amol, on Caspian Sea . . 104 B F d
Amol, on the Amu-Daria R. 104 B G d
Amor, dist. . . . . 4 F c *
Amoun Derness, dist. . . . 60 H c
Ampelus, in Crete . . . . 14 ins.
Amphipyrgos, prom. . . . . 10 B c
Amsterdam, isl. . . . . . 128 C M g
Amsterdam (Carmentine) 128 C ins. D
Amu-Daria River . . . . 104 B G d
Amur River . . . . . . 104 C M b
Anaforta . . . . 168 L D c
Anapa . . . . 139 E g
Anavio . . . . 51 P h
Anchedive Island . . . . 104 B R j
Anchialus . . . . 39 N l
Ancient Prytaneum, in Athens 23 D (10)
Ancient Wall of Athens . 23 D
Ancyle, deme . . . . . 23 D
Andaman (Angaman) Is-
     lands . . . . 104 C J f
Andaraba . . . . 104 B G d
Andijan . . . . 104 B H c
Angaman (Andaman) Is-
     lands . . . . 104 C J f
Angara River . . . . . 104 C K b
Anglo-Norman Colonies &
     Earldoms . . . . . . 70 E c
Anglo-Saxons, people, about
     900 . . . . 57 C c
Angus, dist. . . . . . . 128 F d
Anim . . . . 7 C f
Annaghdown, bp. . . . . 97 B c
Annam . . . . 171 L f
Annan . . . . 128 E f
Annandale, dist. . . . . 128 E e
Annopol . . . . 103 O c
Año Nuevo . . . . 181 U l
Anshan, dist. . . . . . . 4 G c *
Anta-ia (Antioch) . . . . 168 J C b
Antandrus . . . . 9 D e
Antioch, princ. in 1265 . 89 E c
Antofagasta, prov. . . . 216 ins.
Antoninus and Faustina,
     Temple of . . . . . . 24 B (22)
Anzac Cove . . . . . . 168 L D c
Apán . . . . 106 B a
Aphek, near Gebal . . . 6 D a
Aphek, near Joppa . . . 7 B d
Aphnitis Lake . . . . . 9 E d
Aphrodisias . . . . . . 9 D d
Aphroditopolis . . . . . 1 B c
Apollonia, in Cyrenaica . 35 I g
Apollonia, in Guinea . . 128 C ins. D
Apollonia, in Mysia . . . 9 F d
Apollo Patroos, in Athens . 23 D (5)
Apremont . . . . 104 A C b
Apremont-Dun, seign. . . 104 A C b
Apsinthii, people . . . . 9 D d
Aptera . . . . 14 ins.
Apuli, people . . . . . 29 D d
Aquae, in Britain . . . . 51 P h

95

Name	Page		
Aquae Flaviae	38	A	d
Aquae Tarbellicae	38	B	d
Aqueduct of Hadrian, in Athens	23	D	
Aqueduct of Pisistratus, in Athens	23	D	
Arabian Sea	104B	G	f
Arabia Sebba, reg.	104B	E	f
Arabistan, reg.	168K	E	c
Arabs, people	168L	K	i
Aracan, reg.	171	K	e-f
Aragon, march	45	D d (Ar)	
Aragon River	82	B	a
Aramatha	6	E	c *
Aramu, people	4	F	c
Aranjuez	130	C	e
Ararat, mt.	168J	D	b
Aras River	139	G	h
Arbedo	86	G	e
Arbela (Beth Arbeel)	6	D	c
Arbil	99	L	f
Arbocala	38	A	d
Arcadians, people	8	N	i
Arcadians, people	14	leg.	
Archelais, in Palestine	7	C	e
Archelaus, Dominions of	7		
Arches, near Épinal	104A	D	c
Arcis-sur-Aube	104A	B	c
Arctonnesus, isl.	9	B	b
Arda, R.	168L	E	f
Ardabil	139	G	h
Ardahan	139	F	g
Ardasa	168J	C	a
Ardstraw	74	C	a
Arganthonius, mt.	9	F	d
Argennum, prom.	9	D	e
Argentaria	39	I	i
Argentorate (Strasburg)	39	I	i
Arghana Maden	168J	D	b
Argob, reg.	6	D	c
Argonne Forest	168C	C	c
Arguin, isl.	128B	H	d
Argyll and Tarbet, cty.	128	C	d
Aribi, people	5	C	b
Arisba, in Lesbos	9	D	e
Arisbe, in Troas	9	D	d
Arklow	74	C	b
Arlberg Pass	87	H	e
Armagaon	128	B ins.B	
Armagh	74	C	a
Armalec	104B	I	c
Armenia, auton. rep.	168G	N-O	g
Armenia, Lesser, km., in 1265	89	D	c
Armenia, Lesser, km., in 1355	89	J	g
Armenian Christians	168L	leg.	
Armenians, people	168L	L	h
Ar Moab	7	D	f
Aror	53	I	d
Arpad (Tel-Erfâd)	4	C	d
Arran, isl.	128	C	e
Arrancy	104A	C	b
Arrö, isl.	87	H	a
Arsakion, bldg. in Athens	23	D	
Arsila	174	O	n
Artace	9	E	d
Artemea	9	E	d
Artynia Lake	9	F	d
Arve River, in Savoy	91	O	l
Arx, in Munychia	16	D	c
Ascalon	7	D	d
Ascania Lake	9	G	d
Asch	79	H	c
Ashburton	74	J	i
Ashdown	60	I	d
Ashdown, dist.	60	D	d
Asia, Proconsulate of	43	H	f
Asia. Rom. prov. under Trajan	20	C c (I)	
Asiago	168H	ins.	
Askabad	104B	F	d
Asmak River	9	B	b
Asolo near Feltre	87	H	f
Aspara	104B	H	c
Aspinwall (Colón)	214	A	b
Assiniboine River	190	E	a
Assus	9	D	e
Assyrian Empire	5		
Assyrian trade-routes	44	leg.	
Astacus, in Bithynia	9	G	d
Astacus, Bay of	9	G	d
Astae, people	9	F	c
Astaroth	6	E	c
Astrabad	104B	F	d
Astrabad, reg.	139	H	h
Astyra	9	D	e
Åsunden, lake	88	E	c
Atalaya	106	C	a
Atarneus	9	D	e
Athena Street, in Athens	23	D	
Athene, Altar of	23	C	
Athene Hygiaea, in Athens	23	C (4)	
Athenry	74	B	b
Athlone	74	C	b
Atholl, dist.	128	E	d
Athyras River	9	F	c
Atrek River	139	I	h
Augustobriga	38	A	e
Augustus, Arch of	24	B (18)	
Auldearn	128	E	c
Aulon, str., on Andros I.	15	E	b
Auschwitz (Oswiecim)	87	L	c
Aust	60	D	c
Austeravia, isl.	38	D	b
Austerfield	60	D	c
Austria, rep.	168F	H-I	f
Ava	104C	J	e
Ava, reg.	104C	J	e
Avaris	4	ins.	*
Avars, people in Hungary	45	H	c
Avars, people, on the Don R.	45	M	c
Avignon, abp.	94	C c (A.)	
Avioth	104A	C b (Av.)	
Avon River	60	D	c
Awanui	179	I	k
Awarua	179	H	l
Axbridge	60	H	d
Axim	128C	ins. D	
Axos (Oaxus)	14	ins.	
Ayana, reg.	109	V	g
Aylesborough = Aylesb.	60	D	d
Ayotzingo	106	B	a
Ayr	128	D	e
Ayr River	128	D	e
Ayyub, Mosque of	93	G	e
Ayyub, quarter	93	G	e
Azcopatzalco	106	A	a
Azerbaijan, auton. rep.	168G	O	g
Azerbaijan, reg.	67	P	f
Aziziyah	168J	A	b
Azjer	168K	F	d
Baal Hazor	7	C	e
Baal Meon	7	D	e
Baal Salisa	7	C	e
Baba Eski	168L	F	f
Babilu (Babylon)	4	G	c *
Babylon (Cairo)	99	J	h
Babylonian trade-routes	44	leg.	
Bacanore	104B	R	j
Baccanae	35	ins. B	
Bacharach	102	H	c
Bactrus River	19	K	c
Badakshan, reg.	104B	H	d
Badenoch, dist.	128	E	d
Bafk	168K	G	c
Baghché	168J	C	b
Bagistana (Behistun)	5	D	b
Bahrein, isl.	104B	F	e
Baikal, lake	104C	K	b
Bairnsdale	172	K	d
Baither	7	C	e
Bakchiserai	139	D	g
Bakewell	60	I	c
Bakhtegan (Niriz), lake	168K	F	d
Bakkar	104B	G	e
Baku, Sea of	99	N	f
Balasore	137	D	b
Balaton, lake (Platten-See)	87	K	e
Balga, castle	87	M	a
Balkash, lake	104B	H	c
Balkh	104B	G	d
Ballarat	172	D	d
Ballyk	9	B	b
Bam	168K	G	d
Bambilonia (Cairo)	99	J	h
Bamborough	60	D	b
Bamian	104B	G	d
Bampur	168K	H	d
Banana	182	CC	h
Banda Islands	104C	M	h
Banff, cty.	128	E	c
Bangor, in Wales	60	G	c
Banjaluka (Banialuka)	159	I	f
Banjarmasin, reg.	104C	L	h
Bankot	137	B	b
Bannaventa	51	P	h
Banská Bystrica (Neusohl)	103	N	c
Banská Štiavnica (Schemnitz)	103	N	d
Bar (Antivari) abp.	95	F	c
Baramahal, reg.	137	C	f
Barberini, Palazzo, bldg. in Rome	22	A	
Barcelona, march	45	E d (B)	
Barchin	104B	G	c
Barda'a	99	M	f
Bardney, abbey	74	M	f
Bardo, in Posen	159	J	b
Bardo, in Tunis	174	E	a
Bardonis, mt.	26	D	c
Barfurush	168K	L	b
Bargu, reg.	104C	F	b
Bar Harbor	181	U	c
Barkhalikend	104B	H	c
Barkul	104C	C	b
Baroch	104B	R	i
Barra, isl. (Calabria)	31	H	b
Barra, isl. (Hebrides)	128	A	c
Barrow-in-Furness	162	C	c
Baselus (Besor) River	7	B	f
Bashkir, auton. rep.	168G	Q	d
Bashmakli	168L	E	f
Basileus, Stoa	23	D (3)	
Basilica Argentaria, bldg. in Rome	24	A	
Basilica Fulvia, bldg. in Rome	24	A	
Basilica Opimia, bldg. in Rome	24	A (6)	
Basilica Porcia, bldg. in Rome	24	A (5)	
Basing	60	I	d
Bassae	14	B	b
Batanga, Great-	174	E	a
Batavia	128C	N	f
Bateia	9	B	b
Batel	174	D	n
Bath, in England	60	Q	h
Battas, people	104C	J	g
Battle, abbey	74	N	i
Batum	139	F	c
Bauchi	174	E	c
Bauske	88	K	c
Bayazid	168J	R	j
Beaufort, near Stenay	104A	C	b
Beaumont, near Sedan	158	D	d
Beaumont-en-Argonne	104A	B	b
Beaune-la-Rolande	158	D	b
Bedford, in England	60	I	c
Bedmar	83	K	h
Bedr	53	F	d
Bedwin (Bedwyn)	74	L	h
Bedwyn (Bedwin), Great-, parl. bor.	163	M	f
Beer Elim	7	D	c
Behistun (Bagistana)	5	D	b
Beibahan	168K	F	c
Belbeis	150	B	

Belleau Wood . . . . 168 c   B   c
Bellefontaine . . . . 104 A   C   b
Bellenz (Bellinzona) 91   R   l
Benbecula, isl. 128   A   c
Bencoolen (Benkulen) . . 104 c   K   h
Bene Šov (Beneschau) . . 135   H   d
Benevento, march. 45   H d (Be)
Benfleet 60   J   d
Bengala, reg. . . . . . . 104 B   I   e
Benjamin Constant 181   U   h
Bennamarim 7   D   f
Bensington 60   D   d
Berar, prov., 18 cent. . . . 137   D   d
Beraun River 135   G   d
Berbice . . . . 128 B   ins. A
Bere, castle 74   J   g
Bere Alston. parl. bor. . . 163 J g(B.A.)
Bereku . . . . 128 c   ins. D
Berenice, in Egypt 4   F   d *
Berga, in Macedonia 11   E   b
Bergreichenstein 103   K   d
Bergulae 9   E   c
Berkeley, castle 74   K   h
Berlin, Treaty of . . . . 168 L   leg.
Bermudas, isl. . . . . . . 128 B   E   d
Bernau 103   K   b
Bernicia, dist. 60   C   b
Berwick 128   G   e
Berwick, cty. 128   F   e
Besace, La- . . . . . . 104 A B b(L.B.)
Besbicus, isl. 9   F   d
Besika Bay 9   A   b
Besika Tepe 9   A   b
Besztercze (Bistritz) . . . 159   M   e
Beszterczebanya (Neusohl) 159   J   d
Beth Anoth 7   C   e
Beth Arbeel 6   D   c
Beth Emek 6   C   c
Beth Gamul 7   D   f
Beth Garma 99   L   f
Beth Hagla 7   C   e
Beth Maacha 6   D   b
Bethramphtha 7   D   e
Beth Rehob 6   D   b
Beth Thappuah 7   C   e
Betifuli 27   H   f
Beuthen, castle, in Branden-
   burg 85   C   b
Beyshehr . . . . 168 J   B   b
Bezek 7   C   d
Bharatpur (Bhurtpore) . . 137   C   c
Biana . . . . 104 B   H   e
Bias River 14   B   c
Bidar . . . . 104 B   R   j
Biel 91   P   k
Bielaia River 99   O   c
Bielostok (Bialystok) . . . 168 G   J   e
Bielsko (Bielitz) 155   L   b
Bièvres . . . . 104 A C b(Bi.)
Bihach (Bihać) 87   J   f
Bilin 82   J   c
Bilin, castle 79   H   c
Bilma, reg. 174   E   c
Bima, isl. . . . . 128 c   ins. C
Bimlipatam . . . . 104 B   S   j
Birjan . . . . 168 K   H   d
Birkenhead 162   C   d
Birket el Karun (Qurun),
   lake 174   J   j
Birmingport 181   S   d
Birze 138   B   d
Bisanthe 9   E   c
Bishbalk (Urumtsi) . . . 104 B   I   c
Bissao 181   Z   f
Bistonis Lake 9   C   c
Bistriţa (Bistritz) 159   M   e
Bithynia and Pontus, Rom.
   prov. 20   D b (II)
Bitolj (Monastir) 165   B   a
Bit-Yakin, reg. . . , ... 5   D   b *
Blackpool 162   C   d
Black Sea Basin . . . . . 168 J   B   b

Blackwater River, in Ireland 74   B   b
Blagny . . . . 104 A   C   b
Blagoveschensk 171   N   c
Blair Atholl 128   E   c
Blancheville . . . . 104 A   C   c
Blatobulgium 51   O   g
Bleiberg 103   K   e
Blemmyes, people 4   F   d *
Bletchingley 74   M   h
Bne Barak 7   B   d
Boa Vista do Rio Branco . 181   U   h
Bocca do Acre 181   U   h
Bochum . . . . 168 E   E   b
Bodensee (Lake of Con-
   stance) 103   I   e
Bodmin 74   I   i
Boeotians, people 14   leg.
Boer Republics, the 175   N   m
Boghazkoi 4   B   c
Bogou, reg. 174   C   c
Bohun, dist. 74   J   h
Bokhara . . . . 104 B   G   d
Bolerium, prom. 38   A   b
Bolinas 180   O   d
Bolingbroke 74   M   f
Bolzano (Bozen) 103   J   e
Bomba 174   F   a
Bonin Islands 171   P   f
Borgholm 88   G   c
Borgo (di Valsugana) . . 168 H   ins.
Borissow 153   N   g
Bosham 60   I   d
Bosnia, reg. 56   F   d
Bosra . . . . 168 J   C   e
Botanical Garden, in Athens 23   D
Bothwell 128   E   e
Boulevard des Italiens, in
   Paris 149   L
Bourbon, isl. . . . . 128 c   K   g
Bourdon . . . . 104 A   C   c
Bouresches 184   ins.
Bourgneuf, Bay of 102   C   e
Bournemouth 162   E   g
Bovianum vetus 30   D   a
Bozanti . . . . 168 J   B   b
Brabant, duchy, 13 cent. . 104 A   B   a
Bradford, battle 60   C   d
Brahmanabad 53   I   d
Brancepeth 74   L   e
Branchidarum, Oppidum . . 19   K   c
Bränkyrka 88   G   b
Braşov, Brassó (Kronstadt) 159   M   f
Bratislava (Presburg) . . . 103   M   d
Bravonium 51   O   h
Brazhimov 71   P   b
Breadalbane, dist. 128   D   d
Brechin 128   F   d
Brecknock, dist. 60   C   c
Brecon 74   J   g
Bremenium 51   P   g
Bremetennacum 51   O   h
Bressanone (Brixen) . . . 168 H   ins.
Brest-Kujawsk 88   H   e
Brest-Litowsk 155   L   b
Breux . . . . 104 A C b(Br.)
Briantica, reg. 13   D   a
Bribiesca 83   K   g
Bridport, English bor. . . . 60   H   d
Briey . . . . 168 E   A   c
Brigantes, people in England 51   O   g
Brigobanne 39   J   j
British North Borneo, col. 171   L   h
Brixen (Bressanone) . . . 168 H   ins.
Brixillum 26   E   c
Brno (Brünn) 87   K   d
Brocavum 51   O   g
Brocomagus 39   I   i
Broumov (Braunau, in Bo-
   hemia) 135   I   c
Brunanburh 60   H   b
Bruneck (Brunico) . . . . 168 H   ins.
Bruntál = Freudental 72   D   b
Bruttii, people 29   E   e

Bruyères, near Épinal . . 104 A   D   c
Bryges, people 10   C   b
Brzesc (Brest Kujawsk) . . 135   J   b
Brześć (Brest-Litowsk) . . . 159   L   b
Buccaneers, headquaters of
   the . . . . 128 B   ins A
Buchan, dist. 128   F   c
Buckingham, English bor. . . 60   I   d
Budějovice (Budweis) . . . 87   J   d
Budorum, pen. 16   A   b
Budva (Budua), bp. 95   F   c
Buenos Aires 215   D   f
Buenos Aires, audiencia . 215   ins.
Buenos Aires, viceroyalty . 215   ins.
Builth 74   J   g
Bukharest, Treaty of . . . 168 L   leg.
Bulair (Playari) . . . . . . 168 L   D   c
Buleuterium, in Athens . . . 23   D   (8)
Buleuterium, in Olympia . . 9   H   f (1)
Bulgaria, Khanate of 55   I   e
Bulgaria, km. in 1929 . . 168 G   J-K   g
Bulgarians, people, about 500 52   I   d
Bulgarians, people in 1929 168 H   F-G   d
                                   G   c
Bulgars, people on the Upper
   Volga 59   N   b
Bulgurlu . . . . 168 J   B   b
Bunarbashi 9   B   b
Bunarbashi Brook, canal . . 9   A   b
Bungay, castle 74   O   g
Burdur . . . . 168 J   B   b
Burgas . . . . 168 L   F   e
Burgas, Gulf of . . . . . 168 L   F   e
Burgenland, prov. . . . . 168 D   D   d
Burhanpur . . . . 128 B   ins. B
Burma, reg. . . . . 104 c   J   e
Burtas, people 59   M   c
Buryato Mongolia, Autono-
   mous Socialist Soviet Re-
   public 171   L   c
Bury Saint Edmunds (Venta
   Icenorum) 51   Q   h
Bury Saint Edmunds, ab-
   bey 74   N   g
Bute, cty. 128   C   e
Butifilis . . . . 104 B   S   j
Butler, fam. 74   C   b
Butuntum 31   F   a
Bydgoszcz (Bromberg) . . . 87   K   b
Byzantium 9   F   c
Byzdry (Peisern) 79   J   b

Cabyle 39   N   l
Caconda . . . . 128 c   I   f
Caeni, people 9   D   c
Caerleon, castle 74   J   h
Caerphilly, castle 74   J   h
Caesao 26   A   c
Caesar, Statue of 24   B (23)
Café Corazza, in Paris . . 149   B
Cahul 139   C   f
Caicus River 9   E   e
Cailac 92   H   c
Cairo, Calif. of 66   H   g
                       67   K   h
Caistor (St. Edmund) 51   Q   h
Caithness, dist. 128   E   b
Calchedon 9   G   d
Caledonia, reg. . . . . . . 128 B   ins. A
Caledonia Bay . . . . 128 B ins. A (C. B.)
Caleta Buena 216   ins.
Caleta Colosa 216   ins.
Caleta Patillos 216   ins.
Caleti, people 38   C   c
Calgary (Fort La Jonquière) 190   C   a
Califate, The, emp. about 750 53
Calleva Atrebatum (Sil-
   chester) 51   P   i
Calliupolis 9   D   d
Calmar, Union of 77   leg.
Calpán, Ranchos de 106   S   j
Calven, Pass 91   S   l
Calydnae Islands 9   A   b

Camanu, reg. 5   C   b
Cambalec (Peking) . . . . 104 C   L   d
Cambambe, reg. . . . . . 128 C   I   f
Cambodia, reg. . . . . 104 C   K   f
Cambrai (Cambray) 62   B
Cambridge, in England . . 60   J   c
Camerons, fam. 128   C   d
Campbells, fam. 128   C   d
Campo Formio 153   G   c
Campo Militare, loc. in Rome 22   A
Camulodunum (Colchester). 51   Q   i
Canary Islands . . . . . . 128 B   H   d
Canbalec (Peking) . . . 103   L   d
Canberra 172   D   d
Candia . . . . 168 J   D   d
Cannes 157   B   d
Canovium 51   O   h
Cansay 92   M   d
Canterbury, in England (Du-
  rovernum 51   Q   i
Canterbury, bp. 60   E   d
Cantigny . . . . 168 C   B   c
Cantwara, people 51   S   k
Cape Breton Island 212   I   d
Cape Cod 181   U   c
Cape Three Points . . . . 128 C   ins. D
Caporetto . . . . 168 B   F   b
Cappadocia, Rom. prov.
  under Trajan . . . . . . 20 G c (IV)
Capuchins, The, ch. in Paris 149   B
Capuchins, The, mon. . . . 149   B
Caracarum (Karakorum). 104 C   K   c
Carbisdale 128   D   c
Carcer (Prison), in Rome . . 24   A   (4)
Cardia 9   D   d
Cardiff. castle 74   J   h
Cardigan, dist. 60   G   c
Carduniash, reg. 5   D   b *
Caresus River 9   E   d
Carians, people 8   Q   i
Carian Tributary . . . . . . 13 K f (IV)
Carlisle, in England 60   C   b
Carlow 74   C   c
Carmarthen, castle 74   I   h
Carmelites, The, mon. in
  Paris 149   B
Carmentine . . . . 128 C   ins. D
Carnarvon, castle 74   I   f
Carpinteria 216   G   i
Carrick, dist. 128   B   b
Carrion River 83   E   c
Carthaginian trade-routes. . 44   leg.
Cascaes 83   J   h
Casimirs (Kazimierz) . . . 103   O   c
Cassaba . . . . 168 J   A   b
Castellorizzo, isl. . . . . . 168 J   A   b
Castel Sant' Elmo 153   G   d
Castilla 216   ins.
Castlekevin 74   C   b
Castleroe 74   C   a
Castor and Pollux, Temple of 24   A   (21)
Catalauni 38   C   c
Cataonia, reg. 20   F   d
Cathedral (Metropolitan
  Church), in Athens 23   D
Catterick, mon. 60   D   b
Caucasian Gates, Pass . . . 18   F   b
Caucasian peoples . . . . 168 L   L   g
Cauvery River 137   C   f
Cavour, Piazza, loc. in Rome 22   A
Cavour, Ponte, loc. in Rome 22   A
Cavour, Via, street in Rome 22   A
Caystrus 20   D   c
Céa River 83   D   c
Cebrene 9   D   d
Cecryphalea, isl. 15   D   b
Cedrius, mt. 14   ins.
Celestins, The, mon. in Paris 149   B
Celje (Cilli) 159   H   e
Celtae, people 29   C   a
                       B   b
Celts, people, about 900 . . 57   B d/c
Cembalo 99   J   e

Cemetery, in Athens 23   D
Central Australia, state . . 172   C   c
Central Black Earth, eco-
  nomic reg. . . . . 168 F   leg
Central Industrial, eco-
  nomic reg. . . . . 168 F   leg.
Cephisia Street, in Athens . 23   D
Ceramus 13   K   f
Cerata, mt. 16   A   a
Ceraunii Mountains, in Epi-
  rus 17   A   a
Ceraunii Mountains, in Italy 27   H   e
Ceres, Temple of, in Athens 23   D
Ceressus 11   E   d
Ceriadac, deme 23   D
Cernauţi (Czernowitz . . 168 G   D   k
Česká Skalice (Skalitz) . . 159   I   c
České Budějovice (Bud-.
  weis) 103   L   c
Cetinje 165   A   b
Ceuta 174   P   n
Chagatai, Khanate of . . . 92   leg.
Chahar, reg. 171   M   d
Chalcedon 9   G   d
Chalco, lake 106   D   d
Chaldea, in the Middle Ages 99   M   g
Chaldeans, people . . . . 168 L   L   h
Chalish (Karashar . . . . 104 C   I   c
Chalti . . . . 168 J   A   b
Chalybon 20   G   d
Chamonix 91   O   m
Champagne, cty., 13 cent. 104 A   A   c
Champe, reg. . . . . . . 104 C   K   f
Champigny 158   B   d
Chanak Kale . . . . . . 168 L   D   c
Chanchalacas, R. 106   D   a
Chanderi . . . . 104 B   H   e
Changanor . . . . 104 C   L   c
Changchun 179   D   c
Chantraines . . . . 104 A   C   c
Chaones (Chaoni), people . 8   M   g
Chapultepec 106   A   a
Charadra River 16   B   a
Charax(-Spasinu) 44   F   c
Charikar . . . . 104 B   G   d
Charkov (Kharkov) . . . 139   E   e
Charleville (Ardennes) . 168 C   C   c
Charmouth 60   H   d
Charny . . . . 104 A   C   b
Charshembe . . . . 168 J   B   a
Chatalja . . . . 168 L   G   f
Châtenois . . . . 104 A   C   c
Chatham 162   G   f
Chatyn Deirmeni 9   A   b
Chaul . . . . 104 B   R   i
Chaumont - devant - Dam-
  villers . . . . 104 A   C   b
Cheb (Eger) 87   I   c
Cheboksara . . . . 168 G   O   d
Chebreiss 150   B   a
Chechen, auton. area 168 G   O g (2), leg.
Chechen, isl. . . . . . . 168 G   O   g
Chelm 159   L   c
Chełmno (Kulm) 135   J   b
Chełmno (Kulm), bp. . . . 95   F   a
Chełmża (Kulmsee), seat of
  bishopric 95   F   a
Chelsea 60   D   d
Chemin des Dames . . . 168 C   B   c
Chemmis 4   F   d
Cheng-tu-fu . . . . . . 104 C   K   d
Chen-si . . . . 104 C   J   c
Chequamegon, Fort . . . 191   G   e
Cheragan Palace 93   G   e
Cherekli . . . . 168 J   B   a
Cherkasy 139   D   f
Chernigov 71   M   c
Chernoi-Yar 139   G   f
Cherso, isl. 161   J   e
Chersonesus, in Crete . . . 14   ins.
Chertsey, mon 60   D   d
Chesme 165   E   d
Chester, battle 60   C   c

Chester, castle 60   H   c
Chester, County Palatine of 74   K   f
Chester, Palatine Earldom of 65   E   d
Chichester, Engl. bor. . . . 60   I   d
Chico Viejo 106   D   a
Chigrin 139   D   f
Chilen-fu . . . . 104 C   C   d
Chillaw . . . . 104 B   R   k
Chilternsaete, people . . . 60   D   d
Chimkent 170   H   d
Chin, Sea of . . . . . . 104 C   M   e
China, Republic of . . . . 171 J   M   e
Chintabor (Goa) . . . . . 104 B   R   j
Chiny . . . . 104 A   C   b
Chiny, cty. . . . . 104 A   C   b
Chipangu, emp. (Japan) . 104 C   O   d
Chippenham 60   H   d
Chirbury 60   H   c
Chisholms, fam. 128   C   c
Chisinau (Kishinev) . . . 168 G   K   f
Chitor 92   H   e
Chivril . . . . 168 J   A   b
Chocim 139   C   f
Chojnice (Konitz) 135   I   b
Chomutov (Komotau) . . . 87   I   c
Chorillos 216   F   g
Chorlu . . . . 168 L   F   f
Chorum . . . . 168 J   B   a
Choshi 179   E   d
Christchurch, parl. bor. . . 163 M g (Chr.)
Christiania (Akershuus) . . 88   D   b
Christiansborg . . . . . . 128 C   ins. D
Chrysopolis 9   G   c
Chuguiev 139   E   f
Chullu 44   B   c
Churche, people 92   M   c
Chu River . . . . 104 B   G   c
Chuvash, auton. rep. . . 168 G   O   d
Ciando (Shangtu) . . . . 104 C   L   c
Cibalae 39   F   c
Cicones, people 9   C   c
Cieszyn (Teschen) . . . 159   J   c
Cilicia, Rom. prov. under
  Trajan . . . . 20 F d (VI)
Cilician and Syrian Gates,
  pass 20   G   d
Cilician Gates, pass . . . 20   F   d
Cilli, County of 87   J   c
Cimbri, people 38   D   a
Cimmerians, people . . . 5   C   a
Cimolus 15   E   c
Circassia, reg. 164   F   b
Cius 9   G   d
Cius, Bay of 9   F   d
Clackmannan, cty. 128   E   d
Clanoventa 51   O   g
Clare, dist. in Wales . . . 74   J   h
Clausentum (Southampton). 51   P   i
Claverhouse 128   E   d
Cleon, Wall of, in Athens . 23   D
Cleveland, dist. in England 60   I   b
Cleven (Chiavenna) 91   R   l
Clitheroe 74   I   e
Clonmel 74   C   b
Cloppenburg 78   F   b
Cluj (Klausenburg) 159   L   d
Clun, castle 74   K   g
Cluse, La 158   D   e
Clydesdale, dist. 128   D   e
Clysma 4   ins. *
Coatlichán 106   B   a
Cobh (Queenstown) . . . 168 F   D   e
Coburg (Koburg) 79   D   e
Coccium 51   O   h
Cockermouth, castle 74   J   e
Coelaletae, people 9   C   c
Coelesyria, reg. 20   G   f
Coilon (Quilon) . . . . . 104 B   H   g
Colchester (Camulodunum) 51   Q   h
Colchester, abbey 51   N   b
Coleroon River 137   D   f
Colisée, The, bldg. in Paris 149   B
Coll, isl. 128   B   d

Collaguasi . . . . 216 ins.
Collège des Quatre Nations, bldg. in Paris . . . 149 B
Collège Mazarin, bldg. in Paris . . . . 149 B
Collioure . . . . 83 L g
Collytus, deme . . . . 23 D
Colombey . . . . 158 D d
Colonae . . . . 9 D e
Colonia do Sacramento . 128 B F f
Colonia Falisca . . . . . . 27 G e
Colonus Agoraeus, deme . . 23 D
Colonus Hippius, deme . . . 23 D
Cclumbum . . . . 104 B R k
Comedae, people . . . . . 19 L c
Commenda . . . . 128 C ins. D
Compitum of Acilius . . . 24 B
Compludo . . . . 83 K g
Compostela, Santiago de . . 82 A a
Compostela, Santiago de, abp. 94 A c
Conchi . . . . 216 ins.
Conchi, Land of . . . 92 H b
Concord, Temple of . . . 24 A (7)
Conde, Fort (Mobile) . . . 191 H e
Connaught, prov. . . . . 74 B b
Consabura . . . . 38 B e
Constanța (Kustenje) . . . 165 F a
Constantine, Statue of . . . 24 B (15)
Constantinople, Treaty of 168 L leg.
Conway . . . . 74 J f
Conway River . . . . 60 G c
Cophas . . . . 19 J e
Coptos . . . . 1 C d
Corameran River . . . . 104 C K c
Corbilo (Nantes) . . . . . 44 A b
Corbridge . . . . 60 H b
Cordeliers, The, mon. in Paris . . . . 149 B
Cordova, in Alaska . . . . 180 M a
Coreae . . . . 7 C d
Cork . . . . 74 B c
Coron (Koroni) . . . . . . 89 H g
Coronel . . . . 168 A F f
Corpilii, people . . . . 9 C c
Corrib, Lough, lake . . . . 127 H h
Corso d'Italia, street in Rome 22 A
Cortina (d'Ampezzo) . . . . 168 H ins.
Cortona, in Etruria . . . . 27 G d
Cortona, in Spain . . . . . 38 F d
Cosmin . . . . 104 C J f
Côte Lorraine . . . . . 168 C C c
Courland, bp. . . . . . . 88 J c
Courons, people . . . . . . 57 H b
Cours de la reine, in Paris 149 B
Coventry, abbey . . . . . 74 L g
Coyoacán . . . . 106 A a
Cranganur (Cranganore) . 137 C f
Cravant . . . . 86 D e
Crediton . . . . 60 C d
Crediton, bp. . . . . . . 97 N k
Cricklade, bor. . . . . . 60 H d
Crimea, auton. rep. . . . 168 G L f
Croats, people in 1929 . 168 H E c
Cromarty . . . . 128 D c
Cromarty, cty. . . . . 128 C b
Cronos Hill . . . . 9 H f
Crowland, mon. . . . . 60 I c
Cuantitlán . . . . 106 A a
Cuiavia (Kujavia), dist. . . . 79 K b
Culloden Moor . . . . . 128 C c
Cumania, reg. . . . . . . 99 J d
Cumans, people, in Turkestan 53 H b
Cumberland, dist. in England 60 H b
Cumuhi (Cummuhi), reg. . . . 5 C b
Cumukh . . . . 99 M e
Cunetio . . . . 51 P i
Cunningham, dist. . . . . . 128 D c
Cunus aureus . . . . . . 26 D a
Cupar . . . . 128 E d
Curia Julia . . . . 24 B
Cusus River, near Brigetio. 39 C c
Cusus River, near Lauriacum 39 E c
Cuyavia, reg. . . . . 87 L b

Cybistra . . . . 20 F d
Cydamus . . . . 44 C c
Cynia, lake . . . . 10 C d
Cynkali . . . . 104 B R k
Cypsela . . . . 9 D d
Cyrenaica, dist. . . . . . . 174 F a
Cyzicus . . . . 9 E d
Czechoslovakia, rep. . . . . 168 G H/J f
Częstochowa . . . . 135 J c

Dabrath . . . . 6 C c
Dagasira . . . . 19 I e
Daghestan, auton. rep. . 168 G O g
Dahshur, Pyramids of . . . . 4 ins. *
Daibul . . . . 104 B G e
Dai'am . . . . 99 N f
Dalarne (Dalecarlia), dist. . 88 F a
Dalriada, dist. . . . . . 60 F b
Dalwhinnie . . . . 128 D d
Damascus, Kingdom of . . . 5 C b
Damghan . . . . 104 B F d
Damme, near Bruges . . . . 102 F c
Danelagh (Danelaw), The . 60 leg.
Danish Mercia . . . . . . 60 I c
Dannaba . . . . 7 D f
Dannewerk, wall . . . . . 55 Q i
Darab . . . . 168 K F d
Dardania, reg. . . . . . . 17 B a
Dardanus . . . . 9 D d
Darien Colony . . . . . 128 B ins. A
Dascylium . . . . 9 F d
Daulatabad . . . . 104 B R j
Dauphin, Fort . . . . . . 190 E a
Dawston (Degsastan) . . . . 60 C b
Deal . . . . 154 A c
Debir . . . . 7 B f
Dęblin (Ivangorod) . . . . . 159 K c
Debreczén . . . . 159 K e
Decapolis, dist. . . . . . . 7 leg.
Děčín (Tetschen) . . . . . 135 H c
De Clare, earldom . . . . 70 E c (De C.)
De Courcy, earldom . . . 70 E c (De Co.)
Deddington, castle . . . . 74 L h
Dedeagach . . . . 164 D b
Deer . . . . 128 F c
Deerhurst . . . . 60 H d
Dee River, in Wales . . . . 60 C c
Dee River, in Kirkcudbright 128 D f
Dee River, in Aberdeen . 128 F c
Degsastan (Dawston) . . . . 60 C b
Deheubarth, dist. . . . . . . 60 G c
Dei Consentes Portico of the 24 B (7)
Deira, dist. . . . . 60 D b
Deir-ez-Zor . . . . 168 J D b
Dej (Dees) . . . . . . 159 L e
De Lacy, earldom . . . . . 70 E c (De L.)
Delcus . . . . 9 F c
Delhi, Empire of the Sultans of . . . . 104 B H e
Deligun Buldagha . . . . . 92 L b
Delia, reg. . . . . 4 F c (I)
Demonnesi Islands . . . 9 F d
Demarchia, bldg. in Athens 23 D
Denbigh, castle . . . . . . 74 J f
Denisli . . . . 168 J A b
Deogir, reg. . . . . . . 104 B R i
Deorham (Dyrham) . . . . 60 C c
Derat . . . . 168 J C c
Derbent . . . . 139 G g
Derby, danish borough . 60 I c
Derby, cty. . . . . . . 74 L f
Derna . . . . 174 F a
Deshima, isl. . . . . . 128 C O d
Desmond, dist. . . . . . . 74 B c
Deutschendorf . . . . . . 80 G g
Develtum . . . . 39 N l
Deveron River . . . . . 128 F c
Devon, dist. . . . . . . 60 C d
De Vries, route of . . . . 128 C P c
Dhafar . . . . 104 B F f
Dhar . . . . 104 B R i
Dhibat al Mahal, isl. . . 104 B H g

Diagorgan . . . . 99 M f
Diala River . . . . . . 168 K E c
Didyma . . . . 13 E c
Dieppe, near Verdun . . . 104 A C b
Dieuze . . . . 102 H d
Dindymus, mt. near Cyzicus 9 E d
Dinefwr . . . . 60 G d
Dinhaba . . . . 7 D f
Diomea, deme . . . . . . 23 D
Dionysium, Lenaeum and, in Athens . . . . 23 D (12)
Dirk Hartog, isl. . . . . 128 C N g
Disna . . . . 88 M d
Disna River . . . . . . 88 L d
Dium, prom. . . . . . . 14 ins.
Dividing Range, Great . . 172 D c
Divonum . . . . 38 C d
Divrik (Divirigi) . . . . . 99 K f
Divus Julius, Temple of . 24 B (17)
Divus Romulus, Temple of 24 B (21)
Dixcove . . . . 128 C ins. D
Dixmude . . . . 168 C B b
Dnieper River . . . . . 139 D f
Doblen . . . . 88 J c
Doboj . . . . 87 L f
Dobruja, reg. . . . . . . 89 C b
Dodecanesia, isl. . . . . 165 E e
Dodekaschoenos, reg . . . . 4 F d (IV)
Dofar . . . . 104 B F f
Dogger Bank . . . . . . 168 A J b (II leg.)
Doliones, people . . . . . 9 E d
Doljani (Dolyani), bp . . . 95 F c
Dolonci, people . . . . . 9 D d
Domašov (Domstadtl) . . . 135 I d
Domeyko . . . . 216 ins.
Dominion of the Hammadites 66 G g
Dominion of the Karakhitai 92 H c
Dominions of Timur . . . 92 leg.
Dompaire . . . . 104 A D c
Dondra Head . . . . . . 137 D g
Don River, Scotland . . . 128 F c
Doorn . . . . 168 D B c
Doornik (Tournai) . . . . 86 D c
Dorchester . . . . 74 K i
Dore . . . . 60 I c
Dorestad . . . . 45 F b
Doria, Piazza, loc. in Rome 22 A
Dorians, people . . . . . 14 leg.
Doriscus . . . . 9 D d
Dornoch . . . . 128 E c
Dorpat, bp. . . . . . . 88 L b
Dorset, cty. . . . . . . 74 K i
Dosab . . . . 168 K H f
Douaumont . . . . . . 168 C C c
Douglas, in Scotland . . . 128 E e
Dover . . . . 60 J d
Downpatrick . . . . . . 74 D a
Downton . . . . 74 L h
Drač = Durazzo
Drepanum, in Asia Minor . 9 G d
Drewenz River . . . . . 135 J b
Dregoviches, people . . . 57 H-I c
Drevlians, people . . . . 57 I c
Drissa River . . . . . . 88 M d
Drogheda . . . . 74 C b
Droi, people . . . . . 17 C a
Droitwich . . . . 74 K g
Drumclog . . . . 128 D e
Dubica (Dubitza) . . . . 164 B b
Dublin . . . . 60 F c
Dubrovnik (Ragusa) . . . . 89 A b
Dubrovnik (Ragusa), abp. . 95 F c
Dukha, people . . . . . 5 C b *
Dulyebs, people . . . . . 57 H c
Dumbarton . . . . . . 128 D e
Dumbarton, cty. . . . . 128 D e
Dumbrek, R. . . . . . 9 B b
Dumfries . . . . 128 E e
Dumfries, cty. . . . . . 128 E e
Dun (-sur-Meuse . . . 104 A C b
Dunajec River . . . . . 135 K d
Dunbar . . . . 128 F e
Dunblane . . . . 128 D d

Dunblane, bp.	97	J	c
Dundalk	74	C	b
Dundee	128	F	d
Dundram, castle	74	C	a
Dunfermline	128	E	d
Dungarvan	74	C	b
Dunkeld	128	E	d
Dunnottar Castle	128	F	d
Dunwich	74	O	g
Dunwich, bp.	60	E	c
Duos Lucos, Inter, loc. in Rome	24	A	
Duressi = Durazzo			
Durham, Palatinate of	74	L	e
Düren	168 g	B	b
Dürnstein	155	H	d
Durobrivae, near Lindum	51	P	h
Durobrivae, near Londinium	51	Q	i
Durocobrivae	51	P	i
Dur-Samand, reg.	104 B	R	j
Dutch, people in 1929	168 H	C	b
Dutch East Indies, col.	179	B/E	
Duzje	168 J	B	a
Dvina, Gulf of	167 G	M	b
Dvina River	167	N	c
Dwara-Samudra	104 B	R	j
Dyfed, dist.	60	B	d
Dyrham (Deorham)	60	C	d
Earn River	128	D	d
East Africa, British = Kenya, col. and pro.	175	G	d
East Africa, German, Brit. Mand.	175	G	e
East Africa, Portuguese = Mozambique	175	G	g
East Anglia, km.	60	J	c
Eastbourne	162	G	g
East Götland, dist.	88	F	b
East-Kirghiz, economic reg.	170	leg.	
East March, dist.	128	F	e
East Scheldt, R.	168 C	B	b
East Sea	99	G	b
Ebora	38	A	e
Echmiadzin	139	F	g
Echo Hall, in Olympia	9	H	f
École Militaire, in Paris	149	B	
Écuries, in Paris = 1	149	B	
Eddisbury	60	H	c
Edelsland, reg.	128 C	N	g
Edgcott	84	C	c
Edinburgh	128	E	e
Edinburgh, cty.	128	E	e
Edington	60	H	d
Edirne (Adrianople)	93	C	b
Eendrachtsland, reg.	128 C	N	g
Eger (Erlau)	79	L	e
Eger (Erlau), bp.	95	G	b
Egesta	30	B	e
Eggenburg	87	J	d
Egherdir	168 J	B	b
Eglaim	7	D	f
Egnatian Way	10	A	a
		D	b
Egremont, castle	74	J	e
Egrigaia	104 C	K	d
Egyptian Empire	4		
Eichstätt	79	G	d
Eichstätt, bp.	79	G	d
Eiderstedt, reg.	86	G	a
Eifel, mts.	168 C	D	b
Eigg, isl.	128	B	d
Eisenerz	103	L	e
Ekhmim	4	F	d *
Elaeus, in Thrace	9	D	d
El-Arish, in Egypt	67	M	g
El-Arish, in Morocco	174	O	n
Elbasan	165	A	c
El Caney	213	E	b
	(E. C.)		
Elde River	134	B	b
Eleans, people	8	N	i *
Eleutherius, Port of	93	G	e

Elfsborg	88	E	c
El Gezira, reg.	174	G	c
Elgin	128	E	c
Elgin and Forres, cty.	128	E	c
El Hasa, reg.	104 B	E	e
Elizabetpol	139	G	g
El-Jauf	168 J	C	c
El Kab	1	C	e
El Katif	104 B	E	e
El Katr, reg.	168 K	F	d
Ellandun	60	I	d
Elmedsaete, people	60	D	c
Elmham	60	E	c
Elmina (São Jorge da Mina)	128 B	H	e
Elsinore (Helsingör)	103	K	a
El Toco	216	ins.	
Ely, mon., in England	60	E	c
Ely (Hili), in India	104 B	R	j
Ely, Isle of, dist.	74	N	g
El Yemamah	104 B	E	e
Embabeh	150	B	a
Emmerich	168 g	E	c
Empinghan	74	M	g
Empire of the Great Khan	92	leg.	
Empire of the Sultans of Delhi	104 B	H	e
Emporium, loc. in Piraeus	16	D	c
Enaghdun, bp.	74	B	b
English Marches, dis	74	K	d
English Pale, The, dist.	74	C	b
Ennakrounos, in Athens	23	D (11)	
Enneapylon (Pelasgikon) in Athens	23	C	
Entebbe	174	G	d
Enzeli	168 G	O	h
Eordaioi, people	10	B	a
Epamanduodurum	39	I	j
Ephron (Ephrem)	7	C	e
Epirots, people	8	N	h
Eppan	72	C	b
Equins	104 B	H	c
Erbil (Arbil)	99	M	f
Ercavica	38	B	d
Eregli (in Cilicia)	168 J	B	b
Eregli (Heraclea)	168 J	B	a
Eressus (Eresus)	9	C	c
Ergene, riv.	168 L	F	c
Ergines River	9	D	c
Erginul, Erginur	104 C	K	d
Eridanus, River, in Athens	23	D	
Erivan	139	F	g
Erne, Lough-, lake	127	J	g
Er Riad	104 B	E	e
Ersekujvar (Neuhäusel)	135	J	e
Esbus	7	D	e
Esdrelon	6	C	c
Esebon	7	D	e
Eskdale, dist.	128	E	e
Esla River	83	D	c
Essek (Osjek)	77	H	c
Essequibo	128 B	ins. A	
Esthaul	7	C	e
Estonia, rep.	168 G	J/K	d
Estrella Mountains	82	A	b
Esztergóm (Gran)	59	H	d
Esztergóm (Gran), abp.	95	F	b
Etaples	86	C	c
Etea	14	ins.	
Ether (Jattir)	7	C	f
Ethiopia (Abyssinia), reg.	174	G	d
Etropolje	165	C	b
Etrusci, people	29	B	c
Etsch River = Adige River	90	C	b
Eudoses, people	38	D	a
Euesperides = Hesperis	44	D	a
Eule, in Bohemia	103	L	d
Eupen	168 g	A	b
Eureka	180	O	c
Euripides Street, in Athens	23	D	
Europus, in Syria	20	G	d
Evangelismos, bldg. in Athens	23	D	
Ewst River	88	L	c
Eynsham	60	D	d

Eyoub (Ayyub), mosque	93	G	e
Eyoub (Ayyub), quarter	93	G	e
Fairbanks	180	M	a
Fair Island	128	ins.	
Faith, Temple of	24	A (1)	
Faknur	104 B	R	j
Falkenstein, castle, in Swabia	62	E	d
Falkenstein, castle, on the Selke R.	85	F	e
Falkirk	128	E	e
Fansur	104 C	J	g
Fao	168 K	B	e
Farah	104 B	G	d
Far-Eastern, economic reg.	170	leg.	
Far Eastern Region	171	N Q	c
Far Eastern Republic	171	O P	c
Farquharsons, fam.	128	E	d
Fars, reg.	104 B	E	e
Farther India, reg.	104 C	J	e
Faucigny, reg.	91	O	m
Faucilles, Monts	168 C	C	c
Faustina, Temple of Antoninus and	24	B (22)	
Federal Democratic Republic Transcaucasia 1917—1918	168 G	N/O	g
Federal Territory = F. T.	172	D	d
Federated Malay States = F. M. S.	171	L	h
Fehértemplon (Weisskirchen)	159	K	f
Fehmarn, isl.	134	F	a
Felden	79	H	d
Fellin	68	K	b
Ferentis	27	G	e
Ferghana, reg.	104 B	H	c
Ferlech	104 C	J	g
Fern Pass	87	H	e
Ferrières, near Joinville	104 A	C	c
Ferrol	83	J	g
Feronian Grove	35	ins. B	
Ferrybridge	74	L	f
Fetlar, isl.	128	ins.	
Fez, reg., 14 cent.	77	C	f
Fidei Faith), Temple	24	A (1)	
Findhorn River	128	E	c
Fines, Ad, near Volaterrae	26	E	d
Finland, rep.	168 G	K	b/c
Finmark, reg.	138	B	b
Finns proper, people	57	H-I	a
Firando (Hirado), isl.	128 C	O	d
Firebur	104 B	G	d
Firth of Clyde	128	C	e
Firth of Forth	128	F	d
Firth of Lorne	128	C	d
Fismes	168 C	B	c
Fitzgerald, fam.	74	B	b
Flandrina	104 B	R	j
Flaviae, Aquae	38	A	d
Flemings, people in 1929	168 H	B	b
Flevum	38	C	b
Flodden Field	128	F	e
Florent	104 A	B	b
Flushing	168 C	B	b
Foča	87	L	g
Focsani (Fokshani)	153	J	c
Fojnica	103	M	g
Fons, Gate of, in Rome	24	A	
Fonseca Bay	213	D	c
Fontanafredda	150	G	c
Forbes, fam.	128	F	c
Forfar, cty.	128	F	c
Formartin, dist.	128	F	c
Fornham	65	G	d
Fort Albany	128 B	D	c
Fort Amsterdam	128 B	C	c
Fort Bliss	180	Q	d
Fort Chequamegon	191	G	b
Fort Condé (Mobile)	191	H	e
Fort Dauphin, in Canada	190	E	a
Fort Dauphin, in Madagascar	128 C	K	g

Fort de la Reine ..... 190 F a
Fort des Abitibis ..... 191 J b
Fort des Miamis ...... 191 H c
Fort Edward .... 191 K c
Fort Garry (Winnipeg) .. 212 F d
Fort Gibbon .... 180 L a
Fort Hollandia .... 136 I d
Forth River .... 128 D d
Fort James, in Gambia . 128 B H e
Fort Jemseg .... 191 L b
Fort La Tourette ..... 191 H a
Fort Meductic .... 191 L b
Fort Miami .... 191 H c
Fort Michipicoten .... 191 H b
Fort Nachouac .... 191 L b
Fort Perrot .... 191 G c
Fort Pickawillany .... 191 I c
Fort Radisson .... 191 G b
Fortrose, bp. .... 97 I b
Fort Rouge .... 190 F b
Fort Rupert .... 128 B E c
Fort Saint Antoine ... 191 G c
Fort Saint Croix .... 191 G b
Fort Saint Jean ...... 191 L b
Fort Saint Joseph, L. Huron 191 I c
Fort Saint Louis, Alabama R. ..... 191 H e
Fort Saint Nicholas .... 191 G c
Fort Saint Pierre, in Mississippi ..... 191 G e
Fort Sauvage .... 191 I b
Fort Sill .... 180 R d
Fort Tadoussac ...... 191 K b
Fort Trempealeau .... 191 G c
Fortune, Temple of ... 24 A
Fort Victoria .... 137 B e
Fort York (Bencoolen) . 128 C ins. C
Fort Zelandia ...... 128 C O d
Forum Fulvii ...... 26 C b
Forum Piscarium (Fish-market), in Rome .. 24 A
Foula, isl. .... 128 ins.
Fountain Gate, in Rome .. 24 A
Fraserburgh .... 128 G c
Frazers, fam. .... 128 D c
Fredrikshamn .... 138 C c
Freistadt, in Austria .. 79 I d
Freiwaldau (Frývaldov) .. 103 M c
French River .... 191 I b
Freudental (Bruntál) .. 72 D b
Friesians, people in 1929 168 H C b
Friuli (Furlans), people in 1929 ..... 168 H D c
Frouard .... 104 A D c
Frunse .... 170 I d
Fugui (Fu-chau) ..... 104 C L e
Fulford .... 65 F d
Fulginiae (Foligno) ... 27 G e
Fulham .... 60 I d
Fulvian Way .... 26 C c
Fünen (Fyen or Fyn), isl. 88 D d
Furness, dist. ...... 60 H b
Fustat .... 53 F c
Fuzo (Fu-chau) ..... 104 C L e
Fyn (Fünen), isl. .... 88 D d
Fyvie .... 128 F c

Gadara, in Gilead ..... 7 D d
Gadara, in Jair ...... 6 D c
Gaina, reg. .... 51 R k
Galatia, Rom. prov. under Trajan ..... 20 E c (III)
Galava .... 51 O g
Galich .... 138 F d
Galinds, people ..... 57 H c
Galli, people ...... 29 A b
Gallinazos .... 29 ins.
Gallipoli, pen. ..... 168 L D c
Galloway, dist. ..... 60 G b
Galway .... 74 B b
Gambia, reg. .... 128 B H e
Gambrium .... 9 E e
Gambron .... 128 C K d

Gandia .... 88 K h
Ganfu .... 104 C M d
Ganja (Gandja) ..... 139 G g
Ganus .... 9 E d
Garamantes, people ... 34 G h
Garanbi .... 179 D e
Garde Meuble, bldg. in Paris 149 B
Garde Meuble, bldg. in Versailles ..... 149 A
Gardinas (Grodno) .... 168 G J e
Gargamish .... 5 C b *
Gargara .... 9 D e
Gariannonum .... 51 Q h
Garibaldi, Monument of, in Rome ..... 22 A
Garioch, dist. ...... 128 F c
Garma, Beth ...... 99 L f
Garry, Fort (Winnipeg) .. 212 F d
Gata Mountains ..... 82 A a
Gath Hepher ...... 6 C c
Gaulanitis, reg. ..... 6 D c
Gävle (Gefle) ...... 88 G a
Gaza, in Judaea ..... 7 A e
Gaza, in Sogdiana ... 19 K b
Gebalene .... 7 C g
Gebel Silsileh ...... 4 F d *
Gedor, in Gilead .... 7 D d
Gedor, in Jair ..... 6 D c
Gelsenkirchen ...... 168 E B b
Gemauerthof ...... 138 B d
Gembes .... 104 A C a
Gemina, Legio VII ... 38 A d
Gemona .... 154 G e
Genevois, reg. ..... 91 O m
Georgia, auton. rep. ... 168 G N g
Gerbéviller .... 104 A D c
Gerenia (Pylus) .... 14 B c
Gerlos Pass .... 87 H e
German East Africa, Late, Brit. Mand. ..... 175 G e
Germania Inferior .... 39 H h
Germania Magna, reg. .. 38 D b
Germania Superior .... 39 H j
German Ocean ...... 98 D b
German Republic on Volga ..... 168 G O e
German South-West Africa, Late ..... 175 E g
Germany, rep. ...... 166 H e
Germe .... 9 D e
Gérouville .... 104 A C b
Gersif .... 174 Q n
Gerstungen .... 62 E c
Gesoriacum (Boulogne) ... 38 C b
Gex .... 86 F e
Ghat .... 174 E b
Ghel (Ghelan), Sea of .. 99 M-N e
Gheluvelt .... 168 C B b
Gheria .... 137 B e
Gherla (Szamos-Ujvar) .. 159 L e
Ghiseh (Ghizeh) .... 150 B a
Giants, Stoa of the, in Athens 23 D (2)
Gibeah of Benjamin ... 7 C e
Gibeah of Saul ..... 7 C e
Gilbert, route of .... 108 L c
Gilead .... 7 D d
Gilead, reg. .... 7 D d
Gilgal, near Jericho .. 7 C e
Gilgal, near Joppa .... 7 B c
Gilgal, near Ramathaim .. 7 C d
Gilgal, near Shechem .. 7 C c
Gilgenburg .... 87 M b'
Gilyan, reg. .... 139 G h
Gilyan, Sea of ..... 99 N e
Gimso .... 7 B e
Ginaea .... 7 C c
Girba, isl. .... 44 C a
Giurgiu (Giurgevo) ... 165 D a
Giza (Ghizeh) ..... 174 J j
Gjatsk .... 153 O f
Glamorgan, dist. .... 60 G d
Glasgow .... 128 D e
Glastonbury, ab. .... 74 K h

Glastonbury, mon. ..... 60 H d
Glencoe, in Scotland ... 128 C c
Glengarry .... 128 C c
Glenluce .... 128 D f
Glen Shiel .... 128 C c
Gloucester, in England .. 60 H d
Gloucester, abbey ..... 74 K h
Gloucester, cty. ..... 74 K h
Glubokoie .... 153 N f
Glurns .... 91 S l
Gmünd, in Carinthia .. 87 I e
Gnesen (Gniezno) .... 63 I b
Gnesen (Gniezno), abp. .. 95 F a
Gobelins, The, bldg. in Paris 149 B
Göding (Hodonin) .... 87 K d
Godmanham .... 60 D h
Gokcha, lake ...... 168 K E a
Goldap .... 155 L a
Golden Mile-stone, in Rome 24 B (9)
Goldingen .... 88 J c
Gollub .... 87 L b
Golzow .... 85 C b
Gomer (Cimmerians), people 5 C a *
Gomera, bay ...... 174 P n
Gomera, (Peñon de Velez) 136 I c (P.)
Goplo, lake .... 88 E e
Gorales, people in 1929 . 168 H E c
Gordons, fam. ...... 128 D e
Goree, isl. .... 128 B H e
Gorizia (Görz) ..... 103 K f
Gormaz, San Estéban de . 82 B a
Gortscha (Koritza) .... 165 B c
Gortyn .... 14 ins.
Gorze .... 78 E d
Göta River .... 88 E b
Göteborg (Gothenburg) .. 88 E c
Gothia (Crimea) .... 99 J d
Gotland, isl. ..... 88 H c
Götland, East, dist. .. 88 F b
Götland, West, dist. ... 88 E b
Goulfeï .... 174 E c
Gower, dist. .... 60 G d
Gradisca .... 154 G f
Graecostasis, in Rome .. 24 B (9)
Gran (Esztergom) .... 79 K e
Grand Arsenal, bldg. in Paris ..... 149 B
Grand-Failly ...... 104 A C b
Grand Morin, R. .... 168 C B c
Grandpré, in France ... 104 A B b
Grandpré, cty. ..... 104 A B b
Granicus River ..... 9 E d
Grants, fam. ...... 128 E c
Grappa, Monte ..... 168 B F b
Graslitz .... 79 H c
Graupen .... 79 H c
Gravelotte .... 158 C d
Grave of Adam, mt. .. 104 B I g
Grave of Saint Thomas . 104 B I f
Gray League ...... 91 R l
Great Batanga ..... 174 E b
Great Bedwin, parl. bor. . 163 M f
Great Belchen, mt. .. 168 C D c
Great Canal, in China .. 104 C L d
Great Desert ...... 104 C K c
Great Dividing Range ... 172 D c
Greater (Black) Sea ... 99 J e
Greater Zap River ... 168 J D e
Great Gymnasium, in Olympia 9 H f
Great Hungary, reg. ... 92 E b
Great Khan, Empire of the 92 leg.
Great Salt Desert ... 168 K F c
Great Wall, in China .. 104 C K d
Greece, rep. ...... 168 G J h
Greek Orthodox ..... 168 L N g leg.
Greek trade-routes .... 44 leg.
Greencastle, in Ireland .. 74 D a
Greencastle, in Pa. .... 208 ins.
Greenland, reg. .... 128 B F
Greenwich, East, in Rhode Island ..... 18e ins. A
Grenada, isl. ...... 136 ins. A
Grimsby .... 74 M f

Grimsel Pass	91	Q	l
Grójec	135	K	c
Grosser Belchen, mt.	168c	D	c
Gross Friedrichsburg	128B	H	e
Grozka (Grocka)	139	B	g
Grozny	168K	E	a
Grudziądz (Graudenz)	135	J	b
Grünberg, castle in Bohemia	87	I	d
Guadalaviar River	82	B	a
Guadalcanal	83	J	h
Guadarrama Mountains	82	B	a
Guaira, La	214	C	a
Guaranis, reg.	128B	F	g
Guiana, reg.	128B	F	e
Guichet de Marigny, in Paris	149	B	(3)
Gümürdjina	168L	E	f
Güns (Kőszeg)	115	I	e
Güssing, castle	79	J	e
Gwent, dist.	60	C	d
Gwynedd, ter.	60	C	c
Győr (Raab)	87	K	e
Győr (Raab), bp.	95	F	b
Gyrwe, people	60	D	c
Habayes, Les	104A	C	b
Habitancum	51	O	g
Haddington, cty.	128	F	e
Hadersleben (Haderslev)	88	C	d
Hadid	7	B	e
Hadrian, Aqueduct of, in Athens	23	D	
Hadrianopolis, quarter in Athens	23	D	
Hadrianutherae	9	E	e
Hafir	53	G	d
Hafisfiord	45	F	a
Hagia Triada	4	B	b
Haidar Pasha	168J	A	a
Haifa	150	B	a
Haji Chefan	168L	B	b
Hala-I-Bedr	4	F	d*
Haleb (Aleppo)	4	F	c*
Halhul	7	C	e
Halidon Hill	74	K	d
Halil-Eli		B	b
Hallein	79	H	e
Hallstadt, near Bamberg	55	R	j
Hallstatt, near Salzburg	103	K	e
Halonnesos, isl.		C	e
Halwan, near Babylon	5	D	b*
Halwan, near Bagdad	99	M	g
Hamadan	53	G	c
Hamar, in Iraq	168K	E	c
Hamar, in Norway	131	F	a
Hami	104C	J	c
Hamilton in Scotland	128	D	e
Hamm	168E	B	b
Hammadites, Dom. of the	66	G	g
Hang-chau-fu	104C	L	e
Hanifa, people	53	G	d
Hankau	171	M	e
Hanoi (Kesho)	104C	K	e
Hansi	104B	H	e
Hapharaim	6	C	c
Harah (Herat)	104B	D	c
Hardegg	72	D	b
Hardt Mountains	168C	D	c
Harlech	74	I	g
Harmakut, mts.	104B	I	e
Harpessus River	9	C	c
Harplea	14	C	c
Hartmannsweiler Kopf	168C	D	c
Hasa, El-, reg.	104B	E	e
Hastings	60	J	d
Haunts of the Buccaneers	128B ins.	A	
Hay	74	K	g
Haye Sainte, La	156	A	a
Heathfield	60	D	b
Heavenfield	60	D	b
Hecanas (Magesaete), people	60	C	c
Hedon	74	M	f
Hejaz, reg.	170	E	l
Hekatompedon (Temple of Athena), in Athens	23	C	(1)
Helicon Mons, in Attica	23	D	
Helif	168J	D	b
Helles, cape	168L	D	c
Hellespont (Dardanelles), str.	9	D	.d
Hellespontine Phrygia, satr.	17	E	b
Hellespontine Tributary	13	K	d (II)
Helmsdale	128	E	b
Hendrica, dist.	60	D	d
Hephaestia	9	C	e
Heptanomis, reg.	4	F	d (II)
Heraclea (Perinthus) ;	9	E	d
Heracleum, in Crete	14 ins.		
Heraeum, in Olympia	9	H	f (7)
Heraeum, in Thrace	9	E	c
Herat	104B	G	d
Hercules Custos, Temple of	22	A	
Hercules Invictus, Temple of	24	A	
Hercules Pompejanus, Temple of	24	B	
Hereford, Palatine earldom	65	E	d
Hereros, people	175	E	f
Heri-Rud, R.	168K	H	c
Herkend, Sea of	104B	I	f
Hermandad, Santa	83 L h leg.		
Hermes Street, in Athens	23	D	
Hermopolis, in Egypt	1	B	d
Hermopulis, in Greece	165	D	e
Herod Antipas, Principality of	7		
Herodes Atticus, Exedra of	9	H	f (6)
Herodes Atticus, Tomb of	23	D	
Herstal	104A	C	a
Hertford	60	D	d
Hertogenbosch	168E	A	b
Hestiaeotis, dist.	10	C	c
Hexamilion	9	D	d
Hexham, mon.	60	C	b
Hielmar (Hjälmar), lake	88	F	b
Hieraconpolis	1	C	e
Hierapolis, in Asia Minor	20	C	d
Hili (Ely)	104B	R	j
Hilmend, lake	168K	H	c
Himyar, people	53	G	e
Hind	104B	R	j
Hindenburg Line	168C leg.		
Hindukush Mountains	104B	G	d
Hippodrome, in Olympia	9	H	f
Hirado (Firando), isl.	128C	G	d
Hispaniola, reg.	128B ins.	A	
Hissar, in Turkestan	104B	G	d
Hissarlik	9	A	b
Hittites, Kingdom of the	4	C	c
Hixton Down	60	G	d
Hjälmar (Hielmar), lake	88	F	b
Hoang-ho, R.	104C	L	d
Hodonin (Göding)	87	K	d
Hohenzieritz	154	G	b
Holderness, dist.	60	I	c
Holland, dist. in England	60	I	c
Holland, dist. in Friesland	60	C	b
Holme	60	I	c
Holme Saint Benet, abbey	74	O	g
Holwan (Halwan)	53	G	c
Holy Brotherhood	83 L h leg.		
Holyhead	60	G	c
Hooghly	137	E	d
Hooghly River	137	E	d
Hope (Spes), Temple of	24	A	
Hôpital Saint-Louis, in Paris	149	B	
Hořice (Horschitz)	87	J	c
Horonaim	7	D	f
Horsham	74	M	h
Horsham, parl. bor.	163	N	f
Hôtel de Cluny, bldg. in Paris	149	B	
Hôtel de Soubise, in Paris	149	B	
Hôtel Rambouillet, in Paris	149	B	
House of Parliament, in Athens	23	D	
Hoy, isl.	128	E	b
Hradec Kralove (König-grätz)	87	J	c
Hradec Kralove (König-grätz), bp.	95	F	a
Hradisch (Hradiště)	87	K	d
Hsiang-yang	104C	L	d
Hudson, route of	128B	D	c
Hudson Bay Company	128B	D	c
Hudson Bay Territory	133	L	e
Huexotzingo	106	B	a
Hueyotlipán	106	B	a
Hulagu (Dominion of the Ilkhans)	92 leg.		
Humaytá, in Brazil	181	U	h
Hungarian Altenburg	155	I	e
Hungarians, people, on the Theiss R.	45	I	c
Hungary, rep.	168G	I-J	f
Huningue (Hüningen)	157	B	c
Hunkiar Iskelessi	164	D	b
Huns, people, in Hungary	45	I	c
Huns, people, on the Dnieper R.	45	K	c
Huns, people, on the Ural R.	45	N	c
Hunsrück, mts.	168C	D	c
Huntingdon, Dan. bor.	60	I	c
Huntingdon, cty.	74	M	g
Hu-peh, reg.	171	M	
Hushi (Huşi, Hush)	131	I	d
Huzuli, people in 1929	168H	F	c
Hvar (Lesina), isl.	90	F	c
Hwang-Ho (Hoang-ho), R.	92	M	d
Hwicce, people	51	R	k
Hyères	78	E	g
Hyettus	11	E	d
Hyogo (Hiogo, Kobe)	171	O	e
Hythe	74	O	h
Iaca	38	B	d
Iacetani, people	38	B	d
Ibelim	68 ins.	A	
Ibir-Sibir, reg.	104B	G	b
Iça River	214	C	c
Ida Mountains, in Troas	9	D	e
Idle River	60	D	c
Idomene, in Epirus	10	C	c
Idomene, in Macedonia	17	C	a
Idria	103	L	e
Iglau, in Moravia (Jihlava)	79	I	d
Iglau, in Zips (Igló, Spišská Nová Ves)	80	G	g
Igló = Neudorf, in Zips	87	M	d
Ilchester, bor.	74	K	h
Ilebo	175	F	e
Ile (Isle) Bourbon	128C	K	g
Ilipa	38	A	e
Ilium (Troy)	9	B	b
Ilkhans of Persia, Dominion of the	92 leg.		
Ilkley	51	P	h
Illyrii, people	29	D	b
	17	B	a
Ilus, Burial mound of	9	A	b
Imbros	9	C	d
Imbros, isl.	9	C	d
Imeritia, reg.	139	F	g
Imil	104B	I	c
Inauen River	174	P	c
Incurables, The, bldg. in Paris	149	B	
India, Farther, reg.	104C	J	e
Indian Islands, Sea of the	104C	K	g
Indragiri	128C ins.	C	
Ineboli	168J	B	c
Ingushetiya, auton. area	168F leg.		
Inner Ceramicus, deme	23	D	
Inner Tibet reg.	171	K	e
Insulae Nudorum (Nicobar Islands)	104C	J	g
Insular Tributary	13	J	e (V)
Intercontinental Railway	215 leg.		
Inverary	128	C	d
Inverlochy	128	C	d
Inverness	128	D	c
Inverness, cty.	128	B	c

Iona, mon. . . . . 60 F a
Ionians, people . . . . 14 leg.
Ionian Tributary . . . . 3 K f (III)
Ipoly (Eipel) River. . . . . 159 J d
Ipswich, in England . . . . . 60 J c
Iraq, reg. . . . . 67 P g
Irawadi River . . . . 104 C J f
Irina Lagoon . . . . 19 K f
Irish Free State . . . . . . 168 F D e
Iron Gate (Eiserntor Pass) 159 L f
Irtish River . . . . 104 B H b
Isauria, reg. . . . . 20 E d
Isburus River . . . . 30 C c
Isfahan (Ispahan) . . . . . 168 K F c
Ishim River . . . . 104 B G b
Isle (Ile) Bourbon . . . . 128 C K g
Isle of France, march . . . 45 E c (F)
Isles in the Midst of the Sea 4 E c ★
Ismarus, mt. . . . . 9 C d
Isnik Geul . . . . 168 L G f
Isonzo River . . . . 135 G f
Isparta . . . . 168 J B b
Issyk Kul . . . . 104 B H c
Ištip . . . . 165 C c
Istri, people . . . . 29 C b
Itonian Gate . . . . 23 D
Itter, castle . . . . 79 H e
Ivanjica . . . . 165 B b
Ivanovo Voznesensk . . . . 167 N d
Iwaki . . . . 179 F d
Ixhuacán . . . . 106 C a
Ixtacmaxtitlán . . . . . . 106 C a
Iztapalapa . . . . 106 A a

Jabal Shammar . . . . . . 170 E-F f
Jabesh, in Gilead . . . . . 7 D d
Jablonne (Gabel) . . . . . 159 H c
Jacatra . . . . 128 C N f
Jacobabad . . . . 170 H f
Jacobites, people . . . . 168 L L h
Jacob's well . . . . 7 C d
Jaffna (Jaffnapatam) . . . 104 B S k
Jahaz . . . . 7 D e
Jaice (Jajce) . . . . . . 90 F b
Jaik (Ural) River . . . . . 53 H a
Jair, reg. . . . . 6 D c
Jaluit, isl. . . . . 179 H g
Jambi . . . . 128 C ins. C
Jandishapur . . . . 99 M g
Janina (Jannina or Yanina) 89 E d
Janoha . . . . 7 C d
Janus, in Rome . . . . . . 24 A (13)
Japanese Mandate . . . . 179 G g
Japan Sea . . . . 104 C N c
Jardin du Luxembourg, in Paris 149 B
Jaromĕr . . . . 87 J c
Jaszo, mon. . . . . . . 80 G g
Jats, people . . . . . . 128 B ins. B
Jattir (Ether) . . . . . . 7 C f
Java, Lesser, reg. . . . . 104 C K h
Jazoros . . . . 7 C e
Jedburgh . . . . 128 F e
Jedlinsk (Yedlinsk) . . . 155 K c
Jedlnia . . . . 87 M c
Jehud . . . . 7 B d
Jelairs, people . . . . . 104 C L b
Jemseg, Fort . . . . . . 191 E e
Jenghiz Khan, Dominions of 92 leg.
Jenil River . . . . . . 82 B b
Jerablus . . . . 168 J B b
Jesana . . . . 7 C e
Jews, people . . . . . 168 L K i
Jeziret-ibn-Omar . . . . 168 J D b
Jibleam . . . . 7 D b
Jičín (Gitschin) . . . . . 159 H c
Jidda . . . . 168 J C e
Jihlava (Iglau) . . . . . 87 J d
Jilove (Eule) . . . . . . 103 L d
Jogbeha . . . . 7 D b
John of Pian de Carpine,
  Route of . . . . . . 104 B leg.

Jordan River, Source of . . 6 D b
Joscelin, Lordship of . . . 68 C b
Josefov (Josefstadt) . . . 159 I c
Jucar River . . . . . . 82 B b
Judaea, Rom. prov. . . . 7 leg.
Julianehaab . . . . . . 181 W a
Julias (Beth Haran) . . . 7 D e
Jullin . . . . 103 L b
Jumna River . . . . . . 137 D c
Juno, Temple of (on Forum
  Holitorium) . . . . . 24 A
Junonia Falisca, Colonia . . 27 G e
Jupiter Custos, Temple of . 24 A (2)
Jupiter Eleutherus, Stoa of 23 D (4)
Jura, isl. . . . . 128 C e
Jurjan . . . . 104 B F d
Jutes, people, in Britain . 51 R k
Jutes, people, in Denmark . 42 D b
Juturna, Lake of . . . . . 24 A (20)

Kaarta, reg. . . . . . . 174 B c
Kabardia, dist. . . . . . 139 F g
Kabardino-Balgar, auton.
  area . . . . 168 F leg.
Kadah . . . . 104 C K g
Kafche-kue, reg. . . . . 104 C K e
Kafirs, people . . . . . 109 T k
Kai-fong-fu . . . . . . 104 C L d
Kail . . . . 104 B R k
Kaili . . . . 104 C L h
Kaindu . . . . 104 C K e
Kaisarieh . . . . 89 K g
Kakh . . . . 168 K G c
Kakun . . . . 150 B a
Kalaat Sherghat . . . . 168 J D b
Kalat . . . . 170 H f
Kalgoorlie . . . . 172 B c d
Kalhat . . . . 104 B F e
Kalifati . . . . 9 A b
Kalinga, reg. . . . . . . 104 B S j
Kallirrhoe . . . . 7 D e
Kalmar (Calmar) . . . . 88 G c
Kalmyk, auton. area . . . 168 G O f
Kamchatka, pen. . . . . 171 Q c
Kamenets Podolsk . . . . 139 C f
Kamexu (Kan-chau-fu) . 104 C K d
Kammer . . . . 79 H e
Kamon . . . . 6 D c
Kamrup, reg. . . . . . 104 C J e
Kan-chau-fu . . . . . 104 C K d
Kandahar . . . . . . 104 B G d
Kane . . . . 104 B B e
Kanklis, reg. . . . . . 104 B F c
Kansan . . . . 104 C K d
Kaoli, reg. (Korea) . . . 104 C M d
Kao-tai . . . . 104 C K d
Kaphtor (Crete) . . . . . 4 E c ★
Karabagh, reg. . . . . . 139 G h
Karabigha . . . . . . 168 L F f
Karachal, mts. . . . . . 104 B H d
Karachaevo Cherkises,
  auton. area . . . . . 168 F leg.
Karagach . . . . 168 L F f
Karajan . . . . 104 C K e
Karajan, reg. . . . . . 104 C K e
Kara-Kalpak, Autonomous
  Socialist Soviet Area . . 170 H d
Karakhitai, Dominion of the 92 I c
Karakhitai, reg. . . . . 104 B H c
Karakhoja . . . . . . 104 C J c
Karakorum . . . . . . 104 C K c
Kara Korum Mountains . . 170 I c
Karashar . . . . . . 104 C I c
Kara Su River . . . . . 168 J D a
Karatepe . . . . 168 K E b
Kardis . . . . 138 C d
Karelia, auton. rep. . . . 168 G L/M c
Karelians, people . . . . 57 J a
Karlovac (Karlstadt) . . . 159 H f
Karlovci (Carlowitz, Karlo-
  witz). . . . . 159 J f
Karlovy Vary (Carlsbad) . . 158 G c
Karlskrona . . . . . . 168 F I d

Karnaim . . . . 6 E c
Karnata, reg. . . . . . 104 B R j
Karun, R. . . . . . . 168 K E c
Karun, Birket el, lake . . 174 J j
Kaschau (Košice). . . . . 79 L d
Kashan . . . . 104 B F d
Kashgar . . . . 104 B H d
Kashimghar . . . . . . 104 B H d
Kashmir (Keshimur), reg. 104 B H d
Käsmark (Kešmarok) . . . 79 L d
Kašperské Hory (Bergreichen-
  stein) . . . . 103 K d
Kasrkand . . . . 168 K H d
Kassa (Kaschau) . . . . . 87 M d
Kassala . . . . 174 G e
Kassim Pasha, quarter . . . 93 G e
Kassubs, people in 1929 . 168 H E b
Kastelorizo, isl. . . . . . 168 J A b
Katanga . . . . 175 F f
Katia (Katieh) . . . . . 168 J B c
Katif, El- . . . . . . 104 B E d
Kaunas (Kovno) . . . . 168 G K d
Kavak, near Constantinople 168 L G f
Kavak, near Gallipoli . . 68 L D c
Kaveri (Cauvery) River . . 137 C f
Kavsa . . . . 168 J C a
Kayalik . . . . 104 B I c
Kazakskaia, Autonomous
  Socialist Soviet Repub-
  lic . . . . 170 G I d
Kazerun . . . . 104 B F e
Kazimierz . . . . 103 P c
Kazvin . . . . 168 G P h
Kedemoth . . . . 7 D e
Kelkid Irmak . . . . . 168 J C a
Kelso . . . . 128 F e
Kelyub . . . . 150 B a
Kemkemjuts, people . . . 104 C J b
Kemmel, mt. . . . . . 168 C B b
Kempsford . . . . . . 60 I e
Kenchak . . . . 104 B H c
Kenilworth, castle . . . . 74 L g
Kennedys, fam. . . . . . 128 D e
Kentyre (Kintyre), dist. . . 128 C e
Kenya, col. . . . . . . 174 G d
Kepoi (Gardens), in Athens. 23 D
Keraits, people . . . . . 104 C K c
Kerch . . . . 89 E a
Kerkhah, R. . . . . . 168 K E c
Kerman . . . . 104 B F d
Kerman, reg. . . . . . 53 H d
Kermanshah . . . . . 168 K E c
Kert River . . . . . . 174 Q n
Kerulen River . . . . . 104 C L c
Kesh . . . . 92 D d
Keshan . . . . 168 L F f
Keshimur (Kashmir), reg. 104 B H d
Kesho . . . . 104 C K e
Kesmacoran, reg. . . . 104 B G d
Kesmark (Kežmarok) . . . 103 O d
Kesteven, dist. . . . . . 60 I c
Keuprikeui . . . . . . 168 J A a
Khabiri, people . . . . . 4 F c ★
Khaf . . . . 168 K H c
Khaibar . . . . 53 F d
Khalkas, people . . . . 104 C K c
Khalman (Haleb) . . . . 5 C b
Khamil (Hami) . . . . 104 C J c
Khanate of Chagatai . . 104 B G-I c
Khanate of Persia . . . . 104 B F d
Khanate of the Crimea . 139 E f
Khanate of the Golden Horde 99 K d
Khanbaliq (Peking) . . . 104 C L d
Khanfu . . . . 104 C M p
Khanikin . . . . 168 K E c
Khansa . . . . 104 C M d
Khanu . . . . 168 K G d
Kharesm . . . . 53 I b
Kharesm (Khiva), reg. . . 104 B F c
Kharesm, Sea of (Aral Sea) 104 B F c
Kharluks, people . . . . 104 B H c
Kharput . . . . 168 J C b
Khatanga River . . . . . 104 C K a

Khatti 4	F	c	*
Khatti (Hittites), people . . . 5	C	b	*
Kheir . . . . 168 K	F	d	
Kheta, people 4	F	c	*
Khilakhu (Cilicia), reg. . . . 5	C	b	*
Khilikhi (Cilicians), people . 4	F	c	*
Khingan-Mountains . . . . 104 C	L	c	
Khiva, reg. . . . . 104 B	H	c	
Khmer, reg. . . . . 104 C	K	f	
Khoi . . . . 168 K	E	b	
Khojend 170	H	d	
Khokand . . . . 104 B'	H	c	
Khoper River 139	F	e	
Khorab 175	E	f	
Khotan . . . . 104 B	H	d	
Khumdan . . . . 104 C	K	d	
Khur . . . . 168 K	F	c	
Khuram . . . . 104 B	H	c	
Khurma, near Basra . . . 168 K	E	c	
Khurma, near Mecca 170	E	f	
Khusistan (Khuzistan), reg. . 53	G	c	
Khwarazm (Khiva), reg. . . 104 B	H	c	
Kiangning-fu . . . . 104 C	L	d	
Kia-yu-kwan . . . . 104 C	J	d	
Kidwelly 74	I	h	
Kiel Canal . . . . 168 D	B	c	
Kien-chang-fu . . . . . . 104 C	L	e	
Kiev, in 864 45	K	b	
Kifane 174	Q	n	
Kij Mekran, reg. . . . . . 104 B	G	e	
Kilid-Bahr . . . . 168 L	D	c	
Killiecrankie Pass 128	D	c	
Kilmallock 74	B	b	
Kinana, people 53	F	d	
Kincardine, cty. 128	F	d	
Kin Dynasty 92	K	d	
King's Stoa, in Athens . . . 23	D	(3)	
Kingsze 92	M	d	
Kinross, cty. 128	E	d	
Kinsale 74	B	c	
Kintyre (Kentyre), dist. . . 128	C	e	
Kipschak, khan. 99	L	d	
Kirchholm 88	K	c	
Kirghiz, people on the			
Yenisei R. . . . . 104 C	I	b	
Kirghiz, Autonomous So-			
cialist Soviet Republic. 170	I	d	
Kiriath Arba 7	C	e	
Kirioth 7	D	e	
Kirkagach . . . . 168 J	A	b	
Kirkcudbright 128	D	f	
Kirkcudbright, cty. 128	D	e	
Kirk-Kilisse . . . . 168 L	F	f	
Kirkuk . . . . 168 J	D	b	
Kirkwall 128	F	b	
Kish 4	D	c	
Kishinev 139	C	f	
Kishm, isl. . . . . 104 B	F	e	
Kittim, people 4	F	c	*
Kizil Uzen, R. . . . . . . 168 K	E	b	
Kizlya . . . . 168 K	E	a	
Klaipeda (Memel) . . . . 168 G	J	d	
Klatovy (Klattau) 135	G	d	
Klek 157	D	d	
Klepsydra, Spring of 23	C		
Kliszow (Klissow) 135	K	c	
Ključ 87	K	f	
Klosterzeven 134	E	b	
Knights of the Sword 80	I	b	
Koburg 79	B	c	
Kobylka 135	K	b	
Kochak Bay . . . . 168 G	P	g	
Kočevje (Gottschee) . . . 168	D	d	
Koil . . . . 104 B	H	e	
Koja Chai, R. . . . . 168 L	D	c	
Kokenhusen 88	K	c	
Koko-Nor, lake . . . . . 104 C	K	d	
Kolachel . . . . 104 B	R	k	
Kolozsvár (Klausenburg,			
Cluj) 159	L	e	
Kolymsk, Nizhne - 171	R	b	
Komarom (Komárno, Ko-			
morn) 159	J	e	

Komotau (Chomutov) 87	I	c	
Kong, reg. 174	C	d	
Konia (Konieh, Iconium) . . 89	J	g	
Königgrätz, bp. 95	F	a	
Konitza 165	B	c	
Konkan, reg. . . . . 104 B	R	j	
Konkan-tana . . . . 104 B	R	j	
Konstantsa (Constantsa) . 168 G	K	g	
Koporye 88	M	b	
Kora 137	D	c	
Korčula (Curzola), bp. . . . 95	F	c	
Korčula (Curzola), isl. . . . 90	F	c	
Koreish, people 53	G	d	
Koritza 165	B	c	
Körmöczbanya (Kremnitz) 159	J	d	
Koroni (Coron) 89	H	g	
Kors, people 57	H	b	
Korusko 4	F	d	*
Košice (Kaschau) 79	L	d	
Kosmidion, quarter 93	G	e	
Köszeg (Güns) 135	I	e	
Kotor (Cattaro) 89	A	b	
Kotor (Cattaro) abp. . . . 95	F	c	
Kotrobah (Sokotra). isl. . 104 B	F	f	
Kotylaion (Cotylaeum), mt. 11	E	d	
Koura (Kura) River . . . 168 G	O	g	
Koweit (Kuwait) . . . 168 K	E	d	
Kowel 159	M	c	
Koźmin (Koschmin) . . . 159	I	c	
Krajina, dist. . . . . . . 168 D	C	a	
Kraków (Cracow) 87	L	c	
Krasnodar . . . . 168 J	C	a	
Krasnokokshaisk . . . . 168 G	O	d	
Kratovo 165	C	b	
Kremenchug 139	D	e	
Kremnitz (Kremnica) . . . 79	K	d	
Kremsier (Kroměříž) 87	K	d	
Krithia . . . . 168 L	D	c	
Kriviches, people 57	I-J	b	
Krnov (Jägerndorf) 135	I	c	
Kroja (Kruja) 89	G	f	
Kroměříž (Kremsier) 87	K	d	
Kronstadt, in Transylvania			
(Brașov, Brassó) 159	M	e	
Krumlov (Krumau) 135	H	d	
Krupanj 103	N	f	
Ksar-el-Kebir 174	O	n	
Książ (Xions) 159	I	b	
Kuba, in Daghestan . . . 139	G	g	
Kublai Khan, Empire of the 92	leg.		
Kucha . . . . 104 B	I	c	
Kuchan . . . . 168 K	G	b	
Küchük Derbend . . . . 168 L	E	f	
Küchük-Kainarji 139	C	g	
Kuen-lun Mountains . . . 104 B	I	d	
Kufa 53	G	c	
Kughi . . . . 104 B	G	e	
Kujavia (Cuyavia), dist. . . 79	K	b	
Kulevcha 164	D	b	
Kulja . . . . 104 B	I	c	
Kulpa River 87	J	f	
Kum . . . . 168 K	F	c	
Kum-Kale . . . . 168 L	D	c	
Kum Kioi 9	A	b	
Kummeh 4	F	d	*
Kunduz . . . . 104 B	G	d	
Kupferberg 79	I	c	
Kuprikeui . . . . 168 B	L	c	
Kur (Kura) River 43	L	e	
Kuraiat . . . . 104 B	F	e	
Kurds, people . . . . . 168 L	L	h	
Kurna . . . . 168 K	E	c	
Kurnegalle . . . . 104 B	S	k	
Kustenje (Constanța) . . 165	F	a	
Kutaia 165	F	c	
Kut-el-Amara . . . . . 168 K	E	c	
Kuti, people 4	G	c	*
Kutná Hora (Kuttenberg) . 135	H	d	
Kuwait (Koweit) . . . 168 K	E	d	
Kuyavia (Cuyavia), reg. . . 87	L	b	
Kwei-lin-fu . . . . 104 C	L	e	
Kyakhta 171	L	c	
Kyle, dist. 60	B	b	

Kyll River . . . . 104 A	D	b	
Kyūshū, isl. 171	O	e	
La Bassée . . . . 168 C	B	b	
La Besace . . . . . 104 A	B	b	(L.B.)
La Central 216	ins.		
Lacetani, people 38	C	d	
La Cluse 158	D	a	
Laconians, people 8	O	i	
Lac Saint Joseph 191	G	a	
Lactodorum 51	P	h	
Ladins, people in 1929 . 168 H	D	c	
Lagosta, isl. 161	K	f	
Lagunas 216	ins.		
Lahari . . . . 104 B	D	c	
Laighin (Leinster), dist. . . . 60	A	c	
Laing's Nek 175	N	l	
Laknaoti . . . . 104 C	I	c	
Lametz . . . . 104 A	B	b	
Lamzai (Yang-chau-fu) . 104 C	M	d	
Lanark 128	E	e	
Lanark, cty. 128	E	e	
Lancaster, in England 74	K	e	
Lancaster, County Palatine of 74	K	f	
Lan-chau-fu . . . . . . 104 C	K	d	
Land of Conchi 92	G	b	
Lands of the Generality,			
dist. 134	C	c	
Lanercost mon. 97	O	g	
La Neuveville - devant-			
Nancy . . . . 104 A	D	c	
La Neuveville-lès-Raon . 104 A	D	c	
La Neuville-au-Pont . . . 104 A	B	b	
Langa 83	E	c	
Langeais 86	C	e	
Langres, Plateau of . . . 168 C	C	d	
Lang-son 171	L	f	
Lankavi-Island . . . . . 104 C	J	g	
Lanzarote, route of 108	O	e	
Lapis Niger, in Rome 24	A	(11)	
La Plata, reg. . . . . . 128 B	F	g	
Lapsaki . . . . 168 L	O	c	
Larache 174	O	n	
Laranda (Karaman) 20	E	d	
Lasa 7	D	e	
Lastingham 60	,D	e	
Las Virgenes, Cape 108	K	e	
Latakia . . . . 168 J	C	b	
Latin America . . . . 180 Q	f-U	k	
La Tourette, Fort 191	H	a	
Latvia, rep. . . . . . . 168 G	J-K	d	
Latvis, people 57	I	b	
Lauderdale, dist. 128	F	e	
Laugona (Lahn) River . . . 39	J	h	
Laun 87	I	c	
Lau River 174	P	n	
Lauro 38	B	e	
Lausanne, Treaty of . . . 168 L	leg.		
Lavatrae 51	P	g	
Laxenburg, castle 79	J	d	
Lebecii (Libici), people . . . 26	C	c	
Le Cateau . . . . . . 168 C	B	b	
Ledre 45	B	b	
Ledstone (Loides) 60	D	c	
Leepaja (Liebau) . . . . 168 G	J	d	
Leganes 83	K	b	
Legiolium 51	P	g	
Legio VII Gemina 38	A	c	
Leibnitz 87	J	e	
Leicester (Ratae) 51	P	h	
Leicester, bp. 60	D	e	
Leicester, cty. 74	L	g	
Leicester, danish borough . 60	D	c	
Leighton Buzzard 60	I	d	
Leinster (Laighin), dist. . . 60	A	c	
Leinster, prov. 74	C	b	
Leipzig 63	G	c	
Leipzig, univ. 100	H	d	
Leith 128	E	d	
Leitomischl (Litomyšl) . . 79	J	d	
Leitomischl, bp. 95	F	b	
Leix, dist. 74	C	b	
Le Maire, route of . . . . 128 B	E	h	

Le Marais, quarter in Paris 149   B
Lemba 7   D   e
Lenaeum and Dionysium, in
    Athens 23   D (12)
Lena - Transbaikal, econo-
    mic reg. 170   leg.
Lenczica 87   L   b
Leninakan (Alexandropol) 168 J   D   a
Leningrad (Petrograd, St.
    Petersburg) . . . . . . 168 G   L   d
Leninsk 170   H   e
Lenkoran 139   G   h
Lennox, dist. 128   D   d
Lenzin . . . . 104 C   L   d
Leonidaeum, in Olympia . . 9   H   f
Le Pas 180   Q   b
Lerma 83   K   g
Lerwick 128   ins.
Les Habayes . . . . 104 A   C   b
Lesser Armenia , km. in
    Cilicia 89   D   c
Lesser Java, reg. . . . . 104 C   K   h
Lesser Phrygia, reg. 9   E   d
Lesser Zab, R. . . . . . 168 J   D   b
Leszno (Lissa) 135   I   c
Létanne . . . . 104 A C b (Le.)
Leucas (Leukas), isl. 10   B   d
Leucas (Santa Maura) . . 10   B   d
Leucates, prom. 10   B   d
Leucos Limen 4   F   d *
Leuchtenburg, castle 79   H   d
Leutschau (Levoča) 79   L   d
Lewes, engl. bor. 60   J   d
Lewes, castle 74   M   i
Lewis, isl. 128   B   b
Liang-chau 92   K   d
Liao-ho, R. 171   M   d
Liao-tung, pen. 171   N   d
Libba 7   D   e
Liberec = Reichenberg, in
    Bohemia 135   H   c
Liberta, Piazza della, loc. in
    Rome 22   A
Library, in Athens 23   D
Liburni, people 27   I   c
Lichtenberg, castle 78   E   d
Lidisdale, dist. 128   F   e
Liechtenstein, castle 91   R   k
Lienz 79   H   e
Ligures, people 29   A   b
Lijdzaamheid . . . . . . 128 C   ins. D
Limerick 74   B   b
Limnae, in Thrac. Cherson. 9   D   d
Limonum 38   C   c
Lin-ching . . . . 104 C   L   d
Lincoln, bp. in England . . 60   I   c
Lincoln, cty. 74   M   f
Lincoln, danish borough . . 60   I   c
Lindisfarne, bp. 60   I   b
Lindiswara, reg. 51   R   k
Lindsays, fam. 128   E   d
        F   e
Lindsey, dist. 60   D   c
Lingah . . . . 168 K   F   d
Linlithgow 128   E   d
Linlithgow, cty. 128   E   c
Lin-tsing-chau . . . . . 104 C   L   d
Liptau (Liptó, Liptov) . . 87   L   d
Lipotvár (Leopoldstadt) . . 159   I   d
Lisht, Pyramids of 1   B
Lissa (Leszno) 115   I   c
Lita (Litani) River . . . 6   C   b *
Lithuania, reg. . . . . . 168 G   F   a
Lithuanians, people in 1829 168 H   F   a
Litoměřice (Leitmeritz) . . 135   H   c
Litomyšl (Leitomischl) . . 87   K   b
Litomyšl (Leitomischl), bp. 95   F   b
Littau (Litove) 72   D   b
Little Entente 168   F   leg.
Litvas, people 57   H   c
        J   b
Livia and Tiberius, Posses-
    sions of . . . . - 7

Livias 7   D   e
Ljubljana (Laibach) 135   H   f
Ljungby 88   G   c
Llandovery 74   J   h
Llan Elwy (Saint Asaph) . 60   H   c
Llanos 106   C   a
Lleyn, dist. 60   G   c
Llobregat River 82   C   a
Loanda . . . . 128 C   I   f
Lob . . . . 104 C   I   c
Locac, reg. . . . . . . 104 C   K   g
Lochaber, dist. 128   C   d
Loch Leven 128   E   d
Loch Linnhe 128   C   d
Loch Ness, lake 128   D   c
Lochstädt 87   L   a
Loch Tay 128   D   d
Locrians, people 8   O   h
Lodomeria, reg. 139   B   f
Loides (Ledstone) 60   D   c
Łomża (Lomzha) 159   L   b
London, in England . . . 60   I   d
London, abbey 74   N   h
London, Treaty of . . . . 168 L   leg.
Long (Makra) Stoa 23   D
Loos . . . . 168 C   B   b
Loreto 103   K   g
Lorne, dist. 128   C   d
Lothian, dist. 60   H   b
Lough Rea, lake 127   J   h
Lourenço Marques 175   G   j
Lovosice (Lobositz) 135   G   c
Lower Egypt, reg. 4   F c (1)
Lower Lorraine, duchy,
    13 cent. . . . . 104 A   A   a
Lower Nairi Sea 5   D   b
Lower Tunguska River . 104 C   J   a
Lower Volga, economic reg. 168 F   leg.
Low Germans, people
    in 1929 . . . . 168 H   C—E b
Lo-yang . . . . 104 C   L   d
Loznica 165   A   a
Lubango 175   E   f
Łubawa (Löbau) 155   J   b
Lucani, people 29   D   a
Luck 139   C   e
Lucuci, bp. 99   K   d
Lud (Lydians), people . . . 4   E   c *
Ludgershall 74   L   h
Ludgershall, parl. bor. . . 163   M   f
Ludsen 88   L   c
Lueitha 7   D   f
Luga River 88   M   b
Lugoj (Lugos) 168   H   d
Luhith 7   D   f
Lule Burgas . . . . . 168 L   F   f
Luna, in Spain 83   K   g
Lunda, reg. 175   F   e
Lundenburg (Břeclav) . . 168   E   b
Lungara, Via della, loc. in
    Rome 22   A
Luris, people . . . . . . 168 L   M   i
Lussin, isl. 161   J   e
Luxemburg, cty., 13 cent. 104 A   D   b
Luzienské, Pass 91   R   k
Lwów (Lemberg) 159   L   c
Lycaonia, dist. 20   E   c
Lycia and Pamphylia, Rom.
    prov. . . . . 20 D d (V)
Lycopolis 4   F   d *
Lydian Empire 8   Q   h
Lynn Regis 74   N   g
Lyons, univ. 100   F
Lysanias, Principality of . . 7
Lysimachia, on the Propontis 9   D   d
Ma'bar, reg. . . . . . . 104 B   R   j
Macallisters, fam. 128   C   e
Macassar . . . . . . 128 C ins. C
Mac Carthy, fam. 74   B   c
Macdonalds, fam. . . . . 128 A c   C   e
Macdona lds of Clanranald
    fam. 128   C   d

Macdonalds of Glencoe,
    fam. 128   C   d
Macdonalds of Glengarry,
    fam. 128   C   c
Macdonalds of Keppoch,
    fam. 128   D   d
Macedonians, people 8   N   g
Macestus River 9   F   e
Macgregors, fam. 128   D   d
Machin 139   C   f
Maciejowice 135   K   c
Macina, reg. 174   C   c
Macintoshes, fam. 128   D   c
Mackays, fam. 128   D   b
Mackenzies, fam. 128   C   c
Maclachlans, fam. 128   C   d
Macleans, fam. 128   B   d
Macleods, fam. 128   B   c
Mac Mahon, fam. 74   C   a
Mac Murrough, fam. . . . 74   C   b
Macnabs, fam. 128   D   d
Macneills, fam. 128   A   d
Macphersons, fam. 128   D   d
Mačva, reg. 87   L   f
Madain 53   G   c
Madrigal 83   J   g
Madytus 9   D   d
Magesaete (Hecanas), people 60   C   c
Magharis . . . . 168 L   E   c
Magnae 51   O   h
Magnetes, people 8   O   h
Maguire, fam. 74   C   a
Magyars, people, on the
    Dnieper R. 45   K   c
Magyars, people, on the
    Theiss R. 45   I   c
Magyars, people, south of
    the Don R. 45   L   c
Magyars, people in 1929 . 168 H   E-F   c
Mahdchin (Canton) . . . 104 C   L   c
Mahrattas, people . . . . 128 B   ins. B
Maidan - i - Naphtun . . 168 K   E   c
Maidos . . . . 168 L   D   c
Maikop . . . . 168 J   C   a
Mailapur . . . . 104 B   S   j
Maimachin 171   L   d
Mainland, isl., Orkney Isl. . 128   E   a
Mainland, isl., Shetland Isl. 128   ins.
Mairie, in Paris 149   B
Majdan 103   M   f
Makatea, isl. 180   M   i
Makhach Kala (Petrovsk) 168 G   O   g
Makra (Long) Stoa 23   D
Malatia (Malatiyeh) . . . 168 J   C   b
Malborghet 154   G   e
Malea, prom. in Lesbos . . 9   D   c
Malene 13   E   b
Malians, people 8   O   h
Malines 81   M   g
Malmesbury, bor. 74   K   h
Malmesbury, mon. 60   H   d
Malpas 74   K   f
Malton, castle 74   M   e
Mamre 7   C   e
Mangaseya . . . . . . 128 C   M   b
Manias Geul . . . . . 168 L   F   f
Manresa 83   L   g
Mansura, in India . . . 104 B   G   e
Mar, dist. 128   F   c
Marabout 150   A   a
Marais, Le, quarter in Paris 149   B
Marburg, in Hesse 122   E   c
Marburg, in Styria (Maribor) 168   D   c
Marcher Earldoms 74   J   g
Marco Polo, Route of . . 104 B   leg.
Marea 4   ins.   *
Mare Majus 99   J   e
Mare Maurum 99   K   e
Maresa 7   B   e
Mari, auton. area . . . 168 G   O   d
Mariana, in Corsica . . . 26   D   e
Mariana, in Spain 38   B   e
Maribor (Marburg, in Styria) 168   D   c

Marienburg castle, in Livonia 88 L c
Marion . . . . 181 T c
Maritsa (Maritza) River . . 139 C g
Marlow . . . . 74 M h
Marmarice (Marmaris) . . 165 F e
Marne-Rhine Canal . . . . 168 E B c
Maronea . . . . 9 C d
Maronites, people . . . 168 L K i
Maros Vasarhely (Osorhej) 168 I c
Marquette and Jolliet . . 128 C leg.
Marshall, dist. in Wales . 74 I h
Mars-la-Tour . . . . 158 C d
Martaban . . . . 104 C J f
Martinsberg, mon. . . . . . 80 E h
Marton, battle . . . . 60 I d
Marville . . . . 104 A C b (Ma.)
Marylebone, parl. bor. 163 N f (Maryleb.)
Maserfield (Oswestry) . . 60 C c
Mask, Lough-, lake . . . 127 H h
Masphate . . . . 7 D d
Massawah . . . . 174 G c
Mastusia, prom. . . . . 9 D d
Masurian Lakes . . . . . . 168 B H a
Masurs, people in 1929 . 168 H F b
Matadi . . . . 175 E e
Mater Matuta, Temple of . . 24 A
Mathons . . . . 104 A C c
Matthane . . . . 7 D e
Mauerbach, mon. . . . . . . 79 J d
Mauritania, reg. . . . . . . 174 B c
Maurits-tad (Pernambuco) 128 B G f
Mauthausen . . . . 155 H d
Mawarannahr, reg. . . . . . 53 I b
Maybole . . . . 128 D e
Meath (Midhe), dist. . . . . 60 A c
Medaba . . . . 7 D e
Medershampsted, mon. . . . . 60 D c
Medias (Mediasch, Medgyes) 159 M e
Medina . . . . 53 G d
Medina de Rioseco . . . . 83 J g
Medjidia . . . . 165 F a
Meduacus . . . . 27 G b
Meductic, Fort . . . . . . 191 L b
Meenen (Menin) . . . . . . 134 B c
Megaron, in Olympia . . . . 9 H f
Meknes . . . . 174 P n
Melas, gulf . . . . 9 D d
Melcombe Regis, bor. . . . . 74 K i
Meliapur . . . . 104 B S j
Melibar, reg. . . . . 104 B R j
Melinde (Malindi) . . . . . 128 C K f
Melrose . . . . 46 F b
Melrose, mon. . . . . 60 C b
Memel River . . . . 88 J
Menado . . . . 128 C ins. C
Mendeli . . . . 168 K E c
Mendereh, R. . . . . 168 L D d
Menderes River(Maeander R.) 89 I g
Menderes River(Scamander R.) 9 D d
Meng-tse . . . . 171 L f
Menin (Meenen) . . . . . . 134 B c
Menteith, dist. . . . . 128 D d
Menzala, lake . . . . 174 K i
Menzies, fam. . . . . 128 D d
Meonwara, people . . . . 60 D d
Merano (Meran) . . . . . 103 J e
Merchant Adventurers,
  seats . . . . 88 B-De (M. a.)
Mercia, Duchy of . . . . . . 60 leg.
Mercia, km. . . . . 60 D c
Merians, people . . . . . . 59 M b
Merkits, people . . . . 104 C K b
Mernis, dist. . . . . 128 F d
Meroë . . . . 4 F e *
Mers (Merse), dist. . . . . 128 F e
Mersina . . . . 168 J D d
Meserib . . . . 168 J C c
Meshed, in Iraq . . . . . 104 B E d
Meshed, in Khorasan . . 104 B F d
Meshra-Klila . . . . 174 Q n
Meskene . . . . 168 J C b
Messenians, people . . . . 8 N i
Messines Ridge . . . . 168 C B b (M.)

Mesta, R. . . . . 168 L E f
Mestre . . . . 103 K f
Methurides Islands . . . . 16 A b
Methymna . . . . 9 D e
Metronia Gate, in Rome . . 22 A
Metropolitan Church, in
  Athens . . . . 23 D
Metroum, in Olympia . . . 9 H f(4)
Metroum, in Athens . . . 23 D (6)
Metsovon (Metzovon) . . . 165 B d
Meurthe River . . . . . . 104 A D c
Mezen River . . . . 138 G c
Mezre . . . . 158 J C c
Miami, Fort (on L. Erie) 196 ins. B
Miami, Fort (on Maumee R.) 191 H c
Miamis, Fort des (on
  L. Michigan) . . . . . . 191 H c
Mianeh . . . . 99 M f
Michael, Saint, parl. bor. . 163 I g
Michelau, reg. . . . . 87 L b
Michipicoten, Fort . . . . 191 H b
Middel Zee (Zuider Zee) . 102 G b
Middle Angles, people . . 60 D c
Middle Egypt, reg. . . . . . 4 F d (II)
Middle Empire see Khanate
  of Chagatai . . . . . . 104 B G-I c
Middle Germans, people
  in 1929 . . . . 168 H C c - E b
Middleham . . . . 74 L e
Middle India, reg. . . . . 104 B E f
Middle March . . . . 128 E e
Middlesex, parl. dist. . 163 N f (Midd.)
Middle Volga, economic
  reg. . . . . 168 F leg.
Midhe (Meath), dist. . . . . 60 A c
Midhurst, bor. . . . . 74 M i
Mien . . . . 104 C J e
Mikhailovsk . . . . 170 G d
Mikulov (Nikolsburg) . . 135 I d
Milassa (Milas) . . . . . 168 J A b
Milborne Port, parl. bor. 163 L g (Milb.)
Milden (Moudon) . . . . . . 86 F e
Miletopolis . . . . 9 F d
Milford, castle . . . . 74 H h
Milos, isl. . . . . 165 D e
Milton, in Kent . . . . . . 60 J d
Ming Dynasty, in China . . 92 K e
Mingio (Ning-po) . . . . 104 C M e
Minibar, reg. . . . . 104 B R k
Ministero della Guerra, bldg.
  in Rome . . . . 22 A
Minoa, on Siphnus I. . . . 15 E c
Minoa, pen. . . . . 16 A b
Minster, mon. . . . . 60 E d
Miraflores, in Chile . . . . 216 ins.
Mirapolis . . . . 104 B S j
Misco River . . . . 27 H d
Missinaibi River . . . . . 191 I b
Mitanni, dist. . . . . 4 D d
Miteretane Sea . . . . 98 D f
Mitrovica Kosovska . . . . 165 B b
Mitrovica (Sremska) . . . . 87 L f
Mittenwald . . . . 103 J e
Mitylene, on Lesbos I. . . 9 D e
Mitylene (Lesbos), isl. . . 168 J A b
Mixquic . . . . 106 B a
Mizpa, in Gilead . . . . . . 7 D d
Mlada Boleslav (Jung-
  Bunzlau) . . . . 135 H c
Mobar, reg. . . . . 104 B R j
Modena, univ. . . . . 100 H f (M.)
Modon (Methoni) . . . . . . 89 H g
Modruš (Modrush), bp. . . 95 F b
Moffat . . . . 128 E e
Mogaung . . . . 104 C J e
Mohilev . . . . 153 O g
Moidart . . . . 128 C d
Mojaisk . . . . 153 P f
Molat (Meleda), isl. . . . . 90 F c
Moldavia, auton. rep. . . 168 G K f
Molossians, people . . . . 8 N h
Money changers, Arch of the 24 B
Mongol Baltic trade-route . 98 leg.

Mongol Dynasty, in China . 92 L d
Mongols, people . . . . 104 C L c
Monjuich . . . . 83 L g
Monmouth, castle in Eng-
  land . . . . 74 K h
Monomotapa, reg. . . . . . 109 T i
Monserrat . . . . 83 L g
Monte Caseros . . . . . . 216 H i
Montecatini . . . . 79 G e
Montfaucon (en - Argonne),
  mon. . . . . 95 D b
Montfaucon, near Château-
  Thierry . . . . 184 ins.
Montfort (-l'Amaury) . . . 76 D b
Montfort, near Langres . 104 A C c
Montmélian . . . . 86 F f
Montpellier, bp. . . . . . . 94 C c
Monts Faucilles . . . . . 168 C C c
Monzon . . . . 83 L g
Morava (March), R. . . . 168 D D d
Moray, dist. . . . . 128 D c
Mordvins, people, about 900. 57 L c
Morena Mountains . . . . 82 A b
Moresnet . . . . 168 E A b
Morges . . . . 168 C O c
Morhange . . . . 168 C D c
Moridunum . . . . 51 O i
Morin, Grand, R. . . . . 168 C B c
Morlaks, people in 1929 . 168 H E d
Mortimer, dist. . . . . 74 J g
Moson (Wieselburg) . . . 159 I e
Mossi, reg. . . . . 174 C c
Mosychlos . . . . 9 C e
Motho . . . . 7 D f
Moudon . . . . 86 O l
Mountain Territory . . . 168 K E c
Mount Kemmel . . . . . 168 C B b
Mouree . . . . 128 C ins. D
Mucheon Come . . . . 7 D f
Mudania . . . . 168 G K g
Mukačevo (Munkács) . . . 168 H b
Mulehet, reg. . . . . 104 B F d
Mul-Java (Malacca), pen. 104 C K f
Mülheim (on the Ruhr) . 168 E B b
Mull, isl. . . . . 128 C e
Mumford . . . . 128 C ins. D
München-Gladbach . . . 168 E B b
Municipal Theatre, in
  Athens . . . . 23 D
Munster, prov. in Ireland . 74 B b
Murad Su, R. . . . . 168 J D b
Murano . . . . 103 K f
Murghab (Pasargadae) . . 19 H d
Murghab, R. . . . . 168 K H b
Murmansk . . . . 182 E E a
Muromans, people . . . . 59 M b
Murrays, fam. . . . . 128 D b
Mürz River . . . . 87 J e
Murzuk . . . . 174 E b
Musa Keui . . . . 168 L B a
Muscat . . . . 104 B F e
Mush . . . . 168 J D b
Mussur (Egypt), emp. . . 5 C c *
Mustafa Pasha . . . . . . 168 J A a
Mutatili (Mutapili) . . . 104 B S j
Mygdones, people . . . . 9 C e
Mynyw (St. Davids), bp. . 60 B d
Myoshormos . . . . 4 F d *
Myrina, in Lemnos . . . . 9 C e
Myrina, in Lydia . . . . . 17 E b
Myrlea . . . . 9 F c
Myrtilis . . . . 38 A e
Mysians, people . . . . . . 8 Q a

Nablus . . . . 150 C h
Nachouac, Fort . . . . . 191 L b
Nacrasa . . . . 9 E b
Nador . . . . 174 Q n
Nagy Szeben (Hermann-
  stadt) . . . . 159 M f
Nagy Szombat (Tyrnau) . 155 I d
Naharini, dist. . . . . 4 F c
Naimans, people . . . . 104 C J c

Nairi, dist.	5	D	b
Nairi Sea, Lower	5	D	b
Nairi Sea, Upper	5	D	b
Nairn, cty.	128	E	c
Nakhichevan	99	M	f
Nakhichevan, auton. rep.	168 G	O	h
Nang chang-fu	104 C	L	e
Nandurbar	104 B	R	i
Nanking	104 C	L	d
Narenta River	103	M	g
Narvik	168 F	I	b
Nasamones, people	18	B	d
Nascivan	99	M	f
Nassau, on Gold Coast	128 C	ins.	D
Natuna, isl.	104 C	K	g
Naupactus (Naupaktos)	10	C	d
Nauru Island	179	H	g
Navalia (Shipyards), loc.	24	B	
Navarre, march	45	D d	(N)
Naworth	74	K	d
Naxus (Naxos), in Sicily	30	E	e
Nazionale, Via, street in Rome	22	A	
Neandria	9	D	e
Neath, castle	74	J	h
Nechtansmere	60	C	a
Necuveran Islands	104 C	J	g
Negeb, reg.	7	B	f
Negumbo	128 B	ins.	B
Nehawend	53	G	c
Nejd, reg.	53	G	d
Nejed (Nejd), Sultanate of	170	F	f
Nejef (Meshed). in Iraq	99	L	g
Nekheb	4	F	d *
Nekhen	4	F	d *
Nemea River	15	C	b
Némecký Brod (Deutsch-Brod)	87	J	d
Nenagh	74	B	b
Nepomuk	79	H	d
Neptune, Temple of, on Sunium Prom.	16	C	b
Nerchinsk	171	M	c
Neuberg, in Styria	79	I	e
Neudorf (Spišska Nová Ves, Igló)	79	L	d
Neuhaus, castle in Bohemia.	79	I	d
Neuhausen, in Livonia	88	L	c
Neuilly (near Paris)	168 D	A	d
Neuilly, Treaty of	168 L	leg.	
Neuilly Wood	168 C	B	c
Neusatz (Novi Sad, Ujvidék)	159	J	f
Neusiedl, lake	103	M	g
Neutra (Nitra. Nyitra)	79	K	d
Neuve Chapelle	168 C	B	b
Neuveville-devant-Nancy, La	104 A	D	c
Neuveville-lès-Raon, La	104 A	D	c
Nevada Mountains	82	B	b
Neva River	88	N	b
Neville's Cross	74	L	e
Neviodunum	27	J	b
New Albion, reg.	107	E	d
New Bern	193	F	d
New Britain, reg.	136	Q-S	d
Newcastle, in Leinster	74	C	b
Newcastle, in Ulster	74	C	a
New Castile, reg.	108	J	i
New Edinburgh	128 B	ins. A	(N. E.)
New England, reg.	128 B	E	c
Newfoundland, isl.	186	N	d
New Galicia, prov.	190	E	g
New Guinea, Territory	179	F	h
Newport, in Monmouth	162	D	f
New Republic	175	N I	(N.R.)
New Shops, bldg. in Rome	24	A	(17)
New Zealand, Dominion of	172	F	d
New Zealand (Statenland)	128 C	Q	h
Nganking	104 C	L	d
Nicobar Islands	104 C	J	g
Nicomedia (Ismid)	168 J	B	a
Nicoverra Islands	104 C	J	g
Nidisdale, dist.	128	E	e

Nied River	104 A	D	b
Nijmegen (Nymegen, Nimwegen)	117	D	c
Nijmegen (Nymegen, Nimwegen), Hans. cy.	99	ins.	B
Nikh	168 K	H	c
Nikopoli	165	D	b
Nilawar	104 B	S	j
Nimrim	7	D	f
Nimwegen, Nimeguen see Nymegen (Nijmegen)			
Nin (Nona) bp.	95	F	c
Ning-hia	104 C	K	d
Ning-po	104 C	M	e
Ninua	5	D	b
Niriz	168 K	F	d
Niriz (Bakhtegan), lake	168 K	F	d
Niš (Nish)	165	B	b
Nishapur	104 B	F	d
Nisibin	168 G	N	h
Nisibin, metropol.	99	L	f
Nitra (Neutra)	79	K	d
Nizhne Kolymsk	171	R	b
Nizhne Udinsk	179	A	b
Nizhni Kamchatka	128 C	Q	c
Nizhni-Novgorod	138	F	d
Noain	83	K	g
No-Amon (Thebes)	4	F	d *
Nogent (-sur-Marne)	158	B	d
Nogent (-sur-Seine)	69	I	f
Nordstrand, isl.	86	G	a
Norfolk, dist.	60	E	c
Norfolk, cty. in England	74	N	g
Norham	74	K	d
Northallerton, parl. bor.	163	M	c
North Australia, state	172	C	b
North Caucasus, economic reg.	168 F	leg.	
Northeast, economic reg.	168 F	leg.	
Northern Ireland, reg.	184	B	b
Northern Long Wall, in Athens	23	D	
North Folk (East Angles), people	51	S	k
North Osset, auton. area	168 F	leg.	
North Osset Territory	168 J	D	a
North Riding, dist.	60	I	b
North Sporades, isl.	165	C	d
North Uist, isl.	128	A	c
Northumberland, duchy.	60	H	b
Northumbria, km.	60	C	b
Northwest, economic reg.	168 F	leg.	
Northwestern Greeks, people	14	leg.	
Norumbega, reg.	108	K	c
Nosairians, people	168 L	K	h
Nossibé	175	H	f
Noteborg	138	D	d
Notley, mon.	127	P	h
Nottingham, danish borough	60	I	c
Nottingham, cty.	74	L	g
Nová Ves (Neudorf)	79	L	d
Nové Město (Neustadt, in Moravia)	135	I	d
Novgorod, about 840	45	K	a
Novi Pazar	165	B	b
Novi Sad (Neusatz, Ujvidék)	159	J	f
Novo-Cherkask	139	F	f
Novorossisk	168 J	C	a
Nowe Miasto	155	K	c
Nowy Port (Neufahrwasser)	168 D	D	c
Nowy Sącz (Neu Sandec)	135	K	d
Nowy Targ (Neumarkt, in Galicia)	135	K	d
Nubia, reg.	4	F	e *
Nukha	168 K	E	a
Nutmeg Islands	128 C	ins.	C
Nyborg	88	D	d
Nyeman River	168 G	J	d
Nyitra (Neutra)	155	J	d
Nyitra (Neutra), bp.	95	F	b
Nymburk (Nimburg)	135	H	c
Nymegen (Nijmegen)	55	Q	i

Nyon	91	O	l
Oakley	60	J	d
Oaxus	14	ins.	
Oberhausen	168 E	B	b
Oberland, reg., in Berne	91	P	l
Obi River	104 B	G	a
O'Brien, fam.	74	B	b
Observatory, bldg. in Athens	23	D	
Ocean Island	179	H	h
Ochakov	139	D	f
O'Connel, fam.	74	A	c
O'Connor, fam.	74	B	b
Odar (Oder), R.	168 D	D	c
Ödemish	168 J	A	b
O'Dempsy, fam.	74	C	b
Odeum of Herodes Atticus, in Athens	23	C	
Odiham, castle	74	M	h
O'Dogherty, fam.	74	C	a
O'Donnel, fam.	74	C	a
O'Donoughue, fam.	74	B	b
O'Dwyer, fam.	74	C	b
Oeum, in Attica	16	B	a
Oeum, in Lacedaemonia	14	C	b
O'Farrel (Ferral), fam.	74	C	b
Offaly, cty.	74	C	b
Offa's Dyke	60	C	c
O'Flaherty, fam.	74	B	b
O'Hara, fam.	74	B	a
Ohrid (Okhrida)	165	B	c
Ohud, mt.	53	D	g
Oikanga	182 E	E	a
Oirat, Autonomous Socialist Soviet Area	170	J	c
Okas	53	F	d
O'Kelly, fam.	74	B	b
Okhrida (Ohrid)	89	B	b
Olbia (Astacus)	9	G	d
Old Babylonian Empire	4		
Old Calabar	136	J	d
Oldenburg, in Holstein, bp.	95	C	a
Old Sarum, bp.	97	P	j
Old Shops, bldg. in Rome	24	A (16)	
Oliva, in Spain	83	K	h
Olomouc (Olmütz)	87	K	d
Olomouc (Olmütz), bp.	95	F	b
Olovo	103	N	f
Oltu (Aluta), R.	168	I	d
Olvera	83	J	h
Olympene, reg.	9	F	e
Olympia, Plan of	9	H	f
Olympus, mt., in Lesbos	9	D	e
Olympus Mysius mt.	9	G	d
O'Malley, fam.	74	B	b
Oman, Gulf of	104 B	F	e
Oman, reg.	104 B	F	e
Oman, Sea of	104 B	G	f
Omiš (Almissa), bp.	95	C	f
O'More, fam.	74	C	b
Onchestus	11	E	d
O'Neill, fam.	74	C	a
Onon Kerule	92	L	b
Onon River	92	L	c
Opava (Troppau)	159	I	d
Ophrynium	9	B	c
Oppidum Branchidarum	19	K	c
Oradea Mare (Grosswardein)	159	K	e
Orange in Afrika, Guinea Coast	128 C	ins.	D
Orăştie (Broos)	159	L	f
Ordovices, people	51	N	h
O'Reilly, fam.	74	C	b
Orford	74	O	g
Orkhon River	104 C	K	c
Ormuz, Gulf of	168 K	G	d
Ormuz, isl.	104 B	F	e
Ormuz, km.	104 B	F	e
Ormuz, Strait of	168 K	G	d
Ornas (Otrar)	104 B	G	c
Ornas (Tana)	99	K	d
Ornes	104 A	C	b
Oropesa	83	L	g

O'Rourke, fam. 74 B a
Orphan Asylum in Athens 23 D
Ortenburg, castle 79 H d
Ortiz de Retes, route of 110 FF h
Ösel, bp. 88 I b
Osezaki 179 D d
O'Shaughnessy, fam. 74 B b
Osiek, near Thorn 159 J b
Osjek (Essek) 159 J f
Oslo 46 I a
Osmanie 168 J C b
Osorhej (Maros Vasarhely) 168 I c
Osseg (Osiek, near Thorn) 159 J b
Ossetes, people 67 O e
Ossory, dist. 74 C b
Ostrołęka (Ostrolenka) 135 K b
Ostyaks, people 138 K c
O'Sullivan, fam. 74 B c
Oswestry (Maserfield) 60 C c
Oswiecim 87 L c
Otford 60 E d
Otočac (Otoschatz), bp. 95 F c
O'Toole, fam. 74 C b
Otrar 104 B G c
Otterburn 74 K d
Ottoman Empire, 1451-1481 93
Ottoman Empire, 1481-1683 128A
Ottoman Empire, 1683-1913 164
Ottoman Empire till 1920, 1922 168 J B b
Oudle, mon. 60 D c
Oulu Kishla 168 J C b
Ourcq River 168 C B c
Our River 104 A D a
Outer Ceramicus, deme 23 D
Outer Tibet, reg. 170 J e
Oxus River 19 J c
Oxyrhynchus 4 F d *
Oxyrhynchus, patr. 43 I h
Oykell River 128 D b

Pactye 9 D d
Padang 168 A O e
Padstow, mon. 60 G d
Pagan 104 C J e
Pagi Islands 104 C J h
Palace Garden, in Athens 23 D
Palace of the Crown Prince, in Athens 23 D
Palaeo-Kastro (Besika Tepe) 9 A b
Palaeo-Kastro (Ophrynium) 9 B a
Palaestra 9 H f
Palam 104 B H e
Palazzo Barberini, bldg. in Rome 22 A
Palazzo Senatore, bldg. in Rome 22 A
Palembang 128 C ins. C
Palermo, univ. 100 H g
Palmaria, isl., in Liguria 26 D d
Palmaria, isl., Pontiae Isls. 30 B b
Palmyrene, reg. 20 H e
Palo Alto, in California 180 O d
Palo Alto, in Texas 201 F d
Pampa Central 216 ins.
Panactum 16 A a
Pan-American-Railway 215 leg.
Pancrazio, Porta San, loc. in Rome 22 A
Panderma 168 J A a
Panormus in Achaia 14 B a
Panoramus, port, in Tenos I. 15 F b
Panthéon, ch. in Paris 149 B
Papremis 4 ins. *
Papua, Territory of 172 D a
Parganas, 24 (Twenty four) 137 E d
Parisi, people in Roman Britain 51 P h
Parium 9 E d
Parrett River 60 C d
Partition of Guiana and the Westindies 128 B ins. A
Pashat 104 B H d

Passarowitz (Požarevac) 131 H e
Passavant (-sur-Aisne) 104 A B c
Passchendaele Ridge 168 C B b (P.)
Patani 104 C K g
Patroclus, Burial mound of 9 A b
Pattan 104 B R i
Patzinaks, people 47 M-O d
Pechelbronn 168 E B c
Pechenga 168 G L b
Pécs (Fünfkirchen) 159 J e
Pécs (Fünfkirchen), bp. 95 F b
Pécs (Fünfkirchen), univ. 100 J c
Pecsaete, people 60 D c
Peebles, cty. 128 E e
Pegu 104 C J f
Pegu, reg. 104 C J f
Peisern (Pyzdry) 79 J b
Peking 104 C L d
Pelagonia (Heraclea) 10 C a
Pelagonia, dist. 10 C a
Pelasgikon, in Athens 23 C
Pelopium 9 H f (5)
Penjdeh 168 K H b
Penjhir 104 B G d
Penner River 137 C f
Peñon de Velez, bay 174 P n
Penselwood, battle 60 C d
Pentan, reg. 104 C K g
Pentland Firth 128 E b
Penzance 102 B c
Peraeum 15 C a
Percote 9 D d
Pereiaslav 139 D e
Pereiaslavl-Saleski 138 E d
Pergamum 9 E e
Perinthus 9 E d
Perperene 9 D e
Perrhaebians (Perrhaebi), people 8 N h
Perrot, Fort 191 G c
Persepolis, ruin 168 K F d
Persia, khan. 104 B F d
Persia, reg. 53 G-I c
Persia, Sea of 99 M h
Persian Gates 19 H e
Perth, in Scotland 128 E d
Perth, cty. 128 D d
Petapoli 128 B ins. B
Peterborough, abbey 74 M g
Peterborough (Medeshampsted), mon. 60 D c
Peterborough, Soke (Abbey) of 74 M g
Peterhead 128 G c
Petersfield, bor. 74 M h
Pétervárad (Peterwardein) 159 J f
Petitjean 174 P n
Petrikau (Piotrkov) 79 K c
Petrograd (Leningrad, St. Petersburg) 168 D G b
Petrovaradin (Peterwardein) 87 L f
Pettau, March of 72 D b
Pevensey 60 E d
Pfirt 91 P k
Phabra, isl. 16 B b
Phalasarna 14 ins.
Phaleric Wall, in Athens 23 D
Pharaton 7 C d
Pharygae 16 F e
Phelleus, mt. 16 B a
Pherae in Messenia 14 C b
Pherae in Thessaly 11 D c
Philaedae 16 C b
Philiphaugh 128 F e
Philippeum, in Olympia 9 H f (8)
Philippus, Principality of 7
Phinopolis 9 G c
Phocians, people 8 O h
Phoenician trade-routes 44 leg.
Phreattys 16 D c
Phrygian Empire 8 Q h
Phrygian Kingdom 5 B b
Piazza Cavour, loc. in Rome 22 A
Piazza Colonna, loc. in Rome 22 A

Piazza Dante, loc. in Rome 22 A
Piazza della Libertà, loc. in Rome 22 A
Piazza del Popolo, loc. in Rome 22 A
Piazza di San Pietro, loc. in Rome 22 A
Piazza Doria, loc. in Rome 22 A
Piazza Navona, loc. in Rome 22 A
Piazza Risorgimento, loc. in Rome 22 A
Piazza Venezia, loc. in Rome 22 A
Piazza Vittorio Emanuele, loc. in Rome 22 A
Pica 216 ins.
Pickawillany, Fort 191 I c
Pictones (Pictavi), people 38 B c
Picts, people, 8 cent. 60 B a, b
Picts and Scots, Kingdom of 60 G a
Pietro in Montorio, San, ch. in Rome 22 A
Piety (Pietas), Temple of 24 A
Pindasus, mt. 9 E e
Ping-yang, in China 104 C L d
Pinkie 128 F e
Piraeus Street, in Athens 23 D
Pirate Cove 180 L b
Pireathon 7 C d
Pisagua 216 ins.
Pistoia 90 L j
Pisuerga River 83 E c
Pityonnesus, isl. 15 D b
Pizzo 161 K h
Place de l'Opéra, in Paris 149 B (2)
Place of Concord, loc. in Athens 23 D
Place of Constitution, in Athens 23 D
Place Royale, in Paris 149 B
Plana 103 O g
Pläswitz 155 I c
Plateau of Langres 168 C C d
Platten See (L. Balaton) 87 K e
Playari (Bulair) 168 L D c
Pleasant Island 179 H g
Plöcken Pass 79 H e
Plovdiv (Philippopolis) 93 C b
Plympton, bor. 74 I i
Plzeň (Pilsen) 103 K d
Poemanenum 9 F e
Poikile, Stoa-, in Athens 23 D (1)
Pointe (Point) de Galle 137 C g
Pointe Noire 182 C C h
Pokrovsk 168 G O e
Poland, rep. 168 G J e
Polangen 88 I d
Polesie, reg. 55 J c
Poles, people in 1929 168 H E—F b
Polianovka 138 D d
Policlinic, bldg. in Rome 22 A
Polish Corridor 168 D D c (P. C.)
Polock (Polotsk) 71 M b
Polock, princ. 71 L b
Polumbum 104 B H g
Pomaks, people in 1929 168 H F d
Pomerania-Stettin, duchy 79 H b
Pomerania-Wolgast, duchy 79 I b
Pomesania, bp. 95 F a
Pomfret, mon. 97 P h
Pommat (Formazza) 168 H C c
Pompey 104 A D c
Ponape, isl. 168 A R d
Poniec (Punitz) 135 I c
Pontafel 79 H e
Ponta Grossa 215 E e
Pont-à-Mousson 104 A D c
Pont de Grammont, in Paris 149 B
Ponteamas 104 C K i
Ponte Cavour, loc. in Rome 22 A
Ponte Garibaldi, loc. in Rome 22 A
Ponte Sisto, loc. in Rome 22 A
Ponte Umberto I, loc. in Rome 22 A

Ponte Vittorio Emanuele, loc.
in Rome 22   A
Pontia, isl. 30   B   b
Pont Marie, in Paris . . 149   B
Pont-Saint-Vincent . . 104 A   D   c
Pontus, reg. under Trajan . 20   G   b
Poopo, lake . . . . 216 ins.
Porchester, bor. 60   I   d
Pordenone 154   G   e
Porolissa 44   D   b
Porrentruy 91   P   k
Porta del Popolo, loc. in Rome 22   A
Porta Flumentana, in Rome 24   A
Port Alfred 175   M   m
Porta Maggiore, loc. in Rome 22   A
Porta Pia, loc. in Rome . . 22   A
Porta Portese, loc. in Rome 22   A
Porta San Giovanni, loc. in
Rome 22   A
Porta San Lorenzo, loc. in
Rome 22   A
Porta San Sebastiano, loc. in
Rome 22   A
Port Desire 108   K   l
Portendik 136   I   d
Porte Saint-Antoine, in Paris 149   B
Porte Saint-Bernard, in Paris 149   B
Port Harcourt 174   D   d
Port Moresby 179   F   i
Port Nelson 180   R   b
Porto Belgrano 181   U   k
Porto Rose . . . . 168 D   D   d
Porto Velho 181   V   i
Port Royal (Kingston) in
Jamaica . . . . . . 128 B ins. A
Portus, loc. near ancient Troy 9   A   a
Portus Lemanae 51   Q   i
Port Vila 179   H   i
Posidium, prom., Propontis 9   F   d
Postumia (Adelsberg) . . . 159   H   t
Powis (Powys), dist. 60   H   c
Poyang Lake . . . . 104 C   L   e
Požarevac (Passarowitz) . . 139   B   g
Požega (Pozsega), in Sla-
vonia 159   I   f
Požega (Pozhega), in Servia 87   L   g
Poznań (Posen) 66   J   d
Poznań (Posen), bp. 95   F   a
Pozo Almonte . . . . 216 ins.
Pozsony (Presburg, Bratis-
lava) 79   K   d
Pozsony (Presburg), univ. 100   I   e
Prachatice (Prachatitz) . . . 87   I   d
Praesus . . . . 14 ins.
Praha (Prague) 87   J   c
Praha (Prague), abp. 95   E   b
Praïa 181   Y   f
Predil, Fort 154   G   e
Predil Pass 79   H   e
Presburg (Pozsony, Bratis-
lava) 87   K   d
Prestonpans 128   F   e
Priapus 9   E   d
Přibyslav (Pribislau) 87   J   d
Prinkipo (Princes) Islands 168 L   G   f
Pripet River 55   J   a
Prison (Carcer), in Rome . . 24   A   (4)
Priština 165   B   b
Prizren 165   B   b
Proconnesus 9   E   d
Proëdria, in Olympia 9   H   f
Prome . . . . 104 C   J   f
Pronectus 9   E   d
Propontis (Sea of Marmora) 9   E   d
Propylaeum, in Olympia . . 9 H f (11)
Providence Islands . . 128 B ins. A
Pruntrut (Porrentruy) . . . 91   P   k
Prusa 9   G   d
Prussi (Prussians), people . 57   H   c
Prymnessus 20   E   e
Prytaneum, in Olympia . . 9   H   f(9)
Prytaneum, Ancient, in
Athens 23   D   (10)

Psillium 9   G   c
Pszczyna (Pless) 135   J   d
Ptuj (Pettau) 103   L   c
Pudefitani . . . . 104 B   R   j
Puerto Escocés . . . . . . 128 C leg.
Pulicat . . . . 104 B   S   j
Pulo Condore Island . . . 171   L   h
Punt, reg. 4   F   e *
Puschlav (Poschiavo) . . . 91   S   !
Puszta, reg. 103   O   e
Putlam . . . . 104 B   S   k
Putumayo River 214   B   c
Pyhrn Pass 87   J   e
Pylus vetus 14   B   b
Pyrgi 27   F   f
Pyrgus 14   B   b
Pyrrha 9   D   e

Qemt (Egypt), emp. 4   F   d *
Quai Dauphin, in Paris . 149   B
Quai des Théatines, in
Paris . . . . . . 149 B (Q. d. Th.)
Quai d'Orsay, in Paris . . 149   B
Quais, isl. . . . . 104 B   F   e
Qu'Appelle River 190   E   a
Quengian . . . . 104 C   K   d
Quiahuiztlán 106   D   a
Quilon . . . . 104 B   R   k
Quiros, route of . . . . . 128 C   P   f
Qurun, Birket el, lake . . 174   J   j

Raab (Györ), in Hungary . . 72   D   b
Raabs, in Austria 72   D   b
Rabaul 179   G   h
Rabbit Islands . . . . . . 168 L   D   d
Raby 74   L   e
Racconigi 161   F   e
Racionsh 87   L   b
Raciawice 135   K   c
Radcot Bridge 74   L   h
Radimiches, people 57   J   e
Radisson, Fort 191   G   b
Radstädter Tauern, pass . . 87   I   e
Radziejow 79   K   b
Raeti, poeple 29   B   a
Ragnit 103   P   a
Rai (Ragy) 99   N   f
Rakow (Annopol) 103   P   c
Ramoth 6   E   c *
Ramsbury, bp. 60   I   d
Ranchos de Calpán . . . 106   B   a
Ras (Novi Pazar) 89   G   f
Ras-el-Ain . . . . 168 J   C   b
Ratnapura . . . . 104 B   S   k
Rauden, mon. 80   F   f
Ravendan 68   C   b
Rawitsch (Rawicz) 155   I   e
Rayak . . . . 168 J   C   c
Rea, Lough, lake 127   J   h
Reading, in England 60   I   d
Recklinghausen . . . . . 168 E   B   b
Reculver, mon. 60   E   d
Redesdale, march 74   K   d
Red Tower (Rotenturm Pass) 159   M   f
Reged, dist. 60   C   b
Reghinul Săsesc (Szasz-Re-
gen) 159   M   e
Regia, bldg. in Rome 24   A   (18)
Reichenstein 87   K   c
Reigate, castle 74   M   h
Reikiavik 166   A   c
Reine, Fort de la 190   F   a
Remeth 7   C   d
Renfrew, cty. 128   D   e
Repgow 85   G   e
Rephaim 7   E   e
Reppichau 85   G   e
Repton 60   I   c
Resengo . . . . 104 C   K   h
Resion, Gate of 93   G   e
Resvojo, R. . . . . 168 L   F   e
Rethondes . . . . 168 C   B   c
Retz, in Austria 87   J   d

Retz, in France, seign. . . . 76   C   c
Rhaedestus 9   E   d
Rhaeto-Romanians, people
in 1929 . . . . 168 H   C   c
Rhebus 9   G   c
Rhegion, Gate of 93   G   e
Rhesus River 9   D   c
Rethondes . . . . 168 C   B   c
Rhizarion, bldg. in Athens 23   D
Rhodius-River 9   D   d
Rhoeteum 9   B   b
Rhoeteum, prom. 9   B   a
Rhone-Rhine Canal . . 168 E   B   c
Rhuddlan 74   J   f
Rhyndacus River 9   F   e
Riadh . . . . 104 B   E   e
Riberalta 181   U   i
Richmond, castle near York 74   L   e
Riff, the, reg. 174   D   c
Rimnik 139   C   f
Rio do Padrão 108   R   h
Ripen (Ribe) 88   C   d
Risan (Risano), bp. 95   F   c
Risorgimento, Piazza, loc.
in Rome 22   A
River-gate, in Rome 24   A
Riyadh 170   F   f
Road to Marathon, street in
Athens 23   D
Robertsons, fam. 128   D   d
Rochefort, near Langres 104 A   C   c
Rohitsch (Rogatec) 79   I   e
Romagne . . . . 104 A   C   b
Roman Baths, in Athens . . 23   D
Roman Empire, under Diocle-
tian 34, 35
Roman (Romanula) Gate . . 24   A
Roman Market, in Athens . 23   D
Roman trade-routes . . . . . 44 leg.
Roman Wall, in England . . 60   C   b
Rome-Ostia Railway Station 22   A
Romney 74   N   i
Romulus, Grave of 24   A   (11)
Ronas Peninsula . . . . . 128 ins.
Roncal 83   K   g
Roosebeke 78   C   c
Roratonga, isl. 180   L   j
Ros (Rurik), House of . . 138 leg.
Roscrea 74   C   b
Rosenau 80   G   g
Rosenberg, castle 79   I   d
Rositten 88   L   c
Ross and Cromarty, cty. . . 128   D   c
Rossieny 88   J   d
Rostra, loc. in Rome . . . 24   A   (10)
Rostra Julia 24   B   (17)
Roubaix . . . . 168 C   B   b
Rouge, Fort 190   F   b
Rousay 128   E   a
Rovno 168   J   a
Roxburgh 128   F   e
Roxburgh, cty. 128   F   e
Royal Palace, in Athens . . 23   D
Royal Palace, Ancient, in
Athens 23   C   (2)
Royal Stables, in Athens . . 23   D
Ruanda, reg. 175   F   e
Rubruquis, Route of . . . 104 B leg.
Rudeshur, R. . . . . 168 K   F   b
Rudnik 103   O   f
Rue de Grenelle, street in
Paris 149   B
Rue de Sèvres, street in
Paris 149   B
Rue de Vaugirard, street
in Paris 149   B
Rue du Bac, street in Paris 149   B
Rue Montmartre, in Paris. 149   B
Rugians or Rugii, people . 16 H b, G c
Ruhrort . . . . 168 E   B   b
Ruhr Valley . . . . . . 168 D B c (R. V.)
Rullion Green, battle . . . 128   E   e
Rum, isl. 128   B   d

Rumania, princ. till 1881 . 164 Cb - Da
Rumania, km. 1882 .... 164 Cb - Da
Rumania, km. 1918 .... 168 G J-K f
Rumanians, poeple .... 168 H F-G c
Rupert's Land .... 212 E-I c
Rupt .... 104 A C b
Rurik, House of ...... 138 leg.
Rus'chuk .... 165 E b
Russia in Europe, 1300—1796 138—139
Russia (R.S.F.S.R.) ... 168 F leg.
Russian River .... 190 A d
Russian Socialist Federal
    Soviet Republic ... 168 G L-R d
Ruthenia, dist. ...... 168 D E d
Ruthenians, people in 1929 168 H F-G c
Ruthin, castle .... 74 J f
Ruza .... 138 E d

Saalabbin .... 7 B e
Saar Basin .... 168 E B c
Saargemünd (Sarre-
    guemines) .... 168 E B c
Saaz (Žatec) .... 87 I c
Sabina, Santa-, ch. in Rome 22 A
Sabini, people, north-east
    of Rome .... 27 G e
Sabzawar .... 92 F d
Sachion (Sha-chau) .... 104 C J c
Sächsisch Reen (Szasz-
    Regen) .... 159 M e
Sacred Road, to Eleusis .. 23 D
Saffi .... 174 C a
Saffron Walden ..... 127 Z o
Sagitaria (Tahiti) .... 128 B A f
Saida (Sidon) ...... 168 J C c
Saint Albans, mon., in
    England .... 60 D d
Saint Andrews, in Scotland 128 F d
Saint-Antoine, Fort .... 191 G c
Saint Asaph (Llan Elwy), bp. 60 H c
Saint-Aubin du Cormier .. 86 B d
Saint Bartholomew, isl. . 128 B ins. A
Saint Charles, in Quebec 191 K b
Saint Croix, in Quebec . 191 K b
Saint Croix, Fort, in
    Wisconsin ...... 191 G b
Saint David, castle ..... 74 H h
Saint Davids (Mynyw), bp. . 60 B d
Saint Demetrius ...... 9 A b
Saint Domingue, col. .. 128 B E e
Saint Eustache, ch. in Paris 149 B
Saint Eustatius, isl. ... 213 F c
Saint Fr. Xavier ...... 191 H c
Saint Germain l'Auxerrois,
    in Paris .... 149 B
Saint Gotthard, mon. .. 80 E h
Saint Jean, Fort ...... 191 L b
Saint Joseph, Fort (L.Huron) 191 I c
Saint Joseph, Fort (L. Michi-
    gan) .... 191 H c
Saint Joseph, Lac- ..... 191 G a
Saint-Julien-sur-Rognon . 104 A C b
Saint Louis, in Gambia . 128 B H e
Saint Louis (São Luiz do
    Maranhão) ...... 128 B F f
Saint Louis, ch. in Paris . 149 B
Saint Louis, Fort in
    Alabama .... 191 H e
Saint Marcel, ch. in Paris 149 B
Saint Martin, ch. in Jeru-
    salem .... 68 ins. B (10)
Saint Martin, ch. in Paris 149 B
Saint Medard, ch. in Paris 149 B
Saint Michael, parl. bor. . 163 I g
Saint-Mihiel .... 168 E B c
Saint Naoum .... 168 D E e
Saint Nicholas, Fort .. 191 G c
Saint Osyth, mon. ..... 127 Q h
Saint Paul, Pribilof Isl... 180 K b
Saint Peter's Railway Sta-
    tion, in Rome ...... 22 A
Saint Pierre, Fort (Rainy L.) 191 G b
Saint Pierre, Fort (Yazoo R.) 191 G e

Saint (San) Sebastian .. 128 C ins. D
Saint Sulpice, ch., in Paris 149 B
Saint Thaddeus .... 99 L f
Saint Thomas, Grave of 104 B I f
Saint Thomé, Jesuit mis-
    sion .... 128 B ins. A
Sairam .... 104 B G c
Sakkara, Pyramids of .. 4 ins. *
Sala .... 44 A c
Salacia .... 38 A e
Salahiyeh .... 150 B a
Salbai .... 137 C c
Salbke .... 85 F d
Salces .... 83 L g
Salinas .... 181 W h
Salsette Island ..... 137 B c
Saltash, parl. bor. .... 163 J g
Salwin River ...... 104 C J e
Samaga .... 7 D e
Samara River ..... 139 H e
Samarra .... 168 B L e
Sambhal .... 104 B H e
Sambhal, reg. ..... 104 J H e
Samir .... 7 B f
Samland, dist. ..... 87 M d
Samnites, people ... 29 D d
Samothrace ...... 9 C d
Samothrace, isl. .... 9 C d
Samoyeds, people, in Asia 104 C J a
Samoyeds, people, in Europe 138 H b
Sana .... 104 B F f
San Clemente, in Spain .. 83 K h
Sanday, isl. ...... 128 F a
Sandjy, Sea of ..... 104 C L f
Sandu .... 104 C L c
Sandwich, in England ... 74 O h
Sandy Sea, desert .... 104 B F d
San Estéban de Gormaz . 82 B a
Sanf, reg. .... 104 C K f
San Gerónimo, near Córdova 83 J h
San Giovanni in Laterano,
    ch. in Rome .... 22 A
Sangpo, R. ...... 104 B I e
Sangüesa .... 83 K g
San Juan Hill .... 213 E b (S. J.)
Sankt Andrä ..... 87 J e
Sankt Andreas (Sassandra) 128 B H e
Sankt Eustatius, isl. .... 213 F c
Sankt Martin, isl. .... 213 F c
Sankt Veit, in Carinthia . 87 J e
San men Bay ..... 171 N f
Sanoah .... 7 B f
San Pietro in Montorio,
    ch. in Rome .... 22 A
Sanquhar .... 128 D e
San Stefano, Treaty of . 168 L leg.
Santa Cruz (Saint Croix),
    isl, West Indies ..... 105 H c
Santa Hermandad ..... 83 L h leg.
Santa (Saint) Lucia, isl. . 213 F c
Santa Maura (Leucas), isl. . 10 B d
Santa Sabina, ch. in Rome 22 A
Santiago de Compostela . 82 A a
Santiago de Compostela,
    abp. .... 94 A c
Santi Quaranta ..... 164 B b
Santo (San) Stefano .... 164 D b
São Agostinho, Capo ... 108 N h
São Jorge da Mina (Elmina) 128 B H c
São Roque, cape .... 214 F c
São Salvador (Bahia) ... 108 N i
São Thomé, Cape ... 108 M j
Sapaei, people .... 9 C c
Sapera .... 104 B R i
Saphir .... 7 B e
Sapolye .... 88 M b
Sarai, Sea of ..... 99 N f
Sarakhs .... 104 B G d
Sarepta, in Phoenicia .... 6 C h
Sarepta, in Russia .... 139 F f
Sargasso Sea ..... 108 K e
Sari .... 104 B F d
Sari Bair .... 168 L D c

Sari Kamish .... 168 J D a
Sarkel .... 45 L c
Saros, Gulf of ...... 168 L D c
Saros Islands .... 168 L D c
Sarpedonium, prom. .... 9 C d
Sarrebourg (Saarburg) . 168 E B c
Sarum, Old, bp. ..... 97 P j
Saseno, isl. ...... 168 F I g
Sassandra (Sankt Andreas) 128 B H e
Sassanids, Dominion of the,
    8 cent. .... 53 G c
Satganw .... 104 B I e
Satu Mare (Szatmar Nemeti) 80 H h
Saturn, Temple of ..... 24 A (15)
Sauer, R. .... 168 E B c
Sauerland, dist. ..... 168 E B b
Saulces - Montclin .... 104 A B b
Saulxerotte ...... 104 A C c
Sauvage, Fort ...... 191 I b
Sauville ...... 104 A B b
Savah .... 104 B F d
Saverne (Zabern) .... 134 D d
Savigliano ...... 150 D d
Saxons, people in France . 45 D c
Sayville .... 168 A F c
Scalae Gemoniae, loc. in
    Rome ...... 24 A (3)
Scalanova ...... 168 J A b
Scalloway ...... 128 ins.
Scamander River .... 9 B b
Scandian Islands ... 38 E a
Scatinavia (Scandinavia) . 38 E a
Scepsis ...... 9 D c
Schauenburg, castle in
    Baden .... 142 B c
Schaumburg, castle in Lippe 72 B a
Schaunberg, castle in Austria 79 H d
Schauenberg (Schaumberg),
    cty. .... 79 H d
Scheggia Pass ..... 27 G c
Schemnitz (Banská Štiavnica,
    Selmeczbánya) .... 79 K d
Schneeberg (in Saxony) . 87 I c
Schouten, route of .... 128 B F h
Schwarzena River ... 135 I d
Schyl (Jiu), R. .... 168 H d
Sciri, people ...... 39 G b
Sciron, loc. in Athens .. 23 D
Sciron River ..... 23 D
Škodra (Scutari), bp. .... 94 F c
Scone ...... 60 H a
Scotch Harbor .... 128 C leg.
Scotra (Sokotra), isl. . 104 B F f
Scots, people, about 900 . 57 B c-b
Scotts, fam. ...... 128 c
Sea of Chin ..... 104 C L e
Sea of England .... 98 D b
Sea of Herkend .... 104 B I f
Sea of Kharezm (Aral Sea) 104 B F c
Sea of Oman .... 104 B G f
Sea of Persia and the
    Indies ...... 104 B F e
Sea of Sandjy ... 104 C L f
Sea of the Indian Islands 104 C K g
Sea of the Indies .... 104 B G f
Sebatum ...... 27 F a
Sebu River ..... 174 P n
Secondi ...... 128 C ins. D
Sedd-el-Bahr .... 168 L D c
Sefid Rud=Amardus River 44 G c
Segeberg, castle .... 88 D e
Segesvar (Schässburg,
    Sighişoara) ...... 168 I c
Segobriga, near Saguntum . 38 B e
Segobriga, near Toletum . 38 B e
Segodunum .... 38 C d
Segor (Zoar) ...... 7 C f
Segura River ..... 82 B b
Segu Sikoro ...... 174 C c
Sehwan ...... 104 B G e
Seihun River .... 168 J C b
Seilan (Ceylon), isl. . 104 B S k
Seille River ..... 104 A D c

Seistan, reg. . . . . . . 104 B G d
Selenga River . . . . . 104 C K c
Selestat (Schlettstadt) . . . 134 D d
Selke River . . . . 85 F e
Selkirk . . . . 128 F e
Selkirk, cty. . . . . . . 128 E e
Selmeczbánya (Schemnitz) . 87 L d
Selsey, bp. . . . . 60 D d
Seluan . . . . 174 Q n
Selymbria . . . . 9 F c
Selymbria, Gate of . . . . 93 G e
Semender . . . . 45 N d
Semigallia, dist. . . . . . 88 K c
Semigallians, people . . . . 57 I b
Semiscant (Samarkand) . 104 B G d
Semlin (Zemun) . . . . . . 87 M f
Semnan . . . . 168 K F b
Semneh . . . . 4 F d *
Senaculum, bldg. in Rome . 24 A (8)
Senatorio, Palazzo, bldg. in Rome . . . . . . 22 A
Senj (Zengg) . . . . 72 D c
Senj (Zengg), bp. . . . . 95 F b
Senjirli . . . . 5 C b
Sennabris . . . . 6 D c
Senussi, people . . . . . 174 F b
Septimius Severus, Arch of 24 B (11)
Seraijik . . . . 168 L D d
Serampur . . . . . . 128 B ins. B
Serbs, people in 1929 168 H E d
Sergin . . . . 168 L F f
Serre River . . . . . 104 A A b
Serrhium, prom. . . . . 9 C d
Sestus . . . . 9 D d
Sevastopol (Cherson) . . . 89 J d
Severians, people about 900 57 J c, I e
Sèvres . . . . 168 D A d
Sèvres, Treaty of . . . . . 168 L leg.
Sézanne . . . . 104 A A c
Shabatz (Šabac) . . . . . . 87 L f
Sha-chau . . . . 104 C J c
Shadwen Island . . . . . . 150 N e
Shaftesbury . . . . . . 74 K i
Shaftesbury, mon. . . . 97 O k
Shaliyat (Calicut) . . . . 104 B R j
Shamaiten (Samogitia), reg. 88 J d
Shamir (Van) . . . . . . 99 L f
Shangtu . . . . 104 C L c
Shatt-el-Arab, R. . . . . 168 K G d
Sheffield, castle . . . . 74 L f
Shemak (Shemakha) . . . . 99 M e
Sheppey, Isle of . . . . . 60 E d
Sherborne, bp. . . . . . 60 C d
Sheriffmuir . . . . 128 E d
Sheshauen . . . . . . 174 P n
Shiahs, sect . . . . 168 L N g, leg.
Shiblak . . . . 9 B b
Shilka River . . . . . . 104 C L b
Shipyards, loc. in Rome . 24 B
Shiraz . . . . 104 B F e
Shirvan, reg. . . . . . . 139 G g
Shkodra (Scutari), in Servia 89 A b
Shoreham . . . . 74 M i
Shrewsbury in England . . . 65 E d
Shrewsbury, abbey . . . . . 74 K g
Shrewsbury, Palatine earldom 65 K g
Shropshire, cty. . . . . 74 K g
Shusha . . . . 168 K E e
Shushtar (Shuster) . . . . . 99 M e
Š benik (Sebenico) . . . . . 87 J g
Sibenik (Sebenico), bp. . . . 95 F c
Siberian, economic reg. . 170 leg.
Sibir . . . . 104 B G b
Sibiu (Hermannstadt) . 159 M f
Sicelia, hill in Athens . . . 23 D
Sidini, people . . . . . 38 E b
Sidnacaester, bp. . . . . . 60 D c
Sieg River . . . . 134 D c
Sierra Gorda . . . . . 216 ins.
Sierra Leone, reg. . . . . 128 B H e
Siewierz . . . . 79 K c
Sigeum . . . . 9 A b
Sighişoara (Schässburg) . . 159 M f

Sigrium, prom. . . . . . . 9 C e
Sikhs, people . . . . . . 137 B b
Si-kiang, R. . . . . . . 104 C K e
Sikkim . . . . 171 J f
Silberberg . . . . 103 M c
Silchester . . . . 51 P i
Silet . . . . 174 D b
Silian (Ceylon). isl. . . . 104 B S k
Silivri, Gate of . . . . . 93 G e
Siljan, lake . . . . 88 F a
Silk-Route . . . . 104 B leg.
Sillein (Zsolna, Žilina) . 155 J d
Sillerie . . . . 191 K b
Sil River . . . . 82 A a
Silsileh, Gebel . . . . 4 F d
Simoeis River (Dumbrek R.) 9 B b
Sin . . . . 104 C L d
Sin-al-Sin (Canton) . . . 104 C L d
Sinclayrs, fam. . . . . . 128 E b
Sine . . . . 168 L D d
Si-ngan-fu . . . . 104 C K d
Si-ning-fu . . . . 104 C K d
Sinkalan (Canton) . . . 104 C L e
Sinob (Sinope) . . . . 89 K f
Sinti, people . . . . . . 17 C a
Sinub (Sinope) . . . . . 168 J J d
Siraf . . . . 104 B F e
Siugui . . . . 104 C M d
Sivas . . . . 89 K g
Siwa Oasis . . . . 174 F b
Skara . . . . 46 I b
Skias (Tholos), in Athens . 23 D (7)
Skofja Loka (Bischoflack) 135 H e
Skoplje (Uskub) . . . . . 89 H f
Skradin (Scardona), bp. . . 95 F c
Skutari . . . . 168 G K g
Slack . . . . 60 C c
Sleat Sound . . . . . . 128 C c
Slesvik. . . . . 78 F a
Slesvik, Duchy of . . . . 78 F a
Slesvik (Schleswig), March of 62 E 1
Sligo, castle . . . . . . 74 B a
Slovenes, poeple, about 900 57 I-J b
Slovenes, people in 1929 168 H Dc, Gd
Sochaczew (Sokhaczew) . 135 K b
Södermanland, dist. . . . . 88 G b
Soer . . . . 104 B F e
Sofala . . . . 128 C J g
Sofia, Treaty of . . . . 168 L leg.
Söke . . . . 168 J A b
Solangas, people . . . . 92 M c
Sole Bay . . . . 125 D b
Solingen . . . . 102 H c
Solon Street in Athens . 23 D
Solovyeva . . . . 153 O g
Solvychegodsk . . . . . 138 G c
Solway Firth . . . . . 60 C b
Soma . . . . 165 E d
Somnath . . . . 104 B R i
Songhar . . . . 104 B R i
Songko River . . . . . . 171 L f
Sorbiodunum (Salisbury) . . 51 P i
Sous, Wadi . . . . . . 174 C a
Southampton in England . 60 I d
Southern Country (Negeb) . 7 B f
Southern Long Wall in Athens 23 D
Southern Sung Dynasty . . 92 K e
South Folk (East Angles), people . . . 51 S k
South Mining, economic reg. 168 F leg.
South Osset, auton. area . 168 F leg.
South Osset, Territory . 168 J D a
Southport . . . . . . 162 C d
South Sea Islands, Japan. Mand. . . . . . 179 G f
South Uist, isl. . . . . 128 A c
Southwark, bor. . . . . 60 I d
Southwest, economic reg.. 168 F leg.
Spa . . . . 168 F G e
Spanish Main (Tierra Firme) . . . . . . 128 B ins. A
Spes (Hope), Temple of . . 24 A
Spey (Spay) River . . . . 128 E c

Spichern . . . . 158 D d
Spišská Stará Ves (Altendorf) . . . . . . 79 L d
Spišská Nová Ves (Igló, Neudorf) . . . . . . 87 M d
Spithead . . . . 127 X p
Spits (Zips), dist. . . . . 168 D E d
Split (Spalato) . . . . . . 89 A b
Split (Spalato), abp. . . . . 95 F c
Spoleto, march . . . . . . 45 G d (Sp)
Spring Gate . . . . 93 G e
Srebrenica . . . . 103 N f
Srebrenik . . . . 87 L f
Sredetz (Sofia) . . . . . . 89 B b
Środa (Schroda) . . . . . 159 I b
Stadium, in Athens . . . 23 D
Stadium, in Olympia . . 9 H f
Stadium, street in Athens . 23 D
Stafford, bor. in England . . 60 H c
Stamford, in England, danish borough . . . . . . 60 I c
Stamford, mon. . . . . 60 D c
Stanimaka . . . . 165 D c
Stanislawow (Stanislau) . . 159 M d
Stará Ves (Spišská-, Altendorf) . . . . . . 79 L d
Stargard, in Holstein . . . 103 J a
Stargardt (in Pomerelia) . . 87 L b
Starhemberg, castle, near Wels . . . . . . 79 H d
Starhemberg, castle, near Wiener Neustadt. . . . 123 I e
Stari Grad (Cittavecchia), bp. 95 F c
Statenland (New Zealand) 128 C Q h
State Treasury, in Rome . . 24 B (8)
Stato degli Presidii . . . 151 I h
Stefano Rotondo, Santo, ch. in Rome . . . . 22 A
Stentoris Lake . . . . . . 9 D d
Stewarts, fam. . . . . . 128 C d
Štiavnica (Baňská-, Schemnitz). . . . . . . 79 K d
Štip (Ištip) . . . . 165 L c
Stirling . . . . 128 D d
Stirling, cty. . . . . . . 128 D d
Stoa, on the Acropolis of Athens . . . . . . 23 C
Stoa Basileios, in Athens . 23 D (3)
Stoa of Attalus . . . . . 23 D
Stoa of Eumenes, in Athens 23 D
Stoa of Hadrian . . . . . 23 D
Stoa of Jupiter Eleutherus 23 D (4)
Stoa of the Giants, in Athens 23 D (2)
Stoa Poikile, in Athens . 23 D (1)
Stockbridge, parl. bor. . . 163 M f
Stockerau . . . . 87 K d
Stolberg (in Harz) . . . . 87 H c
Stolpe River . . . . 135 I a
Strasburg, near Thorn . . 87 L b
Strathclyde, dist. . . . . 60 B b
Strathclyde, km. . . . . 60 G b
Strathearn, dist. . . . . 128 D d
Strathmore, dist . . . . 128 E d
Strathnaver, dist. . . . . 128 D b
Streaneshalch (Whitby), mon. 60 D b
Street of Tombs, in Athens 23 C
Stříbro (Mies) . . . . . 103 K d
Stroganov, Colony of . . . 138 I d
Stryme . . . . 9 C d
Stuhm . . . . 87 L b
Styr River . . . . 168 I a
Suamians, people . . . 57 H-I b
Suardones, people . . . 38 C b
Subeitala . . . . 53 C c
Subotica (Szabadka, Maria-Theresiopel) . . . . 168 F c
Succur (Su-chau) . . . 104 C J c
Su-chau (Siugui) . . . . 104 C M d
Suedia . . . . 168 J C b
Suffolk, dist. . . . . . . 60 E c
Sugd, reg. . . . . . . 92 G c
Sui-chau-fu . . . . . . 104 C K e
Suiones (Sueones), people . 34 G b

Suiyan	171	M	d
Suk-el Arba	174	O	n
Sukhum-kaleh	164	G	b
Sukkot	7	D	d
Suleimanieh	168 K	E	e
Sulu, isl.	104 C	M	g
Sumatia	14	C	b
Sumbal	104 B	H	e
Sumbal, reg.	104 B	H	e
Sumbawa, isl.	128 C	ins.	C
Sumen (Shumla)	165	E	b
Sunarganw	104 C	J	g
Sungari River	104 C	M	c
Sung Dynasty	92	K	d
Sung Dynasty, Southern	92	K	d
Sungerlu	168 J	B	a
Sunian Gate, in Athens	23	D	
Sunium, prom.	15	E	b
Sunnites, sect	168 L	leg.	
Sunzumata	104 C	L	d
Surrounding Sea	104 C	L	g
Sutherland, cty.	128	D	b
Sutherland, dist.	127	P	f
Suthrige (Surrey), dist.	60	D	d
Suvla Bay	168 L	D	c
Suvla Burun	168 L	D	c
Suwali	104 B	R	i
Svensksund	138	C	c
Sverdlovsk (Ekaterinburg)	168 G	R	d
Svienta River	88	K	b
Svitary (Zwittau, in Moravia)	168	E	b
Swanage	60	I	e
Swansea, castle, in Wales	74	J	h
Swansea, in Mass.	189	ins.	A
Sweden and Norway, km. 1815–1905	157	B	a
Swenet (Syene)	4	F	d *
Swiecie (Schwetz)	135	J	b
Syra, isl.	165	E	c
Syra Orda	104 C	K	c
Syrian Gate	20	G	d
Syrmia, dist.	87	L	f
Szabadka (Maria Theresiopel)	159	J	e
Szaszvaros (Broos)	159	L	f
Szatmar Nemeti(Satu Mare)	80	H	h
Szegedin (Szeged)	79	J	e
Székesfehérvár (Stuhlweissenburg)	159	J	e
Szendrö	87	M	d
Szombathely (Steinamanger)	159	I	e
Taanath-Shiloh	7	C	d
Tabal, people	5	C	b *
Tabernae novae, bldg. in Rome	24	A (17)	
Tabernae veteres, bldg. in Rome	24	A (16)	
Tachau (Tachov)	87	I	d
Tacna, prov.	216	ins.	
Tacuba	106	A	a
Tadoussac, Fort	191	K	b
Tagong	104 C	J	e
Tahiti (Sagitaria), isl.	128 B	A	f
Taif	53	G	d
Taifur Keui	168 L	D	c
Tain	128	D	c
Tai-yuen-iu	104 C	L	d
Tajik, Autonomous Socialist Soviet Area	170	H	e
Talas	104 B	H	c
Talay River	104 C	K	c
Ta-li-fu	104 C	K	e
Talish, reg.	164	H	c
Tallinn (Reval)	168 D	E	b
Tamerlane (Timur), Dom. of	92	leg.	
Tamworth, bp.	60	D	c
Tanatus Island	51	Q	i
Tanganyika Territory (Late German East Africa)	175	G	e
Tangut	104 C	J	c
Tangut, reg.	104 C	J	c
Tannu-Tubin, rep.	170/171	K	c
Tantamquerry	128 C	ins.	D
Taoce	19	H	e
Tapiau	87	M	a
Tarabulus (Tripoli)	168 J	C	c
Tarapacá, prov.	216	ins.	
Tarbellicae, Aquae	38	B	d
Targovicz (Targovitza	139	D	f
Târgu Mureşului (Maros Vasarhely)	159	M	e
Tarim River	104 B	H	d
Tarsi, people	104 B	I	c
Tarsius River	9	I	e
Tartar, auton. rep.	168 G	P	d
Tartessus River	44	A	c
Tartkul	170	H	d
Tartu (Dorpat)	168 D	F	b
Tashkent	104 B	G	c
Tasman, route of	128 C	O	f
Tasmania (Van Diemen's Land)	128 C	P	h
Tasmanland, reg.	128 C	O	f
Tatar Dynasty in China	92	L	d
Tatars, people in Azerbaijan	168 L	M	g
Tatars, people in eastern Asia	104 C	L	e
Tatars, people in Dobruja	168 H	G	d
Tauchira	44	D	e
Taungu	104 C	J	f
Taungu, reg.	104 C	J	f
Taurirt	174	Q	n
Tavoy	104 C	J	f
Tavoy, reg.	104 C	J	f
Tawalisi, people	104 C	L	g
Taydo (Peking)	104 C	L	c
Taza	174	P	n
Tebez	7	C	d
Tecoac	106	C	a
Tegyra	11	E	d
Tehennu, people	4	E	c *
Tejend, R.	168 K	H	b
Tekrit	168 J	D	c
Tel (Tell) el Kebir	174 J	J	i
Telingana, reg.	104 B	J	i
Tell el Amarna	1	B	d
Tellenae	35	ins.	B
Temesvar (Temisoara)	103	O	f
Templin	87	I	b
Tempsford	60	I	c
Tenasserim	104 C	J	f
Tenduc, people	104 C	L	c
Tepeyac	106	A	a
Teplice(Teplitz, in Bohemia)	159	G	c
Teptunis	4	ins.	
Teruentum	27	I	f
Tešanj	87	K	f
Teschen (czech Tĕšin)	79	K	d
Teschen (Tĕšin) princ.	79	K	d
Teschen (polish Cieszyn)	168	F	b
Tesmelucán	106	B	a
Tête	182 E	E	i
Tettenhall	60	H	c
Teuthrania, reg.	9	E	e
Teutonic Order, 13 cent.	47	K	c
Texcoco	106	B	a
Texcoce, lake	106	B	a
Thaema	44	E	d
Thaenae	44	C	c
Thana	104 B	R	j
Thebais, reg.	4	F	d (lII)
Theocoleum in Olympia	9	H	f
Theodosius, Port of	93	G	e
The Riff, reg.	174	P	n
Thesmotheteum, in Athens	23	D	(9)
Thesprots (Thesprotians), people	8	N	h
Thessalians, people	14	leg.	
Thimnath Serah	7	C	e
Thirsk, castle	74	L	e
Thisb(a)e	11	D	d
Thishe	7	D	e
Thogarma, reg.	5	D	b *
Tholos (Skias), in Athens	23	D	(7)
Thomar	83	J	h
Thomond, km.	74	B	b
Thonne le Thil	104 A	C b(Th.)	
Thonon	91	O	l
Thourout, fair	99	ins.	
Thracian Bosporus, str.	9	G	c
Thracian Tributary	13	J d (I)	
Thracians, people	8	P	g
Thrasyllus, Monument of	23	C (10)	
Three Points, cape	128 C	ins.	B
Thriasian Gate, in Athens	23	D	
Thriplow (Triploe) Heath	127	Z	r
Thsenthung (Tsuen-chau-fu)	104 C	L	e
Thule (Shetland) Islands	34	D	a
Thuria	14	C	b
Thuringia, state	168 D	C	c
Thurso	128	E	e
Thymbra	9	B	b
Thymbrius River	9	B	b
Thyni, people	9	G	d
Thyrea	14	C	b
Tian-shan Mountains	104 B	H	d
Tiberius, Arch of, on the Forum	24	B (14)	
Tibet, reg.	104 B	I	d
Tibet, Inner, reg.	171	K	d
Tibet, Outer, reg.	170	J	e
Tichiussa	17	I	f
Tigranocerta	20	I	c
Tihany, mon.	80	E	h
Timişoara (Temesvar)	103	O	f
Timna	7	C	e
Timur, Dominions of	92	leg.	
Tinnevelly	137	C	g
Tintagel	74	I	i
Tione	168 H	ins.	
Tippermuir	128	E	d
Tiraspol	168 G	K	f
Tireboli	168 J	C	a
Tiree, isl.	128	A	d
Tirmidh	104 B	G	c
Tirnovo (Tirnova)	93	C	b
Tityrus, mt.	15	D	d
Tivertzes, people	57	I	d
Tobol River	104 B	G	b
Tokaj (Tokay)	87	M	d
Tokat	168 J	C	a
Toledo, univ.	100	E	g
Toledo Mountains	82	B	b
Tönsberg	58	F	b
Tor (Sinai Penins.)	150	B	a
Torcy	104 A	G	c
Tordesillas	83	J g (Tordes.)	
Torksey	60	I	c
Torre (Tor), mon.	97	N	k
Torrelobaton (Torrelob,.	83	J	g
Torres, route of	128 C	P	f
Toruń (Thorn)	135	J	b
Toski	174	G	b
Touapse	182 E	E	c
Tougurt	174	D	a
Tovačov (Tobitschau)	159	I	d
Towcester	60	I	c
Tozan, people	104 C	K	d
Tralee	74	B	b
Tramin, castle	79	G	e
Tranquebar	128 B	ins.	B
Transcaucasia, rep.	168 G	N-O	g
Transcaucasian Socialist Federal Soviet Republic (T.S.F.S.R.)	168 F	leg.	
Trans-Jordan, reg.	168 J	C	c
Transoxiana, reg.	53	I	c
Transvaal (South African Republic)	175	M	l
Trastevere Railway Station, in Rome	22	A	
Traun River	135	G	d
Trave River	134	F	a
Treasuries in Olympia	9	H	f
Trebbin, castle	85	C	b
Trebiae	27	G	e
Trebinje (Trebinye), bp.	94	F	e

Trebitsch (Trebič) . . . . . 87 J d
Tregony, bor. . . . . 74 I i
Trempealeau, Fort . . . . . 191 G c
Trenčin (Trencsén, Trent-
schin) . . . . 63 J d
Trentino, reg. . . . . . 168 H ins.
Trikkala . . . . 89 B c
Trimontium . . . . 51 O g
Trincomali (Trincomalee) 137 D g
Trinovantes, people . . . . . 51 Q i
Triocala . . . . 30 C e
Triploe (Thriplow) Heath 127 Z n
Tripods, Street of the, in
Athens . . . . 23 C
Tripolitania, dist. . . . . . 174 E a
Tripolitsa, in Greece . . . 165 C e
Tritaea, in Achaia . . . . . . 14 B b
Trnava (Tyrnau, Nagy-
szombat) . . . . 79 J d
Trnova (Tirnova) . . . . . . 93 C b
Troas, reg. . . . . 9 D c
Trocnov (Troznow) . . . . 87 J d
Trogir (Traú), bp. . . . . . 95 F c
Troian Plain . . . . 9 A b
Troitskaia . . . . 138 E d
Troki . . . . 88 K d
Tropaeum Augusti . . . . . 26 B d
Troy in Asia Minor . . . . . 9 B b
Troyland, reg. . . . . 9 D e
Trucial Oman, reg. . . . 168 K F d
Truns . . . . 91 R l
Truro, mon. . . . . 97 L k
Trutnov (Trautenau) . . . 135 H c
Tsaribrod . . . . 168 G J g
Tsaritsyn . . . . 139 F f
Tsarskoe Selo . . . . . . 138 D d (T.S.)
Tscherlitz (Echallens) . . . 91 O l
Tsi-ning-chau . . . . 104 C L e
Tsuen-chau-fu . . . . . . 104 C L e
Tuapse . . . . 168 J C a
Tuaregs, people . . . . . . 174 D b
Tuat . . . . 174 C b
Tüffer . . . . 72 D b
Tulcea (Tulcha) . . . . . 165 F a
Tun . . . . 168 K G c
Tunguska River, Lower- 104 C J a
Tunguska River, Upper- 104 C J b
Turaba . . . . 170 F f
Turan, reg., in India . . 53 I d
Turcoman Socialist Soviet
Republic . . . . 168 F leg.
Turfan . . . . 104 C I c
Turkestan, economic reg. 170 leg.
Turkestan, East, reg. . . . 170 I e
Turkey, Republic, 1923 . 168 J B b
Turkish (Ottoman) Em-
pire, 1683—1913 164
Turkish (Ottoman) Em-
pire, till 1920, 1922 . . 168 J B b
Turkoman Socialist So-
viet Republic . . . . . . 170 G d-e
Turks, people, 8 cent. . . . 53 H b
Turks, people, 14 cent. . . 89 J g
Turks, people, in 1913 . . 165 leg.
Turriff . . . . 128 F c
Tus . . . . 99 L g
Tutbury, castle . . . . . 74 L g
Tuticorin . . . . 170 I h
Tuxtepec . . . . 216 D d
Tuz Geul . . . . 168 J B b
Tuz-Khurmati . . . . . . 168 J D c
Tuzla . . . . 103 N f
Tweeddale, dist. . . . . . 128 E e
Twyneham . . . . 60 I d
Tyche, Temple of . . . . . 23 D
Tyrconell, ter. . . . . . . 74 B a
Tyre . . . . 168 J C c
Tyria . . . . 168 J A b
Tyrnau (Trnava, Nagy-
szombat) . . . . 79 J d
Tzompantzinco . . . . . 106 B a
Udgir . . . . 137 C e
Uglich . . . . 138 E e

Ugrians, people . . . . . 104 B G a
Uigurs, people . . . . . . 104 C I c
Uirats, people . . . . . . 104 C J b
Uist, North and South, isl. 128 A c
Ujda . . . . 174 Q n
Ujek-Tepe . . . . 9 A b
Ujiji . . . . 175 F e
Ujjain . . . . 104 B R i
Ujvidék (Neusatz, Novi Sad) 168 F d
Ukrainian Socialist Soviet
Republic (U.S.S.R.) . . 168 F leg.
Uladh (Ulster), dist. . . . . 60 A b
Ulala . . . . 170 J c
Ulan-Butor-Khoto (Urga) 171 L d
Ulcinj (Dulcigno) . . . . 165 A e
Ulcinj, (Dulcigno), bp. . 95 F c
Uliasutai . . . . 171 K d
Uliches, people . . . . . 57 J d
Ulster (Uladh), dist. . . 60 A b
Ulster, prov. . . . . . . 74 C a
Ulu-kem River . . . . . 104 C J b
Uman reg. . . . . 104 C J e
Umberto I, Ponte-, loc. in
Rome . . . . 22 A
Umbilicus, in Rome . . . . 24 B (10)
Umbri, people . . . . . . 29 C c
Ume River . . . . 98 G a
Una River . . . . 87 K f
Unie, isl. . . . . 168 F H g
Unghvár (Užhorod) . . . 168 H b
Union of South Africa . . 175 F g
Union of Soviet Socia-
list Republics (Russia) 168 G L-R d
Université, quarter in Paris 149 B
University, in Athens . . . 23 D
University Street, in Athens 23 D
Unst, isl. . . . . 128 ins.
Upland, dist., in Sweden . 88 G a
Upper Egypt, reg. . . . . 4 F d (III)
Upper Germans, people
in 1929 . . . . 168 H C-E c
Upper (Gray) League . . . 91 Q l
Upper Lorraine, duchy,
13 cent. . . . . 104 A C c
Upper Nairi Sea . . . . . 5 D b
Upper Silesia, reg. . . . 168 D D c
Upper Tunguska River . 104 C J b
Uppsala (Upsala) . . . . 88 G b
Ural, economic reg. . . . 170 leg.
Uratu, dist. . . . . 4 G c *
Urci . . . . 38 B c
Urci. bp. . . . . 42 B f
Urfa . . . . 168 J C b
Urgenj . . . . 104 B F c
Urmia . . . . 168 K E b
Urmia, Lake . . . . . . 99 M f
Ursha . . . . 168 L D c
Urumtsi . . . . 104 B J c
Urundi, reg. . . . . . . 175 F e
Ush . . . . 104 B H c
Usk, castle . . . . . . 74 K h
Usk, R. . . . . 60 H d
Uskub (Skoplje) . . . . 89 H f
Üsküdar . . . . 168 L F f
Ussa River . . . . . . 138 J b
Ussuri River . . . . . 104 C N c
Ústí (Aussig) . . . . . 135 G c
Uvejek . . . . 9 A b
Uxellodunum, in Britain . 51 O c
Uxellodunum, in Gaul . . 38 ins.
Uzbek Socialist Soviet Re-
public . . . . 170 H d
Uzes, people, on the
Dnieper R. . . . . . . 99 J d
Uzes, people, on the Ural R. 53 H b
Uzgend . . . . 104 B H b
Užhorod (Unghvár) . . . 168 H b

Vaşcanae (Baccanae) . . . 35 ins. B
Vács (Waitzen) . . . . . . 87 L c
Vács (Waitzen), bp. . . . 95 F b
Vadstena (Wadstena) . . 88 F b
Valencia Island, in Ireland 168 F C e

Vallay of Salt . . . . 7 B f
Valley of the Sweet Waters
of Europe . . . . 93 G e
Val Pusteria . . . . 168 H ins.
Valona (Avlona) . . . . . 164 B b
Val Venosta (Vintschgau),
reg. . . . . 87 H e
Väner (Wener), lake . . . 88 E b
Vangui (Yang-chau-fu) . 104 C M d
Varad, Nagy-(Grosswardein,
Oradea Mare) . . . . . 168 G c
Värälä . . . . 138 C c
Varberg (Warberg) . . . . 88 E c
Varini, people . . . . . . 38 D a
Värmland (Vermland), reg. 45 G a
Varvakion, bldg. in Athens 23 D
Västerås (Westerås) . . . . 88 G b
Vätter (Wetter), lake . . . 88 F b
Vaudemont . . . . 104 A D c
Vaudemont, cty., 13 cent. 104 A D c
Vaux (-devant-Damloup) 168 C C c
Vaux-lès-Laferté . . 104 A C b (V.l. L.)
Vaux-lès-Mouzon . . 104 A C b (V.l.M.)
Vechta . . . . 78 F b
Veldes . . . . 79 I e
Veles . . . . 165 B c
Venta Icenorum (Caistor,
Bury St. Edmunds) . . 51 Q h
Venus, Temple of, near Ardea 35 ins. B
Venus Cloacina, Temple of 24 A (14)
Venus Genetrix, Temple of 24 B (24)
Venzone . . . . 154 G e
Veps, people . . . . . . 59 L b
Veramin . . . . 104 B F d
Verbas River . . . . . . 87 K f
Verneuil (near Evreux) . . 69 H f
Verneuil (near Montmédy) 104 A C b (Ve.)
Versecz (Werschetz, Vršac) 168 G d
Vesle River . . . . 104 A B b
Vespasian, Temple of . . . 24 B (6)
Vesta, Temple of . . . . . 24 A (19)
Veszprem . . . . 87 K e
Veszprem, bp. . . . . . . 95 F b
Veurne see Furnes . . . . 134 B c
Via Appia Nuova, street in
Rome . . . . 22 A
Via Cavour, street in Rome 22 A
Via della Lungara, loc. in
Rome . . . . 22 A
Via di Porta San Sebastiano,
in Rome . . . . 22 A
Viale Ardeatino, in Rome . 22 A
Viale Ostiense, in Rome . . 22 A
Via Nazionale, street in Rome 22 A
Via Nomentana, street in
Rome . . . . 22 A
Viatka . . . . 138 G d
Viatka River . . . . . . 138 G d
Viatka-Vetluga, economic
reg. . . . . 168 F leg.
Via Venti Settembre, street
in Rome . . . . 22 A
Viazma . . . . 138 D d
Viborg (Wiborg) . . . . . 88 C c
Vieille Rue du Temple,
street in Paris . . . . 149 B
Vielun (Wielun) . . . . . 79 K c
Vienna, in Austria . . . . 63 I d
Vigneul-sous-Montmédy . 104 A C b (Vi)
Vijayadurg . . . . 137 G c
Vijayanagar, reg. . . . . . 92 H f
Viking raids . . . . 45 E b
Világos . . . . 139 B f
Viliui River . . . . 104 C L a
Viliya (Wiliya) River . . . 88 K d
Villa Cisneros . . . . . . 181 Z e
Villafranca (Villefranche) 102 H g
Villa Hayes . . . . 216 H h
Villalar . . . . 83 J g (Villal.)
Villanueva, in Spain . . . 83 K g
Villa Medici, bldg. in Rome 22 A
Villareal . . . . 83 K h
Villa Rica de Vera Cruz 106 D a

Villa Rica la Vieja 106	D	a	
Villa Viçosa (Portugal) . . . 83	J	h	
Ville, quarter in Paris . . 149		B	
Villefranche (-de-Rouergue) 76	E	d	
Villefranche (-sur-Mer) . . 102	H	g	
Villers-lès-Mangiennes . . 104 A	C	b	
Vilmanstrand 138	C	c	
Vilnius (Vilna) . . . . . . 168 D	F	c	
Vimy Ridge, mt. . . . . . 168 C	B	b	
Vincennes, in France . . . 86	D	d	
Vincennes, Fort-(Indiana) . 191	H	d	
Vintschgau (Val Venosta), reg. 87	H	e	
Virbalis (Virballen) 159	L	a	
Virginia, reg. 191	I e - L	b	
Viroconium (Wroxeter) . . 51	O	h	
Virzjärv (Wirzjärw), lake . . 88	K	b	
Vis (Lissa), isl. 90	F	c	
Visborg (Wisborg), castle . 88	H	c	
Visby (Wisby) 88	H	c	
Višegrad, in Bosnia 87	L	g	
Visegrad, castle in Hungary 87	L	e	
Visoko 89	A	b	
Vitim River . . . . 104 C	L	b	
Vitry (-le-François) 154	C	d	
Vitry (-en-Perthois) . . . 104 A	B	c	
Vittorio Emanuele, Ponte, loc. in Rome 22	A		
Vittório Véneto . . . . . 168 B	F	b	
Viza 165	E	c	
Vltava (Moldau), R. . . . 168 D	C	d	
Voguls, people 138	J	c	
Voivodina, reg. 159	J	f	
Vordernberg 79	I	e	
Vordingborg 87	H	a	
Voreda 51	O	g	
Vosprus 99	K	d	
Votiak, auton. area . . . 168 G	P	c	
Vots, people 57	I	b	
Vrana 87	J	g	
Vratza (Vraca) 165	C	b	
Vrbas River 161	K	e	
Vredenburg . . . . 128 C	ins.	D	
Vrhbosna (Sarajevo) 87	L	g	
Vršac (Versecz, Werschetz) 168	G	d	
Vychegda River 138	G	c	
Vyschegrad (Wyszegrad), castle (near Bromberg) . . 79	K	b	
Vyšehrad (Wyschehrad), castle (near Prague) . . 79	I	d	
Vytegra . . . . 182 E	E	a	
Wadgaon 137	B	e	
Wadi Halfa 174	G	b	
Wadi Sous 174	C	a	
Wagon Road (Hamaxitos) . 23	D		
Wahabis, people 170	F	f	
Waldenburg, in Saxony . . 79	H	c	
Waldenburg, in Wurtemberg 143	I	g	
Wales, princ. 8 cent. 60	C	c	
Wales, princ. 11 cent. . . . 65	E	d	
Wales, princ., 1200-1450 . . 74	I	g	
Wales in 1832 163			
Wales, North-, dist. 60	H	c	
Wallingford 60	I	d	
Walloons, people in 1929 168 H	B	b	
Walvis (Walfish) Bay . . 175	B	g	
Wanborough 60	D	d	
Wantage 60	I	d	
Warangal . . . . 104 B	R	j	
Ware 127	Z	o	
Warga River 174	P	n	
Warszawa (Warsaw) 87	M	b	
Wartenberg, castle, in Bohemia 79	I	c	
Washington, routes of . . . 195	C	d	
Wassulu, reg. 174	C	d	
Watchet, borough 60	H	d	
Waterford, in Ireland . . 74	C	b	
Waterloo 156	A	d	
Wawat, reg. 4	F	d *	
Wedmore 60	H	d	
Weissenstein, castle, in Esthonia 88	K	b	

Weitenstein, castle 79	I	e	
Weitra 79	I	d	
Wells, in England 74	K	h	
Welsh Marcher Earldoms 70 F c (W.M.E.)			
Welsh Mountains 2	D	c	
Welshpool 74	J	g	
Welsh Principalities . . 70 F c (W. P.)			
Wends, people in 1929 . 168 H	D	b	
Wenlock, mon. 60	C	c	
Werdenfels, castle 79	G	e	
Werfen 87	I	e	
Werschetz (Versecz, Vršac) 168	G	d	
Weset, Kingdom of 4	F	d *	
Wessex, Kingdom of . . . 60	leg.		
West, economic reg. . . . 168	F	leg.	
Westerna, dist. 60	C	c	
Western Euphrates River . . 18	E	c	
Western Samoa, Territory of 172	H	b	
Westerwald, mts. . . . . 168 C	D	b	
West Götland, dist. 88	E	b	
West Hartlepool 162	E	c	
West Kirghiz, economic reg. . . . . 170 G d leg. (B)			
Westmanland, dist. 88	F	b	
West March, dist. 128	C	c	
Westminster, abbey 74	M	h	
Westmorland, dist. 60	H	b	
Westmorland, cty. 74	K	e	
Westmorland, parl. dist. . . 163	L	c	
Westray, isl. 128	E	a	
West Riding, dist. 60	I	c	
West Samoa, Territory . . 180	J	i	
West Saxons, people . . . 60	C-D	b	
West Scheldt, R. . . . . 168 C	B	b	
West Sea (North Sea) . . . 98	D	c	
West Wales, dist. 60	B	d	
Wexford 74	C	b	
Wezzan 174	P	n	
Whalsay, isl. 128	ins.		
Wharfe River 60	D	c	
Whitby (Streaneshalch), mon. 60	D	b	
Whiterne (Whithorn), bp. . . 60	B	b	
White Russian Socialist Soviet Republic (W.R.S.S.R) . 168	F	leg.	
Whithorn 128	D	f	
Whithorn (Whiterne), bp. . . 60	B	b	
Wick 128	E	b	
Wicklow, castle 74	C	b	
Wied, castle 78	D	d	
Wiek, dist. 88	J	b	
Wieringen . . . . 168 D	A	c	
Wigmore, castle 74	K	g	
Wigtown 128	D	f	
Wigtown, cty. 128	D	f	
Wilimow 87	J	d	
Wiliya (Viliya) River . . . 138	C	e	
William of Rubruck, Route of . . . . 104 B	leg.		
Willis Islets 179	F	i	
Wilno (Vilna) 159	M	a	
Wilton, battle 60	I	d	
Winchester in England (Venta Belgarum) 51	P	i	
Windau River 88	J	c	
Winds (Slovenes), people . 56	E	c	
Wing 60	I	d	
Winnebah . . . . 128 C	ins.	D	
Winnipeg River 190	F	a	
Winwaedsfield, battle . . . 60	D	c	
Wirzjärw, lake 88	K	b	
Wisborg (Visborg), castle . 88	H	c	
Wislica 87	M	c	
Witbois, people 175	E	g	
Witham, borough 60	J	d	
Witteland, reg. . . . . . . 128 C	N	g	
Wittgenstein, castle 86	G	c	
Wkra River 135	K	b	
Woèvre Plain . . . . . . 168 C	C	c	
Wolkowysk 155	M	b	
Wollin, bp. 95	E	a	
Wolmar 88	K	c	
Wolodomir 99	H	c	
Wolyn, dist. 139	C	e	

Woodstock, borough 74	L	h	
Worcester, bp. in England . 60	C	c	
Wormser Joch, pass (Stelvio Pass) 86	H	e	
Wörth 158	D	d	
Wrath, cape 128	C	a	
Wreocensaete, people . . . 60	C	c	
Wycombe 74	M	h	
Wye River 60	C	c	
Wyschehrad (Vyšehrad), castle 79	I	d	
Wyszegrad (Vyschegrad), castle 79	K	b	
Wytschaete Ridge . . . . . 168 c B b (W.)			
Xavier, Saint Fr(ancis) . . . 191	H	c	
Xochimilco, lake 106	A	a	
Xocotla 106	C	a	
Xoïs 1	B	b	
Yachi . . . . 104 C	K	e	
Yakut, economic reg. . . . 171 O b (G)			
Yakutat 180	N	b	
Yakutsk, Autonomous Socialist Soviet Republic . 171	M/P	b	
Yala Geul . . . . 168 L	D	c	
Yamburg 88	M	b	
Yamurtalik . . . . 168 J	C	b	
Yandabu 171	K	f	
Yang-chau-fu . . . . . . 104 C	M	c	
Yang-tse-kiang, R. . . . 104 C	K	e	
Yang-tsun . . . . 170 ins. A			
Yanina (Janina) 89	B	c	
Yarkand . . . . 104 B	H	d	
Yarmouth, (I. of Wight) . . 74	L	i	
Yarmouth, Great- (Norfolk) . 65	G	d	
Yarmouth, Great-, parl. bor. 163	P	c	
Yatnan (Cyprus), isl. . . . 5	C	b *	
Yatreb (Medina) 53	G	d	
Yatvegs, people 71	K	c	
Yazvings, people 57	H	c	
Yedlinsk (Jedlinsk) . . . 155	K	c	
Yell, isl. 128	ins.		
Yemama, reg. 53	G	d	
Yemamah, El- . . . . . . 104 B	E	d	
Yenihan . . . . 168 J	C	b	
Yeni Kioi 9	A	b	
Yenisei River . . . . . . 104 C	I	a	
Yeni-Shehr 9	A	b	
Yerkessi 9	A	b	
Yezd 170	G	e	
Yezdi Chast . . . . 168 K	F	d	
York, in England 60	D	b	
York, abbey 74	M	g	
York, Kingdom of 60	I	b	
Yoshino . . . . 104 C	N	d	
Yozgad . . . . 168 J	B	b	
Ypiranga 215	D	e	
Yrac, reg. 99	K	f	
Yser River . . . . 168 C	B	b	
Ystad 103	K	d	
Yttingaford 60	I	d	
Yuan Dynasty 92	I	e	
Yu-ché, people . . . . . 104 C	M	c	
Yugoslavia, km. . . . . . 168 F	I-J	g	
Yung-ning-fu . . . . . . 104 C	K	e	
Zab River 53	G	c	
Zadar (Zara) 168	D	d	
Zafarin Islands 174	Q	n	
Zagreb (Zagrab, Agram) . . 79	J	f	
Zagreb (Agram), bp. . . . 95	F	b	
Zagros Mountains . . . 168 K D b - E c			
Żagubica 165	B	a	
Zaiton (Tsuen-chau-fu) . 104 C	L	e	
Zajeca 103	N	f	
Zamość 155	L	c	
Zampa, reg. . . . . . . 104 C	K	f	
Zappeion, bldg. in Athens . 23			
Zardandan, reg. . . . . 104 C	J	e	
Zarev 139	G	f	
Zarey, abp. 99	M	d	
Zarnowitz 87	L	a	

Žatec (Saaz)	87	I	c
Zator	87	L	d
Zebid	104 B	E	f
Zeebrugge	168 c	B	b
Zeitun	168 K	F	c
Zeitz, bp. (Naumburg-)	95	E	a
Zeklers, people in 1929	168 H	G	c
Zelea	9	E	d
Zemun (Semlin, Zimony)	168	G	d
Zenda Rud, R.	168 K	F	c
Zengg (Senj)	168	D	d
Žepče	87	L	f

Zephat	6	C	c
Zephyrium, prom., in Crete	14	ins.	
Zerenj	104 B	G	d
Zeus, Temple of, in Olympia	9	H	f (2)
Zhagubitza (Žagubica)	165	B	a
Zhaia	104 B	F	f
Zhitomir	139	C	e
Ziegenhain	78	F	c
Ziklag	7	B	f
Zile	168 J	C	a
Zimony (Zemun, Semlin)	168	G	d
Zinjar	77	M	e

Zipangu, emp. (Japan)	104 C	O	d
Zips, County of	87	M	d
Zircz, mon.	80	E	h
Ziza	7	D	e
Znaim (Znojmo)	87	K	d
Zolyom (Zvolen, Altsohl)	159	J	d
Zone of the Straits	168 D	F	e
Zsolna (Sillein)	155	J	d
Zubeir	168 K	E	c
Zuhab	99	M	g
Zvornik (Zwornik)	87	L	f
Zwettl	87	J	d

ADDITIONAL PLACE NAMES AND REVISIONS FOR INDEX SUPPLEMENT

(Ninth edition)

Abu Roash	1	B	b
Adab	4	E	e
Akhetaten	1	B	d
Akhmim	1	B	d
Alalah	4	C	d
Alishar Hüyük	4	C	d
Aniba	1	B	f
Antaeopolis	1	B	d
Armant	1	C	e
Arpachiya	4	D	d
Arrapha	4	D	d
Arwad	4	C	e
Arzawa	4	B	d
Ashmunein	1	B	d
Assiut	1	B	d
Assuwa, reg.	4	A	d
Aswan	1	C	e
Athribis	1	B	b
Azzi, people	4	C	c
Badari	1	B	d
Benha	1	B	b
Beni Hasan	1	B	d
Bersheh	1	B	d
Buhen	1	B	g
Byblos	4	C	e
Chagar Bazar	4	D	d
Crocodilopolis	1	B	c
Damanhur	1	B	b
Dashur, Pyramids of	1	B	c
Dendereh	1	C	d
Derr	1	C	f
Dion	6	D	c
Diospolis Parva	1	C	d
Diyala River	4	E	e
Edfu	1	C	e
Elians, people	8	N	i
Erech	4	E	e
Eshnunna	4	D	e
Esna	1	C	e
Esneh (Esna)	1	C	e
Es-Sebua	1	C	f
Essene Gate	6 ins.	A	
Fara	4	E	e
Fullers Tower, in Jerusalem	6 ins.	A	
Gasga, people	4	C	c

Gebelein	1	C	e
Gebel es-Silsileh	1	C	e
Gerf Husein	1	C	f
Giza, Pyramids of	1	B	c
Gubla	4	C	e
Habur River	4	D	d
Halab (Aleppo)	4	C	d
Hasmonaean Palace	6 ins.	A	
Hassuna	4	D	d
Hatnub quarries	1	B	d
Hattusas	4	B	c
Hyasa, people	4	D	c
Hermonthis	1	C	e
Hu	1	C	d
Isin	4	E	e
Isuwa, people	4	D	d
Jarmo	4	D	d
Jemdet Nasr	4	D	e
Kalabsha	1	C	f
Kalhu (Nimrud)	5	D	b
Kanesh	4	C	d
Kantareh	1	C	b
Kantir	1	B	b
Karatepe	4	C	d
Kedron, Vale of	6 ins.	A	
Khafaje	4	D	e
Kir Hareseth	7	D	f
Kizzuwatna, reg.	4	B	d
Kom Ombo	1	C	e
Kültepe	4	C	d
Kuyunjik	4	D	d
Kystus	6 ins.	A	
Larsa	4	E	e
Leontes River	6	C	b
Lower Zab River	4	D	d
Malatia	5	C	b
Mari	4	D	e
Marqasi	4	C	d
Medamud	1	C	e
Meidum	1	B	c
Meir	1	B	d
Merimdeh	1	B	b
Mersin	4	B	d
Musasir	5	D	d
Musur (Egypt)	5	C	c
Negadeh	1	C	e

Nuzi	4	D	d
Ombos	1	C	d
Philae, isl.	1	C	e
Qatna	4	C	e
Qattunan	4	D	d
Qumran	7	C	e
Qaw el-Kebir	1	B	d
Rakotis	1	A	b
Rapiqu	4	D	e
Ras Shamra	4	C	d
Sagaratim	4	D	d
Sakae, Sakans, people	18	S	h
Sakkarah, Pyramids of	1	B	c
Sam'al	5	C	b
San el-Hagar	1	B	b
Sea Lands, dist.	5	D	b
Sharuhen, Ancient Near East	4	B	e
Sharuhen, in Ancient Palestine	7	A	f
Shuruppak	4	E	e
Sohag	1	B	d
Tabal, dist.	5	C	b
Tell Brak	4	D	d
Tell Agrab	4	D	e
Tell Asmar	4	D	e
Tell el-Yahudiyeh	1	B	b
Tell Halaf	4	D	d
Tell Harmal	4	D	e
Telloh	4	E	e
Tema	8	C	b
Tepe Gawra	4	D	d
Terqa	4	D	e
Tod	1	C	e
Turushpa	5	D	b
Tuttul	4	D	e
Tuwanuwa	4	B	d
Ubaid	4	E	e
Ugarit	4	C	d
Umma	4	E	e
Upper Zab River	4	D	d
Urartu, dist.	5	D	b
Uxians	8	I	e
Wadi Hammamat	1	C	d
Warka	4	E	e
Yamhad, dist.	4	C	d